lonely planet

Ecuador & the Galápagos Islands

Bailey Freeman, Luke Waterson, Joel Balsam, Anthony Ham, Trent Holden, Michael Grosberg, Alex Egerton, Mayra Peralta and Wendy Yanagihara

CONTENTS

FROM TOP: SL-PHOTOGRAPHY/SHUTTERSTOCK, CARLOS G. MARIN/SHUTTERSTOCK

Plan Your Trip

The Guide

Rucu Pichincha, p69

Shrimp ceviche

Toolkit

Storybook

VILLE PALONEN/ALAMY

Manta ray near Los Túneles (p339)

ECUADOR & THE GALÁPAGOS ISLANDS

THE JOURNEY BEGINS HERE

It was love at first volcano – all it took was an afternoon ambling across the golden *páramo* beneath snowcapped Cotopaxi on the back of a horse named Tequila, and I was head over heels for this country of contrasts. The honeymoon phase continued on a ride down the Río Jatunyacu, and became love everlasting when I set foot in the Galápagos archipelago, among the wildlife that launched these tiny islands into a centuries-long scientific conversation.

Bailey Freeman

@the_traveling_b

Bailey is a writer, photographer and circus performer living in the hills of central Tennessee. Bailey wrote the Galápagos Islands chapter.

My favourite experience was watching a group of huge manta rays somersault beneath the clear blue waves on the way to **Los Túneles** (p339).

WHO GOES WHERE

Our writers and experts choose the places which, for them, define Ecuador & the Galápagos Islands.

JOEL BALSAM

Mompiche (p148) is a surf town that sucks you in. Perfect waves that are some of the gnarliest in Ecuador. A tightly knit group of locals passionate about preservation – and community. Adventures to bioluminescent mangrove forests around Isla Portete (pictured; p151), which cradled the country's first Afro-Ecuadorian community. I barely made it out without changing my plans to stay longer.

Joel Balsam

@joelbalsam

Joel is a Canadian freelance journalist based in Rio de Janeiro, Brazil. He's contributed to more than a dozen Lonely Planet guidebooks. Joel wrote the North Coast chapter.

IRENEUKE/SHUTTERSTOCK

Hiking in the spectacular mountains around **Saraguro** (p300) is about more than nature and adventure, it's a cultural experience. Even on a short trek, visitors will be surrounded by tiny Andean farms where Indigenous communities grow ancient crops often using irrigation and terracing that has been around for centuries. Speaking with the Saraguros, one is struck by the pride they show in their history and efforts to protect their traditions in a changing world.

Alex Egerton

X: @alexetravel

Alex is a journalist based in the mountains of central Colombia writing about travel, culture and history throughout Latin America and the Caribbean. Alex wrote the Cuenca & the Southern Highlands chapter.

The sometimes rough coastal road north of Playas ends in several way-under-the-radar spots, some with seemingly endless stretches of abandoned sandy shores, others with fishing villages like **Puerto Engabao** (p263).

DFLC - MULTMEDIA DESIGNER/SHUTTERSTOCK

Michael Grosberg

likelocal.io

Michael has worked on four editions of the Lonely Planet Ecuador & Galapagos guidebook, as well as books for several other countries in the region. He's the co-founder of travel start-up LikeLocal. Michael wrote the South Coast & Guayaquil chapter.

If ever there was a time I realized how far from home I was, it came while embarking on the **Quilotoa Loop** (p218). Hiking alone through emerald valleys, I gained an unexpected trekking partner. Not another hiker, but a baby cow who ambled faithfully by my side for over an hour in serene, contented silence.

SL-PHOTOGRAPHY/SHUTTERSTOCK

Trent Holden

Instagram: @hombreholden

A writer for Lonely Planet for nearly 20 years, Trent's covered destinations as diverse as Brazil, Rwanda, India and Mongolia – and now Ecuador twice. Trent wrote the Central Highlands chapter.

Intag Valley (p122) is like an Eden unfurling before you. It boasts everything from coffee tours to cloud-forest retreats to archaeological sites and thermal baths. It's also a great spot to relax: sitting on the veranda before green tree-clad hillsides.

LUKE WATERSON

Luke Waterson

lukeandhiswords.com

Luke is a novelist, travel writer and loving father to his daughter, Eira. He specializes in adventures (especially hikes and trips to historical sites) across Latin America, Scandinavia and the UK. Luke wrote the Northern Highlands chapter.

SASHA_GERASIMOV/SHUTTERSTOCK

Parque Nacional Yasuní (p184) is my idea of the perfect adventure – remote, filled with wildlife and far from the tourist crowds. There's nothing better than drifting down an isolated river close to sunset.

Anthony Ham

@AnthonyHamWrite

Anthony writes about the wild places of our planet from the deserts of Africa and the Arctic to the Amazon. He has written two books of narrative non-fiction, including The Man Who Loved Pink Dolphins, *which is set in the Rio Negro Basin of the Amazon. Anthony wrote the Oriente chapter.*

NANCY PAUWELS/SHUTTERSTOCK

Although I've lived half of my life in the city, I'll never cease to be amazed by **Quito** (p50), a city so full of contrasts and contradictions that it perfectly captures the spirit of Ecuador – both colonial and contemporary, cold and burning hot, welcoming and yet sometimes distant.

Mayra Peralta

Instagram: @lesjoursemay

Mayra is a pop-culture-loving journalist and editor based in Latin America, who never travels without a carefully curated playlist. She's also the founder of No Manners Magazine. *Mayra wrote the Toolkit chapter.*

JON CHICA/SHUTTERSTOCK

One of my favorite little streets in Quito is **Junín** (p64) in Barrio San Marcos, a corner of the Centro Histórico that feels like a secret, partly because it's hidden behind the massive Monasterio Santa Catalina de Siena. It feels intimate – when I stopped to look at the menu of a little cafe, a neighbor across the street called out that I should go in, it's good!

Wendy Yanagihara

@wendyyanagihara

Wendy is a writer and artist who has contributed to around 70 guidebooks for Lonely Planet. Wendy wrote the Quito chapter.

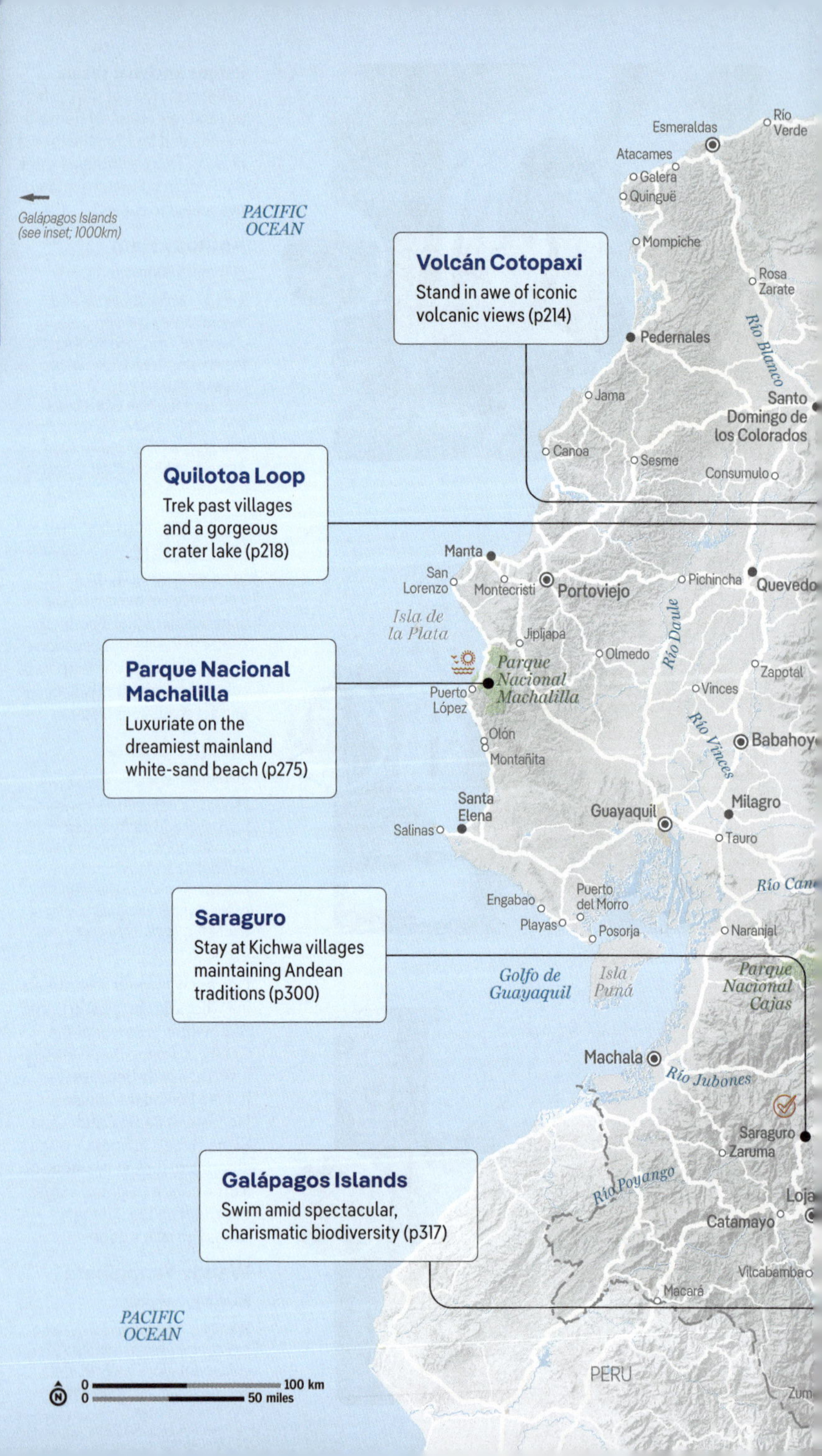

Volcán Cotopaxi

Stand in awe of iconic volcanic views (p214)

Quilotoa Loop

Trek past villages and a gorgeous crater lake (p218)

Parque Nacional Machalilla

Luxuriate on the dreamiest mainland white-sand beach (p275)

Saraguro

Stay at Kichwa villages maintaining Andean traditions (p300)

Galápagos Islands

Swim amid spectacular, charismatic biodiversity (p317)

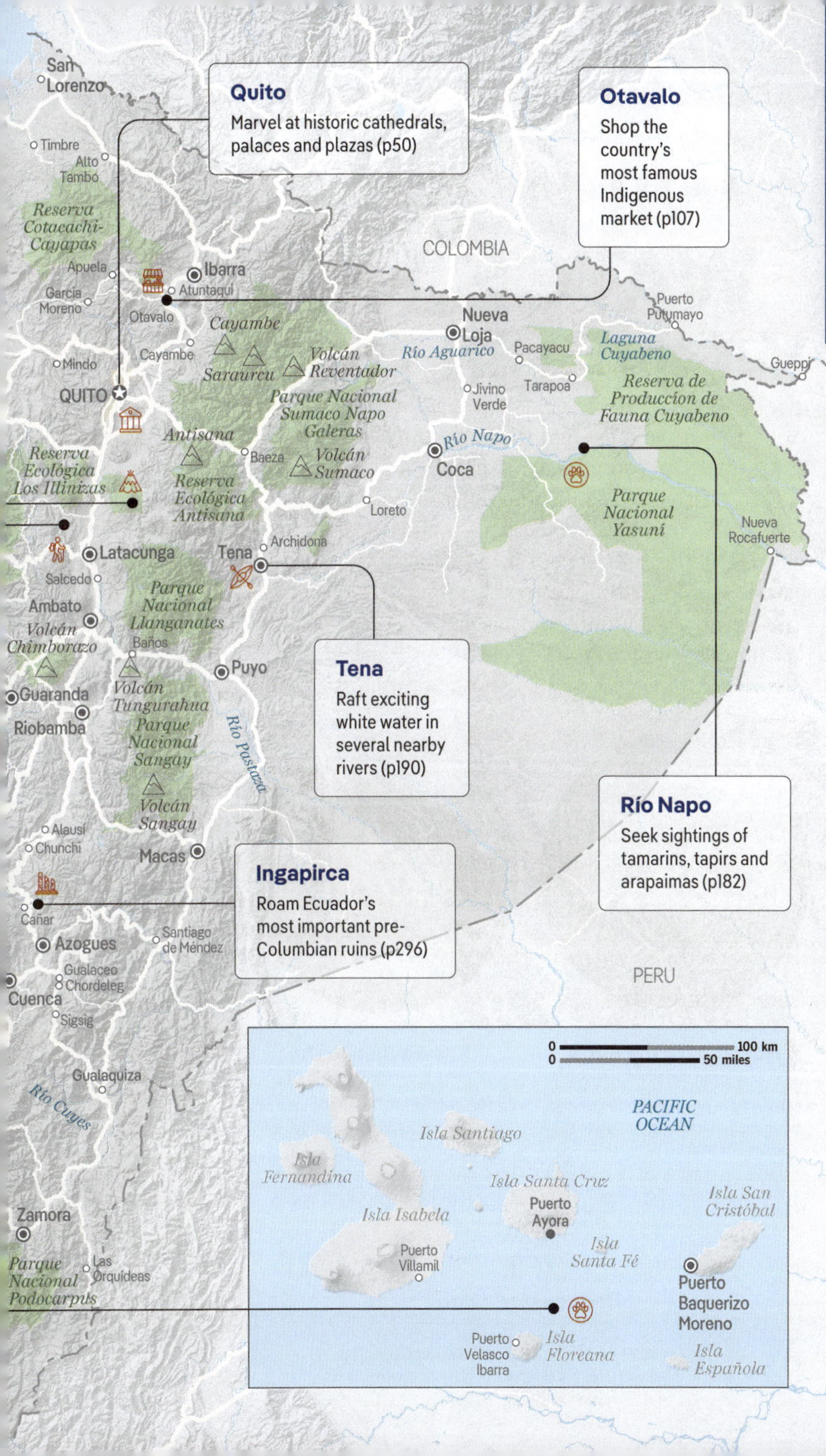
Quito
Marvel at historic cathedrals, palaces and plazas (p50)
Otavalo
Shop the country's most famous Indigenous market (p107)
Tena
Raft exciting white water in several nearby rivers (p190)
Río Napo
Seek sightings of tamarins, tapirs and arapaimas (p182)
Ingapirca
Roam Ecuador's most important pre-Columbian ruins (p296)
San Lorenzo
Timbre
Alto Tambo
Reserva Cotacachi-Cayapas
Apuela
García Moreno
Ibarra
Atuntaqui
Otavalo
Cayambe
Cayambe
Saraurcu
Volcán Reventador
Mindo
QUITO
Parque Nacional Sumaco Napo Galeras
Antisana
Baeza
Volcán Sumaco
Reserva Ecológica Los Illinizas
Reserva Ecológica Antisana
COLOMBIA
Nueva Loja
Río Aguarico
Pacayacu
Laguna Cuyabeno
Puerto Putumayo
Güeppí
Reserva de Producción de Fauna Cuyabeno
Tarapoa
Jivino Verde
Río Napo
Coca
Loreto
Parque Nacional Yasuní
Nueva Rocafuerte
Archidona
Latacunga
Tena
Salcedo
Parque Nacional Llanganates
Ambato
Volcán Chimborazo
Baños
Puyo
Guaranda
Volcán Tungurahua
Riobamba
Parque Nacional Sangay
Río Pastaza
Volcán Sangay
Alausí
Chunchi
Macas
Cañar
Azogues
Santiago de Méndez
Gualaceo
Chordeleg
Cuenca
Sigsig
PERU
Gualaquiza
Río Cuyes
Zamora
Parque Nacional Podocarpus
Las Orquídeas
0 100 km
0 50 miles
PACIFIC OCEAN
Isla Santiago
Isla Fernandina
Isla Santa Cruz
Puerto Ayora
Isla San Cristóbal
Isla Isabela
Puerto Villamil
Isla Santa Fé
Puerto Baquerizo Moreno
Puerto Velasco Ibarra
Isla Floreana
Isla Española

WILDLIFE-WATCHING WONDERLAND

Catch multiple once-in-a-lifetime wildlife-watching encounters in a single trip, from pink river dolphins to rare spectacled Andean bears, equatorial penguins and giant Galápagos tortoises. Ecuador may be modest in size, but it bursts with spectacular biodiversity in both remote and populated corners of the country. Rich flora and fauna live on the islands where Darwin's theory of evolution sparked into existence, as well as on the mainland.

FROM LEFT: SL-PHOTOGRAPHY/SHUTTERSTOCK, ROBERT HARDING VIDEO/SHUTTERSTOCK, ANIMALGRAPHY/SHUTTERSTOCK

Not Just for the Birds

Even if you're not a certified twitcher, bringing a pair of binoculars to the Amazon or Mindo (pictured) adds to the excitement of crazy-cool bird and wildlife sightings.

Know When to Go

The wildlife in the Galápagos moves to nature's rhythm – if you've got a bucket-list animal you want to see, check migration patterns and seasons before booking tickets.

Underwater Video

Many snorkeling guides have underwater cams and share video with guests afterward, but not always. BYO if video footage is a priority.

Sea lion, Isla Fernandina (p340)

BEST WILDLIFE EXPERIENCES

Frolic with sea lions, marvel at giant tortoises and find blue-footed boobies in the mythic islands of the ❶ **Galápagos** (p317).

Travel the lower ❷ **Río Napo** (p182) into the Amazon jungle to look for golden-mantled tamarins, prehistoric-looking hoazin and pink river dolphins.

Check a few birds off your list in ❸ **Mindo** (p126), which has more than 500 species, including cock-of-the-rock, quetzal and rare Leydebamba antpitta.

Hike in ❹ **Maquipucuna Reserve** (p131) for a great chance to sight rare spectacled bears, most readily seen from August to November.

Board a whale-watching boat from ❺ **Puerto López** (p273) during humpback migration season to see these majestic cetaceans.

HIKING & TREKKING THE ANDES

More than 20% of Ecuador's land is protected in natural reserves or parks, and 10 of its peaks top out above 5000m. Experienced mountaineers will find plenty of tempting challenges to tackle, while avid hikers are spoiled for choice with day hikes and longer treks ranging from sea-level lava fields to cloud forest and *páramo* (high-altitude grassland). Move through this breadth of ecosystems on foot to absorb Ecuador's abundant natural beauty.

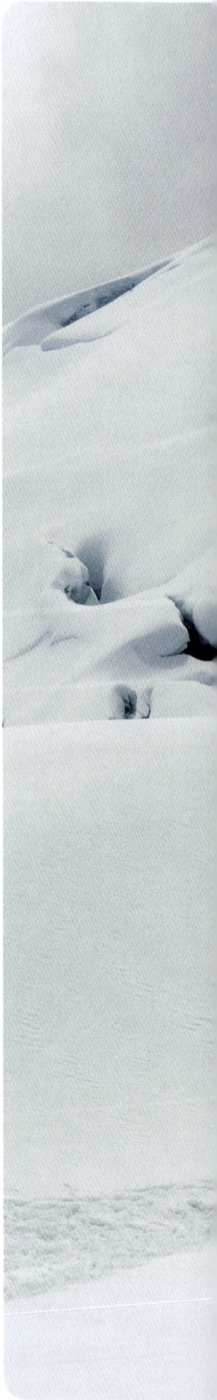

Acclimatize

Allow a day or two to acclimatize to the altitude (p43) before setting out on a multiday trek, especially on serious mountaineering expeditions.

Summitting Not Required

If you're not on a peak-bagging mission, you can still hike kilometers of spectacular trails on the slopes and bases of Ecuador's volcanoes.

Check Changing Conditions

Check conditions on arrival – Volcań Cotopaxi reopened in 2024 following a closure spurred by a 2022 eruption, but conditions can always change.

Volcán Cotopaxi (p214)

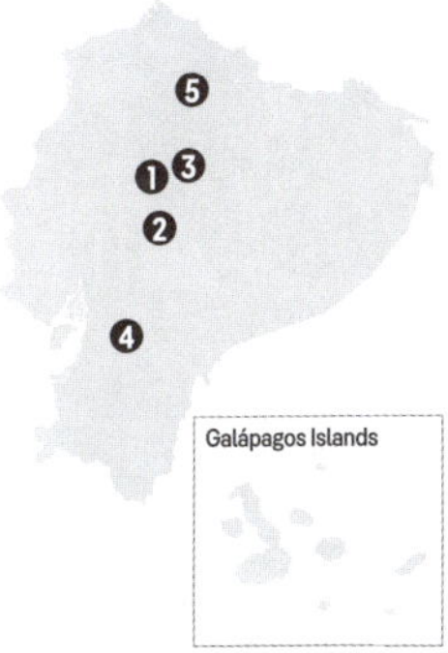

BEST HIKING & TREKKING EXPERIENCES

Trek the 1 **Quilotoa Loop** (p220) through indigenous villages and artist communities, past Laguna Quilotoa, which local people believe to be bottomless.

Summit the closest terrestrial point to the sun with a climb on 2 **Volcán Chimborazo** (p238) – for experienced mountaineers only.

Admire the perfectly conical 3 **Volcán Cotopaxi** (p214) from the plains below or make your way up its snowcapped peak.

Hike through delicate Andean moors at 4 **Parque Nacional Cajas** (p295), winding around shimmering lakes and through mist-covered dwarf forests.

Circumnavigate the rim of 5 **Laguna Cuicocha** (p110) for gorgeous views of the crater lake and islands.

JON CHICA/SHUTTERSTOCK

Catedral de la Inmaculada Concepción (p287), Cuenca

COLONIAL BUILDINGS

Anchoring Ecuador's cities with large central plazas, the elaborately wrought cathedrals and churches established by the Spanish date back as far as the 16th century. Highlighting their Andean cities, the well-trodden plazas and parks often spill out onto nearby streets filled with colonial facades and cobblestone alleys, while some house regional or art museums.

Sacred Sites

Many of Quito's churches were built on top of sacred indigenous sites, including **Iglesia y Convento de San Francisco** (p63).

Quito Vertigo

Brave the climb to the top of the tower at the **Basílica del Voto Nacional** (p57) for a vertiginous 360-degree view of Quito.

BEST ARCHITECTURE EXPERIENCES

Rove the plazas, palaces, cathedrals and monasteries of Quito's UNESCO-listed ❶ **Centro Histórico** (p56), some of which were centuries in the making.

Soak up the sociable atmosphere of ❷ **Cuenca's** (p286) photogenic historic center, awash with centuries-old churches and plazas.

Wander the cobbled streets, colonial churches and plazas of ❸ **Latacunga** (p224), enhanced by the dramatic backdrop of Volcán Cotopaxi.

Visit ❹ **Riobamba's** (p240) historic parks and churches, including the neoclassical basilica.

Stroll ❺ **Loja** (p304), the far south's largest city, where the narrow streets of its colorful colonial heart are lined with meticulously renovated old mansions.

COASTAL LEISURE

Beaches may not be Ecuador's top attraction, but it has its share of gorgeous shoreline. The country's most beautiful mainland beach has all the soft sand and turquoise waters of dreamy, jungle-fringed beach fantasies, and the Galápagos Islands are pocked with sandy coves where you'll sunbathe and swim alongside unfussed local wildlife.

FROM LEFT: UWE-BERGWITZ/GETTY IMAGES, CHAMSKI/SHUTTERSTOCK

Weekday Lull

Ecuadorian families and friend groups love hitting the beach on weekends, so you're more likely to find smaller crowds on a weekday.

Hydrate Well

Bring plenty of water with you, as you'll often have to hike under the hot sun to reach your beach of choice.

Rainy-Season Rules

Rainy season from December through May is actually the best time to hit the beach – skies are clear between rains, with fewer clouds and less humidity.

BEST BEACH EXPERIENCES

Hike through the dry tropical forest of Parque Nacional Machalilla to ❶ **Los Frailes** (pictured left; p276), the long, white beach considered the most beautiful on mainland Ecuador.

Grab an empanada and walk down Isla Isabela's massive ❷ **Puerto Villamil Beach** (p336) for a perfect sunset stroll.

Take a dip in a white-sand cove sheltered by a lava headland at uncrowded ❸ **Puerto Chino** (p335) on Isla San Cristóbal.

Traverse the arid landscape dotted with palo santo and opuntia cactus to the wild stretch of ❹ **Tortuga Bay** (p325) on Isla Santa Cruz.

Surrender to beachside relaxation in ❺ **Mompiche** (p148), a charming surf town known for its low-key vibes.

PRE-COLUMBIAN HISTORY

Though some extant Inca ruins remain, the Inca presence was preceded by other communities, the earliest being the Valdivia, who settled along the Santa Elena Peninsula more than 5500 years ago. Most of what modern visitors can experience of pre-Columbian history exists in artifacts and archaeological interpretation, but it's still possible to walk in ancient places and listen for whispers of the Cañari, Puruhá, Quitus and Omagua people who came before.

Coastal Habitation

Although the majority of indigenous people today live in the highlands and the Oriente, Ecuador's coastline supported the densest populations in pre-Inca times.

Poetic Injustice

Manco Capac, the last Inca ruler, staged one of the greatest revolts against the Spanish. He was killed by a Spaniard whose life he had saved.

Vast Inca Empire

At the height of its empire, the Inca ruled more than 12 million people across some 1 million sq km.

FROM LEFT: ARNE THIELENHAUS/SHUTTERSTOCK, UNIVERSAL ART ARCHIVE/ALAMY, ROBERT GIBSON Z/SHUTTERSTOCK

Parque Arquelógico Cochasquí (p106)

BEST PRE-COLUMBIAN HISTORY EXPERIENCES

Visit ❶ **Ingapirca** (p296), Ecuador's most important pre-Columbian ruins, built by the Cañari and later expanded by the Incas.

Wander through the history of Ecuador's indigenous cultures at the ❷ **Museo del Banco Central Pumapungo** (p290), which backs onto Inca ruins.

Encounter remnants of the Río Napo's Omagua civilization at the ❸ **Museo Arqueológico Centro Cultural Orellana** (p188).

Hear the story of buried lovers and the Las Vegas and Valdivia cultures at the ❹ **Museo los Amantes de Sumpa** (p265), just outside Salinas.

Roam northern Ecuador's largest pre-Columbian complex at ❺ **Cochasquí** (p106) and learn about the Carranqui people's huge solar and lunar observatories.

Volcán Cotopaxi (p214)

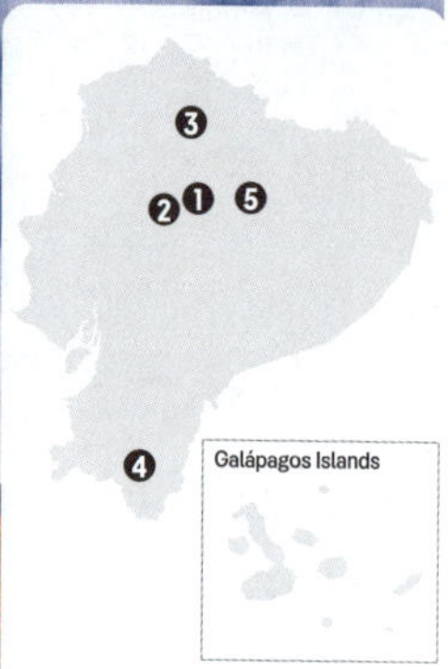

ECUADORPOSTALES/SHUTTERSTOCK

DYNAMIC OUTDOORS

Smoldering, glacier-topped Andean volcanoes loom out of the landscape across Ecuador. From literally breathtaking heights, their slopes transition into windswept *páramo,* while further below, tropical cloud forest sips from fog and sustains a delicate system of biodiversity.

Volcanic Eruptions

Of the eight volcanoes in Ecuador that have erupted in the past 20 years, three – Fernandina, Reventador and Sangay – erupted as recently as 2024 and 2025.

A Complex River System

Ecuador's Amazon basin is largely defined by the Río Napo, the country's main tributary of the Amazon River, which originates in the Andean highlands.

BEST OUTDOOR EXPERIENCES

Take in iconic views of ❶ **Volcán Cotopaxi** (p214) – which may or may not be erupting – for snowcapped Andean drama.

Marvel at the deep, reflective colors and stunning mountain setting of ❷ **Laguna Quilotoa** (p220), the crater lake considered Ecuador's most beautiful.

Watch mist swirl through the Andean cloud forests of the ❸ **Intag Valley** (p122), a biodiversity hot spot for endemic orchids and frogs.

Trek on foot or horseback in the forested mountains around ❹ **Vilcabamba** (p310), among the loveliest settings in the Ecuadorian Andes.

Climb the steep, gravel-covered slopes of Ecuador's most active volcano, ❺ **Volcán Reventador** (176), for front-row views of its explosions.

ARTISANS & MARKET DAYS

Artisan traditions are alive and well in Ecuador, jamming market stalls with pieces and sustaining workshops throughout the country. Find hat makers creating classic Montecristi (aka Panama) hats in Cuenca shops, Kichwa weavers hand-looming fine textiles in highland Gualaceo, and the Shuar community beading seed jewelry in the Oriente.

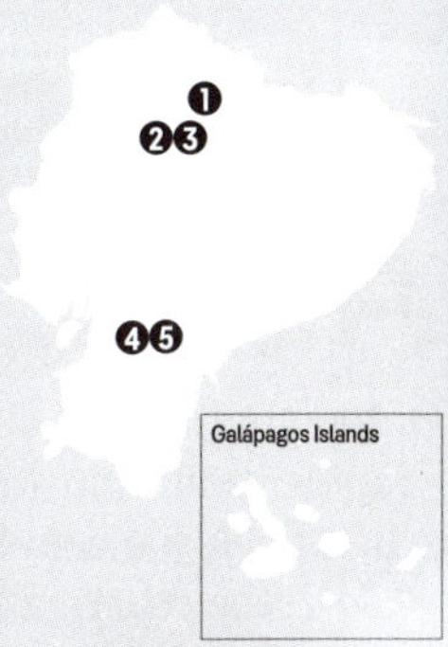

FROM LEFT: ANGELA MEIER/SHUTTERSTOCK, JOEL BALSAM

Catching Market Days

If you're walking the Quilotoa Loop, time your circuit to hit the weekly craft markets (p218) at the villages along the way. Don't miss Guamote's vibrant Thursday market.

Montecristi Hats

You can still find a handmade *sombrero de paja toquilla* (don't call it a Panama!) in the place of its origin – coastal Montecristi.

Pretty Poison

The attractive little red-and-black *huayruro* seed, used extensively in indigenous jewelry in the Oriente, is toxic when ingested. Keep away from children and pets.

BEST ARTISAN EXPERIENCES

Delight your senses with the vivid energy of the Saturday market in ❶ **Otavalo** (p107), where indigenous artisans and tourists converge.

Peruse the hundreds of stalls in Quito's ❷ **Mercado Artesanal La Mariscal** (p70) for handmade artisanal souvenirs amid the mass-produced stuff.

Wander Cuenca's many bustling ❸ **marketplaces** (p292) to pick up some unique handmade souvenirs, such as *cuy* roasters or more practical ceramics and basketry.

Watch ❹ **Cuenca's** (p292) master hat makers turn fibers into fine *sombreros de paja toquillo*, Ecuador's famed headwear.

Poke around tiny ❺ **Gualaceo, Chordeleg and Sigsig** (p299), each with its own specialty handicrafts made using age-old techniques.

ADRENALINE ADVENTURES

Outdoor adventure abounds in the ocean swells, river rapids, mountainsides and jungles across Ecuador. In a week you could conceivably surf a few breaks along the coast, raft one of the rivers out of Tena, mountain bike down the slope of Volcán Chimborazo or Cotopaxi and go canyoning in the jungles of the deep southeast. Even if you can't do it all, it's easy to fit in an epic adventure or two along your journey.

FROM LEFT: VICTOR CAICEDO TOBAR/SHUTTERSTOCK, BARNA TANKO/SHUTTERSTOCK, KAMRAN ALI/SHUTTERSTOCK

Outdoor Mindo

Mindo (p126) is beginning to rival Baños for outdoor adventures such as tubing, quad riding and mountain biking, and a cable car whirring over the jungle canopy.

Camping by Horseback

For a lower-speed, high-payoff wilderness adventure, go horse trekking and camping in the rugged mountains outside Vilcabamba (p310).

Adrenaline Hangover

Nurse your adrenaline comedown and sore muscles with a soak in the thermal spring waters of Papallacta (p174).

La Casa del Arbol (p234)

BEST ADRENALINE EXPERIENCES

Cruise the south coast's Ruta del Surf in search of the perfect wave, starting in ❶ **Montañita** (p269).

Raft the rivers around ❷ **Tena** (p190), which offer both exhilarating runs and gentle floats through scenic countryside.

Get your gravity on with zip-lining, bungee jumping and rafting around ❸ **Baños** (p231), Ecuador's outdoor-adventure capital.

Mountain bike down the side of an active volcano for an exhilarating experience of ❹ **Volcán Cotopaxi** (p214).

Pedal across the top of the cloud-forest canopy on a skybike at ❺ **Mashpi** (p132) lodge outside Mindo.

INDIGENOUS CULTURAL IMMERSION

Indigenous culture is a vibrant entity in Ecuador. Though the Kichwa make up the great majority of the country's indigenous population, the beautiful diversity of tiny groups between the coast, Andes and Amazon illustrates the importance of supporting their cultural preservation. Seek out Indigenous-led tourism projects where communities share their culture and knowledge on their own terms, while giving insight into their long-practiced traditions and deep connections with their lands.

Ecuador's Indigenous Communities

Fourteen distinct indigenous communities reside in Ecuador: the Achuar, Andoa, Awa, Chachi, Cofán, Epera, Kichwa (pictured), Secoya, Shiwiar, Shuar, Siona, Tsáchila, Waorani and Zápara.

Tour Local

Community-based tourism is baked into Amazon lodge stays, but indigenous-led experiences can also be arranged in coastal and highland communities.

Photo Permissions

Always ask permission before taking pictures of anyone. If they decline, be respectful and refrain.

Artisan, Tena (p190)

BEST INDIGENOUS CULTURAL EXPERIENCES

Learn some of the traditional ways of the Otavalo Kichwa from a woman's perspective at a village homestay in ❶ **La Calera** (p113).

Visit the town of ❷ **Salasaca** (p230), where the predominantly Kichwa community carries on traditional wool-spinning and hand-weaving.

Go off-grid to overnight in ❸ **Kichwa villages** (p300) around Saraguro, where self-sufficient mountain communities maintain a traditional Andean way of life.

Travel down the ❹ **Río Napo** (p204) to a riverside indigenous village deep in the rainforest to discover its timeless traditions.

Take a trip into Yasuní with the Huaorani-owned ❺ **Otobo's Amazon Safari** (p187), learning all about the area's wildlife and cultural history.

ECUADOR'S LIFE AQUATIC

The Galápagos Islands are on the bucket lists of many divers and snorkelers for good reasons, among them curious sea lions and serene sea turtles unfazed by human visitors. The equatorial marine ecosystem 1000km off the coast teems with life, seasonally infused with even richer biodiversity from cold upwellings of the Humboldt and Cromwell currents. If your travels aren't taking you to the islands, there's great snorkeling at the 'Little Galápagos' off the mainland south coast.

Seasonal Conditions

Galápagos waters are warmer and calmer from January to June, though the cold, nutrient-rich Humboldt Current attracts greater numbers of wildlife from July to December.

Wetsuit Weather

In the Galápagos' hotter season, water temps average 24°C (swimsuits suffice). Opt in when snorkeling tours offer wetsuits in cool season.

Liveaboard or Land-Based

Divers are best booking dedicated liveaboard dive trips, while snorkelers will see lots of wildlife on land-based day trips.

FROM LEFT: NPAVLOV/SHUTTERSTOCK, ALEKSEI KORNEV/SHUTTERSTOCK, MICHAEL NOLAN/ALAMY

Galápagos penguin, Isla Bartolomé (p329)

BEST DIVING & SNORKELING EXPERIENCES

Cross paths with speedy Galápagos penguins – if you're lucky – in the shadow of Isla Bartolomé's ❶ **Pinnacle Rock** (p329).

Wall dive at ❷ **Kicker Rock** (p334) to look for hammerhead sharks, sea turtles, and whitetip and blacktip sharks.

Explore the submerged lava caves of ❸ **Los Túneles** (p339) to chill with sea turtles, sleeping reef sharks and camouflaged seahorses.

Let the current carry you around ❹ **Devil's Crown** (p345) amid colorful reef fish and sharks.

Dive with giant manta rays at ❺ **Isla de la Plata** (p276) – the best season is July to early October, coinciding with the humpback migration.

REGIONS & CITIES

Find the places that tick all your boxes.

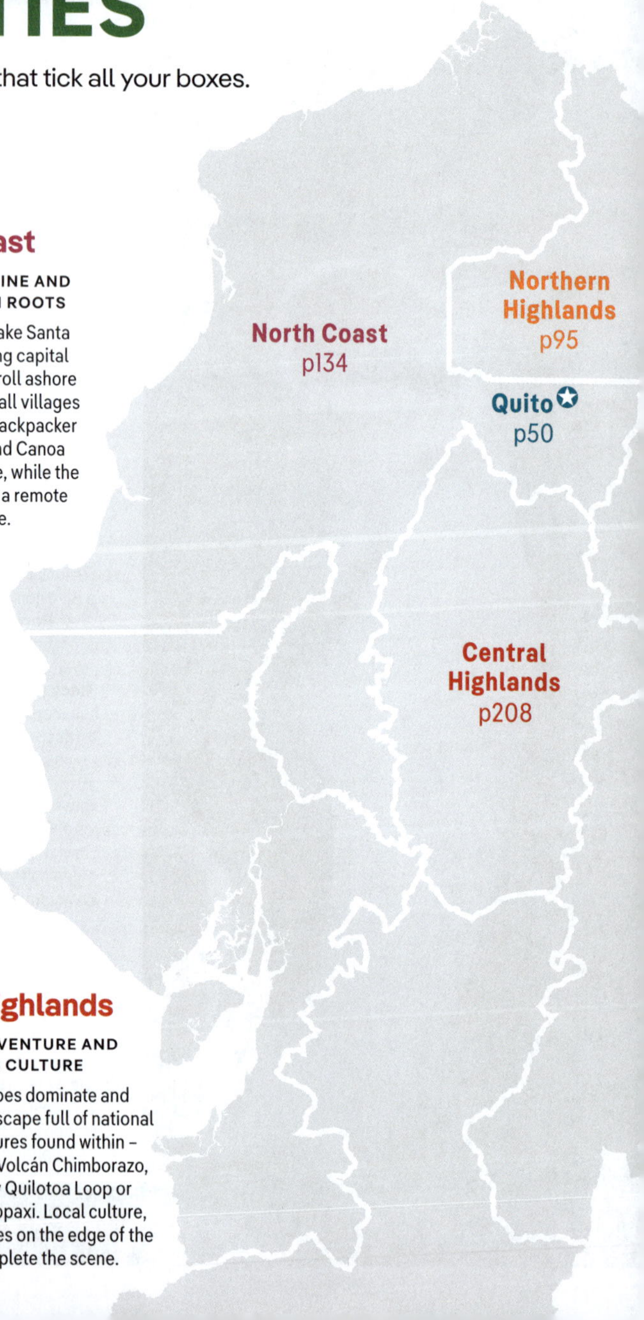

North Coast

UNSPOILED COASTLINE AND AFRO-ECUADORIAN ROOTS

Surf's up. The winds make Santa Marianita the kitesurfing capital of Ecuador, and breaks roll ashore along the coast near small villages or verdant jungle. The backpacker towns of Mompiche and Canoa keep the party vibe alive, while the steamy lowlands offer a remote tropical reserve.

Central Highlands

VOLCANOES, ADVENTURE AND INDIGENOUS CULTURE

Glaciers and volcanoes dominate and shape this soaring landscape full of national parks and the adventures found within – mountain biking down Volcán Chimborazo, trekking the multiday Quilotoa Loop or summiting Volcán Cotopaxi. Local culture, historic towns and slopes on the edge of the Amazon Basin complete the scene.

Northern Highlands

STRONGHOLD OF TRADITIONAL HIGHLAND LIFESTYLE

Most famous for Otavalo's traditional markets, which burst with colorful textiles, the Northern Highlands might represent peak Ecuador. From glacier-topped Volcán Cayambe to the crater lagoon of Cuicocha, the Andes define the landscape. Lower-altitude appeals include cloud-forest bird-watching around Mindo and the rural way of life in the Intag Valley.

Quito

ECUADOR'S HIGH-ALTITUDE, CULTURE-RICH CAPITAL

At 2850m above sea level, Quito climbs partway up the slopes of Volcán Pinchincha and the surrounding hills. Large metropolitan parks, museums and the colonial architecture of its World Heritage–listed Old Town provide for plenty of urban exploration, complemented by diverse international cuisine, nightlife and traditional Ecuadorian markets.

The Oriente
p169

The Oriente

WILDLIFE, INDIGENOUS CULTURE AND DEEP FOREST IMMERSION

The steamy tropical sprawl of the Oriente covers more than one-third of the country, sloping from the eastern Andes to the Amazon Basin. The thermal pools of Papallacta and the white water of Tena spill down to vast tracts of spectacular biodiversity, accessible via river lodges at Cuyabeno and Parque Nacional Yasuní.

REGIONS & CITIES

Find the places that tick all your boxes.

Galápagos Islands (see enlargement; 1000km) ←

Galápagos Islands

LIVING, BREATHING BIRTHPLACE OF DARWINISM

A field trip to the natural lab of evolutionary theory, where equatorial penguins, swimming iguanas and giant centenarian tortoises actually exist. These islands embody balance between human habitation and environmental conservation. Hike a volcano, snorkel your heart out and watch sea lions show off.

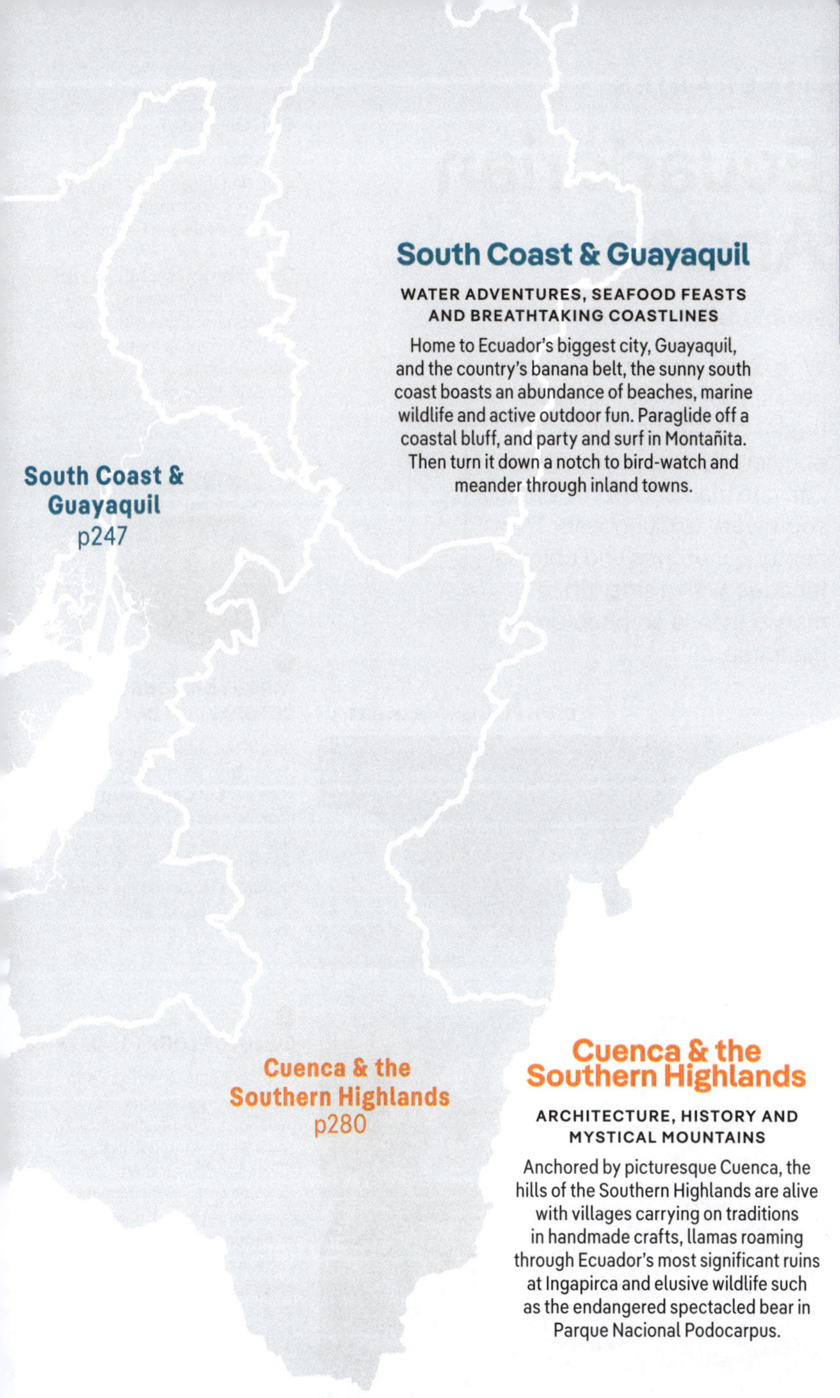

South Coast & Guayaquil

WATER ADVENTURES, SEAFOOD FEASTS AND BREATHTAKING COASTLINES

Home to Ecuador's biggest city, Guayaquil, and the country's banana belt, the sunny south coast boasts an abundance of beaches, marine wildlife and active outdoor fun. Paraglide off a coastal bluff, and party and surf in Montañita. Then turn it down a notch to bird-watch and meander through inland towns.

Cuenca & the Southern Highlands

ARCHITECTURE, HISTORY AND MYSTICAL MOUNTAINS

Anchored by picturesque Cuenca, the hills of the Southern Highlands are alive with villages carrying on traditions in handmade crafts, llamas roaming through Ecuador's most significant ruins at Ingapirca and elusive wildlife such as the endangered spectacled bear in Parque Nacional Podocarpus.

ITINERARIES

Ecuadorian Andes

Allow: 10 days **Distance**: 767km

With Quito nestled in Andean peaks, your intro to Ecuador begins at altitude. Take in ebullient Andean color at the Otavalo market before heading southward to Cuenca for 17th-century churches and colonial facades, with a side trip to marvel at Inca architecture at Ingapirca.

Cuenca's historic center (p286)

1 QUITO 1 DAY

In **Quito** (p50) spend a day exploring the architecture of the Old Town, such as the Iglesia y Convento de San Francisco, and viewing exquisite pre-Columbian artifacts at Casa del Alabado. In the evening, enjoy Ecuadorian cuisine with a view at Vista Hermosa followed by salsa, clubbing or cocktails in Mariscal Sucre or La Floresta.

2 PARQUE NACIONAL COTOPAXI 1 DAY

Take in the sublime *páramo* landscapes and mighty snow-cone peak of **Cotopaxi** (p212) – best enjoyed on foot, horseback or even from a hot tub! But for the ultimate view, put on the crampons to summit the world's highest active volcano.

3 QUILOTOA LOOP 3 DAYS

Hike the iconic **Quilotoa Loop** (p220) from Latacunga, slow traveling the old-fashioned way. You'll wander through highland villages, indigenous art galleries and weekly markets, if you time your trek right. The undulating route meanders through cloud forests and valleys, with views of Quilotoa's spectacular crater lake to top it all off.

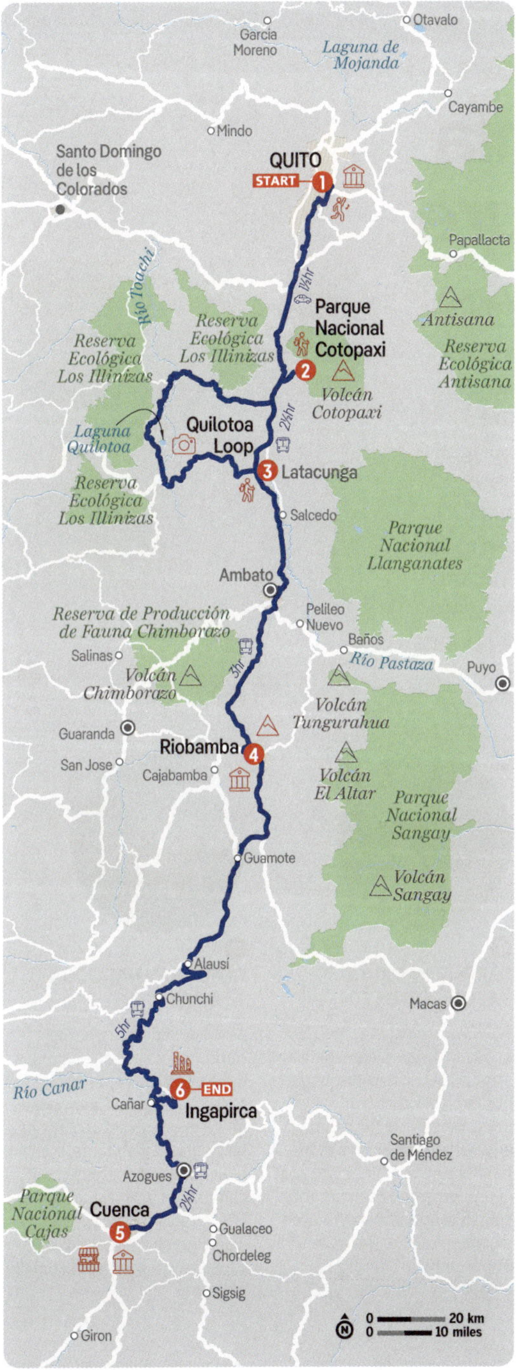

4

RIOBAMBA ⏱ 2 DAYS

Continue southward through the highlands to **Riobamba** (p240), rich with indigenous culture and historic colonial architecture. This appealing Andean city is worth a couple of days, and is an excellent base for high-altitude adventures to Volcán Chimborazo, whether to hike up the slopes of Ecuador's highest peak or bomb down them on a mountain bike.

5

CUENCA ⏱ 2 DAYS

Unabashedly pretty **Cuenca** (p286) invites a wander for its colonial architecture, plazas and cathedrals, and riverside atmosphere. Visit the Museo Pumapungo and shop the low-pressure Cemuart craft market, fueling your walks with the city's diverse cuisine, craft beer and ice cream.

6

INGAPIRCA ⏱ 1 DAY

The archaeological site of **Ingapirca** (p296), Ecuador's best-preserved Inca ruins, lies two hours northwest of Cuenca. Now reduced to stone-wall remnants and the Temple of the Sun, the site was originally established by the Cañari people, while the grassy spaces between are now roamed by grazing llamas. Return to Cuenca to fly back to Quito.

ITINERARIES

Amazonía Adventure

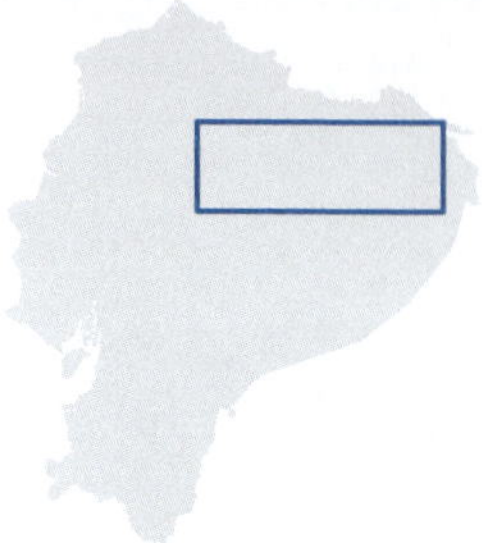

Allow: 9 days **Distance:** 490km

Fly into tropical, lowland Coca to board a canoe into the Amazon Basin. Explore the Parque Nacional Yasuní jungle, introduced by its indigenous communities and filled with otherworldly wildlife. Then road trip back to Quito, climbing into the highlands to raft white water and soak in mountain hot springs.

1

COCA ½ DAY

Fly from Quito to **Coca** (p182), gateway to the Amazon Basin. Coca is a real-deal Amazonian hub, where the road ends and guarded terrestrial access to rainforest oil fields begins. Before heading down the Río Napo to your river lodge, make a point to stroll the small-town *malecón* (waterfront) and visit the excellent Museo Arqueológico Centro Cultural Orellana.

2

PARQUE NACIONAL YASUNÍ 4 DAYS

From your river lodge, you'll head out to this biodiversity **hot spot** (p184) deep in the jungle in search of wild parrots at clay licks, monkeys in the canopy and perhaps an elusive tapir. From the canoe, you might spot half-submerged caimans, the splash of an arapaima, or even a giant river otter. Take the opportunity to stay in a Kichwa village.

3

LAGUNA PAÑACOCHA ½ DAY

As a side trip down the Río Napo, or if your lodge happens to be based there, the still waters of **Laguna Pañacocha** (p189) might reveal some of its fascinating inhabitants: hoatzin, piranhas and hopefully some glimpses of pink river dolphins. The lagoon, sheltered in lush jungle greenery, feels like an especially pristine pocket of the Amazon.

FROM LEFT: CURIOSO.PHOTOGRAPHY/SHUTTERSTOCK, SL-PHOTOGRAPHY/SHUTTERSTOCK, FOTOS593/SHUTTERSTOCK

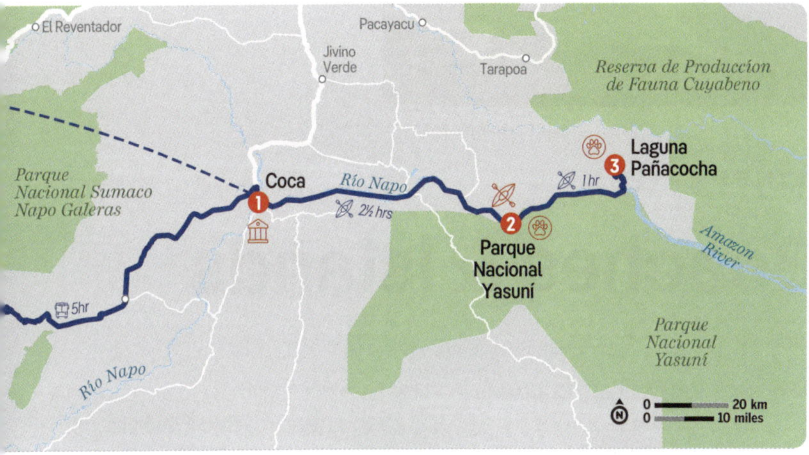

4

TENA 2 DAYS

Catch a bus from Coca to **Tena** (p190) and post up at a *hostal* (small hotel) in this friendly and pleasant town, at its best in the evenings along its riverfront center. Tena makes a great base for rafting trips, as it's positioned near several rivers and has well-established rafting outfitters ready to take you on gentle jungle floats and white-water adventures.

5

BAEZA 1 DAY

Bus north from Tena to **Baeza** (p180), the crossroads of mountain passes and a quaint base for more rafting in a less urban setting. For nature lovers, this is a step up from Tena in both atmosphere – think sparse montane village – and altitude. Hike and bird-watch, enjoy the cool mountain air in Baeza Antigua and kayak exciting Class III+ white water on the Río Quijos.

6

PAPALLACTA 1 DAY

End your trip with a hot-spring soak before heading back to Quito. The thermal springs of **Papallacta** (p174) steam away within the mountains about an hour's drive from Quito's airport, making it a reasonably convenient spot to relax ahead of a long flight. Day passes are available at Termas de Papallacta, the largest, most developed resort – you can also lodge here overnight, or at other nearby *hostals*.

FROM LEFT: ANGELA N PERRYMAN/SHUTTERSTOCK, ANGELA N PERRYMAN/SHUTTERSTOCK, SL-PHOTOGRAPHY/SHUTTERSTOCK

NPAVLOV/SHUTTERSTOCK

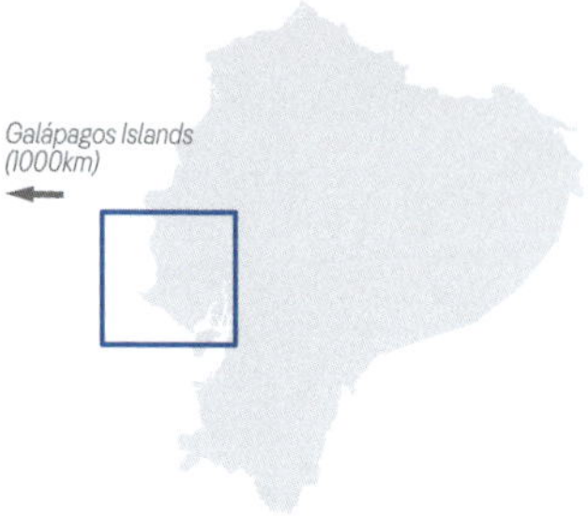

Isla Bartolomé (p329)

ITINERARIES

Beaches & Islands

Allow: 8 days **Distance:** 1500km

Hike, surf and chill at Ecuador's inviting beaches, with a dose of jungle and beach parties, before flying west to the near-mythic Galápagos Islands. Spend four days minimum in the archipelago, but extend that visit as long as you can for maximum wildlife encounters in this once-in-a-lifetime locale.

1

SALINAS 1 DAY

For a more Miami Beach kind of experience, head west to admire the crashing ocean at mainland South America's westernmost point, **La Chocolatera** (p266), before living it up and crashing for the night in **Salinas** (pictured; p261).

Detour: *On the way to Salinas from Guayaquil, spend a couple of hours enjoying a seaside lunch and nearly empty beach at* ***Playa Engabao*** *(p263).*

2

MONTAÑITA & OLÓN 1 DAY

Move up the coast to **Montañita** (pictured; p267) to play – surf your heart out, recover with some yoga and recharge with cocktails and dancing in Ecuador's coastal party capital. If you're keeping it simple and just want to surf or chill on the beach, opt for nearby **Olón** for a more peaceful vibe.

3

PARQUE NACIONAL MACHALILLA 1 DAY

Continue north to the fishing village of Puerto López, your base for visiting **Parque Nacional Machalilla** (p275) or Isla de la Plata – also known as Little Galápagos – if you're not moving on to the actual islands. At the national park, hike to, and revel in, the gorgeous beach and water at Los Frailes (pictured).

FROM LEFT: IRENEUKE/SHUTTERSTOCK, FOTOGRIN/SHUTTERSTOCK, ELISA LOCCI/SHUTTERSTOCK

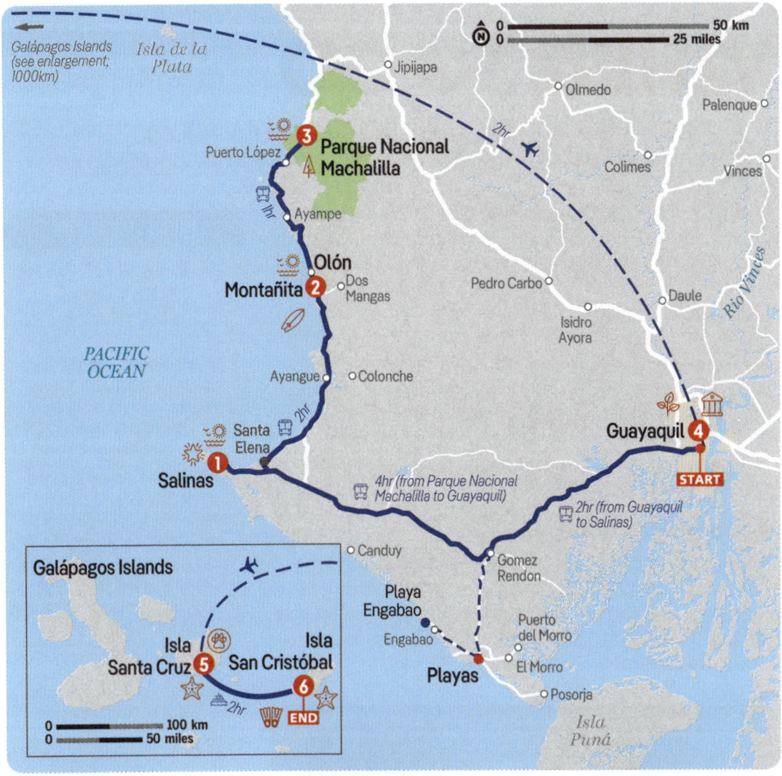

4

GUAYAQUIL ⏱ 1 DAY

Return to **Guayaquil** (p252) and stroll the Malecón 2000 to soak up some coastal urban vivacity. Enjoy the energy of *guayaquileños* in the waterfront parks, playgrounds and gardens, and learn everything about the history and origins of chocolate at Museo del Cacao, snagging a taste of the sweet at a nearby cafe. Then prep for your morning flight to the Galápagos Islands.

5

ISLA SANTA CRUZ ⏱ 2 DAYS

On **Isla Santa Cruz** (p322), your intro to this wildlife wonderland begins with meadows of grazing giant tortoises and urban sea lions napping on the *malecón*. Take a day trip to an outlying island such as Bartolomé or Seymour Norte to hike through lava landscapes and snorkel with sharks and sea turtles.

6

ISLA SAN CRISTÓBAL ⏱ 2 DAYS

Ferry or fly to **Isla San Cristóbal** (p330), downshifting to a slower pace, and walking to beaches and the lovely bay at Las Tijeretas to snorkel with sea turtles, sea lions and reef fish. Take the 360° tour day trip to Kicker Rock to swim above hammerhead sharks and walk on the pearly sands of Bahía Rosa Blanca.

FROM LEFT: LEONID ANDRONOV/SHUTTERSTOCK, NATASHAFA/SHUTTERSTOCK, SL-PHOTOGRAPHY/SHUTTERSTOCK

WHEN TO GO

Very generally speaking, Ecuador has two seasons: dry and rainy, with weather varying markedly between the coast, Andes and Oriente.

Along the coast, the rainy season from December to April brings regular showers that leave the air fresh when the sun comes out again. The surf is best during this season, before Ecuadorians flock to the beaches around the Easter holidays, July and August.

The highlands start drying out in May, and are warmest from June through September. Weather cools down, with afternoon clouds and rain, from October to May.

In the Amazon, the seasons are rainy – and rainier. It's driest and hottest (with intermittent rain) from December to February. Rainy season means higher water, lusher flora and more active fauna, with heaviest rainfall in May and June.

Accommodations

Room rates are highest throughout Ecuador around Christmas and New Year, around Semana Santa (Easter week) and during July and August. They also peak during local fiestas. Hotels along the coast sometimes charge higher rates on weekends.

I LIVE HERE

NESTING QUETZALS

Alicia Noboa Imboden is co-owner of Agora Tours, located on Isla Isabela in the Galápagos. *@alicia_gps*

My favorite time is during the changing seasons, around November–December and April–May. That's when I love camping on the edge of the Sierra Negra Volcano. The sky feels impossibly clear and the sunset over the western side of the island is breathtaking. On perfect evenings, the full moon rises over the edge of the crater just as the last light fades – it feels like the most peaceful place on Earth.

Volcán El Altar, Parque Nacional Sangay (p243)

TROPICAL GLACIERS

Though endangered by climate change, Ecuador's tropical glaciers cap eight of the country's peaks, including Cotopaxi, El Altar and Sangay. The Antisana glacier (at higher than 5700m) represents a crucial percentage of Quito's water supply.

Weather through the Year: Quito

JANUARY	FEBRUARY	MARCH	APRIL	MAY	JUNE
Avg. daytime max: 21°C	Avg. daytime max: 21°C	Avg. daytime max: 20°C	Avg. daytime max: 21°C	Avg. daytime max: 21°C	Avg. daytime max: 21°C
Days of rainfall: 10	Days of rainfall: 11	Days of rainfall: 15	Days of rainfall: 15	Days of rainfall: 13	Days of rainfall: 7

WHERE CURRENTS CONVERGE

Five major ocean currents converge around the Galápagos Islands, affecting seasonal weather and wildlife. The cold, nutrient-rich Humboldt Current flows up the coast of South America, while the south-flowing Panama Current brings warm water from Central America. The rest flow east to west.

Major Festivals

Carnaval One of the best places to experience this is Ambato (p229), where Catholic tradition collides with the Fiesta de Frutas y Flores in a profusion of color and foamy water fights in the streets. **February/March**

Semana Santa (Holy Week; p293) Pageantry and processions fill the streets with rich color; traditions vary from town to town. **March/April**

Inti Raymi The Kichwa Festival of the Sun is celebrated in the Andes at the summer solstice with cleanses, feasts, music and dances. Larger celebrations happen in Otavalo and Ingapirca. **June**

Fiesta de la Mamá Negra (p224) Blending pre-Columbian, *criollo* and Catholic religious traditions, this Latacunga festival invokes the Virgen de las Mercedes and involves shamans spitting *aguardiente* at procession onlookers in *limpiezas* (cleanses). **September** and **November**

I LIVE HERE

WHALE-WATCHING

Luis Malave is a fishing guide, Spanish teacher and surf instructor who leads tours along Ecuador's South Coast. *outdoorecuador.com*

I've spent my entire life living on the coast of Olón, Ecuador, where the tropical climate lets me live and work outdoors year-round. On a misty July day we set out before dawn for a full day of fishing and surfing, navigating through pitch-black waters that shimmer with bioluminescence as humpback whales surface around us.

Humpback whales, Puerto López (p275)

Local Celebrations

Chonta Festival In Macas (p203), the most important Shuar celebration of the year honors the abundance of nature and is marked by the harvest of the chonta fruit, signaling a new natural cycle. **May**

El Día de la Virgen del Cisne The pilgrimage honors the Virgin Mary where she is carried from El Cisne, 70km west of Loja, to the departmental capital in one of the country's biggest religious festivals. **August**

El Retorno al Palenque de Libertad (p152) This festival celebrates the first community of African descendants in Ecuador with marches, bonfires and music. **November**

Fiestas de Quito (p65) This weeklong shindig celebrates the foundation of the city in 1534. Quito's Old Town is the hub of festivities, though they spread out over the city's neighborhoods. **December**

GALÁPAGOS WEATHER

Calmer ocean coincides with warmer, wetter weather from December to May, when water temps average 24°C. Waters are rougher and temps cooler from June to December, but wildlife is more abundant. Shoulder season from August to October sees fewer crowds.

JULY	AUGUST	SEPTEMBER	OCTOBER	NOVEMBER	DECEMBER
Avg. daytime max: 22°C	Avg. daytime max: 22°C	Avg. daytime max: 22°C	Avg. daytime max: 22°C	Avg. daytime max: 21°C	Avg. daytime max: 21°C
Days of rainfall: 5	Days of rainfall: 5	Days of rainfall: 11	Days of rainfall: 14	Days of rainfall: 11	Days of rainfall: 11

Volcán Sierra Negra (p341)

GET PREPARED FOR ECUADOR

Useful things to load in your bag, your ears and your brain.

Clothes

Rain jacket There's a good chance you'll encounter some rain, even in drier seasons. You can get by with a lightweight, water-repellent layer for most parts of the country, but if you're spending any time in the rainforest (rain is built right into the name!), you'll need a solid rain jacket with a hood for Amazon deluges.

Layers As Ecuador's climate can vary dramatically from lowlands to highlands in any season, think in terms of layers. Quito and the rest of the highlands can get chilly even in the daytime, so bring a sweater or fleece and a jacket that fits over a bulkier layer. Mountaineers will know to bring burly, waterproof gear.

Hat Here at the equator, you're closer to the sun, especially at elevation. Bring a hat for sun protection.

Manners

Polite greetings customarily precede any interaction. Start with *'Bueno/as días (tardes/noches)!'* before asking directions or how much something costs.

Bargain gracefully at local markets. Simply walk away if you feel a price is too high, but remember that vendors are trying to make a living.

Tip guides and drivers for good service. Tips (propinas) are not expected at restaurants that include service charges.

READ

The Villagers (Jorge Icaza; 1934) Seminal novel detailing the story of a landowner and his exploitation of indigenous villagers.

The Mapmaker's Wife (Robert Whitaker; 2004) True story of Amazon hardships faced by an Ecuadorian woman in the 1700s.

Cockfight (María Fernanada Ampuero; 2018) Short stories steeped in contemporary Ecuadorian politics, religion and class.

Carnaval Fever (Yuliana Ortiz Ruano; 2022) Follows a young girl growing up in the Afro-Ecuadorian community of Esmeraldas in the 1990s.

Words

Hola (o-la) Hello.
Buenos días (bwen-os *dee*-as) 'Good morning,' but can also mean 'good day.'
Buenas tardes/noches (bwen-as *tar*-des/*no*-ches) Good afternoon and good evening; you could also use the latter to say goodbye for the evening, as in 'good night'.
Hasta luego (as-ta *lwe*-go) Literally 'until later', this is a more casual goodbye when parting ways, especially if you will see the person again.
Adiós (a-*dyos*) A more formal 'goodbye'. People in some regions may say 'adiós' as a passing greeting on the street.
¿Qué tal? (ke tal) How are you?
Bien, gracias (byen, *gra*-syas) Fine, thank you.
Gracias (*gra*-syas) Thank you.
De nada (de *na*-da) You're welcome.
Sí (see) Yes.
No (no) No.
Disculpe (dee-*skool*-pe) A polite way to say 'excuse me' to get someone's attention, or before asking a question.
Perdón (per-*don*) The way to say 'excuse me' in a more casual way, or if you've bumped into someone.
Lo siento (lo *syen*-to) I'm sorry.
Por favor (por fa-*vor*) Please.
La cuenta, por favor (la *kwen*-ta, por fa-*vor*) 'Check, please', at a restaurant or cafe. Using the universal gesture of writing something in the air is commonly understood to mean the same thing if you catch your server's eye.

WATCH

The Porcelain Horse (Javier Andrade; 2012) Examination of middle-class privilege, drugs and family dynamics.

How Much Further (Tania Hermida; 2006; pictured) Two young women road trip through Ecuador.

Rats, Mice, Petty Thieves (Sebastián Cordero; 1999) Action-drama about a small-time street punk and his criminal cousin.

In the Name of the Girl (Tania Hermida; 2011) A girl visiting her grandparents begins questioning everything she knows.

Women Wearing Shoulder Pads (Gonzalo Cordova; 2025) Stop-motion show set in 1980s Quito about a Spanish woman starting a business involving guinea pigs.

LISTEN

Exitos de Julio Jaramillo (JJ; 2010) The legendary Guayaquil-born JJ *('jota jota')* sang pop, *pasillo* and other traditional folk music.

Ishkay Llakta (Los NIN; 2023) Latest album from the indigenous hip-hop group (*'nin'*, in the group's name, means 'to say' in Kichwa).

La Corriente (Mirella Cesa; 2017) The 'mother of Andipop,' Mirella Cesa, integrates Andean elements into her catchy Latin pop.

Blanca (La Máquina Camaleón; 2023) Dreamy Ecuadorian psychedelic-tinged pop from a band whose experimental sounds continue to evolve.

JOEL BALSAM

Ceviche (left) and *encocado de pescado* (right)

THE FOOD SCENE

From the Pacific coast to the Andes and the Amazon, the threads of Ecuadorian cuisine tie the national identity together.

Ecuadorian cuisine is an adventure unto itself – from coastal catches to Andean staples and Amazonian fare, the country's culinary traditions naturally stem from the bounty of its vastly varying landscape. Many classic Ecuadorian dishes blend Spanish and indigenous influences, echoing the cuisine in neighboring Andean countries.

Culinary novelty abounds, as Ecuadorian chefs make creative and delicious use of corn and yuca (cassava), goat and *cuy* (guinea pig) and even the protein-packed larvae of the chonta palm. On the coast, seafood plays the starring role, with the usual sides of plantain prepared 1000 ways. Ceviches with coconut milk and peanut sauce provide twists on the basic dish, while fish and seafood also appear in other Ecuadorian favorites. Inland, meat and poultry take the stage alongside robust sides of rice and potatoes. Though the names might be the same, dishes can differ quite surprisingly from region to region, making the tasting adventure part of the joy of traveling in Ecuador.

Andean Traditions

Ecuador's dominant physical feature – the equatorial Andes – is an omnipresent influence on the national cuisine. Mountain fare like potatoes, corn and quinoa feature in numerous traditional dishes served across Ecuador. The rainbow of potato varieties are key to Ecuadorian specialties such as *llapingachos* and *locro de papas*, the creamy potato soup served with avocado and cheese, or *yaguarlocro*, potato

Best Ecuadorian Dishes

CEVICHE
Raw or steamed fish or shellfish marinated with lime juice, onions and chilies.

ENCEBOLLADO
Tuna soup with pickled onions and yuca – breakfast of champions.

LLAPINGACHOS
Potato fritters stuffed with cheese and fried until crispy.

BOLÓN DE VERDE
Fried breakfast dumpling of mashed plantain stuffed with cheese or meat.

and blood-sausage soup. Corn is equally ubiquitous, forming the basis of everything from salty street snacks to spiced highland desserts. Large grains of *choclo* (Peruvian corn) often round out soups in whole or pureed form, or accompany plates of *fritada* or *menus del día*. Ground fresh corn can be stuffed with cheese and steamed in its own husk to make *humitas* – akin to tamales – or the sweet version of *quimbolitos*.

Coastal Pleasures

Though ceviche can be found in much of Ecuador, it tastes best closest to the source. The most common version is made with shrimp (raw or steamed) marinated in lime or lemon juice with sliced onions, peppers and perhaps tomatoes and cilantro. Regional variations of ceviche read like a flavor map, as do variations of *cazuelas de mariscos* (seafood stews) and *encocado de pescado* (fish in coconut sauce). Have fish for breakfast also, especially in case of hangover, in the form of *encebollado*, the soul-saving tuna soup festooned with piquant pickled onions and hunks of stomach-soothing boiled yuca.

Indigenous Amazonía

In the Amazon Basin, yuca complements the wilderness bounty of river and jungle. Yuca is most widely prepared in the Oriente as flatbread – the cassava root is ground on a mortar, wrung of moisture and pan-cooked like a tortilla. Protein in the Amazon comes mostly from wild-caught river fish and larvae harvested from the chonta palm. *Maito* (fish wrapped in bijao leaf and cooked over fire) is a typical Oriente dish. Also destined for the grill are the *chontacuros* (beetle larvae), skewered for open flame or simply eaten raw.

Yuca

FROM LEFT: FOTOS593/SHUTTERSTOCK, ROBERT GIBSON Z/SHUTTERSTOCK

FIESTA DEL YAMOR

This colorful weeklong festival in Otavalo (p107) celebrates *yamor*, a traditional indigenous drink made with seven different kinds of corn unique to the Kichwa people of the region. Held at the beginning of September, the fiesta draws people from all over Ecuador for festivities that include dancing, live music, parades, games and the crowning of a Reina del Yamor (Yamor Queen). There's also ample opportunity to sample *yamor* and other local delicacies. The fiesta stems from pre-Columbian harvest traditions to show gratitude to Pachamama, the Inca Earth Mother. Over time, the celebration incorporated the Catholic faith into the mix, honoring Otavalo's patron saint, the Virgin of Monserrat, along with Pachamama.

TIGRILLO
Breakfast scramble of fried plantain, eggs and cheese.

HUMITAS
Fresh ground corn cakes stuffed with cheese and steamed in corn husks.

FRITADA
Braised or fried pork chunks served alongside yuca, potatoes or hominy.

CAZUELA
Hearty Ecuadorian seafood stew traditionally cooked in a clay pot.

Specialties

Street Snacks

Empanadas de viento Airy fried empanadas stuffed with cheese.
Empanadas de verde Plantain-dough empanadas stuffed with cheese.
Chifles Crispy fried plantain chips.
Tostado Crunchy toasted Andean corn.
Chochos Toasted lupini soybean, sometimes mixed with tostado or made into vegan ceviche.

Sweet Treats

Helado de paila Fresh fruit-juice sorbet whipped up in a pan over ice, said to have been invented in Ibarra.
Bizcochos A Cayambe specialty; eat these biscotti-like cookies the traditional way, paired with *queso de hoja* (string cheese) and dipped in *dulce de leche* (caramel).
Quimbolitos Steamed in taro or banana leaves, these corn cakes are often flavored with anise and studded with raisins.
Espumilla Fluffy, fruit-flavored meringue scooped into ice-cream cones from street carts.

Drinks

Guayusa Energy-giving tea from a leafy tree native to the Amazon.

Quimbolito

Canelazo Hot, sweet cinnamon tea mixed with fiery *aguardiente*.
Aguardiente The nation's choice of firewater, made with fermented sugarcane.
Mishki/Miski Agave-sap beverage served warm as a breakfast drink, or fermented and distilled into a spirit.

Super Specialties

Cuy Highland restaurants might have it on the menu, but often you'll spot *cuy* being grilled at street stalls or markets.
Chontacuros The larvae of the chonta palm beetle is the height of sustainable protein in the Amazon.
Chicha In the Amazon, you may be invited to try this highly nutritious drink, the fermentation of which starts with yuca or chonta palm.

MEALS OF A LIFETIME

Somos (p87) One of Quito's most celebrated restaurants, Somos turns out inventive takes on traditional Ecuadorian food, such as *cuy* dumplings, alongside cocktails accompanied by its own playlists.
Nuema (p78) One of the world's top 100 restaurants, with beautifully presented and creatively executed multicourse tasting menus that show off Ecuador's regional and seasonal bounty.
ShamuiCo (p302) Chic modern takes on traditional Andean dishes in a tiny mountain town.
ØY (p324) Elevated Ecuadorian dishes with a Galápagos twist – fresh ingredients beautifully presented alongside delightful wine pairings.

THE YEAR IN FOOD

SPRING

Find crab dishes during the wet season along the coast. During Semana Santa, traditional dishes like *fanesca* – a fish soup made with 12 beans, grains and vegetables representing Jesus' disciples – are eaten.

SUMMER

Try all the fruits, from refreshing *guanábana* (soursop; pictured) juice to *guayaba* (guava) ice cream and *guaba* (ice-cream bean), the fluffy fruit in a pod that melts in your mouth.

AUTUMN

The non-alcoholic, deep-purple *colada morada* (made with blackberries and other fruit, spices and purple corn flour) is typically shared around the Day of the Dead (November 2) holiday season.

WINTER

Rompope is Ecuador's answer to eggnog made with *aguardiente* and cinnamon. A non-alcoholic alternative is *morocho,* a drinkable corn pudding with cinnamon and raisins.

TOP: FOTOS593/SHUTTERSTOCK; FROM LEFT: FABIAN PONCE GARCIA/SHUTTERSTOCK, RENIAR KA/SHUTTERSTOCK, JORGE ANTONIO SION REYES/SHUTTERSTOCK, MARCOS CASTILLO/SHUTTERSTOCK

IRENEUKE/SHUTTERSTOCK

Lago Toreadora (p297), Parque Nacional Cajas

HOW TO... Avoid Altitude Sickness

Ecuador's mountainous spine spans much of the country's most visited regions, which means you'll likely encounter high altitude even if you're just on a Quito city break – the capital sits at 2850m (9350ft). The country is even home to the mountain that's the closest point on Earth to the sun, Volcán Chimborazo, which towers at 6263m (20,549ft). So knowing how to navigate altitude and avoid the ailments that can accompany it is crucial.

What Is Altitude Sickness?

Altitude sickness is a series of symptoms that occur when your body doesn't have time to adjust to lower amounts of oxygen in the atmosphere than it's used to. It's triggered when you move into high-altitude places too quickly and is easily exacerbated by physical activity. Usual symptoms include headaches, nausea, dizziness, fatigue and trouble sleeping, but altitude sickness sometimes can trigger deadly complications (pulmonary edema, cerebral edema). Altitude sickness can affect anyone regardless of physical fitness, but those with pre-existing conditions should take extra care.

Acclimatize

When arriving in a high-altitude place (anywhere over 2440m), don't jet off immediately to start your itinerary. Give yourself a couple of days to acclimatize before moving on to physical activity or higher altitudes. If your journey is taking you higher than Quito, the general rule of thumb is to not increase your altitude more than 300m (1000ft) per night. For every 300m gain, spend an extra night in that location to acclimatize.

Hydrate

Rule #1 of any high-altitude adventure: drink plenty of fluids. Not only are you in a low-humidity environment, but your body has to work harder at higher altitudes, which leads you to breathe harder and expire more moisture more quickly.

Go Slow

On the trail, slow your pace to make sure you don't outpace your oxygen supply. If you start experiencing any symptoms (even if they seem minor), pause any ascent until they go away.

MEDICATIONS

General advice is to avoid anything that can slow your breathing (and, consequently, your oxygen intake) – most commonly sleeping pills, narcotics and alcohol. If you've experienced altitude sickness before or experience health conditions that put you at higher risk, consider obtaining some acetazolamide (Diamox) before your departure. Ibuprofen is also a good standby if you can't get your hands on Diamox. That said, Diamox is considered a diuretic, so take extra care to stay hydrated if you decide to go that route. Consult a doctor before your trip for more detailed information.

FROM LEFT: ECUADORPOSTALES/SHUTTERSTOCK, GERA GUZMAN/SHUTTERSTOCK

Volcán Fuya Fuya, Lagunas de Mojanda (p114)

THE OUTDOORS

This land of jungle rivers, Andean highlands and palm-shaded beaches offers unparalleled outdoor adventures, all in an area just a little larger than the UK.

Ecuadorians are proud to live in a country where you can wake in the jungle, lunch beneath snow-covered volcanoes, enjoy an afternoon surf session and fall asleep amid unique wildlife on an equatorial island. Vast rainforest wildernesses, scores of spectacular volcanoes (many active), immense protected areas and more than 2200km of coastline make this one of the world's most appealing outdoor playgrounds.

Volcano Climbing

Volcán Cotopaxi (5911m), traditionally the holy grail for volcano-baggers in Ecuador, reopened in 2024 after an eruption-induced hiatus that began in late 2022. Many climbers are also turning their attention to other iconic monsters such as Carihuairazo, Imbabura and Cayambe – the highest point on the equator – and, the daddy of them all, Chimborazo, the country's highest peak at 6263m.

You should definitely allow time to acclimatize to high altitudes (p43), but volcano climbing in Ecuador needn't always be about pushing your boundaries in strenuous thin-air slogs: Cubilche and Fuya Fuya (in the northern highlands), Tungurahua (central highlands), Volcán Alcedo and Sierra Negra (Galápagos) make for unique experiences that are challenging enough for bragging rights back home. Volcán Pichincha (near Quito) has the benefit of

Other Adventures

MONKEY TREKKING
Listen to bellowing howler monkeys as you trek through the 'howling jungle' in **Reserva Bosque Seco Lalo Loor** (p161).

SURFING
Take baby steps in the shore break at **Canoa** (p154), or shoot the curl at the world-famous point break in **Montañita** (p269).

HORSE RIDING
Saddle up for a horseback jaunt (or three-day expedition) into the buffer zone of **Parque Nacional Podocarpus** (p307) from Vilcabamba.

FAMILY ADVENTURES

Take a hike in **Parque Nacional Cajas** (p295) and **Lagunas de Mojanda** (p114), which both offer relatively easy *páramo* options for junior hikers, with the added excitement of chances to cool off in nippy highland lakes.

Try tubing on the **Río Bombuscaro** (p309) or some family-friendly rafting runs on the **Río Anzu** (p191).

Keep an eye out for the famous 'Paddington Bear' (the Andean spectacled bear) in his native habitat. For that, you need to head to **Maquipucuna Reserve** (p131), home also to zipping squadrons of magical fairy-like hummingbirds.

Snorkel in the Galápagos Islands, and perhaps see humpbacks during breeding season, from June to October, in **Atacames**, **Mompiche** and **Puerto López**.

the TeleféríQo cable car, which carries you to within 4km of the 4680m summit.

Walking & Hiking

The 40km Qhapac Ñan (in the southern highlands) is widely said to be Ecuador's most spectacular hike, with most trekkers covering the so-called Camino del Inca to the impressive ruins of Ingapirca in three days. Adventurous walkers can take their pick between high-altitude mountain tracks, haunting cloud forests or riotous lowland rainforest. The trail around Laguna Cuicocha (northern highlands) is one of many scenic day hikes and the iconic Quilotoa Loop (central highlands) offers some wonderful routes connecting rural communities.

In the Galápagos, you'll find a few interesting half-day or shorter walks that can be done independently and show off the volcanic landscape in thrilling detail, such as the Playa Baquerizo trail on San Cristóbal, the Sendero de los Pulpos on Floreana and the paved path to Tortuga Bay on Santa Cruz.

ACTION AREAS

For the best outdoor locations, see p46

Toucan, Mindo (p126)

Bird-Watching

With an astounding 1600 species, Ecuador boasts almost twice as many types of birds as all of Europe. The most difficult decision for bird-watchers is choosing which habitat to focus on: jungle canopies, cloud forests, *páramo* (high-altitude Andean grasslands), mangroves or Pacific forests.

The little town of Mindo, in a tropical transition zone at around 1500m, is the epicenter of Ecuadorian bird-watching, but lesser-known Maquipucuna Reserve (an hour from Mindo) and Intag Valley are also spectacularly rich in birdlife. Lower Río Napo is a renowned bird-watchers' paradise in the Amazon, and Isla Santa Cruz is home to many of the Galápagos' 28 endemic species.

The Andean condor, Ecuador's national bird, is rarely seen in the wild these days, but it can sometimes be seen in flight at the highly informative Parque Cóndor (p109).

BEACH
Bracketed by dramatic headlands and featuring a curving arc of perfect white sand, **Los Frailes** (p276) is among the world's finest beaches.

SNORKELING & DIVING
Snorkel among seahorses, turtles, whitetip sharks, rays and sea lions at **Los Túneles** (p339) on Isla Isabela.

CYCLING
Enjoy a roller-coaster, adrenaline-rush descent down **Cotopaxi** (p214), one of the world's most active volcanoes.

EXTREME SPORTS
Zip lines, cable cars, suspension bridges, bungee jumps and canyoning routes lure thrill seekers to **Baños** (p231).

ACTION AREAS

Where to find Ecuador's best outdoor activities.

Surfing

1. Montañita (p269)
2. Mompiche (p148)
3. Canoa (p154)
4. Same (p145)
5. Isla San Cristóbal (p330)

Walking/Hiking

1. Qhapac Ñan (p297)
2. Quilotoa Loop (p220)
3. Laguna Cuicocha (p110)
4. Lagunas de Mojanda (p114)
5. Parque Nacional Podocarpus (p307)

Birdlife/watching

1. Mindo (p126)
2. Intag Valley (p122)
3. Isla Corazon (p159)
4. Parque Cóndor (p109)
5. Isla Santa Cruz (p322)
6. Parque Nacional Cajas (p295)

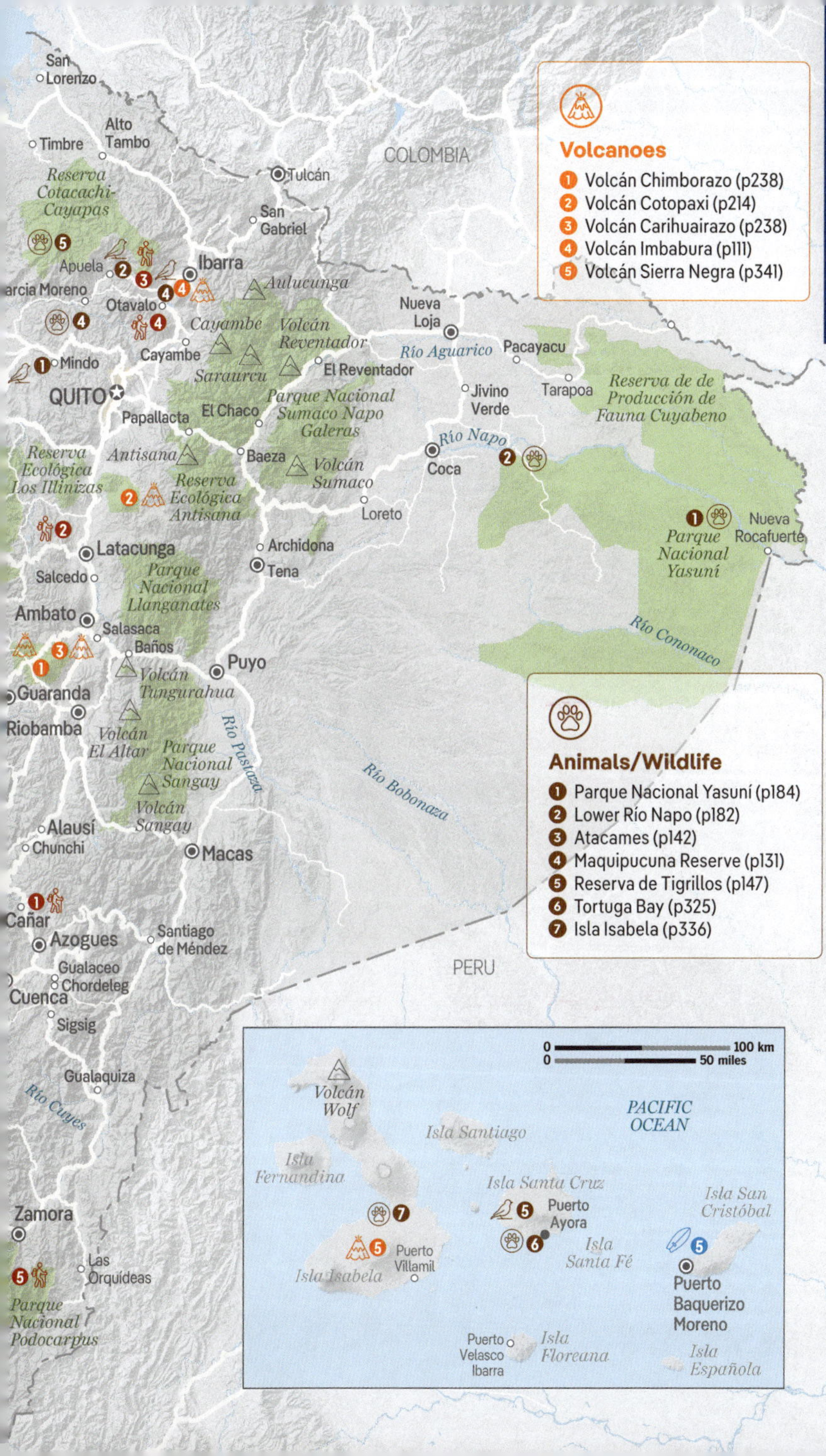

Volcanoes
1 Volcán Chimborazo (p238)
2 Volcán Cotopaxi (p214)
3 Volcán Carihuairazo (p238)
4 Volcán Imbabura (p111)
5 Volcán Sierra Negra (p341)
Animals/Wildlife
1 Parque Nacional Yasuní (p184)
2 Lower Río Napo (p182)
3 Atacames (p142)
4 Maquipucuna Reserve (p131)
5 Reserva de Tigrillos (p147)
6 Tortuga Bay (p325)
7 Isla Isabela (p336)
COLOMBIA
PERU
San Lorenzo
Timbre
Alto Tambo
Tulcán
San Gabriel
Reserva Cotacachi-Cayapas
Apuela
Ibarra
Aulucunga
García Moreno
Otavalo
Cayambe
Volcán Reventador
Mindo
QUITO
Saraurcu
El Reventador
Nueva Loja
Río Aguarico
Pacayacu
Jivino Verde
Tarapoa
Reserva de de Producción de Fauna Cuyabeno
Papallacta
El Chaco
Parque Nacional Sumaco Napo Galeras
Reserva Ecológica Los Illinizas
Antisana
Baeza
Volcán Sumaco
Río Napo
Coca
Reserva Ecológica Antisana
Loreto
Latacunga
Archidona
Tena
Nueva Rocafuerte
Parque Nacional Yasuní
Salcedo
Parque Nacional Llanganates
Ambato
Salasaca
Baños
Río Cononaco
Volcán Tungurahua
Puyo
Guaranda
Riobamba
Volcán El Altar
Parque Nacional Sangay
Río Pastaza
Río Bobonaza
Volcán Sangay
Alausí
Chunchi
Macas
Cañar
Azogues
Santiago de Méndez
Gualaceo
Chordeleg
Cuenca
Sigsig
Gualaquiza
Río Cuyes
Zamora
Las Orquídeas
Parque Nacional Podocarpus
0 100 km
0 50 miles
Volcán Wolf
PACIFIC OCEAN
Isla Santiago
Isla Fernandina
Isla Santa Cruz
Puerto Ayora
Isla San Cristóbal
Isla Santa Fé
Puerto Villamil
Isla Isabela
Puerto Baquerizo Moreno
Puerto Velasco Ibarra
Isla Floreana
Isla Española

ECUADOR & THE GALÁPAGOS ISLANDS

THE GUIDE

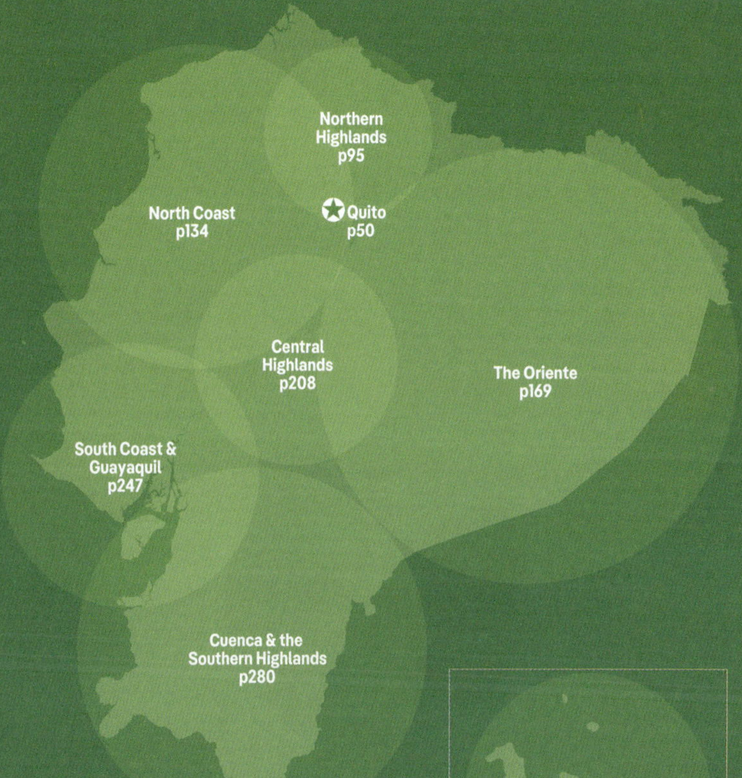

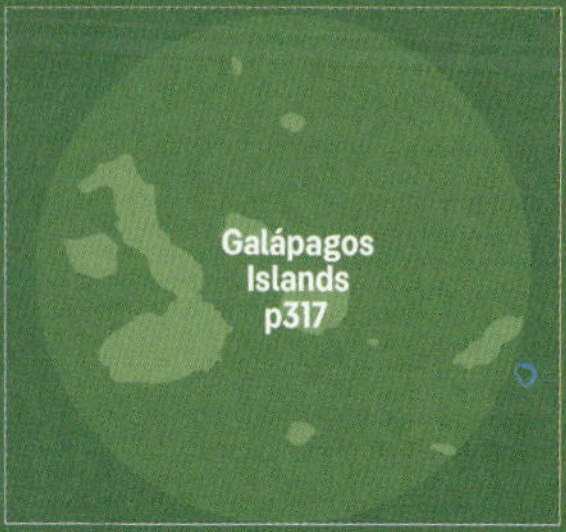

Chapters in this section are organised by hubs and their surrounding areas. We see the hub as your base in the destination, where you'll find unique experiences, local insights, insider tips and expert recommendations. It's also your gateway to the surrounding area, where you'll see what and how much you can do from there.

Rucu Pichincha (p69)

ECUADORPOSTALES/SHUTTERSTOCK

Researched by
Wendy Yanagihara

Quito

Sitting in the foothills of the Andes, this World Heritage city captivates with its 17th-century architecture, indigenous art and cosmopolitan food scene.

It could be the altitude talking, but for us Quito's among the world's most breathtaking capitals – and not only because of its dramatic valley location at 2850m in the foothills of the Andes, but also because of its enchanting 17th-century Centro Histórico, or 'Old Town'. In fact, Quito is so immaculately preserved, it was the first city to be granted UNESCO World Heritage status.

Many travelers to Ecuador see Quito (population 2.5 million) mainly as a gateway to the Galápagos, the Andes and the Amazon. Given the allure of these world-famous attractions, that's fair, but Quito is very much a destination in itself.

ECUADORPOSTALES/SHUTTERSTOCK

The city's crown jewel is undoubtedly its resplendent Centro Histórico, a historical quarter of elegant cobbled plazas and ornate baroque and neoclassical buildings, with some of the most extravagant cathedrals you'll ever see. An abundance of museums tell of its rich history and culture, but this is not a city stuck in the past; it's abuzz with local marketgoers, cafes filled with office workers and palm-filled squares where residents gather to gossip.

Quito's charisma extends beyond the Centro Histórico. Head north to discover the bohemian *barrios* of La Floresta and Marical Sucre, artsy neighborhoods with crumbling mansions near parks, street art, university culture and cool gastronomy scenes. Further north, high-rise development and the business district represent modern-day Quito, leading onward to the equator, a celebrated geographical marker since ancient times.

This region was once home to the indigenous Quitu people, from whom the city derives its name. It was later absorbed into the Inca Empire in the 15th century before they razed its temples to prevent from them falling into the hands of the Spanish conquistadors. Today, as the city strives to come to terms with its colonial past, Quito has become the epicenter of significant protests from various ethnic groups advocating for issues like the cost of living, social justice and cultural preservation. Dynamic yet relaxed and easily navigable, this Andean capital invites lingering.

THE MAIN AREAS

CENTRO HISTÓRICO
Quito's superb, well-preserved old town. **p56**

CENTRAL QUITO
Museums, artisan markets and edgy nightlife. **p69**

LA FLORESTA & AROUND
Creative hub, great gastronomy and cool bars. **p74**

NORTH QUITO
Gardens and contemporary urban living. **p84**

THE EQUATOR
The equator, museums and ecotourism. **p89**

For places to stay in Quito, see p93

ECUADORPLANET/SHUTTERSTOCK

Left: Mitad del Mundo (p89); above: Centro Histórico (p56)

Find Your Way

Thanks to Quito Metro and inexpensive rideshare and taxis, Quito is a pretty easy city to navigate. The three bus systems, Trolebús, Ecovía and Metrobús, are cheap but crowded and prone to pickpockets. Neighborhoods are very walkable but require transportation to get from one to another.

FROM THE AIRPORT

Quito's **Mariscal Sucre International Airport** is 37km northeast of the city. A taxi (from $26) to your accommodation is the most practical means. Public buses to the Río Coca Terminal in north Quito or Quitumbe Terminal in the south take 60 to 90 minutes and cost around $2.

QUITO METRO

After a few false starts, Quito's metro system was finally unveiled in late 2023. At a super-cheap $0.45 per ride, whether from one station to the next or end to end, it's a convenient way to travel the main north–southneighborhoods in the city.

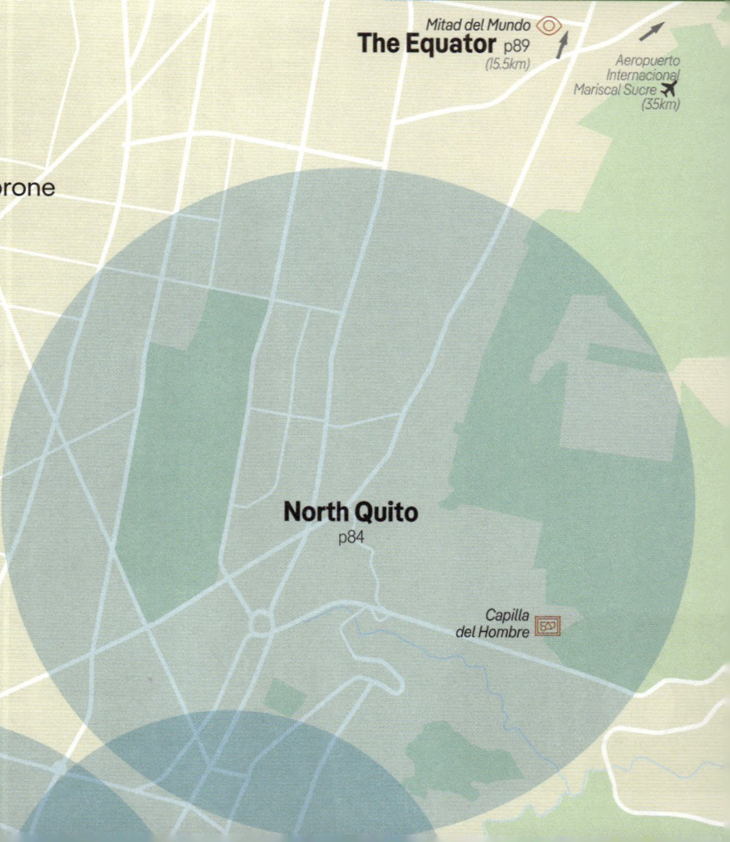

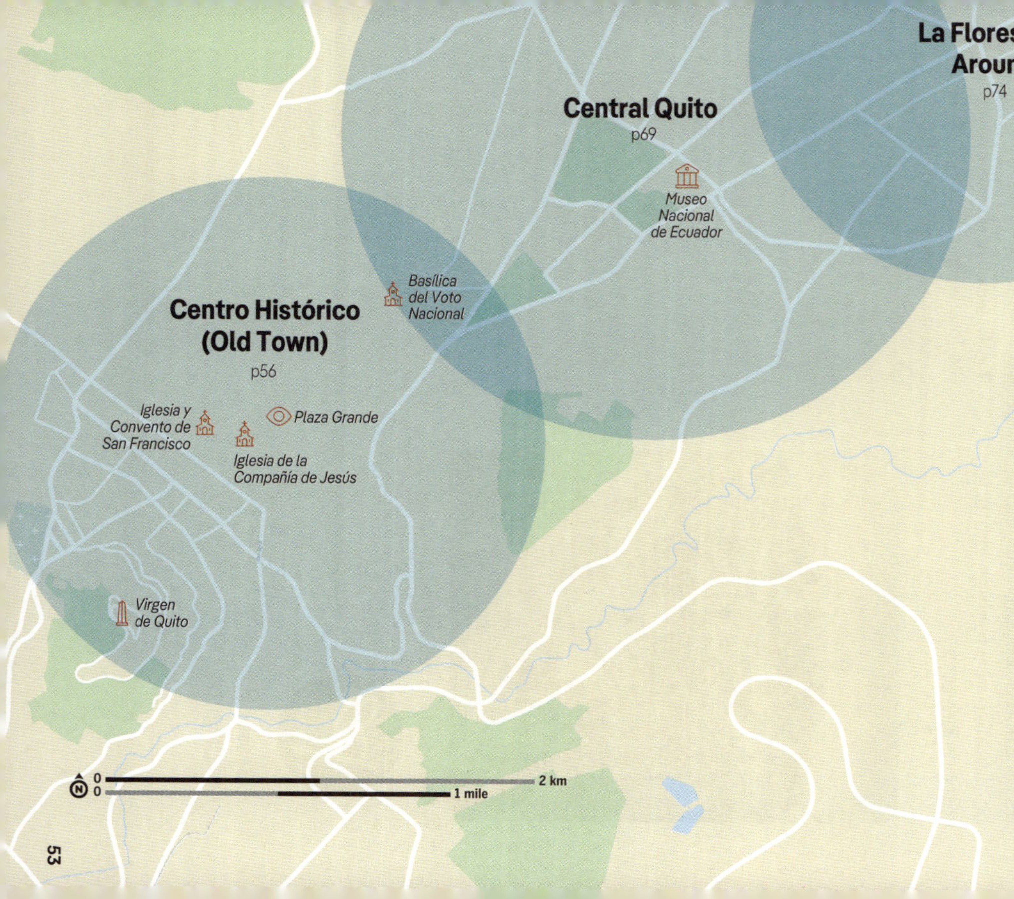

TAXI & RIDESHARE

Taxis and Uber are both inexpensive and readily on call, making them the best option for short trips around Quito. For safety, it's highly recommended you use these at night. Official taxis are yellow with the registration number displayed on the exterior and inside the car.

BUS

It's possible to get around on the bus systems, which cost around $0.30 per trip, depending on your destination. Be aware that they are often crowded and are targeted for opportunistic theft, but they may have stops nearer your destination than the metro.

Plan Your Days

Count on two to five days in Quito. As well as needing that time to see and experience the city's highlights, adjusting to its location at 2850m will help acclimatize you for high-altitude regions beyond.

JON CHICA/SHUTTERSTOCK

Quito street with Virgen de Quito (p56) behind

Day 1

Morning

- For optimal outlooks, head up to **El Panecillo** (p56) in the morning for volcano vistas and city views, before refreshing with a coffee at **Dulcería Colonial** (p63) overlooking **Plaza Grande** (p60).

Afternoon

- After orienting yourself with an Old Town **walking tour** (p64), grab lunch at **La Bodega de Cantuña** (p57) at Plaza San Francisco before taking a more in-depth look inside the plaza's magnificent **cathedral** (p63). Nearby **Casa del Alabado** (p65) is a must for pre-Columbian artifacts.

Evening

- Take in panoramas of the Centro Histórico with a rooftop meal at **Vista Hermosa** (p66). If it's a weekend, swing by **Calle La Ronda** (p63) for a fun night of dancing and revelry.

Seasonal Highlights

JAN

Marking the end of the Christmas season, **Día de Reyes** is celebrated with a parade of dancers and musicians through the Centro Histórico on the weekend near January 6.

FEB

Carnaval (p65) celebrations in mid-February bring color, joyous music and booty-shaking parades drawn from the syncretism of indigenous traditions and Catholic rituals.

APR

Concentrated in the Centro Histórico during **Good Friday** (p65), one of the more visually arresting sights is the procession of purple-hooded and -robed *cucuruchos*, penitents who may also be carrying heavy crosses.

Day 2

Morning

- Start the day with a ride on **TelefériQo** (p69) before continuing to explore the Centro Histórico, ticking off museums such as **Museo de la Ciudad** (p65). Wander the cobblestone streets, admiring **Iglesia de la Compañía de Jesús** (p62) and **Catedral Metropolitana** (p61), then lunch in **Palacio Arzobispal** (p61).

Afternoon

- Drop by **Basílica del Voto Nacional** (p57), check out contemporary art at **Centro de Arte Contemporáneo** (p68), then head into the 'new town' to take in stunning artworks at **Capilla del Hombre** (p86) and **Casa Museo Guayasamín** (p87).

Evening

- Enjoy modern Ecuadorian at **Somos** (p87) before checking out bars around **La Floresta** (p74).

Day 3

Morning

- Take an excursion to the equator at **Museo Intiñan** (p90), followed by views over **Volcán Pululahua** (p91) and lunch at **Santana Brewing Company** (p91).

Afternoon

- Back in Quito, look for hummingbirds at **Jardín Botánico** (p84) in Parque La Carolina before heading to La Floresta to walk around checking out **street art** (p78). Squeeze in time for last-minute souvenirs at **Mercado Artesanal La Mariscal** (p70).

Evening

- Treat yourself to dinner at one of the world's top 100 restaurants, **Nuema** (p78), or be enchanted by valley views with a pizza from **Ananké** (p83) in Guápulo. Then dance some **cumbia** (p62) or chill out with a craft beer in **La Pradera** (p80).

AUG

Ecuador's **Independence Day** (Día del Primer Grito de Independencia, p65) is celebrated with a military parade, concerts and cultural events on August 10, centered around the Palacio del Gobierno on Plaza Grande.

AUG & SEP

The fluffy blossoms of the **Arupo trees** burst into bloom all over the parks and streets of Quito, adding puffs of pink delight to the urban landscape.

NOV

Leading up to the citywide Fiestas de Quito, the free, annual music festival known as **Quito Fest** (p88) kicks off the winter holiday season with inclusive, non-religious dancing and music accessible to all.

DEC

Beginning the last week of November, **Fiestas de Quito** (p65) culminate on December 6. Festivities include live music, dancing, *chivas* (cruising busloads of celebrants), parades and neighborhood parties.

Centro Histórico

ORNATE CHURCHES | ARCHITECTURE | PRE-COLUMBIAN ART

TOP TIP

If walking up a few stairs is leaving you breathless, or you're feeling unusually fatigued, you're probably suffering symptoms of mild altitude sickness (p43). You'll acclimate after a day or two, but stay well hydrated. Many swear by the benefits of chewing coca leaves or sipping *té de coca* (coca-leaf tea).

As you stroll the cobblestone streets of Quito's Old Town, known as the **Centro Histórico**, taking in its treasure trove of magnificent basilicas, grand plazas, elegant palaces, museums and monasteries, it will come as no surprise that this was the first city to receive UNESCO World Heritage status.

What further impresses is that this is no open-air cultural museum showpiece filled with tacky souvenir stores; instead, it's very much a pulsating commercial and religious hub without a whiff of tourist trap. Despite the lavish heritage backdrop, here it's very much about the present – the plazas, cafes and restaurants are packed with chatty locals in what remains the capital's political and cultural heart. *Quiteños* (Quito residents) relax on the plaza in front of the presidential palace, the seat of Ecuador's government, and attend mass at the monumental, opulent churches anchoring this well-preserved historic center.

THE OV (ORIGINAL VIRGEN)

Visit the small but significant Virgen at the main altar of **Iglesia y Convento de San Francisco** (p63) to see the inspiration for the iconic Virgen on the hill.

Visitations to La Virgen de Quito

Quito's guardian angel

Standing high on Quito's **El Panecillo** hill is the city's emblematic 41m-tall **Virgen de Quito** *(Virgin of Quito; statue interior $1)*. Though perhaps not as evocative as Brazil's Christ the Redeemer, this statue is a

GETTING AROUND

Exploring the Centro Histórico on foot is the best way to navigate and acclimate to this high-altitude capital. Consider starting your first day with a walking tour (p64), often free through your accommodations. A guided stroll through the key sites is a great introduction to the Old Town and its pleasures, and you can ditch the tour if something catches your fancy along the way. If you're heading to Central or North Quito, it's unbelievably cheap and convenient to hop on the **Quito Metro** from Plaza San Francisco in the heart of the Centro Histórico.

KATH WATSON/SHUTTERSTOCK

Basílica del Voto Nacional

beloved icon visible from most parts of the city, even at night when she glows like a rave-lit beacon. First commissioned in 1892, she wasn't completed until 1976 and features a crown of stars, angelic wings and a chained dragon, all built from a patchwork of aluminum sheets.

The interior of the statue features black-and-white photographs documenting the monument's construction, while at the top of the spiral staircase you can step out on the walkway encircling the statue for staggering 360-degree vistas. Aim for an early morning visit for your best chance of volcano views.

As appealing as it may look to walk here via the stairs, muggings are common, so a taxi is definitely the way to go.

Climb the Towers of Basílica del Voto Nacional

Quito's iconic neo-Gothic basilica

There's no shortage of grand churches in Quito, but none is bigger or more imposing than the **Basílica del Voto Nacional** *(church only/church & towers $2/4)*. Sitting atop a hill north of the Old Town, this massive, awe-inspiring Catholic church is the largest neo-Gothic basilica in the Americas.

continues on p62

COCA LEAF

Buying some coca leaf may help alleviate symptoms of altitude sickness, although chewing the tough leaves might feel awkward and uncomfortable as you have to gnaw on them for a while to get any effect. Sipping coca tea may be a more palatable way to experience the leaf. If you do buy either the leaves or tea, be careful to jettison any remainders when leaving South America. Laws vary depending on individual countries, but it is illegal to bring it with you into the US or EU, for example, and it's best to assume that carrying coca leaf into your home country is considered smuggling.

EATING IN THE OLD TOWN: ECUADORIAN CLASSICS

San Agustín: Double-story colonial house packed with locals for *seco de chivo* (goat stew) and homemade ice cream. *10am-4pm* **$$**

La Bodega de Cantuña: Delicious Ecuadorian dishes, including lamb stews and Galápagos cod. *10am-5pm Sun-Thu, to 10pm Fri & Sat* **$$**

La Exquisita: Good spot to sample traditional working-class local cuisine, with cheap and filling *almuerzos* (set lunches). *8:45am-3pm* **$**

Leña Quiteña: Deliciously sauced and presented Ecuadorian dishes, including *cuy* (guinea pig) and slow-braised pork. *noon-9pm Tue-Sat, to 7pm Sun* **$$**

CENTRO HISTÓRICO (OLD TOWN)

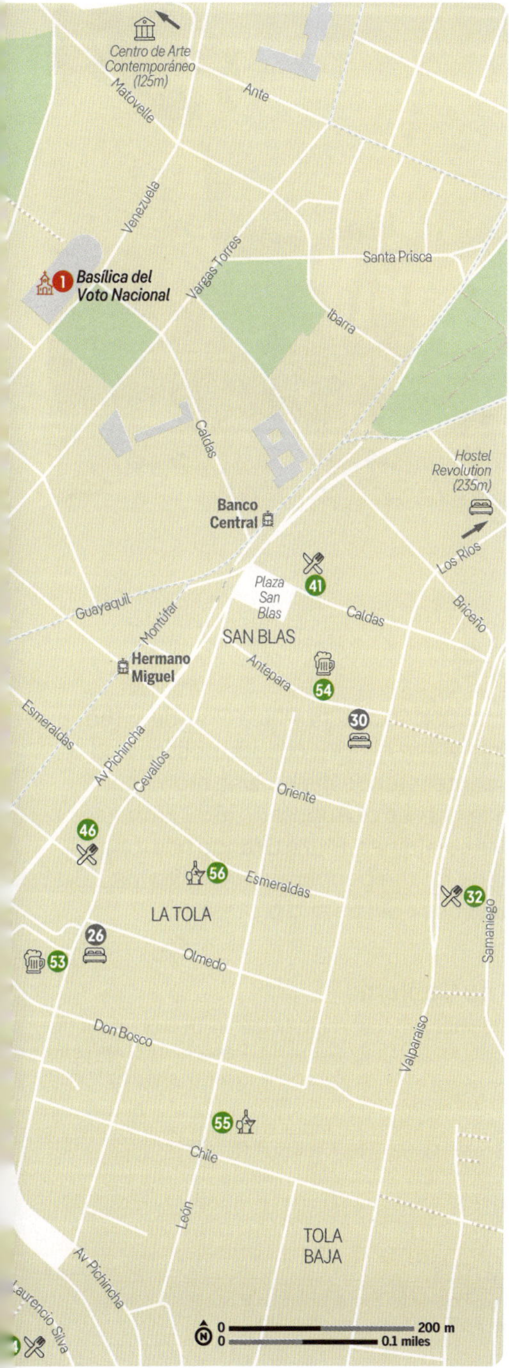

HIGHLIGHTS
1 Basílica del Voto Nacional
2 Iglesia de la Compañía de Jesús
3 Iglesia y Convento de San Francisco
4 Plaza Grande
5 Virgen de Quito

SIGHTS
6 Calle La Ronda
7 Casa del Alabado
8 Casa Museo María Augusta Urrutía
9 Catedral Metropolitana
10 El Panecillo
11 Iglesia La Merced
12 Museo Alberto Mena Caamaño
13 Museo Camilo Egas
14 Museo Casa de Sucre
15 Museo de Arte Colonial
16 Museo de la Ciudad
17 Museo del Pasillo
18 Museo Manuela Sáenz
19 Museo San Francisco de Quito
20 Palacio Arzobispal
21 Palacio de Gobierno
22 Plaza de Santo Domingo
23 Plaza San Francisco

SLEEPING
24 Carlota
25 Casa Gangotena
26 Community Hostel
27 Friends Hotel & Rooftop
28 Hotel San Francisco de Quito
29 La Casona de la Ronda
30 Secret Garden
31 Viajero Hostel Quito

EATING
32 Café Mosaico
see 25 Café Quiteño
33 Cafetería Modelo
34 Dulcería Colonial
35 El Ladrillo que Faltaba
36 El Ventanal
37 Govindas Gopal
38 Kitu
39 La Bodega de Cantuña
40 La Caponata
41 La Exquisita
42 La Vid
43 Las Cuevas de Luís Candela
44 Laurita Buena
45 Leña Quiteña
46 Mercado Central
47 Pim's
48 Pizza SA
49 San Agustín
50 San Ignacio
51 Vista Hermosa

DRINKING & NIGHTLIFE
52 Andes Brew Pub
53 Bandido Brewing
54 La Oficina
55 Palenque Casa
56 Sereno Moreno

ENTERTAINMENT
57 Teatro Bolívar
58 Teatro Sucre
59 Teatro Variedades Ernesto Albán

SHOPPING
see 39 Ecuador Shops

INFORMATION
60 Tourist Information

TRANSPORT
61 Estación San Francisco

FIIPHOTO/SHUTTERSTOCK

TOP EXPERIENCE

Plaza Grande

Officially known as Plaza de la Independencia, Plaza Grande is the Centro Histórico's main square, where history, culture, politics and everyday life converge. At its center stands the rousing monument dedicated to the independence heroes of August 10, 1809. Home to some of Quito's most significant buildings, Plaza Grande has long been the central gathering place for the people: where *quiteños* congregate to relax, gossip, discuss politics and protest.

DON'T MISS

- Domes of Catedral Metropolitana
- People-Watching on the Plaza
- Changing of the Guard
- Palacio del Gobierno
- Plaza Arzobispal

Palacio de Gobierno

The monumental building fronting the northwest side of the **plaza**, Ecuadorian flag flying, is the **Palacio de Gobierno** (Carondelet Palace), the residence of Ecuador's president. Visit at noon on a Tuesday for the changing of the guard, a 30-minute ceremony featuring military horsemen and band in full regalia, and during which the president often appears. It's not unusual for the ceremony to be followed up with organized protests, giving insight into current political concerns. When

PRACTICALITIES

● catedraldequito@yahoo.com ● 9am-5pm ● museum & domes / museum only $4/2 tours are running, you can visit **Museo de la Presidencia**, which takes in parts of the palace, including a brilliant mosaic by Oswaldo Guayasamín. At the time of publishing, tours were booked out six months ahead; email *ucultural@presidencia.gob.ec* to reserve in advance.

People-Watching on the Plaza

Plaza Grande is Quito's ground zero for people-watching. From animated discussions taking place beneath the statue, families posing for special-occasion photo shoots on the steps of Catedral Metropolitana, shoeshiners parked along Palacio Arzobispal and vendors selling *espumillas* (meringue cones), it attracts folk from all walks of life. Weekends feel particularly relaxed and festive as couples stroll, street magicians perform and even Spiderman may appear. At the base of the church, you'll find a row of alfresco cafes perfect for soaking up the square's atmosphere, including Dulcería Colonial (p63) built into its stone vault.

Catedral Metropolitana

To the southwest, **Catedral Metropolitana** offers guided tours ($2) of the works by artists from the Quito School within its grand interior. You'll find unique interpretations of the Last Supper, with Christ and his disciples feasting on *cuy* (guinea pig), and a Nativity painting featuring a llama peering over the newborn Jesus, the native fauna and geographical backgrounds serving as familiar and relatable features to the local congregants. The cathedral houses the tomb of independence hero Antonio José de Sucre, along with an adjoining museum of religious relics and a small library. Tickets for the complete tour ($4) also grant access to the green-and-yellow checkered domes, which involve ascending its very narrow, labyrinthine stairs (not for claustrophobes) to the rooftop for splendid views of the plaza and its surroundings.

Palacio Arzobispal

On the plaza's northeast side stands **Palacio Arzobispal**, the former archbishop's palace, which has been transformed into a row of shops and a dining precinct. You can have your shoes shined or buy a snack from roving vendors along the front portico, while the interior is essentially a *quiteño* food palace replete with appealing balconies, sunken patios and the odd shop. The upmarket **La Vid** restaurant offers views over the plaza and a romantic experience, while further inside **El Ladrillo que Faltaba** occupies a light-filled atrium within the palace and offers burgers, *seco de chivo* (goat stew) and local craft beers on tap.

City Hall

At the south end of the plaza, you'll find the relatively nondescript city hall, a modern concrete building that houses an excellent **tourist information office**, open from 9am to 6pm, and from 9:30am to 4:30pm on Sundays. The office space includes a souvenir shop, a chocolate cafe and a tour desk in the back.

MUSEO DEL PASILLO

If Palacio de Gobierno tour slots are booked out during your visit, the presidential office offers a kind of cultural consolation prize – a tour of **Museo del Pasillo** (p67), showcasing the art of *pasillo*, the Ecuadorian musical genre designated by UNESCO as an Intangible Cultural Heritage of Humanity. It's two blocks from Plaza Grande and offers a musical angle on Ecuadorian pride and psyche.

TOP TIPS

- Take the 'complete' tour of Catedral Metropolitana to admire Plaza Grande from the terrace of the domes above; you won't get to linger up top beyond 15 minutes, and it's not for claustrophobes.
- Show up at least half an hour early for the changing of the guard if you'd like to score a good viewing spot – prime property is the palace-facing end of the patio of Catedral Metropolitana, giving a higher vantage point.
- In addition to helpful, multilingual tourist advice at the tourist information office at the southeastern corner of the plaza, you'll also find a clean public toilet.

COMMUNITY MASS

Quito's many grand churches receive thousands of visitors for their spectacular architecture and artworks; however, it's important to remember that these are active places of worship for *quiteños,* who come for meditation, prayer, comfort and community. Mass *(misa)* times are posted at church entrances, and visitors are asked to refrain from coming at these hours to respect these religious ceremonies – although they are welcome to attend mass themselves. It's perfectly acceptable to stand at the back and observe quietly, but respect the parishioners and solemnity and come back another time for photos.

SERGE YATUNIN/SHUTTERSTOCK

Iglesia de la Compañia de Jesús

continued from p57

Construction began in 1892, and it's still being built today, making this a local version of Gaudi's Sagrada Família in Barcelona: a perpetually unfinished project that legend says if ever completed will mean the end of the world.

Instead of gargoyles, you'll find protruding from the facade delightful guardians representing Ecuadorian wildlife, including iguanas, tortoises, caimans, jaguars, dolphins and armadillos. Similarly, the stunning stained glass of the basilica's front side features a colorful design emblazoned with native orchids.

The highlight of your visit, however, is ascending the basilica's **towers** (115m tall) from the main roof via steep stairs and ladders (with solid handrails). It's a long, breathless climb to its clock towers, but it guarantees some of Quito's best views.

Be Dazzled by Iglesia de la Compañia de Jesús

Quito's most beautiful church

If you think the intricately carved, volcanic rock facade of the Jesuit **Iglesia de la Compañia de Jesús** is impressive, wait till you step inside. Gleaming with 23-carat gold leaf (amounting to about 23kg worth), its Latin American baroque interior bedazzles with decorative splendor that's a whirl of Spanish, Moorish and Inca architectural styles.

DRINKING IN SAN BLAS: DRINKS & DANCING

La Oficina Brewpub: Cavernous brewpub offering a bohemian vibe, tasty beers, wood-fired pizzas and live music as well as DJs. *5-11:30pm Wed, to midnight Thu-Sat*

Sereno Moreno: A happening rooftop bar shows off sparkling city views and *chicha* on tap, an indigenous alcoholic drink. *4-11pm Mon & Tue, to midnight Wed-Sat*

Bandido Brewing: The Old Town's first and best microbrewery, occupying a building dating to the 1850s and bedecked with religious art. *4-11:30pm Tue-Fri, from 2pm Sat*

Palenque Casa: For late-night shenanigans, this inclusive culture hub is where it's at if you want to hit the dance floor. *6pm-3am Thu-Sat*

Construction began in 1605 and took some 160 years to complete. Guided tours highlight the details of what is one of Latin America's finest churches, including its indigenous symbolism, the impressive trompe-l'œil staircase, grand nave and masterful paintings and sculptures by artists of the Quito School.

There's an extra fee for a guided visit to the **cupola**, where you can step through a small door in the dome to admire up close the molding work, the murals and the splendid church nave from above. From this vantage point, you're treated to a view over Plaza San Francisco and the city.

Calle La Ronda

Salsa and good vibes

Quito's Centro Histórico isn't known for its nightlife, but the cobblestoned and romantically lit 17th-century **Calle La Ronda** is one exception. Lined with colonial houses, this pedestrianized thoroughfare was once the domain of artists, writers and political activists. After falling into disrepair in the latter decades of the 20th century, it has been revived in the 21st as a spot to head Thursday, Friday and Saturday nights for its fiesta vibe of salsa bars (along with bachata, merengue and *reggaetón*). Live music brings people spilling into the alley, warming cups of *canelazo* (*aguardiente* with hot cider and cinnamon) in hand.

In the afternoon and early evening, chocolate and handicraft shops are open for business, while restaurants advertise their truly gigantic empanadas with samples on trays held by mannequins dressed in traditional festival costume. Grab some ice cream or find dinner in atmospheric old buildings, some with attractive interior courtyards.

If you're dining solo, consider leaving by 6:30pm to catch a rideshare or taxi, as the last couple of pedestrian-only uphill blocks above La Ronda's stone archway are dark, shuttered and empty at the end of the day.

Iglesia y Convento de San Francisco

Expansive religious complex filled with surprises

Just when you think you've seen the best of the Old Town's cathedrals, you stumble upon the granddaddy of them all, the **Iglesia y Convento de San Francisco**. Dating back to 1534, the first bricks of Quito's oldest church were laid just months after the Spanish took control of the city.

The Iglesia y Convento de San Francisco is the largest religious complex in Latin America. Set over four blocks, it's not

STREET NAMESAKES

Main streets in the Centro Histórico are named after independence heroes and major political figures.

Antonio José de Sucre: The hero of Ecuadorian independence, assassinated in 1830.

Juan José Flores: Founding president of Ecuador in 1830, serving also as its third and fourth president.

Vicente Rocafuerte: President who established the public school system and formalized greater protections for its indigenous peoples.

Gabriel García Moreno: President assassinated after winning a third term, as a military dictator.

Víctor Mideros: Painter whose works can be viewed at Iglesia La Merced.

EATING IN THE CENTRO HISTÓRICO: QUITEÑO CAFES

Dulcería Colonial: Cafe famed for *pernil* (pork) sandwiches paired with well-made coffees and freshly piped cannoli, right on Plaza Grande. *8am-7pm* $

Cafetería Modelo: Old-school 1950s cafe serving coffee, ice cream and traditional snacks, such as *empanadas de verde*. *8:30am-7pm Mon-Sat, to 5pm Sun* $

Café Quiteño: Treat yourself to a lavish, Ecuadorian-style high tea at Casa Gangotena, with platters of sweet and savory delights. Call to reserve. *4-6pm* $$

San Ignacio: Sit on the patio and people-watch over a *churrasco* (steak) or a cappuccino and *tamal quiteño*. *8am-9pm Mon-Thu, to 10pm Fri & Sat, to 7pm Sun* $$

STROLL THE OLD TOWN

Orient yourself with a stroll around the Centro Histórico, pausing at any enticing stop for a deeper look.

START	END	LENGTH
Plaza San Francisco	Calle La Ronda	2.6km; 2hr

Begin by taking in ❶ **Iglesia y Convento de San Francisco** (p63), and the plaza where little kids and dogs chase pigeons. From here, walk along Sucre to the grand facade of ❷ **Iglesia de la Compañia de Jesús** (p62), whose real splendor lies within. Continue to ❸ **Plaza Grande** (p60), the heart of Quito. After people-watching at the plaza, pause along ❹ **Calle Venezuela** to look uphill to the towers of Basílica del Voto Nacional (p57) and downhill for a view of La Virgen de El Panecillo. Then treat your palate to a chocolate tasting at ❺ **Kitu**.

If lunch sounds more appetizing, browse ❻ **Mercado Central** (p66) for a cheap, delicious Ecuadorian specialty. Or walk down to the appealing, hidden-in-plain-sight ❼ **San Marcos neighborhood**, where cafes, shops and museums along the cobblestoned Calle Junín lead to a peaceful pocket plaza and parish church.

Cross ❽ **Plaza de Santo Domingo**, admiring the church's exterior, and ramble down the cobbled blocks of Guayaquil, which intersects with ❾ **Calle La Ronda** (p63). Shops here will be opening up in the afternoon, but this historic quarter really comes alive at night.

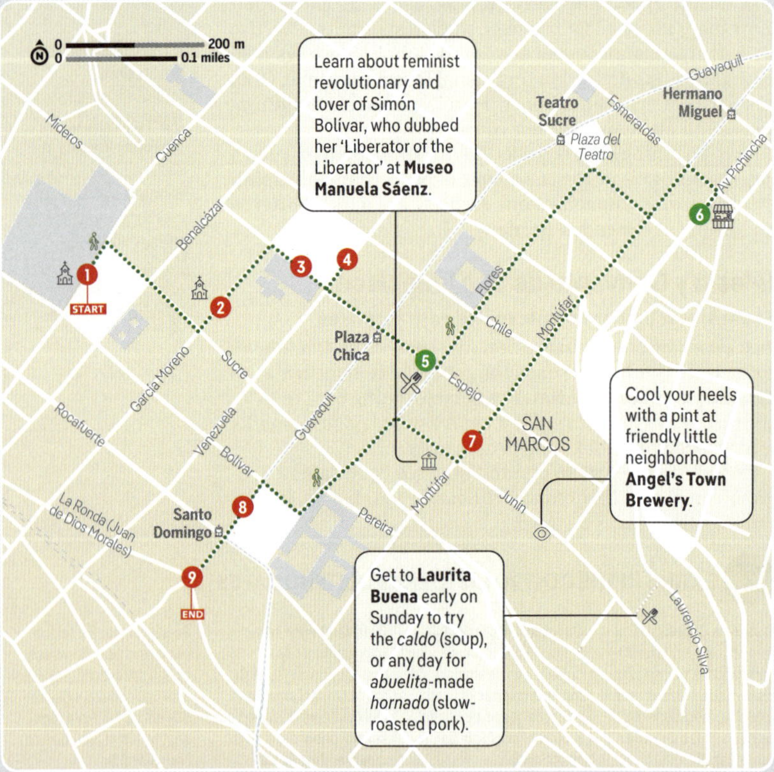

only a monastery but has several chapels, catacombs, palm-filled Andalucian-style cloisters, a museum and the original (retired and restored) brewery where you can buy beer on the weekends. The convent is still home to 11 monks, ranging in age from 40s to 90s.

The interior of the main church is a sight to behold, with its lavish baroque gilding and soaring dome. This is the birthplace of the **Quito School of Art** (Escuela Quiteña), so you'll be treated to much fine art, including works by indigenous artists, who themselves were prohibited from entering the main doors. Look for Bernardo de Legarda's diminutive (30cm tall) wooden Virgen sculpture enshrined at the church's main altar, known as the *Virgen Bailarina* (Dancing Virgin) due to her unusual dynamic pose. If she looks vaguely familiar, it's because sculptor Agustín de la Herrán Matorras later modeled the Virgen de Quito (p56) on this lovely sculpture.

The **Museo San Francisco de Quito** *(museosanfrancisco dequito.com; adult/child $6/2)* is arguably the main highlight of a visit here. Free, guided tours (tips greatly appreciated) lead through galleries displaying exquisite artworks and treasure rooms containing an extensive collection of 3500 pieces from the Quito School of Art before ending up at the bell towers affording lovely city views.

With its mountainous backdrop, the cobblestoned **Plaza San Francisco** itself is one of Centro Histórico's most picturesque squares. Its origins are pre-colonial, this same space having functioned as a major marketplace of the Quitu people before being reconstructed by the Incas. Linger over lunch at La Bodega de Cantuña (p57), built into the church's stone basement. Adjacent, **Ecuador Shops** also occupies old rooms and nooks within the church's underground passageways, and offers high-quality gift items from around the nation.

Stunning Artifacts of Pre-Columbian Indigenous Culture

Pre-Columbian and pre-Incan history

Among the Centro Histórico's splendid heritage buildings are plenty of dedicated museums to help contextualize Quito's rich past, including the pre-Inca societies of the Paleoindian period, dating as far back as 10,000 BCE.

Museo de la Ciudad *(@museociudaduio; adult/child $8/4)*, closed on Monday, is a natural starting point for an overview of Quito's history. A former hospital dating to 1565 (and used until 1974), the museum houses well-presented exhibits chronicling Quito's history. Artifacts and interpretive displays explore the agriculture, customs and trade between indigenous peoples before and during the Inca period (with signage in Spanish).

The museum ties nicely into the next stop, the stellar **Casa del Alabado** *(alabado.org; adult/student $10/5)*, open Wednesday to Sunday. Set within

BEST QUITO FESTIVALS

Feast of the Virgin of La Candelaria: On February 2, the cobbled alleys of hillside Guápulo are bedecked with flowers and candles for the religious procession to the church.

Carnaval: In mid-February, Carnaval celebrations bring colorful parades and traditions drawn from both Catholic and indigenous cultures.

Good Friday: A sea of *cucuruchos* – penitents in purple robes and pointed hats – walk in the procession of Jesús de Gran Poder.

Independence Day: Celebrated with a military parade, concerts and cultural events on August 10.

Fiestas de Quito: Live music, dancing, parades and neighborhood parties begin the last week of November, leading up to Quito Foundation Day on December 6.

QUITO FEST

Quito Fest (p88), the city's best free music festival, coincides with the Fiestas de Quito in late November.

MARÍA AUGUSTA URRUTÍA

Blessed with a life of privilege, María Augusta Urrutía married at 20 and was widowed by the age of 30. Following this personal tragedy, she focused her life on social work and philanthropy. In addition to feeding Quito's vulnerable children, she founded the **Fundación Mariana de Jesús** in 1939, for the purpose of making education, health and housing accessible to those who most needed it. Through the foundation, she donated land in the south of the city that became Solanda, Quito's first housing development, whose homes were given to those in need. In the north, she created another housing development offering affordable housing, and nearby, donated land that included what became the urban refuge that is now **Parque La Carolina** (p84).

DANIEL CONSTANTE/SHUTTERSTOCK

Encebollado

a gorgeously restored colonial house, one of the first residences in Quito, this privately run museum displays a superb collection of pre-Inca artifacts dating back to 4500 BCE. It's beautifully presented and features priceless ceramics, monolithic carved stones and decorative gold pieces from some 20 indigenous cultures across Ecuador.

MORE PRE-INCA DISCOVERIES

Explore the actual sites where Quito's past civilizations lived, and see their artifacts and ritual remnants at the fascinating **archaeological museums** (p87) of North Quito.

Mercado Central

Authentic Ecuadorian cuisine on the cheap

Few places offer a more authentic glimpse into local life than a city market, and Quito's **Mercado Central** makes the perfect stop for exactly that. The food is the main highlight here, so bring your appetite and a shopping list if you're self-catering. Roam the covered market and choose from an array of traditional local specialties done right. If you've yet to try it, go for *encebollado* (fish stew), an Ecuadorian classic, but otherwise,

EATING IN QUITO: FOOD WITH A VIEW

Vista Hermosa: Ecuadorian dishes and international fare served at a rooftop space overlooking Quito. *noon-midnight Mon-Sat, to 9pm Sun* $$

El Ventanal: Creative Ecuadorian cuisine enjoyed high up within the glassed-in terrace of a converted cable-car station. *5-10pm Tue-Sat* $$

Café Mosaico: Parque Itchimbia bistro with superb views offering burgers, sandwiches, Greek appetizers and vegan options. *noon-11pm Mon-Sat, to 10pm Sun* $$

Pim's: Downhill from the Virgen, treat yourself to an elegant meal with stupendous views of the city from El Panecillo. *noon-10pm Mon-Sat, to 6pm Sun* $$$

there are *corvina* (seabass) dishes, *fritada* (fried chunks of pork, served with hominy) and *locro de papas* (potato soup served with avocado and cheese).

There's an abundance of tropical fruits, sold not only within the market but on the surrounding streets themselves. Perfectly stacked pyramids of mangoes, dragonfruit, pineapple and other in-season produce crowd sidewalk baskets and stands.

An easy 10-minute walk from the heart of the Centro Histórico, the market is a fantastic local stop for an inexpensive, authentic lunch between the churches and museums of the Old Town. It's open daily from 7am to 3pm.

Glimpses into Quito's Colonial History

Step into historic spaces

For a glimpse into the privileged lives of Quito's colonial elites, the Centro Histórico delivers with some beautifully restored and maintained former homes. There's no more lavish setup than **Casa Museo María Augusta Urrutía** *(@fmdj.ecuador; adult/student $4/1.50)*, the 19th-century Andalucian-style home of aristocrat and philanthropist María Augusta Urrutía (1901–87). The ground floor was used to feed up to 50 needy children a day, one of many acts of social service Urrutía contributed to the community.

The **Museo Casa de Sucre** *(museosquito.gob.ec; free)* is another beautifully restored 19th-century home. It was the family residence of Mariscal Antonio José de Sucre, the hero of Ecuadorian independence, who was assassinated in 1830 before he got to live here. History buffs may find it more interesting than most; for others, a wander through should suffice. Both museums are closed on Monday.

For a more engaging presentation of history, head over to the **Museo Alberto Mena Caamaño** *(@museodeceraamc; adult/child $1.50/0.50)*, across from the presidential palace. Displays of wax figures depict the city's key historic events, including the massacre of August 2, 1810, when some 200 independence-seeking *quiteños* were executed. Guided tours are given in Spanish; closed Monday and Tuesday.

The less-visited **Museo del Pasillo** *(museopasillo.gob.ec; museodelpasillo@presidencia.gob.ec; 098-245-6797; free)*, set inside a handsome old bank building (c 1907), charts the history of music in Quito, with a particular focus on *pasillo* (a traditional Ecuadorian music style) from the 19th century to today. There's even an opportunity to sing some, karaoke-style, at the end of the tour. Reservations are required; allow for a 90-minute visit.

Exploring the Old Town's Art Scene

Old Town's dedicated art museums

If the wealth of 17th-century ecclesiastical masterpieces throughout Centro Histórico churches isn't

BEST LIVE-PERFORMANCE VENUES

Teatro Bolívar: Film screenings, plays, orchestral and symphonic performances at this beautiful art-deco landmark (1933).

Teatro Sucre: Featuring dance, music and theatrical performances, this neoclassical theater opened in 1886.

Teatro México: A wide variety of dance and live music, ranging from the traditional indigenous to the avant garde.

Teatro Variedades Ernesto Albán: Art-nouveau theater that hosts stage plays, opera, puppet theater, films and stand-up comedy.

Quito Jazz Club (p73): Immerse yourself in a live performance in this historic house in Mariscal Sucre.

OSWALDO GUAYASAMÍN

If you're here to check out local modern art, you must visit **Capilla del Hombre** (p86) and **Casa Museo Guayasamín** (p87), the gallery and home featuring the works of Ecuador's most famous painter, Oswaldo Guayasamín.

THE QUITO SCHOOL OF ART

Mestizo artists like Bernardo de Legarda and Vicente Albán trained in European baroque-style painting and sculpture at the Quito School of Art (p65), established in 1552 at El Colegio de San Andrés. The Catholic Church converted the indigenous people throughout the Americas either by violence or the gentler strategy of arts education. By training local nobility in the arts, including choral singing and playing musical instruments, the Church influenced the indigenous community through its leaders. These artists, many of whose work went unattributed to them, went on to incorporate familiar imagery, such as local flora and fauna, into the religious paintings adorning the ornate churches of the Centro Histórico.

CHRIS HOWARTH/ECUADOR/ALAMY

Centro de Arte Contemporáneo

enough for you, **Museo de Arte Colonial** *(museosquito.gob.ec; adult/child $1/free)* has a divine collection featuring famous sculptures and paintings of the Quito School. Visitors suffering from museum fatigue can safely skip it.

Check out something more current at the **Centro de Arte Contemporáneo** *(fundacionmuseosquito.gob.ec; free)*, one of Quito's premier modern art spaces. Set within a sprawling site that was a former sanatorium for tuberculosis patients before becoming a military hospital, it now hosts avant-garde exhibits by local and international artists covering anything from photography to cutting-edge digital and mixed-media installations. A light-filled atrium has mats on the floor with a children's play area, where you may find an arts-and-crafts activity happening.

For mid-20th-century modern art, don't miss **Museo Camilo Egas** *(@museocamiloegas; free)*, which showcases the work of *quiteño* artist Camilo Egas (1889–1962). Not only is he one of Ecuador's and Latin America's most famous artists, but he's also a pioneer *indigenista* (indigenous-led movement) painter as renowned in New York as in Quito. Other events in the museum, set inside a small colonial home, include temporary exhibitions of contemporary artists, talks and screenings.

EATING IN CENTRO HISTÓRICO: GLOBAL DINING

Las Cuevas de Luís Candela: Atmospheric vaulted cellar serving authentic Spanish tapas and mains since 1963. *10am-6pm Mon-Sat* $$

Pizza SA: Italian favorite cooking up medium-crust pizzas, with loaded salads and international beers. *11am-9:30pm Mon-Thu, to 10pm Fri & Sat, 11am-8pm Sun* $$

Govinda Gopal: Hare Krishna restaurant popular for its cheap and tasty Indian veg dishes in a converted heritage building. *12:30-6pm Mon-Sat, from 11:30am Sun* $

La Caponata: Sicilian pizza and comfort food, including a good selection of vegetarian and vegan choices, in a welcoming, inviting setting. *noon-10pm* $$

Central Quito

HERITAGE MUSEUMS | ARTISAN MARKETS | EDGY NIGHTLIFE

Where the old town of Centro Histórico ends, the 'new town' begins, bringing about a whole new scene and set of adventures. And after days of trudging along cobblestones and through endless churches, it can offer a welcome change as you move from the 16th century to the current day. But that doesn't mean there's a lack of sights to see here – among several interesting stops is its cultural precinct, home to Ecuador's national museum.

Further north is the bohemian enclave of Mariscal Sucre, one of Quito's liveliest neighborhoods, which is known for its raucous nightlife. Until recently, this was ground zero for backpackers – so much so it was nicknamed 'Gringolandia' – but since the pandemic, the area has fallen out of favor as it struggles to recover from the downturn in tourism, leaving a grittier and edgier vibe. It's still worth visiting, and perfectly safe during the day, but if you're here to party, it's best to arrange a ride home after dark.

Riding High on TelefériQo

Cable car climbing to 4000m

One of Quito's premier tourist attractions is the **TelefériQo** *(teleferico.com.ec; adult/child $9/7)*, a cable car that climbs 2.5km along the lower slopes of Volcán Pichincha to Cruz Loma station (4000m). As one of the world's highest aerial lifts, it unsurprisingly delivers spectacular views. Aim to visit in the morning before the clouds roll in.

From the station, head up the trail to the *mirador* **Columpio en las Nubes** (Swing in the Clouds) at 4100m. Though the swings are invigorating, be courteous about your time so other visitors can enjoy the swoop and scenery.

Though this is as far as most venture, serious hikers use the TelefériQo as an access point to summit the dormant **Rucu Pichincha** (4680m). The round-trip hike is over 10.5km and takes four to five hours from the summit station. Make sure you've acclimatized in Quito for a few days; it's best to bring a guide, though you can hike it independently with proper preparation.

GETTING AROUND

Like most big cities in Latin America, Quito isn't necessarily the safest place to explore on foot at night. In Central Quito, the areas around La Mariscal and Plaza Foch in particular are sketchy after dark, so do visit and enjoy, but travel by licensed taxi or take an Uber at night. Getting here via Quito Metro is super convenient from the Centro Histórico – hop off at **Estación El Ejido**, which drops you into Parque El Ejido, a short walk from Mercado Artesanal La Mariscal.

TOP TIP

Several universities are based in this neighborhood, so during the day allow the vibrant student energy to recharge your batteries, but stay mindful of your environs and belongings while cruising La Mariscal after dusk.

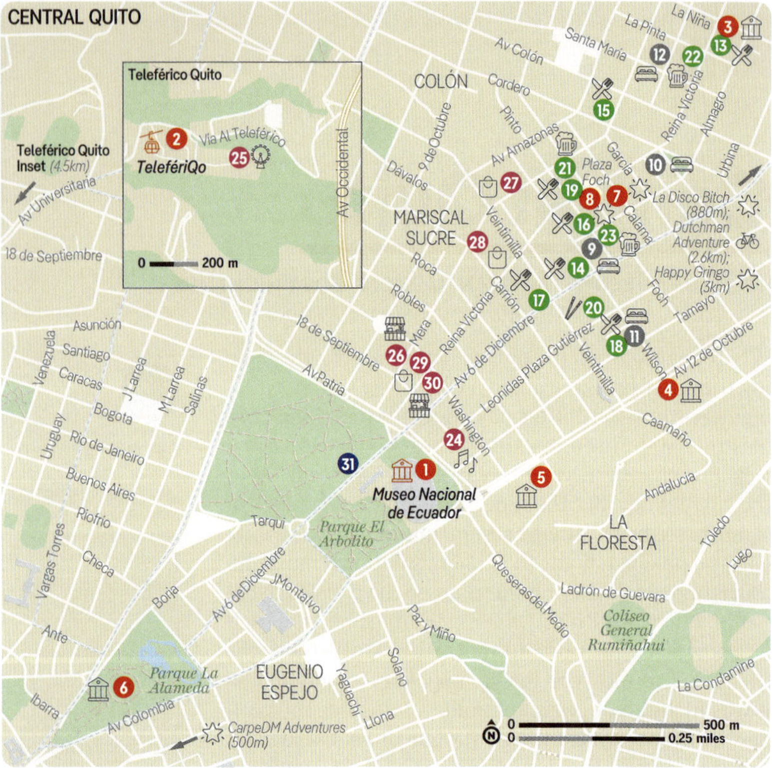

HIGHLIGHTS
1 Museo Nacional de Ecuador
2 TelefériQo

SIGHTS
3 Mindalae
4 Museo Abya-Yala
5 Museo Weilbauer
6 Quito Observatory

ACTIVITIES
7 Desafio Salsa School
8 Gulliver

SLEEPING
9 Blue House
10 Cayman Hotel
11 Ikala Quito Hotel
12 La Rábida Hotel Boutique

EATING
see 10 Achiote
13 Apu Wasi Gastro-Cultura
14 Baalbek
15 Chandani Tandoori
16 El Maple
17 Hacienda de los Arrieros
18 Marcando El Camino
19 Miskay
20 Namu

DRINKING & NIGHTLIFE
21 Corner Pub
22 Django Laboratorio de Cerveza
23 Finn's Irish Pub

ENTERTAINMENT
24 Quito Jazz Club
25 Vulqano Park

SHOPPING
26 Galería Artesanal Mitad del Mundo
27 Galería Latina
28 La Bodega
29 Mercado Artesanal La Mariscal
30 Plaza Artesanal Reina Victoria

TRANSPORT
31 Estación El Ejido

If you've got kids in tow, **Vulqano Park** *(vulqanopark.com; entry free, rides from $1.50)* is a welcome diversion, with bumper cars and basic rides just down the road from the base station.

Shopping Mercado Artesanal La Mariscal

From ponchos to panpipes

If you can't make it to Otavalo, then the sprawling **Mercado Artesanal La Mariscal** *(@mercadoartesanal.mariscal)* is a pretty good alternative, with around 200 stalls selling handicrafts from across Ecuador. Though there's plenty of kitsch, it's packed with alpaca-wool blankets, ponchos and scarves, Andean musical instruments, leather goods, jewelry and art handmade by indigenous craftspeople. A few stalls offer Ecuadorian coffee, chocolate and other edibles that make great souvenirs, making this market an easy one-stop shop for gifts.

Across the way, **Galería Artesanal Mitad del Mundo** *(@galeriaartesanalmdm)* offers a slightly more refined experience with its shopfronts and price tags, and a more curated array of art and handicrafts. It opens at 10am and is closed on Sunday.

Facing the market on the other side of La Mariscal is **Plaza Artesanal Reina Victoria** *(@plazaartesanalreinavictoria)* with a similar setup to La Mariscal, with more indie sellers and a food court if you need to refuel for a longer-than-expected shopping expedition.

The markets are an easy 10-minute walk from Estación El Ejido on the Quito Metro.

For goods beyond alpaca knitwear, **Galería Latina** *(galerialatina.com)* should be on your radar, with its classy, hand-sourced textiles, clothing and handicrafts from across South America. It's open every day but Sunday, as is **La Bodega** *(@labodegaexportadora)*, a fabulous choice for those wanting to browse an eclectic range of Latin American vintage items, from antique jewelry to vinyl. Both are located closer to Plaza Foch.

Ecuadorian Heritage at MuNa

Ancient artifacts and colonial narrative

You may not have time to hit many of Centro Histórico's spectacular museums, but you can take in both indigenous pre-Hispanic artifacts and 20th-century modern art at **Museo Nacional del Ecuador** *(MuNa; muna.culturaypatrimonio.gob.ec; free)*, part of Casa de las Culturas Ecuatorianas. Among its beautifully presented collection of artifacts from Ecuador's varied cultures and regions are exquisite ceramic sculptures and relics dating as far back as 12,000 BCE. Also represented are some of the country's finest artists, with original works by *mestizo* masters Oswaldo Guayasamín and Camilo Egas. This permanent collection is a very manageable amount of space for squeezing a primer on Ecuadorian cultural history into a short visit. Temporary exhibitions also rotate through regularly.

MARKET BARGAINING

When shopping at markets where prices are not listed, as at Mercado Artesanal La Mariscal, expect to do some bargaining as part of the purchase process. Consider starting with an offer at about 50% of the price you're quoted initially and go from there. Keep it friendly and light; vendors are trying to make a living and most aren't out to fleece you. Simply walk away if you feel the price truly doesn't work for you.

Of course, do remember that what to you may be a few dollars' difference may represent quite a significant amount to the vendor, especially on a slow day, week or season.

EATING IN CENTRAL QUITO: ECUADORIAN FAVORITES

Marcando El Camino: Classy bistro enticing foodies with its gastronomic Ecuadorian and international cuisine. *9:30am-9:30pm Tue-Fri, 8:30am-4:30pm Sat* $$

Achiote: Upmarket Ecuadorian dishes accompanied by live music in an inviting space built around a 60-year-old magnolia. *6-9pm Thu-Mon* $$$

Miskay: Overlooks Plaza Foch and offers inventive takes on traditional Ecuadorian food. A good spot to try *cuy*. Reserve ahead. *noon-10pm* $$$

El Maple: One of the area's best spots for vegetarians and vegans to sample Ecuadorian cuisine. *11am-9pm Tue & Wed, from 8am Thu-Sat, 8am-5pm Sun* $

QUITO'S BEST TOUR OPERATORS

CarpeDM Adventures: Experienced, well-priced, thoughtful. Popular for Cotopaxi and equator day trips, as well as the Amazon and beyond.

Happy Gringo: A long-established British/Dutch company offering authentic, tailor-made tours, particularly to the Galápagos and Amazon.

Dutchman Adventure: Ecuador's pioneer mountain-biking operator, with a reputation for excellent tours (and not just cycling).

Free Walking Tours: The 'free' tours (tips always expected) departing Community Hostel (p93) are among the best Quito walking tours.

Gulliver: Dependable, knowledgeable operator offering outdoor adventures in the Andes.

ECUADORPOSTALES/SHUTTERSTOCK

Quito Observatory

More indigenous archaeological treasures await nearby at the compact **Museo Weilbauer** *(puce.edu.ec/centro-cultural/museo-weilbauer; free)* within Pontificia Universidad Católica del Ecuador (PUCE). Reserve ahead to confirm that an English-speaking guide is available for your visit; the museum is closed on weekends.

Gazing up at Quito's Night Sky

South America's oldest observatory

Established in 1873, **Quito Observatory** *(oaq.epn.edu.ec @oaq_ecuador; adult/child $3/1.50)* is South America's oldest astronomical observatory. Ecuador's felicitous position on the equator makes it ideal for observing the skies of both the northern and southern hemispheres. Located in the center of Parque La Alameda, the Victorian-style observatory was modeled after the Bonn Observatory in Germany, designed in the shape of a Greek cross. Now a museum (open on weekdays) and part of the astronomy research institution of Escuela Politécnica Nacional (EPN; National Polytechnic School), the observatory is worth a visit for its 19th-century astronomy and meteorology instruments. The main highlight is its giant German-built Merz telescope, which dates back to 1875 and is open in the evenings by reservation for equatorial stargazers.

EATING IN CENTRAL QUITO: MULTICULTURAL BITES

Hacienda de Los Arrieros: Hearty, cholesterol-heavy Colombian cuisine that will tide you over for the entire day. Veg options available. *11am-11pm* **$$**

Baalbek: Authentic Lebanese serving a mix of meze platters and delicious falafel since 1998. *12:30-4pm Mon-Sat & 6-9:30 Thu-Sat, 12:30-4:30pm Sun* **$$**

Chandani Tandoori: Good place to mix things up with tasty vegetarian and non-veg Indian dishes. *noon-9pm Thu-Sat, to 8:30pm Mon-Wed, to 4pm Sun* **$**

Namu: Get a fix of bulgogi, bibimbap and K-pop at this authentic Korean restaurant. Decor is utilitarian but the atmosphere welcoming. *10am-6pm Mon-Sat* **$**

Mindalae – Ethnographic Handicrafts Museum

Spiritual insights into indigenous artifacts

A superb museum for those interested in indigenous Ecuadorian culture, **Mindalae** *(Museo Etnográfico de Artesanía de Ecuador; mindalae.com.ec; $5)* is open Monday through Saturday. Though you can reserve guided tours ($25 for an English-speaking guide), you can also take a self-guided visit with an introductory rundown of the museum's setup. Inside is a wealth of pre-Hispanic artifacts belonging to indigenous ethnic groups from the Amazon Basin, the Andes and Afro-Ecuadorian coastal communities.

Mindalae has in an unlikely location among restaurants and bars to the north of Mariscal Sucre, but it's well worth the visit for insight into the spiritual beliefs behind the art. The museum is run by the not-for-profit fair-trade organization Fundación Sinchi Sacha, and there's an excellent shop selling indigenous crafts from across Ecuador.

La Mariscal by Night

Late-night dance floors

Mariscal Sucre *was* long the go-to spot where backpackers and *quiteños* converged for late-night dancing. But the post-pandemic years have been brutal for La Mariscal, with many bars, clubs and hostels closing down, letting a sketchier, down-trodden vibe creep in. On evenings out, keep to the main streets with lots of foot traffic and stay alert.

The scene centers around **Plaza Foch**, from where rock bars, *reggaetón* clubs and brewpubs branch out. Walk around this area in the late afternoon for a vibe check and you'll hear the *reggaetón* already thumping loud. Expat hangouts such as **Finn's Irish Pub** *(@finnsquito)* and Dutch-owned **Corner Pub** *(thecornerpubquito.com)* are popular with those looking for a pool table, pub food and live sports on the telly.

Apu Wasi Gastro-Cultura *(@apu.wasi.gastro)*, a cool spot at the northern end of the neighborhood, has an all-vegan menu, local craft beers on tap and an art-filled courtyard. It frequently hosts cultural nights of anything from live music to poetry readings. A block down, brewpub **Django Laboratorio de Cerveza** *(www.djangocerveceria.com)* offers another relaxed spot away from rowdy Plaza Foch. At the southern end of La Mariscal, change it up with a high-quality jazz performance at the intimate **Quito Jazz Club** *(@quitojazzclub)*.

When heading out to a club, expect a cover and bring your passport, as an official ID is often required for entry. Always keep an eye on your drink – surreptitious spiking with scopolamine can be a problem, causing disorientation and memory loss to facilitate robbery. Get to and from your destination by licensed taxi or using a rideshare app, and be sure to test-drive your app in the daytime to make sure you don't run into two-factor authentication or other issues late at night.

BEST DANCE SPOTS

Bongó Dance Center: If you're not super confident with your salsa game, taking a few lessons is a fun way to get your basic step down.

Desafio Salsa School: Tune up your salsa skills and other dance styles before hitting the dance floor.

Salsoteca Lavoe: This popular club in North Quito's Iñaquito neighborhood is a reliable bet for good music and dancers. They also run class series like bachata bootcamps to ramp up your skills.

Safaera: Attracts a younger crowd Thursday through Saturday nights in the Iñaquito area.

La Disco Bitch: Gay club pulling everyone in on Fridays and Saturdays – typically skews younger.

OTHER NIGHTTIME SPOTS

If Mariscal Sucre sounds too edgy for your taste, other areas to check out include **La Floresta** (p74) or **La Pradera** (p80) for a more relaxed bar scene, while downtown **San Blas** (p62) and **La Ronda** (p63) also offer live music and dancing.

La Floresta & Around

CREATIVE HUB | GASTRONOMIC RESTAURANTS | COOL BARS

GETTING AROUND

La Floresta is a great neighborhood to walk around, with a strip of cafes, restaurants and bars clustered along Andalucía. The neighborhood lies adjacent to Mariscal Sucre, through which you can walk (during the day) to the Quito Metro Estación El Ejido in about 25 minutes. At night, catch an Uber from anywhere, or find licensed taxis near the corner of Andalucía and Salazar.

For those who prefer to get their hit of local culture through cool bars, bespoke boutiques, indie record stores and coffee shops rather than from churches, monasteries and cobblestone plazas, be sure to check out La Floresta. Not far from the Old Town, this laid-back, community-minded *barrio* is where *quiteño* creatives hang out, and among its street art and neoclassical mansions (both restored and crumbling), you'll find Quito's most innovative restaurants, a contemporary art scene, and hip bars and cafes.

Established in 1917, this once ritzy neighborhood fell into disrepair. Low rents in the 1990s brought in squatters, filmmakers, artists and writers, who set up its flourishing local arts scene. Like many similar cool neighborhoods around the world, of course, gentrification has seen property prices skyrocket. Among the yuppified elements, it retains its edgy vibe with a liberal, tight-knit community hell-bent on preserving La Floresta's original character.

La Floresta's Coffee Culture

Specialty coffee and cafes

Bohemian neighborhoods and coffee culture go hand in hand, so it's no surprise that La Floresta has some of Quito's best cafes. Here you'll be spoilt for choice for third-wave micro-roasters where expert baristas pour specialty single-origin brews using sustainably sourced Ecuadorian beans.

Local favorite **Nero** *(@nerocafe_)* is your classic neighborhood spot. Pull up a stool at its windowside counter to sip your macchiato and nosh on breakfast. Come back to hang with the cool kids for evening cocktails and DJ sets.

One for coffee and design aficionados alike is **Roveta** *(@roveta.ec)*, a nano-roaster set within a glassed-in coffee lab with a blond timber interior that feels like you've entered a two-story tiny house. It features an intriguing hydraulic lift to deliver superbly made filtered coffees using local beans roasted on-site.

TOP TIP

With its vibrant culinary and bar scene, La Floresta is a great area in which to base yourself. It also happens to be one of Quito's safer neighborhoods, and a short Uber ride away from all the action elsewhere in Quito.

BEN PIPE/ALAMY

A cafe in La Floresta

Located on a busy roundabout, **Coati's** *(@coatis.coffee.house)* is another must-sip venue doing anything from Aeropress, V60 and Chemex filter coffees to flat whites and espresso brewed with local beans by a chatty barista who'll greet you like an old friend. **Cabra Negra** *(cabranegra.com)* is another roaster that takes its coffee very seriously, in terms of both quality and upholding its sustainable ethos.

A few blocks north of La Floresta is **Fankør Coffee** *(fankorcoffee.com)*, a Nordic-inspired cafe specializing in single-origin beans bought directly from coffee farms, which offers tastings of its different light-roasted coffees. It also bakes its own bread, which is a feature of its excellent sandwich and brunch menu.

Glorious Gastronomy

Unpretentious fine dining

Led by a new generation of chefs who have embraced ancestral culinary traditions to create innovative, modern Ecuadorian cuisine, La Floresta's epicurean scene is one no self-respecting foodie will want to miss. Reservations highly recommended.

continues on p78

DE LA FLORESTA

Community organization **De La Floresta Colectiva Cultural** *(delafloresta.com)* is a great starting point for exploring the neighborhood. This collective of cafes, shops and cultural spaces represents the breadth of richness that La Floresta has to offer. Though by no means exhaustive – there are loads of local artists, cafes and other businesses who are not part of the collective – it presents plenty of entry points to this densely abundant *barrio*.

You can pick up printed maps at participating businesses, but there's also an interactive map on its website, and even a Vive La Floresta app.

EATING IN LA FLORESTA: BRUNCH & BAKERIES

Chakra: Healthy food, including pastries and desserts to satisfy the sweet tooth but leave you feeling virtuous. *8am-4pm Mon-Sat* $

Un Pite Dulce: Try something sweet at this bakery making quality breads and pastries that incorporate sourdough. *8:30am-7pm Mon-Fri, to 2pm Sat* $

Dough: Lovely spot for all-day dining, with items varying from *tigrillo* to croque madame to avocado toast. *8am-8pm Mon-Fri, to 6pm Sat & Sun* $

Quito Deli: European-style patisserie and bakery for a sit-down lunch, freshly baked bread and beautiful pastries to take away. *7am-7:30pm Mon-Sat, to 7pm Sun* $

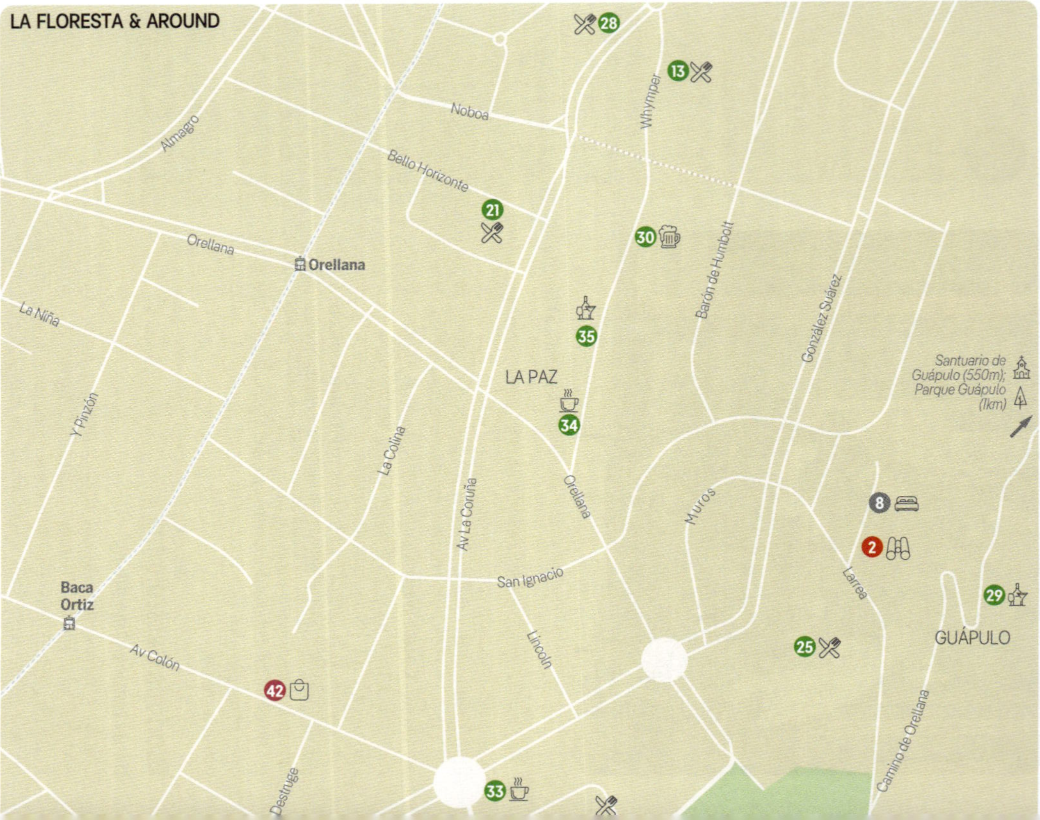

SIGHTS
1 Casa Museo Trude Sojka
2 Mirador de Guápulo
3 N24 Galería de Arte
4 Nudo Street Art Project
5 Quito Publishing House

ACTIVITIES
6 Chawar

SLEEPING
7 Casa Aliso
8 Stubel Suites & Café
9 Swissôtel

EATING
10 Banh Mi
11 Casa Warmi
12 Chakra
13 Chez Jérôme
14 Clara
15 Dough
16 Frida Tacos
17 La Briciola
18 La Cleta Bici Café
19 La Ñora
20 Las Delicias de Doña Anita
21 Nuema
22 Ocho Cafe
23 Quito Deli
24 Segundo Muelle
25 Techo del Mundo
26 Un Pite Dulce
27 Urko
28 Z-Food

DRINKING & NIGHTLIFE
29 Ananké
30 Bandidos Del Paramo
31 Cabra Negra
32 Cela Gastro-Cervecería
33 Coati's
34 Fankør
35 Katari
see 16 La Mezcalería
36 Nero
37 Roveta
38 Sinners Micro-cervecería
39 Tres Pintas Floresta

ENTERTAIN-MENT
40 Ochoymedio

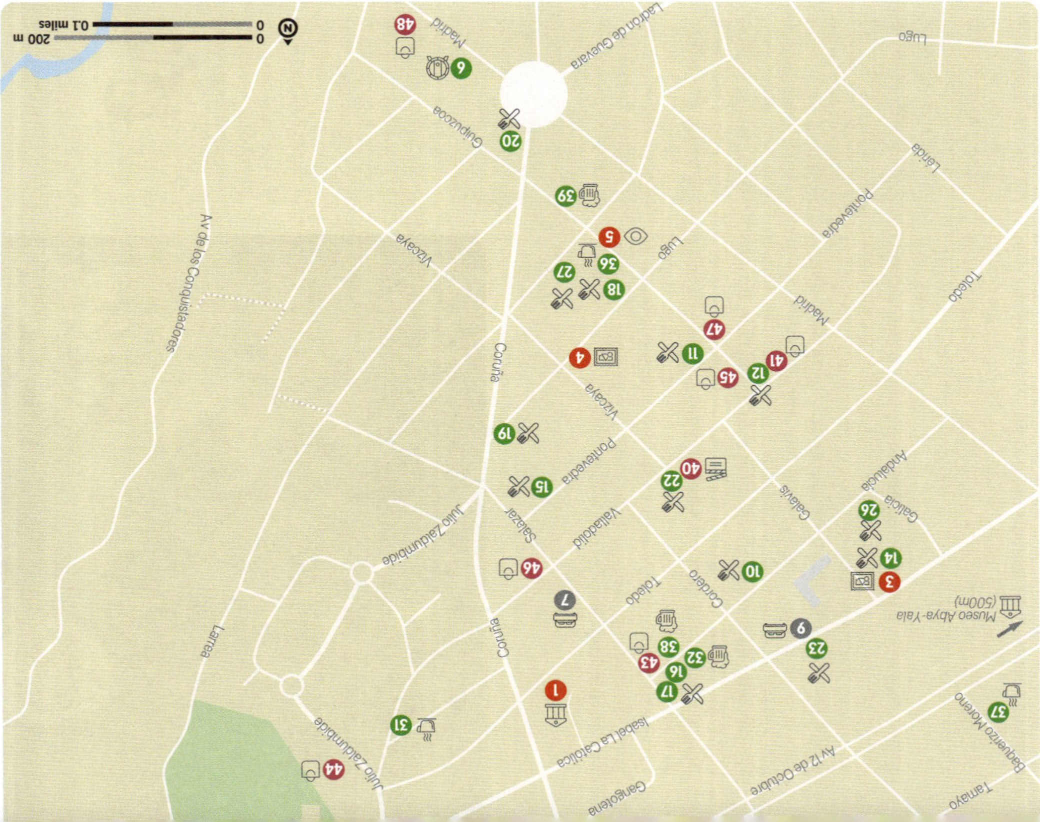

● **SHOPPING**
41 Arte Rayuela
42 Folklore Olga Fisch
43 La ImagiNativa
44 Lava Records
45 Mane Silva
46 Shamuna
47 Sphera
48 Villa Fauna

BOHEMIAN LIVABILITY

Mane Silva, clothing designer and dancer *@manesilvadesign*

After studying fashion design at university, I had the opportunity to work in industrial pattern-making in Italy. While living there, I loved riding my bicycle and walking to get everywhere, never even taking the bus. In 2005 I returned, visiting family in Chile and Argentina, and I saw this movement of many young people in emerging design setting up their own workshops in city centers, renting these big, old houses among other artists. I came back to Ecuador with the idea of doing that too, wanting to find that same rhythm of life that I liked, and I found it in La Floresta. Without thinking twice, I would invite visitors to walk around and explore what was historically a *barrio* of artists and continues to be a lovely neighborhood with so much to enjoy.

continued from p75

One of the city's hottest gastronomic stops, **Nuema** *(nuema.ec)* made #10 in Latin America's 50 Best Restaurants 2025. Run by a husband-wife team, this is a celebration of Ecuador's biodiversity with its 14-course tasting menus taking you on a creative and seasonal journey through the region's flavors.

Nearby is the casual upmarket seafood restaurant **Z-Food** *(zfoodquito.com)*, which is all about sustainable, responsible fishing techniques. Its menu varies from ceviche and seafood stews to good ol' fish and chips.

Chez Jérôme *(chezjeromerestaurante.com)* offers French-Ecuadorian fine dining where you'll get anything from duck confit and foie gras sandwiches to *carrillera de res* (beef cheeks braised in red wine and cacao served with *aligot* made with Yanayacu cheese).

His former restaurant, **Urko** *(urko.rest)* is a Quito institution. Here, current chef Daniel Maldonado's creative seasonal tasting menus follow indigenous agricultural cycles. Expect anything from guinea-pig belly to smoked Amazonian *cachama* fish, all gorgeously plated.

After a few years on the scene, **Clara** *(clara.ec)* has earned its reputation as a high-caliber Ecuadorian restaurant founded by a trio of chefs creating modern twists on traditional cuisine. Wonderful festive ambience and cocktails complement the dishes made for sharing.

Street Art & Murals

Epicenter of urban art

Attracting creatives of all stripes, La Floresta is a vibrant urban gallery of murals, mosaics, paste-ups and stencils.

Here you'll find street-art pieces by local names such as La Suerte, Apitatán and Balseca, along with many works

SOLEDAD ROSALES - WWW.INSTAGRAM.COM/ROSITASOLEDADES

Tasting dishes, Nuema

by visiting artists from around Latin America, in a vibrant urban gallery. Subjects focus heavily on sociopolitical, indigenous and environmental issues faced today, and amid the punk ethos, you'll also find plenty of whimsical pieces incorporating humor and portraits of Andean landscapes and wildlife.

A good place to start a neighborhood ramble is from Ochoymedio (p81), across from which stands a crumbling old building that's become a de facto **street gallery**, tagged with murals, posters, stickers and even some yarn-bomb elements. Some of our favorite murals by visiting artists like Peruvian Elliot Tupac or ERRE from Colombia grace the walls. Also visit **Nudo Street Art Project** *(@nudostreetartproject)*, a space exhibiting more countercultural prints by talented locals and international names. Find artwork, clothing and stickers for sale here, so buy a limited-edition print if it grabs you.

Meet La Floresta's Local Makers

Creativity-nourishing *barrio*

Indie designers flourish in La Floresta – you'll find stuff here you won't find anywhere else.

WHY I LOVE LA FLORESTA

Wendy Yanagihara,
Lonely Planet writer

Staying in La Floresta feels like staying in a hip friend's neighborhood – everything is human-scale, walkable and full of creative life. I love walking around and discovering street art I hadn't noticed before, from small murals to tiny stickers in incongruous places. Stopping for a meticulously prepared coffee in a local joint, browsing an indie designer's shop or bar-hopping on a weekend night all bring me closer to the rhythms of the regulars. In this bohemian mix of *quiteños* both well-traveled and hyper-local, visitors passing through and international inhabitants, the pace feels perfect for starting relaxed conversations and exploring where the artsy set goes to chill.

EATING IN LA FLORESTA: INTERNATIONAL PICKS

Segundo Muelle: Upscale, modern Peruvian with ceviche and Japanese-Peruvian fusion. *noon-4:30pm & 6-10pm Mon-Sat, noon-5pm Sun* **$$$**

La Briciola: Traditional Italian fare with wood-fired pizzas, vegan and vegetarian pastas and salads, and an Italian wine list. *noon-11pm Mon-Sat, to 10pm Sun* **$$**

Banh Mi: Stylish Asian fusion spot serving pho, *pad kra pao llama* and KFC bao to pair with Southeast Asia–inspired cocktails. *lunch & dinner Tue-Sat* **$$**

Frida Tacos: Hip Mexican spot doing authentic, regional dishes with a good veg selection, plus a classy mezcal rooftop bar. *1-10:30pm Tue-Sat, to 5pm Sun* **$$**

LIVE MUSIC & CULTURE EVENTS

Sadly, Quito lost many of its favorite live-music venues during the pandemic, and since then, it's a scene that can be hard to crack. Gigs are often spread across different places as one-off events, so checking the socials of local bars may be your best strategy for catching live music. If you're roaming around La Floresta, stop into Lava Records (p82) to ask what's on while you're in town.

Live music runs the gamut, with Latin genres like salsa, merengue and bachata fueling dance floors, while rock, pop, folk and Afro-Caribbean tunes reflect the diversity of local talent. Thursday through Sunday tends to be your best bet to hear live music.

KAROL KOZLOWSKI PREMIUM RM COLLECTION/ALAMY

Ochoymedio

A contemporary, eclectic assortment of items made by artisans from across Ecuador awaits at **La ImagiNativa** *(laimaginativa.com)*, run by two sisters. Along with clothing, skincare products and gifty items, you'll also find a ceramics workshop in back where you can purchase a blank piece that you can paint yourself – some pieces don't require another firing and can go home with you the same day. For bespoke knickknacks including whimsical handmade wooden toys, hand-printed art cards and pottery, pop into **Arte Rayuela** *(@arte_rayuela_ec)*.

Check out **Villa Fauna** *(@villa.fauna)* for the highly regarded ceramic work of Natalia Espinosa, which includes handmade vessels, homewares and art, as well as jewelry and clothing. Find more threads at the sustainable-fashion boutique of **Mane Silva** (*manesilva.com*; p78), who sells vintage clothing and creates one-of-a-kind pieces upcycling old garments and other textiles into cleverly designed, fun new garments.

Hunt for more secondhand clothing treasures and local artwork at **Sphera** *(@sphera.ec)*, a tiny consignment shop run by local street artist, Antis. Nudo Street Art Project (p79) is a great spot to pick up cool prints and T-shirts by Quito's leading street artists, while **Shamuna** *(shamuna.ec)* sells upmarket streetwear inspired by Ecuador's outdoors that is designed and manufactured in Ecuador.

A Night out in La Floresta

Craft beer, mezcal and music

If you're hankering for quality craft beer, you've come to the right place.

Sinners Microcervecería *(sinners.beer)* is one of Quito's best – the original is in La Pradera, and there's another **branch** on Plaza San Francisco in the Centro Histórico. Along with its award-winning core beers, it brews up seasonals, and the food here doesn't taste like an afterthought.

Across the road is **Cela GastroCervecería** *(@celacerveza)*, the Quito arm of this equator-based brewery (p91), with a cozy enclosed patio and basic pub snacks. The friendly bartenders are happy to offer small tasters to help you decide between current choices on tap.

On Guipuzcoa, the mural-splashed **Tres Pintas Floresta** *(trespintas.ec)* is a convivial neighborhood gastropub serving a meat-heavy menu, including flaming Ukrainian sausages and smoked mutton.

It's well worth the 10-minute walk to Calle Whymper to **Bandidos Del Páramo** *(@bandidos_del_paramo)* – the second branch of Quito's first microbrewery – where its Oregonian owners nail hoppy Pacific Northwest ales to enjoy paired with solid pub grub. Down the road is **Katari** *(kataribeer.com)* where, with its self-serving taps, beer and wine drinkers will be like kids in a candy store – what could ever go wrong?

Not into beer? Rooftop bar **La Mezcalería** *(@lamezcaleria.ec)* specializes in quality mezcals and cocktails to enjoy with authentic Mexican from Frida Tacos (p79) downstairs. For the Ecuadorian version of agave-based alcohol, hole-in-the-wall **Chawar** *(@chawar_miske)* is a small-batch producer of *miske*, the traditional agave-based spirit made by an all-women harvesting co-op using ancient techniques.

Cinema, Coffee & Cocktails at Ochoymedio

Arthouse cinema and cafe

In the heart of La Floresta lies its cherished arthouse cinema, **Ochoymedio** *(ochoymedio.net)*, founded in 2001 by a group of filmmakers and artists with the intention of promoting cinematic culture. This indie theatre screens both local and international films, including current releases as well as cult classics and older obscurities, and hosts several film festivals. Screenings are subtitled in Spanish, so there's no dubbing. Check out what's on and buy tickets at the website.

You can enjoy the creative energy even if you're not here to see a movie – the cool **Ocho Café** *(@ochocafeuio)* operates front of house daily, from morning to late in the evening (opening at noon Sunday and Monday).

UNIVERSITY ENERGY

Around La Floresta and Mariscal Sucre are about half a dozen universities – Pontificia Universidad Católica del Ecuador (PUCE), Universidad Central del Ecuador, Universidad Politécnica Nacional to name a few.

Which is why, along with the bohemian flavor of La Floresta and the rougher edges of Mariscal Sucre, there's the buzz of student energy and knots of young people throughout. Clustered around street vendors selling snacks, oblivious in the bubbles of makeout sessions on quieter blocks, and packing cafes, the youthful element is palpable. In the late afternoon and early evenings, that weekend energy starts ramping up around La Mariscal, and then spilling out into late-night cheap eateries.

EATING IN LA FLORESTA: NEIGHBORHOOD FAVES

La Ñora: Traditional fare like *llapingachos*, *encebollado* and ceviche with a creative twist. Lunch specials are a great deal. *9am-4:30pm* **$**

Las Delicias de Doña Anita: Popular spot for *bolón*, empanadas, *muchines* (yuca fritters stuffed with cheese or pork), *fritada* and *seco de pollo*. *6-11pm Mon-Sat* **$**

La Cleta Bici Café: Cafe with decor assembled from bicycle parts. Beer, coffee, sandwiches and pizza. *11:30am-10pm Mon-Fri, 5:30-11pm Sat* **$$**

Casa Warmi: Stellar women-run cafe offering traditional Andean dishes, salads and sandwiches in a light-filled interior. *9am-9:30pm Wed-Sat, to 3:30pm Sun & Tue* **$$**

LAVA RECORDS

Short for La Venganza del Análogo (The Revenge of Analog), **Lava Records** *(lava-records.com)* is primarily a music store selling vinyl, CDs and even cassette tapes (!). The shop was established in 2020 by and for music lovers, particularly fans of old-school media formats.

Since it carries a lot of music from local bands, it's a killer shop at which to uncover your new favorite *quiteño* tunes. But it's also a great place to hang out a while with fellow audiophiles. Here you can order coffee, snacks, craft beer or *canelazo* (spiced *aguardiente* served warm) and kick back to the sounds of whatever indie tunes they're spinning in what's one of the coolest record stores you'll find anywhere in the world.

JOPSSTOCK/SHUTTERSTOCK

Santuario de Guápulo

Dip into La Floresta's Artistic Roots

Galleries and cultural history

La Floresta has had a significant Jewish population since WWII, and at **Casa Museo Trude Sojka** *(trudesojka.museum; adult/student from $3/2)* you can see the gallery of Holocaust survivor Trude Sojka (1909–2007). This celebrated Czech-Ecuadorian artist was an established painter and sculptor whose works were displayed in Berlin before she was sent to Auschwitz. Fortunately, she managed to flee and arrived in Guayaquil in 1946. Today, her daughter, a designer herself, guides tours of what was once her home and is now a gallery and moving space educating future generations about the atrocities of the Holocaust. Reservations required.

Another who fled Nazi persecution in Europe was Hungarian Bauhaus designer Olga Fisch (1901–90), who escaped the Nazis in 1939, arriving in Ecuador and embracing her adoptive land. Especially taken with indigenous art, she incorporated Ecuadorian folk culture into her own designs and set up her store, **Folklore Olga Fisch** *(olgafisch.com)*. The flagship store remains *the* place to go for high-quality tapestries, clothing, homewares, jewelry and accessories, made in close collaboration with its artisans in a fair-trade relationship. You'll also find a small museum displaying pre-Hispanic artifacts.

While the *barrio* is famous for its street art (p78), another must for avant-garde art lovers is **N24 Galería de Arte** *(@n24galeria)*. This former jazz club (and factory before that) is a wonderful space see to exhibitions of emerging and established alternative artists.

Incongruous to its surrounds is the contemporary six-story **Quito Publishing House**. Despite it being an ecofriendly 'green building' designed to incorporate sustainability and energy efficiency, this landmark was fiercely opposed by the

La Floresta community, who feared that their neighborhood – filled with beautiful neoclassical mansions – would soon be consumed by high-rise development.

Museo Abya-Yala

Intriguing diversity of Amazonian culture

The underrated **Museo Abya-Yala** *(@museoabyayala; free)* shines a fascinating, indigenous-centered spotlight on Amazonian cultures. Set within Universidad Politécnica Salesiana (UPS; Salesian Polytechnic University), self-guided tours with an English-language booklet (or guided tours in Spanish) take you through rooms exhibiting the more conventional examples of grinding stones, vessels for food and drink, and sculptural pieces from ancient cultures such as the Huapula, Valdivia and Jama Coaque.

The exhibits then move on to living Amazon cultures and their various spiritual beliefs, family structures, shamanic rituals and daily practices, with examples of cooking and hunting tools (including a full-sized canoe), ceremonial garments, everyday adornments and musical instruments.

One of its most unusual exhibits is a collection of 19th-century shrunken heads, the result of a meticulous, if gruesome, cultural practice. Though relatively compact, this less-visited museum has a well-organized and insightful collection.

Guápulo's Under-the-Radar Charm

Dramatic views and village church

Flowing on from La Floresta is the adjoining *barrio* of **Guápulo**, one of Quito's most scenic and relaxed neighborhoods.

Take in vistas stretching across the forested hills of the Cumbayá and Tumbaco valleys at **Mirador de Guápulo**. On clear days, you can easily see the snowcapped peak of Volcán Cayambe. The graffitied *mirador* draws couples at the rosy-lit sunset hour, and there's even a 'love lock' phenomenon happening on the fence, with padlocks testifying to true love.

Stop by for the breakfast buffet in the lovely morning light at **Techo del Mundo** *(Roof of the World; @restaurantetechodelmundo; buffet adult/child $15/8)* inside Hotel Quito, then wander down the hillside park below the *mirador* to the steep, winding cobblestoned roads of Guápulo. At the bottom of the stairway past the park, take Pasaje Iberia to another stellar viewpoint. Or turn right along Orellana to round the hairpin turn downhill, and you'll happen upon fan-favorite **Ananké** *(@anake3microclimas)*. Unassuming from the outside, this converted rabbit warren of a house opens up to spectacular panoramas, best enjoyed with a glass of wine, delicious pizza, fireplaces and occasional live music.

Continue zigzagging down to check out the 17th-century **Santuario de Guápulo**. Guided tours lead you through this neoclassical domed church with museum and original masterpieces of the Quito School. Nearby **Parque Guápulo** is an expansive green space set over 47 hectares with walking and cycling trails – hot tip: bring mosquito repellent.

GREENERY & SUSTAINABILITY

In 2024, a wildfire broke out in Guápulo, prompting evacuations and resulting in the incineration of homes and businesses. At the time, multiple other fires were burning across Quito during a season of drought, greatly exacerbating the city's poor air quality. In the city's worst fire in 30 years, 193 hectares – much of it forested land – were decimated.

While reforestation efforts continue, the fire served as a reminder that urban forests are the lungs of the city. Organizations such as **Fundación Entrejardines** *(@entrejardines.ec)* are working to manage the organic waste in Quito through composting initiatives, as well as promoting sustainability awareness at the neighborhood level with tree-planting projects and community gardens.

North Quito

URBAN GREENERY | HIGH-END EATERIES | ARCHAEOLOGICAL SITES

GETTING AROUND

Taxis and rideshares from the Centro Histórico to North Quito take 15 to 20 minutes, and longer during rush hour. Even more convenient is the Quito Metro, except during weekday rush hours when it is jammed and sweaty. The Metro's Estación La Carolina is at the south end of Parque La Carolina, while Estación Iñaquito serves the park's north end. Once you're there, walking is the best way to experience the park and surrounding avenues.

TOP TIP

If creaky colonial houses where lots of things go bump in the night sound like a sleepless nightmare to you, the comfortably modern, more soundproofed hotels of North Quito might be a better base for your Quito adventures.

Heading north from the bohemian enclaves of Mariscal Sucre and La Floresta brings you to Quito's central park and business district, both known as La Carolina. The modern and more moneyed side of the city resides here, its high-rises and financial institutions complemented by the people's green space, established by a *quiteña* heiress-philanthropist of the late 19th century. Within Parque La Carolina, the botanical garden is a a great spot to catch a glimpse of Ecuador's biodiversity, while outside the park, the district is home to some of the city's best places to eat.

You'll also find the stunning gallery and former home of Ecuador's most famous artist, Oswaldo Guayasamín, which is unquestionably one of Quito's must-see sights, adjacent to the city's largest metropolitan park. Pre-Inca ruins, a thriving craft-brewery scene and a soccer (football) stadium are among the contemporary pleasures to be found in 'new town' Quito.

Hanging out in Parque La Carolina

Botanical gardens, active pursuits and street food

Relax with the locals in the expansive **Parque La Carolina**, the 165-acre urban park anchoring North Quito. On weekends, it's packed with *quiteños* of all demographics, here for its street-food stalls, picnicking and active pursuits.

During the week there's less action, making it a great time to jog the 3.9km **loop trail** around the park's perimeter or the many paths within, or to roam the **Jardín Botánico de Quito** *(jardinbotanicoquito.com; adult/child $4/2)*. Habitats represented at the botanical garden include *páramo* (high-altitude Andean grasslands), cloud forest and wetlands, and the gardens include an *orquideario* (orchid greenhouse), an ethnobotanical garden (exploring the plants used by indigenous groups), an Amazonian greenhouse with carnivorous plants, a bonsai collection and a magnificent cactus garden. Bejeweled hummingbirds flit and feed here year-round.

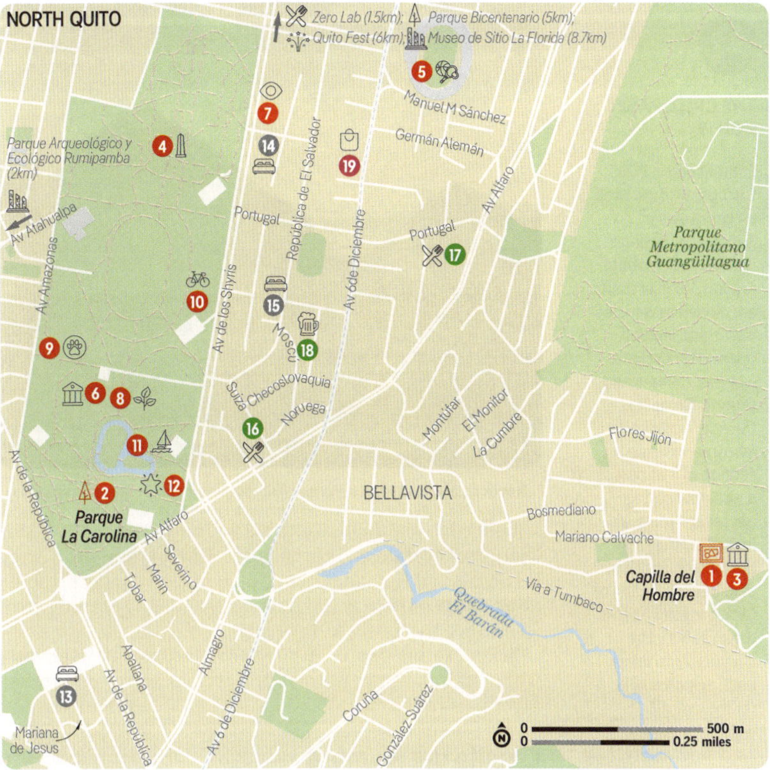

HIGHLIGHTS
1 Capilla del Hombre
2 Parque La Carolina

SIGHTS
3 Casa Museo Guayasamín
4 DC-6
5 Estadio Olimpico Atahualpa
6 Instituto Nacional de Biodiversidad
7 IQON Building
8 Jardín Botánico de Quito
9 Vivarium

ACTIVITIES
10 BMX track
11 Paddleboats
12 Skate park

SLEEPING
13 Hotel Casa Q
14 Hotel Finlandia
15 Le Parc

EATING
16 De La Llama
17 Somos

DRINKING & NIGHTLIFE
18 VIVA Cerveza!

SHOPPING
19 Confederate Books

Next door to the botanical garden is the **Instituto Nacional de Biodiversidad** *(INABIO; inabio.biodiversidad.gob.ec; adult/child $4/2.50)*, a natural-history museum open on weekdays. It illustrates Ecuador's biodiversity and is a repository of current research with taxidermied Ecuadorian species (including Andean spectacled bear and condor) and the fossilized remains of a mastodon, which roamed this area some 20 million years ago. For a hands-on experience, head to the **Vivarium** *(vivarium.org.ec; $4/2.50)* in the park's western section, where you can get acquainted with South American reptile friends, Tuesday to Sunday.

Nearby, rent **paddleboats** *(30min $6)* at the park's lagoon, making a lap or two around the concrete waterway under

THE CICLOPASEO ROUTE

Established in 2003, Ciclopaseo descends on Quito every Sunday. Following a north-to-south route, around 30km of roads are closed to vehicle traffic and instead opened for cyclists, walkers, runners and skaters. Some ride the entire course, but many people ride a section of it as part of a weekend outing.

In recent years, a lack of funding saw the municipality hand over administration of Ciclopaseo to a private organization. The city has since taken back responsibility for the event, but without adequate funding for safety officers and route barriers, the event is currently in a state of flux. Ask locally about developments during your visit.

CRETAN NOMAD/SHUTTERSTOCK

Replicas of ancient huts, Parque Arqueológico y Ecológico Rumipamba

a footbridge and fountain. It's also fun to watch little kids charging the dips and turns at the **BMX track** near Av de los Shyris and Holanda, and if you brought your deck, there's also a **skate park** near Shyris and Eloy Alfaro, another a great spot to see the local skaters' skillz.

Pickpocketing can be a nuisance here, so enjoy the park while taking all the normal precautions you would in any other part of the city.

Capilla del Hombre

The life and works of Quito's favorite son

The world-class gallery and modernist home of Ecuador's most famous artist, Oswaldo Guayasamín (1919–99) is not to be missed. Featuring the essential collection of his work under one roof, the formidable **Capilla del Hombre** *(Chapel of Man; @fundacion.guayasamin; adult/child $10/5)* is much more than a gallery: it's Guayasamín's final masterpiece.

Paying homage to one of Latin America's greatest expressionist painters, this grand, cathedral-sized space blends modernist and pre-Columbian architectural styles in a monolithic building constructed from volcanic rock and topped with a cylindrical pyramid. A design conceived by the artist himself, construction commenced in 1995 and was not completed till 2002 – three years after his passing.

Many of his powerful, giant canvases explore themes of social injustice throughout Latin America, particularly among oppressed indigenous communities (Guayasamín himself was of *mestizo* heritage) and their struggles against colonialism. The gallery's soaring domed interior features Guayasamín's unfinished masterpiece, a mural of floating skeletal figures gravitating toward the light.

Behind the gallery are the amazing pre-Inca tombs that were discovered during the construction of Capilla del Hombre.

Enclosed within a glass walkway, you can view the tombs and remnants of offerings within.

Equally impressive is **Casa Museo Guayasamín**, the artist's former residence, left largely untouched since his passing. Tours lead through this modernist stunner, which was constructed in 1976. It's decorated with Guayasamín's prized collection of pre-Columbian artifacts, religious works (despite his staunch atheism), and art-filled rooms featuring his workspace and photos of luminaries he called friends, including Fidel Castro.

Cruising Contemporary La Carolina

Quito's central business district culture

You've probably not come to Quito for the new, shiny side of the city, but the streets of La Carolina are worth a wander.

Av República de El Salvador is the main thoroughfare and unlike anything else you'll encounter in Quito. It's modern and affluent, and has an array of Westernized retail and eating options. Have an awesome Ecuadorian craft beer at **VIVA Cerveza!** *(facebook.com/VIVACervezaEc)*, a rock 'n' roll brewpub with live bands and DJs on Wednesday and Saturday, and a good place for solo travelers on Tuesday for its English exchange nights.

Speaking of English, if you're after a good page-turner, the well-hidden **Confederate Books** has a wealth of secondhand English-language titles; open Monday to Saturday.

The 133m-high **IQON building** brings the city into the 21st century for contemporary design. Overlooking Parque La Carolina, it's the capital's tallest building, and with its pixelated facade and cascading balconies, it's a standout among the city's otherwise drab high-rises.

As everywhere in South America, attending a football (soccer) match in Quito is a phenomenal cultural experience. Packing in 35,000 fans, **Estadio Olímpico Atahualpa** can have an electric atmosphere, and it's worth checking out a game if you're in town.

The Layered Archaeology of Quito's Culture

Quitu Archaeological Museums

For those interested in the ancestral culture of the indigenous Quitu (Quillaco) people who founded Quito some 4000 years before the Inca arrived, you'll find a few small pre-Inca archaeological sites around the city.

Parque Arqueológico y Ecológico Rumipamba *(museos quito.gob.ec; free)* intermittently conducts archaeological digs on-site. Guided tours (call ahead to confirm the availability of

QUITO AIRFIELDS

Before Aeropuerto Internacional Mariscal Sucre existed in its current Tababela location, Quito's airport had operated since 1960 at the city's northern edge. Hemmed in by urban sprawl, and increasingly hazardous as a high-altitude airport hosting heavier international air traffic, the old airport ceased operations in 2013. In a laudable civic move, the city repurposed the old airport grounds into the metropolitan **Parque Bicentenario**, with playgrounds, soccer fields, basketball and tennis courts, trails and old tarmac now used for cycling and jogging.

But predating even the old airport, Parque La Carolina had been used as an airfield since the 1920s. As a nod to that history, there's a retired **DC-6** in the northern sector of the park.

EATING & DRINKING IN NORTH QUITO: OUR PICKS

Andes Brew Pub: In La Pradera, Andes stands out for its vibrant setting, tasty food and wonderful beers. *5-11pm Mon, 4pm-midnight Tue-Thu, 2pm-1am Fri & Sat* $

De La Llama: Ecuadorian food, good cocktails, contemporary decor and an attractive outdoor courtyard. *12:30-10pm Tue-Fri, 11:30am-4pm Sat & Sun* $$

Somos: Chef-owner Alejandra Espinoza whips up inventive dishes inspired by flavors spanning the Andes, Amazon and coast. *lunch & dinner* $$$

Zero Lab: Award-winner serving *cuy* stuffed with smoked pork belly and Andean salmon confit. Reserve ahead. *12:30-11pm Tue-Sat, to 9:30pm Sun & Mon* $$$

HOLES IN HISTORY

Daniel Ávila, Research Assistant at Parque Arqueológico y Ecológico Rumipamba

Having assisted the archaeologists on digs in my six years here, I realized how deep a hole we have in our understanding of Quito's beginnings. *Quiteños* know our own basic history, in that our city didn't suddenly appear when the Spanish conquered these lands. But we still have so little knowledge about the people who chose this location 3300 years ago and survived here coexisting with volcanoes.

There's so much amazing history under our feet, like postholes beneath the surface suggesting the existence of a sedentary culture at this very site. Ceramic pieces uncovered here matched others from the Cotocollao culture, the oldest settlement of the city.

INGOLAI-PHOTOGRAPHY/SHUTTERSTOCK

Dancers at a festival in Quito

English-speaking guides) lead you through Quito's natural history, early civilizations and artifacts on display before heading outdoors to the 32 hectares protecting various archaeological sites. Archaeological discoveries at the park show evidence that multiple cultures over several periods since 1500 BCE have dwelled here; a fascinating **mini-museum** focuses on death customs, including recreations of burial chambers found here.

The wooded park includes a verdant *quebrada* (ravine), whose creek made the site ideal for habitation, and a re-creation of a *culunco*, part of a pre-Incan trail system following natural drainages sheltered by foliage, creating natural corridors.

There's another small archaeological museum in the outer suburb of La Florida, where a necropolis dating back to 400 BCE was discovered in the 1980s. On this site, the wonderful **Museo de Sitio La Florida** *(museosquito.gob.ec; free)* displays various pieces unearthed from its 15m-deep funerary chambers, including ceramics and clothing made of spondylus shells. It also has a recreated example of the chambers found here. As at Rumipamba, call to check if an English guide is available during your visit.

Quito Fest

Local and international music

Quiteños kick off the holiday season in November with what seems like an endless stream of neighborhood fiestas well before Christmas. Arriving during the excitement of the multiday Fiestas de Quito (p65) in late November comes **Quito Fest** *(quitofest.com; free)* in Parque Bicentenario. This joyful, annual, independent music festival falls on the last weekend of November, bringing in local and international acts who perform over three days and range across genres, from indigenous, hip-hop and *cumbia* to metal and pop. Emerging Ecuadorian artists can audition for one of some dozen spots for a chance to perform, making it a fantastic place to hear up-and-comers as well as favorite Latin American artists.

The Equator

LATITUDE ZERO | QUIRKY MUSEUMS | GRASSROOTS ECOTOURISM

Though the equator passes through 13 countries, slicing through Africa, Asia and South America to divide the northern and southern hemispheres, no country celebrates this geographical feature more than Ecuador. And given it's named after the equator (*ecuador* is Spanish for 'equator'), that's no great surprise.

The equator is accessible from Quito. In fact, it's a popular trip, not just for the equatorial line itself but for the many cultural attractions, including monuments, museums and the stunning inter-Andean valley landscapes. You can't come here and not get that kitschy photo of you standing in two hemispheres at once, but a visit here also adds meaning, given the symbolism it has to the nation.

Long before the 18th-century Spanish-French astronomers arrived on a mission to mark the equator, pre-Inca indigenous people had already identified it. Unlike the arc measurements of Europeans – whose readings were off – the Quitu had correctly located it down to the exact dot of today's GPS technology through tracking the sun's path for what's believed to be agricultural, navigational and ritual purposes.

GETTING AROUND

Organized day trips from Quito are cheap, convenient and easy to come by if you want to hit the equatorial headliners. But if you're interested in some of the culture and landscape beyond the museum stops, which range from agave-spirit tasting, a homegrown nature reserve in town or hiking to the floor of a volcanic caldera, you'll need to book a taxi for the day for around $50. Be sure to establish where you'd like to go when you negotiate the fee, as sites like Cerro Catequilla are a little off the usual day-tripper circuit.

The Middle of the World

Equatorial monument and cultural displays

The equator's centerpiece attraction is **Mitad del Mundo** *(Middle of the World; mitaddelmundo.gob.ec; adult/child $5/2.50)*, a cultural museum built in the late 1970s to commemorate the spot where the 18th-century Spanish-French Geodesic Mission arrived to mark the 'middle of the world'. Awkwardly, it was later discovered to be about 200m off. Despite the error, crowds flock for selfies along the yellow line marking the not-quite equator, and to scale its 30m-high, stone trapezoidal monument. Among the restaurants and microbrewery are various small museums dedicated to anything from beer to chocolate. The sprawling site has a bit of

HIGHLIGHTS
1 Mitad del Mundo
2 Reserva Geobotánica Pululahua

SIGHTS
3 Casa Agave
4 Cerro Catequilla
5 Museo de la Luna
see 1 Museo Intiñan
6 PomasQuinde
7 Templo del Sol
see 2 Volcán Pululahua Mirador

SLEEPING
8 El Crater
9 La Pedregoza
see 9 Pululahua Hostal

EATING
see 1 Balcón al Mundo
see 2 Cafetería El Mirador
see 1 Calima
see 8 Restaurante El Cráter
see 7 Sabor de Pululahua

DRINKING & NIGHTLIFE
see 1 Cela Cerveza Artesanal
10 Santana Brewing Company

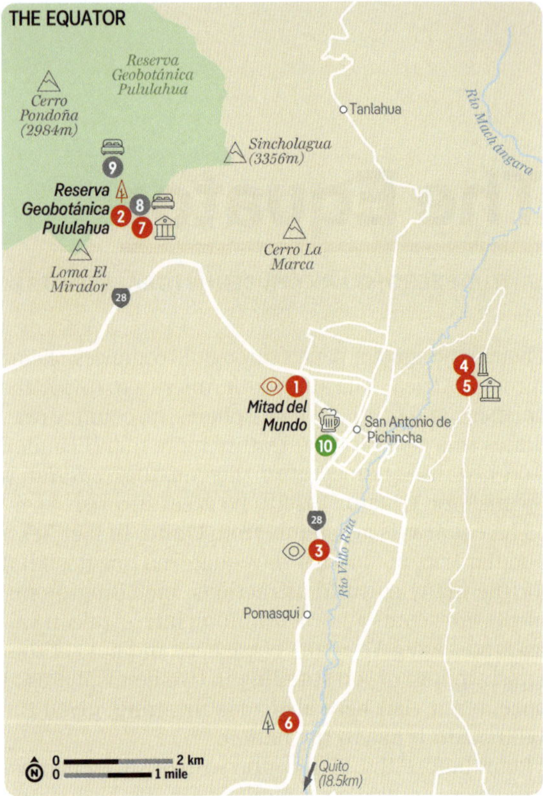

a tacky theme-park feel, but embracing the hokeyness for a quick walkaround and pics is part of the fun.

Museo Intiñan

Whimsical equator museum

A favorite among day-trippers, the quirky **Museo Intiñan** *(@museo_intinan; $5)* prides itself on being the real location of the equator. Guided tours take you to a 19th-century 'solar chronometer,' which shows precise astronomical and conventional time and the month, day and season – all by using rays of the sun. But the main attractions are its weird and wacky demonstrations and 'challenges' illustrating the natural phenomena at latitude zero. Like an illusionist magic show, they will leave you as intrigued as dubious. Tours walk you through the cultural museum, which includes an original house on the premises dating to 1875 with insulating adobe walls, traditionally woven sleeping mats and period tools. Other buildings house displays of Amazon culture, including poison-dart gear, a canoe and ceremonial red powder made from the achiote seed. You'll also see – perhaps a bit close for comfort – actual specimens of shrunken heads, as well as a sample of the dreaded candiru fish.

TOP TIP

If you only have time for a half-day excursion, leave Quito around 8am. Have a look from the Volcán Pululahua Mirador, visit Museo Intiñan and follow up with a stroll through PomasQuinde or a drive up Cerro Catequilla (p92) before returning to Quito for a late lunch.

Peer into Volcán Pululahua

Misty magic of an inhabited volcano

A 4km drive north from La Mitad del Mundo takes you to the stunning **Reserva Geobotánica Pululahua** *(free),* where you'll be treated to magical views over the crater of dormant Volcán Pululahua, one of only two inhabited calderas in the world.

Most day tours to Mitad del Mundo stop here for a quick look from the **mirador**, but if you're visiting independently, plan for a hike down the 1.7km-long **Ventanillas Trail** to the caldera floor to the agricultural community of Pululahua (population: around 60). You can even stay overnight in one of the local lodgings, like Pululahua Hostal (p93), where you can stargaze from the hot tub.

If you're day hiking, take note of the trail's steepness, as the climb out will take about twice the time of your descent; allow 90 minutes for the round trip. On weekends and holidays, it's possible to take a **horse ride** between 10:30am and 5pm; call 096-989-6405 or 098-124-6681 for more info.

Near the viewpoint is the **Museo Templo del Sol** *(adult/child $4/2),* a re-creation of an Inca temple. While the architecture and artwork is interesting, the price of admission buys you a tour serving mostly as a sales pitch for the products inside.

Refresh in an Inspiring Urban Jungle

Grassroots ecotourism at its finest

Just 23km north of the capital on the road to Mitad del Mundo, you'll find a unique oasis in the town of Pomasqui where Rolando Luna and his father undertook a massive effort to reforest their backyard and transform it into **PomasQuinde** *(@pomasquinde; adult/child $4/2),* a mini urban jungle. From the outside, it looks like any other suburban house, but beyond it lies a bird-filled ravine – formerly a rubbish dumping ground. Hummingbirds are among the 32 species, lured by feeders and birdbaths, that you'll see as you're led on a tour, finishing with meditation in a cave, from which you emerge energized and enchanted by the passion of this unique place. Donations beyond the modest admission fee fund this family-run labor of love.

Drop in for a Drop at Casa Agave

Traditional Andean spirit

On a mission to revive Ecuador's ancestral past is **Casa Agave** (*@casa_agave.ec*), a *miske* distillery set up by its passionate

DRAWING A LINE

Though we may think of the equator as an exact, fixed line clearly delineating the hemispheres, it actually shifts ever so slightly throughout the year. In relation to the Earth's poles, the equatorial plane drifts within a range of 9m as the planet's rotational axis wobbles during its orbit, due to forces of the planet's magnetic and electrical fields. According to NASA, the effects of climate change, global distribution of water from glacial melt and tectonic activity may all contribute to tinier shifts in the location of the poles. All of which is to say, not even the equator is set in stone.

EATING & DRINKING AT THE EQUATOR

Santana Brewing Company: Microbrewery with a lawn patio for enjoying ales and Ecuadorian cuisine. *noon-5pm Wed-Fri, 9am-5pm Sat, to 4pm Sun* **$$**

Calima: Part of the Mitad del Mundo complex, this charming little bistro festooned with flowers has served traditional Ecuadorian cuisine since 1987. *9:30am-6pm* **$**

Cela Cerveza Artesanal: Nanobrewery with beers you can sample at the Museo de la Cerveza bar at Mitad del Mundo. *9am-5pm Mon-Fri, to 6pm Sat & Sun* **$**

Balcón al Mundo: Part of the Mitad del Mundo complex. Has balcony dining with Ecuadorian fare and country views. *9am-5pm Mon-Fri, to 6pm Sat & Sun* **$**

owner, Diego Mora, who's added a museum and restaurant to showcase the local agave-based spirit. It's not tequila, nor is it mezcal, but rather a traditional spirit made from the agave sap called *chawarmisqui*. Though tours are a little pricey ($17), they're worth it for fascinating insights into the ancient production process and the multipurpose uses of agave itself, as well as the tasting at the end. Two-hour tours are offered Tuesday through Sunday at 11:30am, 1:30pm, 3pm and 5pm. If you don't have time for a tour, drop in between 10am and 5pm to enjoy a creative *miske* cocktail.

Ceremonial Cerro Catequilla

Ancient hilltop equatorial site

Offering a serene alternative to the more commercial equator sights, this pre-Inca mountaintop monument (2638m) rewards visitors with a more poignant and authentic cultural experience. Unlike the others, GPS data shows this to be exactly 0°0'0", where the equatorial line passes through the hill's summit.

What makes **Cerro Catequilla** all the more remarkable is that it predates European data and is linked to the indigenous Quitu people, who, it's believed, used this as an astronomical observatory. The name Catequilla is derived from Kati Killa, Kichwa for 'the one who follows the moon.'

Cerro Catequilla is notable not only for its cultural significance as a sacred site, but also because it's a rare island of xerophytic scrubland. On this isolated hill, the flora here is adapted to survive in this high-altitude, low-rainfall environment. As you drive up the road, you'll notice the yellow or red birdlike tillandsia shooting up amid the scrub, as well as cacti and spiky succulents, including agave. Once you're walking around atop the peak, notice the hardy plant life at your feet – you may spot the tiny blue blossoms of azulita trepadora, or hot pink pescadito waving in the wind.

The site is accessed via a steep dirt road approximately 7km east of the town of San Antonio. You'll spot the hilltop's monolithic sculpture as you drive up the road; up close, you'll see that it's a series of segments, representing the 12 months of the year. At the northwestern corner of the site, you'll find a pre-Incan stone disk.

Give it a miss if it's been raining – the narrow dirt road is the width of one vehicle most of the way, with precarious drop-offs in some sections.

Below the summit, the **Museo de la Luna** *(museodelaluna.com)* is currently under construction; visit the website for information on occasional events held atop this sacred peak.

RESERVA GEOBOTÁNICA PULULAHUA

The melodious name Pululahua is Kichwa for 'cloud of water' – the aptness of this name will be evident to visitors who arrive around midday and witness the fog flowing in over the valley. Declared a national park in 1966, Reserva Geobotánica Pululahua covers 3383 hectares within the crater of Volcán Pululahua. Later in 1978, its status was re-designated as a geobotanical reserve, due to its geological uniqueness and biodiversity. The reserve contains lava domes, a thermal (though not hot) spring with mineral mud, cloud forest and a multitude of hummingbird and orchid species representing some of the more colorful fauna and flora in this volcanic paradise.

EATING & DRINKING IN PULULAHUA & POMASQUI

Restaurante El Cráter: Enjoy an elegant Ecuadorian lunch at the restaurant of El Cráter Hotel, with gorgeous views of the reserve. *lunch & dinner* $$

Sabor de Pululahua: Warm up with a delicious bowl of *locro*, empanadas or hot *canelazo* at this cozy spot next to the reserve's parking lot. *8am-6pm Fri-Sun* $

Cafetería El Mirador: On the edge of the crater, the terrace is a picturesque perch for a spot of coca tea, but come for the views and not the food. *9am-5pm* $

Casa Agave: If the *miske* tasting whets your appetite, pair it with the creative Ecuadorian fare also served here. *10am-5pm Tue-Sun* $$

Places We Love to Stay

$** Budget **$$** Midrange **$$$ Top End

Centro Histórico (Old Town)
MAP p58

Viajero Hostel Quito Tasteful hostel with immaculately renovated rooms and mixed dorms in a sprawling mansion. **$**

Community Hostel Perennially popular backpacker with a rooftop hangout, friendly staff, renovated private rooms and dorms. Also offers popular tours and has a rooftop restaurant. **$**

Secret Garden Great location and great vibes in this happening night spot. Stunning rooftop views and social atmosphere to go with a good mix of dorms and rooms. **$**

Hostel Revolution Sitting between Centro and Mariscal Sucre, this hostel will suit those looking for some breathing space; breakfast included. **$**

Carlota One for design enthusiasts, this ecofriendly hotel mixes innovation with sophistication. Rooftop terrace and stylish restaurant, too. **$$$**

La Casona de la Ronda A converted boutique hotel dating from 1738 that lands you right on one of the Old Town's most famous strips. **$$$**

Casa Gangotena Luxury accommodations in one of the oldest homes in Quito, now a boutique hotel. **$$$**

Friends Hotel & Rooftop Another cozy hotel in an old house in the San Marcos neighborhood; breakfasts are served with views of El Panecillo. **$$$**

Hotel San Francisco de Quito In one of Quito's oldest houses (dating back to 1698), this heritage hotel has original frescoes and multiple levels of terraces. **$$$**

Central Quito
MAP p70

Blue House Long-standing, social and friendly Mariscal backpacker with a good selection of rooms, including pod dorms. **$**

La Rábida Hotel Boutique Charming boutique hotel in the more appealing northern part of Mariscal, offering elegant rooms and great service. **$$**

Cayman Hotel Tucked down a leafy residential street, this quiet guesthouse sits within a converted house with a lovely small garden. **$$**

Ikala Quito Hotel Four-star boutique option mixing old and new with a good location straddling Mariscal Sucre and La Floresta. **$$$**

La Floresta & Around
MAP p76

Casa Aliso Converted 1930s home turned into a cozy guesthouse with garden-view rooms and fireplace, perfectly placed amid La Floresta's restaurant scene. **$$**

Swissôtel This well-positioned five-star offers great facilities for business travelers, including executive floors with exclusive amenities, quality on-site restaurants and city views. **$$$**

Stubel Suites & Café If you're after views and a relaxed location with full amenities, this quiet spot between La Floresta and La Pradera is a great choice. **$$$**

North Quito
MAP p85

Hotel Casa Q In La Pradera's happening epicurean scene is this vibrant, modern three-star hotel with city views and a rooftop hangout. **$$**

Le Parc If you're not into Quito's heritage hotels, then this slick La Carolina business hotel has all the modern comforts and conveniences you need. **$$$**

Hotel Finlandia Modern high-rise hotel with comfortable rooms in the heart of La Carolina's dining and business precinct. **$$$**

The Equator
MAP p90

Pululahua Hostal A memorable location within Pululahua's crater hosts this ecolodge that offers trekking, mountain biking and horse riding, among other ecotours. **$$**

La Pedregoza Magical zone at the bottom of the crater with A-frame cabins, campground, Jacuzzi and charming common areas – a great spot for families and solo travelers. **$$**

El Cráter Whether you're here to stay in one of its attractive rooms or pop in for lunch, the views overlooking the volcanic crater are utterly superb! One not to miss. **$$$**

For places to stay in Northern Highlands, see p133

LUKE WATERSON

Above: View from Mashpi (p132); right: Pambamarca (p105)

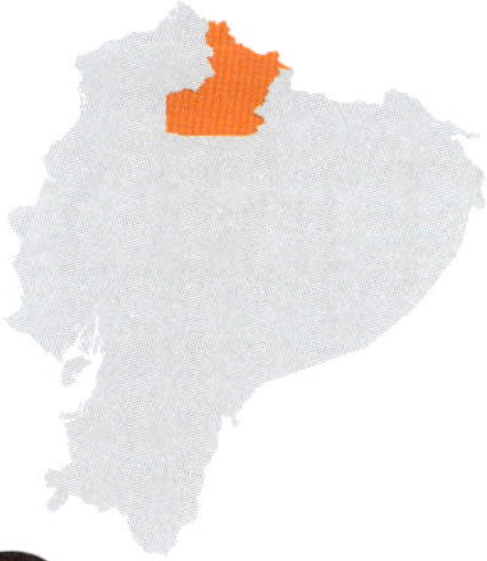

Researched by
Luke Waterson

Northern Highlands

STRONGHOLD OF TRADITIONAL HIGHLAND LIFESTYLE

Some of the best-preserved, most charismatic indigenous culture in South America brightens this breathtaking mountain wilderness.

In all the Northern Highlands' glimmering green, mountain-studded terrain, visitor attention rightly zones in on Otavalo and the continent's largest handicrafts market. But, superlative souvenirs aside, the market's biggest achievement is in vibrantly conserving indigenous culture, done region-wide to striking effect.

The Otavalo people may justifiably be Ecuadorian cultural talismans for their tenacity in maintaining traditional values. But Cayambe's citizens have created a remarkable network of attractions preserving this area's distinctive identity. Intag Valley locals have successfully fought for decades to protect their landscape, arguably Ecuador's prettiest, against mining. Mindo area is a trailblazer in environmental conservation, safeguarding cloud forest comprising some of the planet's best bird-watching.

LUKE WATERSON

The backdrop is intoxicating too: many of Ecuador's loftiest volcanoes, twinkling crater lakes, cloud-forest-cloaked slopes and the country's most fertile farmland. And the Northern Highlands has received recognition for its outstanding scenery. The Reserva Ecológica Cotacachi-Cayapas, beginning northwest of Otavalo, is Ecuador's largest protected area. Parque Nacional Cayambe-Coca guards the region's southeast. Imbabura province, which includes most of the Northern Highlands' sights, has UNESCO Global Geopark status. Hiking and climbing, therefore, are first-class. Stand atop Ecuador's third-highest summit, equator-bisected, snowcapped Volcán Cayambe, and you will be at the point of the planet that rotates fastest. You can relish enjoying the outdoors here, just as much as celebrating centuries-old customs.

THE MAIN AREAS

CAYAMBE
Traditions, ancient sites and volcano climbing. p100

OTAVALO
Resilient culture among looming volcanoes. p107

IBARRA
City class, ice cream, thermal baths. p116

INTAG VALLEY
Spectacular cloud forests and idyllic communities. p122

MINDO
Cloud-forest-surrounded bird-watching and ecohub. p126

Find Your Way

Distances are minimal in the northern Sierra. You could drive from Quito to the Colombia border in five hours. Some travelers opt to skip the capital altogether, heading straight to Otavalo – almost as close to the airport – instead.

BUS

All cities and towns, and most villages, are well connected by comfortable, reliable buses (usually with reclining seats and air-conditioning). Buses can be flagged down on the road, but in practice it's usually easiest to head to the main bus terminals.

TAXI

Taxis can be hailed on the street, though not as readily as they can be in neighboring Peru or Colombia. They're good options for visiting locations within a city and just beyond the city limits.

TOUR BUS

This is a common means of seeing the region, given its small size and the fact attractions can be distilled into a day or two-day tour. Remote locations beyond the public-transport network can be included, and you benefit from a knowledgeable guide.

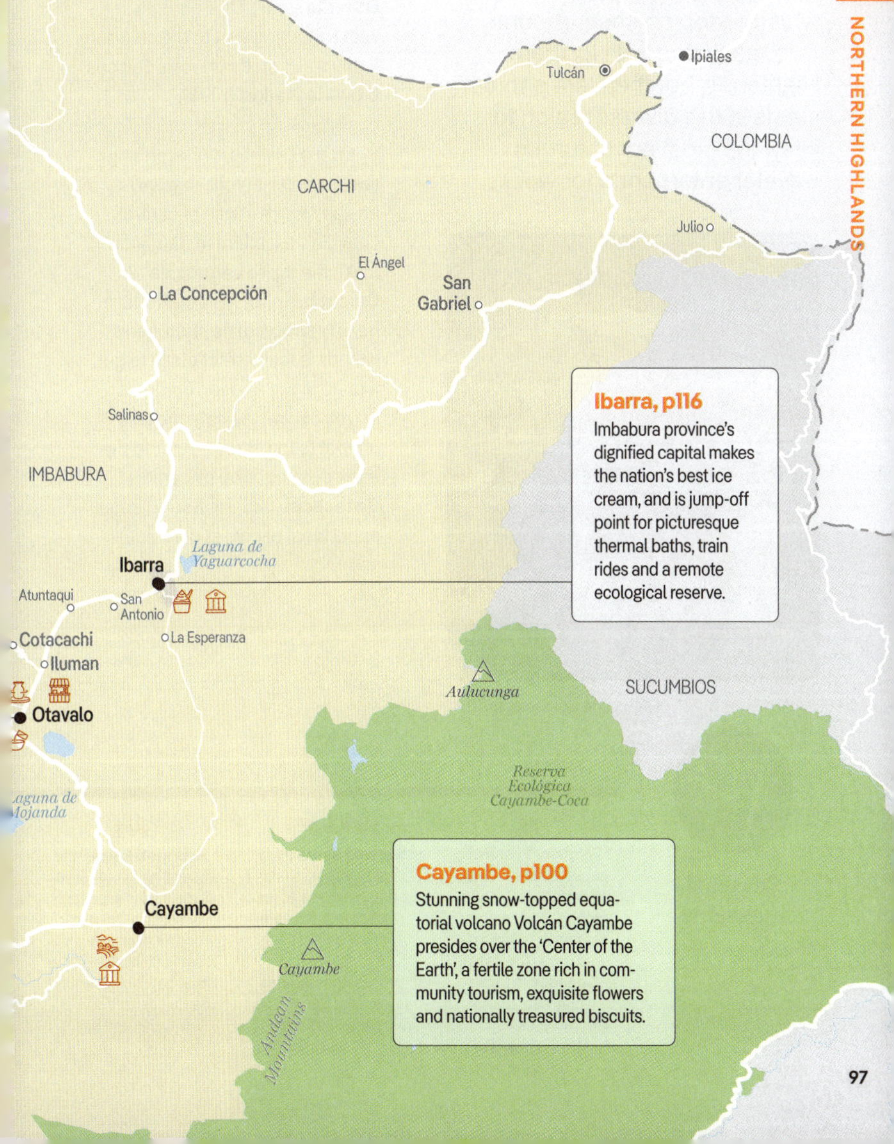

Ibarra, p116

Imbabura province's dignified capital makes the nation's best ice cream, and is jump-off point for picturesque thermal baths, train rides and a remote ecological reserve.

Cayambe, p100

Stunning snow-topped equatorial volcano Volcán Cayambe presides over the 'Center of the Earth', a fertile zone rich in community tourism, exquisite flowers and nationally treasured biscuits.

Plan Your Days

Otavalo is all too often the token whistle-stop on fleeting jaunts through Ecuador's Northern Highlands, but there are enough sights in this diverse region to keep the most adventurous traveler entertained for weeks.

LUKE WATERSON

Laguna de Cuicocha (p110)

Pressed for Time

- One day to experience the Northern Highlands? Avoid an unnecessary layover in Quito by taking a road transfer (75 minutes) from the airport directly to **Otavalo** (p107). Dive straight in with a morning visit to the colorful handicrafts stalls of world-famous **Otavalo Market** (p108).

- After a few hours of exploring and souvenir-purchasing and an early lunch at one of central Otavalo's excellent restaurants, make the trip to **Laguna de Cuicocha** (p110). This crater-lake beauty spot with its photogenic islands is the perfect place to get a taste of the Andean outdoors as you circumnavigate the lake on foot (allow three hours). In the early evening, stop by comely **Cotacachi** (p115) for a stroll about and a feast of *carnes coloradas*.

Seasonal Highlights

FEB

February's carnival parades are a chance to dance, eat festival foods...and sample fermented *chicha de jora* drink. **Carnaval Coangue** in Chota valley near Ibarra, incorporates regional Afro-Ecuadorian traditions.

MAR & APR

Semana Santa (Holy Week) processions bring members of the rural communities in from the countryside. Expect solemn processions bearing replicas of Christ. The rainy season is coming to an end.

JUN

June's **Inti Raymi** (the ancient Inca celebration of the sun) is especially vibrant in Otavalo. Another interesting Inti Raymi celebration is the ritual bathing at Laguna de Cuicocha. Weather is sunny and dry.

Seven Days in Sierra Norte

- On the way to Otavalo, linger in **Cayambe** (p100) to visit compelling equator museum **Quitsato Solar Museum** (p100) and **Hacienda Guachalá** (p103), Ecuador's oldest ranch. See some of the many other sides of Otavalo: a guided day hike in Ecuador's ethereal lake district **Lagunas de Mojanda** (p114), and a stop-off to see rehabilitating Andean condors at **Parque Cóndor** (p109).

- Next, make the dramatic descent into the **Intag Valley** (p122) and spend two days soaking up rural life in charming riverside lodgings – at **Termas de Nangulvi** (p122) or at a cloud forest bird-watching lodge like **Siempre Verde** (p123).

- End your week in ecotourism hub **Mindo** (p126), enjoying the best bird-watching on Earth and getting your pulse pounding on a zip line or river tube.

Two Weeks to Explore

- **Cayambe** (p100) has one of Ecuador's best **community tourism projects** (p103), archaeological sites like **Pambamarca** (p105), and climbs up **Volcán Cayambe** (p104) to waylay you on the journey north.

- In **Ibarra** (p116), savor phenomenal **ice cream** (p116), take the thermal waters at **Termas de Chachimbiro** (p121) and enjoy a fish lunch at **Laguna de Yahuarcocha** (p117). Next day, get active by exploring solitary mountainside sanctuary **Reserva Ecológica El Ángel** (p121) with its trippy *frailejones* plants.

- Try a homestay at **La Calera** (p113) near Cotacachi for an authentic experience of indigenous culture. Add in **Maquipucuna Reserve** (p131) after Mindo or Intag Valley to spot Andean spectacled bears, plus a two-night wildlife-watching stint in high-end cloud-forest lodge **Mashpi** (p132).

SEP

Fiesta del Yamor, Imbabura province's biggest festival, is a celebration of harvest and of Otavalo's patron saint, the Virgin of Monserrat. Ibarra parties with a parade during **Fiesta de Los Lagos**. Migratory bears arrive in Maquipucuna Reserve.

OCT & NOV

Rainy season begins; you'll see fewer travelers and enjoy lower prices. In November, Ibarra celebrates the **Mes de Afroecuatorianidad** (Afro-Ecuadorian Month) in honor of the city's significant Afro-Ecuadorian population and their culture.

DEC

Head to Mindo for the National Audubon Society's **Christmas Bird Count** (p126). Mindo routinely records world-beating numbers of bird species (often 400+ in a 24-hour period); participate in a potential bird-watching world record!

Cayambe

ANCIENT RUINS | BISCUITS | EQUATORIAL ENIGMAS

GETTING AROUND

Most of Cayambe's key sights, including Quitsato Solar Museum and Hacienda Guachalá, lie about 7km southwest on the main Carretera Panamericana (Pan-American Hwy) toward Quito, in Guachalá. Simply stroll to the nearest main-road bus stop to hail a bus anywhere between Cayambe, Guachalá and Quito; you're unlikely to have to wait more than 10 minutes. Outlying sights like Cochasquí ruins require your own wheels; taxis from central Cayambe cost about $30. Cayambe city center itself is easily walkable. The main bus terminal is 1.75km north of Parque Central; buses north to Otavalo and beyond depart from here.

Cayambe is a curious place. Snow-bedaubed 5790m Volcán Cayambe, Ecuador's third-highest peak, dramatically dominates the skyline. Cayambe is also renowned for its cultivated flowers – especially roses – and enjoys the world's optimal growing conditions (nutrient-full volcanic soil, dependably mellow days and year-round guaranteed sunlight). As you explore, floral fragrances mingle with the aroma of the city's other famous product, nationally relished cookies called *bizcochos,* Cayambe's location at the center of the world has spawned its biggest attraction, Quitsato Solar Museum, an excellent monument and information center marking the equator's exact line. The surrounding hills host numerous archaeological sites too, while Guachalá, outside Cayambe, has launched one of Ecuador's most innovative community tourism projects.

Yet central Cayambe is inexplicably chaotic and lackluster. Stay outside, such as in countrified suburb Guachalá, to experience this destination at its best.

Myth Meets Science at Equatorial Ground Zero

Straddle the equator at Quitsato

Quitsato means 'middle of the world' in the Tsa'fiki indigenous language, and **Quitsato Solar Museum** *(facebook.com/Elmuseosolar; $5)* in Guachalá (to Cayambe's southwest), offers much more than the usual clichéd Ecuadorian opportunity to stand with a foot in each hemisphere. Open 8.30am to 5.30pm, this is the only one of Ecuador's eight equator monuments correctly located on the exact line.

You won't find the usual pseudo-scientific gimmicks, like swirling basins where water circles in different directions either side of the equator. Instead, there are fascinating, informative, interactive exhibits. Meanwhile, museum guides will note the lack of logic in atlases being produced with north

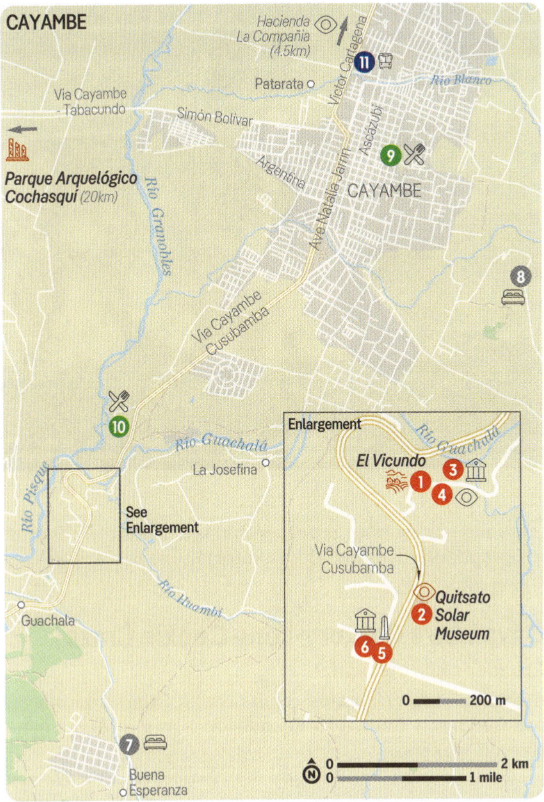

HIGHLIGHTS
1 El Vicundo
2 Quitsato Solar Museum

SIGHTS
3 Cueva de Leyendas
4 El Campo
5 La Bola de Guachalá
6 Museo del Bizcocho

ACTIVITIES
see 3 Stargazing

SLEEPING
see 1 El Vicundo
7 Hacienda Guachalá
8 Hostería Loma Larga

EATING
see 6 Cafetería Ecuatorial
9 Fabrica de Bizcochos San Pedro
see 7 Hacienda Guachalá
10 La Doña Hacienda

TRANSPORT
11 Bus Terminal

uppermost – one museum room exhibits maps (including a whopper covering the entire floor) that are orientated west-east, according to the direction the Earth rotates.

Exhibits in a second room display early geographical theories about the equator (from pre-Columbian sun-worshipping cultures, 18th-century French geographers and space-age calculations). Interestingly, nearby pre-Columbian ruin Pambamarca was a key triangulation point used by the French to calculate the equatorial line in the 1730s. The museum centerpiece is a 10m-high, 54m-diameter sundial which, modern technology now calculates, stands on the world's precise waistline. The black-and-white cobbles are designed to show up on thermal-imaging equipment from space.

Quitsato is the ideal place to come to understand a region where (according to museum literature) 'the days never vary, where there are no seasons and where, twice a year, there are no shadows.'

To get here, ask bus drivers for *'la bola'* (coming from Quito, it's 7km before Cayambe). **La Bola de Guachalá** *(free)*, 200m along the road from Quitisato, is a stone sphere constructed in 2006. It replaced a 1930s-built monument that

TOP TIP

Northern Highlands buses run regularly (every 10 minutes on the Quito–Cayambe–Otavalo–Ibarra route). But from Cayambe toward the Oriente/Amazon, transportation becomes ponderous. Oyacachi, served by twice-daily bus from Cayambe, has access deeper into the Oriente. But it's more efficient to backtrack to Quito for regular Oriente transport via Papallacta. Purchase tickets for buses at Cayambe bus terminal.

ECUADOR'S FLOWER-POWER CAPITAL

Ecuador is one of the most blessed countries in the world for flowers. But Cayambe is regarded as Ecuador's flower capital because – as the sea of greenhouses around town reveals – of its European rose-growing industry.

Roses only arrived here in the early 1980s, but you don't wander far around Cayambe before catching the scent of the 50-odd varieties now grown here. Thanks to the perfect cultivation conditions – fertile volcanic soil, year-round warmth and direct equatorial sunlight – Cayambe's biggest producers grow several million stems each year. If you want to see equatorial rose cultivation in action, beautiful 100-year-old **Hacienda La Compañía** is best set up for visitors.

(erroneously, it now appears) marked where the French geographers calculated the equatorial line to be three centuries ago.

Cayambe's Century-Long Cookie Craze

Ecuador's biscuit capital

Cayambe is so celebrated for its cookies that *cayamberos* are frequently known in Ecuadorian slang as *bizcocheros* (biscuit makers).

There are more than 80 families of *bizcocheros* in Cayambe, where *bizcochos* have been a nationally revered institution since 1928. The warm aroma of cookie dough, and the eucalyptus smoke in which all true *bizcochos* should be baked to infuse them with their distinctive flavor, pervades the city. Deliciously buttery, flaky-pastry *bizcochos* are invariably served with *queso de hoja* (mozzarella-like 'string cheese') and a lathering of dulce de leche (caramel).

Fabrica de Bizcochos San Pedro *(facebook.com/bizcochosanpedro; free)*, open 7:30am to 7pm, by Cayambe cemetery is the most historic family-run business. But **Museo del Bizcocho** *(behind Cafetería Ecuatorial at Bola de Guachalá; free)* offers a perfect opportunity to sample the finest products while discovering the intricacies of Cayambe's baking

EATING AROUND CAYAMBE: CAFES & RESTAURANTS

Fabrica de Bizcochos San Pedro: The Morales family has been producing delicious *bizcochos* for 50-odd years. *7:30am-7pm* $

Cafetería Ecuatorial: This bang-on-the-equator cafe is popular for brunch, thanks to its wood-fired *bizcocho* oven. *7:30am-7:30pm Fri-Wed, from 9am Thu* $

La Doña Hacienda: Commendable empanadas, grills, chicken and pork dishes. Scenic rural setting 5km southwest of center. *8am-6pm* $$

Hacienda Guachalá: This 16th-century hacienda's courtyard is the place to tuck into the likes of trout *guachaleña* with shrimp sauce. *noon-3pm* $$$

BEN PIPE/ALAMY

Bizcochos, **Fabrica de Bizcochos San Pedro**

traditions. It's open 7:30am to 7:30pm, Friday to Wednesday; and from 9am Thursday.

You might not think there's much to baking a humble biscuit. But Cayambe's *bizcochos* are still made faithfully to home recipes, entailing up to five hours of preparation and baking. The biscuits trace their origins back to early Spanish immigrants.

Guachalá's Community Tourism

Vibrant insights into Highlands village life

Despite its flowers and flavorsome biscuits, Cayambe's center is not particularly appealing. So it's a boon that its center-of-the-world suburb, Guachalá, should also be the cradle of one of Ecuador's exemplary community tourism projects. Under the super-friendly guidance of the community of **El Vicundo** *(alvarocoyaguillo@gmail.com)*, Cayambe is now much more for dallying in than driving through.

The community has bolstered the appeal of Quitsato Solar Museum (p100), founded Museo del Bizcocho, and also set up several smaller absorbing attractions. The nexus is **El Campo**, a community hub featuring a homely restaurant dominated by the huge ceramic *chimenea* (chimney) common to traditional Andean homes, and the chance to try on traditional costumes. Nearby **Cueva de Leyendas** is an informative interactive experience where you can learn about local myths and legends.

Another home has telescopes for **stargazing** on the equatorial line; it's special, as stars from both hemispheres are visible. Community members also arrange guided bird-watching trips plus hikes and visits to other nearby sights, like Pambamarca ruins. Best of all, you can overnight within the community through homestay options (or a grassy campsite), hanging out with villagers during atmospheric traditional dinners.

ECUADOR'S OLDEST HACIENDA

Hacienda Guachalá was built in 1580 and, though it's been renovated several times, it remains a masterpiece and a talisman of Ecuadorian history. French geographers from the 1736 mission stayed here when they (slightly erroneously) triangulated the equator, as did former president Gabriel García Moreno.

The chapel, which was built on the site of an Inca temple, contrasts the ancient traditional lifestyle with the colonial era. The hacienda (which also offers horseback excursions) has a small herd of alpacas, llamas and *guarisos* (llama-alpaca hybrids). Today, Hacienda Guachalá is an atmospheric lunch stop and hotel. However, you might want to avoid room 5, said to have been the old jail and torture chamber for 'misbehaving' servants.

Beyond Cayambe

Some landmark archaeological sites and the serrated, snow-coated profile of Volcán Cayambe make standout reasons to explore.

Places

GETTING AROUND

While Cayambe is well connected with Quito, Otavalo and Ibarra, discovering its surroundings involves ditching public transport. For Volcán Cayambe, you'll likely need to charter transportation and organize guided trips through a Quito agency. Cochasquí archaeological site is around a $30 taxi ride from central Cayambe. Ask folks in the Guachalá Community Tourism Project for help visiting Pambamarca.

Oyacachi (served by twice-daily buses from Cayambe) is the best springboard for forays further into the Oriente.

Flower-growing and biscuit-making are relatively modern developments in Cayambe. The area has an ancient soul. And this is laid bare on steep hillsides above the lush farmlands, watered by snowmelt from Ecuador's third-highest mountain – Volcán Cayambe – and caught between stark *páramo* (high-altitude treeless plateau) and the Oriente's forested valleys. The spiritual significance of this place for pre-Columbian indigenous populations is only now becoming understood. Experts now believe that, long before modern science grasped this equatorial zone's geographical importance, large populations were living and worshipping the sun in the region still known as Mitad del Mundo (Center of the World).

The ruins of these civilizations make memorable hikes; clambering up Volcán Cayambe is a tougher endeavor.

Volcán Cayambe

TIME FROM CAYAMBE: **1HR**

Climb the Northern Highlands' high point

The 4000-sq-km Parque Nacional Cayambe-Coca spreads across four provinces, but **Volcán Cayambe** is the park's – and the Northern Highlands' – highest peak. Legend imparts that Cayambe was left standing at the altar by Taita (Father) Imbabura after he fell for Mama Cotacachi (Imbabura and Cotacachi are two other lofty regional volcanoes). These precipitous icy slopes are best described visually by the Ecuadorian phrase *vestida de novia* (in bridal dress). This is one of the few equatorial volcanoes with a permanent glacier, and there are several ways to the top, each of them a significant but doable challenge.

The main route first entails a one-hour drive via unpaved road from Cayambe city (followed by a 20-minute hike). This gets you to Refugio Ruales Oleas at 4600m, the base camp for ascents. Many climbers are happy to go only as far as this southern flank's 4600m mark, the highest point on the planet through which the equator passes. It is an unusual experience to find yourself standing on the equator and yet be ankle-deep in snow. Just under a 1km climb from the refuge is the spectacularly green lake, Laguna Solitaria. Then it's on over the snow and ice to the summit at 5790m. It takes around seven hours for reasonably fit hikers/climbers to reach the top from the refuge; descent time is three hours.

JAMES MORGAN/ALAMY

Volcán Cayambe

Most operators suggest two days and one night for climbing Cayambe, which allows for the necessary acclimatization and basic preliminary training. You'll depart in the early hours of the morning from the refuge on summit-scaling day. Be aware that this is a serious undertaking. Yes, it is only Ecuador's third-highest peak but the climb is considerably tougher than the more frequented trail up Cotopaxi.

Quito-based **Andean Face** *(andeanface.com; tours per person $2970)* specialises in guided trips up Ecuador's volcanoes and includes a two-day Cayambe ascent in its 14-day Volcanoes Expedition. Whichever company you travel with, an experienced guide, 4WD transport for access to the mountain and decent equipment are essential.

Pambamarca

TIME FROM CAYAMBE: **1HR**

Hike to the remnants of an ancient sun-worshipping culture

At over 4000m of elevation, wind-blasted **Pambamarca** *(free)* is one of Ecuador's best-preserved pre-Inca hill forts. Legend has it that the indigenous Cayambe people, under siege from the Inca, retreated to this hilltop and so successfully defended their position that the Inca were obliged to retreat. The summit is sculpted into six concentric rings and its alignment with the sun on summer and winter solstices has led many experts to question whether Pambamarca was first and foremost an ancient site for solar observation.

During the 1735 French Geodesic Mission to the equator, scientist Antonio de Ulloa discovered the Ulloa's halo phenomenon, commonly called a glory, while on Pambamarca. This optical illusion casts the resemblance of a halo upon the shadow of the observer's head. The summit is an extraordinary viewpoint, with Volcán Cayambe to the east and another archaeological site, Quitoloma, lying just south. The shimmering oblongs spread across the valley sides are the greenhouses nurturing Cayambe's blooming marvellous rose-growing industry.

UNFORGETTABLE HIGHLAND CULINARY SPECIALTIES

Seco de chivo: Dried goat stew. The goat meat is braised with onion, garlic, oregano, peppers, annatto (a sweet nutty South American seed) and the fermented Andean corn drink *chicha*.

Locro de Papas: A potato stew made especially flavorsome, as it's combined with cheese, cumin, onions and annatto.

Sancocho: A hearty, warming soup made with yuca, plantains and, usually, chicken.

Llapingachos: Ideal comfort food in the form of potato and cheese fritters, sometimes served with fried eggs. Often served for breakfast.

Mishqui: Served warm as a breakfast beverage, a sort of glutinous agave sap. (The fermented alcoholic form is known as *guarango*).

OYACACHI & PARQUE NACIONAL CAYAMBE-COCA

Parque Nacional Cayambe-Coca, the national park that spreads out to the southeast of Cayambe and encompasses Volcán Cayambe, is interesting because it includes two very different terrain types within its 4000 sq km. Spectacled bears, as well as Andean condors and creatures (such as the tapir and cougar), can be found here. Although the main access to the park is from the south near Papallacta (p174), the welcoming little highland town of Oyacachi marks the park's northern access point. Oyacachi, further along the road that runs to Hacienda Guachalá, is 46km south of Cayambe. It also has waterfalls and thermal springs to discover.

ANGELA N PERRYMAN/SHUTTERSTOCK

Parque Arquelógico Cochasquí

It is a two-hour trek from the nearest road up a labyrinth of lanes southwest of Guachalá. You won't find the way without a guide; the obliging folks at El Vicundo (p103) in Guachalá can arrange trips here.

Cochasquí

TIME FROM CAYAMBE: **45MIN**

Northern Ecuador's largest archaeological complex

The peaceful, grassy **Parque Arquelógico Cochasquí** *(Cochasqui Archaeological Park; parquecochasqui.mitaddelmundo.gob.ec; adult/child $1.50/1)* is one of the country's most extensive archaeological sites. Open 8am to 4:30pm, the 15 *ushnus* (pyramids) and 21 *tolas* (funerary mounds) known to exist here span an area of 84 hectares. Excavation on the site has been limited, and many pyramids still remain under cover. The highlight is the pyramid at the back of the complex, bearing two huge pre-Inca observatories. The larger one was dedicated to the sun; the smaller to the moon. Invaluably, the site is graced by a small, informative museum that exhibits several site findings. Cochasquí was constructed by the Carranqui peoples, who flourished between 800 CE to about 1500 CE: an alliance between local chiefdoms that would have included both the Otavalo and the Cayambe peoples.

Get here via your own wheels from Cayambe: taxis will charge about $30 one-way. Spot the turn-off on the Cayambe-Quito Hwy 288, next to a small blue-and-white chapel 10km southwest of Tabacundo.

The ruins are also on a back road to lovely lake district and hiking area Lagunas de Mojanda (p114), a further 14km northeast. And cyclists do incorporate both sights on a hilly 40km daylong circuit from Tabacundo. But because the lakes are primarily about hiking and it is highly advised to hike there on a guided tour, it is better to visit them from Otavalo, where agencies offer the excursion.

Otavalo

HANDICRAFTS | INDIGENOUS CULTURE | MOUNTAINSIDE HIKES

Culturally captivating, the city of Otavalo is an enriching place to visit. Some 70% of its inhabitants (known generally as *otavaleños*) are indigenous people of the 'Otavalo' group, inhabiting this region since its oldest archaeological sites were built. Surely among the continent's most successful entrepreneurs, the Otavalos have turned their city's vibrant market into a daily event, making it a highlight of any South America trip.

But Otavalo is no sight to be quickly ticked off. Explore far beyond the market and you'll reach quarters inhabited by poncho-clad men – sporting the distinctive *shimba* (braided hair) – and women wearing traditional *polleras* (skirts) and brightly hued shawls; dress has barely changed since Inca times.

Otavalo's location in spectacular Valle del Amanecer (Valley of the Dawn) is also part of its irresistible charm. Take traditional cooking classes, learn more about indigenous culture in a fascinating museum or visit surroundings characterized by indigenous-run homestays, handicraft-making artisans and gleaming mountain-bound lakes.

GETTING AROUND

With its grid layout fanning around the Plaza de Ponchos and its vast market, central Otavalo is easily navigable on foot. Attractions just beyond the center, including Museo Viviente Otavalango, Kawsaymi cooking school in Quichinche, Peguche, El Lechero, Parque Cóndor and Lago San Pablo, and are all 2km to 3km from Plaza de Ponchos, reachable within about an hour's walk (the altitude, ups and downs make the walk tiring). Local taxis within the city are widely available and well-priced; it's $4 to $5 to the aforementioned destinations.

indigenous Cultural Insights at Museo Viviente Otavalango

The Otavalo people showcase their history

For a greater grasp of Otavalo indigenous culture, **Museo Viviente Otavalango** *(otavalango.wordpress.com; $5)* is an invaluable resource. Turning history on its head, on the site of a former textiles factory that exploited indigenous labor, some 20 local families of Otavalos have founded a museum showcasing their culture as they believe it should be portrayed. Here you will see costumes and get entertaining explanations of customs; many are extremely touching. In an Otavalo burial, you learn people are interred with the things

TOP TIP

The word 'Otavalo' refers to the city as well as to the indigenous Kichwa-speaking group that has called the area home for centuries. However, the word *otavaleño* merely refers to an inhabitant (from whatever cultural group) of Otavalo.

TOP EXPERIENCE

Plaza de Ponchos Crafts Market

For its sheer sprawling size, vitality and array of items, South America's largest, most famous market (on Otavalo's central square) is surely one of Latin America's greatest everyday fiestas. From tapestries to tagua-nut jewelry, socks to sweaters, ponchos to paintings, this throng of exquisite handicrafts, of deals being struck and street food being devoured, is a sight to behold.

LUKE WATERSON

TOP TIPS

- Some bargaining is expected, but don't overdo it: many stallholders struggle to make a living.
- Plaza-facing cafes and restaurants with upper-level terraces have bird's-eye market views.
- Otavalo people have used the market for business deals and social interactions since before the Incas arrived.

PRACTICALITIES

- free
- 7am-6pm
- Otavalo Bus Terminal, served by regular direct buses from Quito, is a 500m walk northeast of Plaza de Ponchos.

Center of the Action

The market's nexus is the Plaza de Ponchos, bounded by Calles Quiroga, Sucre, Salinas and Jaramillo. Every day from about 7am, this central city square is a lively mass of handicrafts and street-food stalls. Earlier is always better to visit, as many stallholders start packing up at 5pm. But on Saturday (and, to a lesser extent, Wednesday) the market spills out through the surrounding streets in a vibrant, clamorous shopping extravaganza.

Handicrafts Galore

The plaza is jam-packed with several hundred stalls, where the main wares sold are handicrafts, especially Otavalo region's renowned weavings. Expect exquisite handwoven carpets and intricate tapestries depicting typical highland scenes, people and customs. Similar designs feature on the many clothing items sold: ponchos through to sweaters and socks. Then there is the jewelry, fashioned from semiprecious stones or tagua nut (sometimes called vegetable ivory), wood carvings from San Antonio near Ibarra, leather goods and more. Among a cornucopia of street-food stalls, you can try highland specialties like *chicha* (fermented corn drink), *hornado* (roast pork) and *locro de papas* (potato stew) in between stall-hopping.

believed to help them most in life's next chapter. Children are laid to rest with musical instruments; adults get fruit and vegetables. But as those who show you around concede, this is not strictly a museum. Exhibits are not artifacts from a bygone people but representative of a culture that continues to thrive. The best bit here is chatting to Otavalos about their own culture.

Come by taxi: it's 2km north of Plaza de Ponchos and open 9am to 5pm, Monday to Saturday.

Make Ecuadorian Culinary History at Kawsaymi

Traditional cooking school

Discover the sierra through your taste buds at the cozily furnished family home of **Kawsaymi** *(kawsaymi.com; cooking classes $30-60)*, where you can learn about and cook a wide variety of ancestral highland cuisine under head chef Claudia's friendly stewardship. You'll be following recipes that are often centuries old. To grasp preparing a complete Ecuadorian meal, plump for the three-course option: you'll make *sopa* (soup), a *plato fuerte* (main) like Cotacachi marinated-pork specialty *carnes coloradas,* and a *postre* (dessert).

You get to eat it all afterwards and it's an excellent means of meeting fellow travelers while getting valuable insights into Andean life. Ensure Claudia takes you to her traditional Andean *tulpa:* a hearth made of stones, where some cooking gets done. With one day's notice you can order traditional meals to eat in the restaurant; and the pretty property in Quichinche, a $4, 10-minute taxi ride from central Otavalo, also has rooms for guests too full to move after class!

Textiles in Peguche

Otavalo's weavings hub

Plaza de Ponchos might be where most visitors buy their woven souvenirs, but tranquil suburb Peguche is where many of the best actually get woven. Alpaca and sheep wool are naturally dyed and handwoven on looms in private houses and workshops throughout the village to create astoundingly intricate textiles.

Workshops open to the public include master weaver **José Cotacachi** (behind Peguche's church), beavering away on his latest work most days. He transforms scarlet dye from crushed

THE PLIGHT OF ECUADOR'S CONDORS

Despite being Ecuador's national bird, only 100-odd Ecuadorian Andean condors remain in the wild. Habitat loss and illegal poaching are key reasons why.

Otavalo's **Parque Cóndor** was established as an educational center serving to counteract the disastrous actions that led to the near-extinction of condors and other raptors, and offers unique insights into Ecuador's endangered national treasure. Almost 80% of this center's rescued birds have been injured by gunshots. Wherever possible, they are rehabilitated to the wild, in hopes that this will sustain Ecuador's condor population. Visitors can observe them here (open Wednesday to Sunday) in their spacious aviaries and at twice-daily feeding sessions.

EATING WITH A VIEW IN OTAVALO

Puerto Lago: Smart restaurant, plus glass-sided garden cabin for vista-blessed Lago San Pablo dining. Plentiful fresh fish options. Look for the mock lighthouse. *9am-9pm* **$$**

Cabañas del Lago: Thatched restaurant besides water-sports complex nudging Lago San Pablo lakeside. Serves carnivorous grills and trout. *noon-8pm Mon-Sat, to 5pm Sun* **$$**

Hacienda Pinsaqui: Elegant hacienda once hosted Simón Bolívar, liberator of Ecuador. Its Ecuadorian restaurant abuts picturesque gardens. *noon-5pm & 7-9pm* **$$**

Hacienda Cusín: Idyllic hacienda near Lago San Pablo's southeast end. Delectable lake trout served in charming 17th-century restaurant. Booking essential. *noon-3pm* **$$$**

CIRCUMNAVIGATE LAGUNA DE CUICOCHA ON FOOT

The Laguna de Cuicocha trail is one of the area's most beautiful and accessible: a beguiling volcanic crater lake circled by a walking path at 3000–3500m elevation.

START	END	LENGTH
Hostería Laguna Cuicocha	Hostería Laguna Cuicocha	12km; 4–5hr

The trailhead is a 45-minute drive from Otavalo. Bus the Otavalo–Cotacachi section then grab a taxi ($6) from Cotacachi's Parque San Francisco past Reserva Ecológia Cotacachi-Cayapas park entrance to lakeside Hostería Laguna Cuicocha (still over 3000m altitude). Follow the road back 300m to 1 **Centro de Interpretación (visitor center)**. The path begins with steep steps on the paved 2 **Ruta Sagrada (Sacred Route)**, so-called for its part in indigenous rituals and featuring a reconstructed giant sundial, offering site and ritual bathing spot. From here, the lakeside circuit (Gorky Campuzano in Kichwa) affords increasingly dramatic views over the 3km-wide crater lake. You pass three *miradores* (lookouts) to reach trail high point 3 **Mirador de Laguna** (3480m) after two hours' hike. Just west, 4 **Mirador Laguna Cuicocha** has a shelter and makes the ideal picnic stop. This is the perfect angle for observing the channel between the lake's two islands, Canal de los Ensueños (Channel of Dreams). It's another hour to muddy 5 **Quebrada Los Vicundos** valley, a rare chance to refill water bottles. Two more steep hills and a long, slow descent deliver you down to what is known as 6 **Last Viewpoint**, with excellent views of Isla Teodoro Wolf. This double-humped island, named after a German naturalist, supposedly resembles a *cuy* (guinea pig).

Lake access is free. Bring your passport for registering at the park entrance.

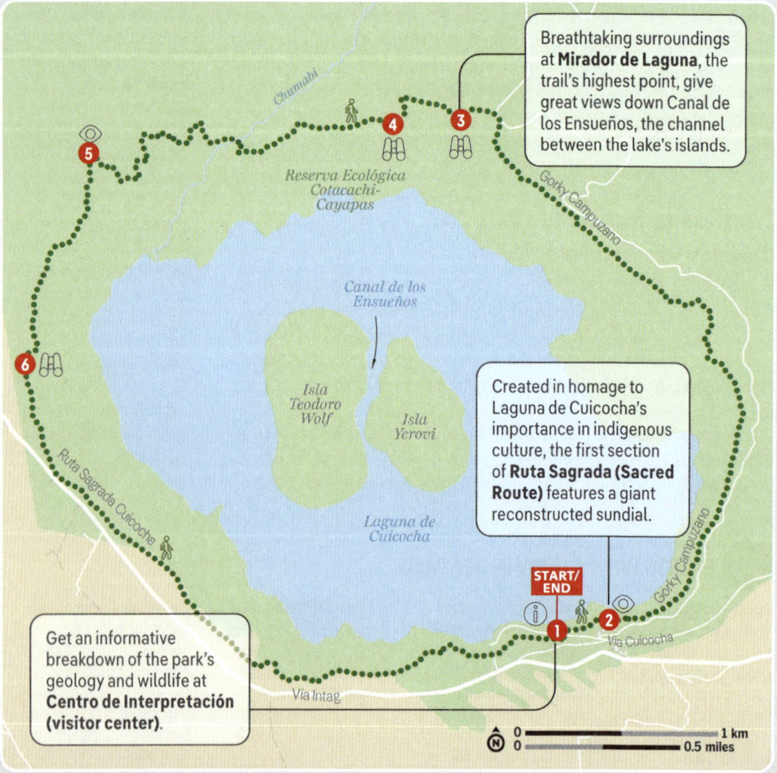

cochineal beetles into kaleidoscopic colors by adding lemon, ash, sulphur or walnut. Urine was once used to fix dyes; today, a mix of lemon, rock salt and vinegar is preferred!

A block west down the hill, **Taita Gundo** *(facebook.com/taitagundo)*, open 8am to 8pm, is another extraordinary workshop where the owner hand-makes traditional Andean musical instruments and obligingly gives visitors a rendition on each. Visit Peguche's workshops independently or get shown the highlights on tours like those run by Metropolitan Touring *(metropolitan-touring.com)*.

Peguche's Magical Cascades

Waters with special powers

Below the suburb of Peguche, the waters of **Cascada de Peguche** *($0.50)* weave their own magic. Locals will tell how the waterfall is purportedly charged with positive energy; some claim this is because the forefathers of the Otavalos once washed their precious textiles here. It's a 30-minute, 2km walk from Peguche church down Facchi Ñan to the biggest waterfall (open to visitors 8am to 6pm), the last stage on a well-kept woodland trail. The 20m-high cascade, squeezed between wooded hills, is beautiful, and there are rustic places to eat nearby.

Lakeside Antics at Lago San Pablo

Water sports and special views

This inviting body of water, sprawled below the crinkled crags of **Volcán Imbabura** (4609m) and visible on the approach to Otavalo from Quito, is one of Ecuador's largest lakes, with its surface area about 7 sq km. It is encircled by shimmering green farmland dotted by rural homes. You will still see locals paddling traditional vessels made from bunched reeds here. Getting to the edge of **Lago San Pablo** and (why not?) out on the water is an appealing way to spend an afternoon. In the right light, Volcán Imbabura's rocky profile is reflected on the lake's surface.

OTAVALO'S SACRED TREE

A 2km uphill walk from Otavalo town center brings you to the community of Pucara Alto and the sacred tree known as **El Lechero**. You can still see the remains of walls surrounding a *pucara* (Inca fortress) but the site was also a cemetery for *niños limbos* (babies 'in limbo', who died before baptism). The original tree, supposedly 400 years old, was destroyed by fire, and a new tree (two in fact) planted alongside the original's stump. Harvest festivals in honor of Pachamama (Mother Earth) are still held here.

Legends aside, the site is worth visiting for the breathtaking panoramas across Lago San Pablo and to the Imbabura and Cotacachi volcanoes.

EATING IN OTAVALO: OUR PICKS

Cafe Pachamama: The delight of this vast, slightly out-of-center place is its beautiful garden – and its vegetarian food, like peppers stuffed with lentils and cheese. *7am-8pm* $

Sumak Rasu: Diminutive charmer with rustic decor (corn husks, coffee sacks, Panama hats) and first-class coffee and homemade ice cream. *7:45am-10pm Mon-Sat, to 7pm Sun* $

Quinde Bistro: Prime Plaza de Ponchos views, four floors up. Try a mouthwatering cheese and meat platter, with a *jugo de mora* (blackberry juice) or icy beer. *noon-midnight* $

Maytushka: Ecuadorian restaurant specializing in Amazonian fare. Try *maytu de tilapia*, Amazonian fish cooked in jungle leaf. *11:30am-8pm Sun-Thu, from 10:30am Fri, from 7am Sat* $

Tatya Wasi: For cake- and coffee-lovers, this is top choice. The chic, shiny wood-and-glass premises is great for idling, people-watching, bagels and waffles. *8am-9pm* $

Alpa Nayra: Suave Brazilian-style grill house that also serves excellent locally grown coffee. *noon-9:30pm* $$

Restaurant Árbol de Montalvo: Homely spot with wood-fired pizza oven and local specialties with rare twists (Ecuadorian-style Dutch *slavink* sausages). *7am-9pm Tue-Sun, to 6pm Mon* $$

Mi Otavalito: A little touristy, but a cozy, nicely presented place with its murals of highland scenes and delicious predominantly grilled meat dishes. *9am-9pm* $$

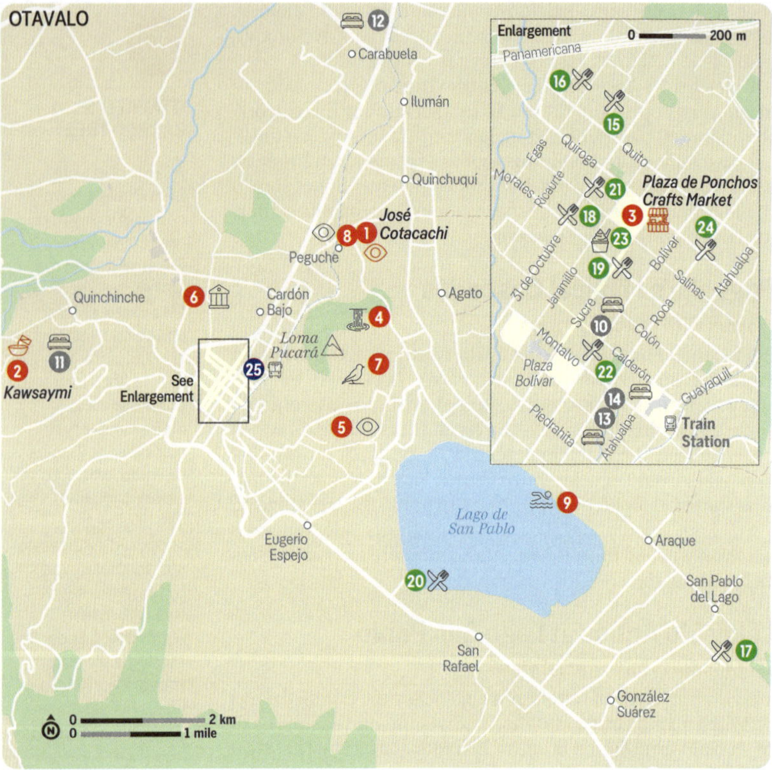

HIGHLIGHTS
1 José Cotacachi
2 Kawsaymi
3 Plaza de Ponchos Crafts Market

SIGHTS
4 Cascada de Peguche
5 El Lechero
6 Museo Viviente Otavalango
7 Parque Cóndor
8 Taita Gundo

ACTIVITIES
9 Cabañas del Lago

SLEEPING
10 Flying Donkey Hostal
11 Hacienda Otavalo
12 Hacienda Pinsaqui
13 Hostal Riviera Sucre
14 Hotel Otavalo

EATING
15 Alpa Nayra
see 9 Cabañas del Lago
16 Cafe Pachamama
17 Hacienda Cusín
see 12 Hacienda Pinsaqui
18 Maytushka
19 Mi Otavalito
20 Puerto Lago
21 Quinde Bistro
22 Restaurant Árbol de Montalvo
23 Sumak Rasu
24 Tatya Wasi

TRANSPORT
25 Bus Terminal

There is a raft of water sports available at **Cabañas del Lago** *(cabanasdellago.com.ec; $10-50)*, including kayaking and paddleboarding, boat trips and aquatic motorbikes. Access is via Peguche on the lake's northeast side, 9km outside central Otavalo.

You can also enjoy a phenomenal overview of the lake from above at viewpoints like El Lechero sacred tree and Parque Cóndor (p109). These are respectively a 3km and 3.5km walk or taxi ride up from Plaza de Ponchos, southeast of center.

Beyond Otavalo

UNESCO cited the dozen volcanoes when declaring Imbabura province a Global Geopark: 25-odd lakes and indigenous cultural experiences are also major draws.

Otavalo is an ideal launching pad for a spectrum of Ecuadorian adventures in Imbabura province. The beguiling lakes, mountains and volcanoes particularly lure hikers. Laguna de Cuicocha is one of the region's most-visited natural sights; seldom-visited lake district Lagunas de Mojanda is an equally enticing trekking area.

Neighbouring Cotacachi (just 15 minutes' drive away) near Laguna de Cuicocha makes another appealing hangout. However, an influx of foreign residents (mostly from the US and Canada) means the town sometimes feels overrun with outsiders. Meanwhile, the little agricultural town of La Calera might be Ecuador's best place for getting to know the Kichwa-speaking people who have called this place home since long before even the Incas arrived.

Places

La Calera p113
Lagunas de Mojanda p114

La Calera

TIME FROM OTAVALO: **30MIN**

Homestay in a traditional Otavalo community

The community of **La Calera** *(quichuatours.com)*, outside Cotacachi, is a traditional district of Kichwa-speaking Otavalo people. La Calera lets you grasp indigenous cultural intricacies more profoundly by lodging here overnight.

Quichua Native Travel *(quichuatours.com)* is the community-run organization concentrating on uplifting rural people through locally-beneficial community tourism; it is your first point of contact if this cultural immersion appeals. It works with English-speaking female guides, providing insight into village life from a *warmi* (indigenous women's) perspective.

Women don traditional garments to explain fascinating craft traditions, focusing on embroidery, jewelry and food preparation (guests can participate). Nearby Cotacachi is famous for its quality leatherwork, and La Calera even has a workshop where bespoke leather goods are still handcrafted. As you explore, the women can tell you about traditional outfits, including the all-important *mama chumbi* sash worn as a protective talisman. It's refreshing to see indigenous female guides carving a career in tourism, a business that has traditionally been male-dominated hereabouts.

GETTING AROUND

Otavalo is well-connected to its surroundings (and the entire Northern Highlands) by efficient buses. Head to the main terminal (where you can purchase tickets) and ask for the next bus to your destination. La Calera and Cotacachi are both less than 30 minutes away on the same bus route.

Taxis can be easily flagged and are a relatively inexpensive time-saving option. There's no public transport to Laguna de Cuicocha (visit by bus/taxi instead) or Lagunas de Mojanda (visit by guided tour with Otavalo agencies).

OTAVALO'S YACHAKUNA

Otavalo area is known for its *yachakuna*. While this Kichwa word implies 'shamans', *hombres sabios* (wise men) is the most accurate translation.

Otavalo's Carabuela and Agato districts are especially associated with *yachakuna*. Many believe a *yachak* (the singular form) can treat conventionally incurable diseases, but more commonly, people visit *yachakuna* to resolve problems in their love or work life, or to request charms. Working alleged miracles can usually be done for a little more money. A *limpia* (spirit-cleansing ritual) is among the most popular services. Do not attempt to visit any *yachak* without an introduction. Better, if you have no introduction, would be to attend a spiritual center that has (or arranges for) its own *yachak*.

ECUADORPOSTALES/SHUTTERSTOCK

Traditional medicine is alive and well here, too. You'll learn, for example, how canna plant leaves allegedly speed up childbirth, or how Peruvian ragweed counteracts curses.

Nor will you rough it. You'll be served healthy, hearty country food at comfortable, welcoming homestays, often outshining accommodation in Cotacachi.

Lagunas de Mojanda

TIME FROM OTAVALO: **45MIN**

Spectacular hiking

Lagunas de Mojanda, south of Otavalo, ranks among Ecuador's most spectacular hiking areas. It's a less challenging proposition than many of the country's high-altitude Andean 'highlights'.

The pastoral blend of these three lakes, grassy summits and extinct volcano Volcán Fuya Fuya (4263m) is serenely beautiful.

A fairly easy circular trail zigzags south from the tourist complex on the southern side of the biggest lake, Kari-Cocha ('male lake' in Kichwa), to Laguna Chiquita (Little Lake). It skirts 4260m Cerro Negro (Black Peak) to a breathtaking lookout over Laguna Negra (Black Lake). Stroll back by road to Kari-Cocha. Climbing Volcán Fuya Fuya is a steeper prospect, doable in two hours from the parking lot on Kari-Cocha's northwest side.

Lagunas de Mojanda

With all of the spectacular scenery in the Northern Highlands and no specific restrictions on wild camping, it's tempting to think of overnighting out in the wilderness under canvas. Consider whether you do so or not very carefully. There have been a few reports of independent travelers getting robbed and assaulted in the Lagunas de Mojanda area in particular. It is a far safer option to come to these beauty spots either for the day only (with a tour or independently) and camp out only if you are doing so with an experienced tour operator and they deem it safe to do so. Tours organized by Otavalo's **Flying Donkey Hostal** *(kyjuan_89@hotmail.com; per person $60)* include transport (no public transport exists) and several hours of hiking.

EATING IN COTACACHI: CAFES & CARNES COLARADAS

Esther Moreno de Unda: Esthercita began concocting *carne colorada* – Cotacachi's fabled 'red meat' or marinated, sun-dried beef – here in 1930. *10am-6pm* **$**

Cafe Río Intag: Ex-hacienda with a delightful enclosed courtyard. Coffee (from the highly regarded Río Intag producer), paninis and salads. *8am-10pm* **$**

Red Rabbit Coffee Lounge: On Parque San Francisco, this terraced cafe has fine coffee, imaginative paninis and cakes. *7:30am-9pm Mon-Fri, to 10pm Sat & Sun* **$**

Subs: Breakfasts, fresh-baked bread, hamburgers and paninis (try the falafel-stuffed one!) on Parque San Francisco. *9am-6pm Mon-Sat* **$**

Ibarra

ICE CREAM | THERMAL BATHS | TRAIN RIDES

GETTING AROUND

Yellow taxis are ubiquitous; flag them down easily on the street. They'll head to out-of-town places as far as Chachimbiro's thermal baths for $40. The Indrive app works well – with this app, you have to 'bid' for a taxi fare.

Buses are inexpensive, connecting most of the interesting destinations outside the city – including Laguna de Yahuarcocha and handicrafts hub San Antonio – to the main bus terminal (where you can buy tickets), 1.5km southwest of center. The train – albeit spectacular – doesn't connect to anywhere useful.

Ibarra is chilled: super chilled. With the main diversions being feasting on world-class ice cream, lounging by its heart-shaped lake with a fresh fish lunch, taking a gorgeous countryside train ride and lolling in dreamy thermal baths, this is somewhere you'll need to learn how to relax. Larger, more cosmopolitan and yet less touristy than Otavalo, Ibarra is urbane without getting worked up about it. Centered on two pretty main squares, it has a multicultural population of *indígena*, *mestizo* (partly Spanish) and Afro-Ecuadorians (mostly descendants of enslaved people who moved here from Ecuador's coast).

Refounded after an earthquake in 1872, this is Ecuador's newest city. Nevertheless, it is rich in tradition and a deep-seated sense of community. There's a wider array of things to do around Ibarra than there is in any other Northern Highlands destination, and you may find locals greeting you with nods of familiarity on just your second day here.

Indulge in the World's Best Ice Cream

Ibarra's divine helados de paila

One unforgettable highlight of a sojourn in Ecuador's ice-cream capital is visiting some of the famous *heladerias* (ice cream shops) that specialize in handmade *helados de paila* ice cream.

A paila (a wok-like copper dish) is spun by hand on a bed of ice set within insulating straw. In just a few minutes, the pure fruit juice – sightly sweetened and sometimes containing a smidge of egg white – turns to ice cream (or sorbet) and can be scooped up with a wooden spoon. In the old days, the ice used was brought down from the mountains on mules, but otherwise, little has changed since Rosalía Suárez opened **La Bermejita**, Ibarra's first ice cream shop, in 1896.

Today, descendants of Doña Rosalía still run La Bermejita by Ibarra's Parque La Merced. Open 8:30am to 9pm, it is

HIGHLIGHTS
1 La Bermejita
2 Museo y Centro Cultural

SIGHTS
3 Carranqui
4 Casa de Arte Talleres
5 Galería Luis Potosi
6 Iglesia de la Merced
7 Iglesia de Santo Domingo
8 Laguna de Yahuarcocha
9 Murals
see 4 Ricardo Villalba Madero de Arte
10 Yahuarcocha

SLEEPING
11 Finca Sommerwind
12 Hotel Barcelona

EATING
13 Cava Caran
14 El Buen Café
see 1 La Esquina
see 10 Restaurante Doña Blanquita
15 Stella Rooftop
16 Vinila Lounge

a city institution, with ice-cream-making demonstrations around midday. **La Esquina**, open 7:30am to 7:30pm, and right next door is equally popular, but if you order a sundae local-style, know that it will arrive topped with grated cheese!

At either joint, and at others around the center, an overwhelming assortment of flavors awaits; all are intensely delicious, being made with the real, fresh ingredients, not their powdered equivalents. *Mora* (blackberry) is supposed to be the most traditional, while soursop and *taxo* (a type of passion-fruit, here mixed with banana) are also incredibly good. To say Ibarra's *helados de paila* rivals Italy's finest gelato is no understatement; you got the scoop here first!

Enjoying the Good Life at Laguna de Yahuarcocha

Fish banquet at the lake of blood

Laguna de Yahuarcocha (10 minutes by taxi from Ibarra) is a favorite hangout for *ibarreños* (Ibarra folks). The 'Lake of Blood', to give its translation from Kichwa, is a heart-shaped

TOP TIP

Andean and Afro-Ecuadorian traditions have vibrantly mingled around Ibarra. The city's November *Mes de Afroecuatorianidad* (Afro-Ecuadorian Month) showcases these traditions with music performances, talks and more. The Chota valley, northeast of Ibarra, is another hub of Afro-Ecuadorian culture, famous for its *bomba* music and handcrafted masks.

INCAS IN IBARRA

Ibarra's buildings might be relatively modern, but this area's history goes back to long before the Spanish arrived. The name of Laguna de Yahuarcocha derives from a Kichwa phrase meaning 'lake of blood'. Legend has it that the waters turned red after 30,000 Caranqui warriors were slaughtered here by forces of Inca emperor Huayna Capac, with their bodies tossed into the depths. Huayna Capac's son, the last Inca emperor Atahualpa, was also supposedly born just outside Ibarra at Inca Huasi in the suburb known, ironically, as Caranqui. The archaeological site purported to be his birthplace was closed at the time of research, but a monument to the last Inca stands in the district's Parque Atahualpa.

recreation zone on Ibarra's northeastern edge. You can reach the shore of the lake along a dirt track through avocado and mango orchards from strung-out settlement **Yahuarcocha** at the lake's southern end.

Yahuarcocha is also where you'll encounter the most popular attraction: the chain of dining venues on Paseo Yahuarcocha. This almost-daily culinary festival serves up several tons of tilapia fish to hundreds of locals and is a colorful window into social life. **Restaurante Doña Blanquita**, with its humungous *comedor* (eating hall), is among the most popular of these *pescaderías* (fish restaurants). It's open 8am to 6pm Monday to Friday, and until 7pm on Saturday and Sunday. Save space for the excellent deep-fried banana empanadas!

Operating on a smaller scale during the week, Yahuarcocha village erupts into life on weekends when people from across Imbabura province flock here for lunch and a *paseo* (stroll) through the market that sets up on the lake access road. This is not exactly your peaceful Andean lake – there's even a racetrack on the northern shore – but it is culturally fascinating.

Burn off some calories after your binge on tilapia by walking the lovely path that runs for 14km around the lake. The German

EATING IN IBARRA: OUR PICKS

El Buen Café: Cavernous, chandelier-hung place; serves Ibarra's best breakfasts, featuring eggs, coffee, *humitas* and fresh juice. *7am-8pm* $

Stella Rooftop: Avocado toast, burgers, *picadas* (nibbles) and cocktails three floors up at this trendy open-sided restaurant-bar. *4-10pm* $

Cava Caran: Best-known for its artisan microbrewed beers, also produces crowd-pleasing carbs like potato wedges, tacos and fat burgers. *9am-11:30pm* $

Vinila Lounge: Soaring arches, columns, plant-bedecked spaces. Pay for its sophisticated atmosphere and dishes like octopus with balsamic reduction. *8.30am-10pm* $$

BARNA TANKO/SHUTTERSTOCK

Artisan painting a hand-carved wooden statue, San Antonio

beer garden, food and rustic lodgings at **Finca Sommerwind** *(finca-sommerwind.info; restaurant 8am-6pm Sun-Wed, to 10pm Thu-Sat)* is ideally located about 4km, heading anticlockwise around the lake, from Yahuarcocha.

Ibarra's 'Magical Village'

Meet San Antonio's artisans

In 2020, San Antonio, on the outskirts of Ibarra (20 minutes by bus), was listed as a *pueblo magico* on the Ministry of Tourism's list of 'magical villages' with natural or cultural appeal. San Antonio's specialty is ornate woodwork, and there are many workshops where you can observe handicrafts being made.

Within 100m of turning into thoroughfare Calle Antonio Jose de Sucre, San Antonio's magic unfolds in a series of beautiful **murals**. Keep heading south four blocks and you see a sign reading **Casa de Arte Talleres** *(tiktok .com/@casadeartetalleres)* on what appears to be a turn-of-the-century townhouse (another illusion, since it is newly built). Here, Gabriel Garcia Portillo, master sculptor, works his own magic. Don Gabriel will happily take time to give you an insight into the four-month process involved in perfecting his wooden creations (drawing, carving, painting, gold-plating). It's open 8am to 6pm.

Two blocks northeast, on Parque Francisco Calderón, more outstanding gallery-workshops beckon: **Galería Luis Potosi** *(facebook.com/escultorluispotosiecuador)*, open 8am to 6pm, the village's most famous exponent of wooden sculptures; and **Ricardo Villalba Madero de Arte**, open 9am to 6:30pm.

Otavalo might come out on top for handicrafts overall, but San Antonio is the winner when it comes to wood!

IBARRA'S BEST HISTORIC SIGHTS

Museo y Centro Cultural: In central Ibarra, this is a mesmerizing place to gain a better understanding of the area's rich archaeology.

Iglesia de la Merced: On Parque La Merced, the latest incarnation of this church was completed in 1945, a rebuild after the devastating 1868 earthquake.

Iglesia de Santo Domingo: This quaint church on Parque Santo Domingo features *La Virgen del Rosarío,* a painting by famous artist Diego de Robles, on its altar.

Carranqui: The Ibarra suburb of Carranqui has a park with a monument to Inca emperor Atahualpa and the remains of the Inca Huasi archaeological site (closed at the time of research, but you can still peep through the fence on Calle Huiracocha), where Atahualpa was purportedly born.

Beyond Ibarra

Off-the-radar for most, Ibarra is ideally based for exploring the sierra's far north, where there is much to see without equal elsewhere in Ecuador.

Places

GETTING AROUND

Ibarra has good road infrastructure and bus networks if you stick to main roads: you can easily travel north to Tulcán and the Colombia border (2½ hours) or south to Cayambe (1½ hours).

Off the main highways, going is slower: reaching Reserva Ecológica El Ángel takes two hours, despite being barely 50km from Ibarra. Unless you're set on crossing into Colombia by land, it's advisable to maintain distance from the frontier, where organized crime is prevalent.

The sierra's green, mountain-swept terrain sweeps right to the Colombian border. Heading north from Ibarra, fun relaxation awaits, with a tourist-train ride (one of South America's most scenic, if it's running) between Ibarra and Salinas; and Ecuador's most bewitchingly located thermal springs, Termas de Chachimbiro. East of Salinas, the Río Chota valley is the main center of Afro-Ecuadorian culture away from the coast.

For a sterner test of your adventurous spirit, journey further north to the *páramo* of Reserva Ecológica El Ángel. This vast, remote reserve is famous for its giant *frailejones*: tall, hairy-leafed, bulbous plants so-called because of their supposed resemblance to Franciscan friars wearing their trademark hooded robes.

Salinas

TIME FROM IBARRA: **2HR**

The Liberty Train to Salinas

The Tren de la Libertad (Train of Liberty) trundles from Ibarra to backcountry town Salinas. It's only a 30km journey, but the round-trip excursion – about six hours – has ample atmosphere and picturesque scenery, despite a distinct lack of speed.

This little 54-passenger locomotive traverses splendid mountain-dotted highland landscapes. It heads into the wooded Río Tahuando valley, rattles through seven tunnels and over spectacular bridges, then descends through sugarcane plantations toward Salinas. A phalanx of motorbike-mounted security officers normally ride ahead to ensure the track is obstacle-free. This excursion is about the journey, not the destination; Salinas itself has a dilapidated feel.

Departures from Ibarra are scheduled for 10:30am Thursday to Sunday, with the train returning from Salinas at 3pm. The round-trip journey costs $30 if you buy tickets for the ride at **Ibarra train station**, open 8am to 4pm. You can get further information, and purchase far pricier tickets, including debatable perks like a visit to Salinas' salt museum, at Ecuador Rail *(ecuadorrail.net)*. At the time of research, track repairs were nearing completion and expectations were high that trips would recommence in spring 2026.

LUKE WATERSON

Termas de Chachimbiro

Chachimbiro

TIME FROM IBARRA: **1HR**

Relaxing thermal baths

Squeezed between tree-clad hills, **Termas de Chachimbiro** *(santagua.com.ec; $10)*, open 7am to 11pm, has the loveliest location of any of Ecuador's natural thermal baths. It lacks the grandeur of Termas de Papallacta near Quito, but this collection of pools – featuring toasty water temperatures of 35–55°C and numerous medicinal properties – are blessed with well-maintained facilities. The **lower recreation area** *($5)* is a kids' splash-about pool. Proceed up steps and along walkways to the main pools and the terracotta-roofed surrounding buildings containing the spa, restaurant and accommodations. Spa treatments promise stress alleviation, as does simply arriving at this serene, seldom-visited oasis. Buses leave Ibarra's bus terminal at 7am, 7:45am and 12:30pm, returning from Chachimbiro at 1pm, 3:30pm and 5pm.

El Ángel

TIME FROM IBARRA: **2HR**

Spot unusual flora and fauna at a nature reserve

Reserva Ecológica El Ángel *(tours per person $150)* is a mesmeric place to become acquainted with the natural treasures of Ecuador's *páramo*. This zone of bare mountainside plain only truly exists in three countries: here, Peru and Colombia. The reserve's icons are the tall, hairy-leafed *frailejones*, plants early explorers named 'little friars' for their resemblance to Franciscan friars with hooded habits. Endemic to the Northern Andes, the bizarre *frailejones* protrude from hills dotted by forests of *Polylepis*, one of the world's highest-altitude trees. El Ángel also attracts the likes of Andean foxes; Andean spectacled bears; and Andean condors, among the 320 bird species.

The reserve abuts the Colombia border: get up-to-date advice on security here, especially if you're hiking in lonelier reaches. The reserve office is in El Ángel, 1¼ hours' drive from Ibarra; it's 17km north via rough road to the reserve entrance. You'll need your own wheels. Hiring a vehicle from Ibarra costs $150–200.

GHOST-FACED BATS

If you're traveling in the north country, the detour to Gruta de la Paz (Cave of Peace) will certainly repay you in spectacle. This speleological sight is perhaps the most popular tourist attraction in Carchi, Ecuador's northernmost province, in a lonely location off the Ibarra–Tulcán highway, but the 150m-deep cave and shrine is special for being one of the few dwelling places in Ecuador for the rare ghost-faced bat. With the protruding flaps of skin on their foreheads and their undeveloped noses, the bats' faces have an uncanny caved-in (ghost-faced) appearance. Their high body temperatures mean that they quickly get hypothermia if exposed to temperatures that are lower than 10°C.

Intag Valley

COUNTRYSIDE CHARM | COFFEE PLANTATIONS | BIRD-WATCHING

GETTING AROUND

The dramatic descent from Otavalo or Cotacachi to Intag's main town, Apuela, takes 1½ hours. Buses ply these routes around five times daily, continuing through the valley to Chontal, at Intag's western end. Here buses link to Nanegalito for onward connections to Mindo and Quito. Since lodgings are mainly outside Apuela, ensure bus conductors alert you when yours is getting close. Local 'taxis' are 4WD pickup trucks, known as *carros*. Accommodations providers may also have transportation to help you get about.

For its beguiling blend of subtropical forests, sheer foliage-blanketed hills, thunderous rivers and unspoiled rural communities, the balmy Intag Valley is up there with Ecuador's – if not South America's – most scenic subregions. Here, the Northern Highlands lays on its humble charm most thickly.

The valley's beauty is due to its diversity. It straddles altitudes of 600–3500m, thus sporting a fabulous range of terrains and appealing to an array of wildlife. This is not an urban destination in its own right but a collection of relatively isolated highland communities; and the main attractions, though numerous, are spread over a distance of 60km or more.

The spectacular winding descent into Intag Valley from Otavalo would be reason enough to make the journey here. But this neck of the woods is also fabled for its once-in-a-lifetime bird sightings, evocative countryside lodges and hiking trails across enchanting cloud-forested hillsides, where bears and pumas roam.

Plant to Coffee Pot

World-class coffee-plantation tours

Intag has ideal conditions for cultivating arabica coffee, with steep slopes and misty conditions that nurture a slow maturation of the coffee cherries. The coffee farm that plonked Intag on the world stage was Finca Soledad, above Apuela, where Instinto Coffee – Ecuador's most celebrated boutique coffee producer – is based. In 2023, Instinto Coffee won 5th place (among producers from 38 countries) in the World Barista Championships, and the prestigious Sprudgie Award for Most Notable Producer.

Yet Intag has many highly regarded coffee producers. Most are hard to reach. But one of the region's best (and friendliest) is **Finca San Rafael** *(instagram.com/fincasanrafaelintag; coffee tour $5)*, just 3km from the centuries-old thermal springs **Termas de Nangulvi** on the Peñaherrera road. The tour includes a walk around the river-bounded estate, tastes of the

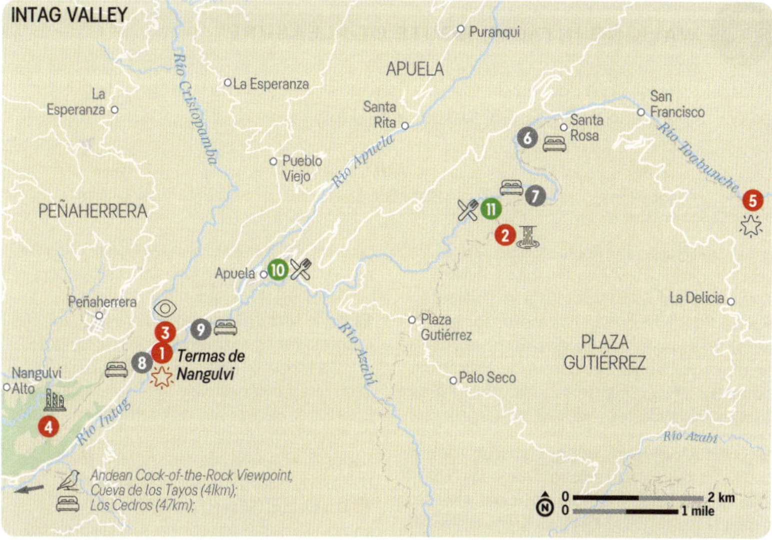

HIGHLIGHTS
1 Termas de Nangulvi

SIGHTS
2 Cascada el Placer
3 Finca San Rafael
4 Gualimán

ACTIVITIES
5 Siempre Verde

SLEEPING
6 El Refugio de Intag
7 Finca Orgánica San Antonio
8 Hosteria La Isla
9 Pachecho Farmhouse
see 1 Willka Eco Farm

EATING
10 Cafe y Restaurant Sol y Mar
11 Casa de los Turas
see 7 Finca Orgánica San Antonio
see 4 Gulimán Restaurante
see 11 Kinde Sacha
see 1 Willka Eco Farm

coffee cherries and a cup of the fine finished product under an awning in the garden, as the owner himself explains the whole process of taking coffee beans from tree to cup. For $15, lunch is included.

Bird-Watching in Cloud-Forest Hideaways

Intag's jungle havens

Stationed at either end of the Intag Valley are two exceptional cloud-forest bird-watching lodges.

About 1.5km east of Santa Rosa at Intag's northeast end, a long and winding road (walkable in two hours) concertinas up to **Siempre Verde** *(Always Green; siempreverde.org; lodging incl guided bird-watching hike $35)*. This remote cloud-forest

TOP TIP

Travelers often ponder which part of Intag Valley to stay in. Overnighting somewhere near the Termas de Nangulvi hot springs puts you close to the best choice of lodgings and centrally located for visiting valley sights. You will have thermal waters to relax in after your excursions, too.

EATING IN INTAG: OUR PICKS

Finca Orgánica San Antonio: On the Ruta del Placer hike, this farm serves delicious creations with ingredients grown right outside. Reserve in advance. *9am-8pm* $

Willka Eco Farm: Ecuadorian-Italian cooking at the valley's best lodgings is first-rate; fish and pasta dishes stand out. Reserve in advance. *9am-8pm* $

Cafe y Restaurant Sol y Mar: Cute little spot in Intag's 'capital', Apuela, with Río Intag coffee, ice creams and great-value Ecuadorian-style food. *8am-8pm* $

Gulimán Restaurante: The archaeological site's restaurant, serving coffee and fruit, plus the likes of local fried fish with *llapingachos* (cheesy potato cakes) *7am-7pm* $

WALKING INTAG'S 'ROUTE OF PLEASURE'

This bucolic ramble alongside the Río Toabunche, a tributary of the Intag, is an easy introduction to the valley's excellent hiking.

START	END	LENGTH
Santa Rosa	Plaza Gutiérrez	7km; 6–8 hr

La Ruta del Placer (The Route of Pleasure) is a specially designed walking trail tracing the Río Toabunche from Santa Rosa, 10km northeast of Apuela. Reach the start by bus or *carro* (pickup truck); return from Plaza Gutiérrez by *carro*. The route is walkable in two hours, but there are ample distractions. From Santa Rosa, a noticeboard beside a schoolyard indicates where the trail begins.

1 **El Refugio de Intag**, with its upmarket wooden cabins, restaurant and guided hikes, is the first stop. Proceed 1.75km down the trail and, after a trout farm, you'll find 2 **Finca Orgánica San Antonio**, a 12-hectacre organic farm and lodging, where owner Marisol happily shows you around gardens where she produces vegetables, coffee and world-class honey, then cooks scrumptious meals for guests. A further 1km further on, 3 **Kinde Sacha** (Hummingbird of the Forest), has cabins where you can order a refreshing plate of edible crickets! Neighboring 4 **Casa de los Turas** offers home-cooked traditional highland Ecuadorian meals. The trail continues on, passing the house of renowned Cuban conservationist Carlos Zorrilla, who has been fighting to protect these forests for three decades. Cool down at 5 **Cascada el Placer** (Pleasure Falls) as the path enters a secluded tract of moss-draped, orchid-sprinkled forest. The route afterwards continues 4km on a zigzagging route to Plaza Gutiérrez.

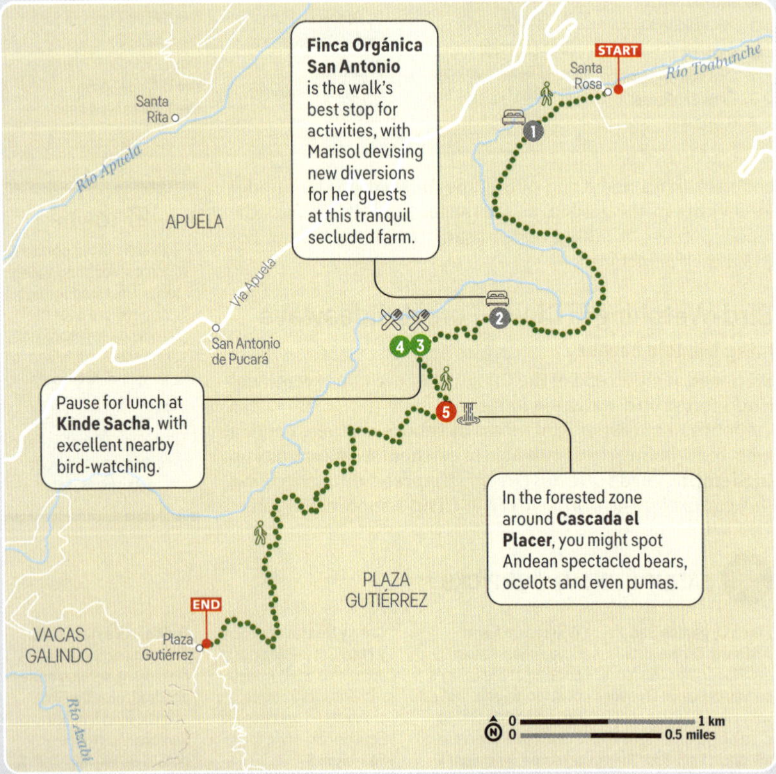

reserve lies in the sort of picture-perfect jungle valley that normally only exists in movies.

The lodge is now a world-renowned research center. Local bird-watching guide David Ruiz *(davidrruiz99@hotmail.com)* can arrange transportation up from Apuela, and leads trekking and bird-watching tours through the pristine rainforest here. Paths run to a quartet of waterfalls – at one, you splash through the veil of water into a cave where you can see the nests of chestnut-collared swift hatchlings – and to the reserve's upper reaches at almost 3500m.

The viewing platform has vistas right across the canopy. On the 280-strong bird list are the plate-billed mountain toucan, collared Inca, red-hooded tanager, tiger heron and famous Andean cock-of-the-rock. Once-in-a-lifetime sightings of the incredibly rare *Leydebamba antpitta* are also possible. Bird-watching complete, relax in the commodious common area and library where meals are served, and sleep in a simple well-maintained cabin.

From Chontal, in Intag's southwest, a 15-minute, $10 pickup-truck ride up the Río Magdalena valley brings you to Magdalena Alto. Here, transfer to mule or foot for the two-hour climb by trail to **Los Cedros** *(reservaloscedros.org; lodging incl guided tours $80)*. The sense of adventurous isolation is equal to that at Siempre Verde, and wildlife-watching is often superior. Here, 350-odd bird species plus pumas, ocelots and hundreds of reptiles, insects and plants can be spotted.

Both the above require at least an overnight visit. But for bird-watchers in a hurry, two further spots are of note. Three kilometers before Chontal on the road from Apuela, a driveway on the left marks the stop-off for the rough trail to Intag's best **Andean cock-of-the-rock viewpoint**. You'll climb before dawn for 20 minutes and may need to wait around an hour to see these gaudy red birds, as they arrive looking for mates.

Continuing toward Chontal, just before the village, a sharp left-hand track brings you in 1km to **Cueva de los Tayos**, a murky chasm where you can observe *tayos* (oilbirds). These birds fly at night through echolocation, like bats. Arrange a guided visit to both spots through **Willka Eco Farm** *(2-person min, per person incl food $40)*. It's impossible to visit independently; you need a guide to show you the way.

Become Your Own Indiana Jones at Gualimán

Intag's archaeological site

On a verdant, ribbed ridge above the Intag river, **Gualimán** *(gualiman.com; $5)* is a group of truncated pyramids harking back to the Caranqui culture, who likely used it as a ceremonial center. Without major excavations, the site's history is shrouded in mystery; those who venture here will feel they are going where few have gone before. There is a small archaeological museum, a restaurant and a zip line. The site also sells its own organic coffee. Gualimán is 7km above Termas de Nangulvi (2½ hours' walk), with the turnoff just before Peñaherrera village.

MY FAVORITE PLACES IN INTAG

María Belén Rodríguez Altamirano, owner of Willka Eco Farm *(willkaecofarm-ec.com)*

Campo Colibrí At this restored forest, hiking and breathtaking landscapes blend seamlessly. I love the stunning orchid-viewing. There is also zip lining and a Tarzan swing.

Gualim án This is an 84-hectare archaeological site: I love the mountaintop scenery as much as the pre-Incan pyramids.

Farm Tours Intag is famous for its permaculture farms. You can volunteer at some and learn about regenerative agricultural practices, such as at Finca Abundancia, where Kerry Klages also offers farm tours, including lunch.

Siempre Verde Of all the places to observe wildlife, this is my favorite. It shelters thousands of native species of animals and plants, with waterfalls and trails perfect for nature lovers.

Mindo

BIRD-WATCHING | ADRENALINE SPORTS | LODGE STAYS

GETTING AROUND

Most visitors reach Mindo directly from Quito (two hours by bus or taxi). Buses usually halt at the junction on Hwy E28, the Quito–Santo Domingo road; here, *colectivos* (shared taxis) ferry passengers down into Mindo (a further 10-minute drive). Buses also connect Mindo to the Intag Valley (via Nanegalito and Intag Valley village Chontal) for travel across the Northern Highlands without backtracking through the capital. Most visitor destinations are within 5km of Mindo's central plaza (pickup-truck taxi $5).

For ornithologists, ecotourists and adrenaline junkies, Mindo rules the roost. There is debate over precisely how many bird species inhabit these cloud-forest-covered hills, but most estimations reckon on 400 to 500. Mindo has led the world in bird counts (species recorded in one 24-hour event) for multiple years and, if all the surrounding Western Andean slopes are factored into calculations, 900-odd avian species could be glimpsed here.

At possibly the planet's top bird-spotting destination, you can go bird-watching on guided trips at private reserves (often only if you are staying overnight here) or on self-guided scenic forest trails. Mindo's motley-but-likeable tin-roofed homes have also been the vanguard of Ecuadorian ecotourism for decades, and provide heart-in-mouth thrills, such as one of Ecuador's best canopy tours.

Beyond Mindo, on the way to Intag Valley, the Maquipucuna Reserve (the world's best Andean spectacled bear habitat) and Mashpi Lodge (Ecuador's finest cloud-forest bird-watching refuge) entice wildlife-watchers into tantalizingly isolated territory.

Bird-Watching World Records

Mindo's myriad bird-watching possibilities

Ecuador is home to almost 1600 bird species; almost twice as many as you'd find in all Europe. The area directly around the town of Mindo has between 400 and 500 species routinely recorded, with local events like National Audubon Society's annual **bird counts** regularly tallying up more than 400 sorts of avians within 24 hours (come to town in December, and you can participate in the bird count). Such stats cement Mindo as Ecuador's, and often the world's, number-one spot for bird-watching.

From the moment you reach the junction on the E28 highway where public buses stop and spot the giant Andean

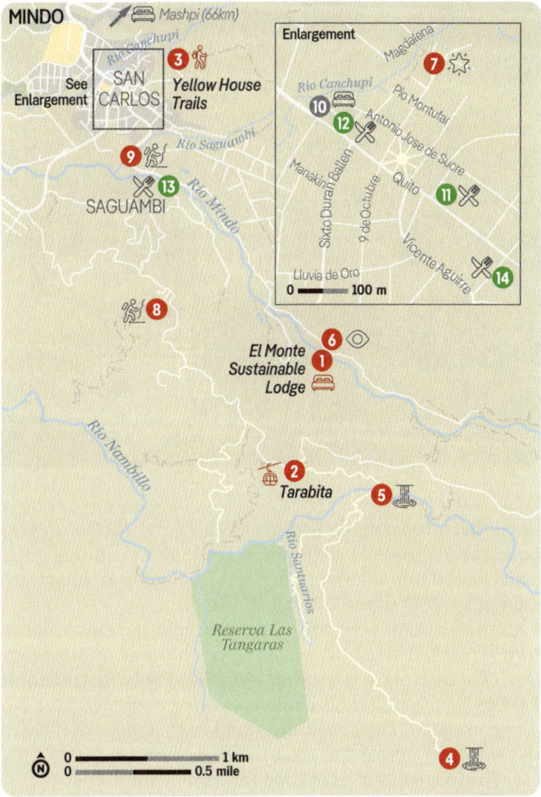

HIGHLIGHTS
1 El Monte Sustainable Lodge
2 Tarabita
3 Yellow House Trails

SIGHTS
4 Cascada la Reina
5 Cascada Nambillo
6 Mariposario Mariposas de Mindo

ACTIVITIES
7 El Quetzal de Mindo
8 Mindo Canopy Adventure
9 Mindoextreme

SLEEPING
10 Hostal Zafiro

EATING
11 Mindo Forest Coffee & Tea
12 Persian House
13 Ristorante Pizzeria del Cavallino
14 Sisakuna

cock-of-the-rock statue, you'll begin to suspect that you're entering a town somewhat obsessed with birds. Another oversized hummingbird statue in Parque Central and the bird-watching tours advertised all along Av Quito (the town's main street) are added confirmation that a large proportion of townsfolk and tourists here are dedicated bird enthusiasts.

Many kilometers of cloud-forest trails can be walked without a guide. The most extensive are at Hacienda San Vicente's **Yellow House Trails** *(ecuadormindobirds.com; $6)*, which is a good option if you're pressed for time, cash or both. Each of these five pretty trails bisecting hilly cloud forest close to town take between one and three hours to walk: highlights include the view of Mindo on Trail 3 and sightings of Andean cock-of-the-rocks on Trail 5. Hike here independently, remembering that since bird-watching is best around dawn, the hours after sunrise are usually busiest on the trails. Alternatively, hire an expert local bird-watching guide (per day $60 to $120). One of the best is **Julia Patiño** *(Juilaguideofbirds@yahoo.com)*, Mindo's first female bird-watching guide, but there is no shortage of accredited bird-watching guides around

TOP TIP

Though there are bus connections from Intag Valley, it is easiest to approach Mindo direct from Quito. The Maquipacuna Reserve and Mashpi Lodge usually arrange their own shuttles for guests.

MINDO'S ENVIRONMENTAL MOVEMENT

Mindo is not just a pretty cloud forest. The community has fought hard over many decades to conserve their land. While Mindo-Nambillo Ecological Reserve, safeguarding 19,200 hectares of regional forest, was established in 1988, the haven faced significant early obstacles. In 2002, the local response to proposals to run the Oleoducto de Crudos Pesados (OCP) oil pipeline through the reserve was almost three months' peaceful occupation of cloud forest along the pipeline route, attracting much international publicity. The protestors were removed and the pipeline built. But the stand Mindo folks made set the precedent for modern Ecuadorian environmental activism, and established Mindo as the movement's powerhouse. Indirect consequences of the protests also included creation of mini-reserves around Mindo at Río Silanche, Milpe and Tandayapa.

town. **Mindoextreme** *(mindoxtreme.com, bird-watching tours per 1-3 people $60)* is one of the longest running, most experienced tour operators, and it offers bird-watching tours among a raft of other local adventure fixes.

Another option is to stay in a lodge that benefits from its own reserve, where bird-watching can be done on the premises. One such place is the wonderful **El Monte Sustainable Lodge** *(ecuadorcloudforest.com; guided bird-watching per day from $60)*. The adventure starts with a piece of theater: the cable car across the river to the 45-hectare tract of forest. The lodge has a reputation for employing the services of many of Mindo's top guides.

Tarabita to Mindo's Most Scenic Experience

Terrific views and trails to tumbling waterfalls

Mindo may bait adventure-lovers, but the cable-car ride high above the canopy across the Río Nambillo valley to tranquil Santuario de las Cascadas (Sanctuary of the Waterfalls) in Mindo's **Tarabita** *($5)* gives you superlative natural beauty without expending very much effort at all. You are transported across (and 150m above) a dramatic cloud-forest-draped river valley in a motor-powered wire basket with a slow-but-steady chug. It operates 8:30am to 4pm.

This is only the first chapter of the odyssey. Once on the other side, you enter a protected area of steep-sided forest containing three hiking trails to a series of entrancing waterfalls. You can swim at some of the falls, too. The closest waterfall is **Cascada Nambillo**, at the end of 20-minute Trail 1. Trail 2 culminates in the highest waterfall, supreme **Cascada la Reina**, after 50 minutes of walking, while Trail 3 features no fewer than five waterfalls on its 35-minute route. You could spend a day ambling these three trails, pausing for swims as you go.

SALLY ANDERSON/ALAMY

El Monte Sustainable Lodge

Remember your swimming costume, some water and the fact that it's a 5km uphill walk (or $7 taxi ride) from central Mindo.

Swoop Through Mindo's Magical Canopy

Four kilometers of forest thrills

Constructed by the people who built the zip lines in Costa Rican cloud-forest adventure playground Monteverde, **Mindo Canopy Adventure** *(mindocanopy.com; per zip-line route $10-20)* is the town's hottest adrenaline fix. It's also Mindo's original and best zip-line experience, and was among Ecuador's very first canopy tours. Of the three different routes, the main one with its 10 lines is the one to try, taking 1½ hours to complete. All routes together comprise 3800m of cableways. The entrance is 2.75km up Via a las Cascadas – the road that goes to the Tarabita – from Mindo.

Brighten Your Day at Butterfly Paradise

Mindo's marvellous mariposario

There are many *mariposarios* (butterfly sanctuaries) scattered across South America, but travelers regularly opine that this butterfly farm and conservation center is among the best

WHY I LOVE MINDO

Luke Waterson,
Lonely Planet writer

For me, Mindo is much more than just another spectacular tract of Ecuador's scenery. It is one of the reasons why so much of the country has stayed looking spectacular. Drives to protect nature here have spearheaded campaigns to protect it elsewhere in Ecuador. This place has soul as well as good looks: just watch locals turn out to tally up bird species for counts that regularly show Mindo has greater avian variety than anywhere else on Earth. Nor is Mindo a one-trick pony. I love that there is always something new to try here, from bird-watching walks at dawn to chocolate-making to dunking yourself (my overall favourite!) in one of umpteen different waterfalls.

EATING IN MINDO: OUR PICKS

Persian House: Bargain-worthy Ecuadorian Middle Eastern food in a flower-bedecked little enclave on Mindo's main street. *9am-9pm* $

Mindo Forest Coffee & Tea: Locally grown coffee, omelets and cheesecake in a large, chic premises a block off Parque Central. *8am-10:30pm* $

Sisakuna: Breakfasts like smashed plantains with cheese and eggs; chicken with *maracuya* headlines some innovative mains. *7am-9pm* $$

Ristorante Pizzeria del Cavallino: First-rate pizzas and lasagnes. Photogenic locale, on Via a las Cascadas amid cloud forest 1.75km southeast of center. *noon-9pm* $$

MINDO & ITS ORCHIDS

Ecuador is home to a mind-boggling 4500 types of orchids, and over 400 have been recorded in Mindo and its surroundings. The humidity of the cloud-forest climate helps these beautiful plants to thrive. The Jardín de Orquídeas (orchid garden) at Cabañas Armonia in Mindo grows over 200 orchid varieties. On a tour, you can discover more about the uniqueness of these plants, their importance in an ecosystem and other surprising stats, such as that one in every four plants you clap eyes on in Ecuador will be an orchid. Yet many of Mindo's orchid species, you will also learn, have been threatened by human activity, and work continuously needs to be done here to conserve the rich diversity of these flowers.

MARIPOSAS DE MINDO

***Morpho peleides* butterfly, Mariposas de Mindo**

they have seen. **Mariposas de Mindo** *(mariposasdemindo.com; adult/child $8.50/5)* is an impressive facility that serves as an excellent introduction to over 25 of Ecuador's native species of butterflies. More than 1000 of the pretty winged things can be observed here in the greenhouse and nursery, where you'll stand every chance of observing a butterfly emerge from its chrysalis! Some butterflies will even land on you if you entice them with a little of the tropical fruit available (staff will show you how): a humbling and graceful experience. Glimpsing one of the blue morphos, the biggest butterflies here, is a sight that will stay with you long after your trip. It's open 9am to 4pm, Thursday to Monday; and to 2pm on Tuesday and Wednesday.

Unwrap the Secrets of Chocolate-Making

Bean-to-bar on Mindo's sweetest guided tours

Ecuador is deservedly known worldwide for its high-quality chocolate. And while most of the stuff for international consumption is grown close to the coast, it is not usual to have a chocolate-production facility in the same place the cacao is cultivated (the coast is warm; the chocolate would melt). Unless that place is Mindo, of course, where the climate is balmy enough to grow cacao yet sufficiently cool to stop the chocs from turning straight into goo. Mindo, therefore, is one of Ecuador's best spots to take a bean-to-bar chocolate tour. **El Quetzal de Mindo** *(elquetzaldemindo.com; 1½hr tours per person $18)* has been making chocolate in Mindo since 2009. On a tour, you will see cacao plants growing; participate in the grinding, peeling and roasting entailed in transforming cacao fruit into paste; choose flavors to make your own bar and – of course – taste the chocolate. Several other businesses in Mindo coordinate tours with variations on the same sweet theme.

Beyond Mindo

Go scouting for Andean spectacled bears or cocoon yourself away in a cloud-forest retreat.

The cloud-forest-clad hills soar far beyond Mindo in waves of green. This is a fabulously remote zone, broadly encompassing the area north of Mindo and west of Intag Valley. As the scenic beauty heightens, civilization fades and wildlife-watching opportunities increase. You can forge into this verdant oasis to observe South America's only native bear species, the Andean spectacled, at Maquipucuna Reserve. Alternatively, continue by increasingly rutted road to the environmentalists' utopia of Mashpi. Ecuador's premier lodge for cloud-forest wildlife-watching is set in a protected 1214-hectare reserve: a place to experience exceptional bird-, reptile-, insect- and plant-spotting or take on other adventures, such as sky-biking or a cable-car ride high above the canopy.

Places

Maquipucuna Reserve
p131

Maquipucuna Reserve

TIME FROM MINDO: **1HR 15MIN**

The world's premier place to see spectacled bears

From about August to November, Andean spectacled bears migrate from the highlands to bulk up on the oil-rich wild avocados, making **Maquipucuna Reserve** *(maquipucuna.org; 2 days & 1 night from $160)* a unique bear habitat.

Among South America's rarest wildlife sightings, one or more of the 50 or so resident bears in this 5600-hectare cloud forest haven *can* be spotted year-round. But in avocado season, guests may clock several in a morning's hike with Maquipucuna's experienced guides. You'll forget you're 30km as the condor flies from Quito, trekking pristine forest searching for Ursidae family members and other wildlife, or watching hummingbirds flutter like squadrons of fairies.

Just one hour from bird-watching epicenter Mindo, Maquipucuna promises unspoiled remoteness. **Maquipucuna Lodge** has appealing accommodations, great food, a research center and guided reserve wildlife-watching walks, so it's recommended to visit on its overnight package. Brave the bumpy road here from Mindo, Intag Valley (three hours' drive) or Quito (two hours by the reserve's shuttle).

GETTING AROUND

Along with the rest of civilization, the roads fade away too. With both of this region's highlights, it takes long enough to reach them from Mindo that an overnight stay becomes necessary. Maquipucuna Reserve and Mashpi are roughly equidistant from either Mindo or from the Intag Valley, and you can arrange your trip out from either place. But most visitors use the complimentary shuttles laid on by the lodges to visit direct from Quito.

TOP EXPERIENCE

Mashpi

There is no lovelier location in Ecuador for immersion in splendid cloud-forest isolation than Mashpi. Inside, this trailblazing ecolodge combines low-impact luxury, dining outshining most high-end Quito restaurants, shopping and wellness. Outside, it is a vast wildlife reserve, with knowledgeable guides, invaluable research projects, hiking trails and other adventure activities.

COURTESY OF METROPOLITAN TOURING

TOP TIPS

- Getting here direct from Quito (three hours' drive) is simplest: transport is included in all packages.
- Come for a minimum of two nights to fully appreciate what the lodge and reserve offer.
- Book stays either direct with the lodge or through official operators Metropolitan Touring *(metropolitan-touring.com)*.

PRACTICALITIES

- mashpilodge.com
- daily
- 2 days & 1 night from $738

Dramatic Beginnings

It is a theatrical approach, corkscrewing increasingly deeper into lonesome hilly cloud forest, to reach Mashpi. The epic journey prepares you for something basic and far-flung, but Mashpi is its own classy, buzzing entity. Spot the stylish lobby with its shop, seminar rooms for lectures on rainforest life and views to the stunning atrium restaurant, and you will scarcely believe this cleverly constructed space – with its 24 bedrooms and suites, spa, gourmet dining and floor-to-ceiling glass throughout – could have been created without a single tree being felled.

Resplendent Reserve

You could spend days appreciating Mashpi from within but, with the jungle looming enticingly, you will soon wish to explore outside. Some of Ecuador's best naturalist guides take you on wildlife hikes through the 1214-hectare wilderness in search of 500+ bird species, pygmy boas, flora (including the reserve's magnificent 40m-high namesake tree, magnolia mashpi), numerous frogs and insects. Then there is the sky-bike (a hair-raising cable-suspended pedal above the treetops), a 2km-long canopy gondola, a 42m-high observation tower, waterfalls to swim beneath, a butterfly farm...there are enough forest adventures for a week – or more.

Places We Love to Stay

$ Budget $$ Midrange $$$ Top End

Cayambe

MAP p101

El Vicundo One of the country's best community homestay projects, near Guachalá, could see you staying in a fairy-tale-like cabin or on a pretty campsite. Unbeatable for getting to know the Ecuadorian people. $

Hacienda Guachalá In one of Ecuador's oldest haciendas (c 1580) you can sleep in huge rooms with parquet floors and fireplaces, or enjoy the pool, restaurant, animals and horse riding. It's 10km south of Cayambe. $$

Hostería Loma Larga A real treat, this horse-riding center is 5km southeast of Cayambe city; some suites come with Jacuzzis. $$$

Otavalo

MAP p112

Flying Donkey Hostal With a friendly, clued-up owner, this place is great for learning about the indigenous culture of the Otavalo people. Clean rooms, large shared kitchen and a pretty roof terrace. $

Hostal Riviera Sucre Long-serving, brightly painted, friendly guesthouse with 20 rooms abutting multilevel comely courtyards in central Otavalo. Hammock areas, book exchange and breakfast included. $

Hotel Otavalo For upmarket central Otavalo digs, this is the top choice: a renovated 100-year-old mansion, where an impressive atrium opens onto rooms with exposed brick or stone walls, hardwood floors and various objets d'art. $$$

Hacienda Pinsaqui Huge property edging countryside, 6km north of Otavalo, offering two restaurants and delightful grounds, plus cooking and musical-instrument classes. $$$

Hacienda Otavalo Paradisal self-catering home in a gated community in Quichinche, 3km above Otavalo to the west. $$$

Cotacachi

La Mirage Garden Hotel & Spa One of Ecuador's finest lodgings: a five-star hotel on the grounds of a 200-year-old hacienda, with haute cuisine dining and a world-class spa. $$$

Ibarra

MAP p117

Hotel Barcelona Three floors of rooms arranged around a cozy patio overlooking one of Ibarra's central squares, Parque La Merced, make this one of the region's best budget options. $

Finca Sommerwind Camping, cabins and a restaurant specializing in German food and beer on the serene far side of Laguna de Yahuarcocha. $

Hacienda Zuleta A 17th-century hacienda, retaining much of the regal luxury from when it was a presidential home. It's 20km south of Ibarra on the back road to Cayambe. $$$

Intag Valley

MAP p123

Pachecho Farmhouse Alongside the tumbling Intag River 1km northeast of Termas de Nangulvi, this friendly B&B is a mine of local information, with simple but homely rooms. $

Hosteria La Isla The valley's best-value backpacker option, 1km southwest of Termas de Nangulvi, with small, simple wood-and-brick rooms in lush, expansive riverside grounds. $

Willka Eco Farm Intag Valley's best hostelry: impeccably crafted cabins in expansive, balmy riverside gardens, with a pool and divine cooking. The Ecuadorian-American owners help with everything you might want to do in the area. Right by Termas de Nangulvi. $$

Mindo

MAP p127

Hostal Zafiro Pretty three-floor wooden chalet with a well-regarded restaurant abutting the river in central Mindo. $$

El Monte Sustainable Lodge Super-stylish, two-floor lodges scattered through the trees in a 45-hectare cloud-forest expanse, 3km outside Mindo. The Ecuadorian-American owners are immensely knowledgeable bird-watchers. $$$

Mashpi Ecuador's most luxurious wildlife-watching lodge, sequestered in hills between Mindo and the Intag Valley. $$$

Researched by
Joel Balsam

North Coast

UNSPOILED COASTLINE AND AFRO-ECUADORIAN ROOTS

Catch some sun and waves on the beach-lined Pacific coast, meet Afro-Ecuadorian communities and taste outstanding seafood.

Pristine beaches with highly surfable waves, flavor-packed seafood and Afro-Ecuadorian culture, plus almost no international tourists. That's Ecuador's North Coast. Though paradise comes with caveats.

The last decade has been particularly rough on the northwestern coast, with a devastating earthquake in 2016 followed by a COVID-19 pandemic lull and an uptick in narco-trafficking-related violence in Esmeraldas and Manabí provinces – the two states covered in this chapter. The result has been that most international visitors are (understandably) scared off, and the tourism industry is struggling. But if you have the time and the will to travel here, the laid-back (and safe) beach towns on the North Coast can easily wiggle their way into your heart.

JOEL BALSAM

The pearl of the North Coast is tiny Mompiche, one of the best surfing spots in Ecuador, with a passionate community of internationals and Afro-Ecuadorians who stand up for their mangrove- and fauna-filled slice of paradise. Next is Canoa, a town especially hard hit by the earthquake, with waves as easygoing as its people.

Atacames and Manta, areas hardest hit by violence, are still accessible and safe if you stick to the tourist areas. Atacames is great for boating out to see migrating humpback whales, while the Manta area is renowned for its Panama hats (originally from here), world-class kitesurfing and paragliding.

No, traveling the North Coast isn't always easy, and the tension in the air is palpable. But this is a place where your tourist dollars can have a real effect.

THE MAIN AREAS

ATACAMES
Old-school beach town with whale-watching.
p142

MOMPICHE
Surf town surrounded by forests.
p148

CANOA
Laid-back surf town.
p154

MANTA
Base for kitesurfing and hat shopping.
p162

For places to stay in North Coast, see p167

KATH WATSON/SHUTTERSTOCK

Left: Playa San Mateo (p165); above: Isla Portete (p151)

Find Your Way

Starting from Atacames makes the most sense if traveling from Quito. Or start in Manta if traveling from the South Coast or Guayaquil. Alternatively, head straight for your beach town of choice directly via overnight bus.

Mompiche, p148
Arguably Ecuador's best surf town, with a freight-train point break and a community of quirky international migrants who flock here to escape society.

Atacames, p142
Aged beach town, best for tasting Esmeraldas seafood and setting off on a boat tour to see migrating humpbacks.

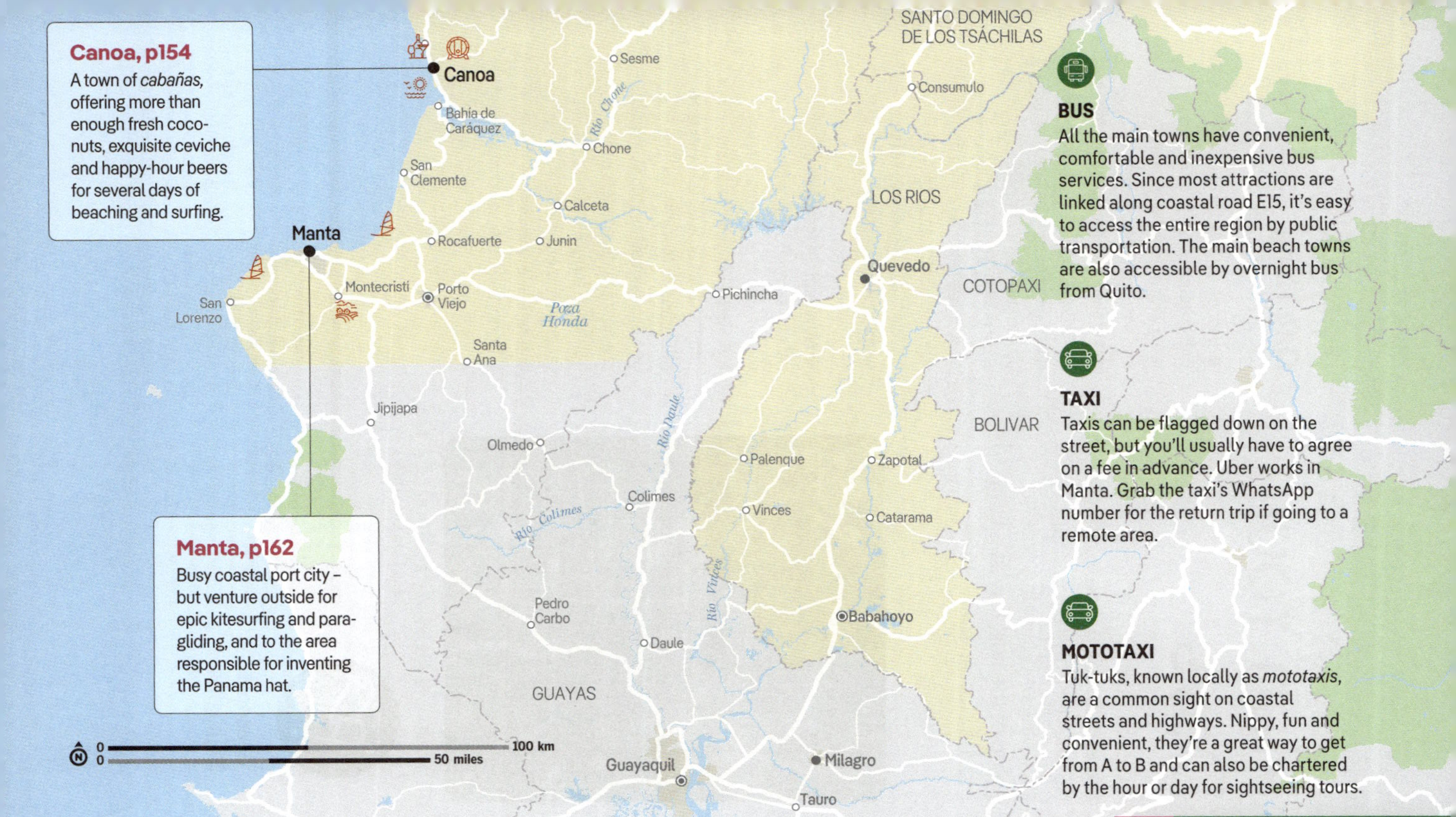

Canoa, p154

A town of *cabañas,* offering more than enough fresh coconuts, exquisite ceviche and happy-hour beers for several days of beaching and surfing.

Manta, p162

Busy coastal port city – but venture outside for epic kitesurfing and paragliding, and to the area responsible for inventing the Panama hat.

BUS

All the main towns have convenient, comfortable and inexpensive bus services. Since most attractions are linked along coastal road E15, it's easy to access the entire region by public transportation. The main beach towns are also accessible by overnight bus from Quito.

TAXI

Taxis can be flagged down on the street, but you'll usually have to agree on a fee in advance. Uber works in Manta. Grab the taxi's WhatsApp number for the return trip if going to a remote area.

MOTOTAXI

Tuk-tuks, known locally as *mototaxis,* are a common sight on coastal streets and highways. Nippy, fun and convenient, they're a great way to get from A to B and can also be chartered by the hour or day for sightseeing tours.

Plan Your Days

It would take nine hours to drive the entire North Coast highway, but we'd highly recommend stopping and sticking around some of the surf towns – time moves slower 'round here.

NATURE PICTURE LIBRARY/ALAMY

Golden howler monkey, Reserva Bosque Seco Lalo Loor (p161)

If You Only Do One Thing

- Escape society by heading to **Mompiche** (p148), a surf town with astonishing waves and a passionate community of international migrants devoted to preserving this tiny paradise. After catching some waves and soaking up the surf-town atmosphere, walk to **Playa Negra** (p150) – a beach that shimmers with metallic volcanic sand – and meet other travelers at a **capoeira, salsa, yoga or Pilates class** (p150).

- Now explore Mompiche's wild natural surroundings with a half-day boat tour of the mangrove forests and Afro-Ecuadorian communities around **Isla Portete** (p151), and to Muisne's natural pools, **Las Positas** (p153). A night in a hilltop nature reserve for a nocturnal **jungle walk** (p152) will teach you about medicinal plants and what it's really like to live in an off-grid, self-sufficient homestead.

Seasonal Highlights

JAN–MAR

Height of the surfing season, with big waves powering onto the coast in places like Mompiche. Despite it being in Ecuador's rainy season, you won't ever see much rain on the North Coast.

FEB/MAR

Carnaval (dates vary) processions are largest in Esmeraldas city, but you'll still catch the energy, and some colorful parades, in nearby Atacames (where it's safer).

APR

Kitesurfing season kicks off again in Santa Marianita, as **Kite Ecuador** (p166) reopens its doors after taking February and March off. In places like Canoa and Mompiche, surfing waves are at their lowest.

If You Have A Week

- **Canoa's** (p154) seemingly endless beach is one of the best places to learn to surf, and it's worth spending an afternoon mountain biking or taking a taxi to its excellent craft brewery – **Beerkingo** (p156) – in a rural community. Head south to San Vicente for a gastronomic experience at **Iche** (p158), which promotes ancient Manabí foodways; and to **Isla Corazón** (p159) for a cruise around the mangroves and seabird colonies. Further south is a **sports bar** (p160) making a positive contribution to a community going through some rough years; and **Playa San Clemente** (p160), a family-friendly beach that's popular with locals and expats.

- North of Canoa, hike forested trails in **Reserva Bosque Seco Lalo Loor** (p161), and hear its famed howler monkey scream.

A Month or Two in the North

- Take a boat tour in Atacames to see **whales** (p142) or a **bird island** (p143), and **eat seafood with Afro-Ecuadorian flair** (p144). Then jump into a monthlong volunteer experience in the coastal forest south of Atacames to take care of sea turtles at a **sanctuary** (p147). If you have another month to volunteer, learn the ins and outs of **regenerative farming and how to make chocolate** (p147).

- North of Atacames, **Reserva de Tigrillos** (p147) is a remote forest filled with rare birds like great green macaws, five-colored barbets and even the extremely rare Baudo Guan. Take a bird-watching tour and you'll also get a chance to meet an Afro-Ecuadorian community that's been living in a remote forest for centuries.

JUN–SEP

Meet homecoming giants during humpback-whale breeding season. Boat captains along the coast, particularly in Atacames, can take you to see the majestic mammals for less than $20 per person.

OCT

End of the whale-breeding season. Enjoy the shoulder-season sunshine with fewer crowds and more reasonable prices. Instead of boating for whales, consider a mangrove, snorkeling or bird-watching tour.

NOV

On November 6, celebrate Ecuador's African descendants at **El Retorno al Palenque de Libertad** (The Return to the Palenque of Freedom, p152) on Isla Portete. The event features a march, traditional food and marimba dancing.

HELP ME PICK:

North Coast Beaches

Sink your toes into the sand and sip coconut water straight from the drupe – the North Coast is lined with gorgeous beach after beach, each with its own unique vibe and swells. Narrow down which beach to spread your towel on by first deciding on your favorite activity. Want to learn to surf or kitesurf? Or maybe your target is seeing the humpback whale migration? Here's a guide to help you pick.

Where to Beach if You Love...

Surfing

Consistent waves from November to May and sandy shorelines make Ecuador's North Coast an idyllic spot for surfing. Grab your board and beach-hop along the coast from one empty beach to the next. Or get to one of the surfing hubs, which are busier but never crowded.

Playa de Mompiche (p148), in Esmeraldas province, delivers both the most legendary barrels on the North Coast and some fun beginner-friendly swells. Catch a wave on its perfect point break, and you might be enticed to become the next international visitor to call this place home. Or head to **Playa de Canoa** (p155), where the waves are as chill as the beach town's laid-back vibe. Learning in Canoa is a pleasure, and the sandy floor means you won't risk any rock scrapes when you fall (just beware of being smacked in the head by your board, as this writer was).

STRUCTURED VISION/SHUTTERSTOCK

Kitesurfing & Paragliding

Kitesurfing has become a global phenomenon in recent years, and **Playa Santa Marianita** (p165) is the best place in Ecuador to catch some waves. Rent equipment and learn from its reputable schools, and wave at passing humpback whales during their migration season (the best chance to see them here is from August to October). Or catch some wind from the top of a hill in **Crucita** and soar down gracefully in a 15- to 20-minute paragliding flight. Both are day-trippable from Manta or Guayaquil.

Whale-Watching

From June through October, Ecuador's Pacific coast becomes a highway for one of the world's great migrations, as hundreds of humpback whales travel between Antarctica and the Caribbean. Most beach towns on the North Coast run whale-watching tours in small motorboats, and prices per person are around $20. No need to plan ahead – just speak to a boat captain on beaches in towns like Atacames, Mompiche, Canoa and Manta to arrange a tour.

Relaxing

The North Coast is hot and humid year-round, so don't feel pressured to overexert yourself. Unwind with a relaxing beach day – many beaches here have hammocks underneath umbrellas for really kicking back. Long **Playa San Clemente** (p160) has slow, kid-friendly waves – perfect for a calm beach day; while **Playa Muisne** (p153) has warm, natural pools at low tide that feel like taking a bath.

PAUL KENNEDY/ALAMY

Left: Playa de Canoa (p155); above: Playa Santa Marianita (p165)

HOW TO

Before you go
Plan how to get to your desired beach, as bus times aren't frequent and you may need to change.

When to go
The great thing about the North Coast is that any month can be beach weather, as temperatures hover around 25°C (77°F) year-round.

Equipment
Surf schools teach beginners and rent boards in Canoa (**Happy Kiki Surf**; p155) and Mompiche (**La Peña**; p150). **Kite Ecuador** (p166) is the spot for kitesurfing in Santa Marianita.

Stays
Most accommodations in Canoa, Mompiche, and Santa Marianita are simple *cabañas,* with little to no hot water in the shower. Manta, San Clemente and **Tonsupa** (p143) have the most comfortable hotels.

Hiring a Boat

Boat captains walk along beaches in Atacames, Mompiche, Canoa and Manta offering whale-watching tours for $15 to $20 per person. Outside whale-watching season, they offer tours to remote beaches and caves inaccessible by road to go snorkeling and to see rare birds (including rare blue-footed boobies) for prices as low as $5 per person. It doesn't hurt to haggle if they quote you more, and if you're a larger group.

The North Coast is also home to huge mangrove forests (both in territory and plant size) – a diverse ecosystem home to seabirds and plump shrimp (Ecuador is the world's largest producer of the critters). From Mompiche, take a mangrove tour with local guide Ramon Cotera *(@ramons_jungletours)* south to **Isla Portete** (p151), an island with a fascinating Afro-Ecuadorian history, and jump into bioluminescent water. The tour also visits uninhabited Isla Júpiter. Or combine a tour of the mangroves around Mompiche with a visit to Playa Muisne's natural pools, **Las Positas** (p153). Local captain Juan (+593 98 020 8133) can take you there.

South of Canoa near San Vicente, there's another mangrove boat tour around heart-shaped **Isla Corazón** (p159). It's run by local octogenarian Francisco Reyes (+593-99-938-4425) alongside Ecuador's Ministry of Environment, and features thousands of frigate birds along with a canoe tour of mangrove tunnels at low tide.

Atacames

MARINE LIFE | SEAFOOD | BEACH BARS

TOP TIP

The Northern Esmeraldas region has seen security issues centered around the transborder activities of international drug cartels and criminal gangs. The town of San Lorenzo (close to the Colombia border), in particular, is best avoided; and if traveling along the coast, avoid overnighting in Esmeraldas city and taking overnight buses.

You're unlikely to see many international travelers in Atacames, but if you like the idea of hanging out with Ecuadorian vacationers, this is the place.

Atacames is an old-school South American beach hangout, complete with some of Ecuador's best seafood and vendors parading the sand, selling churros, beer, fresh fruit, ice cream and coconut milk. On weekends, bars on Atacames' *malecón* (beach road) blare with *reggaetón* and salsa music, as *serranos* (people from the highlands) swarm down to catch up on their beaching and, to some extent, boozing.

Between June and October, Atacames might be the most affordable place in the world to see huge pods of breeding humpback whales; the rest of the year, boat captains lead tours to see sizable populations of birds that crowd near an offshore island.

If loud music isn't your jam, stay in neighboring Tonsupa or Same for a more peaceful day at the beach.

Watch Breeding Humpbacks

Whale-watching boat tour

From June to October, Ecuador's Pacific coast is the site of one of the world's longest animal migrations, as humpback

GETTING AROUND

Atacames' beach area is small enough to be easily walkable, and it's generally considered safe to do so (word has it that local cartels prohibit robbing tourists). Tuk-tuks, known here as *mototaxis*, that buzz down the *malecón*, can take you to neighboring Tonsupa or Súa and up to the **Peñón del Suicida** (p145) viewpoint, for less than $3.

Buses are inexpensive and run frequently to Esmeraldas (the main hub further north), and 30 minutes south to calmer beach town, Same. Long-distance buses, including to/from Quito (eight hours), serve Atacames at bus companies' headquarters, as there's no central bus terminal.

whales travel nearly 8000km from Antarctica to breed in warmer Caribbean water – and Atacames might be one of the best, and cheapest, places to witness it.

Talk to boat captains on Atacames (p145) or **Tonsupa** beaches for an hour-long tour that takes you around 10km offshore to see not just humpbacks, but possibly Bryde's whales, orcas (killer whales), pilot whales and several species of dolphin. With up to 25 passengers per boat, and often screaming children, whale-watching tours here aren't exactly peaceful, but you'll be compensated by the fact that they cost just $15 to 20 per person. Consider chartering a private boat for some tranquility.

HEART-SHAPED MANGROVE ISLAND

See thousands of frigate birds and venture inside mangrove-forest tunnels on Isla Corazón, an aptly named island that will take your heart. Find out how to take a **boat tour** (p159).

See Dozens of Seabirds

Boat tour to Bird Island

Outside of whale-watching season, boat captains on the beach lead tours for just $5 per person to **Isla de los Pájaros** (Bird Island), a huge rock 200m offshore that attracts large populations of frigate birds, pelicans, black-headed gulls, whimbrels and the iconic (though rare) blue-footed boobies. You'll pass a

HIGHLIGHTS
1 Cevicheria Brisas del Mar
2 Isla de los Pájaros
3 Peñón del Suicida

SIGHTS
4 Playa de Atacames

SLEEPING
5 Cielo Azul
6 El Marqués
7 La Aldea

EATING
8 Encebollados El Tauro
9 Kike's
10 La Ramada
11 Las Delicias del Marisco
12 Los Bolónes del Parque
13 Niño Manuelito

WHALE-WATCHING TOUR ETHICS

Seeing migrating humpbacks on a cheap boat tour is the main reason to visit Atacames – but are these tours okay for these huge mammals? The answer is complicated, and depends on your boat captain.

Clearly, being chased by gas-guzzling boats that howl underwater isn't great for humpbacks. It could even be dangerous for them if boats get too close. However, whale-watching tours are generally okay if the captains cut their engines when close to avoid any interference and to let the curious mammals approach. This usually happens in Atacames, but not always. It's also worth considering that these tours give locals an economic incentive to keep humpbacks alive. Without them, who knows?

There's no clear-cut answer here, so do what feels right for you.

WORLDWIDE PHOTO/ALAMY

Ceviche

series of caves beneath trees painted with *guano* (bird poop), including Cueva de los Milagros (Cave of Miracles), which is only accessible at low tide – guides quip that 'courting couples enter two by two and emerge as three.' You'll also see a nudist beach allegedly popular with foreign tourists – if only there were any.

For more bird-spotting, you'll often see *gallinazos* (black vultures) hovering on afternoon thermals above Playa de Atacames, along with semipalmated plovers, reddish turnstones and sandpipers at the quieter southern end of the 4km-long beach. Or wander along the river that cuts through town and you may see herons, egrets and kingfishers.

Sample Seafood

Flavor-packed Esmeraldas cuisine

The cuisine in Esmeraldas province is distinct from the rest of the country. Here, the collision of Afro-Ecuadorian, indigenous and Hispanic foodways, and the region's range of herbs, spices and coconuts, creates some truly scrumptious dishes – especially if you like seafood.

Fresh clams, shrimp, langoustines and octopus overflow from bowls of well-spiced ceviche in a broth that's less soupy than in Quito. There are two ceviche markets on Atacames' *malecón*: **Cevicheria Brisas del Mar** and **La Ramada**, each with more than two dozen stalls. Or eat ceviche made from huge oysters on Playa de Tonsupa (p143) at **Ceviche Antoneta**, a tent in front of Pichos Bar.

Encocado (seafood slow-cooked in coconut milk with herbs and spices, turning a vibrant orangey-red) is Esmeraldas' marquee dish. Find it at any sit-down restaurant in Atacames.

View from 'Suicide Rock'

A viewpoint with a story

For the best views of Isla de los Pájaros and over Atacames, hire a *mototaxi* to take you up to **Peñón del Suicida** (Suicide Rock), a viewpoint with a *Romeo & Juliet*–like story behind it.

As legend goes, tribal royalty Prince Tonsupa and Princess Súa (the namesakes of present-day beach towns) were in an intense love affair, only to have it cut short when the prince was sent off to war.

When news came that the prince had been killed, the princess was heartbroken and flung herself off the 80m-tall cliff. The thing was, the news was wrong, and the prince wasn't dead.

When the prince returned, he too jumped from the rock to meet his lover in the afterlife.

Party Beachside

Salsa and swigs

Despite its privileged stretch of Pacific, and waves that tend to be much calmer than further down the coast, Atacames is best known as a party destination. Neon-lit bars with similarly incandescent drinks line the *malecón*, blasting music well into the night – avoid staying anywhere close by if you want to get any shut-eye. Umbrellas and chairs on **Playa de Atacames** should cost you $5 a set.

For a calmer beach day, take a *mototaxi* 10 minutes north to Tonsupa, lined with upscale hotels and apartments on its northern edge. Tonsupa's vintage **Pichos Bar** *(@pichos_bar)* is great for drinks and takes song requests.

Súa, bordering Atacames to the south, has a rockier beach and is thus much better for lunch on its *malecón* than lounging – **Kike's** is our favorite.

Same, 20 minutes from Atacames on any southbound bus, has cuter beach-town architecture than Atacames and surfable waves, though Mompiche (p148), 1½ hours south, is a much better bet for surfing.

THE SPONDYLUS

Walk around enough shops in Atacames, and you'll see spiky red conches selling for ridiculous prices – as much as $5000. This 'spiny oyster,' aka the *Spondylus*, was a highly sought-after currency for thousands of years, used in ceremonies (it was believed that it brought rain and power) and traded for some of the most valuable goods leading up to Spanish Conquest. To find *Spondylus* in South America, divers – many of whom were Manteños in modern-day Ecuador – would have to risk their lives by plunging as deep as 30m.

Today, more than being a cool collectible, the mollusc is the namesake for Ruta Spondylus, a tourist trail from Esmeraldas down to northern Peru. Tour a segment of it on the South Coast (p271).

EATING IN ATACAMES: OUR PICKS

Breakfast tigrillo (mashed plantains) is also outstanding.

Encebollados El Tauro: Serves traditional Albacore and onion soup *mixto* (with shrimp) in a broth bursting with flavor. Three locations in Atacames. *7am-1pm* $

Los Bolónes del Parque: Makes Manabí's fried green plantain balls, only with way more seafood, meat and cheese. *7am-1pm* $

Niño Manuelito: Superb fried fish with *manestra* (lentil soup) and seafood bathed in sauces like *al ajillo* (garlic) and *al mostaza* (mustard). *8am-7pm* $

Las Delicias del Marisco: *Malecón* restaurant known for Esmeraldas favorites like *encocado* (fish or seafood in coconut milk) and prawn ceviche. *7am-10pm* $$

Beyond Atacames

Rare birds, volunteering opportunities and remote villages await in Esmeraldas province, an area that's well off the tourist trail.

Places

Reserva Marina Galera-San Francisco p146
Reserva de Tigrillos p147

With the help of a guide or in-the-know locals, there are memorable experiences to take you well off the beaten track and into the embrace of unspoiled nature. However, it isn't a great idea to venture around Atacames on your own, especially to Esmeraldas city and the areas north toward Colombia, due to the chance of being caught up in cartel violence.

South of Atacames, two conservation programs in a coastal forest reserve help protect baby turtles and teach best practices for soil regeneration and homesteading. East in the Choco Biosystem, go on an adventure of a lifetime to see rare birds, *tigrillos* (ocelots) and visit a remote Afro-Ecuadorian community living far from the rest of society.

Reserva Marina Galera-San Francisco

TIME FROM ATACAMES: **1HR**

Protect sea turtles

The chunk of green space south of Atacames and west of the coastal highway is home to the country's last remaining coastal rainforest, which has been designated a national marine reserve since 2008. On the way from Atacames, you'll pass isolated beaches known to few but fisherfolk and local surfers.

Many of the beaches in Reserva Marina Galera-San Francisco might be isolated, but that doesn't mean sea turtles – who lay

GETTING AROUND

Atacames doesn't have a central bus terminal, but there are plenty of buses that stop on the highway leading north or south.

If traveling south to the Reserva Marina Galera-San Francisco via public transportation, you'll need to take a bus from Atacames to Tonchigüe, and then wait for a pickup truck (only three a day) to take you to Estero Del Platano or Quinguë, close to where the turtle project and permaculture farm are located. Renting a car or taking a taxi is more reliable, but note that it is not possible to come to Reserva Marina Galera-San Francisco from Muisne in the south due to a broken bridge. Speak to either conservation project before attempting to go on your own.

To get to Playa de Oro, you'd need to take a 7am bus from Esmeraldas for a few hours to Selva Alegre, and then wait to be picked up by a 10-person motorized canoe for a one-hour journey, and then 30 minutes' drive from there to Reserva de Tigrillos. Avoid the hassle (and safety risk) by booking a tour with Juan Carlos Calvachi (+593 99 966 4503).

some 120 nests here – are safe. Plastic pollution, fishing nets and other predators put the rare (and cute) reptiles at risk. Nonprofit **Punta Tortuga Wildlife Conservation** *(puntatortuga.org)* is working to protect both the reserve and the sea turtles by patrolling and building wire borders to safeguard nests and hatchlings, cleaning up plastic waste and conserving the forest.

Volunteer for a couple of days (per day $40), or long-term (per week $175) at the remote lodge situated close to a stunning view of the Pacific. The highly reviewed **Worldpackers** *(worldpackers.com/es/positions/66346)* program includes three meals a day, internet, and a bed in a shared cabin, though you can pay extra for a private room.

Learn regenerative farming

For Jorge Fletcher and Cris Reyes, former guides in the Amazon, it wasn't enough to speak about sustainability on their tours – they wanted to 'walk the talk.' So, the Peruvian and Ecuadorian couple bought land near Quinguë and spent decades becoming leaders in permaculture, regenerative farming and seed saving in Ecuador. Spend months (two minimum) volunteering at **Finca Chagüisa** *(@fincachaguisa; +593 99 793 8371; per day $15)* to learn how regenerative farming techniques can heal soil after years of unsustainable agriculture. They also teach how to make chocolate and honey (including tasty cacao honey) with the farm's cacao trees, and can show you what it takes to have your own homestead. Or come for a couple of days of activities, including bird-watching (Jorge has spotted 300 species on his property), snorkeling, fishing with a string, whale-watching, and herping night tours to see frogs and snakes. Jorge speaks English and Cris speaks French. Ask about pricing for activities and day visits.

Reserva de Tigrillos

TIME FROM ATACAMES: **4HR**

Bird-watching and remote village

It isn't easy to get to, nor advisable on your own, but the Choco biosystem that includes the 10,000-hectare **Reserva de Tigrillos** is one of the most diverse habitats in Ecuador – and also among the most isolated.

Experienced English-speaking guide Juan Carlos Calvachi *(juancarloscalvachi1@gmail.com)* leads 10- or 12-day tours that take visitors around Reserva de Tigrillos and Playa de Oro in forests where tree canopies can tower 30m. You'll be on the lookout for rare birds, including great green macaws, five-colored barbets, Choco poorwills, sapayoa, tooth-billed hummingbirds, ocellated antbirds, rose-faced parrot, streak-chested antpittas and even the extremely rare Baudo guan. You'll also have a chance to see *tigrillos* (ocelots), jaguarundi and the weasel-like tayra.

Three of the nights are spent at **Reserva de Tigrillos Jungle Lodge** in Playa de Oro, a village inaccessible by road that's mostly inhabited by descendents of the Afro-Ecuadorians who arrived here 500 years ago to pan for gold, where you'll have a chance to meet locals who live much as they've always lived: hunting, collecting jungle produce and medicine, and existing in harmony with nature a long way from society. The tour costs $300 per day for groups of two to six people, or $500 for solo travelers.

MARIMBA MUSIC

Marimba is much more than a music genre and dance from Esmeraldas and southwestern Colombia. Inscribed on UNESCO's Intangible Heritage List in 2015, marimba is an expression of Afro-Ecuadorian culture and community, dating back to *palenques* (fugitive communities of escaped slaves) and to Africa.

Characterized by palm and bamboo xylophones and drums known as *bomba* and *cununo*, marimba remains of tremendous cultural significance here, and is still a way of transmitting stories, legends and codes of life from the elders to the younger generation.

The best place to see marimba is at Esmeraldas Carnaval – the greatest celebration of the province's Afro-Ecuadorian heritage (in February/March). However, we wouldn't recommend going until cartel violence simmers down.

Mompiche

SURF | COMMUNITY | AFRO-ECUADORIAN HISTORY

If you pick one stop on the North Coast, pick Mompiche.

Two decades ago, there was no road into town and no electricity. Nowadays, buses run directly to Mompiche from Quito and along the coast, there's fiber-optic internet, and several excellent restaurants serving international food. But Mompiche hasn't lost its magic, and is far less of a party hub than Montañita down the coast.

Despite just a few strips of sand and no big-name hotels (and no hot water for showers), travelers come from far and wide to surf some of Ecuador's best waves. Many come for a few days, but plenty stay much longer, pulled in by Mompiche's slow-going beach lifestyle and friendly community members who do monthly beach cleanups and teach yoga, salsa and capoeira year-round.

However long you plan to spend in Mompiche, consider doubling it, but be careful; you might never leave.

Surf Ecuador's Longest Left-Hand Wave

Surfers' paradise for all levels

Most Ecuadorian surfers agree that **Playa de Mompiche** has the country's best waves. On a good day, it's a sapphire-tinged, cut-crystal barrel, often over 3m in height, which breaks off the end of the headland, ripping with freight-train power for up to 500m across the bay. Don't let the high waves faze you, though. This sort of scenario only comes together a few times each year and, even then, there's usually a sheltered spot to appeal to novices. Crowds are rarely a problem since, on an average day, cruise-y waves are breaking all along Mompiche's 1km-long arc of sand. The river mouth at the northern edge of Mompiche catches the best of this beach-break swell with an A-frame (left and right) wave that is perfect for learning, thanks to the sandy bottom.

The swell breaks most consistently from January to March, with February often the optimum month. Groups of international surfers (many regular visitors) tend to appear when significant swells line up. Although the left-hand point break is the icing on the cake, there's a good mix of reefs, beach breaks and river mouths near the town and on neighboring islands, especially Isla Bonita (p153), Muisne (p153) and Isla Portete (p151).

GETTING AROUND

Mompiche is small enough to stroll around barefoot on its dirt roads. If you want to go a bit further afield, there are always *mototaxis* near the beach and boats that can be chartered for exploring neighboring islands, inlets and mangrove forests.

One or two daily buses connect Mompiche with Atacames and Canoa down the coast, as well as to Quito. Ruben Espinosa (+593 95 970 2481) drives travelers to and from the Quito airport in his van for $160, which can be split among 10 passengers.

TOP TIP

Mompiche lives by the tide – and that's not just for surfing. At low tide, you can walk or take a *mototaxi* north on the beach to one of several seaside hotels, or south to a viewpoint and cemetery. At high tide, the beach mostly disappears. Plan accordingly.

MOMPICHE BEACH WALK

Skim the sand on your way to a traditional cemetery, viewpoint, bar and beach with some of the blackest volcanic sand you'll ever see.

START	END	LENGTH
Mompiche	Playa Negra	1.5km; 1hr

At low tide, or within a few hours, leave Mompiche and walk west on the beach, perhaps past a couple of fishing boats and crowds of black vultures. When you reach the trees, look for a sign pointing to the *cementerio* and climb up the rocks to a wooded trail. Follow it to a small, traditional Catholic 1 **cemetery** that's still in use.

A few steps past the cemetery, a steep trail leads down to the water – hold onto the rope for safety. Volcanic rocks and the best 2 **viewpoint** of Mompiche will greet you at the bottom.

Hop along the rocks back toward town, past a gorgeous strip of sand that only appears at low tide, before stopping for a cold beer at 3 **El Chiringuito** (p150), a seafood restaurant with stunning sea views.

Follow the trail behind the restaurant for about 10 minutes until you hit a main road. Veer right and keep walking. You'll come to a sign leading to 4 **Playa Negra**, a beach with shimmery black volcanic sand – the shine is due to high concentrations of metals such as titanium and iron.

Make your way back to Mompiche on foot, or call a *mototaxi* driver like Romel (+593 98 458 4302) to take you back to town.

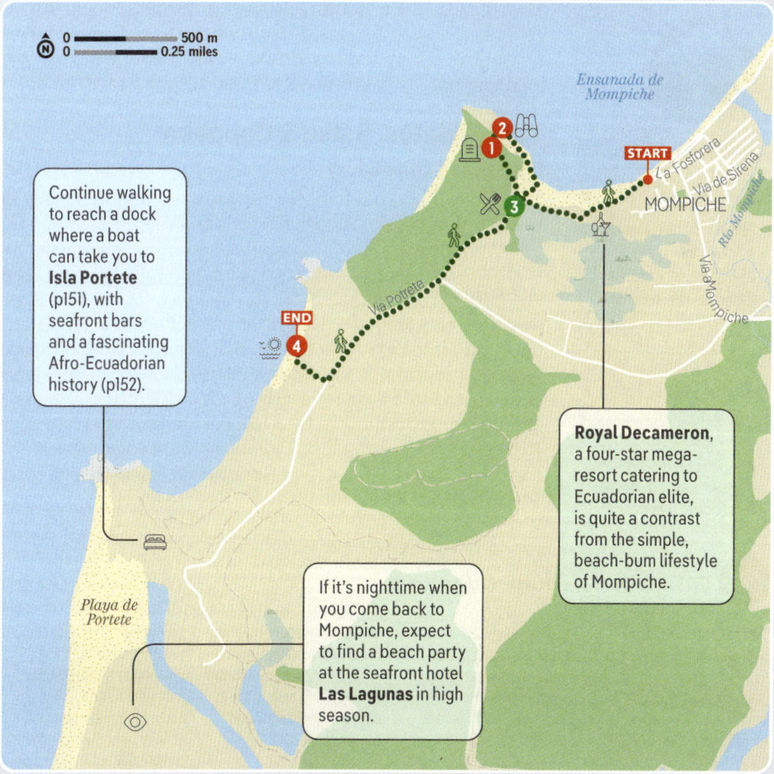

HIGHLIGHTS
1 La Peña
2 Playa de Mompiche

ACTIVITIES
3 Ground Wellness
4 Ubuntu

SLEEPING
5 La Caleta
see 3 La Facha
6 Mudhouse
7 Onda
8 Santo Antonio

EATING
see 8 La Facha
9 Madre Selva
10 Secret Garden Mompiche

DRINKING & NIGHTLIFE
11 Las Lagunas

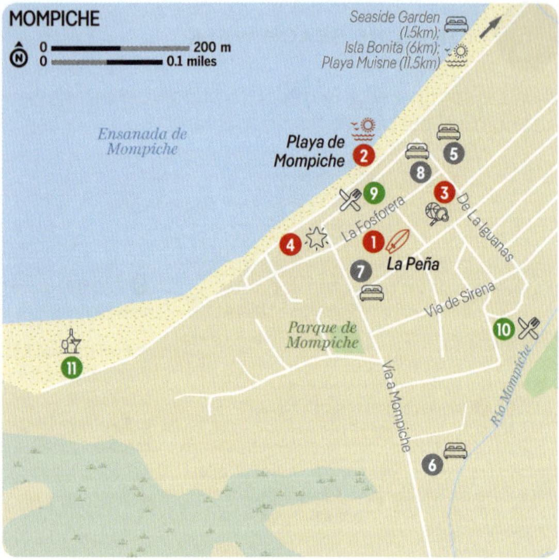

WHY I LOVE MOMPICHE

Joel Balsam, Lonely Planet writer

Mompiche is the kind of place where a weekend washes into a week, then a month, then a lifetime. Just ask the town's cast of colorful characters.

The day-to-day life of whole foods, jungle walks, wellness, volunteering, friends and surfing is difficult to resist. Within hours, I felt I could live here.

There are several surf schools and board-rental outlets in Mompiche. At **La Peña** *(@lapenasurfschool)*, local surfer Jefferson Panezo has good-quality boards and runs classes for surfers of any level. A 1½-hour surf lesson will cost you $25, and board rentals are $20 for a full day or $15 for half.

Yoga, Pilates, Salsa & Capoeira

Fitness and community

Mompiche might not have paved roads, but it has an array of wellness activities to keep both locals and visitors busy and fit.

Above **Ubuntu** *(@ubuntumompiche)* – a bar that opened in late 2025 serving *tacocones* (fried plantains stuffed with chicken and basil mayo) – former professional dancer Maria José Vélez teaches lively group salsa classes (no partner necessary) on Tuesdays and Thursdays from 5pm to 6pm for $5. The same space is used for morning yoga and mat Pilates classes ($5) by experienced instructor Mariana Pasarisa. Or try a free capoeira Angola (a slower, more traditional form) class with Brazilian Waldemar Henrique *(@g.c.a.palmares_mompiche)* on Wednesdays or Fridays from 7pm to 9pm at gym **Ground Wellness**, which costs $40 to workout for the month and includes a fitness assessment.

EATING IN MOMPICHE: OUR PICKS

Secret Garden Mompiche: Tasmanian-born Roni's treehouse kitchen has vegan, gluten-free and FODMAP meals. WhatsApp ahead (+593 96 405 8132). *8am-10pm* $

Madre Selva: Mompiche's unofficial 'third place', where locals hang out over burgers, pizza, ravioli and beers. *9am-2pm & 5-10pm Wed-Mon* $

El Chiringuito: The only restaurant on the beach, with idyllic views over the waves, fried fish, shrimp ceviche and cold Club beers. *9am-5pm* $

La Facha: Chef Tito Calle serves flavorful dishes like honey shrimp at this restaurant/hotel. Ask to taste his house-roasted coffee beans. *8-10am & 6-11pm* $$

Beyond Mompiche

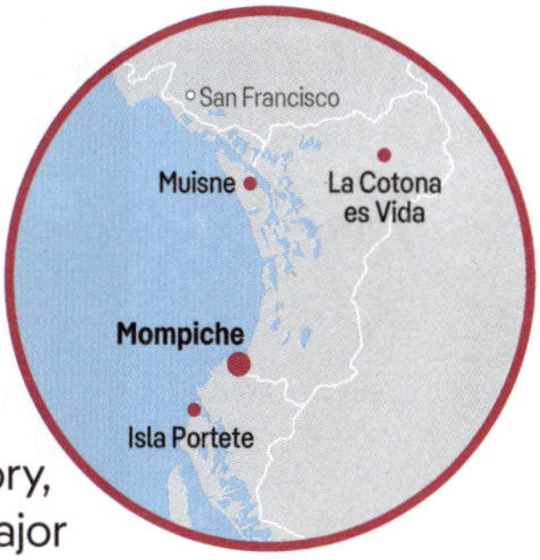

Stuck out on a secluded coastal promontory, Mompiche's wilderness surrounds are a major part of the town's magic.

Places

A short trip by three-wheeled *mototaxi* or boat can take you on unforgettable adventures that are essential if you plan to spend more than a day or two in Mompiche.

South of town, see where the country's Afro-Ecuadorian community began, and ride a boat through mangrove forests to an uninhabited island (at least in terms of humans, as there are tons of crabs). Close to the Mompiche highway turnoff, wake up to the soundtrack of howler monkeys, after hiking in the jungle on the lookout for incandescent insects. Or, about 6km of unbroken and unspoiled white sand stretches to the north of Mompiche on the way to a stunning beach that might be one of the coast's finest.

GETTING AROUND

For Isla Portete, hop on a *mototaxi* to the inlet opposite Portete's beach and flag down a motor launch ($0.50). Or, better still, take a three-hour boat tour.

La Cotona es Vida is a short *mototaxi* ride from town.

A private boat (per person $30) can take you to Muisne. If you bus, you'll need to get off the E15 highway and take a *mototaxi* to the beach. Direct buses go to Muisne from Atacames.

Isla Portete

TIME FROM MOMPICHE: **15MIN**

Illuminating mangrove tour

Just outside of Mompiche, **Isla Portete** and neighboring Bolívar house communities of fisherfolk – many of them descendants of enslaved Africans who escaped a Spanish shipwreck in 1553. You can get over to Isla Portete by boat launch and stay for lunch at one of its waterside restaurants, or take an evening tour through the mangroves to swim with bioluminescent plankton.

While the mangrove trees here may not be quite up to the scale of the giants near San Lorenzo (the world's tallest), many are over 100 years of age. Their tangled roots over glassy turquoise water provide critical habitats for shrimp, molluscs and bioluminescent plankton that beam blue when you swish the water. They're also home to an incredible diversity of waterbirds, including cormorants, frigate birds, pelicans, ibis and egrets.

See this fascinating ecosystem on a three-hour night tour with experienced guide **Ramon Cotera** *(@ramons_jungletours; per person $25)*. The tour starts at the Isla Portete boat launch and wades through a mangrove tunnel to a park with a bust commemorating Afro-Ecuadorian leader Alonso de Illescas. You'll then pass riverside villagers in Bolívar, where Cotera grew up, on the way to Isla Júpiter, an uninhabited island that feels like another planet. After chasing some crabs around, you'll return to the mangroves with a chance to spot – and even swim with – bioluminescent plankton. This swim could easily be your North Coast highlight.

THE FIRST AFRO-ECUADORIANS

In October 1553, a Spanish ship transporting enslaved Africans from Panama to Peru stopped in the mangroves by Isla Portete and was wrecked by a storm. Nearly two dozen enslaved Africans managed to escape, including future *palenque* leader Alonso de Illescas.

Ecuador's first community of African descendants is memorialized every November 6 at **El Retorno al Palenque de Libertad** (The Return to the Palenque of Freedom), a festival where hundreds march in traditional clothing before celebrating around a bonfire. Expect drumming, marimba music and dancing, poetry, and to dine on traditional *tapao* (fish stew with coconut milk and spices). Contact Afro-Ecuadorian culture organization Muisne Desne Adentro *(@muisne desdeadentro)* if planning to go, or to partake in Afro-Ecuadorian experiences the rest of the year.

While Ramon only speaks Spanish, the tour is still worth it if you don't.

La Cotona es Vida

TIME FROM MOMPICHE: **30MIN**

Night in the forest

Ever wonder what it'd be like to escape society and go live up on a mountain? Heed the howler monkey's call and see for yourself with a man who did just that by spending a night in the jungle at La Cotona es Vida.

Off coastal highway E15, a few hundred meters from the turnoff to Mompiche, **La Cotona es Vida** is a reserve owned and protected by local guide Ramon Cotera *(+593 98 445 8012; per person $35)*. It's also his home. Ramon managed to have his property officially registered as a reserve in 2018.

At his mountaintop home made of wood and bamboo, you'll eat simple, vegetarian food cooked over an open fire, sleep in (surprisingly comfortable) beds under a mosquito net and follow machete-wielding Ramon on night and morning hikes to look for huge, incandescent and/or venomous insects and reptiles in this extremely diverse ecosystem.

Among the wildlife in La Cotona es Vida are armadillos, various types of snakes (as evidenced by the 2m skin laid out on Ramon's table), rainbow crickets, blue morpho butterflies, tiger spiders (among the world's most venomous arachnids), tree frogs (including glass frogs that resemble transparent crystal beads) and the distinctive strawberry poison-dart frogs. You'll also see and learn (a translation app can help if you don't speak Spanish) about medicinal plants and have the option to partake in a gratitude ceremony beneath a spring. Especially if you've spent time traveling in loud buses or in cities, the night in the jungle should have you feeling refreshed and calm.

JOEL BALSAM

Ramon Cotera at La Cotona es Vida

Word of warning: don't bring large suitcases, as you'll have to walk 15 minutes up to the hill through the grass and mud.

Muisne

TIME FROM MOMPICHE: **45MIN**

Natural pools and beach tour

Playa Muisne is legendary in these parts (at least according to their frequency in dreamy poetry readings in Mompiche). Its sand is spotless. There are gorgeous palm trees lining the *malecón,* and it has warm natural pools on its north end. But few arrive outside of Sundays, when in-the-know locals flock here. If you go, hire a three-wheeled *mototaxi* to take you from rough-and-tumble working-class town of Muisne over the pedestrian bridge to the beach. Also hire a *mototaxi* to take you along Playa Muisne's heart-wrenchingly beautiful 6.5km stretch of sand. *Mototaxi* drivers charge $6 per person for 40 minutes.

At the southern end, you'll see **Isla Bonita**, a mini bay that's a paradisal place to swim (you can see Mompiche from here, and even walk over in about an hour if you time the tide right). At the northern end, melt into **Las Positas**, warm natural pools that emerge at low tide.

There are a few restaurants on Playa Muisne's *malecón*. Your best option is old-timey **Las Palmeras**, which serves freshly caught fish and seafood as ceviche, and also *encocada* (seafood in coconut milk) along with pitchers of coconut water.

Boat ride to the beach

If you plan to travel to Muisne from Mompiche, a chartered boat (taking about 40 minutes) can save hours on what can be a convoluted journey. It's also an exciting experience, since you'll travel through protected mangrove forests, Mompiche's long, sandy beach, and shrimp farms to emerge at Playa Muisne.

Local captain Juan (+593 98 020 8133) can take you over in his relatively modern boat for $30 per person.

WHY PROTECT PACHAMAMA?

Ramon Cotera *(@ramons_jungletours)*, guide/protector of La Cotona es Vida reserve, shares why it's important to conserve the forest around Mompiche.

This humid forest is home to a wealth of flora, including various medicinal plants. It was also inhabited by ancestors of the indigenous Chachi people, and wildlife here is abundant. We have ocelots, armadillos and howler monkeys; birds including toucans, parrots and chachalacas; snakes, spiders and the world's most poisonous ant. Visiting places like this is very important because it allows you to gain a different perspective on life. Spiritually, it's about living in complete harmony with nature and respecting every species found within it. Mother Earth, Pachamama, is pure love. She takes such good care of us, so let's take better care of her.

Canoa

SURFING | HAPPY HOUR | SWIMMING

TOP TIP

Bizarrely for such a busy, boisterous beach town, there's not a single ATM in Canoa that works for international cards. Plan in advance or you'll be forced to make the 20-minute bus ride south to the ATMs in San Vicente.

Days in this ultra-chill beach town have a particular rhythm. Wake up for an *encebollado* (Albacore tuna soup), surf some of the most consistent waves around, eat a $3 *almuerzo* (lunch) or bowl of fresh ceviche, then find a stool alongside welcoming locals for happy-hour drinks into the night. Repeat the next day, or, as is the case with many American retirees who've settled in Canoa and in nearby San Clemente, for the rest of your life.

After Mompiche, Canoa is the most worthwhile beach town on the North Coast, and is considered safe, despite safety issues in nearby Bahía de Caráquez and Manabí state.

While there's little to do here but surf, chill and drink – including at a beloved microbrewery within biking distance – it's worth coming for a few days to unwind on beach time and share some travel stories.

Learn to Surf

Ecuador's most consistent surf break

Canoa's unobstructed westward-facing expanse of white sand attracts waves year-round in a way that more celebrated (but more sheltered) spots like Montañita and Mompiche rarely do. This means that even in the 'flat season' (April to October),

GETTING AROUND

Canoa is small enough to be easily walkable, but taxis and three-wheeled *mototaxis* are always within hailing distance. If none are around, you'll find some at the corner of Calles Javier Santos and Ramón Centeno.

Hostels Coco Loco (p167) and Rutamar (p167) rent bikes for $15 per day. Use one to get to the Beerkingo craft brewery, or bike along the coast to San Vicente, nearly 18km away.

There's no bus terminal in Canoa, but buses stop in front of **Lunarcito** restaurant. Buy tickets from the restaurant, and Whatsapp the owner (+593 99 762 2943) to confirm bus times.

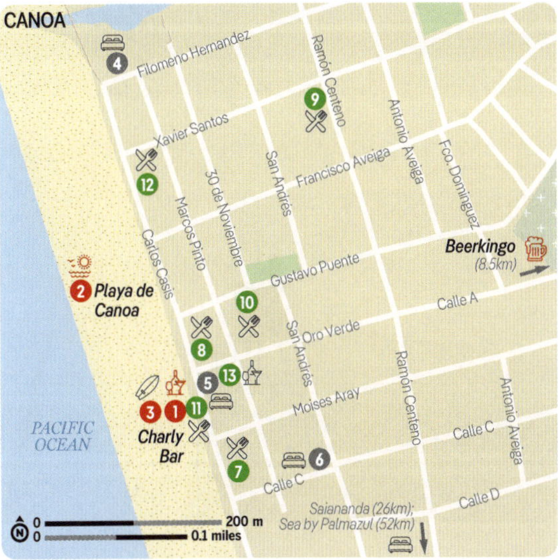

HIGHLIGHTS
1 Charly Bar
2 Playa de Canoa

ACTIVITIES
3 Happy Kiki Surf

SLEEPING
4 Bambú
5 Coco Loco
6 Rutamar

EATING
7 Delicias del Pacifico
8 La Casa del Camotillo
9 Lunarcito
10 Pinches Tacos
11 Saborearme
12 Surf Shak

DRINKING & NIGHTLIFE
see 4 Bambú
13 Coco Loco

you're almost certain to find surfable waves at Canoa. The sandy bottom (entirely free of rocks) and sheer space at **Playa de Canoa** (what's claimed to be Ecuador's longest beach at 13km) means ample room to play. This stretch of beach is particularly terrific for learning, as the waves rarely get very high and the sand cushions falls.

Kick off your surfing career, or hone your skills, with a gentle and friendly push from **Happy Kiki** *(@happy.kiki.surf; +593 98 418 1341),* aka Manuel Nevarez. The Canoa-born instructor started surfing shortly after he could walk, using the wooden plank underneath the bed at his grandmother's house to ride his first waves. After losing his shop and boards to the 2016 earthquake, Kiki left for Quito – but the waves, and the dream of helping local kids get into surfing rather than drugs and cell phones, pulled him back.

Contact Kiki for a lesson, as he doesn't have a fixed shop. A 1½-hour introductory class from the centre of Canoa's beach costs $25 and is full of smiles, as Kiki, who speaks only Spanglish, teaches proper form before helping you catch your first waves. The boards you'll be riding were handcrafted by Kiki himself using ultralight balsa wood. Rentals cost $3 per hour or $15 a day.

Tour a Cave & Isolated Beach

Offbeat adventures

About every eight days, when the tide is at its lowest, a beautiful cave within walking distance of Canoa is revealed. Surf instructor Happy Kiki can take you there on a two- or three-hour walking tour for $5 per person. If you're lucky, there'll be sea lions and blue-footed boobies hanging out in the cave.

2016 EARTHQUAKE

On April 16, 2016, tectonic plates shifted in the Pacific, triggering a 7.8-magnitude earthquake that devastated Ecuador's North Coast. Nearly 700 were killed, more than 16,000 injured, and an estimated 35,000 homes were destroyed or damaged. The worst hit was Pedernales, 80% of it reduced to rubble; but Canoa, an hour south, was badly affected as well.

You'll be hard-pressed to find a local here untouched by the quake; some had homes or businesses crushed. Others were severely injured or lost loved ones. A decade on, its effects remain – compounded by COVID-19 and narco-related security fears in Manabí. Once buzzing, this beach town is now a sleepy stop with an air of sadness. It's also a place where your tourism dollars can make a real difference.

Kiki can also arrange a boat tour to take you to **Cabo Pasado**, a peninsula north of Canoa with virgin beaches only accessible by sea. Ask about the option of spearfishing with a megalodon-tooth-tipped spear, snorkeling and staying a night at the beach. Prices depend on activities and group size.

Rural Craft Brewery

Swim, shoot hoops and drink

'Haga frio, haga calor, una beerkingo siempre es mejor' (Whether it's cold or hot, a Beerkingo is always better) – that's the catchy slogan at **Beerkingo** *(@beer.kingo)*, an artisanal brewery located 20km inland from Canoa's beach in a rural settlement. The brewery has established itself as having one of the best brews on the North Coast, and makes for a terrific afternoon break from the beach.

The impressive brewery compound is equipped with swimming pools, a basketball court, simple cabins for staying overnight if you drink too much (per night $15) and several tasty beers on tap, including a red fruit cider, 12% golden lager and a stout. The easiest way to get here is via taxi

EATING IN CANOA: OUR PICKS

Pinches Tacos: Take a break from seafood with Mexican-style tacos a couple of blocks from the *malecón* (beach road). *3-10pm Wed & Thu, to 11pm Fri-Sun* $

Saborearme: Four brothers have virtually taken over the Canoa coastline with four restaurants by the same name. This one is known for its ceviche. *7am-10pm* $$

Delicias del Pacifico: Three decades of experience on Canoa beachfront; potentially the best place to sample *ceviche de concha* made with sea-snail conches. *8am-9pm* $$

La Casa del Camotillo: Super-friendly, family-run place that serves fantastic *ceviche mixto* (with everything). Grab a beer and a hammock at sundown. *7am-10pm* $$

JOEL BALSAM

Happy Kiki (p155), Playa de Canoa

(one way $6). Make sure to grab the driver's number for a ride back.

Bike to Beerkingo

Adventure away from the beach

Go on a mountain-biking adventure by renting a bike from Coco Loco (p167) or Rutamar (p167) hostels for $15 per day. Bring plenty of water and make sure you know the directions beforehand, though the route is well marked, so you won't need a guide. The dirt track is three blocks from Canoa's beach area and leads into the Río Canoa valley past the rural settlement. The way is mostly uphill and the only traffic you'll see is from snarling dogs (which are, admittedly, really terrifying).

RETIREE HOT SPOT

While you won't find many international tourists in Canoa, you'll run into plenty of Canadian and American so-called expats at beachside bars during happy hour. Attracted by the warm weather, relaxed vibes, US dollar and affordable healthcare, retirees are common across the North Coast in Canoa, Tonsupa, San Clemente and Crucita.

To retire in Ecuador, you need to apply for a Visa de Pensionado (Pensioner's Visa), which involves proving that you receive a monthly guaranteed income (from a pension, rental property or investments). You also need health insurance (abroad or with Ecuador's public system) and a clean criminal background check.

If interested, check out Facebook groups like Ecuador Expats, or consider a multiday introductory tour with **Ecuador Expat Journeys** *(ecuadorexpatjourneys.com)*.

DRINKING IN CANOA: OUR PICKS

Charly Bar: Hang with locals at happy hour (4pm to 5pm), then return in the morning for *encebollado* and watermelon juice. *7:30am-8pm Wed-Sun*

Coco Loco: Sit at the bar for happy hour (6pm to 7pm) at this beachfront hostel, and stick around for occasional live music. *8am-10pm*

Bambú: The bar area in the sand at this beachfront hotel has a romantic, low-lit ambience that's better than the food and service. *8am-9pm*

Surf Shak: Severely earthquake-damaged, American-owned bar opens for Wednesday-night trivia, Sunday brunch and NFL games. *5:30-10pm Wed, 10am-5pm Sun*

Beyond Canoa

While off most itineraries, the towns around Canoa have some of the most fascinating off-beach experiences on the North Coast.

Places

San Vicente p158
San Clemente p160
Jama p161

GETTING AROUND

Turismo Manabí, Tosagua and Reina del Camino buses travel along the E15 highway every 30 minutes or so throughout the day.

Taxi Maccar *(+593 98 578 5769)* is a solid option if you don't mind sharing a taxi, or you can grab a private yellow taxi from the stop in Canoa at Calles Ramón Centeno and Javier Santos.

Leave sleepy Canoa to explore upper Manabí state, a region rich in history, culinary traditions and under-appreciated landscapes.

South of Canoa, taste and tour what's easily the North Coast's finest restaurant on the coast or embark on a boat tour through mangrove tunnels teeming with frigate birds. Southbound also features a sports bar with a hell of a story, and a family-friendly beach town beloved by expats. Northbound, hike in a reserve that echoes with the call of howler monkeys.

Violence, particularly in Bahía de Caráquez, means that traveling south of Canoa at nightfall isn't recommended – you'll barely see any cars on the road if you do, and taxi drivers might even be too scared to venture to your destination.

While just a cluster of 10 or so blocks, shrimping hub San Vicente is the busiest town around, especially when combined with vacation hub Bahía de Caráquez, now linked by a modern bridge that survived the 2016 earthquake.

San Vicente

TIME FROM CANOA: **20MIN**

Manabí food lab

Few states in Ecuador demand more praise for their cuisine than Manabí. In 2026, the International Institute for Gastronomy, Culture, Art and Tourism (IGCAT) named the state a World Region of Gastronomy – and we can see why. Here, salty, creamy peanuts accent soups, ceviches and *bolónes* (fried plantain balls), while achiote (a shrub used to make a natural condiment), Creole corn and clay-oven-cooked meats work their magic elsewhere.

Down a long and winding road, up a hilltop and along a candlelit path, find **Iche** *(@iche.ec)*, a cutting-edge food laboratory and restaurant devoted to preserving Manabí's ancient culinary traditions. Built in 2021 as a way to uplift the region after the devastating 2016 earthquake, Iche is both a school that trains underprivileged youth in Manabita-cooking and a foodie restaurant inside a striking wooden-and-glass building.

Come to taste award-winning chef Valentina Álvarez's cuisine via the eight-item tasting menu ($48) or order à la carte

JOEL BALSAM

Francisco Reyes, Isla Corazón

($15 to $25). Menu standouts include the carpaccio topped with peanut-butter ice-cream, and melt-in-your-mouth pork ribs. And don't skip its creative craft cocktails and *currincho* (sugarcane liquor), which is distilled here.

Before or after dinner, ask for a tour to see Iche's vegetable garden, traditional Manabí grill (a clay pit topped by removable grills), distillery and distilled liquors, and its cutting-edge classroom.

Hidden world of mangrove forests

Before the 1998 El Niño weather event, life had been relatively easy for the inhabitants of the 24 communities surrounding the mangrove-fringed lagoon around the Río Chone river mouth. The nets were heavy with fish and prawns and there was plenty of work to be had at the busy Portobello harbor. But in less than a year, the river silted up, going from 40m in depth to less than 9m. The fish and the cargo boats disappeared.

Tourism provided a solution. There had been a long history of the community protecting **Isla Corazón** *(Heart Island; islacorazon.com)*, a fish-spawning ground; one community currently runs boat tours in collaboration with the Ministry of the Environment. Expert local guide Francisco Reyes (+593 99 938 4425) leads two-hour tours (at 10am and 2pm) for $20 per person.

Tours start with a visit to its small museum of taxidermied reptiles and monkeys, before embarking in a motorboat on the lookout for 83 native and migratory bird species, including pelicans, blue herons, kingfishers and the colony of 20,000 to 25,000 frigate birds that roost here. These majestic birds are at their most spectacular during the July–September mating season, when the males sport their distended scarlet-colored throat pouches. There's also a chance to see pink-hued roseate spoonbills and white egrets, known to locals as *gansa nivea*

BIG SHRIMP

Along Ecuador's Pacific coast, you're bound to see constructed shrimping pools – evidence of the country's world-leading shrimp-farming industry. Ecuador is blessed with shrimp, due to having the largest mangrove forest in the South Pacific, and selling it is a major source of income for residents here and the country as a whole. The thing is, shrimp farming can be terrible for the environment, as shrimpers often rip out mangrove forests to get to the critters, destroying an important ecosystem and shelter from weather events.

Recently though, Ecuador has promised to clean up its act. In 2022, it became the first country to agree to halt habitat conversion for shrimp farming. Whether or not that's being enforced is another question.

LOCAL EXPERT TIPS

Jessica Meza, owner of the Sea by Palmazul *(theseabypalmazul.com)*, shares her favorite spots.

Japotó Museum This newly opened museum features artifacts from the Manteño people who lived here from the 1st century CE to Spanish arrival.

Playa San Clemente Every morning, you can see the fishermen taking out their nets and actually help them drag their nets out. To thank you, they'll give you some fish.

Manabí food Here we cook everything with peanuts and I highly recommend tasting as many dishes as you can.

Paseo Comunitario Manglar La Boca Just south of San Clemente, the Portoviejo River Delta is amazing for bird-watchers, with lots of different species.

(their feathers are the same color as Nivea cream). You'll get off the boat to walk along a short timber walkway into the mangrove forest, and sing a local serenade with the help of octogenarian Francisco, who sees the mangroves as his children. If the tide is low enough, you'll also have a chance to switch to a canoe and paddle through a mangrove tunnel.

Sports bar with a story

Across the water from San Vicente, Bahía de Caráquez has long been an Ecuadorian vacation spot, complete with high-rise apartment rentals and a small urban beach. Recently, though, it's become a hot spot for violence, especially in the Leonidis Plaza neighborhood, turning it into a ghost town at night.

If you find yourself here, stop by **H Sports Café** *(facebook.com/hsportscafe#)* to watch a game on one of its many TVs, eat some hearty food (tacos Tuesdays are awesome) and chat with the bar's do-gooder owner, expat Henry Wonsey. A former parachute rescuer with the US Army during the Iraq War who retired at 29 and moved to Bahía de Caráquez on a whim (he spun a globe and moved where his finger landed), Henry sees his business as more than a sports bar. It's a 'third place' for locals who suffered so much during the 2016 earthquake, and a place where his employees can learn important skills like English, accounting and customer service, as well as make some cash. It's open day and night, including for a fairly priced Ecuadorian *almuerzo* (lunch with soup).

San Clemente

TIME FROM CANOA: **1HR**

Family-friendly beach

Twin towns San Clemente and San Jacinto are generally off the tourist trail, but make for a relaxing stop for some beach time, seafood and hanging out with expats.

Unlike most other beach towns on the North Coast, San Clemente isn't known for its surf breaks. You won't typically find any surfers, kitesurfers, paragliders or any other adventure-sport lovers for that matter.

Here, the waves gently brush against the sandy shore, and you can stand in the water without swimming. That, along with the long, not busy shoreline and general lack of noisy partiers, makes **Playa San Clemente** popular among families and North American retirees – some 1200 expats are said to be living here.

EATING IN SAN CLEMENTE: OUR PICKS

Has live music on Sundays.

Meier's: This German-owned pizzeria at the north end of San Clemente is a favorite among expats. *noon-10pm Tue-Sun* $

Hotel San Jacinto: Old-school hotel on the beachfront in San Jacinto, serving $3.50 *almuerzo* and beers on its concrete terrace overlooking the sea. *9am-5:30pm* $

Asadero Doña Costilla Ahumada: If you're sick of seafood, this might be the best barbecue joint on the North Coast. *noon-3pm & 6-9:30pm Mon-Sat* $$

Cocomar: The restaurant and bar at the Sea by Palmazul hotel specializes in sea-to-table fish and steak, served from its lovely rooftop terrace. $$

Earthstar fungus, Reserva Bosque Seco Lalo Loor

Come spend a day at the beach and eat at one of its solid restaurants, many of them specializing in sea-to-table cuisine. Or, spend a few nights at its best hotel, the Sea by Palmazul (p167).

Jama

TIME FROM CANOA: **1HR**

Hike in the 'howling' jungle

Accessible from Canoa or Mompiche, Jama is home to a nature reserve known for its howler monkeys.

The pristine Pacific coast woodlands of **Reserva Bosque Seco Lalo Loor** *(reservalaloloor.com; $5)* are named after Eudaldo 'Lalo' Loor, the Ecuadorian dairy-farmer conservationist who worked to preserve this dry forest ecosystem. Recognized as a nature reserve in 2019, these dry forests are a terrific place to see – and, more spectacularly still, to hear – awesome howler monkeys.

Lalo Loor, a particularly rich and diverse transition zone between the tropical forests of Choco region and the drier southern woodland (which stretches into Peru), is worth visiting for its 9km network of forest hiking trails, including a 4km loop (about two hours). The reserve features more than 200 bird species, including toucans, parrots and hummingbirds; and the astoundingly beautiful blue morpho butterflies (indigenous jungle dwellers thought they were fallen pieces of heaven) are hard to miss. For a deeper insight into the reserve's insects, reptiles and amphibians, you'll need the experience – not to mention the sharp eyes – of one of the reserve's expert Spanish-only **guides** *(+593-99-006-7089; $20)*.

There is accommodations in the reserve in simple eco-cabins.

LOS COLORADOS

Northeast of Canoa, in the Lowlands around Ecuador's fourth-largest city, Santo Domingo, members of the indigenous Tsáchila community continue to practice their ancient customs, wear traditional clothing and paint their hair in their emblematic scarlet skullcap. According to oral history, the Tsáchila were being killed off by smallpox in the 17th century when a shaman's vision during an *ayahuasca* ceremony led him to the achiote berry, and to painting his hair with its juice as a way to ward off disease. The community followed, leading the Spanish to name the Tsáchila 'los Colorados' for their dyed red hair.

Few members of the Tsáchila community remain, but some work as *curanderos* (shaman healers), hosting *limpiezas* (spiritual cleansings involving traditional plants, blown tobacco) and *ayahuasca* ceremonies.

Manta

MONTECRISTI HATS | BEACH CITY | SEA SPORTS

TOP TIP

Safety-wise, Manta often makes headlines for narco-trafficking-related violence, but the Playa Murciélago area, where you'll likely stay, is generally fine. Keep your wits about you, and take Ubers to get around.

You'll have caught the scent from the fishing port long before the gigantic statue of a tuna swimming above a tin can confirms that Manta – the fifth-largest city in the country and the capital of Manabí province – revolves around the Pacific coast fisheries. Once upon a time, it was also a major shipping port for Montecristi hats – the original Panama hat.

There's little point in making a deliberate trip to Manta, but it has a couple of decent beaches, a small museum with exhibits of pre-Columbian culture and terrific Manabita-style seafood. Manta is primarily a convenient hub for visiting the hat-producing town of Montecristi (10km to the south), as well as Santa Marianita and Crucita – world-renowned destinations for kite-surfing and paragliding.

There are several decent hotels to choose from if you stay a night or two, including top international brands, along the coastline near Playa Murciélago and Plaza La Quadra mall.

PARTY BEACH TOWN

Continue south down Ruta Spondylus, aka La Ruta del Sol (Sunshine Route), to the South Coast where you'll find Montañita, Ecuador's backpacker party and surf spot (p267).

Manta's City Beaches

Sunshine time with locals

The sand at **Playa Murciélago**, Manta's main and most popular beach, is a hard-packed mix of brown and grey volcanic

GETTING AROUND

Manta is well served by yellow taxis and Ubers around town and from its busy bus station, **Terminal Terrestre de Manta**, and airport next door, **Eloy Alfaro International Airport** (MEC). Taxis or Ubers to Playa San Mateo and Santa Marianita shouldn't cost more than $10–20. Buses are plentiful from the bus station to Montecristi and Crucita, or you can take a taxi. Bus company Reina del Camino can take you up the coast or to Guayaquil ($7.25, three hours). Many of Manta's hotels are located close to the waterfront, where it's easy to walk around – though avoid walking at night for safety reasons.

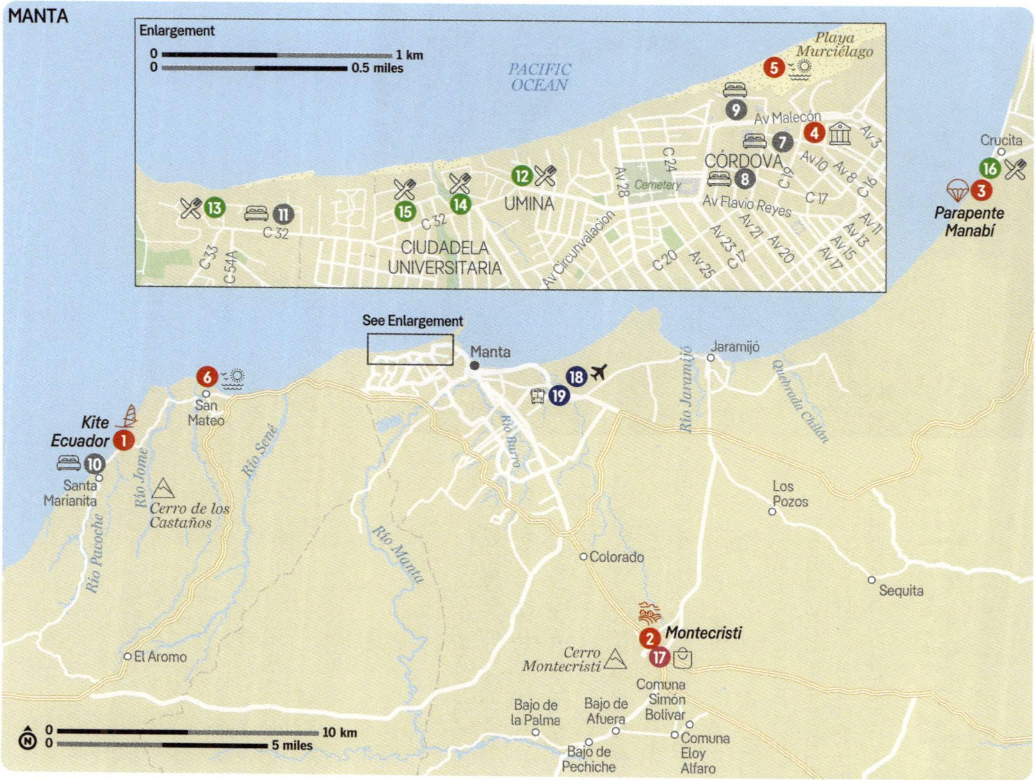

HIGHLIGHTS

1 Kite Ecuador
2 Montecristi
3 Parapente Manabí

SIGHTS

4 Museo de Manta
5 Playa Murciélago
6 Playa San Mateo
see 1 Playa Santa Marianita

SLEEPING

7 Balandra
see 1 Donkey Den
8 Manakin
9 Oro Verde
10 Soga
11 Wyndham Manta Sail Plaza

EATING

see 1 Cabaña Leidy
12 Cevicheria Umiña
13 Iche
see 3 La Loma De Crucita
14 Lúpulo Beer Garden
15 Martinica
16 Omega 3

DRINKING & NIGHTLIFE

see 1 Tatú

SHOPPING

17 Modesto Hats
see 17 Toquifina

TRANSPORT

18 Eloy Alfaro International Airport
19 Terminal Terrestre de Manta

TOP EXPERIENCE

Montecristi

Sombreros de paja toquilla, known internationally as Panama hats, gained popularity in the early 20th century when US President Theodore Roosevelt wore one during the construction of the Panama Canal. Contrary to the name, Panama hats are originally from Ecuador. Visit Montecristi, 10km south of Manta, to see hat artisans hard at work.

BRYAN FRANCO HATS/SHUTTERSTOCK

TOP TIPS

- Check the label to make sure it's made in Montecristi.
- The hat should fit slightly loose around your head, as Montecristi hats shrink over time.
- Get a box to keep its shape as you travel.

See Hats Being Made

Bus or taxi to Montecristi's Calle 9 de Julio to find a line-up of shops selling Montecristi hats. Many of the shops sell sombreros you'll find elsewhere – some of which are made in China – but there are authentic shops where artisans have been weaving hats for generations.

One of them is **Modesto Hats**, where Modesto Mero Pachay, a fourth-generation hatmaker, and his son weave and mould each hat into shape. Ask for a demonstration (he speaks English) to see some of the painstaking 28-step process that goes from the toquilla straw being slapped and split from the branch, to weaving, ironing, smashing with wood and molding into a hat. Another terrific authentic hat shop is **Toquifina**.

Buy One for Yourself

The quality and durability of each Montecristi hat are determined by the number of weaves per square inch. A hat woven so tightly that it looks smooth can take eight months to make and cost up to $25,000, though Modesto sells ones for as low as $30.

Tour the shop for a hat that attracts you – the classic black-band fedora-type Montecristi hat is the classic, but there are beautiful options in many different shapes and colors.

PRACTICALITIES

- Modesto Hats (modestohats.com), Toquifina (toquifina.com)
- Modesto: 8am-6pm Mon-Sat, 10am-3pm Sun; Toquifina: 8:30am-5pm Mon-Fri, 9am-4pm Sat & Sun
- free

sand – so, not the prettiest – but it's worth seeing for a taste of local Manabi life. Grab an umbrella and chair, sheltered 360-degrees around, and try giant coconuts, bananas coated in chocolate, *ovos* (an olive-shaped fruit that's both sweet and salty) and *corviche* (plantains and peanut fritters that encase fish). The beach is also lined with restaurants serving giant platters of grilled seafood.

During humpback-whale-migration season from June to October, boat captain Richard (+593 96 058 1951) leads whale-watching tours for $20 per person. Otherwise, you can book his boat for snorkeling or to check out the fishing port.

Playa San Mateo, a 20-minute taxi ride west, is a fishing village with a more idyllic strip of sand. The beach is quite small for the North Coast, but it has plenty of well-kept beach tents (some with hammocks) and a lineup of humble restaurants.

Proud Manteño History

Beachside archaeology museum

Across the road from Playa Murciélago, **Museo de Manta** *(@museomanta)*, houses more than 800 artifacts from the indigenous groups that lived in the region before Spanish contact. On the 3rd floor, see 'Giants' – imposing anthropomorphic clay and ceramic figures that reflect ritual symbolism crafted by the Bahía culture between 500 BCE and 650 CE. On the 4th floor is an exhibit on the Manteño people, the last indigenous group on the coast before Spanish contact.

The museum also houses 65 contemporary art pieces and a collection of quirky fishing paraphernalia. It's open from 8:30am to 5pm Monday to Friday, and 10am to 4pm on weekends.

Ecuador's Best Kitesurfing

Catch some wind in Santa Marianita

Surfing is so passé. These days, kitesurfing is all the rage around the world, and Santa Marianita, a 30-minute Uber or taxi ride west of Manta, is considered the best place in Ecuador to catch some wind.

Warm water, thermal winds, a sandy, 4km-long beach free of rocks and a general absence of crowds in this laid-back town draw in-the-know kitesurfers to **Playa Santa Marianita** from everywhere, but particularly the US and Canada. Kitesurfing is possible year-round, but the best months are from June through December, when winds are 15 to 20 knots. If you come between August and October, you'll have a chance to kitesurf alongside migrating humpback whales.

INDIGENOUS ANCESTORS

By the time the Spanish arrived, the Manteño were a thriving, sophisticated culture stretching from Bahía de Caráquez down the coast to Guayaquil. Emerging around 600 CE, the Manteño were skilled at sea, using large balsa-wood boats with sails to trade, fish and carry heavy cargo as far north as Mexico. Their society was highly organized, with powerful chiefs and shamans who sat in U-shaped stone seats – symbols of authority that helped inspire these people to resist Incan expansion.

Today, while the Manteño are not officially registered as an indigenous group – many died from disease and conflict – they didn't disappear. Their legacy is clear in locals' maritime knowledge, autonomy and food culture rooted in pre-Columbian ingredients like fish, peanuts, plantains and corn.

EATING IN MANTA: OUR PICKS

Cevicheria Umiña: Locals' favorite for different types of ceviche, including *concha* (sea snail conch) and *cangrejo* (crab). *8am-4pm* $$

Iche: Taste Manabita food like Jipijapa ceviche (with peanut sauce) and *arroz caldoso de mariscos* (creamy, seafood rice). Unrelated to the Iche in San Vicente. *8am-9pm* $$

Martinica: Romantic, upscale dining room with excellent seafood and grilled meats. *noon-11pm Wed-Sat, to 3pm Sun* $$

Lúpulo Beer Garden: For a break from seafood, try the hot wings, burgers and pizzas with a pint of one of its intriguing craft brews. *5:30-11pm Mon-Wed, to 2am Thu-Sun* $$

TROPICAL FRUITS OF THE COAST

Guanábana: Ecuador's national fruit (known as soursop or custard apple) makes a thick, creamy and refreshing juice.

Tomate de árbol: Literally tree tomato (sometimes called *tamarillo*), these oval fruits taste more like a kiwi than a tomato. They're a key ingredient in *ají casero* (chili sauce).

Naranjilla: Called 'little orange', though it isn't actually related to an orange. The pulp is bright green and it tastes like a mix of pineapple, lime and rhubarb.

Ovo: Olive-shaped green fruit that's both sour and sweet, typically topped with salt or fruit syrup in Manabí.

Babaco: Looks like an unusual combination of star fruit and papaya, but tastes of strawberry and pineapple.

CARVINCES/SHUTTERSTOCK

Paraglider, Crucita

Rent boards and kites from **Kite Ecuador** *(kiteecuador.com; per hr $15-25)*, or take lessons. A 14-hour beginner course costs $487, or you can take two-, four- or eight-hour courses to get started ($85, $160 and $297). Courses can be combined with stays in a dorm room at kitesurfer-favorite **Soga** *(sogahostal.com)*. You can also rent or learn how to use a wing-foil *(three-hour course $170)*. Kite Ecuador is open 10am to 5pm every day for the wind season, from mid-April through the beginning of February.

When you're not on the water, Santa Marianita has plenty of beachfront restaurants and bars to choose from.

Paragliding Paradise

Fly off a mountain in Crucita

Crucita, an hour's drive north of Manta, is a beach town with a perfectly curving arc of sand, and sunset bars popular with weekend warriors from Manta and Guayaquil, along with retirees from the US and Canada. For travelers, Crucita is best known as an ideal place to jump off a cliff – and glide gracefully to the ground.

Book a paragliding flight with the certified pilots at **Parapente Manabí** *(@parapente_manabi; $60)*. The flight takes 12 to 15 minutes once the pilot takes you down off the hill, and includes 10 videos from the pilot's GoPro. It's a good shot of adrenaline, and an easy day trip from Manta, though there are plenty of hotels to choose from if you plan to spend the night.

EATING & DRINKING IN SANTA MARIANITA & CRUCITA: OUR PICKS

Cabaña Leidy: One of a lineup of seafood-serving tents over Playa Santa Marianita, perfect for fish soup and watching kitesurfers. *8:30am-5:30pm* $

Omega 3: Towering plates of seafood rice and Manabí *bolónes* (fried plantain balls), a block from Crucita's *malecón*. *6:30am-5:30pm* $

La Loma De Crucita: Watch the paragliders soar off the cliff from this seafood-and-burger restaurant next to the jumping-off point. *10am-8pm* $

Tatú: One of a growing number of sleek beach bars in Santa Marianita slowly turning this into a destination for upper-class urbanites. *11am-8pm Thu-Sun*

Places We Love to Stay

$ Budget $$ Midrange $$$ Top End

Atacames

MAP p143

La Aldea Thirty rooms, two pools and direct access to the beach, along with a parking lot in the back. Most importantly, it's cleaner than anything on the *malecón*. $

Cielo Azul Curvaceous colonial-style hotel painted in gold and terracotta directly on the beachfront, a safe distance from the blaring music – but it'll cost you. $$

El Marqués The most upmarket location in Atacames, with a great pool and fantastic cocktail bar/cafe (with some seriously good coffee) in front of the promenade. $$$

Beyond Atacames

Hosteria Marina Same town also has a calmer vibe compared to Atacames, especially within this Argentine-owned bamboo lodge a block from the beach. $

Castellmar This single-level motel in Tonsupa feels like an oasis of calm compared to loud Atacames, with a tranquil pool, cool wooden furniture and clean rooms. Dogs allowed. $$

Mompiche

MAP p150

Mudhouse This Dutch-owned hostel is a backpacker favorite, with eight- and four-bed dorms, three private *cabañas*, an apartment and a fun bar. The drawback is it's outside of town, 10 minutes' walk from the beach. $

Onda Another backpacker favorite, this hostel is much closer to the beach and has a large, fenced-off chill area with a ping-pong table. $

La Caleta A couple of well-kept private *cabañas* next to the Portuguese and Ecuadorian owners' jungle-like home and steps from the beach. Cold showers only $

Seaside Garden Hire a *mototaxi* at low tide to take you to this hotel on volcanic black sand, with rooms that have floor-to-ceiling windows. Otherwise, it's a 45-minute walk. $$

La Facha The coolest designed hotel in Mompiche, along with a great restaurant, upstairs terrace and location on Mompiche's surfer street make this a firm favorite. $$

Santo Antonio The tallest hotel on Mompiche's beach (which isn't saying much), located on the surfer drag. One of the few places in Mompiche to have hot water. $$

Canoa

MAP p155

Rutamar Canoa's most idyllic hostel, with psychedelically curved branches and round windows housing 12 rooms. Also has excellent breakfasts. Find it a few blocks back from the beach. $

Coco Loco Long-time go-to hostel on the promenade across from the beach with welcoming staff and a fun bar in the sand. Great place to meet people during high season. $

Bambú Several two-story cabins back from the beach and a low-lit bar (with, unfortunately, subpar food) make for the most romantic location in Canoa. $$

Beyond Canoa

Saiananda Ecolodge overlooking the river, just outside Bahía de Caráquez, by Peruvian biologist and Sathya Sai Baba follower Alfredo Harmsen. Ask about singing bowl ceremonies, stand-up paddleboard and kayak rentals, nature walks and romantic specials. $$

Sea by Palmazul San Clemente's finest accommodation features a tranquil pool and hot tub facing the sea (day passes are $12.50) and an excellent rooftop restaurant with live music on Sundays. $$$

Manta

MAP p163

Manakin Converted one-story house with a friendly cafe (open to nonguests), and 10 nicely furnished rooms. Those committed to their fitness routines will love its outdoor gym. $$

Balandra Great for kids, with a playground, trampoline, arcade and pretty pool area. Its 55 rooms are spread over several buildings, including private Swiss-style bungalows. $$$

Oro Verde The only hotel directly on the beach, with a resort-like pool area and 105 rooms, including bungalows, as well as a spa with massages and a sauna. $$$

Wyndham Manta Sail Plaza A worthwhile upgrade, with a pool and all the facilities you'd expect from a big-name hotel brand. Rooms have sea views, but no beach access. $$$

Beyond Manta

Donkey Den Seemingly stuck in time since the hippie days, this Santa Marianita guesthouse attracts artists young and old to to paint, read and pet dogs. $

Soga Go-to for kitesurfers, with a miniature pool; great for refreshing after catching some wind. It's a solid 25-minute walk to the main beach area. $

For places to stay in the Oriente, see p206

Above: jungle hut, Tena (p190); right: market, Puyo (p198)

Researched by
Anthony Ham

The Oriente

WILDLIFE, INDIGENOUS CULTURE AND DEEP FOREST IMMERSION

Welcome to the wild. If the Galápagos is where we came to understand how nature works, the Oriente is where nature's biodiversity explodes into life. All you have to do is explore.

The Oriente has gravitas. Sparsely populated, dripping wet and full of mercifully untamed nature, the vast and deeply forested lowlands of the Oriente promise seemingly infinite possibilities for adventure.

The stage is set from the moment you descend into the region of the Andes, accompanied by swollen rivers that become powerful waterfalls as they tumble down off cliffs and toward the plains below. These rivers are the lifeblood of the region and eventually merge to form majestic wide waterways that trade speed for volume and flow relentlessly eastward toward the Amazon, blanketed by walls of jungle, at once impenetrable and mysterious. Along the way, they pass pristine nature reserves and traditional indigenous communities that have called these lands home for millennia and safeguard the secrets of the forest.

CURIOSO.PHOTOGRAPHY/SHUTTERSTOCK

The variety of wildlife is astonishing. Whether paddling blackwater lagoons in search of enormous caimans, pink dolphins and hyperactive river otters, scanning treetops for mischievous monkeys, or watching brightly plumed macaws descend to drink from mineral-rich springs, the animals and landscapes of the region feel plucked straight from an HD natural-history documentary.

There's plenty here for active travelers too, with river tubing, thrilling rafting and kayaking, and challenging hikes, with Ecuador's most inviting thermal baths ready to soothe tired muscles afterwards as your reward.

THE MAIN AREAS

Find Your Way

The Oriente covers around half the Ecuadorian mainland, yet once you leave the Andean foothills there are far more rivers than there are roads. Getting around requires advanced planning, and most trips here will involve at least some boat travel.

Northern Oriente, p174

Easily accessible from Quito, the northern Oriente is home to the wildlife-rich Río Cuyabeno, as well as great hiking and soothing thermal baths.

Coca & Lower Río Napo, p182

The rainforest-covered lowlands of the Río Napo shelter Ecuador's finest ecolodges and most pristine national park, as well as timeless indigenous villages.

Tena, p190

The gateway to exhilarating adventures in nature, with wild rivers to run, dramatic caves to explore and hikes through unspoiled nature reserves.

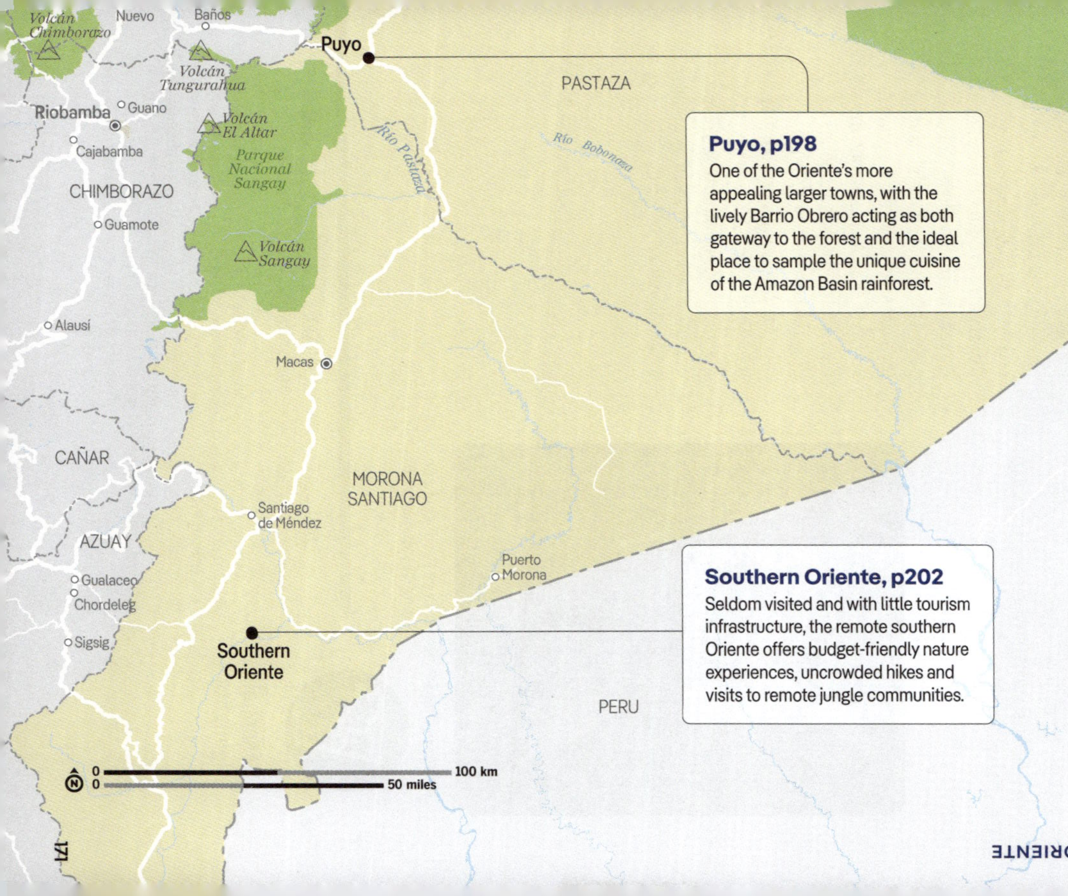

Puyo, p198

One of the Oriente's more appealing larger towns, with the lively Barrio Obrero acting as both gateway to the forest and the ideal place to sample the unique cuisine of the Amazon Basin rainforest.

Southern Oriente, p202

Seldom visited and with little tourism infrastructure, the remote southern Oriente offers budget-friendly nature experiences, uncrowded hikes and visits to remote jungle communities.

BOAT

The rivers of the Oriente are often the only connection between remote villages and jungle lodges and the rest of the country. Most lodges run their own boats to ports accessible by road, while public canoes, riverboats and speedboats serve riverside towns.

BUS

In western areas of the Oriente, buses are the workhorses of the Oriente's roads, running frequently between major towns along the Troncal Amazónica highway. Services from towns to rural communities are often irregular and conditions rough.

PLANE

A few ecolodges are so deep in the jungle the only way to get in is by chartered flight on a small aircraft. Commercial flights to the region's main airport at Coca are convenient for trips on the lower Napo.

Plan Your Days

The Oriente covers a vast area, so breaking it up into manageable chunks makes it easier to enjoy – get to know a few areas well, rather than trying to do everything at once.

ANTON SOROKIN/ALAMY

Pygmy marmoset, Reserva de Producción de Fauna Cuyabeno (p178)

If You Only Do One Thing

- For an action-packed weekend of wildlife-watching, drive down into the Oriente from Quito and spend the night at the base of **Volcán Reventador** (p176) to observe the clouds of ash above Ecuador's most active volcano. Get an early start to reach Lago Agrio in time to pick up a tour to the **Reserva de Producción de Fauna Cuyabeno** (p178), where you can pass a couple of peaceful days (or a considerably longer period if you have the time) exploring the blackwater rivers and lagoons to observe pink dolphins, caimans, otters and monkeys. On your way back to the capital, climb high into the Andes at **Papallacta** (p174) for mountain hiking followed by a soak in soothing thermal baths.

Seasonal Highlights

JAN

The dry season sees lagoons dry up in Cuyabeno, drawing wildlife such as caimans and anacondas out of the forests; conversely, it's more difficult to see dolphins, manatees and otters at this time as they head downriver.

APR

The rains begin in earnest across the Oriente. While locals may celebrate, travelers will need a raincoat, mosquito repellent and lots of patience, as some rural roads and hiking trails become impassable.

JUN

Macaws and other parrots are active in the forest canopies of northern Oriente. It's wet season, a time of great abundance in the forest; as water levels rise, river wildlife returns to the lagoons.

A Week in the Jungle

- Begin your jungle adventure in **Tena** (p190). From here you can take a day trip to **Cotundo** (p192) to explore impressive caves and canyons before returning for a cocktail by the river. Next, head to **Misahuallí** (p194) to meet the town's famous monkeys followed by a hike to see more wildlife in the **Reserva Biológica Jatun Sacha** (p196). Travel along the Río Napo's southern bank to **Coca** (p182) to board a boat to an ecolodge downstream, from where you can explore the pristine wilderness of **Parque Nacional Yasuní** (p184) as well as visit an indigenous community for a meal harvested directly from the forest. Time spent in Yasuní, one of the Amazon Basin's true wildernesses, is precious so stay longer if you can.

If Time Is No Constraint

- After exploring Tena and the area around Parque Nacional Yasuní, take a boat down the Río Napo to remote **Nueva Rocafuerte** (p189), right on the border with Peru. From here, one of South America's most isolated frontiers, you can organize an adventure deep into the jungle at **Laguna Jatuncocha** (p189), or get up close to pink river dolphins, giant river otters and other wildlife at the mouth of the **Río Cocoya** (p189). Ride a speedboat back to **Coca** (p182) before picking up a bus south to **Puyo** (p198) to learn about indigenous Shuar medicine and enjoy top-notch rainforest cuisine. Finish in sleepy **Gualaquiza** (p205), exploring the waterfalls, canyons and forest-clad swimming holes that surround the town.

JUL & AUG

Generally dry weather and firm ground make for the best hiking around Papallacta and Parque Nacional Cayambe-Coca. Also good for bird-watching in the foothills of the western Oriente.

OCT & NOV

Rafting season begins in earnest around Tena, with great conditions on many rivers surrounding the town. More widely, it's a terrific time for river travel, with high water levels and generally fine conditions.

DEC

Heavy rain in the mountains above Baeza attracts kayakers from around the globe looking to ride the wild rapids. Down below, it's dry and some rivers become impassable due to low water levels.

Northern Oriente

PRISTINE WILDERNESS | OUTDOOR ADVENTURES | VOLCANO CLIMBING

TOP TIP

Attractions in the mountains and foothills along the road from Quito to the Oriente are quiet during the week, but fill to capacity on weekends when families from the capital head out to explore. If you can only visit on a weekend, book accommodations well in advance, especially in Papallacta.

Home to Ecuador's most accessible jungle wilderness, the northern Oriente is a land of rushing rivers, restless volcanoes and hidden blackwater lagoons that offers nonstop adventure just a few hours' drive from the capital.

None of the many approaches to the northern Oriente are quite so soul-stirring as the road from Quito to Lago Agrio. Along the way, a dramatic sampling of Ecuador's diverse ecosystems unfurls to the far horizon, carrying travelers across windswept, moor-like *páramo* (high-altitude grassland), through Andean cloud forest, and then down into sultry lowland rainforests. You could drive to Lago Agrio in one day – what a day! But take your time to explore forested foothills, soak in thermal baths, spot rare birds and run river rapids along the way.

And once you're here, the pristine Reserva de Produccion de Flora y Fauna Cuyabeno has blackwater lagoons and flooded forests inhabited by pink dolphins, caimans and large populations of monkeys.

High-Altitude Relaxation

Soak in Ecuador's best thermal baths

Close to Quito and yet a world away, the misty mountain village of **Papallacta** is known around Ecuador for its piping-hot thermal baths, which are set among enchanting green hills high in the Andes. The town's proximity to Quito and the airport make

GETTING AROUND

Regular express buses link Quito with Papallacta, Baeza, Reventador and Lago Agrio. It's also possible to reach Papallacta by taxi driving yourself, or as part of a guided tour.

In recent years, various stretches of the Troncal Amazónica highway north of El Chaco have collapsed due to erosion of the riverbanks, occasionally causing road closures. Even when the road is open, it may not be suitable for all vehicles – check the latest at *ecu911.gob.ec/consulta-de-vias* before setting out, and be prepared to take longer than you expect.

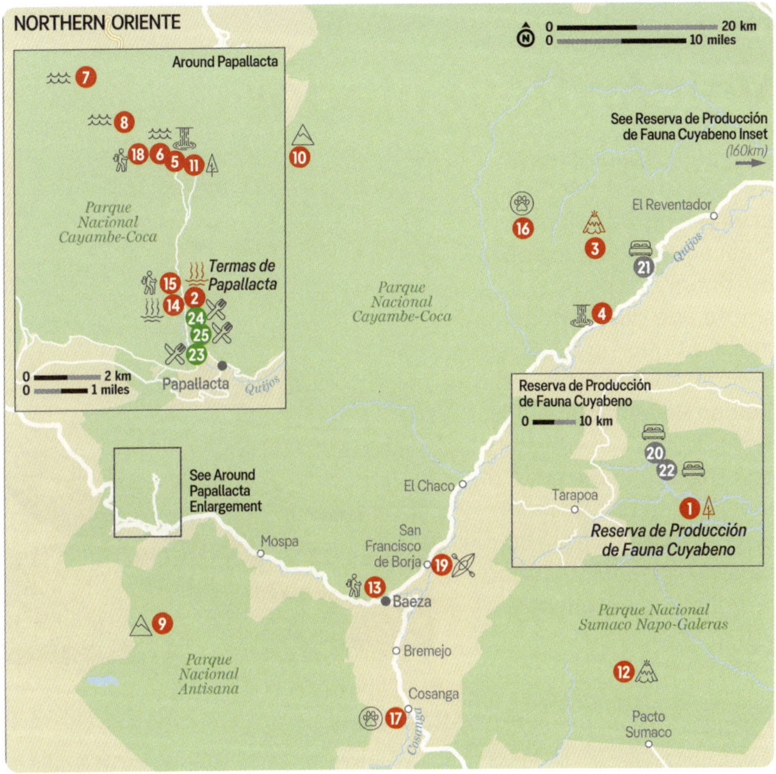

HIGHLIGHTS
1 Reserva de Producción de Fauna Cuyabeno
2 Termas de Papallacta
3 Volcán Reventador

SIGHTS
4 Cascada Mágica
5 La Cascada Milagrosa
6 Laguna de Baños
7 Laguna Parcacocha
8 Laguna San Cristobal
9 Nevado Antisana
10 Nevado Cayambe
11 Parque Nacional Cayambe-Coca
12 Volcán Sumaco

ACTIVITIES
13 Baeza Antigua Trailhead
14 Balneario
15 Rancho del Cañon
16 Reserva Alto Coca
17 San Isidro Lodge
18 Sendero Agua y Vida
see 18 Sendero El Oso
19 Small World Adventures
see 2 Spa

SLEEPING
20 Bamboo Lodge
see 20 Cuyabeno Lodge
21 Hostería Reventador
22 Jamu Lodge
see 22 Tapir Lodge

EATING
see 13 Gina's
see 13 Hard River Restaurant Mirador
23 La Choza de Don Wilson
see 13 Pizzeria Kopal
see 13 Quinde Huyaco
24 Restaurante El Refugio
see 2 Sucus
25 Termas El Arriero

it the perfect place to stop and sooth tired muscles at the end of a trip. And if you can't imagine being cold enough in Ecuador to really enjoy a hot bath, you'll soon change your mind on arrival in Papallacta, which sits at an altitude of 3300m above sea level.

There are a number of thermal complexes, and several hotels also have their own pools, but the main attraction is the **Termas de Papallacta** (*termaspapallacta.com; adult balneario/spa $10.50/24, child $5.25/16*), an inviting retreat with a range of different spa pools nestled below the mountains just north of town.

Unlike many thermal baths in Ecuador, which feature plenty of concrete and feel a little like a hospital, the construction

TOP EXPERIENCE

Volcán Reventador

As natural spectacles go, it's hard to beat the rush of watching Ecuador's most active volcano spew out enormous clouds of smoke and dust. Since a major eruption in 2002, it's been impossible to summit Volcán Reventador, but fit and adventurous travelers can still hike to the edge of the volcano to admire its daily explosions from up close. It's a fabulous, once-in-a-lifetime experience.

ECUADORPLANET/SHUTTERSTOCK

TOP TIPS

- Stay overnight to see the lava glow in the dark.
- Hosteria Reventador has simple rooms at the base of the volcano; watch the show through their large windows.
- While the volcano is in Parque Nacional Cayambe-Coca, the 5km trail begins at the Hosteria Reventador on the Quito-Lago Agrio road.

PRACTICALITIES

- Hosteria Reventador (hosteriaelreventador.com)
- trail access guests/nonguests free/$3

A Front-Row View

One of South America's best volcano experiences begins at **Hosteria Reventador**, which has comfortable rooms beside a rushing river lined with smooth swimming holes carved into the rock. Within the hotel grounds, trails lead up to half a dozen lookout points with sweeping panoramas of the Río Quijos Valley and partial views of the volcano.

To get a better look at El Reventador, follow the steep access path covered with perilous loose gravel for 5km up through the cloud forest. You'll need quality boots and hiking poles to maintain your footing – the path is particularly tricky on the way down. It takes about three hours in each direction. Nonguests can pay to use the trail.

A Different Perspective

Another great place from which to observe El Reventador's rumblings is the **Reserva Alto Coca** *(altococa.com)*. This privately owned cloud-forest reserve, set between 1500m and 2000m, backs onto Parque Nacional Sumaco Napo-Galeras across the other side of the valley. Access is via a tough four- to five-hour hike, but the reward is pristine nature and spectacular views.

at Termas de Papallacta makes use of stone and wood and feels much more in harmony with the surrounding nature.

The complex has two distinct sets of baths, both filled from the same source. The cheaper **Balneario** has 10 hot pools of varying temperatures, in addition to a few ice-cold contrast pools all set around pretty gardens beside a bubbling river. During the week it's rarely crowded, but on weekends it can fill with day-trippers from Quito.

Turning the luxury up a notch, the **Spa** is pricier, so it pulls less of a crowd. It has five hot pools (and one cold pool) with massage jets around the edges and plenty of seating areas in a series of garden gazebos. There's a smart restaurant and the changing rooms are first class. Admission to the Spa also includes access to the Balneario pools.

On paying admission, you'll be given a wristband and can come and go freely – it's well worth returning at night for a soothing soak under the stars.

Hiking the Páramo of Papallacta

A backdoor to Cayambe-Coca

While most visitors come to Papallacta with just relaxation on their mind, the town is also the gateway to some wonderful hikes through stunning *páramo* sprinkled with mystical lakes high in the Andes. Smart travelers with time will hike first, then relax in the thermal springs afterwards.

You don't have to go far out of town to start exploring the wilderness. Adjoining the Termas de Papallacta, the 200-hectare **Rancho del Cañon** (free) nature reserve is run by a hotel complex and has a number of guided trails ranging in duration from one to eight hours. The shorter trails weave through primary forest and *páramo* alongside the Río Papallacta, eventually reaching a series of pretty waterfalls. Longer treks reach high into the mountains, from where it's possible to observe the snowcapped peaks of **Nevado Antisana** (5753m) and **Nevado Cayambe** (5790m) as well as the attractive symmetrical cone of Volcán Sumaco (p197) rising from the jungle-covered plains.

More pristine wilderness can be found 5km north of the baths along a fairly good unpaved road to the **Parque Nacional Cayambe-Coca** entrance at a chilly 3700m. From the guard station, a gentle, albeit often muddy, trail leads about 800m uphill to **La Cascada Milagrosa** before continuing a further 1km along fairly flat terrain to the mirror-like **Laguna de Baños**, which is actually two adjoining lakes surrounded by

continues on p180

THERMAL ETIQUETTE

When immersing yourself in Ecuador's soothing thermal baths, you'll be expected to follow some basic rules.

Attire: Most baths require visitors to have a proper swimsuit. In reality, any shorts that don't go below the knees are usually OK; however, T-shirts are frowned upon.

Swimming caps: All visitors are usually required to wear a swimming cap over their hair – this usually applies even to those who are bald! Cheap cloth caps are normally for sale on site – hang on to it for later in your travels.

Bandages and wounds: Thermal baths may deny access to visitors with visible wounds or obvious bandaging.

Showering: It's customary to shower before entering the pools.

EATING IN PAPALLACTA: OUR PICKS

Restaurante El Refugio: Cheap and cheerful place serving well-prepared Ecuadorian plates just outside the baths. *7am-6pm* **$**

La Choza de Don Wilson: Most visitors to Papallacta call in here for delicious river trout washed down with shots of *aguardiente*. *8am-10pm* **$$**

Termas El Arriero: As so often in these parts, river trout (whole or filleted, grilled or in a mushroom sauce) is the star, along with chicken soup. *7am-10pm* **$$**

Sucus: Fine dining with an international menu within the confines of the Termas de Papallacta hotel. *noon-3pm & 6-9pm* **$$$**

ANTON SOROKIN/ALAMY

TOP EXPERIENCE

Reserva de Producción de Fauna Cuyabeno

Little known outside the country, the flooded forests, winding rivers and jungle-shrouded lagoons of the Reserva de Producción de Fauna Cuyabeno are home to mainland Ecuador's best wildlife-watching.

DON'T MISS

- Staying at a lagoon lodge
- Staying at a riverside lodge
- Nighttime lagoon swim
- indigenous encounter
- Wildlife-watching

The Cuyabeno Backstory

Over the years, the boundaries of the reserve have shifted with the political winds, but the area (6000 sq km) is substantially larger than it was originally. The reserve was created in 1979 to protect rainforest, conserve wildlife and provide a sanctuary in which the indigenous inhabitants – the Siona, Secoya, Cofán, Kichwa and Shuar – could lead customary ways of life.

Cuyabeno is indeed home to a number of different indigenous groups, but its protected status notwithstanding, Cuyabeno

PRACTICALITIES

● There is no entry fee for the reserve, but it is not possible to visit without a confirmed lodge reservation ● facebook.com/reservacuyabeno

was opened to oil exploitation almost immediately after its creation. The oil towns of Tarapoa and Cuyabeno and parts of the trans-Ecuadorian oil pipeline were built within the reserve's boundaries. But under more recent protections, Cuyabeno has survived.

The area dedicated to tourism is the homeland of the Siona people, who own the land on which most lodges are built and exclusively run all transport within the reserve.

Wonderful Wildlife

Seasonally flooded by heavy Amazonian rains, the reserve spreads across both sides of the chocolatey Río Cuyabeno in a maze of waterways that shelter an incredibly diverse array of aquatic species, forest foragers and birdlife.

From the moment you board the small boat that carries you into the heart of the reserve, the striking beauty and utter tranquility of Cuyabeno quickly takes hold. Scores of colorful butterflies flutter through the air, guiding the way downstream to the wetlands where towering ceibas and macrolobium trees jut from the tannin-rich black waters.

The reserve is the most accessible place in Ecuador to spot pink river dolphins, which can be seen frolicking in the lagoons and rivers in front of the reserve's unobtrusive jungle lodges. While the playful cetaceans may be the reserve's star attractions, the supporting cast is equally impressive, with anacondas, manatees, giant river otters, macaws, toucans, enormous caimans and tapirs often observed.

Then there's the monkeys. Ten different species are found in the reserve's forests, and even on a short visit it's possible to encounter most of them, swinging from the trees, jumping across narrow rivers or chilling high in the jungle canopy.

How to Visit

It's simply not possible to visit the reserve independently, and those without reservations through a lodge won't be permitted to board a boat at the Cuyabeno Bridge. Tours generally leave from Lago Agrio.

Most lodges offer similar activities, including hikes, boat trips through the lagoons and flooded forest, a visit to a local Siona community and night walks, all usually accompanied by bilingual guides. In the evening, most lodges take guests out into the middle of Laguna Grande for a magical sunset swim. Before diving in, your guide will assure you that the caimans and anacondas are only found around the lagoon's edge, while piranhas really are tranquil and totally misunderstood.

Recommended lodges with extensive experience in all of the necessary arrangements include Cuyabeno Lodge (p206), Jamu Lodge (p206), Bamboo Lodge (p206) and Tapir Lodge (p206). Each has strong ties to local indigenous communities and inhabits prolific wildlife areas.

WHEN TO VISIT

Around the end of January the lagoons dry up, forcing dolphins, manatees and otters downriver, but the shrinking waters draw caimans and anacondas out of the forest, making this a fruitful time for reptile lovers. Around June you'll often see incredible birdlife, including scores of parrots and macaws, while a few months later, large troupes of monkeys are common.

TOP TIPS

- Rooms throughout the reserve are less luxurious than rustic but they're comfortable enough.
- Where accommodations differ greatly is in guest capacity and density of buildings.
- Choose your accommodations based on location, rather than levels of luxury.
- Riverside lodges are remote but don't afford the sweeping views and great bird-watching that a lagoon location can give.
- Stay alert at all times in the reserve. The jungle's pristine nature means you'll have close encounters with wildlife on hikes and boat trips, but also while relaxing in your lodge.

WHY I LOVE CUYABENO

Anthony Ham, Lonely Planet writer

For me, nowhere in Ecuador carries quite the same level of excitement and possibility as Cuyabeno. The landscapes carry their own drama – the mystery of the lagoons and what lies beneath, the endless variety of the riverbanks. But it's the wildlife that seals the deal. I have travelled all over the Amazon, and Cuyabeno is one of my favorite Amazonian experiences – just knowing that giant otters, pink dolphins, lumbering manatees and charismatic monkeys could appear at any minute sets my heart racing. And I never want to sleep. Even at night, the jungle is alive.

continued from p177

rugged rocky bluffs. Don't underestimate the altitude here – carry plenty of water, pace yourself in the thin Andean air and listen to your body: altitude sickness is real and possible above 3000m, and it can be dangerous.

From the lookout above the waterways, the path splits into the 8km **Sendero Agua y Vida**, which skirts **Laguna San Cristobal** before reaching immense **Laguna Parcacocha**, and the 5km **Sendero El Oso**, which passes a series of smaller *lagunas*.

On the longer trails, after you leave the crowds behind, keep an eye out for grazing tapirs and the shy Andean spectacled bear, both of which inhabit the area.

Both trails eventually end up on the Quito Hwy, from where you can hail a bus back to Papallacta.

Take to the Water in Río Quijos

White-water rafting and kayaking

When it comes to rafting and kayaking, the **Río Quijos Valley** is one of South America's best, yet most underrated, adventure hubs. Accessed from the cute little gateway town of **Baeza** on the Quito–Tena road, the dramatic valley of the Río Quijos is cut through by some of Ecuador's wildest white-water runs, attracting hardcore kayakers and rafting enthusiasts from across the globe.

During the wet season, the narrow rivers that flow into the Quijos, such as the Sardinas, Oyacachi and Cosanga, fill with tricky, fast-churning waters that thrill even experienced paddlers. It's not the place for beginners, and several incidents have occurred over the years, meaning even experienced kayakers should consult – or, better still, travel with – local guides.

The Río Quijos itself has some top kayaking runs, including the 5km-long 'Cheese House.' It's also the destination of choice for rafting trips due to its fun rapids and spectacular canyon scenery. Trips can be organized in the small riverside towns of **Borja** and **El Chaco**, which are also home to some great riverside lodges that will appeal to paddlers and nature lovers alike.

You could try making the arrangements through local lodges, but you'll save time (thereby allowing you to spend more time on the river instead of making the arrangements) if you take a tour. With an office just up the road in San Francisco de Borja, **Small World Adventures** (*smallworldadventures.com*) runs kayaking and rafting trips through the Río Quijos valley, Its programs include the paddle up to its very own riverside lodge, and some continue on to the Tena (p190) and Misahuallí (p194) areas.

MORE CAYAMBE-COCA

The main entrance to Parque Nacional Cayambe-Coca is near the town of **Cayambe** (p100), from where a seven-hour trail leads to the summit of the extinct volcano that gives the park its name.

Hike the Río Quijos Valley

Walking and waterfalls

You don't have to be an adrenaline hound to enjoy the Quijos Valley; the valley is so spectacular that good hiking, top bird-watching and some fine waterfalls are all easily accessible from the region's towns.

From Baeza Antigua, the most charming (and oldest) part of Baeza, popular **hikes** climb up to the radio masts above town for spectacular valley views, and down to a pair of attractive cascades on the **Río Machangara**, the latter of which drops down a vegetation zone into tropical forest.

Then even more spectacular, around 120km northeast of Baeza by road, the high-volume **Cascada Mágica** pours over a verdant cliff near the town of San Carlos.

Bird-Watching at San Isidro Lodge

Wildlife-watching at a jungle lodge

An excellent example of sustainable conservation, the 2000-hectare **San Isidro Lodge** *(sanisidrolodge.com)* is an important biological corridor between Parque Nacional Antisana and Parque Nacional Sumaco Napo-Galeras.

Set amid spectacular cloud forest at 2000m, the area surrounding the lodge is prime bird habitat and the owners are highly skilled bird-watchers with unparalleled local knowledge. Rare animal species, including mountain tapirs and spectacled bears, have also been spotted within the reserve.

Staying here includes access to more than 10km of trails that wind through primary forest to waterfalls and rushing rivers, as well as the chance to explore the forest in a canoe.

At the end of the day, guests can relax in the heated pool or around the outdoor fireplace before retiring to their comfortable *cabañas* with forest views.

Taking the Path Less Traveled to Colombia

From one top wildlife-watching zone to another

The fairly unattractive Oriente oil town of **Nueva Loja** (known locally as Lago Agrio) is most often visited by those on their way to the Cuyabeno, but the settlement is also the jumping-off point for the remote border crossing to Colombia at San Miguel, around 60km north of town.

While once off-limits due to security concerns, the area is now considered fairly safe for travelers, though the border here still sees far less traffic than the Andean crossing at Tulcán. For nature lovers and bird-watchers, the crossing is convenient as it leads from one of Ecuador's best wildlife-watching zones to the wonderfully biodiverse Putumayo region of Colombia.

A DISAPPEARING ACT

Almost overnight in early 2020, Ecuador's most famous waterfall, the 131m-high Cascada San Rafael (between El Chaco and Simón Bolivar along the E45) simply stopped flowing, leaving a dry rock face where there was once a thunderous torrent. Instead of cascading over the precipice, the river had shifted to move through a sinkhole in the mountain.

Ecologists blamed the Coca Coda Sinclair dam, built upstream just four years earlier. The dam had already reduced the flow of water to the falls during the dry summer months. But a government investigation ruled that the event was the result of natural erosion. Either way, the incident has once again led to debate over the true costs of infrastructure projects in once-pristine areas of the Oriente.

EATING IN BAEZA: OUR PICKS

Gina's: Atmospheric wood-plank restaurant plastered with rafting stickers, serving trout cooked every which way and other hearty local favorites. *7am-10pm* **$**

Pizzeria Kopal: A charming little pizzeria with a peaceful porch out back serving great pies and Oriente's best burritos. *9am-5pm Mon & Tue, to 7pm Wed-Sun* **$**

Quinde Huyaco: Your best bet for breakfast in Baeza, with filled bagels and proper strong espresso. *7am-7pm* **$**

Hard River Restaurant Mirador: A fine place where the empanadas and mixed-grill platters are the best order. Fabulous views. *8.30am-9pm Mon-Sat, 9am-5pm Sun* **$$**

Coca & Lower Río Napo

AMAZON ADVENTURES | INDIGENOUS ENCOUNTERS | JUNGLE WILDLIFE

TOP TIP

Don't turn up in Coca and expect to make a lodge and boat-transfer reservation for the following day – book well in advance online or through offices in Quito.

The Lower Río Napo is where many of Ecuador's best Amazon adventures become possible. The wide, powerful waters of the lower Napo are the highway that leads visitors into the lowland jungles of eastern Ecuador, some of the most accessible rainforests in the Amazon Basin.

These are the classic jungles and remote rivers of Amazonian lore, home to magnificent wildlife and ancient rainforest cultures. In short, the Napo jungles are among the world's most biodiverse places. The unavoidable gateway to this immense wilderness is the noisy, rather uninspiring city of Coca, a once-sleepy dirt-road port town transformed by the discovery of petroleum downstream.

Beyond Coca, the Napo flows slowly but with unstoppable momentum eastwards to join the Amazon in northern Peru. From here, you'll be entering the remote heart of the continent. It's an area where independent travel can be difficult – book a stay at one of the many fine jungle lodges and immerse yourself in rainforest life.

continues on p188

GETTING AROUND

Most lodges include river transport from Coca in their packages. Ask when making your reservation.

If you're traveling independently, you can take public river boats from Coca's Puerto Maritimo to communities along the Río Napo. Slow boats, known as *canoas*, leave at 7:30am and take about nine hours to reach Nueva Rocafuerte, including a brief meal and bathroom break at Pañacocha. From Rocafuerte, *canoas* return upriver, departing around 5:30am.

Faster, more expensive express boats leave Coca at 8am and 1pm and take five hours to complete the same journey. From Rocafuerte, express boats return at 6am and noon.

COCA & LOWER RÍO NAPO

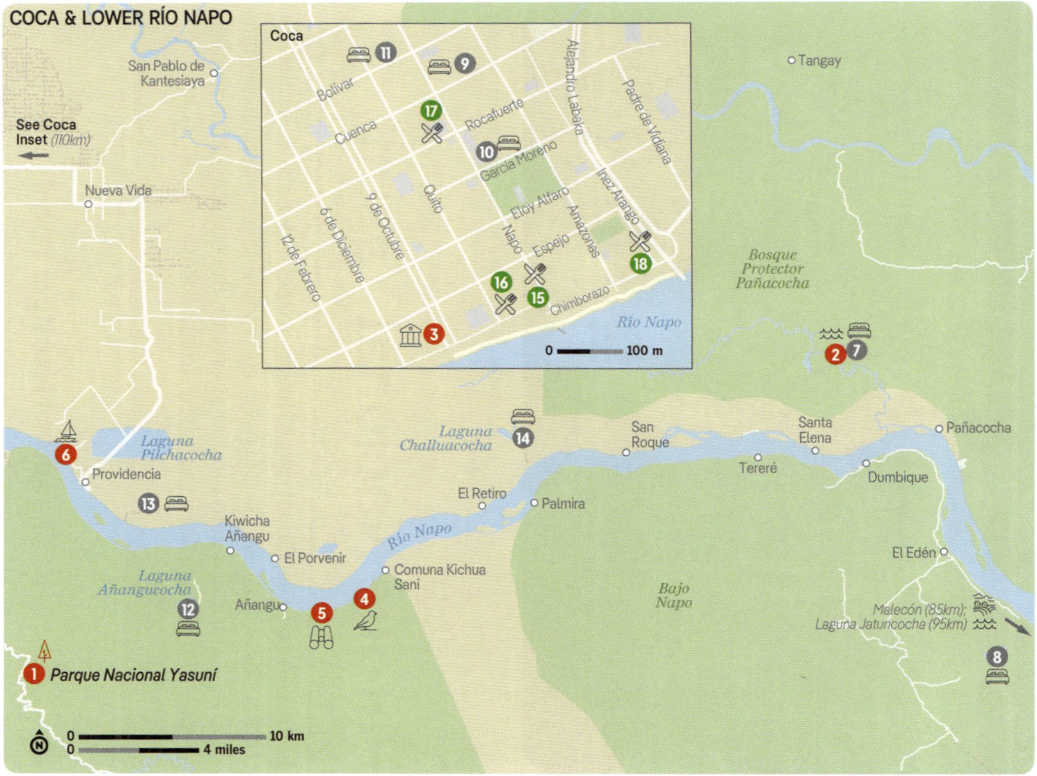

HIGHLIGHTS
1 Parque Nacional Yasuní

SIGHTS
2 Laguna Pañacocha
3 Museo Arqueológico Centro Cultural de Orellana (MACCO)
4 Observation Tower
5 Saladero de Loros

ACTIVITIES
6 Anakonda River Cruises

SLEEPING
7 Amazon Dolphin Lodge
8 Eden Amazon Lodge
9 Heliconias Grand Hotel
10 Hotel El Auca
11 Hotel Río Napo
12 Napo Wildlife Center
13 Sacha Lodge
14 Sani Lodge

EATING
15 El Refugio del Cangrejo
16 La Casa del Maito
17 Tenedor y Bolónes
18 Waysa Pamba

FOTOS593/SHUTTERSTOCK

Above: Parque Nacional Yasuní; right: scarlet macaws

TOP EXPERIENCE

Parque Nacional Yasuní

Seen from above, the Parque Nacional Yasuní is dense jungle as far as the eye can see. Down below, luxury forest lodges and indigenous communities shadow remote rivers as wildlife of astonishing diversity plays hide and seek with travelers beneath the soaring cathedral-like canopy of trees. In short, this is the Amazon Basin as you've always imagined it to be.

DON'T MISS

- Saladero de Loros
- Napo Wildlife Center
- Sani Lodge
- Sacha Lodge
- Eden Amazon Lodge
- Huaorani indigenous Tours

The Ancient Forests of Yasuní

Parque Nacional Yasuní stands today as one of the last true, pristine wildernesses in Ecuador. Dominating the map of eastern Ecuador, this 9620-sq-km national park is the country's largest mainland protected area.

Bordered by Río Napo to the north and Río Curaray to the southeast, the park encompasses most of the watersheds of Ríos Yasuní and Nashiño, as well as substantial parts of Río Tiputini. Its diverse habitats consist of 'terra firma' (forested

PRACTICALITIES

● reservabiosferayasuni.org ● free

MARTIN LINDSAY/ALAMY

hills), which are never inundated even by the highest floods; *varzea* (lowlands), which are periodically inundated by flooding rivers; and *igapó* (semi-permanently inundated lowlands). The park also protects wetlands, swamps, lakes, rivers and tropical rainforest that's remained mostly intact since the last ice age.

In addition to housing more than 600 bird species, jaguars, pumas and other rare jungle species, remote reaches of the park are also home to isolated Tagaeri, Taromenani and Oñamenane indigenous communities that resist contact with the outside world. Park territory has been altered to protect these traditional populations of hunter-gatherers, who vehemently resist contact with the outside world. The nearby Reserva Huaorani contributes as an ecological buffer zone for the national park.

The Parrots of Añangu

Most visitors enter Yasuní near the village of Añangu, where there's a small guard station and short trail. Nearby you'll find one of the park's premier attractions, the **Saladero de Loros** *($25)*, a jungle-covered grotto where, on sunny days, flocks of colorful macaws descend to drink from a mineral-rich pond. Watching masses of fantastically plumed parrots fluttering around at close quarters is one of the jungle's greatest shows. The *saladero* is on community land and the admission fee also gives access to an **observation tower** that rises above the forest canopy. A couple of other *saladeros* that attract smaller green parrots are located on the banks of the Río Napo and can be observed from boats.

A Top Lodge Experience

As the only major lodge deep within Yasuní, the elegant **Napo Wildlife Center** *(napowildlifecenter.com)* has a privileged location for wildlife-watching, making it a favorite among photographers, bird-watchers and serious nature enthusiasts.

TOP TIPS

- Most lodges are found along the heavily forested areas around Yasuní National Park, a couple of hours by boat downstream from Coca.
- Day trips to the park from Coca often involve a lot of travel and little time on the ground.
- When choosing a lodge, location is key – the best wildlife-watching is not found on the Napo itself, but around narrow tributaries and sheltered lagoons.
- Some jungle lodges offer excursions to Yasuní for guests – check the included activities before booking.

A CONTROVERSIAL ROAD

In 1991, the Ecuadorian government gave the US-based company Conoco the right to begin oil exploration. Conoco replaced Maxus Oil Consortium, whose legacy is the Maxus road, which slices 150km into the park. While the road was designed to be lifted up and removed, the forest cut in its wake and the influx of outsiders along the road are not as easily reversed.

SANI LODGE STORY

Sani Lodge has its origins in the arrival of a foreign petroleum company looking for oil on the lands of the Sani Isla community. In exchange for permission to survey the lands, village leaders asked the company to build a lodge they could run. No petroleum was ever extracted, but the lodge was constructed nonetheless.

Owned and operated by the Añangu Kichwa community, the lodge has received numerous awards for its sustainable-tourism model that not only employs many villagers but has also greatly improved quality of life in the area.

One of the greatest thrills of staying here is the arrival itself. From the port on the Napo, guests are paddled for a couple of hours up a narrow blackwater creek where birds, monkeys and otters cavort before the landscape opens out at Añangucocha, an immense mirror-like lagoon, on the far side of which stand the elegant thatched-roofed lodge buildings, looking like some lost jungle palace against the verdant wall of foliage.

Rooms line the lakeshore on both sides of the open-air restaurant with its stunning seven-floor observation tower, and activities, including boat trips, day and night hikes and community visits, are led by highly knowledgeable Kichwa guides.

Other Lower Napo Lodges

With a fantastic position on a narrow lagoon deep in the jungle, community-owned **Sani Lodge** *(sanilodge.com)* is a gem. Built on a small hill overlooking the lagoon, the lodge has great wildlife-watching, especially from the breezy hammock-strung social area by the water. Monkeys, sloths and myriad bird species are regularly seen. Ask about visiting the nearby Sani Warmi women's cooperative and immerse yourself in Kichwa traditions while enjoying an authentic jungle meal.

The closest of the major lodges to Coca, the long-running **Sacha Lodge** *(sachalodge.com)* is a conservation success story and the most luxurious place to stay on the lower Napo. In

DANITA DELIMONT/ALAMY

Sani Lodge

a 2000-hectare private reserve and built around the pretty Pilchecocha lake, a short hike and canoe ride from the Río Napo, the lodge boasts stylish air-conditioned rooms with superb modern bathrooms and large windows onto the jungle. Monkeys swing from the trees and giant river otters frolic in the waters right in front of the restaurant, where gourmet meals are further highlights.

Another excellent lodge is Kichwa-owned **Eden Amazon Lodge** *(edenamazonecuador.com)* with its terrific lagoon-side position on Laguna de Yuturi. With deep ties to local Kichwa communities, it offers guided forest hikes by day and night, as well as fine river trips and wildlife-watching; monkeys, giant river otters and caiman are among the commonly seen species. Rooms are fan-cooled and the restaurant cooks great meals using local forest ingredients.

Huaorani indigenous Tours

By far the most rewarding way to explore Yasuní is in the company of an indigenous guide. With many of the lodges owned and operated by local communities, such experiences are easy to come by. There is also a handful of indigenous-run tour operators, who provide a privileged introduction to life in the forest.

One of these is Huaorani man Otobo Baihua, owner of **Otobo's Amazon Safari** *(otobosamazonsafari.com)*, who for decades has been running tailored trips into his ancestral lands deep within the park. The subject of numerous documentaries about his efforts to protect the forest and his community's tradition's, Otobo is an engaging host who runs multiday trips through Huaorani lands.

Other community members (including Otobo's relatives) run fly-in, fly-out deep-forest camping trips along the Río Cononaco, out of Bameno. Try **Bameno Community Tours** *(bamenocommunitytours.com)*.

Paradise Regained?

Yasuní was declared a national park in 1979 to protect its priceless biodiversity. And for many years, the park's inaccessibility protected it in ways that laws and regulations cannot. However, oil discovery within the park in the late 1980s has complicated Yasuní's conservation success story. Oil concessions were granted throughout the 1990s. In 2007, before large-scale drilling could begin, President Correa launched a ground-breaking initiative whereby the country would leave the reserves untapped in exchange for foreign aid and investment. But the deal collapsed in 2013 when the government, citing a lack of funds received, gave the green light for extraction and big oil moved in, building ports, roads and drilling infrastructure within the reserve.

Ten years later, in response to pressure from ecologists, the Ecuadorian people finally got to vote on the issue and overwhelmingly endorsed a ban on drilling in the park's main oilfield. Whether that means the taps will finally be turned off remains to be seen. The early signs are not promising – as of early 2026, the Ecuadorian government was still delaying the dismantling of the oil-industry infrastructure and oil extraction continued.

SACHA LODGE EXTRAS

At Sacha Lodge, you can enjoy a hanging walkway above the forest canopy and a lookout crane that lifts up visitors for a 360-degree sweep above the treetops. A submerged swimming cage to protect you from caimans means it's possible to take a refreshing dip in the lagoon.

As well as employing and training indigenous people to work in the tourism industry, Sacha has been steadily purchasing plots from Ecuadorian smallholders, and allowing the rainforest to reclaim the land purchased. The lodge sits on 5000 acres of reclaimed land now fully protected for forestation.

continued from p182

An Encounter with the Omagua

Art from a lost civilization

While Coca may be light on for attractions, it does boast one excellent place in which to touch up on the fascinating history of the region while waiting for your boat to depart. A visit here is an essential primer for any visit to Parque Nacional Yasuní (p184), not least because it challenges one of the most enduring myths about Amazonian history: that forest communities were primitive societies who left behind little of enduring value.

The three-level **Museo Arqueológico Centro Cultural Orellana** (*MACCO; macco.ec; adult/concession $3/1.50*) is a slick modern archaeological museum dedicated to the Omagua civilization that resided on the banks of the Río Napo at the time of the Spanish Conquest.

Renowned for the practice of flattening the skulls of their children using tightly fastened wooden boards, the Omagua were expert potters who traded with communities as far away as the shores of the Atlantic.

Through carefully curated displays of artifacts, including intricate anthropomorphic pottery, ceremonial weaponry and stamps used to paint patterns on the skin, the first floors of the museum paint a picture of the culturally rich society that challenged the early European view of the lowlands being inhabited by unorganized hunter-gatherers.

The top floor charts the rapid collapse of Omaguan society under the devastating effects of colonization.

Ride the River in Style

Riverboat magic

Without a doubt, the most luxurious way to see the riverscapes of the lower Río Napo is on a river trip aboard a purpose-built cruising vessel.

Anakonda River Cruises (*anakondaamazoncruises.com*) has two boats, the *Anakonda* and the *Manatee*, with floor-to-ceiling windows that allow passengers to watch life on the river from the privacy of their air-conditioned quarters. Social areas include an observation deck with a hot tub and an open-air lounge.

Itineraries run from four days to just over a week, with longer trips reaching all the way from Coca to Nueva Rocafuerte

A WORLD BENEATH THE WATER

On a wildlife trip deep into the Oriente, some of the most fascinating creatures are below the water.

Pink river dolphins: The largest freshwater dolphins in the world are often spotted frolicking in remote blackwater lagoons and, in drier periods, on main rivers near the mouths of tributaries.

Grey dolphins or tucuxi: Less common and smaller than the pink dolphins, *tucuxis* are found in small numbers in the lower Napo.

Giant river otters: Commonly found living in gregarious family groups in lagoons and narrow rivers.

Amapaimas: These prehistoric-looking fish are considered the world's largest river species.

Piranhas: They're unlikely to devour you like in the movies, but their teeth are still utterly frightening.

EATING IN COCA: OUR PICKS

Tenedor y Bolón: Fill up on a wide selection of delicious Ecuadorian breakfast dishes; it also opens for dinner, with river fish a specialty. *7am-noon & 3:30-8pm* $

La Casa del Maito: Excellent fresh fish *maitos* cooked on a roadside grill. Choose from tilapia or piranha. *7am-7pm Tue-Sun* $

El Refugio del Cangrejo: Busy corner place with filling rice dishes loaded with seafood and perfectly tangy ceviches. *7:30am-5pm* $

Waysa Pamba: Modern riverfront food court with an attached market where tiny stalls prepare snacks and meals sourced straight from the jungle. *7am-3pm Fri-Sun* $

on the border with Peru. Excursions on land, including hikes to get up close to wildlife and visits to local indigenous communities, are included.

Peep Pink Dolphins in Pañacocha

Paddle around the Lake of Piranhas

Magical **Laguna Pañacocha** ('Lake of Piranhas' in Kichwa) is an expansive blackwater lagoon on the north side of the Napo, halfway between Coca and Nueva Rocafuerte, which is famed for its sweeping jungle landscapes and diverse wildlife. Accessed by a long, winding creek that snakes its way through dense jungle, the lake is home to a wonderful array of birds, giant otters and pink river dolphins. It receives few visitors, making it a tranquil spot at which to hole up for a couple of nights surrounded by the sounds of the forest. Simple but well-run **Amazon Dolphin Lodge** (*amazondolphinlodge.com*) is right by the lakeshore.

Local lodges offer all-inclusive packages, but it's also possible to visit Laguna Pañacocha independently by taking a local river boat from Coca to Pañacocha town and contracting a local canoe.

Last Stop: Nueva Rocafuerte

Ecuador's far east

Remote border villages that appear as a tiny dot on the edge of a map are more often than not the kind of place you want to leave as fast as possible. But tiny **Nueva Rocafuerte**, where the Napo bids *adiós* to Ecuador, isn't your average frontier town.

Tranquil Nueva Rocafuerte runs the length of an attractive new **malecón** (waterfront promenade) overlooking the wide, chocolatey waters of the Napo, which are blissfully quiet here. The town is inhabited by an indigenous and *mestizo* community who get around for the most part on bicycles. The only visitors who usually set foot in the town are those seeking to stamp their passport before continuing the long river journey into Peru, but Rocafuerte is a great place to organize DIY jungle adventures. Here, lodges and hotels can put you in touch with a local guide.

Just east of town, groups of pink dolphins often congregate at the mouth of the **Río Yasuní**. Follow the river back to the remote **Laguna Jatuncocha**, where you can pass the night beside the still waters far from civilization. Local guides provide tents, transportation and meals for reasonable prices.

To get even closer to dolphins, charter a boat to the mouth of the **Río Cocoya** beyond the hamlet of Martinica.

FROM NUEVA ROCAFUERTE TO IQUITOS

To reach Iquitos from Rocafuerte, you'll need to get to the tiny Peruvian village of of Pantoja, about 40 minutes downstream on the Río Napo. You can contract a boat for $60 to $100 for an express trip, or wait for a local canoe carrying villagers or supplies (around $20 per person). Whichever you choose, make sure to check the boat before paying – wooden canoes that sit just above the waterline pose a distinct risk to fragile devices. You'll need to get an exit stamp at the migration office in Rocafuerte, and then a stamp into Peru upon arrival in Pantoja.

Slow boats to Iquitos leave Pantoja at 5am on Tuesdays and Fridays – most travelers prefer to stay on the busier Ecuadorian side until close to departure.

Tena

HISTORIC ARCHITECTURE | RIVER RAFTING | RIVERFRONT DISTRICT

GETTING AROUND

Most places of interest in Tena are within easy walking distance of the riverfront hotel and entertainment strip. If you're staying in a rural lodge on the outskirts, taxis are readily available and easy to hail on the street.

Buses to Cotundo leave from opposite the Mercado Central, while those to Misahuallí and other destinations, such as Ahuano and Santa Rosa/San Pedro in the upper Napo, leave from transportation company offices (mostly along Av del Chofer) a block or two from the main bus station.

TOP TIP

If you're in Tena for the rafting, you should be able to head out most months of the year. That said, if you can avoid the rainy season (April to May) do so, as some of the more challenging runs may be classed as off-limits at this time.

At the crossroads of many worlds along the Troncal Amazónica highway, busy little Tena is where the influence of the Andes begins to wane and the classic jungle ambience of the Oriente truly begins.

There's enough in an around the town to hold you for at least a couple of days. Founded in the 16th century, Tena has faint echoes of decaying colonial architecture, while bars and restaurants line Tena's appealing riverside strip, which looks out toward a jungle-covered island connected to the riverbank by a fancy footbridge. And with its own charm as a provincial Ecuadorian town on the cusp of the world of forests and rivers, Tena promises many travelers their first taste of Amazonian culture, landscapes and cuisine. Market days are Friday and Saturday.

Stray a little further and the rewards are rich. Tena is Ecuador's rafting capital, while north of town, around Cotundo, there are wonderful caves, canyons and waterfalls just waiting to be explored.

Riding Tena's Wild Rivers

Big water, spectacular scenery

With a strategic location where the fast-moving waters of the eastern Andes rush down onto the Oriente plains, Tena is Ecuador's rafting capital and the best place to organize trips on rivers throughout the region. Rafting trips range from gentle family-friendly floats down scenic rivers to exhilarating runs through technical rapids in tight canyons.

Serious outfitters (p193) will have everything you would expect – decent life jackets, professional guides, first-aid supplies and throw bags. Many use safety kayakers who paddle alongside the boat in case of capsizings. Kayakers can hire guides or arrange for transportation and put-ins in town.

While the waters around town offer thrills for novice and experienced rafters alike, the mining boom in the surrounding mountains means that operators are often having to take

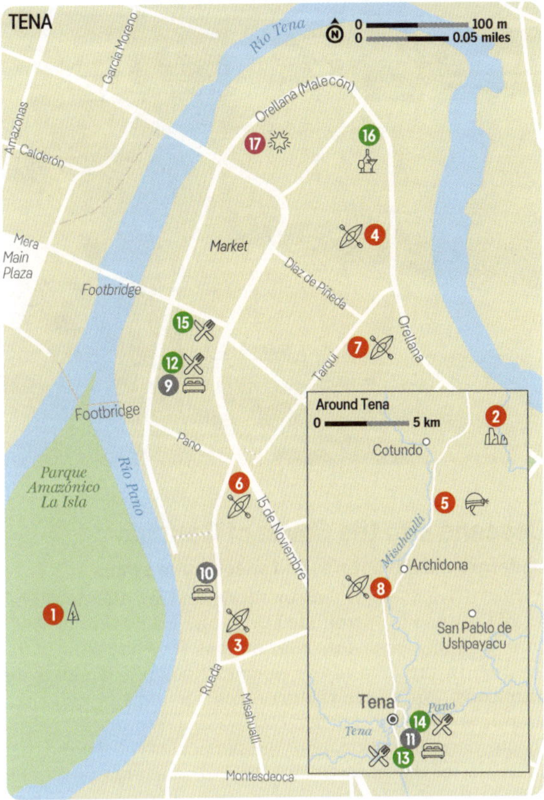

SIGHTS
1 Parque Amazónico La Isla
2 Rayu Pakcha

ACTIVITIES
3 Akangau Jungle Expeditions
4 Caveman Adventures
5 Cuevas de Jumandy
6 Raft Amazonía
7 Rios Ecuador
8 River People Ecuador

SLEEPING
9 Brisa del Río
10 Hostal Los Yutzos
11 Hostal Pakay

EATING
12 Café Tortuga
13 Quiapo Cevicheria
14 Restaurante El Mirador
15 Vilino Albero

DRINKING & NIGHTLIFE
16 Araña de Don Viche Bar Coctelería

ENTERTAINMENT
17 Discoteca La Gallera

groups further afield to find unspoiled runs. One of the most popular is the 25km stretch of the upper **Río Napo** (locally known as Jatunyacu, which means 'big water' in Kichwa), which has a series of Class III+ rapids suitable for rafters of all levels. To push the excitement up a few notches, try the wild Class IV rapids on the **Hollin** and **Jondachi** rivers, both of which are tributaries of the Río Misahuallí, and flow down with force from the slopes of Volcán Sumaco and Parque Nacional Antisana respectively.

Local outfits also arrange trips further afield to the **Río Quijos**, which offers nonstop big water surrounded by a stunning canyon and is only recommended for adult rafters, preferably those with some experience in rafting difficult waters. For a more family-friendly run, the calm upper **Río Anzu** south of town has 18km of gentle Class II and III rapids that are good for younger rafters, with a number of refreshing swimming holes along the way.

REMOTE RAFTING ADVENTURES

For wild rivers deep in nature that see few descents, check out the rafting scene around **Puyo** (p198) in the southern Oriente, where river running is just beginning to take off.

TENA'S HISTORY

The capital of Napo province, Tena was settled by Europeans in 1560 prompting early indigenous uprisings. Jumandy, chief of the Kichwa, led a fierce but unsuccessful revolt against the Spaniards in 1578. The town's strategic location between the Andes and the Amazon, its position at the confluence of numerous navigable rivers, and the fact that the Napo eventually flows into the Amazon meant that Tena worked as an important trading post. In addition to tourism and as a hub for regional river transportation, the city is now known for its cinnamon farms. The anniversary of the town's foundation is celebrated on November 15 with live music and community events.

Descend into the Caves of Cotundo

Underground adventures and spectacular swims

A short drive north of Tena on the Quito Hwy, the tiny hamlet of Cotundo is surrounded by jungle-clad canyons, deep caves and mysterious rock formations. The best-known attraction in the area is the complex known as **Cuevas de Jumandy** *($6)*, where visitors follow an underground river deep into a multi-branched cave system. While the speleothems (cave formations) are not particularly dramatic, the sheer size of the cave – many parts of which have yet to be fully explored – and the tiny swimming holes deep inside make it well worth a trip.

More difficult to access, **Rayu Pakcha** *($7)*, also known as the Gran Cañon, is one of Ecuador's most enchanting swims. Here, a thundering waterfall passes through a hole in the roof of a dark cave before spilling out into a large pool surrounded on all sides by jungle-covered rock walls. Come during the week to enjoy the magic without the crowds; it's around 1.5km east of Mondayacu.

A Malecón Night Out

Riverbank rhythms

Tena's riverbank is one of the more agreeable nightlife zones in this part of the country. Most of the action happens on the east bank, but both sides of the river have fabulous street-food vendors serving pizza, grilled meats and fish. **Araña de Don Viche Bar Coctelería** really cranks up from Thursday to Saturday, and its long list of cocktails is better than most. Of the nightclubs, **Discoteca La Gallera** feels slightly more grown-up than the others, but they're all fun.

Dance floors pulse most nights, open from approximately 8pm to 2am Sunday to Wednesday, and to about 3am Thursday

ALEJO MIRANDA/SHUTTERSTOCK

Tena *malecón*

to Saturday. On most nights of the week, *malecón* bars compete to persuade passersby to stop in for a drink by blaring out *reggaetón* at skull-splitting volumes.

An Island of Tranquility

Explore the urban jungle

Extending out from where the Tena and Pano rivers meet, downtown Tena's main attraction for visitors is the 27-hectare **Parque Amazónico La Isla** *(free)*, which lies in the middle of the Río Tena between the *malecón* (the riverfront promenade) and the town plaza. It's looking a bit rough around the edges these days, and it will all feel rather tame for those who are returning from a genuine Amazon adventure further east. But it's still a pleasant enough way to while away a few hours.

Accessed by a footbridge that also has a spiraling, panoramic **lookout tower**, the park has a partially finished boardwalk network that winds past native plants of the region. Keep an eye out for the troupes of squirrel and capuchin monkeys, and the lonely, free-roaming tapir that spends its days eating bananas from the hands of visitors and bathing in the pond in the center of the island.

BEST RAFTING OPERATORS

Akangau Jungle Expeditions
(akangau.com) Gets consistently good reviews from travelers for its rafting trips and multiday trips.

River People
(riverpeopleecuador.com) Pioneering operator with experienced guides and quality equipment.

Caveman Adventures
(cavemanecuador.com) Professional outfit with good gear. Runs well-organized trips for all skill levels in addition to hikes and cultural activities.

Raft Amazonia
(raftamazonia.com) Owned and operated by a local indigenous family, this small outfitter has friendly licensed guides and also offers trips to nearby caves.

Rios Ecuador
(facebook.com/riosecuador) Repeat visitors and high professional standards make this a good choice for all levels of experience.

EATING IN TENA: OUR PICKS

Cafe Tortuga: A casual riverfront cafe offering great breakfasts, filling fruit shakes and delicious sandwiches and wraps. *7am-9:30pm* $

Quiapo Cevicheria: Hands down the best place in town for seafood, with a small menu of top soups and, best of all, excellent ceviches. *7am-5pm* $

Restaurante El Mirador: Enjoy excellent Mexican food while taking in great views out over the city. Take a taxi there and back. *2-9:30pm Tue-Sun* $

Vilino Albero: The best steak in the Oriente and delicious pasta washed down with a decent selection of wines. *7am-noon & 5-10pm Mon-Fri, 7am-11pm Sat & Sun* $$

Beyond Tena

Let the adventure begin: climb volcanoes covered in cloud forest, float down jungle rivers and immerse yourself in indigenous Kichwa culture.

Places

GETTING AROUND

From Misahualli it's possible to hire boats to travel down the Río Napo, but it's cheaper to travel by bus. Buses from Tena to Ahuano (from where more boats leave) take two different paths: on the north side of the Río Napo, the road is only partially paved and passes through Misahualli, while on the south bank it's paved all the way to La Punta, where the bus will drive onto a barge to reach Ahuano.

Close to Tena, the Río Napo drops down off the Andean hills with some force. But then, once the river hits the bridge at Puerto Napo, it slows and widens, becoming navigable to small boats, opening up a world of lowland jungles in the process.

First port of call downstream is the vibrant little village of Misahuallí with its cadre of capricious monkeys and a fine sandy beach. On the stretch east of Misahuallí, indigenous communities, ecolodges and private nature reserves line the riverbanks, providing an accessible jungle experience.

Northeast of Tena, Parque Nacional Sumaco Napo-Galeras protects a stunning variety of unspoiled ecosystems and is home to one of Ecuador's most rewarding multi-day treks.

Misahuallí

FROM TENA: **30MIN**

Explore a riverside town

Perched on the point where the Misahuallí and Napo rivers merge, the little town of **Misahuallí** was once an important port for travelers and goods arriving from the far-flung reaches of the Ecuadorian Amazon, but it fell into obscurity with the construction of the Tena–Coca road. These days, Misahuallí is a tranquil place during the week with relaxing river views, and many visitors prefer to base themselves here than in larger Tena. On weekends hordes of day-trippers arrive to bathe at the sandy beach at the mouth of the **Río Misahuallí**, go tubing, ride banana boats and drink.

Watch the local wildlife

Misahuallí is best known for the troupe of capuchin monkeys that inhabit a small patch of forest just upstream from the beach. Although their numbers are diminishing, they are usually easy to spot, and local operators usually know where to find them.

Other natural attractions are accessible by road, including the **Árbol Milenario**, a majestic old ceiba that towers above the surrounding forest. It's east across the bridge from Pununo, north of Misahuallí. There's also the **Cascada de Latas**, a wide waterfall that feeds a shallow pool.

While the forests around the town have been encroached upon by people for decades and there isn't much in the way

PETER VAN EVERT/ALAMY

Woman cooking, Misahuallí

of wildlife to spot, boat operators at the beach offer a number of circuits on the Río Napo where sightings of primates and other birdlife are possible. More interesting river and jungle trips can be arranged with the specialized tour agencies around the main plaza.

Visit a riverbank community

One popular destination is **Shiripuno**, a Kichwa community a couple of kilometers downstream, where visitors can sip guayusa tea while watching traditional dance performances. Overnight stays are possible. Ask one of Misahuallí's tour operators about possible village visits further afield for more remote encounters.

Upper Napo

FROM TENA: **1-2½HR**

Sleep in a jungle lodge

If you've been dreaming of an Amazonian river-and-jungle adventure, this is where reality starts to resemble those dreams. Yes, for deep jungle immersion you need to head further downriver to the Lower Napo. But the Upper Napo offers some of the most accessible jungle adventures anywhere in the Amazon Basin.

CHICHA: THE ORIGINAL ENERGY DRINK

Not to be confused with the boiled highland beverage, *chicha* in the Oriente is a thick and highly nutritious drink that's served for breakfast and is an important source of calories in the jungle, where villagers often eat very little. Some locals drink liters of it every day. The drink is made with yuca or chonta palm that's masticated by women (and only women) to form a paste that is then wrapped in leaves, added to water and left to ferment.

When fresh, it tastes mild and yogurt-like, but as time passes, it becomes more alcoholic as bacteria from the saliva turn carbohydrates into simple sugars. While it's usually made with unfiltered water, you're unlikely to have issues from trying a sip.

EATING IN MISAHUALLÍ: OUR PICKS

El Bijao: On the plaza and with smoke from the grills billowing out onto the footpath, come here for fresh fish or chicken *maitos* (grilled in palm leaves). *8am-9pm* $

Papakuna Cafe: Enjoy tasty wings, burgers and grilled beef or prawns, together with ice-cold beers right by the river and fine water views. *3-10pm* $

El Jardín: Take a boat across the river to this upmarket garden restaurant with a soaring thatch ceiling and seasonal gourmet cooking. *noon-4pm & 6-9:30pm* $$

Hamadryade Lodge: A gourmet restaurant offering everything from pizzas to seasonal Peruvian dishes and delicious ceviche. *noon-3pm & 6-9:30pm* $$

FINDING THE RIGHT JUNGLE EXPERIENCE

Accommodations: Lodges offer day trips into surrounding rainforest from a comfortable base, while other tours include camping or sleeping in communities.

Guides: Higher-end tours usually have English-speaking naturalist guides, while cheaper options often group travelers with Spanish-speaking locals.

Location: More expensive tours don't necessarily mean a better wildlife or cultural experience; a camping excursion in the jungle may offer more authentic interactions on both fronts.

Ecological practices: Choose an operator that respects protected-area norms with regard to waste, hunting and feeding animals – look for unambiguous sustainability policies.

GARY IRVINE/ALAMY

Common woolly monkey, AmaZOOnico

The bridge at Puerto Napo, just south of Tena, marks the beginning of the Río Napo proper, which widens as hills begin to flatten and the landscapes start to feel more like the Amazonian realm of your imagination. While the building of roads around the upper Napo has changed wildlife habits for good, and visitors will see fewer animals than deeper in the jungle, the area is nonetheless a good place to get a taste of the rainforest without having to endure a long boat journey.

Best of all, comfortable ecolodges line the riverbanks – even this close to Tena, you'll sleep beneath an astonishing spray of stars and wake to the sounds of jungle and riverbank life. Lodges vary according to levels of luxury and comfort, from budget thatched huts on stilts up to luxurious bungalows with swimming pools and jungle views. Most have hammocks on the balconies and some have hot water. Most serve decent food and have a bar. All offer bird-watching, jungle hiking, tubing, wildlife excursions and cultural activities. Among the excellent options are Misahuallí Amazon Lodge (p207), just across the water from Misahuallí, and Anaconda Lodge (p207), downstream from Punta Ahuano.

Packages usually include transportation, and advance reservations are essential.

Reserva Biológica Jatun Sacha

On the Río Napo's southern bank, just a few kilometers downstream from Misahuallí, the non-profit **Reserva Biológica Jatun Sacha** *($7)* protects some of the upper Napo's most pristine jungle. Spanning 25 sq km from the Tena–Ahuano road back to the Río Arajuno, it's an area of high biodiversity and a number of new species have been discovered here.

Spend any time in the area and you'll quickly see what a treasure this place is. With deforestation in the upper Napo reaching critical levels, the forests of the reserve are an essential haven for wildlife in the area. Visitors can go birdwatching, hike forest trails, check out the botanical garden, or scale the 30m-high observation tower to view the canopy from above.

Visit rescued wildlife at AmaZoonico

Perched on the forested banks of the Río Arajuno, **AmaZOOnico** *(amazoonico.org; adult/child $5/3)* is a rescue and rehabilitation center for jungle animals that have been injured or separated from their habitat to become pets. It has a solid track record in reintroducing species into the wild – reptiles have proven particularly suitable for liberation, but monkeys, tapirs and sloths have also successfully been released deep in the jungle.

Unfortunately, some animals are permanent residents at the center because they've lost the ability to survive on their own, or because of dangerous interactions with local villagers, and you will see animals in cages. Tours around the center are guided by a team of international volunteers.

To visit, you'll need to book in advance by messaging +593-99-414-3395 and organize a boat from Puerto Barantilla – try Don Guido (+593-99-328-420), who resides in the local village. Buses from Tena to Punta Ahuano along the river's south bank will drop you a short walk from the little dock.

Parque Nacional Sumaco Napo-Galeras

FROM TENA: **2¼HR**

Climb a volcano

On the road from Tena to Coca, **Parque Nacional Sumaco Napo-Galeras** *(instagram.com/parquenacionalsumaco)* preserves large tracts of stunning cloud forest that are entirely free of development. The centerpiece of the park is **Volcán Sumaco** (3990m), which can be summited in a tough three- to five-day round-trip trek.

The trail is one of few in the country that traverses the three distinct climatic zones of rainforest, cloud forest and *páramo*, making it one of Ecuador's most rewarding hikes. It's often muddy and nights are spent at three simple wooden refuges along the way. Guides are required for the hike and can be hired in the small village of Pacto Sumaco at the trailhead, 9km north of the Tena–Loreto road, where there are a couple of accommodations options.

Just south of Pacto Sumaco, **Wild Sumaco Lodge** *(wildsumaco.com)* is set atop a hill with sweeping views over the forest and is a wonderful place to relax even if you're not attempting the summit hike. Deep in the forest on the eastern side of the volcano, the **Reserva Biológica Río Bigal** *(bigalriverbiologicalreserve.org)* offers an immersive back-to-nature experience. You'll need to commit to a three-night minimum stay and hike 45 minutes into the lodge, but will be rewarded with some of the region's most breathtaking and unspoiled wilderness.

JUMANDY: REBEL WITH A CAUSE

All around the upper Napo, you'll see landmarks and businesses named after Jumandy. A *cacique* (leader) of the Quijos tribe, Jumandy led an uprising against Spanish colonial rule in 1578, during which his troops burned the cities of Ávila and Archidona – bases from which Spanish authorities in Quito were mounting expeditions to expand their territory in the Oriente. His success inspired rebellions throughout the Oriente, provoking the ire of the conquistadores, who sent thousands of soldiers from Quito to put down the uprising. Jumandy was captured and hauled behind horses through Quito's streets before being decapitated. It wasn't until 2011 that his bravery was officially recognized, when he was named a national hero of Ecuador.

Puyo

RAINFOREST CUISINE | JUNGLE IMMERSION | LIVELY NEIGHBOURHOODS

GETTING AROUND

Puyo is well served by buses from across Ecuador, with buses coming and going from the bus terminal 1km southwest of town. Regular services include Baños (two hours), Tena (two hours), Macas (2½ hours), Ambato (three hours), Quito (5½ hours), Coca (six to seven hours) and Guayaquil (eight hours).

A taxi ride from downtown to the bus terminal or to the Barrio Obrero costs around $1, and no ride within the city should cost much more. Small local buses go to Shell (15 minutes) every half-hour or so from south of the market along Calle 27 de Febrero.

Puyo is an enigma: whereas most towns make efforts to spruce up their centers and leave the outskirts stagnating, this place does the opposite. Dense green jungle flourishes close around the town's edges, and – thanks in part to travelers from Baños making the hour-long drive down to do a rainforest reconnoiter – accommodations are good and plentiful, with some highly recommended jungle-tour operators located here.

Before leaving town, spend some time exploring the outstanding Parque Etnobotanico Omaere, where you get a genuine forest experience, including precious time with a knowledgeable indigenous guide. Take a walk along the banks of the Río Puyo. And head just beyond the town for pristine river swimming. But whenever you're in Puyo itself, you're never far from a great meal – this is one of the best (and most accessible) places in Ecuador to sample indigenous and Amazonian cuisine.

Explore Puyo's Jungle Fringe

Riverside walks and river swimming

As is the case with so many Ecuadorian cities of the interior, first impressions of Puyo can be misleading. For the most part, Puyo is a boisterous provincial town with a largely unappealing, concrete-filled center. And at first glance, it can seem like it's the antithesis of the natural beauty that defines the southern Oriente. Because of this, many travelers stay only long enough to stock up on provisions, arrange a tour or other transport, and head out of town and into the great beyond as quickly as they can. While we understand the impulse, Puyo deserves more than a first glance.

Do what you need to do in the center of town, but it's the Puyo's northern reaches where you'll find a different side to the city altogether.

Around the lively northern neighborhood of **Barrio Obrero**, dense green jungle encroaches on the town edges, and a fine

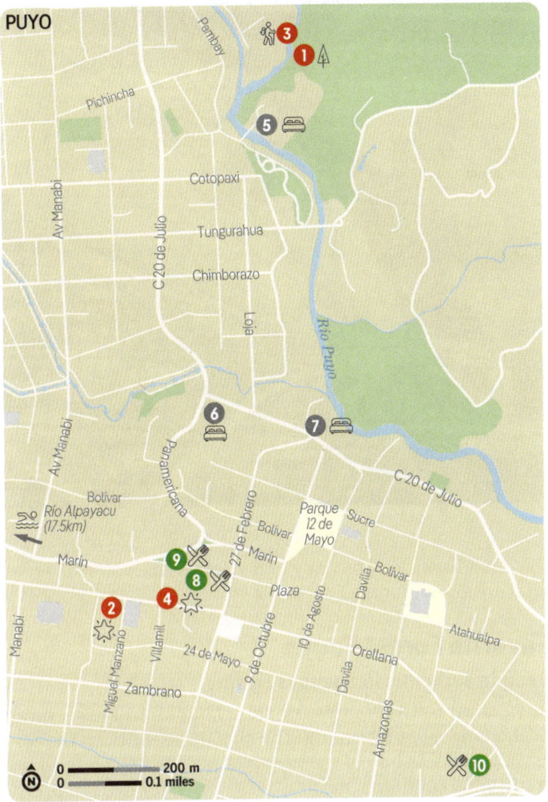

SIGHTS
1 Parque Etnobotánico Omaere

ACTIVITIES
2 Papangu Tours
3 Paseo Turistico
4 Shiran Nantu

SLEEPING
5 El Jardín
6 Hostal Las Palmas
7 Posada Real

EATING
8 El Fariseo
see 5 El Jardín
9 EscoBar
10 Mercado Platano

long walkway, known as the **Paseo Turistico**, runs northward from the family-filled Malecon Boayaku Puyo park for nearly 2km beside the Río Puyo.

While locals swim in the shallow Río Puyo, it's not the cleanest waterway, and we don't recommend joining them. You're better off heading out of town to the **Río Alpayacu** on the Via Shell road, which has crystalline waters surrounded by a wall of greenery.

Discover the Joys of Ethnobotany

Jungle culture and medicine

Across the first footbridge from the Barrio Obrero is the lush **Parque Etnobotanico Omaere** *(omaere.wordpress.com; adult/student/child $3/1.50/0.50)*, protecting 15 hectares of dense forest full of medicinal plants. Founded by indigenous Shuar healer Teresa Shiki and her biologist husband Chris Canaday, the park is as much a cultural experience as a natural one. Entry includes a tour with indigenous guides, who will point out different plants and bird species during a 45-minute to two-hour walk through the forest. And the further you go, the more the sounds and clamor of

TOP TIP

Try the riverside cafes for a typical local dish of *ceviche boquetero*, which is literally 'dumptruck ceviche' – a combination of toasted corn kernels and plantain chips with a can of tuna elegantly dumped on top. It's a surprising mix of smoky and vinegar sharp.

THE RÍO NAPO

Part of the Amazon Basin, the Río Napo flows west to east, like all rivers east of the Andes. Its source lies high in the Andes, down off the slopes of the volcanoes known as Antisana, Sincholagua and Cotopaxi (Ecuador's second-highest mountain). Along the way, it is joined by the Coca and Aguarico rivers, which flow down off the Volcán Cayambe. The further it gets from the Andes, the more the landscape flattens and the slower the river moves. By the time it reaches the Amazon River (of which the Napo is a tributary), 1075km (668 miles) after it began, the Napo can appear sluggish and almost as if it is barely moving.

the outside world ebbs away and you feel like you're deep in an Amazonian forest.

Favorite Forest Foods

Sample authentic indigenous cuisine

Puyo is an unlikely culinary star. Thanks to Puyo's large indigenous population and the city's proximity to the forest, the town is one of the best places in the Oriente to try traditional rainforest meals. And given that Puyo is a pretty untouristy place, the indigenous food here is the real deal, prepared to suit local tastes rather than modified for the traveler diet.

The centerpiece of this genuine rainforest cooking scene is Puyo's **Barrio Obrero** dining district where bright joints selling burgers and wings rub shoulders with local eateries serving *maitos* (fish grilled in palm leaves), cooked using wild-caught river fish, and other Amazonian dishes.

For snacks, you can also get grilled *chontacuros*, a large worm-like larvae found in a palm tree that's full of vitamins and said to have myriad health benefits; sensitive souls might prefer to try them grilled, rather than raw. Less-adventurous palates might want to settle for a refreshing glass of guayusa tea. And everything here comes with an offering of the tortilla-like yuca flatbreads.

For the full local dining experience, head to the Mercado Platano (open sunrise to sunset), not to be confused with the Mercado de los Plátanos (Banana Market). Here you'll find nearly 40 rickety stalls run by indigenous women preparing fish soups and fresh foods brought in daily

MORE TASTY JUNGLE TREATS

Another good place to try Amazonian food is **Coca** (p182), where traditional dishes from the lower Napo are served from dozens of small kitchens in a breezy riverside food court.

APPROVED PHOTOGRAPHY/SHUTTERSTOCK

Chontacuros

from the jungle; avoid dishes like armadillo, agouti or wild boar, as the number of these creatures in the surrounding forest is dwindling. Other decent choices include El Jardín and El Fariseo.

Plan Your Jungle Adventure

Get ready to go wild

Having established that Puyo is not such a bad place to hang out after all, in between the river swims, local meals and tastes of forest life, get yourself organized to go further. Indigenous-run **Papangu Tours** *(papangutours.com)* should be your first port of call. With a focus on community tourism, their day or multiday trips go to **Sarayaku** (a Kichwa community) and **Cueva de los Tayos** (Shuar). Guides are indigenous and speak Spanish and Kichwa, and some of the fees go to participating communities. The tour office is in front of the entrance to the Hostería Turingia.

Shiran Nantu *(facebook.com/shirannantu.agenciadeviajes)* is another recommended option and worth speaking with to learn the possibilities; unusual agrotourism trips to indigenous communities are its specialty.

THE KICHWA

The country's largest indigenous ethnic group, the Kichwa number well over two million. They live in both the Sierra and the Amazon. Those in the mountains subsist on small plots of farmland, raising sheep and cattle, and they're known for their fine textiles and weavings.

Among the best-known Kichwa communities are the *otavaleños*. For men, their unique dress consists of a blue poncho, a fedora, white calf-length socks and a *shimba* (a long braid that hangs down nearly to the waist). Wearing the hair in this fashion probably dates back to pre-Inca times. The women's dress may be the closest to Inca attire worn anywhere in the Andes. White blouses, blue skirts, shawls and jewelry are all ways of outwardly expressing their ethnicity.

EATING & DRINKING IN PUYO: OUR PICKS

Mercado Platano: Heaven for street-food enthusiasts, this lively market is filled with everything you can eat from the forest. *sunrise-sunset* $

El Jardín: Elegant, open-air and some of the best flavor combinations in the Oriente – try the *pollo ishpingo. noon-4pm & 6-9.30pm* $$

El Fariseo: Not much to look at, El Fariseo boasts one of the Oriente's few espresso machines and a very tasty *churrasco* (steak served with a fried egg). *8am-7pm Mon-Sat* $

EscoBar: Serves *patacones* (fried bananas), yuca (cassava) or salads with meat to accompany Ecuadorian microbrews and cocktails. *9am-11pm Sun-Fri, to 11:30pm Sat*

Puyo's coolest place to eat and drink.

Southern Oriente

NATURAL BEAUTY | INDIGENOUS ENCOUNTERS | OUTDOOR ACTIVITIES

TOP TIPS

Tourism is still in its infancy in the southern Oriente and many services lag behind those in other parts of the country. In smaller towns, hotel offerings are limited and many don't list on online booking platforms, so it's good to call ahead before traveling to lock down a room.

Welcome to Ecuador's final tourism frontier. Not many travelers make it to these parts, but those who do are rewarded with endless opportunities for adventure, with thundering waterfalls, crystal-clear rivers, deep canyons and mysterious caves. Such stellar attractions all lie within a short drive of the region's friendly, if not particularly exciting, towns. By coming here, you leave behind the high-end ecolodges, polished tours and backpacker hangouts of the northern rivers. But the southern Oriente is a ravishing world of seldom-explored misty hills falling away into swaths of thick jungle populated by isolated indigenous communities.

Of the towns south of Puyo, bustling Macas affords sweeping views of the Upano River Valley, and makes an excellent base from which to organize trips to remote villages rich in indigenous culture. Further south there's real off-the-beaten-track adventure outside Gualquiza, with rafting, canyoning and remote jungle hikes.

Views of Macas

A picturesque town

Perched atop a plateau overlooking the dramatic wide valley of dark sand carved out by the powerful Río Upano and backed by jungle-covered hillsides, the busy regional capital of **Macas** has a spectacular position. Yes, the town itself faces away from the valley. And yes, once you're in among it, the

GETTING AROUND

Regular bus services ply the Troncal Amazónica, connecting the major towns of the southern Oriente, but getting out to the jungle and more remote attractions takes some planning. Local bus coverage to outlying attractions is at times irregular, with just a few services a day, often inconveniently leaving very early. Make sure to check on return times before setting out. Taxis are found even in smaller towns and are a reasonable way to reach attractions within about a one-hour radius, though you may need to hike in along dirt roads to some sights. Buy tickets at the bus station.

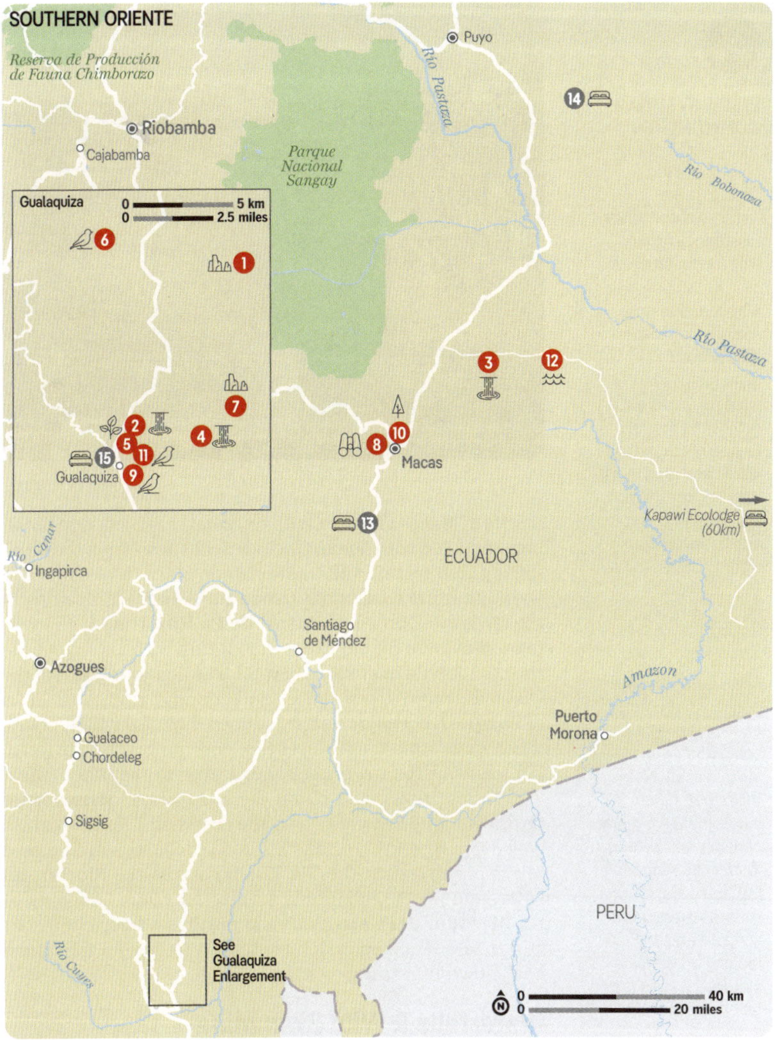

SIGHTS
1 Callejon del Empalme
2 Cascada Las Culebrillas
3 Cascada Yantza
4 Cascadas Kupiamais
5 Jardín Botánico El Gato
6 Jempe Lodge
7 La Dolorosa
8 Mirador de Quilamo
see 8 Mirador del Gato
9 Parque Lineal
10 Parque Recreacional
see 10 Pasaje de La Randimpa
11 Quinta Bellavista
12 Río Colorado

SLEEPING
13 Casa Blanca Hortencia
see 10 Hostal Casa Blanca
14 Huella Verde Rainforest Lodge
15 Posada D'León

EATING
see 15 Asados del Parque
see 10 Copal Bar Restaurant
see 10 La Maravilla
see 15 Los Pinchos

VISITING SHUAR COMMUNITIES

Most of southern Oriente is the territory of the Shuar indigenous group, with a population of over 100,000 in over 600 communities. Also known as the Jivaro, the Shuar community also inhabits the forests across the border in Peru. Until their lands were colonised by the Spanish, the Shuar were semi-nomadic and known as fierce warriors. Even today, the community struggles to maintain its independence: most Shuar communities don't approve of unguided visitors on their lands and some don't want visitors at all. Near the region's main cities, there are many communities offering 'Shuar experiences,' but these are, for the most part, quite scripted and anyone looking for genuine cultural insights may be disappointed.

GORAN ŠAFAREK/ALAMY STOCK

A street in Macas

streets of Macas are lined with unremarkable concrete buildings and filled with honking vehicles. But away from the uninspiring architecture and traffic clamor, Macas is magnificent. To fully admire its superb surroundings, begin by heading to the recently refurbished **Pasaje de La Randimpa**, an inviting walkway on the edge of the mountain with views over the river to the wild mountains beyond. The boulevard ends at the well-manicured green spaces and equally impressive views of **Parque Recreacional** (free), open during daylight hours.

The views from these places face east out beyond the town. For views of the town itself, head over to the other (western) side of town, and climb the road to the **Mirador de Quilamo** for great views over the city with a fine mountain backdrop. To get there, take Eliceo Mancheno, starting west of the airport, then the Via Kilamo across the Rio Jurumbaino and up the mountain for around 1.5km, stopping at the **Mirador del Gato** along the way. It's a steep climb, but best to take a taxi and ask them to wait for you for the return back down into town.

Waterfalls & Wild Swimming

Hike to cascades, bathe in the river

Stirring natural beauty is a recurring theme in the indigenous Shuar lands around Macas, with numerous magnificent waterfalls and clear jungle rivers to explore outside town. You may have to pay a small fee to access some of the sites.

The road west to Taisha, one of the best places to get out among magnificent nature and accessible by local buses, takes you to the **Cascada Yantza**, also known as Musap, where a tall cascade falls over a forested cliff face into a refreshing shoulder-deep pool. The 25-minute walk from the road includes crossing a knee-deep river.

Continue further east to **Río Colorado**, a crystal-clear river with inviting swimming holes surrounded by lush foliage.

Ask the guides at the entrance to lead you to the spectacular nearby waterfall.

Outdoor Adventure in Gualaquiza

Explore canyons and waterfalls

Surrounded by jungle-covered hills that are strewn with waterfalls, caves and canyons, the tranquil little town of **Gualaquiza** is tailor-made for adventurers looking to get off the beaten track and immerse themselves in nature.

A fantastic way to see the magnificent countryside is by rafting the **Río Cuyes**, a 9km, two-hour run through Class II and III (ie gentle) rapids amid remarkable walls of jungle punctuated by rugged rock formations. Turn the adrenaline up a few notches by jumping off a towering suspension bridge.

Even more thrilling is the trip to the **Callejon del Empalme**, a brilliant green-tinged river in a narrow, 30m-deep canyon that runs for 250m before tumbling over an 80m-high waterfall. Visitors must abseil down a sheer wall beside a waterfall and then scale the same rock face at the end.

For a less demanding canyon experience, head to **La Dolorosa**, 14km northeast of town, where stairs leads to a jungle-clad canyon where visitors can wade all the way to a pretty waterfall. Follow the river further downstream to find a deep, dripping-wet cave.

Another place to immerse yourself in Gualaquiza's refreshing waters is **Cascadas Kupiamais**, 7km east of town, where two streams run down the mountainside, forming five different waterfalls, two of which are wonderful swimming holes. If time is limited, the trailhead for the 1km hike to the elegant, narrow **Cascada Las Culebrillas** waterfall is just 3km north of town and can be reached on foot or by taxi.

Bird-Watching in Gualaquiza

Parrots, toucans and tangaras

The Andean foothills around Gualaquiza are a bird-watching hot spot, with the intersection of two key ecosystems attracting colorful toucans and some rare endemic tangara varieties.

Close to town and open during daylight hours, the **Jardín Botánico El Gato** *(free)* is part of a reforestation project and has several trails, a lake and two lookouts offering fine views over town. Other good places for bird-watching include **Jempe Lodge** *(+593-98-723-7506)*, **Quinta Bellavista** and the riverside **Parque Lineal**.

RITUAL BEGINNINGS

Starting the day with a hot caffeinated drink is a worldwide tradition, but in the lowland jungle communities of Ecuador, the beverage of choice is guayusa, made with the boiled leaves of the native *ilex guayusa* tree.

In the Oriente, the morning cuppa begins early – often around 3am – when villagers get up and spend a couple of hours drinking guayusa while reflecting on dreams and knowledge passed down from ancestors before moving onto breakfast – often a large bowl of *chicha*.

Guayusa tea is both a stimulant, with similar amounts of caffeine as coffee, and a powerful antioxidant. In addition to being served as a hot drink in the morning, you'll also find it served cold as a refreshing accompaniment to meals.

EATING IN THE SOUTHERN ORIENTE: OUR PICKS

Asados del Parque: Tasty barbecue served on the porch of one of Gualaquiza's few remaining colonial houses. *2-11pm Mon-Sat* $

Los Pinchos: On Gualaquiza's main square, atmospheric Los Pinchos is a bar that serves skewered grilled meat and veg street-side for a pittance. *noon-11pm* $

La Maravilla: In Macas, this blue casita has *tablas* (cutting boards) of meat and cheese and yuca (cassava) fries. *11am-midnight Mon-Thu, to 2am Fri & Sat* $

Copal Bar Restaurant: Macas spot with a diverse menu, great service and an inviting atmosphere. *7:30-10:30am & 5pm-late Mon-Fri, 10am-1pm & 4pm-2am Sat* $$

Places We Love to Stay

$ Budget $$ Midrange $$$ Top End

Papallacta

Sol de Piedra A bright budget option just a short walk from the main baths complex. **$**

Hosteria Pampallacta Termales Midrange option with fireplaces in the rooms and its own baths out the back. **$$**

Termas de Papallacta High-end hotel attached to the baths with comfortable rooms set around guest-only pools. **$$$**

Baeza & Around

La Casa de Rodrigo An old-school hostel with tidy rooms in Baeza Antigua, run by an affable local kayaking guide. **$**

Cabañas Kopal Beautifully crafted wooden *cabañas* in Baeza Antigua with ample porches and cozy interiors. **$$**

Rio Quijos Eco Lodge An inviting riverside lodge surrounded by lush nature with homely rooms and trails through the trees. **$$**

Cuyabeno

MAP p175

Cuyabeno Lodge The reserve's original lodge and still an excellent choice for nature lovers, with comfortable *cabañas* perched on a small hill overlooking Laguna Grande. **$$$**

Jamu Lodge As luxurious as it gets in Cuyabeno, with stylish and comfortable rooms. The lodge is isolated from other accommodations and the jungle feels close at hand. **$$$**

Bamboo Lodge Close to Laguna Grande, this place looks a treat, with rooms housed in bamboo buildings with thatched roofs and a tremendous lookout tower. **$$$**

Tapir Lodge Features tower lodgings that get guests into the trees. Simple but comfortable rooms come fitted out with screens, mosquito nets, hot water and balconies. **$$$**

Lago Agrio

Hotel d'Mario A good, friendly option in Lago Agrio with tidy air-con rooms. **$**

Hotel Arazá Friendly midrange downtown choice with business-like rooms, a refreshing pool and a gym. **$$**

Gran Hotel de Lago The plushest place to stay in Lago Agrio, with sparkling rooms and a sizeable pool. **$$$**

Coca

MAP p183

Hotel Río Napo Excellent value in the center of town, with spotless, comfortable air-con rooms. **$**

Heliconias Grand Hotel An oasis of tranquility with elegant and spacious faux-colonial rooms and a lovely pool. **$$**

Hotel El Auca Big, light-filled rooms surrounding an ample garden just blocks from the main dock. **$$**

Lower Napo

MAP p183

Sachi Wayra Yasuni Lodge Intimate family-run lodge on the banks of the Napo near the Sani Isla community. **$$$**

Eden Amazon Lodge A well-run community lodge with comfortable *cabañas* and good meals in the Yasuní park buffer zone. **$$$**

Napo Wildlife Center Wonderfully sited Kichwa-owned lodge with incredible wildlife, a great restaurant, terrific activities and deep community connections. **$$$**

Sani Lodge Another community-owned lodge right by a lagoon, with high levels of service and comfort, and plenty of wildlife. **$$$**

Sacha Lodge Accessible from Coca but in its own private reserve by a lake, Sacha has fab rooms with air-con and plenty of wildlife in and around camp. **$$$**

Nueva Rocafuerte

Hostal Chimborazo Right on the *malecón* with wooden fan rooms at the front and concrete air-con rooms at the back. **$**

Sacha Ñampi Ecolodge Just upriver from town, a community-run lodge with thatched-roofed rooms and diverse activities. **$$$**

Tena

MAP p191

Brisa del Rio A bright and spotless budget choice right in the heart of the *malecón* action. **$**

Hostal Los Yutzos Spacious, comfortable rooms set around a delightful riverside garden close to bars and restaurants. **$$**

Hostal Pakay Surrounded by woodland, this fine eco-minded hostel has a rural jungle-lodge atmosphere. **$**

Around Tena

p194

Sinchi Warmi This Río Napo Kichwa women's cooperative

offers all kinds of cultural activities for guests. **$**

Huasquila Lodge Just north of Cotundo, this well-run lodge has cozy rooms and top excursions in the area. **$$**

Hostería El Paraíso de Las Orquídeas Spacious grounds, a huge pool and comfortable *cabañas* make this place near Archidona a good base. **$$**

Reserva Biológica Río Bigal Deep in the forest, this place offers an immersive back-to-nature experience. Commit to a three-night minimum stay and enjoy some of the region's most unspoiled wilderness. **$$**

Anaconda Lodge On a peaceful island in the middle of the Napo, downstream from Punta Ahuano, the well-run Anaconda has comfortable wooden rooms on stilts and a fine restaurant. **$$$**

Liana Lodge Perched beside the Río Arajuno and backed by expansive forest, Liana Lodge has thatched huts with hot showers, porches with hammocks and an inviting open-air bar overlooking the river. **$$$**

Yachana Lodge Inhabiting dense forest close to the Napo, Yachana Lodge is a training center that prepares local residents for careers in conservation. It's a wonderful project. **$$$**

Hamadryade Lodge The stylish and ecofriendly Hamadryade Lodge, upstream from Misahuallí, has luxurious bungalows with jungle-view balconies and a fantastic pool and lounging area. **$$$**

Wild Sumaco Lodge Just south of Pacto Sumaco, Wild Sumaco Lodge is set atop a hill with sweeping views over the bird-rich forest and is a wonderful place to relax even if you're not attempting the summit hike. **$$$**

Misahuallí

El Albergue Español A well-priced and laid-back riverside hostel close to the main plaza. **$**

France-Amazonia On the road into town, this tranquil spot has shady thatched huts surrounding a sparkling pool. **$$**

Misahuallí Amazon Lodge Across the Río Misahuallí, with comfortable cabañas and a pool backed by a private nature reserve. **$$$**

Puyo

MAP p199

Posada Real On quiet grounds just a couple of blocks from the plaza with comfortable rooms decorated with antiques. **$**

Hostal Las Palmas A haven for independent travelers, with bright rooms, a good cafe and a fine terrace for sundowners. **$**

El Jardín A tranquil and luxurious spot surrounded by greenery just over the footbridge from Puyo's dining district. **$$$**

Southern Oriente

MAP p203

Hostal Casa Blanca Easily the best place to stay in Macas, with helpful staff and pleasant rooms surrounding a small pool. **$**

Posada D'León A cheap and friendly no-frills place above a pharmacy right in the heart of Gualaquiza. **$**

Casa Blanca Hortencia Located in sleepy Sucúa with comfortable rooms, a good-sized pool and a warm welcome. **$**

Huella Verde Rainforest Lodge On a bend on the Río Bobonaza, this intimate lodge offers treks through dense jungle, canoe trips with indigenous guides and chocolate-making workshops. **$$$**

Kapawi Ecolodge Ecuador's most remote jungle retreat is also one of its most remarkable. Owned and operated by the Achuar community, the lodge is surrounded by pristine primary forest; the lodge is only accessible by plane. **$$$**

Kapawi Ecolodge

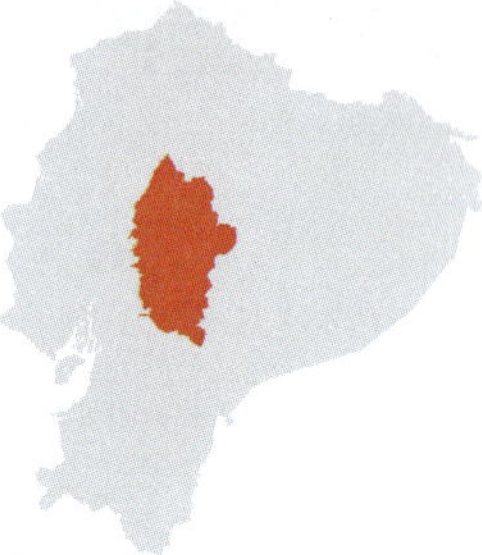

Researched by
Trent Holden

Central Highlands

VOLCANOES, ADVENTURE AND INDIGENOUS CULTURE

Venture into the heart of the Andes for outdoor adventure among stunning landscapes, rich indigenous culture and historical, vibrant cities.

Although the Andes extends 7500km along the length of South America and offers no shortage of highlights, it's in this central Ecuadorian stretch where you'll find some of the range's most dramatic moments. Known as La Avenida de los Volcanes (Avenue of Volcanoes), it's home to one-third of Ecuador's 65 volcanoes, a parade of 5000m-plus glacier-capped peaks that'll leave you humbled by both its stunning beauty and raw power.

With a mix of active, dormant and inactive volcanoes, its biggest attractions include Chimborazo and Cotopaxi, Ecuador's two-highest mountains. Both offer quintessential Andes landscapes, mixing *páramo* (grasslands), grazing llamas and indigenous villages, all set to a mighty backdrop of towering, snowcapped peaks.

JON CHICA/SHUTTERSTOCK

But whether you're a hardcore mountaineer or a day-tripper on a bus tour, you need to acclimatize before setting off gung-ho on any ascents. Altitude sickness isn't something you don't want to take lightly.

For hiking in the picturesque countryside of the Inter-Andean valley, the Quilotoa Loop is hard to beat and culminates at one of the most stunning viewpoints you'll ever see.

Baños is home to Ecuador's outdoor-adventure scene, where in between flinging yourself off bridges and taming white-water rapids, you'll find a scenic, relaxed hub famed for its natural surrounds and hot springs.

Among it all are delightful, relaxed indigenous villages, which when combined with the larger cities provide an intriguing mix of traditional Andean culture and modern-day living.

THE MAIN AREAS

PARQUE NACIONAL COTOPAXI
Biodiversity hub meets smoking volcano. p212

THE QUILOTOA LOOP
Ecuador's premier overland hiking trail. p218

AMBATO
City of rich literary legacy and handsome plazas. p227

BAÑOS
Adventure, relaxation and natural beauty. p231

VOLCÁN CHIMBORAZO
Earth's closest point to the sun. p236

For places to stay in Central Highlands, see p244

CSNAFZGER/SHUTTERSTOCK

Left: Baños (p231); above: Volcán Cotopaxi (p214)

Find Your Way

This central Andes corridor leads you along the Carretera Panamericana (Pan-American Hwy), from where its volcanoes and villages branch off. It's a well-trodden path, typically requiring only two- to three-hour bus journeys between stops.

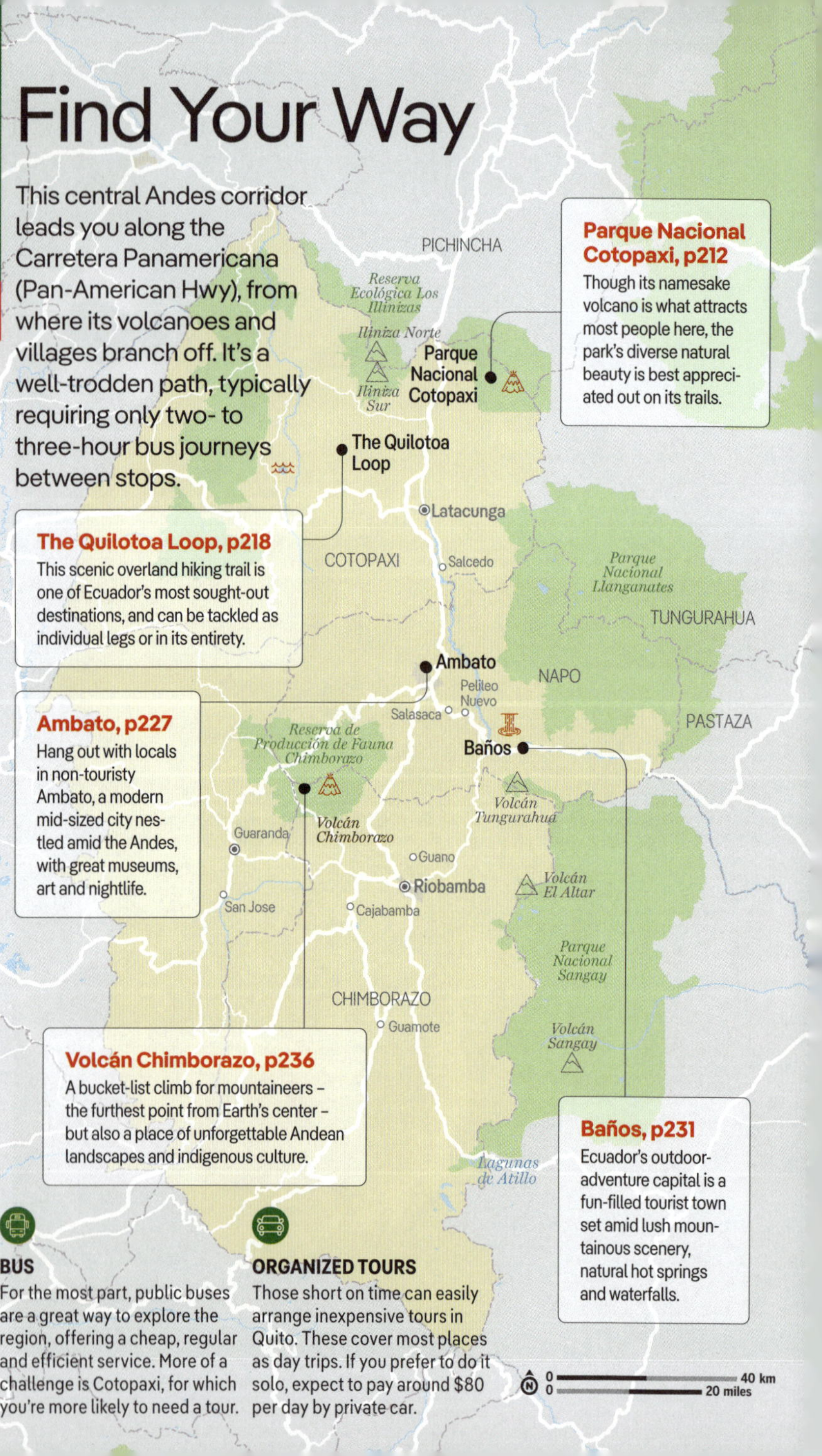

Parque Nacional Cotopaxi, p212

Though its namesake volcano is what attracts most people here, the park's diverse natural beauty is best appreciated out on its trails.

The Quilotoa Loop, p218

This scenic overland hiking trail is one of Ecuador's most sought-out destinations, and can be tackled as individual legs or in its entirety.

Ambato, p227

Hang out with locals in non-touristy Ambato, a modern mid-sized city nestled amid the Andes, with great museums, art and nightlife.

Baños, p231

Ecuador's outdoor-adventure capital is a fun-filled tourist town set amid lush mountainous scenery, natural hot springs and waterfalls.

Volcán Chimborazo, p236

A bucket-list climb for mountaineers – the furthest point from Earth's center – but also a place of unforgettable Andean landscapes and indigenous culture.

BUS

For the most part, public buses are a great way to explore the region, offering a cheap, regular and efficient service. More of a challenge is Cotopaxi, for which you're more likely to need a tour.

ORGANIZED TOURS

Those short on time can easily arrange inexpensive tours in Quito. These cover most places as day trips. If you prefer to do it solo, expect to pay around $80 per day by private car.

AMMIT JACK/SHUTTERSTOCK

Zip-lining, Baños (p232)

Plan Your Time

From climbing and mountain biking down volcanoes to zip-lining across canyons and hiking through the foothills of the Andes to visit indigenous market towns, this is one region that will keep you busy.

Pressed for Time

- If you're here for a good time not a long time, it's hard to pass up on the Cotopaxi–Quilotoa Loop–Baños route. This highlights reel will have you speeding down the slopes of **Cotopaxi** (p214) on a mountain bike, and leave you mesmerized by **Quilotoa's crater lake** (p220) before having you flying across canyons like Superman in **Baños** (p231).

One to Two Weeks

- Strap on the crampons and summit **Cotopaxi** (p214), completing the full **Quilotoa Loop** (p218), then explore the waterfalls around **Baños** (p231) by mountain bike. From there, head to mighty **Volcán Chimborazo** (p238), passing through **Ambato** (p227) and **Riobamba** (p240). Keen climbers should also allow time for **Iliniza Sur** (p226) and **Volcán Tungurahua** (p235).

Seasonal Highlights

JUN–AUG
Prime time for hikes and climbs with minimal rain, moderate temps and clearer skies. Prepare for all weather.

SEP–NOV
Shoulder season is a good time to visit, with fewer crowds, lower prices and, for the most part, optimal weather.

DEC–FEB
A good time to climb Chimborazo and other peaks. Fiesta and Christmas celebrations. Becoming rainy.

MAR–MAY
Rain and snow so avoid climbs, but there are fewer tourists and sunny mornings. Dries up from May.

Parque Nacional Cotopaxi

PEAKS | MOUNTAIN-BIKE DESCENTS | VIEWS

TOP TIP

A trip to Cotopaxi takes you up to heights of 5000m, so altitude will take its effect. Rather than visiting in your first few days, allow a period of acclimatization, and when visiting, drink plenty of water, avoid caffeine and eat before your ascent; coca leaves are also said to help.

Set amid the barren Andean landscapes of high-altitude *páramo* and tundra dotted with flowering shrubs and roaming wildlife is the 334 sq km of protected wilderness that makes up the Parque Nacional Cotopaxi. From its center rises its namesake attraction, the almighty Volcán Cotopaxi – a stratovolcano as picturesque as a giant snow cone. This is one of the world's tallest active volcanoes, and at less than 50km from Quito, it's one of the most anticipated stops on many travel itineraries.

The chance to climb its summit is what draws many, as does the memorable mountain-bike ride down from base camp. Along with other 4000m volcanic peaks, horse treks, hikes and archaeological ruins, there's plenty here to keep you busy.

In the park, keep your eyes peeled for wild horses, llamas, Andean foxes and the seldom-spotted Andean condor, puma and spectacled bear. Listen too for the endangered Andean marsupial tree frog.

A Stroll in the Park

Lakes, archaeological ruins and views

Beyond the many ascents, there's also plenty of hiking on flat ground in **Parque Nacional Cotopaxi**. Located at the base of Volcán Rumiñahui is the 2.6km **Laguna Limpiopungo**, a boardwalk loop that takes around one to 1½ hours to complete. In fine weather you'll see Cotopaxi reflected in its glassy

GETTING AROUND

There's no public transportation within the park, so getting around is only possible via foot, bike, horse, private car or organized tour. Given it's less than 50km from Quito, many visit Parque Nacional Cotopaxi as a day trip. However, it has memorable lodges, and those who stay overnight are rewarded with more reliable morning views and heaps of activities. If arriving from Quito's Quitumbe Terminal, Machachi or Latacunga, take a bus along the Pan-American Hwy, then arrange a local taxi for the final 15km to the park entrance for around $10.

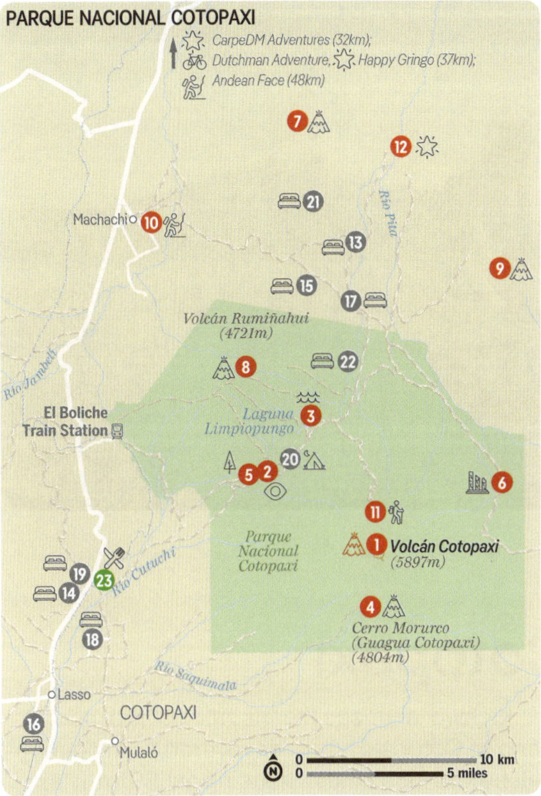

HIGHLIGHTS
1 Volcán Cotopaxi

SIGHTS
2 Centro Visitantes
3 Laguna Limpiopungo
4 Morurco
5 Parque Nacional Cotopaxi
6 Pucará del Salitre
7 Volcán Pasochoa
8 Volcán Rumiñahui
9 Volcán Sincholgaua

ACTIVITIES
10 Andes Climbing
11 Refugio José Rivas
12 Santa Rita Reserva Ecológica & Bike Park

SLEEPING
13 Chilcabamba
14 Cuscungo Cotopaxi
15 El Porvenir
16 Hacienda La Ciénega
17 Hacienda Los Mortiños
18 Hacienda San Agustín de Callo
19 Hotel Cuello de Luna
20 La Rinconada Chagrahuasi
21 Secret Garden Cotopaxi
22 Tambopaxi

EATING
see 13 Chilcabamba
see 11 Refugio José Rivas
23 Rondador Cotopaxi
see 22 Tambopaxi

surface making it a stunning spot for nature photographers – or anyone with a phone, really. Bird-watchers will have plenty to tick off (at least 45 species to be precise), with the Andean lapwing, Baird's sandpiper, Andean coot, caracara, Andean teal, Andean gull and solitary sandpiper all common visitors to the lagoon. Keep an eye out too for the Ecuadorian hillstar, one of the world's highest-altitude hummingbirds.

Another worthwhile spot is the fascinating 15th-century Inca ruins of **Pucará del Salitre**. Don't expect Machu Picchu; this hilltop archaeological site is not much more than stone walls from what is believed to have once been a military fortress. With Cotopaxi as its backdrop, it's an evocative site and a good excuse to head out on foot, bicycle or horseback to explore this remote section of Andean *páramo*.

Most of the lodges including **Tambopaxi** *(tambopaxi.com)*, **Secret Garden** *(secretgardencotopaxi.com)* and **Chilcabamba** *(chilcabamba.com/en)* offer guided hikes and horse treks to the aforementioned places as well as caves, canyons, waterfalls and crystal-clear springs.

continues on p216

ECUADORPOSTALES/SHUTTERSTOCK

TOP EXPERIENCE

Volcán Cotopaxi

With a name that in the Kichwa language means 'neck of the moon', the highly active volcano of Cotopaxi has been revered by indigenous communities since well before Inca times. Standing at 5897m, it is Ecuador's second-highest mountain after Chimborazo. On a day when the weather aligns, this perfectly symmetrical, snowcapped cone is a truly majestic sight.

DON'T MISS

- Peak Summit
- Base Camp
- Mountain Biking
- Horse Riding
- Post-Hike Relaxation

Scaling Ecuador's Most Iconic Peak

Those who wish to summit the glacial peak of **Volcán Cotopaxi** may be in luck. Eruptions in 2015 and 2022 caused its closure for several years, but since late 2024, climbing has recommenced.

Check for the latest updates, but it's a two-day climb that requires an experienced guide and all the gear – ice picks, crampons, ropes, helmets, harnesses – all of which is provided by guide companies. Though you don't need to be an experienced mountaineer to reach the top, the high altitude, freezing temperatures (wind chill of -8°C) and physical demands make it a very challenging endeavor.

PRACTICALITIES

● free entrance, but guests must register on arrival ● 8am-5pm; car access closes 3pm

Also, did we mention ascents take place at night? Most trips set off from base camp around midnight to reach the summit for sunrise. It may sound hardcore, but well-prepared beginners usually make it to the top – and once you do, life-affirming views over the Andes make it all worthwhile.

Reaching Base Camp

If you're not feeling adventurous enough to reach the top, don't worry, you'll still get to enjoy Cotoxpaxi at close range as you make the drive up to its base camp, **Refugio José Rivas** *(facebook.com/refugiocotopaxijoseribas)*, at 4864m. Though the refuge is only a 2km hike from the car park, a 2000m ascent is very different to your normal 2km stroll, so it's a breathless slog that'll take you anywhere from 45 minutes to one hour as you trudge up its volcanic ash trail. Awaiting at the refuge are extraordinary vistas and a **kiosk** with warming mugs of hot chocolate and coca-leaf tea.

Mountain Biking

When it comes to once-in-a-lifetime experiences, tearing down the face of one the world's most active volcanoes on a mountain bike is right up there. It may sound intimidating, but you don't need to be an extreme-sports nut to tackle this: you can take it as slow (or fast!) as you like.

The descent follows a switchback gravel road down to Laguna Limpiopungo and is an activity included on most tour itineraries. Being immersed in these stunning landscapes with the bracing Andes air rushing in your face is as thrilling as it sounds. But remember to go slow: riding on gravel is slippery. Check your brakes before setting out, and take up that offer to wear kneepads! Or you can take the tour bus down and start your ride on flat ground at Cotopaxi's base.

Horse Riding

Horseback is another unique way to experience Cotopaxi. Whether galloping or ambling across the rugged terrain of the high Andean plains, it's a great way to connect with nature as you live out those poncho-wearing *chagra* (Ecuadorina cowboy and cowgirl) dreams. Treks vary from a few hours to multiday expeditions. Tambopaxi (p244), El Porvenir (p217) and Secret Garden (p244), among others, offer tours that cover all corners of the park and are suitable for all levels.

Post-Hike Relaxation

Once you're back from a day of icy, high-altitude adventure, there's nothing better than soothing aching muscles amid the warm cosiness of Cotopaxi's mountain lodges. Guests staying at Secret Garden (p244) can soak in a hot tub perfectly framed by views of Cotopaxi, veg out in trampoline-style hammocks or stretch in a yoga class. Most lodges also feature wood-burning stove heaters either in rooms or communal spaces – ideal for thawing out with a pre- and post-dinner tipple.

RECOMMENDED OPERATORS

Secret Garden Offers summit and base-camp tours, horse riding, and trips to waterfalls and nearby volcanoes.

Andean Face Dutch-Ecuadorian mountaineering company based in Quito.

CarpeDM Adventures Favorite with Quito day-trippers keen to mountain bike from base camp.

Happy Gringo Dutch-English operators offering personalized and group tours from Quito.

Dutchman Adventure Ecuador's pioneer mountain-biking outfit, guiding rides through forests, lakes and Inca ruins.

Andes Climbing Specializes in regional ascents. Based in nearby Machachi.

COTOPAXI'S ERUPTIONS

Volcán Cotopaxi (p214) has a long history of violent eruptions. The poor city of Latacunga has been destroyed several times over the centuries, while in 1877 volcanic mudflows flowed as far as the Pacific in the west and the Amazon in the east. After a lull of more than a century, new eruptions in 2015 saw thousands of locals evacuated. In late 2022, ash plumes soared 1100m and ash falls reached as far as Quito – an eruption that lasted right through till July 2023.

That said, it's also among the world's most monitored volcanoes. Some 60 stations are equipped with seismometers, gas meters, thermal cameras, lahar detectors etc – so vulcanologists are confident about predicting eruptions.

JESS KRAFT/SHUTTERSTOCK

El Porvenir

continued from p213

Getting the Lowdown on Cotopaxi

Eruptions and ecology

Stop by Cotopaxi's **visitor center** (*free; 8am-5pm*) for interesting insights into its geological makeup – including coverage of its volatile past, global warming impacts, and native flora and fauna. It also delves into *chagra* (cowboy) culture and profiles on surrounding volcanoes.

Cotopaxi's Surrounding Peaks

Take your pick of many climbs

Volcán Cotopaxi isn't the only volcano summit within reach of the national park that can be scaled.

Overlooking Laguna Limpiopungo, **Volcán Rumiñahui** (4721m) is the dormant neighbor to Cotopaxi. Named after the Inca warrior who allegedly hid treasure in the nearby Llanganates region, Rumiñahui comprises three peaks of which the central summit (4634m) is the smallest and most straightforward. Though you could do this five-hour hike (one way) independently, it's always best to take a guide for what is sometimes a bit of a scramble. The views from up here, right in the middle of the Avenue of the Volcanoes, are to be savored.

Located 17km north of Cotopaxi, **Volcán Sincholgaua** (4920m) is another extinct volcano and Ecuador's 12th highest. A Kichwa word meaning 'steep upwards', it's an apt name for this pointy-peaked summit. It's a challenging and technical climb requiring full climbing equipment, but it rewards climbers with superb views across to Volcán Cotopaxi.

Other options are **Morurco** (4844m), to the south of the park, a six-hour climb to its summit, while just outside the national park is **Volcán Pasochoa** (4200m). Extinct since the last ice age, this is a perfect choice for climbers looking to get acclimatized; count on around 3½ hours to reach the summit and about two to descend. Treks up Pasochoa are included in the package for those staying at Secret Garden (p244).

Cascades, Camping & Cycling

Waterfalls and mountain biking

Sitting on the northern outskirts of Parque Nacional Cotopaxi, **Santa Rita Reserva Ecológica & Bike Park** *(facebook.com/reservasantarita)* takes in 300 hectares of pristine nature along the forested slopes of Volcán Pasochoa. Visit for waterfall treks (per person $5), mountain-bike trails and a bucolic riverside campground. Call ahead for bike rental.

Stepping Back in Time

A unique place to spend a night

If you can stretch your budget, it's well worth splurging on a night or two at one of the fabulous historic haciendas around Parque Nacional Cotopaxi. Many have been in the same families for generations and are lovingly restored, offering far more than just a place to sleep. Staying here is a complete experience, combining history, atmosphere and adventure: guests can ride horses, hike or mountain bike in the national park, then return to hearty, home-style Ecuadorian cooking by a roaring fire. Some haciendas date back two or three centuries, making a stay feel like sleeping inside a living museum.

Hacienda San Agustín de Callo *(incahacienda.com)* is the most storied: a 15th-century Inca palace used by the French Geodesic Mission in 1748 to measure the equator, and later visited by mountaineers Alexander von Humboldt and Edward Whymper. Dating to 1696, **Hacienda La Ciénega** *(haciendalacienega.com)*, between Cotopaxi and Quilotoa, is palatial, with elegant rooms and refined cuisine. Working ranch **El Porvenir** *(tierradelvolcan.com)* offers rustic luxury, outstanding volcano views, horse riding, cycling and a spa, while **Cuello de Luna** *(cuellodeluna.com)*, a remodeled 18th-century estate, features fireplaces and local produce.

DECLINING SNOWS OF COTOPAXI

Dominating the skyline from afar, few symbols of climate change stand on public display quite like Cotopaxi's giant snowcone. Its glaciers have shrunk by around 50% since the 1950s, making the impacts of global warming visible in real time. Once considered permanent, its snows could eventually vanish altogether as rising temperatures combine with periodic volcanic activity. Cotopaxi is not alone. Tropical glaciers across the Andes are retreating rapidly as warmer oceans and air increasingly bring rain instead of snow. Nearby peaks such as Carihuairazo and Tungurahua have lost their glaciers entirely, while Iliniza Sur retains little or none, placing increasing pressure on water security for ecosystems, agriculture and hydropower.

Has a petting zoo that includes llamas.

EATING AROUND COTOPAXI: BEST FOR LUNCH

Rondador Cotopaxi: Popular bistro doing breakfasts, sandwiches and Ecuadorian mains. Also offers accommodations. *8am-8pm* $

Refugio José Rivas: At 4864m this base-camp cafe serves cheese empanadas, chicken soup, sandwiches, coca-leaf tea and hot choc. *8am-4pm* $

Tambopaxi: The only restaurant inside the park offers a cozy trekking teahouse atmosphere with Ecuadorian mountain fare (go the trout) and stunning views. *8am-8pm* $$

Chilcabamba: Tasteful spot offering a seasonal menu of Andean and international fusion using local produce, including grilled trout with blueberry sauce and walnuts. *8am-8pm* $$

The Quilotoa Loop

VILLAGES | MARKETS | LAKE VIEWS

One of the biggest attractions of the central Andes, if not all Ecuador, this overland village-to-village trekking adventure (p220) immerses you among volcanic craters, cloud forest, farmland and spectacular valleys.

Weekly Markets

Experience authentic Andean highland culture

Sure, we get you're here to trek the Quilotoa Loop, but if your schedule happens to align with one of the region's colorful market days, don't miss this opportunity to experience authentic Andean highland culture. Ordinarily, most of these quiet towns offer limited attractions – until market day, when they erupt with color and commotion as indigenous villagers descend from all corners for their weekly shop. Don't expect tourist trinkets or handicrafts; these markets are the real deal, which, ultimately, is what many tourists to South America are searching for.

Saquisilí is the must-see market on the loop. Regarded as one of Ecuador's best, it attracts villagers from across the region to sell produce, livestock and household goods. Located 22km northwest of Latacunga, Saquisilí was once the starting point for the Quilotoa trek, though today it's rarely visited outside market day.

Tucked away 15km southwest of Tigua, **Zumbahua** hosts a lively Saturday market, which brings in every indigenous man, woman and their llama for an abundance of produce.

On Monday it's the turn of **Guantualo**, a small rural village – accessed via a scenic one-hour valley trek from Isinliví – holding its weekly livestock market (not one for vegetarians) popular with Kichwa-speaking locals in red ponchos and black fedoras.

Pujilí, west of Latacunga, is worth visiting Wednesday or Sunday for pottery, while along the route, **Chugchilán** and **Sigchos** host Sunday markets with a vibrant atmosphere.

Tigua

Discover local indigenous Kichwa art

On the southern slopes of Quilotoa, **Tigua** (elevation 3500m) is a one-street town of galleries featuring the works of local indigenous Kichwa artists. In the 1970s, artist Julio Toaquiza was inspired to use canvases to express the distinctive, colorful style used for many generations to decorate drum skins. Inspired by scenes from Kichwa legends set against the beautiful Andean scenery,

GETTING AROUND

From Quilotoa, many take the bus back to Latacunga to collect their bags. To get to Sigchos or Quilotoa you can take a bus from Latacunga (two hours). The last bus back to Latacunga is 5pm. Otherwise, a taxi from Latacunga to Sigchos or Quilotoa is $50. There are also two daily buses departing from Quito's Quitumbe Terminal Terrestre to Sigchos (3½ hours). A day trip from Quito is another option.

TOP TIP

The good news is the Quilotoa Loop can be hiked year-round. Expect four seasons in one day (or even one hour), so come prepared. Start early, as mornings often bring clear blue skies. Peak season runs from June to October. The rainy season (bringing lush green scenery) generally runs November to May, though rain is intermittent and doesn't usually arrive till the afternoon.

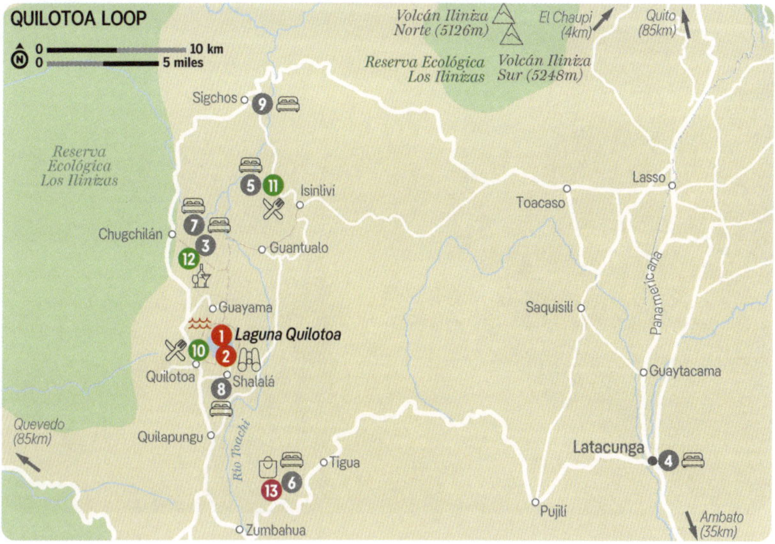

HIGHLIGHTS
1 Laguna Quilotoa

SIGHTS
2 Mirador de Cristal Shalalá

SLEEPING
3 Black Sheep Inn
4 Golden Rest
see 3 Hostal Cloud Forest
see 4 Hostal Tiana
5 Llullu Llama
6 Posada de Tigua
7 Puyu Pacha
8 Shalalá
9 Starlight Mountain Lodge

EATING
10 Kirutwa Mushuc Wasi
11 Taxoloma Saloon

DRINKING & NIGHTLIFE
12 Country Bar

SHOPPING
13 Galería Tío Lobo
see 13 Julio Toaquiza Tigasi
see 13 Kuntur Wasi
see 13 Museo Galería Tigua

Tigua art is a movement in itself – vibrant works featured on canvases and decorative masks. It's continued by generations of the Toaquiza family, including all of Julio's seven children! You'll find the master at work at **Julio Toaquiza Tigasi** *(@juliotoaquiza tigas)*, a space shared with his son Wilson and daughters Magdalena, Luzmila and Targelia. Internationally acclaimed Gustavo Toaquiza is at **Galería Tío Lobo** *(gustavotoaquiza.com)*, Alfredo Toaquiza is at **Museo Galería Tigua** *(facebook.com/artedetigua)* and Alfonso is at **Kuntur Wasi** *(@kunturwasialfonsotoaquiza)* – where you can create your very own Tigua artwork with a hands-on lesson. Alfonso's wife, Anita, is also a painter, as is their son, Sinchi, a third-generation artist who also runs a Ayahuasca healing retreat from here (WhatsApp: +593-99-604-1951).

EATING & DRINKING ON THE LOOP: OUR PICKS

Taxoloma Saloon: Post-trekking heaven awaits in Isinliví with wood-fired pizzas (book in advance), authentic pastas, negronis and espresso. *1-8pm* **$**

Kirutwa Mushuc Wasi: Stunning Laguna Quilotoa vistas and Ecuadorian cuisine (including local trout). Proceeds help support local indigenous communities. *8:30am-9pm* **$**

Posada de Tigua: At this historic farmhouse and working ranch outside Tigua, enjoy homegrown dairy, quinoa, breads and soups by the fire. Call ahead. *noon-2pm* **$$**

Country Bar: The pub the night before a big trek? What could go wrong? Surely one (or two) by the fire in Chugchilán won't hurt... *10am-3am*

FABIO C N/SHUTTERSTOCK

Laguna Quilotoa

TOP EXPERIENCE

Hiking the Quilotoa Loop

Most tackle the loop in a counterclockwise direction, following the Sigchos–Isinliví–Chugchilán–Quilotoa route to finish with astonishing views of the namesake crater lake.

DON'T MISS

- Quilotoa
- The Lake
- Sigchos
- Isinliví
- Chugchilán
- Trekking Lodges
- Weekly Markets
- Tigua

Quilotoa

The pinnacle of the namesake loop hike – **Laguna Quilotoa** – is one of the most astonishing caldera lakes you'll ever see.

Assuming you've trudged up from Chugchilán (p218), a spectacular yet lung-burning 11.4km last leg, the way the lake is unveiled upon arrival is one of the most fitting rewards for a hike we've seen. Nothing compensates for the pain better than a view like this! It's literally breathtaking, taking in the 3km-wide caldera while catching your breath at 4000m.

Fortunately, a rustic kiosk sells coca-leaf tea to help warm you and ward off altitude sickness while you refocus on this awe-inspiring sight before you.

Now dormant, the caldera formed when the volcano last erupted some 800 years ago. In tune with the ever-changing

PRACTICALITIES

● quilotoaloop.com ● per person arriving by bus or car $2

weather, the lake's colors shift dramatically – from emerald to turquoise to slate and everything in between.

Enjoy it and pat yourself on the back for reaching the top, but you're not quite there yet. Somewhat cruelly, there's still another 45-minute trek to the village of **Quilotoa** – quite demoralizing given you think you've already made it. But it's an interesting final stretch, one that follows the rim of the crater while taking you through surreal landscapes of sandy dunes and narrow canyon passes, until you finally reach the village. Phew. Now you really can relax.

This is by far the most touristy village on the loop. Amid selfie platforms, llama photo-ops and restaurants, you'll find stalls selling alpaca ponchos and local artwork. The village also has a small museum, a tourist information office and an ATM. Unfortunately, all accommodations sit across the road, meaning none maximize the lake views.

If you're coming from the other direction or just visiting by bus for the day, don't worry – the views here are equally spectacular, with a viewing deck that allows you to take it all in. Though starting in Quilotoa may mean you avoid the final steep climb of the classic route, do keep in mind the lake sits at an altitude of 3914m, which can be challenging. Therefore it's recommended that you are properly acclimatised before embarking on the direct journey to the lake.

The Lake

There's more to do here than simply gawking at the lake, hence it's worth staying an additional night to explore.

You can walk the entire crater rim on foot in around six hours, though avoid high winds, as conditions can be dangerous.

A 1.6km walk along the eastern edge of the crater brings you to **Shalalá**, a small, community-run indigenous tourism project with one of the nicest lodges in the area (p223). Stop by its art-and-crafts gallery – if you're buying souvenirs, this impoverished community is the place to do it. Shalalá also operates the sleek **Mirador de Cristal Shalalá** *($2)* viewing deck.

You can descend to the lake itself via a steep, zigzagging path (30 minutes down, roughly an hour back up – only attempt this if properly acclimatized). **Kayaks** *(per 30min $3)* can be hired for a paddle, offering an entirely new, spectacular perspective from below. Note: there's no swimming due to volcanic minerals – not to mention it's freezing!

Sigchos

Marking the unofficial start of the Quilotoa Loop is the relaxed market town of **Sigchos** (2850m). It's a pleasant enough place and a good stop to help with acclimatization before building up to Quilotoa at nearly 4000m. Many trekkers start right away, but Sigchos is worthy of one night. In the town center you'll find a market and few restaurants overlooking the plaza where you can take in its languid pace of life. You can also visit a local 'winery' producing local fruit varietals; tours

SAFE TRAVELS

Not actually a loop but a point-to-point trek, there are no rules on how you tackle it: you can walk it, drive it, bus it or mix it up, depending on time, fitness and weather.

The entire trek is around 35km, and for those on foot it takes anywhere between two and five days. For the classic route, distances between towns include Sigchos to Isinliví (14km; three to five hours); Isinliví to Chugchilán (12km; four to six hours); and Chugchilán to Quilotoa (12km; six to eight hours).

For the most part, the Quilotoa Loop is a very safe trail with few risks. But with steep ascents and high altitudes, don't underestimate the physical demands. Most trekkers hike independently, but hiring a guide ($30 per day) isn't a bad idea in case something goes wrong. If trekking solo, aim to inform your guesthouse of your ETA, as there's no phone signal. Dogs can be protective, so avoid entering private property, and if they're aggressive, calmly ignore them by gazing up to the sky to avoid eye contact, or pick up a stone. Cows, especially mothers with calves, should always be given a wide berth.

TOP TIPS

- Trails are mostly signed, but download offline maps such as AllTrails.
- Carry plenty of water; none is available between towns.
- Order packed lunches from lodges; snacks available in villages.
- Start early for reliable weather and relaxed arrivals.
- Travel light and leave main bags at **Hostal Tiana** (p244) in Latacunga.
- Pack sunscreen, hat, rain gear, swimwear, warm layers and dry shoes.
- Bring enough cash; card payments are rare and there's only one ATM in Quilotoa.
- There's no network on the trail; lodges have wi-fi.

best arranged through **Starlight Mountain Lodge** *(facebook.com/starlightsigchos)*.

From here, trekkers embark on the 10.7km trek to Isinliví, winding through scenic farmland set among emerald valleys and dramatic mountain backdrops. Signage can be unreliable – many miss the turnoff – so stay alert and, speaking from experience, don't blindly trust the blue signs! Be sure to download offline maps such as AllTrails. Much of the route is fairly flat, but brace yourself for a brutal steep finish.

Isinliví

A favorite stop for many is the blissfully sleepy village of **Isinliví** (elevation 2900m). The second stop on the 'classic' route, this is the kind of place where days can easily turn into weeks.

Most stay one night here before legging it to Chugchilán, but those with time should linger for day hikes – including to a nearby *pucará* (pre-Inca hill fortress) and to Guantualo for its Monday market. **Llullu Llama** *(llullullama.com)* runs local tours to a cheese factory and woodcarving workshop, along with horse riding, cow milking and a local wine factory. Another unexpected find in this neck of the woods is what's possibly Ecuador's best Italian restaurant, Taxoloma Saloon (p219).

The onward hike to Chugchilán is a 12.4km undulating trail through epic valleys and picture-perfect countryside. Expect poor signage, a sketchy river crossing and yet another steep finish.

MATYAS REHAK/ALAMY

Hostal Cloud Forest

Chugchilán

A welcome sight for weary travelers, **Chugchilán** (3200m) is where most hikers spend their second or third night. Guesthouses with cold beer and saunas play no small part in this, perfect for a bit of rest and recovery!

Surrounded by forest, it's one of the prettiest villages on the loop. While geared toward tourism with plenty of accommodations, cafes and the Country Bar (p219) pub, it retains its relaxed, local village atmosphere.

From here, it's an 11.4km slog to Quilotoa Lake. Start early for what is a punishing but ultimately rewarding ascent.

Trekking Lodges

Trust us, you'll be feeling it at the end of each day's hike, which culminates with hardcore climbs to reach the finish line. But don't worry, lodges know all about it and await to cater to your needs – and for many this is a highlight of the trek. Most have communal dinners, making it easy to meet fellow trekkers for the next day, too.

In Isinliví, Llullu Llama is one of the best lodges on the loop. This Dutch-Ecuadorian-run farmhouse has been transformed into cozy dorms and villas with wood-burning stoves, composting toilets and sweeping valley views. It also offers a hot tub, yoga, spa treatments, sauna, community tours and crafts supporting local female artisans.

Puyu Pacha *(puyupachaadventure.com)* literally sits above the clouds high above Chugchilán, with astonishing, cloud-filled valley views – especially at sunset. Run by a delightful local family, stays include home-cooked Ecuadorian meals, homemade whiskey that's distilled with Andean flowers and enjoyed fire-side, and activities such as milking cows, visits to the local cheese factory and guided valley walks through the forest. There are plenty of hummingbirds in the garden, too. It's off trail, so you'll need transportation here, but it's worth the effort.

Also in Chugchilán, **Hostal Cloud Forest** *(cloudforesthostal.com)* offers some of the warmest hospitality on the trail. The family-run lodge has comfortable, well-priced rooms, fireplaces and a communal restaurant. Guided horse-riding tours are also available. **Black Sheep Inn** *(blacksheepinn.com)* is Chugchilán's classiest option, with strong eco-credentials to go with the sauna, hot tub, yoga, all-vegetarian cuisine and famously good homemade cookies. And yes, there are actually black sheep here, too.

Synonymous with Sigchos, **Starlight Mountain Lodge** *(facebook.com/starlightsigchos)* sits conveniently by the trailhead, rents mountain bikes, and has a pool table and bar, along with great local community-based tours.

LOCAL ADVICE

Edmundo Vega, a founder of the Quilotoa Loop and manager of **Golden Rest** *(goldenrestecuador.com)* in Latacunga.

Tell us about how the Quilotoa Loop Trek came to be. This did not originate as a conventional tourist route, but as a living path historically used by local communities to connect Sigchos, Isinliví, Chugchilán and Quilotoa. Knowing the region deeply, I, with local guides and travelers committed to responsible tourism, helped structure the route while preserving its cultural, human and natural essence.

Why should travelers hike it? Many say the Quilotoa Loop Trek is among South America's most breathtaking and authentic hikes. It is not just a destination, but a life-changing journey about walking slowly, breathing deeply and being connected.

Beyond the Quilotoa Loop

Get off the tourist trail and visit some lesser-known volcanoes and trails before hanging out in the underrated city of Latacunga.

Places

Latacunga p224
Reserva Ecológica Los Ilinizas p226

GETTING AROUND

Latacunga is a very walkable city, making it a convenient, self-contained destination for sightseeing. The bus terminal is about a 15-minute walk from the city; otherwise taxi fares will rarely exceed a few dollars. For Reserva Ecológica Los Ilinizas you'll need to make your way first to El Chaupi. Here you can arrange a pickup truck to La Virgen ($10), from where the rest is on foot as you set off for Refugio Nuevos Horizontes (three hours) – the base camp for tackling one of its twin peaks.

If you're here to do Quilotoa, chances are you'll end up in Latacunga. This attractive Andean city is the 'big smoke' of the region, a relaxed colonial town offering a surprising wealth of sights and restaurants that make it a popular base for travelers in between hikes. Despite being destroyed not once but three times by an erupting Cotopaxi in the 18th and 19th centuries, it still retains a distinct historical feel.

More towering highlights, part of the Avenida de los Volcanes, await in Reserva Ecológica Los Ilinizas. The twin peaks of Iliniza Sur and Iliniza Norte are both enticing options for climbers, while hikers have endless trails amid the *páramo.*

Latacunga

TIME FROM QUILOTOA: **2HR**

Get into the spirit of Fiesta de la Mama Negra

Held twice a year in September and November, Latacunga's famous **Fiesta de la Mama Negra** honors La Virgen de las Mercedes, the patron saint believed to protect the city from Cotopaxi's eruptions. Though a white man portraying a black woman wouldn't fly in most parts of the world, here it's embraced wholeheartedly as part of Latacunga's indigenous, Spanish and African heritage. There's much merry-making with processions, costumes, fireworks, street dancing and Andean music. Locals say September feels more authentic; November includes a bullfight.

Mama Negra's presence is felt throughout the city, emblazoned on murals and restaurants. To learn more about her and other fiesta characters, head to **Casa de los Marqueses**

You can't miss its ostentatious colonnaded facade.

EATING IN LATACUNGA: LOCAL FAVORITES

Pollos Jimmy's: Salivate over juicy charcoal chooks rotating in the rotisserie before digging into Jimmy's famously delicious BBQ chicken. *10:30-9pm* $

Guadalajara Grill: The vibrant Frida Blue facade and Day of the Dead motifs draw in diners for traditional Mexican flavors. *noon-3pm & 5:30-9:30pm Mon-Sat* $

Chugchucaras La Mamá Negra: Serves Latacunga's specialty, *chugchucara*: pork upon pork with plantains, potatoes and toasted corn. *11am-6pm Mon-Sat* $$

El Alabado: Sample a steak at this Argentinian restaurant in a 17th-century building overlooking Parque Bolívar. *12:30-3:30pm & 6-10pm Tue-Sun* $$

CHURCHES & MUSEUMS: LATACUNGA ON FOOT

Latacunga's irresistible charm lies in its cobblestone roads and the historical buildings, museums and markets that line them.

START	END	LENGTH
Hostal Tiana	Mirador de la Virgen del Calvario	3km; 2hr

Starting from ❶ **Hostal Tiana** (p244), wander down this mural-filled passageway draped with colorful umbrellas and turn right to reach grand ❷ **Iglesia de Santo Domingo** (c 1690) to admire its richly painted interior.

Continue north to ❸ **Casa de los Marqueses de Miraflores**, an 18th-century mansion hidden behind high walls that today serves as a museum with Inca artifacts and exhibits on the Fiesta de la Mama Negra.

Follow the mansion walls to reach ❹ **Iglesia Católica La Merced** (c 1797), home to the Virgen de las Mercedes, Latacunga's patron saint and protector from Cotopaxi's eruptions.

Pass a small market and turn left, walking 10 minutes to reach Latacunga's main square, ❺ **El Salto**, and ❻ **Mercado Cerrado**, selling produce and tasty Ecuadorian dishes.

Head south along the river to ❼ **Casa de la Cultura**, an old stone watermill housing ethnographic and art exhibits. Continue east to reach the city's centerpiece, palm-filled ❽ **Parque Vicente León**, framed by ❾ **Catedral Católica de Latacunga** and ❿ **Palacio Municipal**. Cross handsome ⓫ **Parque Bolívar** with namesake statue, then climb to ⓬ **Mirador de la Virgen del Calvario** for city views.

WHY I LOVE THE CENTRAL HIGHLANDS

Trent Holden, Lonely Planet writer

I really love the bigger towns in this central Andes region: Latacunga, Ambato, Riobamba etc. These aren't destinations high on any traveler's list, and perhaps that's part of their appeal, adding a more authentic flavor. Ironically, never have I felt more off the beaten track than in the big towns! They strike just the right balance of being big enough to offer a great array of food and cultural attractions but small enough not be plagued by traffic jams and petty crime. It's the blend of mountainous surrounds, indigenous culture, colonial architecture and contemporary living that makes me feel like I've hit upon the *real* Ecuador.

Refugio Nuevos Horizontes (p244)

de Miraflores *(free)*, which displays history on the festival as well as other artifacts including those dating from Inca times.

Reserva Ecológica Los Ilinizas

TIME FROM QUILOTOA: **2½HR**

Volcano summits and grassland hikes

Cotopaxi, Chimborazo, Quilotoa: there are a lot of volcanoes and hikes vying for your attention in this central stretch of the Andes. However, if you're seeking a different path, **Reserva Ecológica Los Ilinizas** covers 150,000 hectares of *páramo*, cloud forest, lakes and valleys, and offers great rewards. There are endless hiking trails, but the twin peaks of Iliniza Norte and Iliniza Sur lure most people here. Located 55km south of Quito, this protected area extends through to the north of the Quilotoa Loop, and is popular among climbers acclimatizing before tackling Chimborazo or Cotopaxi. **Iliniza Norte** (5126m) is the less technical, but it's still demanding and requires experience and a qualified guide. The glacier-topped **Iliniza Sur** (5248m) is for experienced climbers only, requiring training and full mountaineering equipment. Both trailheads start from Refugio Nuevos Horizontes (p244), a mountain cabin that sleeps 25; BYO sleeping bag and supplies. To get here, it's a two-hour hike from the parking lot at La Virgen shrine, 9km from the village of **El Chaupi**, the main access point to the park.

DRINKING IN LATACUNGA: RELAXED BARS

El Gringo y La Gorda: Hidden away in an atmospheric courtyard, this romantic bar-bistro is perfect for a candlelit glass of vino or two. *4-10pm Tue-Sat*

El Abuelo: Popular drinking den for an evening tipple and meal in a cozy, character-filled bar or front courtyard. *3-11pm Mon-Sat*

Prost Rooftop: Sunset craft beers, cocktails and burgers accompanied by sweeping views. *3-10pm Mon & Tue, noon-midnight Wed & Thu, to 2am Fri & Sat*

Brew Lab: Make the steep climb up to this nanobrewery to taste four ales crafted by the passionate young brewer. Call ahead. *4-10pm Thu-Sat*

Ambato

LITERARY HERITAGE | FOOD | MUSEUMS

If you enjoyed Quito's vibrant art and food scene, chances are you'll like Ambato, too. Sure, it doesn't have the same grandeur or energy as the capital, but it does offer a relaxed stay, where you can observe Andean culture in a contemporary 21st-century setting.

Ambato, the Central Highlands' largest city, was badly damaged by an earthquake in 1947 that flattened a lot of the old city, but it's been rebuilt and is now a sophisticated and culturally rich destination. It has a proud literary heritage, an interesting mix of museums, mural-decorated facades, attractive plazas and botanical gardens. Among it all is a student scene that fuels a lively nightlife to go with some great local food experiences.

Though conveniently located on the main tourist route, Ambato is often bypassed by travelers hell-bent on getting to Quilotoa, Cuenca, Baños or Chimborazo – making it a refreshingly intact and non-touristy stop.

TOP TIP

Right on Ambato's doorstep are quite a few villages that will appeal to those looking to get off the beaten track. Check out Tungurahua's tourism website *(tungurahuaturismo.com)*, which has excellent info on indigenous communities and artisanal towns to visit.

Parque Life

City of culture

At Ambato's heart sits the stately **Parque Cevallos**, shaded by palms and Paraná pine and ideal for sitting and watching local life unfold. It's overlooked by heritage buildings, most notably the monumental Colegio Bolívar, home to the **Museo del Colegio Bolívar** *(free)*. Its eclectic collection ranges from taxidermy displays – including hummingbirds, an Andean condor and enormous tarantulas – to Amazonian ethnology

GETTING AROUND

Ambato's city center is very walkable, which is convenient given many of its main sights are located here. Otherwise there's Uber and an abundance of taxis for cross-town jaunts.

A number of worthwhile day trips to villages are best reached by hired taxi, costing about $10 per 10km (or around $50 a day).

Ambato's **main bus terminal** (Terminal Terrestre), 1.5km northeast of the city center, has buses to Banos, Latacunga, Quito etc. and local 'centro' buses or taxis ($1.50) downtown. If coming from the south, buses may drop you nearer to Terminal Terrestre Sur, 7.5km south of the city – be prepared to hail a taxi to your hotel.

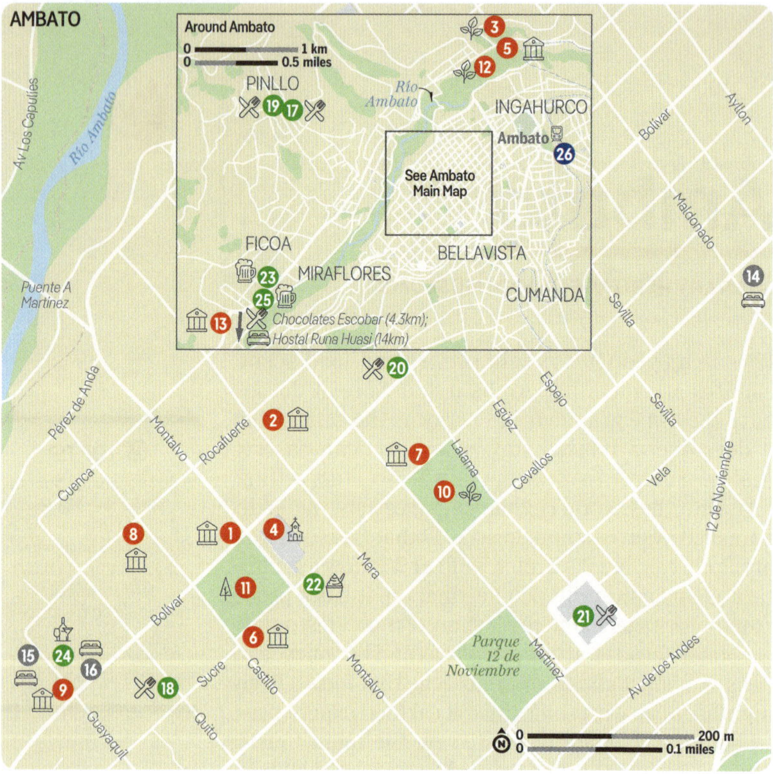

SIGHTS
1 Casa y Mausoleo de Montalvo
2 Hambatu Museo de la Ciudad
3 Jardín Botánico Atocha-La Liria
4 La Catedral
5 Martínez-Holguín House Museum
6 Museo de la Cultura Salasaka
7 Museo del Colegio Bolívar
8 Museo Juan Benigno Vela
9 Museo Pictórico Edmundo Martínez
see 6 Museo Provincial Casa del Portal
10 Parque Cevallos
11 Parque Montalvo
12 Quinta de Juan León Mera
13 Quinta de Juan Montalvo

SLEEPING
14 Hostal Napoles Emperador II
15 Hotel Ambato
16 Hotel Roka Plaza

EATING
17 Casa El Recreo
18 Delicias del Paso
19 El Legítimo Pan de Pinllo
20 La Fuente & Cafetería
21 Mercado Central
22 Ponche Suizo
see 16 Restaurant Roka Plaza

DRINKING & NIGHTLIFE
23 Ficoa Beer Garden
see 16 Lab Bar
24 Manhattan
25 Nünna

TRANSPORT
26 Main Bus Terminal

EATING IN AMBATO: OLD-SCHOOL DELIGHTS

El Legítimo Pan de Pinllo: Dating to the 1890s, this fifth-generation family bakery specializes in namesake wood-fire-baked goodies. *6am-9pm* $

Casa El Recreo: Jump in a cab for iconic Gallinas de Pinllo: wood-fired chicken in peanut sauce, cooked here since 1948. *hours vary* $

Chocolates Escobar: Artisanal chocolatiers using organic wood-fired Ecuador cacao to produce choc 'slabs', hot choc and choc-filled bread. *9:30am-7pm* $

Ponche Suizo: In business since 1952 and known for its sweet eggy, vanilla-y dessert, a recipe that remains tightly guarded. *10am-7pm Mon-Sat* $

and Inca and pre-Inca artifacts, alongside curiosities like a two-headed calf. It's closed on weekends.

A few blocks up is **Parque Montalvo**, a gated green space that's another good place to pause for reflection. A statue of Ambateño writer Juan Montalvo stands in the middle, while on the park's northern edge stands the art deco-styled **La Catedral** *(diocesisambato.org)*. Rebuilt after the original was destroyed in 1947, the church trades traditional ornamentation for minimalist, mid-century straight lines – a classic case of in with the new, out with the old.

On the other side, **Museo Provincial Casa del Portal** *(free)* showcases works by esteemed Ecuadorian artists including Oswaldo Viteri and Luis A Martínez, while next door, the tiny **Museo de la Cultura Salasaka** *(by donation)* displays indigenous artifacts. Note most museums in Ambato close for lunch around 1pm to 2pm.

Getting to Know the City

More museums and galleries

Ambato's new city museum **Hambatu Museo de la Ciudad** *(free; Spanish only)* occupies two levels of well-curated spaces telling the city's story. Engaging exhibits take you from its indigenous roots through to natural disasters and current-day culture. Art and architecture lovers should also head four blocks southwest to the **Museo Pictórico Edmundo Martínez** *(free)*, a historical stone mansion that hosts rotating exhibitions of Ecuadorian masters. Both museums are closed Sunday and Monday.

The Three Juans

Embracing Ambato's literary heritage

The city proudly calls itself the 'Land of the Three Juans', after writers Juan Montalvo and Juan León Mera and lawyer-journalist Juan Benigno Vela. All three are commemorated across Ambato's parks, museums and historic buildings.

We've already met Juan Montalvo (1832–1889) in his namesake Parque Montalvo, but on the park's north side stands **Casa y Mausoleo de Montalvo** *(casademontalvo.gob.ec; $2; Spanish only)*, his former house. It's now both a museum (closed Saturday) dedicated to his life and a grand mausoleum where the writer is interred. His 'countryside' retreat, **Quinta de Juan Montalvo** *($1)*, lies 2km southwest of town, and further honors the author of the satirical *Las Catilinarias* (1880). It's closed Monday and Tuesday.

FIESTA DE LA FRUTA Y DE LAS FLORES

Though the **Festival of Fruit & Flowers** may sound like a ho-hum agricultural event, make no mistake – this is one of Ecuador's most fun and flamboyant celebrations. But this joyous occasion was born out of the city's darkest hours. After the devastating 1949 earthquake, Ambato was a city in desperate need of cheering up, and what better way to defy adversity than by throwing a party? And no ordinary party, but one that lasts two weeks.

In a region famous for volcanic soils and abundance of produce, nothing better symbolizes the city's rebirth than its fertility.

Held every February, it coincides with Carnaval, with the final five days exploding in parades, street parties, bullfights and performances.

EATING IN AMBATO: LOCAL FAVES

Mercado Central: Stop by the market for a plate of *llapingachos* (fried potato patties stuffed with cheese) with eggs, avocado and sausage. *7am-7pm* $

La Fuente & Cafetería: Downtown diner serving home-style Ecuadorian mains, coffees and sandwiches. Has eco-cred, too. *8am-8pm Mon-Sat* $

Delicias del Paso: Old-school city cafe that's a local fave for life's simple pleasures: hearty breakfasts, sandwiches, tamales, cakes and coffee. *8am-9pm Mon-Sat* $

Roka Plaza: Atmospheric courtyard restaurant with signature steaks, good sushi and a great cheeseburger. *7am-10pm Mon-Sat, to 4pm Sun* $$

AMBATO: FOOD CITY

Ambato is blessed with fertile volcanic soils that shape its regional cuisine.

Llapingachos: Originating in nearby Mocha, this carb-on-carb classic of fried potato patties stuffed with cheese is a breakfast staple, served with avocado and chorizo.

Pan de Pinllo: This century-old, wood-fired bread comes in sweet and savory varieties and is baked using generations-old recipes found only in the Pinllo neighborhood.

Gallinas de Pinllo: Also from Pinllo, this wood-roasted chicken is slathered in peanut sauce and served with potatoes – so iconic it has a street named after it.

Cuyes de Ficoa: Cute-animal lovers look away now: guinea pig *(cuy)* appears on menus in the affluent neighborhood of Ficoa.

JEREMY HORNER/ALAMY

Salasaca

Back in the city, **Museo Juan Benigno Vela** *(free; Spanish only)*, closed Sunday to Tuesday, commemorates writer, lawyer and journalist Juan Benigno Vela.

For the third Juan, head 2km north of town to **Jardín Botánico Atocha-La Liria** *($0.50)*. Admission includes entrance to **Quinta de Juan León Mera**, the 1874 residence of the author and politician best known for writing both the lyrics to Ecuador's national anthem and the novel *Cumandá* (1879). The garden itself is a highlight. Dating back to 1849, it's a peaceful place with grand palm-lined paths set on the banks of the jungle-lined Río Ambato. Another museum included in the entrance fee is the **Martínez-Holguín House Museum**, which is dedicated to another Ambato writer; no, not another 'Juan', but Luis A Martínez, author of the novel *A la Costa*. Note the gardens and museums are closed Monday and Tuesday.

Visiting the indigenous Village of Salasaca

Easy half-day trip

For a taste of Andean culture, take a bus (30 minutes) to the indigenous village of **Salasaca**, 14km southeast of Ambato. Though modest in appearance, it's home to a proud Kichwa-speaking community known for artisan crafts and traditional dress – think men in broad-brimmed white hats with long black ponchos over white shirts, and women in colorful shawls and long wool skirts.

DRINKING IN AMBATO: BEST PLACES FOR A RELAXED TIPPLE

Lab Bar: Settle in at Ambato's classiest bar with its enticing menu of well-made original and classic cocktails at Hotel Roka Plaza. *4pm-late Tue-Sat*

Ficoa Beer Garden: Drop by this well-heeled neighborhood for craft beers, cocktails and burgers in an inviting garden. *5pm-midnight Mon-Thu, 4pm-2am Fri & Sat*

Manhattan: Downtown dive bar that's a student favorite for cheap drinks and karaoke. Keep an eye out for two-for-one cocktail specials. *2pm-2am*

Nünna: Pour your own pint, wine or cocktail from DIY dispensers at this industrial-chic bar in happening Ficoa. *5pm-midnight Tue-Fri, 3pm-1am Sat, 3-10pm Sun*

Baños

WATERFALLS | ADVENTURE | RELAXATION

With a majestic backdrop of steep, forested hills and pretty waterfalls, the resort town of Baños (elevation 1820m) enjoys a stunning location. The town itself is a mixed bag, however. It's overrun with an abundance of kitschy theme parks, neon-blaring party buses and tacky souvenir stores, but it's also a town of immense history dating back to 1553, with plenty of character and grandeur.

Not only popular for climbing, hiking and mountain biking, this is also where thrill-seekers come to get their kicks. Bungee jumping, zip-lining, canyoning, paragliding, white-water rafting and rock climbing – you name it, you can do it here.

Perhaps the most extreme thing about Baños, however, is nature itself. Here the mighty Volcán Tungurahua looms ominously over the town. Translating as 'throat of fire', it's one of Ecuador's most active volcanoes, and its perfect conical shape provides a dramatic sight as you approach town.

TOP TIP

As well as the plentiful activities in the area, Baños makes for a good base for day trips further afield. As a gateway to the Amazon rainforest, here you can book a tour into this famed wilderness area on a day excursion, or head to Volcán Chimborazo and be back for a beer by early evening.

Ecuador's Capital for Outdoor Adventure

Adventure, action and adrenaline

When people talk about 'taking the plunge' or 'diving in head first', it's rarely meant as literally as in Baños. But what better way to experience this sublime countryside than flinging

GETTING AROUND

The city center is small enough to explore on foot, and reaching the surrounding areas is easy by mountain bike, public bus or rental car (around $50 per day). Short taxi rides within town rarely exceed $1.50.

For outdoorsy types, a mountain bike is the best option, with rentals (per day $8) widely available from adventure stores, for tackling the popular Ruta de las Cascadas (Waterfall Route).

Public buses are another simple and inexpensive choice, with most major sights accessible for $1 one-way.

Baños' bus terminal is in the town's center and offers regular services to Latacunga, Ambato, Riobamba, Puyo, Quito, Cuenca and Guayaquil.

ROOM WITH A VIEW

Perched on the slopes of Tungurahua, one of the world's most active volcanoes, La Casa del Árbol (p234) is a humble treehouse that was built by a former fireman and self-appointed 'volcano watcher' to monitor the mountain's volatile 'throat of fire'. In 1999, when Tungurahua awoke after an 81-year slumber, the forecast for Baños wasn't rain but ash, toxic gases and falling rocks, forcing about 16,000 residents to evacuate with little warning. Further eruptions in the 2000s and 2010s reinforced the need for constant vigilance, even as modern technology improved early warnings. The swing from the treehouse's platform that its creator added for his grandchildren has today become one of Ecuador's most Instagrammable sights.

yourself across a valley like a superhero, leaping off bridges or rappelling down waterfalls? And that's only the beginning. Baños is a must-visit for adrenaline junkies chasing dizzying highs beyond high-altitude summits.

Here you can expect Ecuador's longest zip line (over 1km), Tarzan pendulums, bridge jumps, rock climbing and tandem paragliding for unrivalled views.

You can also tame Class III and IV white-water rapids, canyon down 30m waterfalls or scale local basalt rock faces. But for the ultimate climb, Tungurahua (p235) remains Baños' big-name peak. More leisurely alternatives include Amazon trips, hiking, horse riding or mountain biking along the Ruta de las Cascadas.

Reliable operators include **Geotours** *(geotoursbanios.com)*, **Wonderful Ecuador** *(wonderfulecuador.com)* and **MTS Adventure** *(@mts_adventures)*.

Exploring the Ruta de las Cascadas

Mountain biking and chasing waterfalls

Stretching 16km east of Baños, the 'Highway of Waterfalls' (Ruta de las Cascadas) cuts through the forested Río Pastaza canyon, where as well as waterfalls, you'll find many adventure operators offering zip lines, bridge walks, cable cars and the like.

Of its dozen or so waterfalls, none is more spectacular than **Pailón del Diablo**. With a name translating as the Devil's Cauldron, this almighty 80m-tall waterfall (Ecuador's second biggest but probably its best) is aptly named given its thunderous surge of water that powers furiously from the cliff face – an extraordinary sight from close range. It's accessed from the village of **Río Verde**, from where there are two separate trails down that offer different experiences. Which is better? Well, they're both pretty awesome, and if you have the time, it's worth doing both.

The original route to **Pailón del Diablo** *(pailondeldiablo.ec; adult/child $3/2; 8am-6pm)* is the longer option, descending a steep trail to a suspension bridge with panoramic views before ducking beneath a rock ledge to experience the thunder of the falls up close.

The newer route **Cascada El Pailón** *(cascadaelpailon.com; adult/child $3/2)* is shorter but equally spectacular, offering multiple viewpoints – none more dramatic than when standing directly alongside the powerful falls engulfed in spray. A third option is a **night visit** *(adult/child from*

EATING IN BAÑOS: OUR PICKS

Cafe Hood: Amicable host Karina has been serving travelers global cuisine for years, including plenty of veg and vegan options. *noon-8pm Thu-Sun* $

Mestizart: A good place to sample homestyle Ecuadorian cooking, from hearty breakfasts to Amazonian fish and vegan mains. *8am-4pm & 6-10pm* $

La Tasca: Classy, cozy Spanish restaurant serving authentic tapas and mains ranging from paella to Galician seafood stews. *1-4pm & 6-10pm Wed-Sat, 1-5pm Sun* $$

La Floresta Restaurante: If you're going to try *cuy* (guinea pig), La Floresta's restaurant is the place to do so, with its signature 24-hour-cooked tacos. *1-9pm* $$

$4/2), between 6pm and midnight, when the falls glow in a kaleidoscope of colors.

Public buses ($1, every 15 minutes) run from Baños to the site, though a car helps if you're wanting to visit the other waterfalls.

The area is also popular with mountain bikers: a 25km trail takes you to all the falls, swimming holes and hidden cascades. Geotours offers popular self-guided tours with maps.

Witness the Miracles of Baños' Patron Saint

Unique religious paintings and cultural displays

In the town center overlooking Parque la Basílica is the striking **Basílica de Nuestra Señora de Agua Santa**. Dedicated to the Virgin of Agua Santa (Virgin of the Holy Water), this decorative church hosts a series of epic paintings depicting the miracles she's performed in the face of an erupting Volcán Tungurahua. The attached **Museo Fray Enrique Mideros** *($1)*

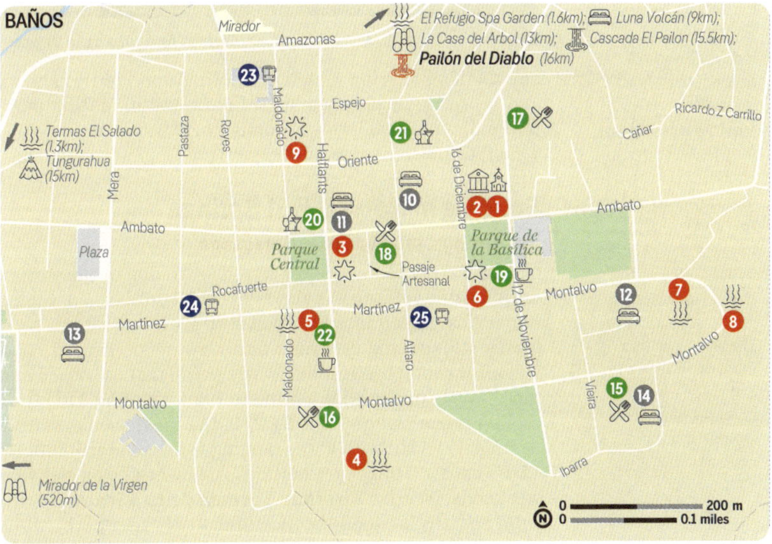

SIGHTS
1 Basílica de Nuestra Señora de Agua Santa
2 Museo Fray Enrique Mideros

ACTIVITIES
3 Geotours
4 Hotel Monte Selva
5 Huellas Natural Spa
6 MTS Adventure
7 Piscinas Termas de la Virgen
8 Termas Antiguas de la Virgen
9 Wonderful Ecuador

SLEEPING
10 El Jardín Escondido Hostel
11 Erupcion Art Hotel
12 Hostal Chimenea
13 Hotel Llanovientos
14 Posada del Arte

EATING
15 Cafe Hood
see 10 F#ckin' Bueno Burger
16 La Floresta Restaurante
17 La Tasca
18 Mercado Central
see 11 Mestizart

DRINKING & NIGHTLIFE
19 Andes Specialty Coffee
20 Azotea740
see 11 Crater Rooftop Bar
21 Leprechaun
22 Libreria Viera
see 10 Soma Beer Garden

TRANSPORT
23 Bus Terminal
24 Bus to Casa del Arbol
25 Bus to Pailón del Diablo

BEST FOR PAMPERING

Luna Volcán *(lunavolcan.com)* Baños' most luxurious spot is in the hills. Volcán's five-star treatments include massage, facials and both natural hot spa and infinity pool overlooking Tungurahua.

El Refugio Spa Garden *(elrefugiospa.com/en)* Another tasteful spa away from the public. Its hot waters aren't natural, but it has by far the best views.

Huellas Natural Spa *(huellasnaturalspa.com)* No views, but it gets glowing reviews for its well-priced range of massage and beauty treatments.

Hotel Monte Selva *(monteselva.com/en/prana-spa)* Baños' most central option is this spa hotel complex of pool, steam rooms and massage therapies.

ANGELA N PERRYMAN/SHUTTERSTOCK

Termas Antiguas de la Virgen

houses more stirring religious paintings, and fairly random and eccentric displays on anything from bullfighting paraphernalia and taxidermy animals (including a stuffed rottweiler) to, most interestingly, superb pre-Columbian artifacts.

Soaking in Natural Hot Springs

Hot springs, mud baths and massage

One of the upsides to living next door to one of the world's most volatile volcanoes is access to luxuriant thermal waters. Baños has tapped into the good stuff with several spa complexes utilizing mineral-rich volcanic waters. These are perfect after a long trek, though expect less Japanese onsen and more rowdy public pool. Dating to 1928, **Termas Antiguas de la Virgen** *(adult/child $4/2)* is the most scenic, set beneath a waterfall with baths ranging from cold to an intense 42°C (118°F). Things get boisterous, however, especially on weekends. Nearby **Piscinas Termas de la Virgen** *(adult/chlld $6/3)* feels equally hectic (think kids' water park), while **Termas El Salado** *(adult/child $4/2)*, 2.5km southwest, offers a lovely canyon setting, but again it's a very local, often over-excited vibe.

Journey into the Hills

Fresh mountain air, hummingbirds and volcano views

A popular short excursion south of town is the steep journey up to **La Casa del Arbol** *(lacasadelarbol.ec; $1)* viewpoint. Though fickle weather means it's always the luck of the draw, on a clear day the views over the valley and Volcán Tungurahua are life-affirming. Among its attractions are a ginormous swing that whooshes you over the precipice, a flying fox, a cafe and a flower-filled garden alive with hummingbirds. A bus up here is the best way, departing every two to three hours from Baños ($0.50; 45 minutes). Otherwise, a one-way taxi will cost $6, or it's a three-hour hike one-way.

There are countless walking trails in the hills surrounding Baños, but one popular option is the sweaty climb up to **Mirador de la Virgen** (40 minutes one-way) for panoramic views over town.

Summiting Tungurahua

Taming volcanos

Looming over Baños like a prehistoric beast is the fire-breathing stratovolcano **Tungurahua** (5023m). Dormant for 80 years, it reawakened in November 1999, triggering the evacuation of some 25,000 residents, many of whom never returned. But despite further eruptions, most recently 2016, Tungurahua remains as enticing as ever to peak baggers.

Although non-technical, Ecuadorian regulations require climbers to hire a licensed guide, and summit attempts depend heavily on weather conditions; good fitness and acclimatization are essential. **Andean Summit Adventure** *(andeansummitadventures.com)* is a recommended operator. The ascent takes one to two days, with a three- to four-hour hike to Refugio Nicolas Martinez (3830m), followed by a 3.5km push to the summit.

If you don't want to make the summit, you can hike to the base camp with Geotours (p232), from where you'll zip down the slopes by mountain bike.

Hitting the Strip

Night out on the town

For many visitors, Baños is all about adventure by day and partying by night. A dedicated nightlife strip sees upper Calle Eloy Alfaro light up with pubs and clubs after dark, of which **Leprechaun** remains a long-time favorite, with several cavernous venues mixing pub, restaurant and salsa dance party.

Craft-beer fans should seek out **Soma Beer Garden** for hoppy ales, while for rooftop drinks, **Crater Rooftop Bar** slings open-air cocktails accompanied by social events such as free salsa lessons (Monday) and bachata and merengue nights (Wednesday). Also head up to **Azotea740** for happy hour overlooking the leafy square and clocktower.

CONQUERING TUNGURAHUA

Elisabeth Gschösser, experienced mountaineer and manager of Andean Summit Adventure. *(andeansummitadventure.com)*

What do you love most about summiting Tungurahua? The view into its deep crater and the steam coming out of cracks in the rock are fascinating. The steep slopes of the volcano are a real challenge to climb.

Given it's an active volcano, is it safe to climb? Yes, monitoring has been very reliable, I'd say, and I consider it safe.

In Baños, how do you like to pass the time? You find lovely cafes in the city, of which my favorite is Café Colibri, where you can admire the surroundings. I also enjoy the hot springs El Salado for relaxing after long days.

EATING & DRINKING IN BAÑOS

Mercado Central: Keeping things real with classic local staples such as *llapingachos* and ceviche. *6am-8:30pm* **$**

Andes Specialty Coffee: Perfect spot to recharge batteries with good Ecuadorian coffees overlooking the square. *8:15am-8:30pm Tue-Sun, to 4:30pm Mon*

Libreria Viera: Part bookstore, part cafe, part hangout for Baños' literati and expats; perfect for conversation over coffee. Established 1958. *9am-7pm Tue-Sat*

F#ckin' Bueno Burger: It's true, the burgers here are f#ckin' good! *2pm-12:30am* **$$**

Volcán Chimborazo

TREKKING | SCENERY | INDIGENOUS CULTURE

TOP TIP

The mountain's extreme altitude and changeable weather mean proper preparation is essential: bring quality gear and allow time to acclimatize. For local info, **Julio Verne Travel** and **Riobamba Tourism** *(riobamba.com.ec)* are reliable sources for activities and treks.

Encompassing all the elements that make the Andes so magical – snowcapped peaks, colorful indigenous culture, llamas, alpacas, vast *páramo* and rolling landscapes – Chimborazo may well be the highlight of your highland adventures.

Standing as the stunning centerpiece to the 58,560-hectare Reserva de Producción de Fauna Chimborazo, the mighty, glacier-topped Volcán Chimborazo (6263m) is Ecuador's highest mountain. But that's not its only claim to fame. Thanks to the bulge along the Earth's equator, its peak is not only the furthest point from the center of the Earth, but also the closest point to the sun – a natural phenomenon that local trekking operators are keen to promote as 'the highest mountain on Earth.'

Neighboring Volcán Carihuairazo (5018m) is another popular climb and also part of this protected wildlife reserve. En route along the flanks of Chimborazo you'll pass through some interesting indigenous villages that predated the Inca civilization by many centuries.

Day Trips to Chimborazo

The rooftop of Ecuador

There are two types who come to Chimborazo: adventurers here to scale its summit, and day visitors here to be

GETTING AROUND

An organized tour or private car is the best way to get around Chimborazo, but there's also a bus from Riobamba that passes the signed turnoff (4370m) for the *refugios* at the park's entrance. Along the way the bus stops off at Pulinguí San Pablo, from where you can embark on treks through the stunning *páramo* wilderness within the region. Another hike starts from **Chimborazo Lodge** (p245) and heads up to the Templo Machay (4700m), an ancient site where indigenous people made offerings to the mountain gods.

Most hotels in Riobamba can arrange a taxi for a day trip to Refugio Carrel for around $70.

HIGHLIGHTS

1 Volcán Chimborazo

SIGHTS

2 Comunidad Palacio Real

see 2 Museo Cultural de la Llama

3 Reserva de Producción de Fauna Chimborazo

4 Volcán Carihuairazo

ACTIVITIES

5 Refugio Whymper

SLEEPING

6 Casa Cóndor

7 Chimborazo Lodge

8 La Moya Community Tourism

9 Refugio Carrel

10 Taytapak Wasi

EATING

see 6 Casa Cóndor

see 8 La Moya Community Tourism

see 9 Refugio Carrel

mesmerized by up-close views of its mighty snowcapped peak. The latter is the larger group, often joining organized tours from Riobamba or from as far away as Baños, Latacunga or Quito.

Bring your passport to register at the entrance of **Reserva de Producción de Fauna Chimborazo**. The park also has a cafe, bathrooms, handicrafts, and an interpretation center on local natural history, indigenous heritage and climbing history. Keep an eye out for Chimborazo hillstars – high-altitude hummingbirds feeding on *chuquiraga* flowers.

From there, make your way to the car park at **Refugio Carrel** (4850m), Chimborazo's base camp, with a restaurant and basic lodging. Tombstones here commemorating climbers' deaths offer a somber reminder that this is no stroll in the park.

From here, day-trippers make the climb to **Refugio Whymper** (5000m), Ecuador's highest lodging (though closed at time of research), named after British mountaineer Edward Whymper, who made the first recorded summit of Chimborazo, in 1880. Though just a 150m gain in elevation, expect a brutal, breathless 45-minute hike.

THE HIGHEST POINT ON EARTH?

When Nietzsche said there are no facts only interpretations, he could well have used Chimborazo as an example. Measured from sea level, it's not even close to being the tallest mountain in the world – Everest has it beat by a whopping 2586m, and in fact, it's only the 39th tallest in the Andes. Nonetheless, Chimborazo's location along the planet's equatorial bulge means its peak is not only the furthest point of land from the center of the Earth, but also the closest point to the sun. So, while calling this the world's tallest mountain may be questionable, it's a geographical quirk Ecuadorians are quick to jump on. Either way, it makes for a good pub-trivia question, and one you're now able to answer.

KYRA DUSHI/SHUTTERSTOCK

Volcán Chimborazo

Many operators, as with Cotopaxi, offer mountain bikes for the descent – an exhilarating way to experience these evocative Andean landscapes. Riobamba-based Julio Verne Travel (p236) is a reputable local operator that can arrange biking tours, or if coming from Baños, Geotours (p232) offers day trips. At the risk of sounding like a broken record, as with any high-altitude mountain, make sure you're acclimatized first.

Keep an eye out for wild vicuña, the llama's smaller, more delicate cousin – though sadly their numbers have declined dramatically in recent years.

Making the Summit

Bagging Ecuador's highest peak

The opportunity to climb to the furthest point from the center of the Earth makes **Volcán Chimborazo** a hard one for peak baggers to pass up on.

However, reaching its glacial summit is no easy feat: it's a technical climb at high altitudes, with unpredictable and often freezing weather, howling winds, snow and steep rock slopes, which means it's one for more experienced climbers. That said, with enough preparation, beginners can also take up the challenge. With the volcano being dormant (for the past 11,000 years, anyway), at least there's little risk of eruption.

You'll need a professional guide and all the proper equipment to make the summit. Riombaba-based Julio Verne Travel (p236) is one of the best operators to arrange climbs, not only for Chimborazo, but also for the acclimatization ascents necessary before tackling Chimborazo (nearby **Volcán Carihuairazo** is the best and most popular option).

Chimborazo comprises four summits – Whymper, Veintimilla, Politécnica and Nicolás Martínez – with Whymper peak being the highest point and the one you'll be tackling over several days. Count on it being around eight to 10 hours to the summit and two to four to return.

As you can probably guess, the panoramas from the top, weather permitting, are absolutely stunning. Here you'll take in views spanning not only surrounding Andes mountains but the Pacific coast too, all while congratulating yourself for making it to the top of the world's highest mountain – or so you can claim, anyway!

Not all summit attempts on Chimborazo are successful. Weather conditions and avalanche risk often force climbers to turn back – sometimes when they're painfully close to the top. Always heed your guide's advice. Guides know the mountain better than anyone, and no chances are taken.

Visiting Villages Around Chimborazo

indigenous communities, unique museums and Andean hospitality

The region around Chimborazo has one of the largest concentrations of indigenous people in Ecuador and is where the Puruhá people have lived for centuries. All communities offer accommodations, food and various cultural activities.

For one of those 'only in South America' moments, head to the small indigenous community of **Pulinguí San Pablo** (3900m), where families still live in the round *chozas* (traditional hut). Here you can stay or eat at **Casa Cóndor** *(per person lodging, meals & tour $40)* among herds of alpaca.

En route from Riobamba is **Comunidad La Moya** *(per person incl lunch $15)*, offering grassroots accommodations, a restaurant and a small **museum** showcasing the *hielero* (ice men; p242) who'd harvest ice from Chimborazo with a pick to sell in Riobamba's market.

Comprising 80 or so indigenous families, **Comunidad Palacio Real** *(lunch $6)* has its **Museo Cultural de la Llama** *($2)* – what we assume to be the world's only llama museum. There's also a restaurant serving llama. It's other claim to fame is that Simón Bolívar once stayed in a hacienda here.

On Chimborazo's western side, the lovely, remote village of **Salinas** is known for its community-based tourism and co-op food producers, most famously Salinerito cheese and chocolate.

THE EMPTY SLOPES OF CHIMBORAZO

Sadly, the Reserva de Producción de Fauna Chimborazo has almost lost its most iconic resident: the wild vicuña. As recently as 2024, the vicuña population in the reserve was estimated at nearly 8000, and it was common to see hundreds grazing Chimborazo's slopes. Today, sightings are rare. This elegant, smaller relative of the llama – once nearly hunted to extinction – was reintroduced in the 1980s through conservation efforts supported by Chile and Bolivia. The vicuña's sudden decline remains unexplained. Possible causes include attacks by feral dogs, agricultural encroachment and mange. The reserve still shelters wildlife such as llamas and alpacas, *páramo* foxes, hummingbirds, pumas, wolves and Andean condors.

EATING AROUND CHIMBORAZO: OUR PICKS

Comunidad La Moya: Between Riobamba and Chimborozo, this Puruhá community offers indigenous dishes, from roasted lamb and guinea pig to veg. *noon-3pm* $

Refugio Carrel: Located at 4850m. The altitude may curb your appetite, but hearty meals are available, or a cup of coca-leaf tea. *8am-2pm* $

Casa Cóndor: A rustic, community-run option overlooking Chimborazo's peak, serving quinoa soups and Andean dishes. *noon-3pm* $

Roxy Cafe: On Chimborazo's western slopes, the town of Salinas is famed for artisanal cheese – best sampled on delicious wood-fired pizzas. *noon-9pm* $$

Beyond Volcán Chimborazo

The area surrounding Chimborazo offers a rich array of sights and experiences that warrant further exploration.

Places

Most travelers to Chimborazo end up in the attractive, culture-filled city of Riobamba. As well as being the gateway to the volcanoes, the city itself offers plenty of sights, along with good restaurants and bars that make it a worthwhile place to spend a few nights.

Riobamba is also an excellent base for exploring surrounding towns, including Guamote for its vibrant indigenous culture, Guano for its curious mummified monk and Colta for Ecuador's oldest church. Further afield lies Alausí, the starting point of Ecuador's last train journey, and the World Heritage–listed Sangay National Park, home to one of world's most active volcanoes and a destination that beckons intrepid travelers.

GETTING AROUND

Riobamba's city center is easily navigable on foot, but otherwise local taxis are a safe, cheap option. Though all villages are reachable by public transportation, if you're short on time, arranging a tour or driver and car is a good way to tick off most places in a day. Riobamba's main bus terminal is about 2km northwest of downtown, with frequent services to Chimborazo, Alausí, Baños, Ambato, Cuenca, Quito, Guayaquil and more.

Riobamba

TIME FROM CHIMBORAZO: 1¼HR

Museum of the Monastery of the Immaculate Conception

While its proximity to Chimborazo is what draws most travelers to Riobamba, like many larger Andean cities, it rewards those who take time to explore it. The capital of Chimborazo Province, Riobamba (population 115,000) was Ecuador's first major Spanish-founded city in 1534 and remains an important trading town with a strong indigenous presence. Its name combines Spanish (*rio*, meaning river) and Kichwa (*rispampa*, meaning plain), reflecting its Puruhá and Spanish heritage. The city features cobbled streets, leafy plazas and colonial buildings, largely rebuilt after the 1797 earthquake.

Set within a still-functioning 18th-century convent, home to around 30 nuns, the **Museo de Arte Religioso** *($4)* holds one of Ecuador's finest collections of 17th- and 18th-century religious art. Displayed in what were nun's cells, highlights include *La Flagelación de Jesús,* a 17th-century painting by an indigenous artist not so subtly condemning colonial abuse.

Within the convent walls visitors can buy natural products through a revolving door, hearing the nuns' voices but never seeing them.

RIOBAMBA ON FOOT

Take in big city Andean culture and charm as you navigate Riobamba's cobbled streets and heritage buildings.

START	END	LENGTH
Mercado La Merced	Lina	4km; 3hr

Ideally begin at lunchtime, when lively hawkers at 1 **Mercado La Merced** (p242) tempt you in with hard-to-resist roast pork. Then stroll a few blocks to leafy 2 **Parque Maldonado**, a relaxed spot to sit, digest and people-watch before heading to the excellent 3 **Museo de la Ciudad**, whose exhibits balance avant-garde art with the city's past. Across the plaza stands the baroque 4 **Catedral Católica San Pedro de Riobamba**, its facade a unique blending of indigenous and Catholic imagery.

Continue through atmospheric neighborhood streets to 5 **Museo de Arte Religioso**, one of the city's premier attractions. Head four blocks to 6 **Parque Sucre**, centered on a fountain of Neptune, and overlooked by the neoclassical 7 **Teatro León** (c 1929). Pass the historic train station 8 **Estación Riobamba** (c 1925), now a tourist office, museum and gallery, then turn north to 9 **Museo y Centro Cultural de Riobamba** to explore the city's heritage.

Head for 10 **Parque 21 de Abril** at sunset for 360-degree mountain views, before returning to the main strip to pass by 11 **Plaza de Toros**, a former bullring. As evening falls, hit Riobamba's boozy strip with beers at 12 **Riobamba Brewing Co** and authentic Mexican at 13 **Lina**.

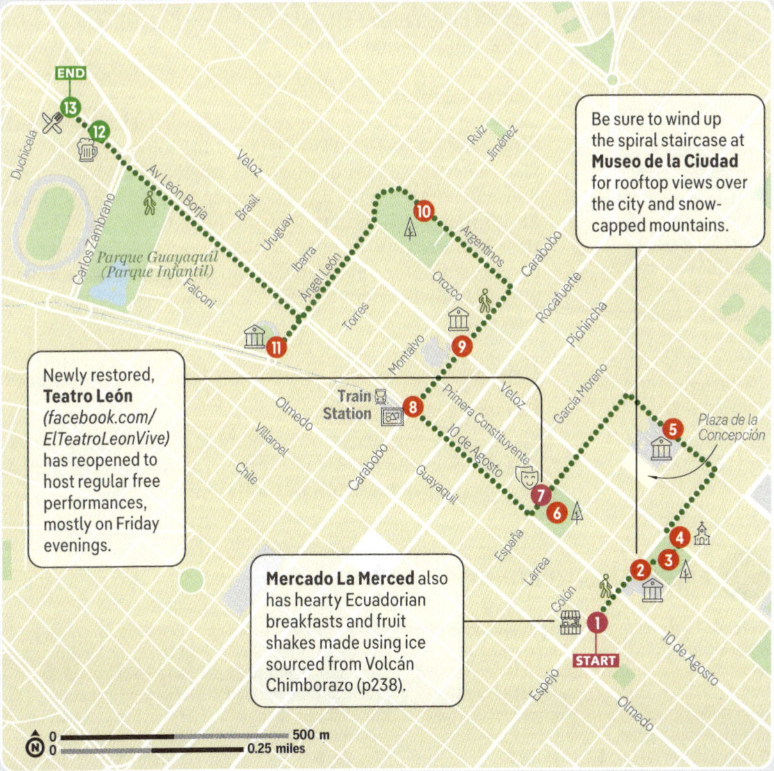

Guano

TIME FROM RIOBAMBA: **20MIN**

Musuems, mummies and monasteries

Just an 8km bus ride north of Riobamba, the picturesque town of Guano makes for a worthwhile half-day trip. Known for its laid-back charm, it offers scenic plazas, monasteries and an authentic Andean ambience – all set against the backdrop of Chimborazo.

The town is best known for **Museo de la Momia** *($2)* and its famous mummy, the remains of a 16th-century Franciscan monk discovered after the 1949 earthquake. It also has a display of pre-Hispanic artifacts and Chimborazo's *hieleros* (ice harvesters). Don't miss the *helados de Paila Baltazar* ice-cream cart outside, made using Chimborazo ice. Next door are the atmospheric ruins of the 1660s **Monastery of the Assumption**.

Guamote

TIME FROM RIOBAMBA: **1HR**

Markets and traditional Kichwa culture

About an hour south of Riobamba, this low-key town attracts few tourists, but once a week it transforms when indigenous Kichwa-speaking Puruhá villagers stream in from the surrounding valleys. If you can rejig your itinerary to free up a Thursday, do so: **Guamote's weekly market** is among Ecuador's best. Spread along the old train line, villagers gather to trade traditional clothing (it's a great place to buy a hat), fresh produce and livestock, creating a vivid snapshot of Andean rural life.

Beyond the market, Guamote is also worth visiting for **Inti Sisa** *(intisisa.com)*. Part of a community tourism project, Inti Sisa (Kichwa for 'sunflower') is a warm, welcoming guesthouse decorated with local artwork. It offers meals (lunch $8; dinner $14), and runs community tours, horse-riding trips and cooking classes. All profits support local healthcare, sustainable development and education, including an on-site kindergarten, all while empowering residents with new skills.

Colta

TIME FROM RIOBAMBA: **25MIN**

Ecuador's oldest church

Some 22km southwest of Riobamba, alongside a highway seemingly in the middle of nowhere, lies what's believed to be Ecuador's oldest church, **La Balbanera**. Dating to 1534,

KEEPING TRADITIONS ALIVE

In the modern world, many time-honored traditions have disappeared. With freezers everywhere, it seems almost impossible that the *hieleros* of Chimborazo – indigenous ice harvesters who climbed the mountain's glaciers to chip out massive blocks of ice for local markets – survived into modern times. Yet until late 2024, they did. Baltazar Ushca (1944–2024), who practiced this grueling trade for half a century, was the last of his kind. Each block, weighing up to 30kg, was wrapped in straw and carried down by donkey to be sold in nearby towns, a livelihood documented in *The Last Ice Merchant* (2012). For romantics, there's still hope: as of 2026, his nephew Juan Ushca has vowed to honor the tradition and keep the legend alive.

EATING & DRINKING IN RIOBAMBA : OUR PICKS

Mercado La Merced: Local institution famous for its delicious *hornado* (roast pork) and *batido* (fruit shakes) made using ice from Volcán Chimborazo. *8am-4pm* $

Casa Rubio Cayfruits: Atmospheric cafe popular for empanadas, sandwiches and steaks, plus coffee, cakes and cocktails. *8am-9pm Mon-Sat* $

Bear Brothers: Brewpub run by three brothers who brew beer and serve up burgers, loaded sandwiches, wings and nachos etc. *5-10pm Tue-Sat* $

El Delirio: Traditional Ecuadorian food in an ambient, candlelit hacienda featuring bullfighting memorabilia and an inviting open fire. *1-10pm* $$

it's also one of the country's first colonial buildings. Much of it was rebuilt after the 1797 earthquake, but original elements remain on the facade, which blends baroque influences with indigenous Incan motifs carved in stone. Don't expect grandeur, instead its humble, minimalist appearance lends it historical charm, while the snowcapped Chimborazo provides a dramatic backdrop.

Alausí

TIME FROM RIOBAMBA: **2HR**

Riding the rails of the Devil's Nose

Long regarded as one of the must-do attractions in Ecuador's central region, Ecuador's legendary train journey is back on track after several years off the rails. Chugging back to life in mid-2025, the dramatic **Nariz del Diablo** (Devil's Nose) ride begins in the Andean town of **Alausí**, 97km south of, and easily reached by bus from, Riobamba. From here it zigzags down hair-raising switchbacks to **Sibambe**, clinging to a sheer 765m rock face carved into the mountainside.

Built in 1908 to connect Quito with the port of Guayaquil, the railway was hailed as an engineering miracle – slashing travel time between coast and highlands from weeks to days and becoming a vital lifeline for trade and travel. The Devil's Nose section was the toughest of all, carved into near-vertical mountainside by hand.

Although the line closed in the 1990s, this stretch survives as a scenic tourist route. The 2½-hour journey includes a stop in Sibambe that showcases cultural performances for passengers.

For schedules and tickets, visit *sialausi.com*. Always check ahead though, as this spectacular line remains challenging to maintain and temporary closures do occur.

Parque Nacional Sangay

TIME FROM RIOBAMBA: **1¼HR**

Lace up your boots for magnificent hikes

As one of the world's most active and volatile volcanoes, the infamous Volcán Sangay (5319m) may be off-limits, but the vast World Heritage–listed park still has plenty to see. Covering 5177 sq km, the park spans glacier-topped volcanoes, cloud forests, lakes, tropical jungles and *páramo*. Most of **Parque Nacional Sangay** is hard to access and seldom visited, but those who do are rewarded with some of the country's most picturesque wilderness landscapes. Highlights include the extinct **Volcán El Altar** (5319m), with its nine jagged peaks and jade crater lake, best reached via the entrance near **Hacienda Releche** *(haciendareleche.com)*, 37km east of Riobamba. There's also the hike to the spectacular *páramo* lakes of **Lagunas de Atillo**, accessed via the Guamote–Macas road.

PARQUE NACIONAL SANGAY

Santiago Cedeño, trekking guide and owner of Hacienda Releche

What makes the trek to El Altar so special? It challenges you physically and mentally, before leading to one of the prettiest places on Earth. El Altar was once South America's highest mountain before a massive stratovolcanic explosion destroyed its summit, leaving only the base. From ground level, it resembles a Catholic church, explaining its name.

Why visit Parque Nacional Sangay? It's one of Ecuador's most biodiverse parks, with *páramo*, forests, volcanoes, wildlife and lots of birds – including high-altitude hummingbirds and a family of Andean condors I've known since I was eight! Plus, there's puma, wolves and even tapir.

Places We Love to Stay

$ Budget $$ Midrange $$$ Top End

Parque Nacional Cotopaxi

MAP p213

Secret Garden Cotopaxi Much-loved backpacker offering plenty of adventure, a hot tub, fireside hangouts and eclectic rooms – think hobbit homes, birdhouses and glamping. Amazing views! $

Cuscungo Cotopaxi Vibrant guesthouse set amid farmland with hammocks and rooftop hangouts to enjoy mountain views. Ideal for those traveling between Cotopaxi and Quilotoa. $

La Rinconada Chagrahuasi BYO everything at this national park campsite with bathroom facilities, 3km from Limpiopungo. $

The Quilotoa Loop

MAP p219

Quilotoa

Hostería Chukirawa There may not be lake views in Quilotoa, but this is a good choice for a cozy trekking-teahouse atmosphere, vibrant rooms and a colorful lounge. $

Shalalá Nestled 1.6km east along the crater rim, this community-run, indigenous lodge offers sustainable tourism, excellent rooms and restaurant – but again, no lake views. $$

Sigchos

Starlight Mountain Lodge Delightfully ramshackle hostel located at the Quilotoa Loop trailhead. Cheap rooms, tasty meals and camping alongside epic views. $

Isinliví

Hostal Taita Cristobal Super-relaxed backpacker offering budget rooms and campsites with stupendous valley views. $

Llullu Llama One of the best lodges along the loop. Cottages with wood burners, cozy dorms, eco-credentials, hot tub, great restaurant and knowledgeable staff. $$

Chugchilán

Hostal Cloud Forest Here staff know what travelers want: comfortable well-priced rooms, fireplaces that keep common areas warm and a social, communal restaurant. $

Black Sheep Inn Tasteful choice with thatched adobe huts, dorms, sauna, yoga, eco-initiatives and an all-veg menu. $

Hostal Mama Hilda Another top option with its cozy, fire-warmed lounge, colorful murals and viewpoints overlooking the valley. Rooms are modern and comfortable. $

Puyu Pacha Come for astounding views above the clouds and stay for warm family hospitality. Offers a memorable array of activities and experiences. $$

Tigua

Posada de Tigua Another reason to visit Tigua is this working dairy ranch, an 1890s farmhouse converted into an atmospheric guesthouse run by a fifth-generation family. $$

Latacunga

Hostal Tiana Vibrant hostel in a colonial building with friendly staff, self-catering kitchen, a heap of travel info and local tours. Head upstairs for rooftop views. $

Hotel Cotopaxi It may not be a heritage building but this functional hotel will put you right in the heart of it. $

Golden Rest Set within a heritage building that's managed by one of the pioneers of the Quilotoa Loop. Great local info. $$

Reserva Ecológica Los Ilinizas

Refugio Nuevos Horizontes Mountain cabin perched at 4700m; BYO sleeping bag and supplies. $

Hostal La Llovizna Good base with cheap rooms. You can arrange guides, as well as mountain bikes and horse riding. $

Hostería PapaGayo Guaranteed memorable stay at this intriguing 300-year-old hacienda 9km northwest of El Chaupi that blends old with new. $$$

Ambato

MAP p228

Hostal Runa Huasi Head to Salasaca 14km south of Ambato for insights into indigenous culture. Run by a local family that offers grassroots tours. $

Hostal Napoles Emperador II In a city lacking budget accom, this no-frills choice is strictly for penny pinchers. Very friendly staff. $

Hotel Roka Plaza Classy boutique city hotel set in an old *casona* (large colonial-era house). **$$**

Hotel Ambato Four-star hotel featuring modern amenities, good natural lighting, swimming pool and valley views. **$$**

Baños

MAP p233

Hostal Chimenea Centrally located backpacker with bright rooms, dorms and rooftop cafe to go with plunge pool, steam baths and kitchen for self-caterers. **$**

Erupcion Art Hotel Set over several floors, here's a contender for Baños best budget stay with its social programs, rooftop bar and comfy mix of rooms. **$**

El Jardín Escondido Hostel Staying at a hostel attached to a microbrewery is either your idea of heaven or hell; for us, it's definitely heaven! **$**

Hotel Llanovientos Relaxed, family-run guesthouse that makes a good choice for those not into the Baños party scene. It's a steep climb here, however. **$**

Posada del Arte Boutique guesthouse just back from the town center, with welcoming hosts and waterfall views. **$$**

Luna Volcán Baños' most luxurious stay offers astounding views from its hilltop location, along with infinity pool and spa. **$$$**

Around Baños

La Casta Located in Patate, 21km northwest of Baños, this atmospheric mountain retreat sits at the foot of Tungurahua. Excellent restaurant, too. **$**

Miramelindo Across from Pailón del Diablo is this relaxed alternative to Baños' commercialized scene, with art-filled rooms, hot tubs, lovely owners and traditional food. **$$**

Hostería Chamanapamba Unique option just outside Baños, with stunning treehouse-style rooms offering views over a canyon. **$$$**

Volcán Chimborazo & Around

MAP p237

Casa Cóndor Experience indigenous Andean culture at this memorable guesthouse at the foot of Chimborazo. **$**

Hotel Roka Plaza

Refugio Carrel Chimborazo's basecamp with dorms for climbers and a restaurant for day-trippers. **$**

Chimborazo Lodge One of the best places to stay in Ecuador, this historical mountaineer lodge delivers the quintessential Andes experience. **$$$**

Taytapak Wasi Opened in late 2025, this rustic lodge features rooms with spectacular Chimborazo views enjoyed by a roaring fire. **$$$**

Riobamba

Villa Bonita Hostel Superb backpacker choice within a historical mansion that delivers both ambience and vibes. Clean dorms and rooms. **$**

Rio Hotel Well priced with plenty of charm and character in a heritage hotel with a prime location in the city. **$$**

Mansión Santa Isabella Beautifully restored mansion with boutique touches throughout. **$$$**

Around Riobamba

Inti Sisa Colorful Guamote guesthouse perfect for those wanting to experience indigenous culture and grassroots community tourism. **$**

Community Hostel Alausí Literally on the train tracks in Alausí, this makes for a convenient stop on the Nariz del Diablo train ride! Modern, friendly, and spotless dorms and rooms. **$**

Parque Sangay

Hacienda Releche This ranch is the base for Volcán El Altar treks, run by expert guides specializing in hiking and horse rides. **$**

For places to stay in South Coast & Guayaquil, see p279

ATOSAN/SHUTTERSTOCK

Above: Cerro Santa Ana (p259); left: surfer, Montañita (p267)

Researched by
Michael Grosberg

South Coast & Guayaquil

WATER ADVENTURES, SEAFOOD FEASTS & BREATHTAKING COASTLINES

Big-city *guayaquileños* mix with Guayas locals at beachfront restaurants, while surfing culture's laid-back ethos draws travelers to low-key coastal towns.

This region, whether known as the Ruta del Spondylus, the Ruta del Sol (Route of the Sun), or the Ruta del Surf, would be as appealing regardless of the nickname. The coastline from river-bound Guayaquil, the country's largest city, to Parque Nacional Machalilla, is dotted with mellow hangouts featuring cosmopolitan cafes, lush mountain-covered cloud forests teeming with unique flora and fauna, big beach resorts, tiny fishing villages and offshore islands ready to be explored.

The three main provinces – Guayas, Santa Elena and Manabí – are where humans first settled in the region. Archaeologists have uncovered vestiges around the Santa Elena Peninsula of La Cultura Las Vegas, the earliest inhabitants, and of the Valdivia, the next people on the scene. The latter left evidence of the region's complex pre-Hispanic history in the form of ceramic carvings and pottery dating back to at least 3500 BCE, and these artifacts are preserved in a few museums.

Outdoors enthusiasts can explore pristine mangrove rivers, beaches of every stripe, and naturalist jungle hikes through protected preserves; those looking for more active thrills can test the region's world-class surf or scuba dive with giant manta rays.

When the sun sets, there's plenty of nightlife to be had, ranging from stylish lounges in Guayaquil and laid-back beach bars nearly everywhere to the backpacker town of Montañita, whose beachfront clubs and cocktail alleys are raucous fiestas year-round.

THE MAIN AREAS

GUAYAQUIL
Modern and historic riverside metropolis. **p252**

MONTAÑITA & OLÓN
Surf-party central and its laid-back little sister. **p267**

PUERTO LÓPEZ & AYAMPE
Cruises, diving and uncrowded beaches. **p273**

Find Your Way

Anchored by Guayaquil, this coastal region stretching all the way to Puerto López in the north, features a stunning diversity of ecosystems. We've focused on the natural preserves and beachfront towns that are easily navigated by car or frequently running buses.

Puerto López & Ayampe, p273

Join travelers focused on surf, yoga and escapism for long days on empty beaches, hikes through protected parks, whale-watching, island excursions and fine food.

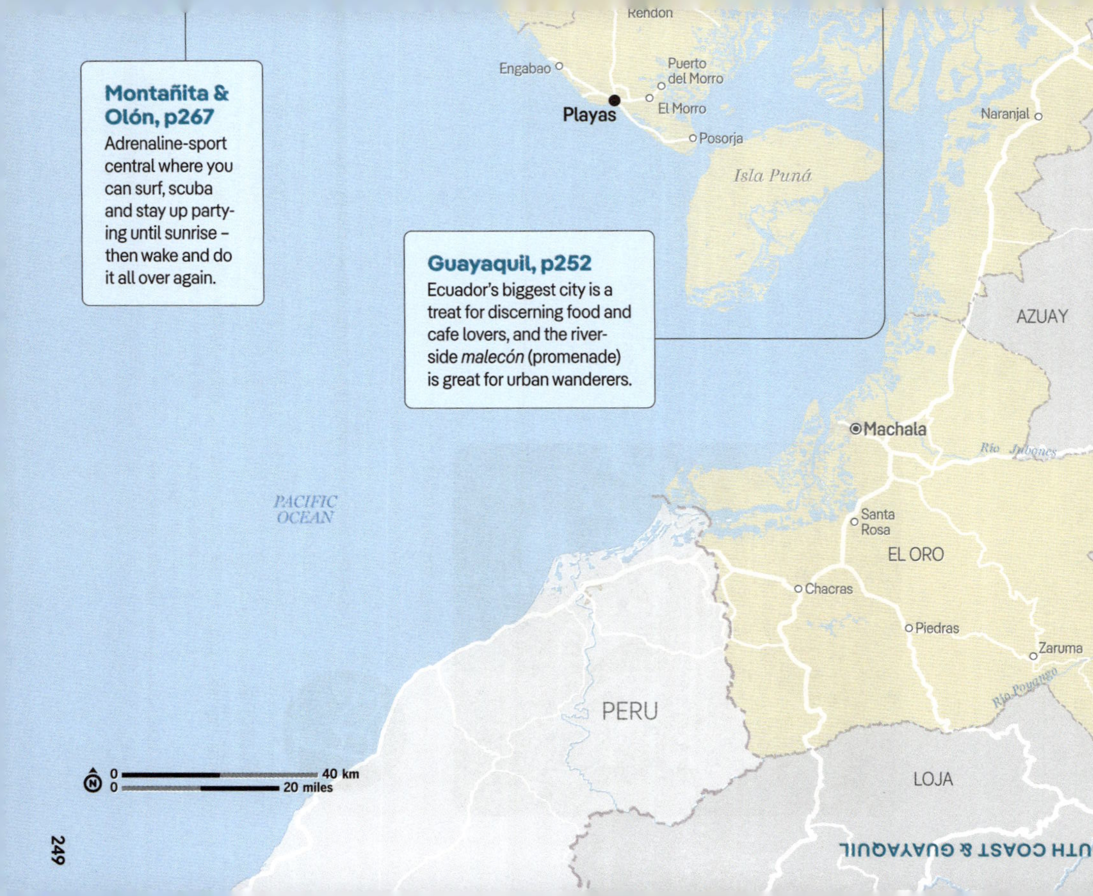

BUS

Buses are frequent, inexpensive and easily accessible from Guayaquil and along the coastal routes. However, they're also crowded and run off schedule. If you're carrying heavy bags, you'll need to grab onward transportation to accommodations in larger towns and cities.

TAXI

Ubers are inexpensive and convenient in Guayaquil. Hiring taxis to go further afield requires negotiation and Spanish language skills. Fares between spots along the coastal roads are generally standardized; ask locals what to expect before hiring.

CAR

To maximize autonomy and flexibility, renting a car is the way to go. Coastal areas have limited road networks and manageable traffic. Splurging on a 4WD expands the territory you can explore. Rent a car from the airport. One caveat: driving out of and into Guayaquil is not for the faint of heart.

Plan Your Days

Explore the coast in a few days between flights, or pick your own beachside idyll to extend your stay for weeks on end.

MICHAEL GROSBERG

Playa Engabao (p263)

A Short Stopover

- If you only have a day or two, your best bet is to stick close to Guayaquil. Chocolate lovers will enjoy a visit to the **Museo Nacional del Cacao** (p259) and a leisurely meal at a Calle Panamá cafe; then wander the **malecón** (p257) and take in a sunset after walking to the top of **Las Peñas** (p252) before dining at a **Puerto Santa Ana** (p259) promenade restaurant.

- On day two, hit the beach with the *costeño* elite in **Salinas** (p261), where Playa de Chipipe and Punta Carnero are the favorites, or visit **Puerto Engabao** (p263), an indigenous fishing village with ocean views, a surf break and a charming beachfront restaurant row just to the south in **Playa Engabao** (p263).

Seasonal Highlights

JAN–MAY
Rainy season, running from January to May, is hot, humid and sunny with occasional downpours. Also, a busy time for beach towns like Salinas.

MAY
Off-season for the coast, the rates listed will drop; ask for discounts if the place has few occupants.

JUN–SEP
Every year from June to September, humpback whales migrate along Ecuador's southern coastline, an event marked by Puerto López's annual **Humpback Whale Festival** (p275).

WeekLong Adventure

● Thanks to an easily navigable coastline, a week is plenty of time to visit the region's main highlights. Make a beeline for **Olon** or **Montañita** (p267), the south coast's surf-party capital. Take a surf lesson or rent a board and enjoy beachfront ceviche carts and cosmopolitan cafes.

● On your way up to **Puerto López** (p273) – the gateway to **Parque Nacional Machalilla** (p275), and home to some of the freshest seafood around – go slow with stops at a handful of fishing villages and at the **Mirador de Salango** (p271) for a breathtaking view. Head offshore for humpback-whale watching (June to September) or a day trip to **Isla de la Plata** (p276), aka 'the little Galápagos.'

Stay Awhile

● The laid-back rhythm of Ecuador's tropical southern coastline always encourages visitors to unwind and stay awhile. Towns like **Olón** (p267) and **Ayampe** (p273) are ideal home bases for surfers and slow travelers interested in temporary roots. Invest in Spanish lessons with **Outdoor Ecuador** (p269), take daily yoga classes and get your scuba certification at a dive center in **Puerto López** (p273) to enjoy the incredible underwater biodiversity. Or simply enjoy leisurely days at one of the area's breathtaking beaches and languid afternoons lounging in a hammock.

● When you need a city fix, the lively cocktail bars and riverfront restaurants of **Guayaquil** (p252) aren't far away.

JUN–OCT
Spot manta rays at offshore diving or while snorkeling sites like Bajo Cope.

NOV
Whether from the shore or deep-sea fishing in a boat, this is a good month to fish for a wide variety of species.

DEC
Heat and humidity do nothing to slow Christmas celebrations, including crowds admiring large-scale decorations on Guayaquil's *malecón*.

Guayaquil

SCENIC VIEWS | HERITAGE MUSUEMS | WINING & DINING

GETTING AROUND

Walking around the tourist zones is considered safe thanks to a fairly heavy police presence. Guayaquil's airport and main bus station, just a few minutes from each other, are only 5km from the city center. They are easy and inexpensive to access by official taxi, bus or rideshare app (which are also by far the best ways to get around town). However, keep in mind that even when covering short distances, heavy and chaotic traffic causes delays.

TOP TIP

Galapágos-bound travelers should build in a day or two (or at least an evening) on either end of their itineraries to get a feel for Guayaquil. After the tropical heat subsides and the sun goes down, bars, restaurants and cafes pack with locals.

The city's *malecón* looks like an elongated amusement park: rides, manicured gardens, food courts and monuments. The pastel-colored picturesque *barrio* (neighborhood) of Las Peñas perches over the northern waterfront as a reminder of the city's origins and a riposte to the massive high-rises being built below. Lively cocktail bars and buzzy restaurants crowd riverfront promenades and pedestrian plazas. Massive local markets hawk delicious seafood. Despite this, the airport or bus station is often all that tourists see of Guayaquil – all flights to the Galápagos Islands stop or originate from the downtown airport.

The country's largest city, its commercial and industrial engine, was strategically founded on the banks of the Río Guayas by Spaniard Francisco de Orellana in 1538 (then relocated three times due to fires). Guayaquil was looted by pirates and invaded by the English, before gaining its freedom from Spain and, later, Peru.

While it's an architecturally nondescript city, a deeper look will reveal how the nearly three million *guayaquileños* who call the city home give it soul.

Catch a Clásico

Fit in with chanting fans

Best to dress in the yellow of Guayaquil's beloved Barcelona, the country's most successful team (they celebrated the 100th year of their founding in 2025) when catching a game at **Estadio Monumental Banco Pichincha** *(barcelonasc.com.ec)*. Ecuador football's crown jewel, the stadium was inaugurated in 1987 with an official capacity of just under 60,000. Since then fans have proved that many more spectators fit in the stadium. In fact, in 1997 a record 91,230 attended a match, making Monumental one of the largest stadiums in South America. Good seats, easily purchased at the stadium for most games, cost around $8. It's located in northern Guayaquil in a working-class neighborhood. Solid Spanish language skills are helpful if attending.

JUAN FDO. VANEGAS/SHUTTERSTOCK

Iguana, Parque Seminario

Catch a 'Clásico del Astillero,' a game between Barcelona SC and their Guayaquil rivals, Emelec. The latter, who are often clad in blue or gray, play in the southern part of downtown at **George Capwell Stadium**, where seating is arranged in dramatically steep rows.

Urban Iguanas

Grab a bench in Parque Seminario

Land iguanas are a startling sight. They're a different species from those found in the Galápagos, and some – over a meter in length – live in downtown Guayaquil's **Parque Seminario** (aka Parque Bolívar, named for the Bolívar monument in the park's center). Certainly, Guayaquil is the only city in the world where these creatures laze the day away among well-maintained fenced-in gardens (perhaps it's the fence, or the dense traffic just outside, that keeps these city dwellers from wandering elsewhere). Enjoy some up-close and personal reptile time (a group of small turtles share the space), but beware if you're keen on having lunch on the grass or a bench – these reptiles aren't shy about getting their share of the snacks.

On the west side of the park is the **Catedral Católica Metropolitana de Guayaquil** *(@catedraldeguayaquil)*, a

continues on p256

SAFETY IN GUAYAQUIL

Guayaquil and the surrounding province of Guayas, as well as the coastal region of Manabí, are considered ground zero in the country's battle with narco-trafficking-related violence. Statistically, as well as anecdotally (with several high-profile events dominating the headlines), the region has experienced an unprecedented rise in assaults and killings. For better or worse, this violence is, by and large, gang-affiliated and targeted. It is also geographically contained within certain areas and neighborhoods, which are easily avoided and not on the itinerary of most travelers. Use common sense, avoid wandering desolate areas at night and ask locals for advice if unsure as to the status of a specific place.

DRINKING COFFEE IN GUAYAQUIL: CAFES

Café Colibri: Occupying a prime daytime people-watching corner of a downtown plaza, with pastries, full menu and hot and frozen coffee drinks. *8am-4pm*

Dulceria La Palma: An atmospheric, old-school place downtown worth visiting for breakfast or snacks like *cachitos* (crispy mini-croissants) or pastries. *7:30am-7pm*

Masamadre – Lomas 316: Fronting an Urdesa office building, deservedly popular for gourmet pastries, croissants, sandwiches and top coffee. *8am-8pm*

Sweet & Coffee: Roomy Puerto Santa Ana branch of widespread chain close to accommodations and with a waterfront setting. *8am-10pm*

HIGHLIGHTS
1 Museo Antropológico y de Arte Contemporáneo

SIGHTS
2 Catedral Católica Metropolitana de Guayaquil
3 Cerro Santa Ana
4 City Cemetery
5 Coliseo Voltaire Paladines Polo
see 3 Fortín del Cerro
6 La Rotonda
see 3 Lighthouse
7 Malecón 2000
8 Museo Nacional del Cacao
9 Olmedo Monument
10 Parque Seminario
11 Torre Morisco

ACTIVITIES
12 La Perla
13 river cruises

SLEEPING
14 Casa las Penas Siglo XXI
see 14 Hotel Boutique Mansion del Rio
15 Hotel Oro Verde

EATING
16 Al Fiume Cucina Italiana
17 Birria Bros
18 Café Colibri
19 Dulceria La Palma
20 Juice Bar
21 La Costeñita
22 Lo Nuestro
23 Malek el Shawarma
24 Masamadre - Lomas 316
25 Mercado del Río
see 8 S&O La Pesca
26 Sweet & Coffee

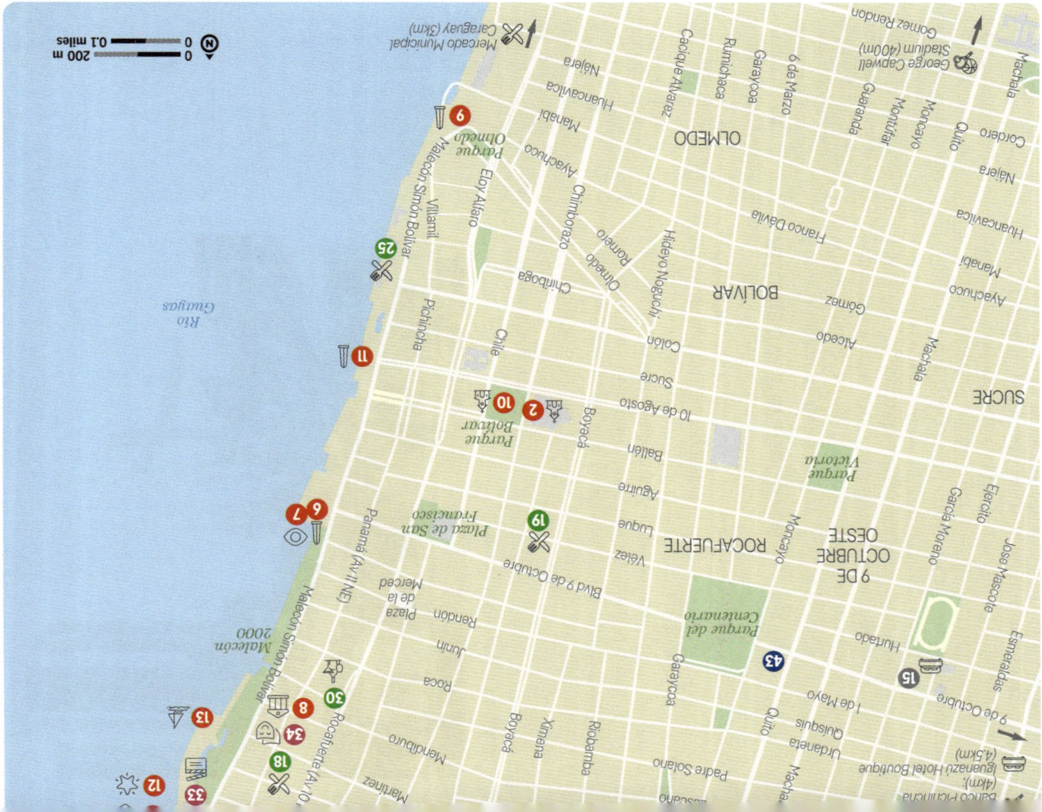

DRINKING & NIGHTLIFE
see 24 City Winery
27 Diva Nicotina
see 8 Juliana
28 La Cueva Jazz Bar
29 Lola Sky
30 Nicanor Casa de Bebidas
31 Santobar
32 Terabithia

ENTERTAINMENT
33 Cinema Malecón
34 Espacio Muégano Teatro
35 MAAC Cine
36 Pop Up Teatro Cafe
see 34 Teatro Casa Zona Escena

SHOPPING
37 Ecua-Andino
38 El Mercado Artesanal
39 Galeria de Mafaldo
40 La Madriguera
41 Solaz
see 39 Woven Straw

TRANSPORT
42 Cuatro Mosqueteros
43 Estación Parque Centenario

CITY CEMETERY

From aloft in the Aerovia, you'll see the 50-acre sprawl of Gayaquil's whitewashed central cemetery. Founded in 1823, the cemetery occupies valuable real estate that the city has steadily encroached upon. It's a mix of massive, grand mausoleums (including the impressive grave of President Vicente Rocafuerte, as well as two other 19th-century Ecuadorian presidents), striking marble statues and thousands of above-ground tombs stacked atop one another, resembling a miniaturized apartment complex more than a final resting place. Visible from the Aerovía is a regal gated entrance along Calle 9 that leads to a wide paved walkway lined with palm trees leading up to the forested slopes of Cerro Carmen.

OCTAVIO PARRA/SHUTTERSTOCK

Market at Guayaquil's *malecón*

continued from p253

neo-Gothic cathedral built in the early 1920s, and renovated in the late 1970s, on the same site where one of Guayaquil's first churches, originally built in 1547, burned down. You can visit the cathedral's 126 stained-glass windows daily from 9am to 5pm. It's also noteworthy as a nice place to cool down and break up a stroll on a hot day.

Both the park and church are watched over by tourist police.

Alternative Perspectives

Aerovía and boat views

While *guayaquileños* hop on and off as commuters, there's no better way to grasp the city's size and geography than grabbing a seat on the **Aerovía** (*aeroviagye.com*), an aerial gondola system that covers some limited territory north of the center.

The most easily accessed station, **Cuatro Mosqueteros**, is located directly across from the Cinema Malecon. The leg from here over the Río Guayas to Duran, oft cited as the most dangerous part of the city, takes 10 minutes each way. Besides the views of the La Perla Ferris wheel and a large swath of the *malecón*, there's a small thrill in passing relatively low over the muddy river. Simply disembark at the **Duran** station, pass

EATING IN GUAYAQUIL: OUR PICKS

Mercado del Rio: Food court offering primarily Ecuadorian-style seafood, with a Mexican, Peruvian and Japanese counter, too. *noon-9pm* $

S&O La Pesca: Small contemporary-style raw bar, specializing in oysters, as well as fresh shrimp, prawns etc. Great ceviche. *10:30am-5pm Tue-Sun* $$

Al Fiume Cucina Italiana: Part of Puerto Santa Ana's lively restaurant row, with wide-ranging menu featuring variety of pastas and pizzas. *12:30-11pm* $$

Lo Nuestro: Housed in a century-old mansion, atmospheric Lo Nuestro serves ceviche, sea bass with crab, and other seafood dishes. *noon-11pm* $$$

through the turnstile and tap your card to enter again for the return trip. Note: while Duran is considered to be dangerous, taking the Aerovía to the Duran station and back is not.

The other route, from Cuatro Mosqueteros then west and south to the downtown's **Parque Centenario** station, is equally worthwhile and scenic, and oft windy. There are fantastic bird's-eye views of the **city cemetery** and of Guayaquil's dense sprawl.

Open between 5:30am and 9pm, the Aerovía is a well-regulated and policed transportation system, with staff on hand to help purchase cards ($2 and $0.75 per one-way trip) and answer questions at each stop.

To get a little wind in your hair, several small-boat cruises ferry you along the Río Guayas. Most frequently, there's a 40-minute **boat ride** *(riverdock.com.ec; per person $4)* between Puerto Santa Ana to the north and the bridge to Isla Santay to the south, leaving from a spot at the northern end of the *malecón*. Less regularly, there's an hour-long sunset trip with drinks and music (reservations required).

Malecón Wander

Stroll the city's riverside showpiece

One of the most extensive urban-renewal projects in South America when it was initiated in 2000, this 2.5km-long gated, policed and well-maintained **promenade** is akin to a riverfront Central Park. It's also where to go to put to rest apocalyptic images of a city under siege by sharing space with *guayaquileños* – including a heavy contingent of families, runners and young couples – enjoying the ordinary daily rhythms of city life. Things are generally more lively from dusk to early evening when temperatures are more comfortable.

Most travelers will likely enter through gates at the *malecón's* northern end, dominated by the **Museo Antropológico y de Arte Contemporáneo** *(MAAC; free)* and its attached **cinema**. The museum, dedicated to pre-Columbian anthropology and archaeology, has a superb permanent collection of artifacts, but can feel partly abandoned when galleries that host temporary art installations go unused.

THE CITY'S ORIGINS

Popular legend has it that Guayaquil's name comes from Guayas, the great Puna chief who fought bravely against the Inca and later the Spanish, and his wife, Quill. Guayas is said to have killed Quill rather than allow her to be captured by the conquistadors, before drowning himself. Several historians claim the city's name actually comes from the words *hua* (land), *illa* (beautiful prairie) and Quilca, one of Río Guayas' tributaries, where the Quilca tribe lived until being wiped out in the 17th century. Under this theory, Guayaquil is literally 'the land like a beautiful prairie on the land of the Quilcas.'

DRINKING IN GUAYAQUIL: OUR PICKS

Lola Sky: Pricey cocktails and spectacular views. A mandatory minimum $21 per person spend. ID required. *5pm-midnight Tue & Wed, to 2am Thu-Sat*

La Cueva Jazz Bar: A cozy hole-in-the-wall with a retro 1960s folk feel on a picturesque cobblestone street. Live jam sessions at 7pm. *to 2am Wed-Sat*

City Winery: The upscale wine bar of Bodega dos Hemisferios, a stylish winery from Santa Elena peninsula. *1pm-1am Wed-Sat, to 11pm Sun-Tue*

Santobar: Puerto Santa Ana waterfront spot serving artisanal cocktails. *5pm-2am Tue-Sun*

Juliana: A sophisticated cocktail bar with twinkling night views of Cerro Santa Ana. *3pm-midnight Mon-Wed, to 2am Thu-Sat*

Nicanor Casa de Bebidas: Craft beers, cocktails, excellent small bites and outdoor plaza seating. *3pm-midnight Wed-Sun*

Terabithia: Classy rooftop cocktail spot in Urdesa with outdoor balcony seating with beautiful sunset views. *5pm-midnight*

Diva Nicotina: At the foot of Cerro Santa Ana. A young crowd packs the house when there's live music. *6:30pm-late Mon-Sat*

SPANISH-LANGUAGE ENTERTAINMENT

Pop Up Teatro Cafe *(popupteatro.com)* A funky micro-theater that draws a hip crowd for short performances.

Teatro Casa Zona Escena *(teatrozonaescena.com)* Downtown cultural center on Calle Panamá plaza, equivalent to downtown off-off Broadway.

Espacio Muégano Teatro *(@mueganoteatro)* Calle Panamá plaza theater with alternative multidisciplinary performances.

Coliseo Voltaire Paladines Polo Hosts big-name stadium performers like Andés Cepeda and Pablo Alborán.

MAAC Cine *(@maaccine)* Modern *malecón*-situated theater for plays, concerts and films, Hollywood blockbusters and South American fare.

FABRICIO BURBANO/SHUTTERSTOCK

La Rotonda

La Perla *(Mon-Thu $3.50, Fri & Sun $5)*, a giant 57m Ferris wheel, the largest in South America, is just to the south. It's worth a spin for views over the city, old town and rivers beyond, especially if you're skipping a ride on the Aerovía gondola. It operates noon to 8pm weekdays and from 10am weekends.

You'll encounter several landmarks while strolling the *malecón*, perhaps most famously **La Rotonda**, one of the city's most impressive monuments, particularly when illuminated at night. Flanked by small fountains, it depicts the historic but enigmatic meeting between Bolívar and San Martín, which took place here in 1822. Where 10 de Agosto meets the *malecón*, you'll see the **Torre Morisco**, a famous 23m-high Moorish-style clock tower. The original was built in 1770, but has been replaced several times since then. And at the far southern end of the *malecón* is the **Olmedo monument**, honoring Jos Joaqun de Olmedo (1780–1847), an Ecuadorian poet and the president of the first Ecuadorian territory independent of Spanish rule.

You can duck into the *malecón's* elongated shopping mall, which covers a good chunk of its southern half. However, it's primarily ordinary clothing, shoe and electronics shops with a smattering of quick eats, ice cream and cafes. Your best bet for a meal, other than fast food and empanada kiosks, is the **Mercado del Río** food court.

Cobblestone City

Old Guayaquil neighborhoods

These historic neighborhoods are among Guayaquil's oldest, with parts untouched by the fires that ravaged the city periodically over the years. Originally settled in the 17th century, the streets and buildings have been restored to a version of a quaint South American hillside village, with brightly painted homes and cobblestone alleyways. The views from the top are spectacular, especially at night.

A handful of small, informal, family-run restaurants, shops and neighborhood bars line the 444 numbered steps of **Cerro Santa Ana**. It's patrolled by security officers, who are also stationed near the bottom gates and the hilltop **Fortín del Cerro**. Cannons, which were once used to protect Guayaquil from pirates, aim over the parapet toward the river and are still fired today during celebrations. If your quads are up for it and you want a little more elevation, climb the **lighthouse** for spectacular 360-degree views, including the high-rises of Puerto Santa Ana just to the north; take a seat in the nearby tiny chapel for a breather and to get out of the sun.

The historic street Numa Pompilio Llona, named after the well-known *guayaquileño* poet (1832–1907), begins at the northern end of the *malecón*, to the right of the stairs that head up Cerro Santa Ana. This narrow, winding street has several unobtrusive plaques set into the walls of some of its houses, indicating the simple residences of past presidents. The colonial wooden architecture has been allowed to age elegantly, albeit with a gloss of paint. Several artists live in the area, and there are a couple of art galleries and craft shops scattered along the lane (and several recommended accommodations).

Keep going along the street and it eventually joins a pleasant paved walkway skirting the river's edge to the massive building development of Puerto Santa Ana. This is one of the city's newest districts and is lined with many lively restaurants and bars.

Both areas can feel sleepy, to the point of abandoned, during the peak of midday heat on weekdays, but the lower portion of Cerro Santa Ana, with a handful of casual bars and eateries comes alive on weekend evenings.

Sweeten Your Day

Tour the Museum of Chocolate

The history of chocolate in Ecuador is a long one. Cultivation began an estimated 5300 years ago, and exports, with Guayaquil at the center, go back half a millennium. So it's hardly surprising there's a **Museo Nacional del Cacao** (*museocacao.com; adult/child $5/free*) in the city. What's startling is that it took until 2021 to open.

It's housed in a regal building built in the 'continental style,' circa late 1920s, typical of European-born chocolate magnates of the time when 20 families owned 70% of cacao haciendas. Several floors of digestible and sophisticated displays and exhibits in Spanish do a fairly comprehensive job of tracing chocolate's cultural and economic primacy, from its pre-Hispanic origins to its role in the country's and world's contemporary

CHOCOLATE CAPITAL

The cacao industry helped build the city of Guayaquil. From 1870 to 1920, Ecuador was the world's largest exporter of the cacao beans. Warehouses and trading shops lined the Río Guayas and nearby streets to such a degree that even now, despite cacao being cultivated in 22 of the country's 24 provinces, nationally the beans are still referred to as 'Cacao de Guayaquil.' At the high point of the industry, there were 80 million cacao trees growing in the country's coastal region, where rainforests provide shade, and bananas and other tropical fruit add a hint of flavor. Relatively recent archaeological finds indicate that cacao originated in the Ecuadorian Amazon and not in Mesoamerica as previously believed.

EATING IN URDESA: CASUAL SPOTS

Malek el Shawarma: One of a half dozen or so Lebanese shawarma spots congregated around this intersection. *10am-1am* $

Juice Bar: Salads, acai bowls and smoothies, personalized to your liking with a choice of proteins and sweeter fixings. *8:30am-9pm* $

La Costeñita: Modestly priced Ecuadorian specialties with a seafood focus, especially bustling at lunchtime. *8am-10pm* $

Birria Bros: Festively decorated Mexican eatery with budget-priced tacos and burritos, massive nachos and strong margaritas. *5-11:30pm Tue-Sat, 2-10pm Sun* $

GUAYAQUIL'S BEST SHOPS

Solaz: Urdesa store selling high-quality sombreros that can be customized and individualized with hand-painted drawings and names.

Ecua-Andino: The main showroom for the popular brand producing stylish reinventions of classic Panama hats.

Woven Straw: Small boutique selling handwoven straw hats, bags and other top-notch small items.

Galeria de Mafaldo: Primarily oil paintings by the eponymous artist, who can create customized works with size, theme and color to your specifications.

La Madriguera: Quirky, independent bookstore in Urdesa; also sells comics, pop-culture figurines and other gifts. It has a small cafe with snacks and coffee.

Calle Numa Pompilio Llona, Las Peñas

economy (Ecuador ranks around seventh in terms of exports, behind a number of West African countries).

Give yourself an hour or more, and pop down to the ground-floor retail space to pick up high-quality hand-crafted chocolate products; staff are happy to answer questions. It's best to visit around lunchtime so you can stroll around the surrounding newly developed pedestrian plaza (off Calle Panamá, which is said to have once been filled with the *aroma a cacao*). It's lined with some of downtown's most appealing cafes and restaurants (most close by 5pm).

Bargain Mercados

Stock up on gifts and gorge with locals

Your best bet for returning home with (admittedly mass-produced) Ecuadorian-'inspired' handicrafts, art, clothing (eg Otavalo-style sweaters), jewelry and other souvenirs is to stroll the stalls of downtown's **El Mercado Artesanal** *(9am-6pm Mon-Sat, to 4pm Sun)*. Bargaining is expected. Nearby, on beautiful Calle Numa Pompilio Llona you'll find a few surviving art galleries, a hat boutique and a souvenir shop.

Less commonly visited due to its location far south of downtown and its hours is the **Mercado Municipal Caraguay** *(3-7am & 8pm-midnight Mon-Sat)*. It's the largest seafood market in the country, with 806 stalls, 315 of which exclusively sell seafood. It also sells fruit, vegetables and other essentials. However, the real draw is the **food court** where cooked-food stalls bring the market alive, offering delicious dishes like *cangrejo criollo* (creole crab), *arroz marinero* (seafood rice) or *encebollado* (seafood soup).

For some of the city's best ceviche and kaleidoscopic piles of produce, head to **Mercado Sauces 9**, Guayaquil's smaller seafood market around 6km north of the airport. It opens early morning and winds down by 3pm.

For the latter two markets, only travel by taxi or Uber and keep your wits about you.

Beyond Guayaquil

Immerse yourself in a rich collection of wildlife-filled landscapes or make a beeline to a beach for downtime between flights.

The destinations outside Guayaquil offer nothing if not variety – whether it's sumptuous spreads at haciendas or wineries, bushwhacking through densely packed native forests, or gliding through placid waters and mangrove mazes. The chorus of bird sounds and throaty barks from monkeys only get louder as you go further into nature. As you escape the last vestiges of urban sprawl to the east, the landscape becomes dry and scrubby, until you reach the year-round sunshine of the Santa Elena Peninsula. Because of their proximity to the big city, the towns of Playas and Salinas are immensely popular with Ecuadorians, who gather at every beachfront *cevicherías* and spare stretch of sand on weekends and holidays. Otherwise, there's no shortage of picturesque shoreline to commandeer.

Places

Dos Hemisférios Vineyard

TIME FROM GUAYAQUIL: **1HR 40MIN**

Wining and dining

Bananas, shrimp, chocolate, coffee, wine... What doesn't fit? Wine lovers know that the best grapes are grown in countries with four seasons, ideally located at temperate latitudes of the globe. Which would make wine produced in Ecuador, a country located where the planet's two hemispheres meet, impossible. Or so it was thought, until the owners of **Bodega Dos Hemisférios** (*doshemisferios.com; tour & tasting/incl lunch per person $69/138*) discovered more than a decade ago the delightful paradox of high-quality wine made in Ecuador.

Visit the vineyard for tours and wine tasting, topped off with an extravagant, three-course, wine-paired lunch.

GETTING AROUND

Getting to Salinas or Playas is an easy short trip from Guayaquil, either in your own rental car (carry cash, preferably coins for tollbooths along the way) or by bus from the central station. In Playas, local buses can take you between towns (Puerto Engabao is a 10-minute bus ride away), or you can hire a taxi for a few dollars to visit less accessible beaches like El Pelado. Check online *(ecuadorbus.com.ec)* for info bus schedules.

CLIMATE COMPLICATIONS

The south coast is generally drier than the north coast, and the rainy season lasts only from January through April. During this time, the coast is oppressively hot and humid, though the water is warm for swimmers and divers. At the same time, it's also sunny, unlike the dry season from May through December, which is often overcast (especially July and August) and pleasantly cool. During the dry season, visitors are often disappointed to find it's a little too cool for sunbathing. Ecuadorians tend to visit the coast during the rainy season and in July and August. What does this mean for you in terms of what to pack? Regardless of the month, bring along a hat, mosquito repellent, sunscreen, rain gear, and water shoes or light rainproof boots if hiking.

LESLIE RUSSUM/SHUTTERSTOCK

Cocoi heron, Reserva Ecológica Manglares Churute

Hacienda la Danesa

TIME FROM GUAYAQUIL: **1HR 30MIN**

Living large on a luxury hacienda

Only 82km east of Guayaquil but world's away in terms of atmospherics, family-owned **Hacienda la Danesa** (*haciendaladanesa.com*) is a working farm, but one with echoes of the grand estates found in Ecuador's highlands. It's also a recommended luxury lodge and a worthy day out from the city. Sloths, ocelots, armadillos and a variety of birdlife call the grounds home. Grab a bike to ride out to the start of a lazy float down a river in a tube past densely vegetated shores (it's 'lazy' because the guide pushes you through the shallows much of the way). Then learn the botanical structure of raw cacao beans and satisfy your sweet tooth at a tasting of Danesa's artisanal chocolates and other products, like jams and jellies.

The full day runs $125 per person, including a gourmet three-course lunch. You'll have to make your own way out there. Not a bad deal if already paying for a rental car, since the price is in the ballpark of guide costs to other cacao plantations in the area.

Bosque Protector Cerro Blanco

TIME FROM GUAYAQUIL: **20MIN**

Into the wild

Understandably, you might have low expectations pulling off the side of the highway only 15km or so west of downtown Guayaquil. The entrance to the **Bosque Protector Cerro Blanco** (*bosqueprotectorcerroblanco.org*) is still amid urban sprawl, and the dirt-road turnoff and gate suggest a construction site rather than over 6000 hectares of privately preserved coastal dry forest.

Birds, insects and rushing water create a wall of sound once you're out on one of the trails. Look up into the branches of massive *matapolo* trees for howler monkeys and be sure to climb to the viewpoint for expansive views. From January to May, there's plenty of water and the plants are green; from June to December (the dry season), the plants flower and it's easier to see wildlife. Ticks and mosquitoes are a nuisance, so best to bring long pants, bug spray and shoes you don't mind getting wet.

Visiting is by reservation only, and guides are mandatory (English-speaking guides might be available). Admission is $10, plus an additional amount, ranging from $15 to $30 per group (up to 10 people), depending on the length of trail you choose. We recommend the 1.5km *sendero canao*, which takes around two hours; the 7km *sendero mono aullador* is longest (give yourself four to five hours; the reserve is open from 8am to 4pm).

Reserva Ecológica Manglares Churute

TIME FROM GUAYAQUIL: **55MIN**

Gliding through mangroves

In the opposite direction is the **Reserva Ecológica Manglares Churute**, a massive preserve of over 55,000 hectares around an hour's drive southeast of Guayaquil. Marvel at the howler monkeys and dozens of endemic bird species, as well as ibises and cormorants during a relaxing (and informative) canoe tour of the mangroves; after registering at the visitor's center a short raised trail leads to the jetty, from which tours depart.

If you choose to head out on foot through one of the reserve's trails through upland dry forest, be sure to guard against mosquitoes with long pants and bug spray. Most conveniently, the El Mate trail begins next to the visitor's center, but be prepared for an uphill slog. Go with a guide, whether pre-arranged through a Guayaquil-based tour company or paid for at the park.

Engabao

TIME FROM GUAYAQUIL: **1HR 50MIN**

Two sides to Engabao, the port and playas

Only a half-hour or so drive north of Playas, there's an end-of-the-road feel to this coastal fishing town. Maybe, it's the rough, potholed roads that peter out into even rougher dirt ones, or the roaming pigs and dogs. More picturesquely, several rows of blue-and-white fishing boats crowd one another along the town beach, best viewed from near a small **lighthouse** just above.

AREA ARCHAEOLOGY

Museo de Valdivia *($2)* Exceptional quality of ceramics housed in a neglected building with some descriptive text in Spanish and English.

Museo las Calaveras Valdivia museum with miniature figurines and jewelry and artifacts of Valdivia, Chorrera, Guangala, and Manteña cultures.

Museo Arqueológico de Salango *($2.50)* Small, well-organized museum of the coastal pre-Hispanic cultures with artifacts, pictures and dioramas (Spanish-language descriptions).

Complejo Cultural Real Alto *(complejocultural realalto.org)* Likely least visited because of its relatively isolated location, built on a neolithic excavation site.

Museo Antropológico y de Arte Contemporáneo Guayaquil museum art and archaeology fans will swoon over.

EATING IN PLAYAS: OUR PICKS

El Algarrobo Crepería: Sweet and savory crepes made with algaroba flour in a Playas cafe near the sea. *3-9pm Thu & Fri, from 11am Sat & Sun* $

Santural: Charming Playas cafe with an open-air bakery. Specializes in sandwiches, waffles and omelets. *8am-9pm Thu-Sun* $

Cecilia Restaurante: Hefty portions of the usual fresh seafood dishes in a thatched-roof dining room just off the beach. *8am-7pm* $$

Parilla del Uruguayo: Sizzling grilled meats, cocktails and a wine selection. Pleasant outdoor dining, too (another location in Salinas). *12:30-11:30pm* $$

SEAFOOD SMORGASBORD

One of the pleasures of traveling Ecuador's southern coastline is the fresh, cheap and delicious seafood, most often served in open-air thatched eateries along the beachfront, or from carts pushed along the beach, like in Montañita. Menus rarely vary, all offering versions of the following with your choice of seafood: *encebollado* (soup with yuca and onion, garnished with popcorn and *chifles*, crispy fried bananas), *encocoado* (cooked in a coconut sauce), *cazuela* (stew) and *ceviche*. Other standards include *cangrejo* (crab), often cooked whole and a Playas specialty, *calamares*, *langosta* (lobster), fish (grilled, fried or cooked with garlic), *camarones* (shrimp), *concha* (shellfish) and *pulpo* (octopus).

VISUAL AND WRITTEN/ALAMY

Puerto El Morro

The proximity of Engabao to Playas and a regular, right-hand point break draw more intrepid surfers. A few beach clubs like **Amoramar** *(amoramar.ec),* which requires $40 worth of food and drinks; **Picones** *(@piconeshouse),* marked by a replica of gaping shark's mouth entrance; and the **Engabao Beach Club** *(engabaobeachclub.com)* all pull a growing number of weekenders. Only 5km south, Playa Engabao's stretch of soft sandy beach has several charming restaurants with a white-and-blue Greek island feel. One such spot is **Cocteles del Paraiso** *(@coctelesdelparaiso),* which is ideal for a long, leisurely meal and cocktails.

El Morro & Puerto El Morro

TIME FROM GUAYAQUIL: 1½HR

One Road to desert and mangroves

An hour and a half from Guayaquil – or a short 20-minute drive from Playas – you'll find the small towns of El Morro and its sister, Puerto El Morro (El Morro Port), only 4km to the northeast.

These are the respective starting points for a stop at **Cerro del Muerto** (Hill of the Dead) and boat tours of **Refugio de Vida Silvestre Manglares El Morro** *(facebook.com/Rvsmanglaresmorro),* a protected mangrove reserve that's a haven for spotting a host of wildlife, including blue and white herons, an immense colony of frigate birds and, most notably, ever-so-friendly bottlenose dolphins. Besides a ride through the ecologically vital mangroves and time spent watching the dolphins play, tours may opt to stop at a small offshore island where a short hike takes you to the site of a gigantic frigate-bird colony.

Simply take the Puerto El Morro road to its literal end at a concrete pier, where there's usually someone around to help arrange a trip. You don't need to book in advance – the

1½-hour tour will leave when the boat is full ($7 per person, maximum six people), or you can pay extra to leave immediately if your group is smaller. Early mornings are best, but you can head out as late as early afternoon.

When back on land, grab a fresh seafood lunch before heading to Cerro del Muerto, a set of three 100m-high hills so named for the silhouette they create when seen from sea – that of a person lying down as if deceased. This zone is popular with outdoor climbers, dirt bikers and hikers. However, for most, a short and gentle climb up to a viewpoint with a religious shrine and horizon-spanning views is enough. Alternatively, scramble to the top for an even more expansive perspective on the surrounding flat and arid scrubland.

Museo los Amantes de Sumpa

TIME FROM GUAYAQUIL: 1¾HR

Buried in an eternal embrace

The Lovers of Sumpa are a pre-Inca and pre-Valdivia couple from the Las Vegas culture buried near the Las Vegas River in a group graveyard, which archaeologists excavated in 1970. In one of 192 graves on-site, the pair of 20-somethings, dated to 4600 to 8000 years ago, became famous for being buried in what appears to be a locked embrace.

The couple sparked numerous cultural creations, including poems by Iván Carvajal Aguirre and Jorge Enrique Adoum, a sculpture by Yela Loffredo and even a folkloric ballad by Juanita Córdova.

The Lovers are the main attraction at their namesake museum, **Museo los Amantes de Sumpa** *(@museoamantesdesumpa; 9am-4:30pm; free; exhibits in Spanish only)* in La Libertad. The museum tells the story of the pre-Hispanic peoples of the Santa Elena Peninsula. It also has a traditional countryside house you can walk through, one of the original balsa boats used to navigate the coastline, numerous other artifacts from the Valdivia, Las Vegas and

MORE ANCIENT ARCHAEOLOGY

Several locally managed museums with displays of ceramics and other artifacts from the country's earliest-known settlements are further north, including in **Agua Blanca** (p277).

EATING IN SALINAS: OUR PICKS

Pedro's Empanadas: Sells fine hand-baked patties a block inland from Chipipe Beach. *8:30am-9pm Thu-Mon* $

Café Jazz: Cozy outdoor space good for inexpensive egg, crepe and waffle breakfasts. *8am-3pm & 6-9pm Tue-Sat, to 1pm Sun* $

Oahu Superfood: Acai bowls with cacao and other toppings in a fast-food-like setting. *8:30am-9:30pm* $

Stonefire: Sidewalk seating at this hole-in-the-wall pizzeria on Salinas' buzziest circle. *3-11pm* $

La Buona Cucina: Homemade pastas, lasagna and pizzas served with artisanal breads. *9am-9:30pm* $$

Mariscos Azul: Peruvian-style seafood with beachfront seating; surcharge when musicians are in the house. *noon-midnight* $$

Umi Sushi Bar: Pint-sized *malecón* spot with Salinas' best Japanese, including a variety of *chirashi* bowls. *5-11pm Tue-Sun* $$

Mar y Tierra: *Malecón* location and an upscale vibe; menu runs from seafood to burgers to pizza. *11am-11pm* $$

WHY I LOVE THE SOUTH COAST

Michael Grosberg, Lonely Planet writer

There's perhaps no better part of the country for having your own wheels and cruising the open road. Ocean views are never far away. Vendors sell fresh coconut and other quick eats alongside the roadways; just give yourself time and cautiously pull to the side. Pristine beaches that barely register on maps dot the coastline. Turn off the main road at almost any tiny town, then drive to the end of a (probably) dirt road, where you'll be often be rewarded by glorious sandy shores that you'll likely have all to yourself. You can finish most days with a sunset stroll along a beach – one of life's great pleasures and greatest cliches – and with a truly authentic seafood meal at a fisherman's shack on the sand.

IRENEUKE/SHUTTERSTOCK

La Lobería

Guangala cultures, and a comparison of burial traditions between pre-Hispanic and modern-day cultures.

La Libertad is several kilometers west of Salinas, the big daddy of south-coast beach-resort towns, where high-rises far along along the beachfront. It's lively in high season, but at other times blowing tumbleweeds wouldn't feel out of place.

La Lobería & La Chocolatera

TIME FROM GUAYAQUIL: **2HR 10MIN**

Sea lions know how to pick 'em

La Lobería and **La Chocolatera**, two adjoining protected areas, are beautifully rough and austere, surprisingly so considering their proximity to Salinas' high-rise development. Both areas are part of the Producción de Fauna Marino Costero Puntilla Santa Elena and are situated past the gates of a naval base (you'll be stopped briefly, and ID is sometimes requested; free).

La Lobería hosts a colony of sea lions, usually found sunning themselves on the rugged rocky shoreline or an outcropping, just offshore. La Chocolatera marks the westernmost point of continental South America with breathtaking views and end-of-the-world vibes, especially when wind and crashing waves pound the shore. Both are good spots to contemplate the vastness of the ocean and also to spot seabirds in flight.

A 2.5km trail just inland from a long half-moon-shaped beach, suitable for walking or mountain biking, connects the two sites. However, keep in mind that it's entirely exposed. There's a kiosk for drinks and ice cream at both. Take a short detour drive up to the **Mirador Puntilla de Santa Elena** for inspiring views of the ocean and Salinas to the south.

Visits are most convenient in your own vehicle, or you can hire a taxi from town, which should run around $15 or so, including wait time. Plenty of locals walk, run or bike from the naval base entrance.

Montañita & Olón

NIGHTLIFE | SURF CULTURE | PEACE & QUIET

Known as much for all-night ragers as great waves, the town of Montañita has evolved, for better or worse, since its early days as a sleepy getaway with a year-round, clean, right-hand point break. There are vestiges of the backpacker and hippie ethos and Rasta vibe that once prevailed, and of course, the surf doesn't die. However, what followed those early days was more building, development and overcrowding – a victim of its own appeal.

These days, Montañita is party central on the Ecuadorian coast, known for its dance clubs and cocktail alley. Locals looking for a more laid-back lifestyle moved a few hundred meters up the coast to La Punta in front of Montañita's main wave, while others 'journeyed' further over the headland to Olón, an expat surf-hipster getaway, more low-key, but going through its own growing pains. An increasing number of cosmopolitan cafes and restaurants line a half-dozen small streets on Olón, while seafood kiosks line the beachfront.

TOP TIP

Don't stress about staying in Montañita proper. Stock up on groceries at **Tía**, the big supermarket in Montañita. Best to buy bus tickets a day in advance. Most restaurants accept credit cards, but not all; there are six ATMs in Montañita.

A Night Out in Montañita

Undisputed party capital

Imagine Mardi Gras, mix in a frat party, add a Latin twist and you have the aptly named **Calle de los Cócteles** (Cocktail Avenue). It's a narrow street lined with stalls all selling the same cocktails, like margaritas and piña coladas, and a nightclub or two pumping out music. If not inebriated, you might

GETTING AROUND

Between 5am and 7:30pm, direct buses ($7) to Montañita leave hourly from Guayaquil's main bus station. A taxi between the two runs around $85 for up to four people. Once you're in town, getting around is easy – both Montañita and Olón are walkable. To travel between the two, hop on the green bus that goes back and forth for less than a dollar each way (tickets sold onboard). Taxis are double the price. There are two daily departures to Quito (5:30am and 8pm) on Transportes Carlos Alberto Aray.

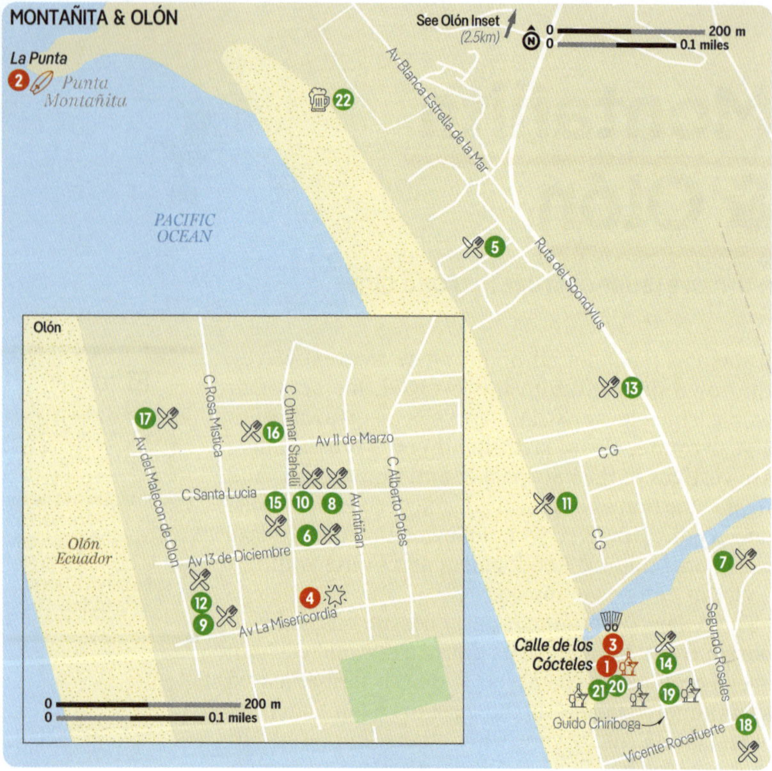

HIGHLIGHTS
1 Calle de los Cócteles
2 La Punta

ACTIVITIES
3 Montañita Surf & Dive
4 Outdoor Ecuador

EATING
5 22 Moon St
6 Benito Café
7 La Teretta
8 Momo
9 Noah Café
10 Pigro
11 Pigro al Sol
12 South Indian
13 Tía
14 Tiki Limbo
15 Tortolos
16 Tortuga Café
17 Vikara Lounge
18 Wave

DRINKING & NIGHTLIFE
19 Alcatraz
20 Caña Grill
21 Lost Beach Club
22 Montañita Brewing Company

feel out of place. And if sleep is of any interest, do not get a room in the vicinity.

Nightlife in Montañita isn't limited to Calle de los Cóteles, however. You could start the night on the avenue at vibey

EATING IN MONTAÑITA: OUR PICKS

22 Moon St: At the beach's north end. Delicious poke bowls, taco salads, veg schnitzel, smoothie bowls and breakfasts. *9am-3pm Wed-Mon* $

La Terreta: Simple family-run spot featuring set menus of beautifully prepared dishes like veg paella, and pita and hummus platter. *noon-10:30pm* $

Wave: T-bone steaks and fried chicken, plus healthy options like vegan burgers and tofu bowls. Situated on Montañita's main drag. *9am-11pm Fri-Wed, to 3pm Thu* $$

Pigro al Sol: Hotel Kundalini's beachfront bistro is good for entrees like grilled yellowtail in black ravioli and smoked plantain. Strong cocktails. *1-10:30pm* $$

Tiki Limbo before venturing further afield to **Montañita Brewing Company** *(montanitabrewingcompany.com)* for a craft beer or tropical cider (apple, mango, passionfruit). When it's time for dancing, Latin music lovers will flock to **Alcatraz** or head to **Caña Grill**, which offers weekly salsa lessons on Fridays from 9pm to 10pm ($4 per class).

But the place to party until the sun comes up is **Lost Beach** *(@lostbeachclub),* Montañita's most famous club. With an open-air beachfront location and five dance floors, it draws globally renowned electronic and techno DJs.

Surf La Punta

Breaking waves everywhere you look

Good year-round surf with breaks every few kilometers have made the south coast a playground for those living the *'pura vida'*. And nowhere else has captured the mantle of the capital of Ecuadorian surf like Montañita. Its early popularity was thanks to **La Punta**, a world-class right-hand point break that turns on from October to April. It's a short 15-minute walk from Montañita's center or a short drive over the headland from Olón.

This epic wave hosts the national surf circuit and some WQS competitions. Best surfed before and after high tide, the wave can get crowded when the swell is on. Off season, the point works irregularly, giving intermediates a chance to dial in their take-offs. Even if you're not a world-class surfer, there are plenty of opportunities for beginners on up to catch a wave on Montañita's beach break or in nearby Olón. Other popular spots nearby are in Ayampe, La Entrada, Río Chico, Las Tunas and La Rinconada.

There's no shortage of board-rental shops (hour/half-day/full-day $7/15/18) and lessons on offer ($20 to $25 for an hour); most accommodations can easily arrange rental and lessons. Beginner surfers can get in touch with **Montañita Surf & Dive** *(@surfdivemontanita)* or **Outdoor Ecuador** *(outdoorecuador.com)* if looking to plan in advance; the latter can also arrange Spanish language lessons and fishing trips.

THE DAY'S CATCH

Luis Malave, local fishing guide *(+593-99-962-4398)*

Fishing is great here. From the shore, you catch snook, corvina and red snapper, best from May to December. For mackerel, jack crevalle, barracuda and sometimes tarpon, the season is November to May. Deep-sea fishing for wahoo, yellowfin tuna, marlin and sailfish is best from June to November. Good shore locations include rocky spots at Punta Montañita, San Pedro, La Rinconada and Ayampe; cliffs at Ayangue; the beach at La Entrada, Salango and its nearby island, and Puerto López's bay. Mornings are best. We don't go out in strong winds and waves.

Sportfishing trips cost $120; capacity of up to three people.

EATING IN OLÓN: OUR PICKS

Tortuga Cafe: Strong, sophisticated espresso drinks, delicious baked goods, and pancake and waffle breakfasts; good place to bring laptop. *8am-8:30pm* **$**	**Benito Café:** Grab a table on the street corner for generous slices of pies and cakes; several other locations along the south coast. *1-10pm Wed-Mon* **$**	**Noah Café:** A whitewashed cafe with pour-over specialty coffee drinks, smoothies, gourmet sandwiches and more substantial mains. *9am-5pm* **$$**	**South Indian:** Unexpectedly authentic Southern Indian cuisine on Olón's beachfront road. Spice levels are taken seriously. *11am-10pm Thu-Tue* **$$**
Pigro: Competing for best Italian around with various pasta dishes, delicious desserts and wine, too. *5pm-midnight Wed-Mon* **$$**	**Tortolos:** Serves up homemade pastas like pumpkin walnut and mushroom ricotta ravioli. *5-10pm Tue-Fri, from 1pm Sat & Sun* **$$**	**Momo:** Upscale, chef-driven, seasonally influenced menu (lamb stew and the like), with wine shop, deli and bar. *noon-10pm* **$$**	**Vikara Lounge:** Hotel cafe serving risotto, quinoa, ceviche, rib-eye etc. *8:30am-8pm Wed, Thu & Sun, to 10pm Fri & Sat* **$$**

Beyond Montañita & Olón

Dive the coast, venture to an upland community-tourism project or explore surf and sand at a string of beachfront villages.

Places

Dos Mangas p270
Ayangue p272

GETTING AROUND

Having your own rental car is the best way to navigate the region. However, buses running north and south operate regularly along the coastal road. You can usually simply stand by the side of the road and pay on-board. Taxis are also widely available, but be savvy negotiating fares.

Inland from Olón, the landscape rises dramatically into a lush cloud forest that climbs over a low coastal mountain range (834m at its highest), part of the Cordillera Chongon-Colonche. Jaguars, howler monkeys and the critically endangered great green macaw all reside here. Deep paths lead into the forest from highland lodges. This area is one of the few places in the world where a beach and a cloud forest are in such close proximity.

But don't overlook lower-profile villages along the coast. Throw a dart at the map and you'll find a beach to day-trip to. On sunny days, the sandy stretch at Ayangue, 22km south of Montañita, gets crowded with local families splashing in the bath-like shallow waters and dining *alfresco* on seafood platters.

Dos Mangas

TIME FROM MONTAÑITA: **20MIN**

Forested walk to a waterfall

Howler monkeys and toucans, and a pleasant enough walk (round trip of about three hours) past a veritable produce section of fruit trees ends in a few small and cool freshwater pools. Don't go to **Dos Mangas** expecting an impressive cascade, but it's a good afternoon excursion if looking for a rural community-tourism experience.

August through October are generally drier months months; otherwise pack rain gear, water, snacks and plenty of insect repellent. Guides (Spanish-speaking only), who are required, point out the flora and fauna along the way; rubber boots can be supplied for the muddy slog in wet weather.

The trail (primarily flat), along a road for a good chunk of the way, begins near the **tourist information center** in Dos Mangas town, and you can opt for riding half the trail on horseback with a guide (per person $32) or guided walking (per person $22) the whole way in. Trips organized through Olón and Montañita hotels and tour companies are available, but you can easily take a taxi ($12) to Dos Mangas and organize a guide on-site to save money.

ROAD TRIP ALONG RUTA DE SPONDYLUS

Whether you're hunting waves, history or just out to explore, road tripping the Ruta is one of the best ways to experience this incredible stretch of coastline.

START	END	LENGTH
Ayangue	Mirador de Salango	61km; 1½hr

Start the drive in the village of ❶ **Ayangue**, marveling at the family-friendly beach scene where soccer-playing kids compete with massive floating playgrounds.

Next is ❷ **Valdivia**, a modern-day town where two humble museums – Museo Las Calaveras (p263) and Museo de Valdivia (p263) – tell the story of some of Ecuador's earliest inhabitants, La Cultura Valdivia.

The town of ❸ **Simón Bolívar** has a main drag lined with shops selling handmade goods and artisan crafts, such as the Montecristi Panama hat, handwoven baskets and hammocks.

❹ **La Entrada** is 25 minutes up the coast, through the crowded towns of Montañita and Olón and over some axle-damaging speed bumps. Brightly painted houses and artistically rendered murals stand against a jungle background.

The road between La Entrada and the turnoff for ❺ **La Rinconada** is a curvy, mountainous stretch. The windy downhill road with breathtaking views ends at a postage-stamp-sized town.

North of La Rinconada, drive slowly and beware potholes. End at ❻ **Mirador de Salango** (p251), a dirt-road-accessed lookout with the best views you'll find along the coast.

ANCESTRAL AYAHUASCA

Tania Duran, owner of Samai Lodge *@samaiholisticliving*

Ayahuasca is an ancestral medicine originating from the indigenous peoples of the Amazon, used for centuries within ritual and ceremonial contexts and a spiritual tradition deeply connected to the rainforest, community life and the oral transmission of knowledge. For many Amazonian cultures, its use facilitates processes of introspection, transformation of consciousness, and personal insight. The experience is usually guided by a *curandero* or shaman, whose role includes chanting *ícaros* (sacred songs). Within this worldview, *ayahuasca*, served as a tea, enables a symbolic dialogue between the individual and the plant, supporting emotional healing and inner growth. *Ayahuasca* preparations have psychedelic properties, so do your due diligence to ensure proper preparation and guidance.

FOTOSS93/SHUTTERSTOCK

Isla Salango (p277)

Ayangue

TIME FROM MONTAÑITA: **30MIN**

Scuba diving the coast

Diving off Ecuador's southern coast is an amazing experience rich with marine life. Here, when in season, you can hear whales singing at nearly every site.

Just a short boat ride from Ayangue Bay, to the south of Montañita, sits a small rocky outcropping known as **El Pelado**, one of the region's fun dive sites. Above water, the rocks are covered with pelicans, seagulls and a few blue-footed boobies, while underwater is a plethora of marine life for divers to enjoy.

The three-pointed rock formation known as **Los Ahorcados**, a sculptural islet seen from the shores of Ayampe and Las Tunas, is another excellent close-to-shore dive site. It has an incredible coral reef below the surface that's home to colorful fish and other marine species.

Twenty nautical miles offshore is **Bajo Cope**, a dive site with crystal clear, warm water and an immense level of marine biodiversity. Sea turtles and octopuses are commonly spotted, along with beautiful corals and colorful fish. The stars of the show, however, are the giant manta rays that stop here every year from June to October.

Considered to be a smaller version of the Galápagos, Isla de la Plata (p276) attracts much of the same marine life that divers see at its larger and more famous counterpart. There are five main dive sites on the island, each with extensive coral reefs and the chance of seeing manta rays, humpback whales, sea turtles, sharks and dolphins, depending on the season.

A short boat ride from Puerto López, Isla Salango (p277), resembles a small slice of Isla de la Plata, minus mantas; the long coral reef in shallow water is good for beginners.

Puerto López & Ayampe

BOAT CRUISES | SURF BEACHES | NATURAL LANDSCAPES

After staying in nearby villages, the bustling town of Puerto López feels like the big city. There's a traffic-clogged main artery, crowded market stalls and buildings that rise to several stories. But there are also dusty streets, blue boats bobbing in the bay, and fishermen gutting their catch in the wee hours of the morning when the air teems with wheeling frigate birds and vultures looking for scraps. Best known as the gateway to the Parque Nacional Machalilla, including offshore islands like Isla de la Plata, there's a thriving hotel scene and a visitor-friendly *malecón* lined with tour companies, shops and seafood restaurants.

Only 17km south in tiny earthy-living Ayampe, unwinding is the name of the game. Thanks to a jungle-backed black-sand beach with consistent surf and a low-key cosmopolitan community, days here follow a slow rhythm. The coastline between Puerto López and Ayampe boasts a stretch of untouched beaches backed by lush rainforest, ideal for flourishing marine life.

TOP TIP

Machalilla is a reminder of what much of the Pacific coast fringing Central and South America once looked like. Created in 1979, it preserves a tiny portion of the vanishing coastal habitat, a combination of tropical dry forest, cloud forest and 20,000 hectares of ocean.

Not Just Flyover Country

Focus on hundreds of avian types

Even non-twitchers can see that the salt ponds, mangroves, dense humid tropical forests and rocky shorelines of the Santa Elena Peninsula and south coast make inviting habitats for

GETTING AROUND

Ayampe and Puerto López are three hours and 3½ hours north of Guayaquil, respectively. You can take a bus from Guayaquil's central bus station to Montañita or Olón, then a local bus up the coast the rest of the way. Driving provides the most flexibility, especially for getting between sites like Los Frailes Beach and Água Blanca, just be alert for potholes and unmarked speed bumps. In either town it's easy to get around on foot or flag down a three-wheeled *mototaxi* in Puerto López.

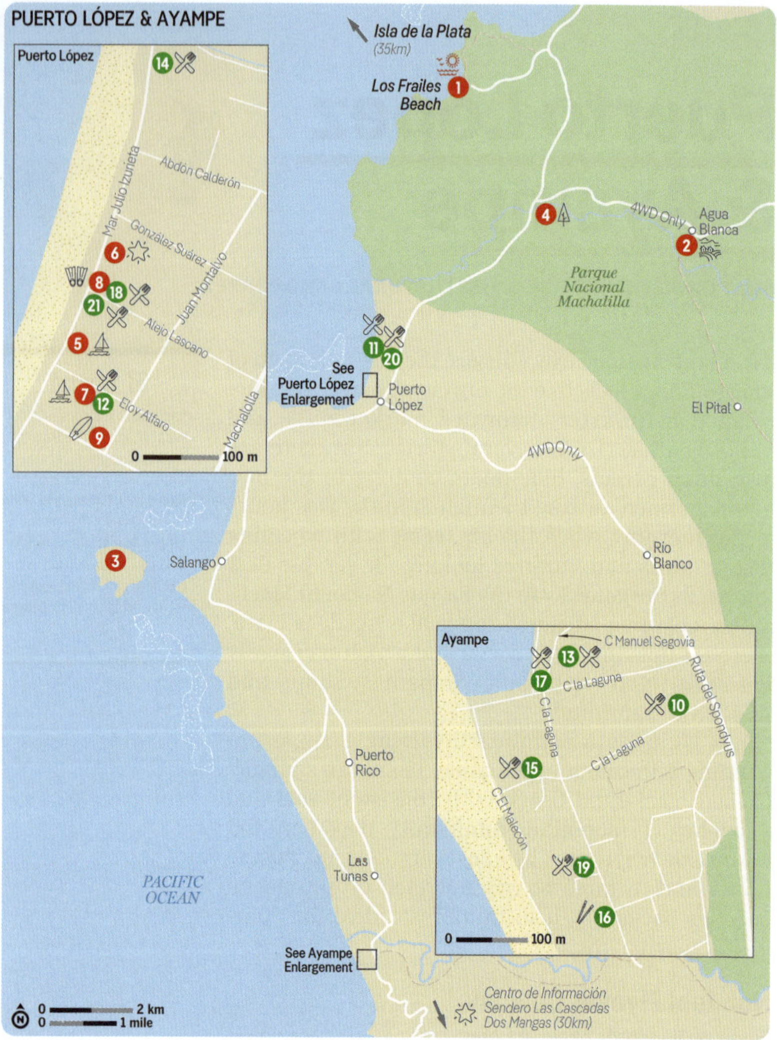

HIGHLIGHTS
1 Los Frailes Beach

SIGHTS
2 Agua Blanca
3 Isla Salango
4 Parque Nacional Machalilla

ACTIVITIES
5 Cercapez Tours
6 Exploramar Diving
7 Fragata Xtreme
8 Native Diving Center
9 Travesía Surf & Bikes

EATING
10 Ayampe Tacos
11 Café Madame
12 Cambalache Pizza
13 Distinto
14 El Nido
15 El Pacay
16 Mali
17 Mulata
18 Nemarch
19 Ohlala Panaderia Francesa
20 Pacha Chocolates
21 Spondylus

birdlife, homebodies as well as those birds making the long migratory journey from northern Canada and other spots. The sheer variety of ecosystems mean there's a niche for hundreds of endemic and non-endemic species.

Ornithological hot spots include the artificial and abandoned industrial salt flats on the outskirts of Salinas. The area around the Ayampe river also sees cormorants, herons and egrets cluster, and the Esmereldas woodstar, a rare and beautiful hummingbird, nests there from December to March. Finally, **Parque Nacional Machalilla** is also a magnet for birdlife, both around communities like Agua Blanca and El Pital's La Bola de Oro (Golden Ball trail) and on Isla de la Plata, where iconic blue-footed boobies, among others, can be spotted.

Casual observers might be satisfied identifying species on their own or via guides on trips elsewhere, including Dos Mangas (p270) or Isla de la Plata (p276). Otherwise, get in touch with **Sandra Plúa** *(www.guiaspnm2008.wixsite.com/sandraplua; per person $50)*, an experienced guide who can tailor trips to your interests.

Giants of the Deep

Get close to breeching humpbacks

Migrating humpback whales can be seen from Súa to Salinas from June through September, from afar on the shore or up close and personal on a whale-watching tour. Boat cruises (2½ hours, per person $25) leave from the docks in Puerto López (11am and 2pm) and are easily arranged through your hotel or one of the tour companies lining the *malecón*. Boats enter the waters of Parque Nacional Machalilla, the epicenter of the breeding grounds.

Going flat out the ride can be rough, so take motion-sickness medication if necessary and bring a light jacket for the wind and spray.

Because of the competition, shop around for your desired language skills and marine biology backgrounds. Snacks and soda are provided, and many include snorkeling around Isla Salango (p277). Trips to Isla de la Plata (p276) stop for whales along the way, in season, so no need to do both.

Local communities love the balletic beasts, and in the canton of Salango, for example, their arrival is celebrated with an annual **Humpback Whale Festival** every June.

GUAYAQUIL TO PERU BORDER

In this edition, we've not included coverage of the area south of Guayaquil. In part, that's because of safety concerns and the travel patterns that result from them. In this region, massive banana plantations surround the dusty city of Machala, a transport hub and the capital of El Oro province. Further inland, the charming old gold-mining town of Zaruma is a revelation, with its narrow, hilly streets and well-kept plaza. Most travelers pass through on an overland journey to Peru. The easiest way to cross into Peru is by road at Huaquillas, about 80km south of Machala, with one of the international bus lines departing from Guayaquil. Alternatively, pedestrians can walk over an international footbridge linking Huaquillas to Aguas Verdes in Peru.

DRINKING IN PUERTO LÓPEZ & AYAMPE: CAFES

El Nido: A cafe with a little Parisian style at the northern end of Puerto López's *malecón*; the four empanadas and two glasses of wine for $10 is a deal. *7am-7pm*

Distinto: Postage-stamp-sized spot in Ayampe serving specialty Ecuadorian roasts. *9am-5pm*

Ohlala Panaderia Francesa: The puffiest, flakiest croissants and other pastries and omelets in a bucolic Ayampe garden setting. *8:30am-6pm Tue-Sun*

Pacha Chocolates: Cocoa temptations in Puerto López: hot choc, choc crepes, brownies and mousse. Call +593-098-202-7351 for factory tours. *10am-7pm*

MORE HUMPBACK FACTS

Each year, a group of humpback whales undertakes one of the longest migrations on earth (around 7000km). The swim from summer feeding grounds in Antarctica to breeding and birthing grounds at the equator takes about five weeks. Once they arrive it's all play – with a purpose, that is. In the quest to breed, males the size of semi trucks (weighing 23,000kg to 36,000kg) romance their sweethearts with blows, acrobatics (each of the half-dozen or so behaviors, including most dramatically, breaching, has a meaning) and songs that amount to one of nature's most phenomenal spectacles. Take a gander oceanward, in season, when traveling along the coastal waters between Isla de la Plata and Salinas.

WILFRIDO LUCERO/ALAMY

Los Frailes

Ecuador's Most Picturesque Beach?

Lazy day at Playa de los Frailes

Generally regarded as the country's most beautiful stretch of sand, **Los Frailes**, a crescent-shaped beach of nearly 2km, is undoubtedly glorious, especially when the sun is out. Marked by dramatic headlands on either side, its protected status as part of Parque Nacional Machalilla (p275) keeps it pristine and undeveloped. Swimmers take care during big swells, as there can be strong undertows.

The well-organized entry includes on-site guards who ensure no food or disposable goods enter the reserve. Access the beach from its main entrance by car (parking is $2) or take the 4km loop hiking trail, which culminates in a breathtaking lookout point a few hundred meters from the water (bring binoculars during whale-watching season). Buses heading north from Puerto López can drop you at the highway entrance or take a *mototaxi* from town ($2 or so); taxis can take you all the way down the semi-rough dirt road to the beach.

Island Cruises

Visit 'little Galápagos'

Not going to the Galápagos? **Isla de la Plata** (Silver Island), nearly two hours by boat from Puerto López, is a reasonably

EATING IN PUERTO LÓPEZ: OUR PICKS

Café Madame: Beachfront cafe with a shaded veranda and menu of crepes, sandwiches, salads and grilled fish and meat specialties. *8am-9pm* $

Cambalache Pizza: Several dozen varieties of pizza and empanadas (we prefer the latter), as well as craft beers on tap. *5:30-11pm* $

Nemarch: Of the plethora of seafood spots, Nemarch is among the best. Offers grilled meat and pasta, too. *8am-10pm* $

Spondylus: Large, brightly lit dining room grilling up the usual seafood, as well as a few pricier whole fish, lobster, prawn and conch specialties. *7am-10pm* $$

accurate facsimile and is frequently referred to as the 'little Galápagos' due to its similar levels of biodiversity. Nearly every tour company in Puerto López offers full-day trips here, including a two-hour guided nature walk, a picnic lunch in the sun and a snorkeling session on an offshore reef.

The origin of the island's name has a couple of explanations – one alludes to claims that Sir Francis Drake buried treasure here, and the other points to the color of the guano-covered cliffs in the moonlight. The island is home to nesting colonies of seabirds: you'll likely see large numbers of blue-footed boobies and frigate birds, as well as red-footed boobies, pelicans, and a variety of gulls, terns and petrels. Critically endangered waved albatross have successfully hatched eggs here (around April to October), and dolphins often pass by.

It's a steep climb from the boat landing to two loop hikes, one to the east and one to the west: the 3.5km Sendero Punta Machete and the 5km Sendero Punta Escalera. Either way, the trail is rough and exposed, so good footwear and plenty of water are essential.

If you don't have a full day to spare, but want to get out onto the water, a 2½-hour boat cruise out to nearby **Isla Salango** ($15 per person; each company usually offers two departures daily around 11am and 1pm) is an enjoyably, leisurely option. You pass a sea colony at Punta de los Piqueros and spend much of the time anchored off a beach for some snorkeling and kayaking.

Rural Idyll

An afternoon in Agua Blanca

Though the indigenous village of **Agua Blanca** *(comunidad aguablanca.net)* itself is really nothing more than a scattering of simple wood-and-bamboo dwellings, it's noteworthy for what's missing: noise and pollution. It's just fresh air, strong breezes and bucolic views of the surrounding countryside.

You'll find the turnoff about 5.5km north of Puerto López on the right. From here it's another 6km down a paved but potholed road to the village. At the turnoff you pay a $5 per person entry fee. This covers museum admission and, theoretically, a guide if requested and available; however, one isn't necessary.

Once there, you can see pre-Columbian art in the small archaeological museum (plus a few excavations of stone wall

BEST PUERTO LÓPEZ TOURS

Exploramar Diving: PADI-certified dive center with 20 years of experience in the Parque Nacional Machalilla and the Galápagos.

Cercapez Tours: Reliable company with an array of regularly scheduled boating tours.

Native Diving Center: PADI-certified dive center based in Puerto López, organizing scuba certifications and fun dives.

Fragata Xtreme: Does the standard boating tours, and offers subwing (underwater snorkeling while pulled by boat).

Travesía Surf & Bikes: The usual Parque Machalilla tours as well as biking, kayaking and stand-up paddleboarding.

EATING IN AYAMPE: OUR PICKS

Ayampe Tacos: Burritos, tacos and quesadillas made with homemade guac and salsa; just off the highway. *8am-10pm* $

El Pacay: Especially good budget-friendly seafood *almuerzos*, daily specials and some of the best ceviche around. *8am-4pm* $

Mulata: Fine dining with a sophisticated menu of dishes like birria and corn with crispy polenta (the beef is cooked for six hours!). *7-10:30pm Wed-Sun* $$

Mali: Funky spot with some tables overlooking the beach, serving Thai specialties like curries, pad thai, mango salad and soups. *8:30am-10pm* $$

PARQUE FLORA

The lowland dry, tropical forests and upland cloud forests of the Parque Nacional Machalilla (p275) are the natural habitat for a wide variety of unique flora, including the palo santo ('the wood of saints' or 'holy stick'). An aromatic tree native to Ecuador and Peru, it has been used in indigenous rituals since the time of the Incas. The smell of burning palo santo, prevalent along the coastline, wards away evil spirits, and the smoke from burning sticks is an effective mosquito repellent. Other common species include the leguminous algaroba, which has green bark and is able to photosynthesize even after losing its leaves; the ceiba (kapok) tree, whose fruit yield a fiber that floats and doesn't get waterlogged; and tall, spindly candelabra cacti and prickly pear.

KIKE CALVO/ALAMY

Agua Blanca (p277)

structures and ceramic urns elsewhere), soak in a sulfur pool and hike the surrounding forest. There's a small, pleasant restaurant across the road from the museum and a basic designated campsite nearby, nothing more than a fenced-off piece of land in the forest. There are several comfortable rooms for rent near the museum.

A fairly delightful, mostly flat one-hour walk (2km) crosses a riverbed, usually dry, and passes through tropical forest. Stop along the way to soak at a 4m-deep **sulfur pool**, where the combination of 70% natural minerals and therapeutic mud are equal to a spa treatment. There's also a small treatment center where you can have **massages** (30 minutes, $15 to $25) with the mud or palo santo oil. A few shops here sell basic snacks and drinks, plus there's a toilet and showers to wash the sulfur and mud off. The area also has hammocks to lounge around in. Close to the end of the walk there's a **viewpoint** with soul-expanding panoramic views to the horizon.

The sun can be merciless during the warmer months – bring a hat, plus plenty of sunscreen and water. Alternatively, those with a 4WD or a willing *mototaxi* can drive the extra 2km to the sulfur pool along a rough dirt track.

Places We Love to Stay

$** Budget **$$** Midrange **$$$ Top End

Guayaquil

MAP p254

Hotel Boutique Mansion del Rio Restored 1920s home, located riverside on a cobblestone street in Las Peñas. Rooms have antique furnishings and original details. Rooftop terrace offers great views. **$$**

Casa las Penas Siglo XXI Go for a balcony room with river views at this contemporarily styled, professionally run boutique occupying prime Las Peñas real estate. **$$**

Hotel Oro Verde A few blocks west of Parque del Centenario. Still among the classiest downtown hotels, as much for its top facilities and several excellent restaurants. **$$**

Iguanazú Hotel Boutique Tranquil oasis with wood-floored rooms, spacious lounge, pool and terrace. Atop a hill a few blocks from busy roads. **$$**

Hotel del Parque Splurge-worthy relocated 19th-century building that's the *crème de la crème* of Guayaquil's luxury accommodations. **$$$**

Playas & Around

Hostel Puerto Engabao Surf Shelter Laid back, well-cared-for hostel, run by surfers who also offer surf guiding and lessons; dorms and private rooms with hammocks. **$**

Ohana Beach Hotel New, fairly nondescript 'high-rise' 4km south of Playas. Across from the beach. Pleasant restaurant. **$$**

Samana Hostal Clean lines, minimalism and Puerto Engabao sea views from nearly every room; plus lovely pool. **$$**

Un Dia Boutique Resort Beachside boutique in El Pelado. Friendly staff, delicious food and on-site bar with live-music evenings. **$$**

Salinas & Around

Chescos Funky *malecón* hostel featuring a TV lounge with swings as seats; small but clean rooms, with minimalist decor and colorful accents. **$**

Hotel Casablanca Chipipe Notable for value and location on Playa Chipipe, less so for its basic rooms and amenities. **$$**

Hostería Farallón Dillon Clifftop inn that's half whitewashed villa, half imaginary ship. The brainchild of an ex-captain, it's filled with seafaring memorabilia. **$$**

Montañita & Olón

MAP p268

Balsa Surf Camp Montañita surf and yoga hideaway with handcrafted two-story bungalows with thatch roofs. It's set in a lush garden across from the beach. **$**

Hostal Kundalini Beachfront spot in Montañita with cozy, well-equipped rooms, top-flight service and good restaurant and bar. **$$**

Samai Lodge Hilltop oasis 15 minutes' drive from Olón, with super views from every room; retreat for yoga, alternative healing and *ayahuasca*. **$$**

Ayampe & Around

MAP p274

Las Golondrinas A stylish oasis just off the beachfront with plunge pool, leafy garden and bar with good food. **$$**

La Buena Vida Friendly hosts, good breakfasts, and an inviting open-sided cafe-bar that's perfect for a sundowner have made this a popular spot. **$$**

Suites La Tortuga Surfer compound of charmingly designed beachside cabins, lovely maintained gardens, pool and super restaurant. **$$**

Ganso & Búho Just off the beach, with wood-floored rooms, tiled bathrooms, balconies and great breakfasts. **$$**

Puerto Lopez & Around

MAP p274

Hospedaje Comunitario Museo Salango Several basic fan-cooled cabins just off the beach; call +593-98-828-8639 or head to the museum for booking info. **$**

Hostería Itapoá Thatch-roofed cabins with a tropical hideaway feel are tucked away in a lush courtyard, opposite the beach. Small restaurant and bar. **$$**

Zutalu Lodge Cozy, charming, well-maintained thatched cabins set back from the quieter northern part of the beach. **$$**

Nantu Hosteria Beachfront Nantu has smart rooms with wooden features, colored accents and thatched cabins. Porch hammocks. **$$**

Nautilus Lodge Boutique, modern property with large rooms, many boasting private balconies with hammocks and couches. Lovely pool and lounge area. **$$**

Hostería Mandala Beautifully designed and ecologically minded cabins in a labyrinthine garden at northern end of main beach. **$$**

Researched by
Alex Egerton

Cuenca & the Southern Highlands

ARCHITECTURE, HISTORY AND MYSTICAL MOUNTAINS

Travel from buzzing historic towns to remote mountain villages steeped in indigenous culture, and to pristine reserves high in the Andes.

Traditional, relaxed and breathtakingly beautiful, the southern expanses of the Ecuadorian Andes are sprinkled with handsome towns framed by majestic peaks, and tiny mountain villages where indigenous culture continues to thrive.

Without a doubt, the place that best represents the region's fascinating mix of cultures is the lively regional capital of Cuenca, which captivates travelers with one of South America's most charming historic quarters. An enchanting cosmopolitan city with proud residents, it's an obligatory stop on any journey through the area.

BOYD HENDRIKSE/SHUTTERSTOCK

Beyond Cuenca, quiet roads branch out to tiny towns known for their ornate handicrafts made using techniques passed down from generation to generation, and onto mysterious ruins left by the Cañari and Inca civilizations.

Further south lie the indigenous homelands of Saraguro, where Kichwa communities cultivate the fertile soils much the same way they always have, the delightful coffee-infused town of Loja, around which Ecuador's best arabica beans are grown, and the new-age hippie magnet of Vilcabamba.

The region's mountains are also home to some of the country's most pristine wilderness, ranging from mist-tangled woodlands and delicate moors to rolling foothills covered in dense jungle. These diverse ecosystems, protected in a network of national parks and private reserves, are home to hundreds of bird species, thousands of plants and many magnificent mammals.

THE MAIN AREAS

CUENCA
Vibrant and cultured historic town.
p286

SARAGURO
Traditional heartland of Andean culture.
p300

LOJA
Gateway to stunning nature.
p304

VILCABAMBA
Tiny village with an international flavor.
p310

For places to stay in Cuenca & the Southern Highlands, see p314

IRENEUKE/SHUTTERSTOCK

Left: Saraguro; above: historic center of Cuenca (p286)

Find Your Way

Most attractions in the southern highlands are within a few hours' drive of Cuenca or Loja, which have the region's commercial airports. Buses are frequent between towns, while taxis are reasonably priced for visiting outlying attractions.

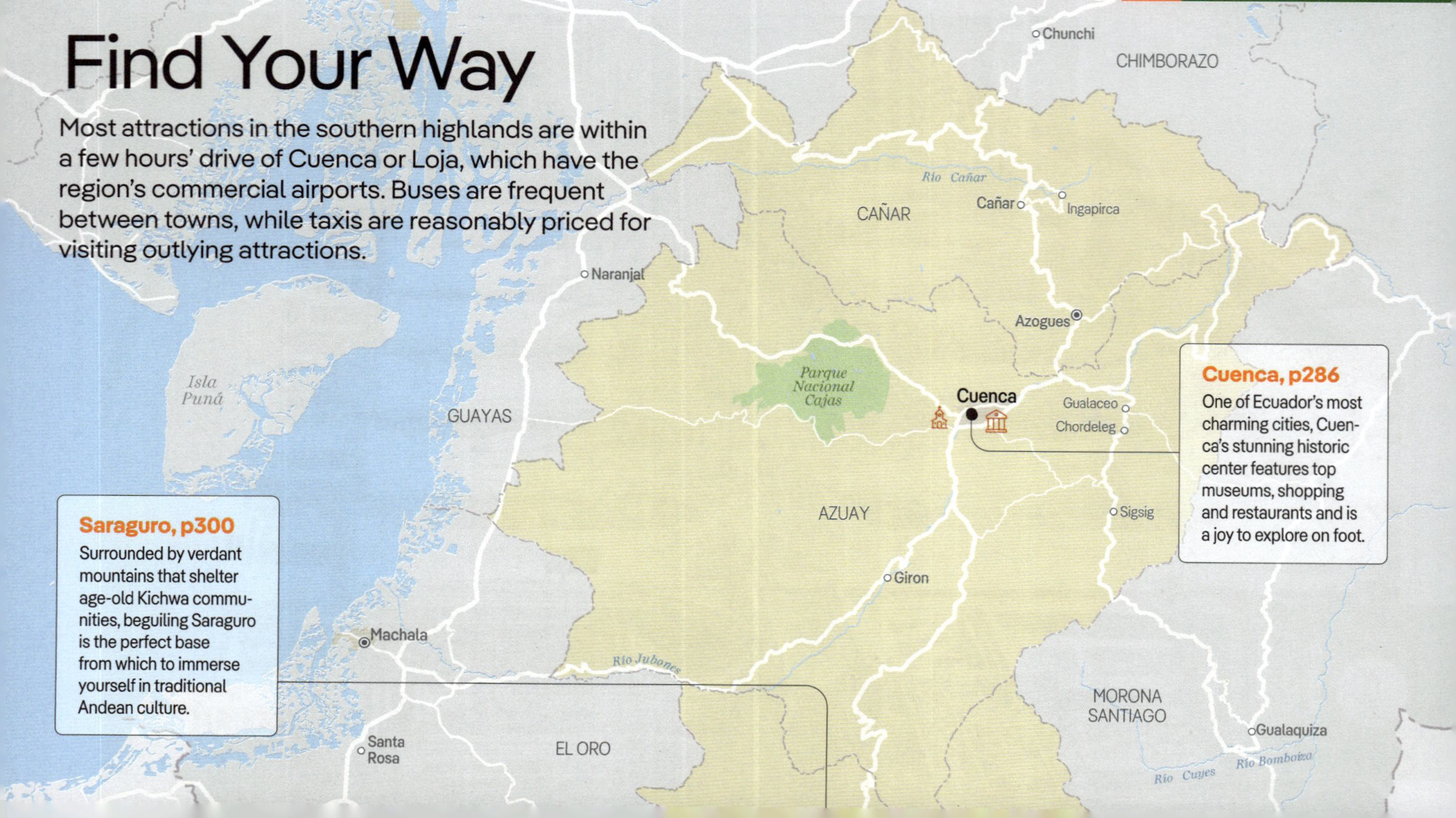

Cuenca, p286
One of Ecuador's most charming cities, Cuenca's stunning historic center features top museums, shopping and restaurants and is a joy to explore on foot.

Saraguro, p300
Surrounded by verdant mountains that shelter age-old Kichwa communities, beguiling Saraguro is the perfect base from which to immerse yourself in traditional Andean culture.

Loja, p304
With a rich history and meticulously restored historic center, this oft-overlooked southern city is home to superb mountain wilderness and the country's best coffee.

Vilcabamba, p310
Recharge in the fresh mountain air of diminutive Vilcabamba, Ecuador's city of eternal youth that's a magnet for expats, travelers and nature lovers alike.

BUS

Fairly comfortable, air-conditioned buses run frequently along the Panamericana (Pan-American Highway) from Cuenca to Loja via Saraguro and are the easiest way to get between the region's major towns. Less comfortable, but also frequent, regional buses link major cities to surrounding towns.

TAXI

In addition to being the easiest way to get around towns and cities, taxis can be hired for reasonable rates for express trips to attractions in the countryside, or even for a whole day of sightseeing, but always agree a total price before departure.

CAR

The southern highlands are a great place to self-drive due to the short distances, good road conditions and generally safe countryside. The best deals are usually found in Cuenca, where there are several major rental companies.

Plan Your Days

Most visits to the southern highlands begin in Cuenca, and while plenty just see the Azuay capital, it's well worth venturing further to discover the fascinating rural communities set in spectacular mountainous landscapes.

CARINA FURLANETTO/SHUTTERSTOCK

Parque Nacional Cajas (p295)

Just a Short Break

- Fly into **Cuenca** (p286) and spend a day taking in the old town's historic buildings and enjoying its excellent international restaurants and lively bars. Visit a few of the city's fascinating museums that focus on the region's pre-Hispanic inhabitants.

- Make a day trip to **Parque Nacional Cajas** (p295) to hike among the shimmering mountain lakes and delicate *páramo* plains before returning to soak your tired muscles in the mineral-rich waters of the thermal baths at **Baños** (p292).

- On your last day, get up early to travel to the Cañari and Inca ruins at **Ingapirca** (p296), where the impressive Temple of the Sun is watched over by a herd of llamas atop a grassy hill surrounded by mountains.

Seasonal Highlights

MAR & APRIL
Holy Week Easter celebrations take over the streets of Cuenca, with daily processions and specialty dishes prepared across the city.

MAY
Coffee harvests begin around Loja department, with interesting visits to working farms showing the process up close.

JUN
Inti Raymi in Saraguro celebrates the solstice harvest with traditional dance and musical performances in the town of Las Lagunas.

A Week in the Mountains

- After spending a few days in **Cuenca** (p286) taking in the sights of the historic center and visiting **Parque Nacional Cajas** (p295), move on to **Saraguro** (p300), booking into a mountain lodge overlooking the town.

- Spend a day hiking to waterfalls and traditional craft workshops before spending a night in the magical community of **Gera** (p302), which overlooks a stunning canyon. Finally, head south to **Loja** (p304) to wander the well-preserved streets lined with colonial-era buildings that connect the city's colorful plazas.

- Finish your trip by downing a few cups of Loja's famous coffee before hiking through the pristine Andean forests of **Parque Nacional Podocarpus** (p307) to spot some of the many exotic bird species.

10 Days in the South

- For your first few days, visit the museums and historic buildings of **Cuenca** (p286) and the surrounding attractions, such as the market towns of **Gualaceo** (p299) and **Chordeleg** (p299) to watch local artisans at work and pick up some interesting handmade souvenirs.

- Next, move south to **Saraguro** (p300) and **Loja** (p304), leaving time for hikes in the mountains before continuing to **Vilcabamba** (p310), where waterfalls, panoramic lookouts and great horse-riding await.

- Double back to Loja to take the bus down the spectacular road to **Zamora** (p308), a tidy and welcoming town surrounded by dripping-wet rainforest.

- Take a trip to the lowland portion of **Parque Nacional Podocarpus** (p307) before finishing with a tubing adventure on the striking **Río Bombuscaro** (p308).

JUL
Mostly dry weather makes for good hiking on trails in the region's high-altitude national parks.

AUG
Devotees of the Virgen del Cisne descend on Loja for one of the country's biggest and most colorful religious celebrations.

NOV
Low season, but generally not too wet, with fewer crowds and good deals on accommodations.

DEC
Join bird-watching aficionados and try to spot rare species during observation days in the rainforests around Zamora.

Cuenca

PRE-HISPANIC HISTORY | GRAND ARCHITECTURE | MOUNTAIN ESCAPES

TOP TIP
Cuenca is slightly more expensive than other destinations in southern Ecuador, but it's not difficult to visit the city on a budget. Many hotels offer much better prices for walk-ins than for online bookings, while eating meals in local markets is a cultural experience and cheap to boot.

The fertile valley of the Río Tomebamba, with its pleasant climes and fetching landscapes, has long charmed visitors. The Incas chose the site for the northern capital of their empire and then the Spanish followed suit, building one of their most important cities at Cuenca. These days the region continues to enamor outsiders, with Cuenca drawing crowds of travelers who descend on the town to wander its architecturally significant streets, visit the excellent museums, sample tasty regional cuisine or take it easy in the many leafy plazas.

The city's UNESCO-listed historic center, with its distinctive skyline of immense domes and towering steeples, dates back to the 16th century. But unlike Quito's historic center, Cuenca's narrow streets are filled with everyday life and are safe to wander day and night, making it the ideal place to immerse yourself in Ecuadorian highland culture.

ECUADOR'S HISTORIC QUARTERS
Find more classic architecture from the colonial era in the historic center of **Quito** (p56) and in the southern city of **Loja** (p304), six hours' drive south of Cuenca.

Historic Cuenca

A city of churches and plazas

Within the boundaries of Cuenca's heart, it can feel like there's a striking church or a handsome plaza with timeworn benches on every corner. The most alluring square

GETTING AROUND

Walking is the best way to explore downtown Cuenca, while taxis are a fairly priced option to cross from one side of town to the other. Fares are metered and the minimum is $1.50. You can hail taxis on the street. During peak hours it's worth downloading the AzuTaxi app to book a ride.

Cuenca's modern tramline is a convenient way to get between the airport/bus station and the historic center. You can buy single tickets at machines at the stops ($1); for frequent use it's cheaper to buy a rechargeable card, available at the bus terminal.

Urban bus lines run out into outlying districts, with the most useful line for visitors being the L12 to Baños. Buses require a different card from the trams – available at shops and kiosks around town.

is found on the historic center's western edge, where **Plaza San Sebastián** is headed by the whitewashed, 19th-century **Iglesia de San Sebastián**, the asymmetrical design of which sets it apart from other Cuenca temples.

Overlooking an ample plaza lined by a colorful mix of old arcaded buildings, the **Iglesia de San Francisco** has a neoclassical design with baroque elements. The interior is dominated by a splendid 17th-century gold-leaf altar. Around the corner, the austere white walls of the **Iglesia El Carmen de la Asunción** contrast beautifully with the riot of color of the fresh flower market held out front every morning.

The immense **Catedral de la Inmaculada Concepcíón**, also known as the 'new cathedral', is a city icon, with sky-blue domes that are visible from all over town. It stands on the west side of the elegant, tree-filled **Parque Calderón**, Cuenca's largest square and main meeting point.

If the cathedral's squat towers look a bit on the short side, that's because they are – a design error meant the building wasn't strong enough to support the intended loftier versions. If you look carefully, you can even see the sizeable crack that appeared when a heavy statue was placed above the main entrance. Climb the 165 steps up one of the towers to the **terrace** *($2.25)* for great views over the rooftops. If you want to see more of the structure, including the rarely visited basements, take one of the in-depth **guided tours** *($5.50)* at 10am, 11:30am and 3pm.

To fully appreciate the cathedral's size, head next door to the 2nd floor of the **Seminario San Luis** *(free)*, a meticulously restored colonnaded seminary now housing cafes and restaurants. Head through the small door in the corner opposite the main entrance to reach the lovely flower-filled internal patio.

Across the park, the prim white **El Sagrario** *(cultura.cuenca.gob.ec, admission $3)*, also known as the 'old cathedral', dates back to the city's founding in 1557. In 1739, its tower was used by La Condamine's expedition to measure the shape of the Earth. It has since been deconsecrated and now hosts a museum of religious art – head to the rear courtyard to check out the fascinating historical photographs of the city.

Wander Through History

Magnificent museums and regal ruins

Unsurprisingly for a city of its historical importance, Cuenca has one of the country's best collections of museums, and most are within a short walk of each other in the historic center.

continues on p290

A TALE OF THREE CITIES

While Cuenca is widely known as a colonial city, its origins reach further back. Upon arriving in the mountains of Azuay in 1557, the Spanish began building their new administrative capital on the ruins of the fallen Inca city of Tumipampa. It was case of history repeating itself, as the Incas under Tupac-Yupanqui had built their northern citadel on top of the defeated Cañari town of Guapondelig in the late 15th century.

Whether due to the climate, fresh water or abundance of available labor, Tumipamba thrived, quickly becoming an important military town. However, fierce battles broke out during the Inca civil war, and by the time the conquistadores rolled into the valley it was mostly reduced to rubble.

EATING IN CUENCA: OUR PICKS

La Maria Cocina Libre: Beautifully crafted gourmet plates, featuring farm-fresh ingredients. Creative cocktails, rural chic ambience. *noon-10pm, closed Sun* **$$$**

El Mercado: Modern, upmarket place overlooking Río Tomebamba. Open kitchen specializes in fusing Andean and international flavors. *noon-10pm, closed Sun* **$$$**

Good Affinity: It's a bit of a walk, but this meat-free diner serves healthy meals and Asian snacks. *11:30am-3:30pm, closed Sun* **$**

Moliendo: Fresh and filling set meals and *arepas* (maize pancakes) topped with all kinds of tasty ingredients draw a crowd to this cafe. Arrive early. *8:30am-7pm* **$**

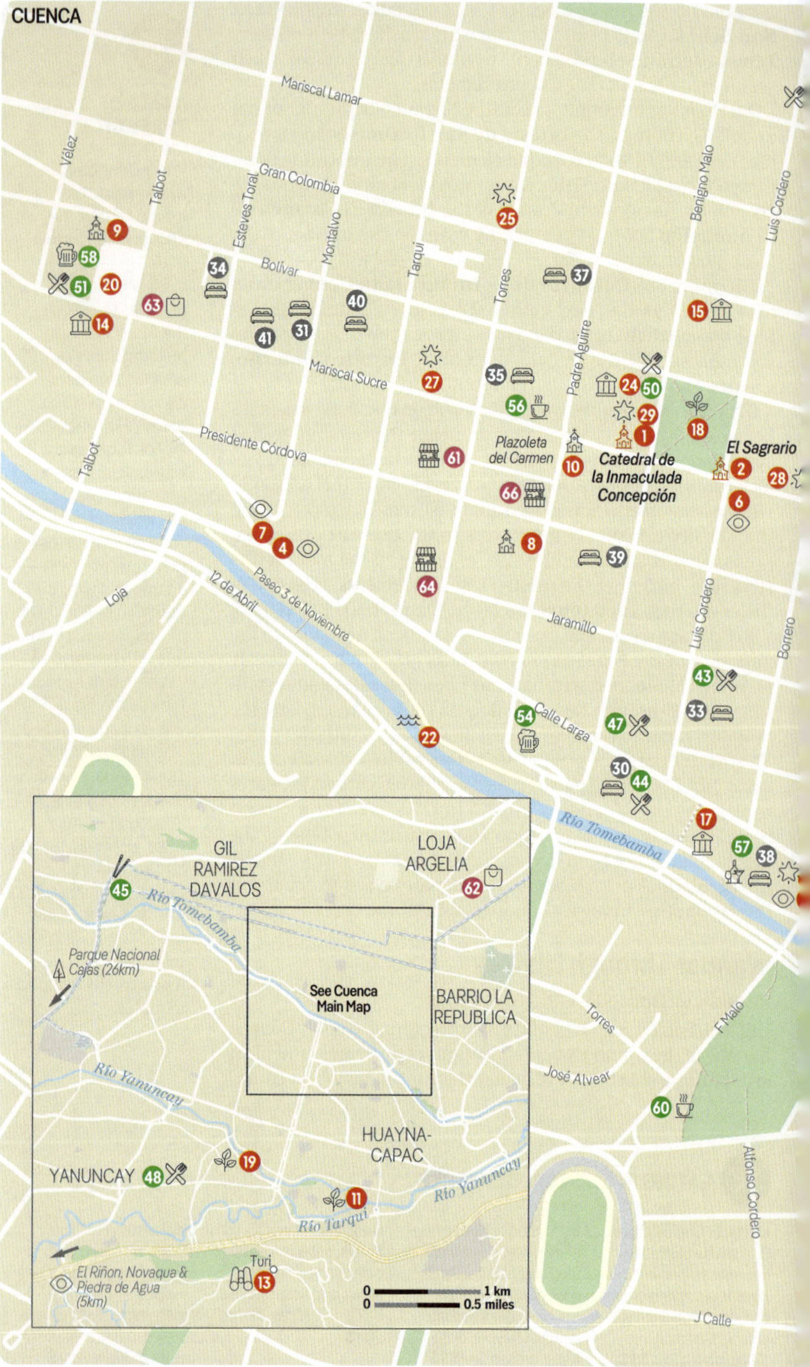
CUENCA
Mariscal Lamar
Gran Colombia
Bolívar
Mariscal Sucre
Presidente Córdova
Vélez
Talbot
Esteves Toral
Montalvo
Tarqui
Torres
Padre Aguirre
Benigno Malo
Luis Cordero
Plazoleta del Carmen
Catedral de la Inmaculada Concepción
El Sagrario
Loja
12 de Abril
Paseo 3 de Noviembre
Jaramillo
Borrero
Calle Larga
Río Tomebamba
F Malo
José Alvear
Alfonso Cordero
J Calle
GIL RAMIREZ DAVALOS
LOJA ARGELIA
Parque Nacional Cajas (26km)
See Cuenca Main Map
BARRIO LA REPUBLICA
Río Yanuncay
HUAYNA-CAPAC
YANUNCAY
Río Tarqui
Turi
El Riñon, Novaqua & Piedra de Agua (5km)
0 1 km
0 0.5 miles

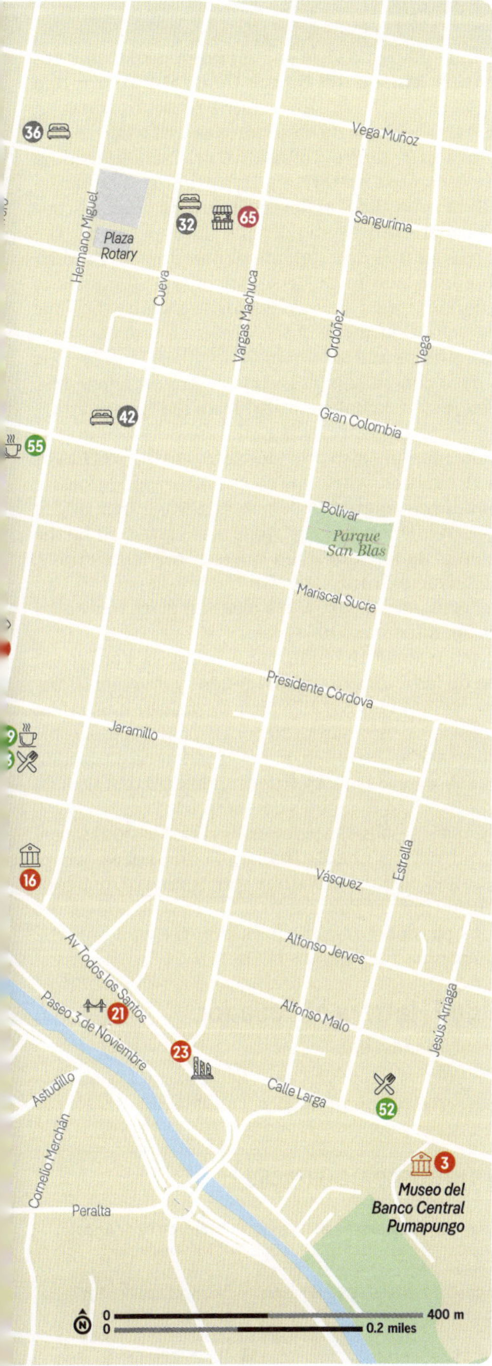

HIGHLIGHTS
1 Catedral de la Inmaculada Concepción
2 El Sagrario
3 Museo del Banco Central Pumapungo

SIGHTS
4 Casa Lira
5 Convento de la Inmaculada Concepcíon
6 Corte Provincial de Justicia
7 El Vado
8 Iglesia de San Francisco
9 Iglesia de San Sebastián
10 Iglesia el Carmen de la Asunción
11 Jardín Botanico
12 La Escalanita
13 Mirador de Turi
14 Museo de Arte Moderno
15 Museo de la Ciudad
16 Museo de las Culturas Aborígenes
17 Museo Remigio Crespo Toral
18 Parque Calderón
19 Parque Lineal Yanuncay
20 Plaza San Sebastián
21 Puente Roto
22 Río Tomebamba
23 Ruinas de Todo Santos
24 Seminario San Luis

ACTIVITIES
25 Center for Interamerican Studies
26 Sampere
27 Spanish Institute
28 Spanish Outdoor
29 Yanapuma

SLEEPING
30 Casa Barranco
31 Casa Montalvo
32 El Cafecito
33 Hostal Yakumama
34 Hostel Posada del Angel
35 Hotel Inca Real
36 Hotel Los Balcones
37 Hotel Morenica del Rosario
38 Hotel Victoria
39 La Posada del Rey
40 Mansión Alcázar
41 Nass Casa del Aguila
42 Pepe's House Hostel

EATING
see 33 Bistro Yaku
43 Bolon Agape
44 El Mercado
45 Good Affinity
46 Guajibamba
47 La Maria Cocina Libre
48 Los Ceviches de Memo
49 Moliendo
50 Raymipampa
51 San Sebas Cafe
52 Tres Estrellas
53 Warmikuna

DRINKING & NIGHTLIFE
54 Aya Uma
55 Café Austria
56 Café de La Sucre
57 Discoteca Nidia
58 Jodoco Belgian Brew
59 Ñucallacta
60 Sinfonia
see 12 Wunderbar

SHOPPING
61 CEMUART
62 Homero Ortega & Hijos
63 MAKI
64 Mercado 10 de Agosto
65 Mercado de Artesanías Rotary
66 Mercado Plaza de San Francisco

continued from p287

If you're only going to visit one museum, make sure it's the fascinating **Museo del Banco Central Pumapungo** *(pumapungo.gob.ec; free)*. Downstairs, there are rotating fine-art and archaeological exhibitions, as well a permanent collection of intricate pre-Columbian artifacts, including elaborately decorated pottery and arrowheads. The museum's highlight is on the 2nd floor, where a detailed journey through Ecuador's diverse indigenous cultures awaits. The stories of the country's original inhabitants are told through colorful dioramas and reconstructions of typical houses of Afro-Ecuadorians from Esmeraldas province, the cowboy-like *montubios* (coastal farmers) of the western lowlands, several rainforest groups and all the main highland groups. The museum's most famous exhibit is right at the end, where rare and eerie *tzantzas* (shrunken heads) from the Shuar culture of the southern Oriente are displayed.

Entry to the museum also provides access to the **Archaeological Park** out back, where you can walk through extensive ruins of buildings believed to be part of the old Inca city of Tomebamba. While most of the stone was carted off by the Spanish conquistadores to build Cuenca, the foundations, canals and terracing running down the hillside are still an impressive sight, and the park is a pleasant place to wander and reflect upon the incredible history of these lands.

Find out more about the indigenous people of Ecuador at the **Museo de las Culturas Aborígenes** *(@museoculturas aborigenes; adult/child $4/2)*, which showcases more than 5000 archaeological pieces from 20 pre-Hispanic groups, some dating as far back as 13,000 BCE. Information cards explain the remarkable everyday items from another era that include obsidian mirrors and ingenious cookware.

Across the road, besides the perpetually closed Museo Manuel Agustín Landivar, lies the **Ruinas de Todo Santos**, where Cañari, Inca and colonial-era stonework is layered, one over the other. It's no longer possible to get in to walk among the ruins but it's possible to have a peek over the wall on Calle Larga and Avenida Todo Santos below.

Unheralded Hatters of Ecuador

Pick up a real Panama hat

The fact that one of Ecuador's most beloved exports has become known around the world as a 'Panama hat' is a source

A PERFECT CUENCA DAY

Benjamin Ordoñez, Ecuadorian circus performer turned brewmaster at Aya Uma Cervecería Artesenal, shares his idea of a perfect day in Cuenca.

I love hiking and adventure sports, so I like to fill up with a big breakfast; and the very best is a good *encebollado* (soup with fish, yuca and onion) from **Los Ceviches de Memo** in Parque Iberia. It has a special taste, big servings and excellent prices.

For me, the very best of Ecuador is the nature, so once fueled up I would head up to Parque Nacional Cajas (p295) to trek around the mountains and lakes.

In the afternoon, I'd take a walk in the historic center before heading down to the **Río Tomebamba** riverside to wind down and drink a beer in one of the bars by the water.

EATING TRADITIONAL MEALS IN CUENCA: OUR PICKS

Tres Estrellas: A long-running restaurant specializing in roast *cuy* (guinea pig); there's also beef and chicken for the rodent-averse. *12:30-3:30pm & 6:30-11pm* $$

Guajibamba: Lovingly prepared local dishes, including *seco de chivo* (rich, slow-cooked goat) and a gourmet *fritada* (fried chunks of pork). *noon-4pm & 6-10pm* $$

Raymipampa: Offering plates from Cuenca and across Ecuador, as well as international flavors, this local institution is a great place to mingle with *cuencanos. 8am-10pm* $$

Mercado 10 de Agosto: Lively market with *comedores* serving all kinds of traditional meals alongside a section devoted to *hornado* (roast pork). *7am-3pm* $

OLD CUENCA ON FOOT

Wander the narrow streets of the historic center to take in the city's unique architecture and observe the buzz of daily life.

START	END	LENGTH
Plaza San Sebastián	Museo de la Ciudad	3.5km; 2hr

Begin on the western side of the city at the Plaza San Sebastián, where the 1 **Museo de Arte Moderno** has a fine collection of Latin American art. Head south on Guillermo Tálbot to reach 2 **El Vado**, one of the oldest neighborhoods in Cuenca. Stop at 3 **Casa Lira**, a centuries-old residence with exposed ancient underground irrigation channels. Continue eastwards along Calle Larga to the 4 **Museo Remigio Crespo Toral**, an immense mansion built in the early 20th century full of antiques and art that is emblematic of El Barranco district, a collection of imposing homes that cling to the steep hillside sloping down to the Río Tomebamba. Just to the east, descend the wide stone stairway known as 5 **La Escalanita** to reach Paseo 3 de Noviembre, where a hiking and cycling path runs along the shady riverbank. Follow the river east to 6 **Puente Roto,** where several striking stone arches have been left behind from a bridge washed away in a flood and now tower over an attractive plaza. Head back up the Bajada de Todos Los Santos and west to Hermano Miguel, to 7 **Convento de la Inmaculada Concepcíon**, founded in 1599. Continue north to Mariscal Sucre and turn left to reach the 8 **Corte Provinicial de Justicia**. Finally head north on Benigno Malo to 9 **Museo de la Ciudad**, one of the town's best-preserved buildings, which now hosts art exhibitions.

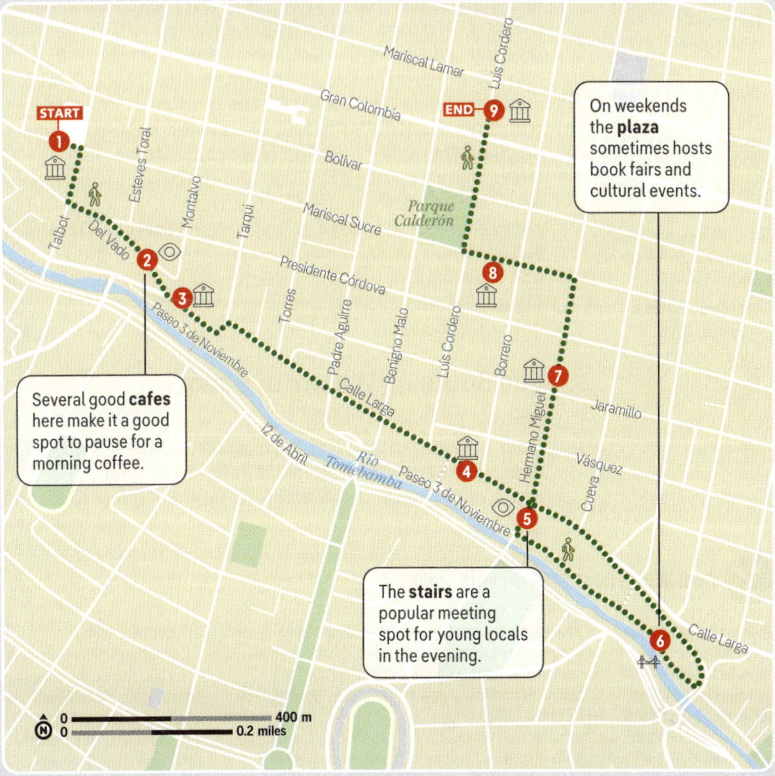

SHOPPING IN CUENCA

Mercado Plaza de San Francisco: Purpose-built modules surrounding the perimeter of this central plaza are a good place to pick up traditional clothing.

Cemuart: More than 100 craft stalls selling handmade musical instruments, embroidered clothing, jewelry and baskets.

Mercado de Artesanías Rotary: Low-key outdoor marketplace, with some lovely handmade crafts among the mass-produced plastic knickknacks.

Maki: Fair-trade gallery shop packed with high-quality crafts from traditional artisans throughout the region: textiles, baskets, clothing and more.

Mercado 10 de Agosto: Best food shopping in downtown Cuenca, with some clothing outlets also on the lower floor.

PRISMA BY DUKAS PRESSEAGENTUR GMBH ALAMY

Homero Ortega & Hijos

of frustration to patriotic Ecuadorians. In Ecuador, the rakish handcrafted fedoras are known as *sombreros de paja toquillo* or simply Montecristis, after the small coastal town where the hats originated (p164). These days, the hub of the country's hat industry is Cuenca, where more *sombreros de paja toquillo* are produced than anywhere else.

Finished hats are graded by the density of their weaves, which generally fall into four categories: standard, superior, *fino* (fine) and *superfino* (superfine). If you hold a real *superfino* up to the light, you shouldn't see a single hole, while the best of them will hold water. To see the differences for yourself, head to hatmaker **Homero Ortega & Hijos** *(homeroortega.com; free)* near the bus station, which has a fascinating museum where you can learn about the history behind the hat and observe each part of the production process.

The Soothing Waters of Baños

Relax in piping-hot baths

On a hilltop southwest of Cuenca, the village of Baños (not to be confused with the town of Baños near Ambato) is nowadays pretty much a suburb of the city and home to several

DRINKING IN CUENCA: OUR PICKS

Jodoco Belgian Brew: Great house beers, imported bottles, delicious bistro food served in a cozy dining room and out on Plaza San Sebastián. *10am-midnight*

Wunderbar: A lively atmosphere and drinks specials make this classic bar on the stairway down from the Calle Larga a popular meeting spot. *3pm-midnight Thu-Sat*

Aya Uma: Bringing life to a once-abandoned alleyway, this microbrewery has tasty house beers (including fine dark ales) and hip cultural events. *noon-1am Wed-Sat*

Discoteca Nidia: Attracting a diverse crowd, the historic center's most boisterous disco plays techno, pop and Latin beats across three floors. *9:30pm-3am Thu-Sun*

thermal-bath complexes that are a great way to soothe aching post-hike muscles. The cheapest and most popular option is **El Riñon** *(+593-72-892-485; adult/child $8/4)*, which is located right above the volcanic source, has one large pool and tends to have the hottest waters. It also has a herb-infused sauna and hot-cold plunge pools. It's not the most aesthetically pleasing of places, but locals swear its waters have the greatest healing power, and it's a good place to mix with *cuencanos* from all walks of life.

Right next door, adults-only **Novaqua** *(novaqua.com.ec; $18)* is more upmarket, with stone walls, green space and loungers, and is rarely overrun. Water is sourced from the same spring as El Riñon and it has one large pool, some indoor plunge pools and a sauna built into the rock face.

The most elegant of all is **Piedra de Agua** *(piedradeagua.com.ec; $20)*, which has three pools protected by low cliffs, well-kept grounds and a full range of spa services, though its water is often tepid, rather than piping hot. It's far more spacious and further from the main road than the other baths, which is a big plus when it comes to relaxation under the stars.

OTHER THERMAL BATHS

There are a number of other inviting thermal baths around the country, including the famous pools at **Baños** (p231) near Ambato and the more luxurious spa at **Papallacta** (p174), high in the Andes close to Quito.

Semana Santa in Cuenca

Traditional Easter festivities

Easter is a big deal in Cuenca, with Semana Santa (Holy Week) processions taking over the streets, beginning on Palm Sunday. From Thursday onwards, the atmosphere ramps up, with devotees calling in at the town's seven key churches. Accommodations should be booked well in advance. The faithful are fueled by special foods, including cheesy *empanadas del viento* and Cuenca's own take on Ecuador's filling Easter soup *fanesca*, which is made with codfish, pumpkin and a dozen kind of beans and grains. It's often followed by a cinnamon-infused rice pudding.

BEST SPANISH SCHOOLS

With a pleasant climate and laid-back atmosphere, Cuenca is a great place to learn Spanish.

Sampere: A popular and highly recommended school close to the river.

Spanish Outdoor: Newer than the others, this popular school focuses on outreach activities, both in the city and beyond.

Spanish Institute: A welcoming and fun school, just a couple of blocks from the central plaza, with flexible study options.

Center for Interamerican Studies: A nonprofit institution offering immersive language programs that include homestays with local families.

Yanapuma: Well-run individual and small-group classes. Also has specialized classes for young learners.

DRINKING IN CUENCA: WHERE TO GET COFFEE

Ñucallacta: A small, friendly old-school coffee place in the historic center with a variety of great brews made from gourmet local beans. *8am-5pm*

Sinfonia: Across the river, this modern cafe roasts its own coffee and is serious about preparation methods. Sells bags of beans. *10am-7:30pm, closed Sun*

Café Austria: A classic European ambience and a good cuppa are guaranteed at this corner institution that also serves traditional Austrian food. *8am-10pm*

Café de La Sucre: Embrace the Ecuador of another era in the central courtyard of a classic old-town house. *8:30am-7:30pm Mon-Sat, to 2pm Sun*

HERBS FOR ALL OCCASIONS

In markets throughout the southern highlands, you'll find stalls selling bunches of fresh herbs that are the key ingredients of traditional Andean medicines. Alongside the leaves, sticks and bark, there are also colorful bottles of premade remedies with catchy labels and wonderful names.

In Cuenca, the best place to find a supposed 'cure' for everything from hangovers to back pain, as well as attract the attention of your secret love, is on the 2nd floor of the Mercado 10 de Agosto (p290), where visitors are greeted by the wonderful aroma of wild herbs sourced from high in the Andes and the jungles below. Be aware that if you sign up for a cleansing procedure, they often involve being spat at with a mouthful of herbal essences – you've been warned.

IRENEUKE/SHUTTERSTOCK

Jardín Botanico

Another Side of Cuenca

A journey to the new town

Located at the confluence of two of Cuenca's waterways, the **Jardín Botanico** *(facebook.com/jardinbotanicodecuenca; free)* is a small slice of lush greenery that makes for a tranquil escape from the busy old center. Well-maintained paths and elevated walkways weave through the grounds past signposted plants and trees from various Ecuadorian ecosystems.

From the gardens, you can follow the Río Yanuncay upstream to the **Parque Lineal Yanuncay**, a quiet riverside park that's a good place to read or enjoy a picnic.

Further to the south, atop the hills overlooking town, the **Mirador de Turi** offers panoramic views of Cuenca's romantic skyline from out front of a humble parish church. It's best to come at sunset to take in the daylight view and then the lights of the city. It's about $5 in a taxi from the historic center.

EATING IN CUENCA: WHERE TO GET BREAKFAST

San Sebas Cafe: From breakfast burritos to bagels, this inviting corner cafe has international breakfasts down pat. Free refills of coffee. *8am-2:30pm* $$

Warmikuna: Flavorful traditional Ecuadorean breakfasts along with tangy fresh juices at this colorful Andean restaurant. *8:30am-7pm, to 4pm Sat, closed Sun* $$

Bistro Yaku: Deep within Hostal Yakumama, this leafy courtyard restaurant serves beautiful farm-fresh breakfasts. *8am-11:30pm, to 1pm Sat, closed Mon* $$

Bolon Agape: A tiny little shop serving the best *bolon de verde* and *tigrillo* in town. The plantain is crunchy and the sauce delicious. *7am-4pm* $

Beyond Cuenca

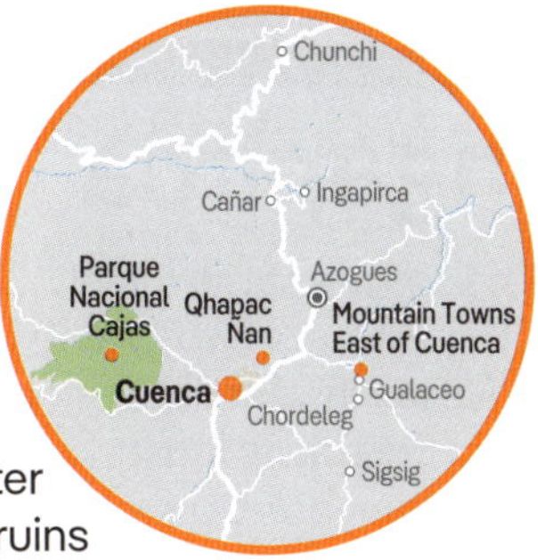

Outside Cuenca, dramatic mountains shelter villages inhabited by artisans, and ancient ruins and epic hikes wind through windswept Andean landscapes.

Sprinkled with market towns, mysterious ruins, traditional craft workshops and immense nature reserves, the mountainous countryside around Cuenca offers ample opportunities for authentic adventure. Roads are good, distances are short and transportation is frequent, making it easy to take in the sights on stress-free day trips and overnight escapes. Shopping is particularly good in the eastern region, where the small towns of Gualaceo, Chordeleg and Sigsig have their own unique handicrafts and are good places to try typical local dishes.

To the west, nature reigns among the not-to-be-missed pristine mountain lakes of misty Parque Nacional Cajas, while to the north the mystical ruins at Ingapirca are Ecuador's most important Inca archaeological site.

Places

GETTING AROUND

For Parque Nacional Cajas, eight daily buses make the one-hour run from Cuenca's Terminal Terrestre up to Laguna Toreadora via the Laguna Llaviucu turnoff. Heading back to town, just hail any southbound bus on the highway. One direct Cooperative Cañar bus to the ruins at Ingapirca leaves the bus station at 9am daily, returning around 1:30pm. Alternatively, take any bus to the town of Cañar, from where frequent local buses run up to the ruins. Frequent buses travel from Cuenca to Gualaceo, Chordeleg, Paute and Sigsig throughout the day.

Parque Nacional Cajas

TIME FROM CUENCA: **1HR**

Chilly mountain wilderness

A magical land of windswept moors, misty tangled forests and glistening mountain lakes, **Parque Nacional Cajas** is one of southern Ecuador's most attractive nature reserves. Less than an hour's drive from Cuenca, it encompasses nearly 3000 sq km of plains and wetlands, ranging in altitude from 3000m to 4300m. The delicate, humid ecosystem is the source of many of the rivers that flow through Azuay and is a vital conservation area for birds, mammals and flora.

The otherworldly landscapes are a dream for hikers, photographers and bird-watchers. The star attractions are the 700-plus lakes and ponds that shine like jewels against the backdrop of golden and pale-green *páramo* vegetation. The cool mountain water is so clear you can make out underwater forests of algae and aquatic plants in the deep from afar. Another highlight is the dwarf forests of

HIKES IN THE ECUADORIAN ANDES

More great Andean highland hikes are in **Parque Nacional Cayambe-Coca** (p177) north of Papallacta, and **Parque Nacional Cotopaxi** (p212) and **Reserva de Producción de Fauna Chimborazo** (p237).

TOP EXPERIENCE

Ingapirca

The striking stone ruins of Ingapirca, a two-hour drive northwest of Cuenca, form Ecuador's most important pre-Columbian archaeological site and are a must-visit for history buffs. Originally built by the Cañari people as an observatory, the Inca later took over and expanded the hilltop complex in the 15th century.

MARCEL HAMONIC/SHUTTERSTOCK

Temple of the Sun

TOP TIPS

- Admission includes a guided tour, departing every 30 minutes. Many guides speak English – ask when purchasing your ticket.
- It's possible to enter independently with a private guide.
- Visit the attached museum before entry for fascinating background about the Cañari civilization.

PRACTICALITIES

● patrimoniocultural.gob.ec/complejo-arqueologico-ingapirca ● adult/child under 12yr $2/free ● 9am-4:15pm Wed-Sun

A Mountain Stronghold

Due to its strategic mountain location and proximity to the Qhapac Ñan (Inca Trail) linking the sacred towns of Peru to new lands further north, Ingapirca, which means 'Walls of the Inca' in Kichwa, soon grew into an important military and administrative center for Inca armies on missions of conquest.

Temple of the Sun

A lot of stone was removed from the site during the colonial period to build nearby towns, and only the foundations of many of the original structures are visible.

Fortunately, the iconic, fortresslike Temple of the Sun has survived mostly unscathed, perhaps due to the Inca's robust construction techniques. It's built from blocks of golden stone that glow in the afternoon sun.

Climb to the temple's elevated viewing platforms to watch the free-roaming llamas grazing between the ruins.

Ritual Baths & Servants' Quarters

In the lower part of the complex, surrounded by terraced farmlands and magnificent rolling green hills, lie the foundations of the *acllahuasi,* where female servants of the elite were housed, along with the ceremonial baths – small rooms with running water, where sacrificial virgins were purified before being led to their fate.

Polylepis trees, with warped limbs linking together to create scenes straight from the pages of a fairy tale.

There are three main recreation areas where you'll find ranger stations and trails of varying difficulty. Before entering the park, you must register your intended itinerary at one of the ranger stations. Groups of eight or more must be accompanied by a registered guide. Even for short hikes, warm, waterproof clothing is essential, as weather conditions can deteriorate very quickly. You can spend the night in the park, but you'll need to bring a tent and sleeping gear; open fires are prohibited.

Most visitors head to **Lago Toreadora**, a picturesque area tucked among handsome peaks, where water flows from one lake to another along stunning crystal-clear streams. It has a number of self-guided trails that hikers can explore at their leisure.

Slightly closer to Cuenca on the same highway, there's another entrance at **Laguna Llaviuco** (Zorrocucho), where a well-maintained path runs along the bottom of a spectacular deep valley, beginning at a glimmering mountain lake. This area of the park has faced some closures for regeneration – check in Cuenca or call the park office before heading out.

The park's remote southern reaches are accessed from the little hamlet of **Soldados**, an hour's drive from Cuenca along a partially unpaved road. Trails here are rarely used and best suited to experienced hikers. A guide is recommended for this area and it's best to organize this in Cuenca before departure. Ask at your hotel or at the tourism office.

Qhapac Ñan

TIME FROM CUENCA: **3HR**

Ecuador's little-known Inca Trail

Far less trodden than the famed portion of the Inca Trail leading to Machu Picchu, the three-day trek along the **Qhapac Ñan** (also sometimes known as the Camino del Inca) to Ingapirca is a wonderful journey through remote mountainous wilderness sprinkled with high-altitude lakes and awash with history.

Beginning in the village of **Achupallas**, the trail runs along a 40km stretch of the Qhapac Ñan, or Andean Main Hwy, that once linked Cuzco with Tomebamba (present-day Cuenca) and Quito. Hiring a guide is recommended to gain insight into the fascinating history of the trail, but it's not strictly necessary. If you go it alone, bring a water filter, food, tent, impermeable boots and cold-weather gear. The trail climbs high into the Andes, where conditions can change quickly.

The first day of the trek ascends steadily for 12km along the valley floor beside the Río Azuay to the shores of **Laguna Yaunavi**,

OVERNIGHTING IN NATIONAL PARKS

It's possible to spend the night in many of the southern highlands national parks, but beyond the ranger stations there are no facilities on the ground, so you'll need to pack the following gear.

Tent: It's windy and there's little shelter in the *páramo*, so a good sturdy waterproof tent is essential.

Mattress and sleeping bag: Temperatures can reach dangerously low levels quickly; you'll need warm sleeping gear.

Water purifier: Clean water sources are plentiful in most parks, but a filter is recommended.

Portable shovel: No toilet facilities on trails. Rangers recommend a dig-and-fill approach to solids.

Gas stove: Open fires are prohibited within the park; bring your own cooking equipment.

EATING AROUND CUENCA: OUR PICKS

Mercado San José: It's not fancy but the best *encebollados* in the mountains (plus many other traditional meals) are at this Paute market. *8am-5:30pm* $

Restaurante Corvel: Top-notch gourmet takes on traditional dishes, served in a relaxed courtyard in the center of Paute. Reserve ahead on weekends. *11am-10pm* $$

Casa Vieja: Traditional mountain house with adobe walls just outside the Cajas checkpoint. Wholesome mountain food. *noon-10pm* $$

Paradero de La Montaña: A haven from the cold, this chalet beside the highway in Cajas has good sandwiches and hot drinks. *8am-10pm* $

DRIVE INTO THE MOUNTAINS

Head out into the rolling green hills north of Cuenca to reach seldom-visited traditional towns.

START	END	LENGTH
Cuenca	Cañar	30km; 4hr

The timeless villages in the mountains around Cuenca remain the center of traditional southern highlands culture. Head east out of town on Hwy 40; then, just after crossing the Puente Europa, you'll come to 1 **El Cabo**, a village famed for its cuisine – it's a great place for a filling breakfast. Follow the highway north to reach 2 **Paute**, an endearing little town tucked among dramatic mountains, with an attractive plaza and breezy riverside park. The hills around the town are crisscrossed with trails that will appeal to both cyclists and hikers. From Paute, head north past the guinea-pig farms on Avenida Antonio Mancilla to reach the highway to 3 **Azogues**, the buzzing capital of Cañar province that is watched over by the impressive twin-towered Santuario de la Virgen de la Nube.

Rejoin Hwy 35 for the short drive northwest to 4 **Biblián**, where the magnificent neo-Gothic stone church of the Santuario de la Virgen del Rocio clings to the side of Monte Zhalao. It's worth climbing the steep stairs behind the temple for 360-degree views of the surrounding countryside. A further 30-minute drive north leads to the the dusty city of 5 **Cañar**, where the inhabitants are proud of their distinctive traditional dress, the centerpieces of which are white woolen hats and distinctive *chumbis* (handwoven belts).

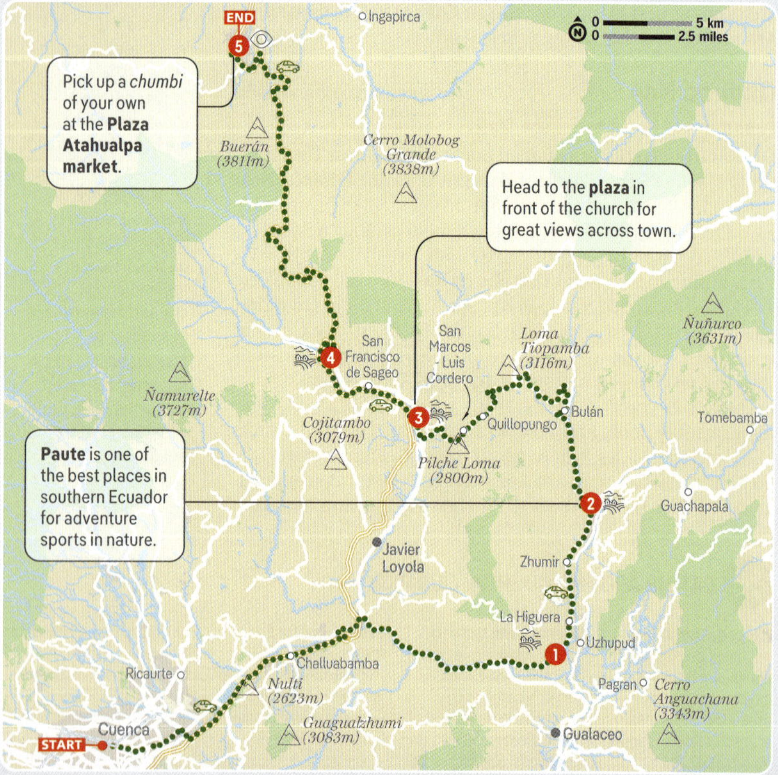

where there is a dedicated camping area beside a stream. On the second day, the hike climbs for about 3km to **Las Tres Cruces**, where various branches of the Qhapac Ñan come together, before reaching the high point of the journey, a 4458m-high peak overlooking **Laguna Sontzahuin**. From here the trail narrows and descends steeply to the Río Sontzahuin valley before climbing gently to the archaeological site at **Paredones**, where some ancient stone walls remain standing. The final day of the trek is the longest but also the least strenuous. It's mostly downhill for the 10km stretch to the little village of **San Jose de Culebrillas** and then another 7km descent to Ingapirca.

Mountain Towns East of Cuenca

TIME FROM CUENCA TO GUALACEO: **45MIN**

Ramble around colorful market villages

The mountain towns to the east of Cuenca are famed for their handicrafts, with even small villages often having their own unique specialties. In addition to colorful clothing, the region's markets also sell woven baskets, fine gold- and silver-filigreed jewelry, woodwork, pottery, musical instruments and ikat textiles made using a pre-Columbian technique of weaving tie-dyed threads.

Perched on the banks of a pretty river, the little town of **Gualaceo** is the place to go for ikat weavings, which are often turned into stylish *makanas* – elegant shawls with macramé fringes. Most *makanas* are made in the rural community of Los Olivos on the road into town, where you'll find the excellent **Casa Museo de La Makana** *(@casa_museo_de_la_makana; free)*, run by the affable José Jiménez – a 5th-generation master weaver – and his children, who are keeping the tradition alive. In the center of Gualaceo, the busy marketplace is a great place to try traditional country meals.

About 10km south of Gualaceo, the hilltop town of **Chordeleg** has been a center of fine jewelry since pre-Inca times, with local artisans producing intricate filigree earrings, necklaces and bracelets. Be aware that fakery is not uncommon, so an expert opinion is recommended before major purchases.

The most southerly and smallest of the market trifecta, **Sigsig** is a slow-paced mountain town known for its handcrafted *sombreros de paja toquillo*. You may see elderly women weaving hats around town, but the best place to see artisans at work and pick up a hat is at the **Asociación de Toquilleras María Auxiliadora** in the old hospital building south of town.

FINDING THE RIGHT TOUR

When choosing excursions to attractions around Cuenca, quality varies among operators. Group size is one of the most important factors. A smaller group means more interaction with your guide and less hanging around once you're done. Many outfitters offer bilingual guides but then proceed to mix groups between Spanish and English speakers, with commentary constantly changing between the two. Find out if your tour will be conducted exclusively in your language before booking.

Another area of difference is in the type of transportation. The best (and most expensive) tours include transportation in comfortable SUVs, while cheaper options usually involve less luxurious minivans.

EATING IN THE MARKET TOWNS: OUR PICKS

Plaza Restaurante: Overlooking the Gualaceo plaza, with a good set meal and wide menu, this bistro offers rest for tired shoppers. *noon-10pm* $$

Mercado 25 de Junio: This market is your one-stop destination for all kinds of traditional country meals, including *hornado*, *cuy* and *encebollados*. *8am-4pm* $

Restaurante Tinaja: Friendly place behind a jewelry market in Chordeleg. Economic meals and more hearty mains, including trout and steak. *10am-5:30pm* $

Tos Tón Restaurante: Tiny place, big portions. Perhaps the most diverse menu in Gualaceo, with dozens of seafood, chicken and meat dishes. *9am-10pm* $

Saraguro

INDIGENOUS CULTURE | FERTILE FARMLANDS | WILD WATERFALLS

TOP TIP
Learning a few words of Kichwa is a great way to open doors and make friends in traditional villages around Saraguro. You can take classes in some communities here and then head out into the countryside to practice. Even if your vocabulary is limited, locals very much appreciate the effort.

Surrounded by rolling green hills that shelter timeless Kichwa communities, the tiny little town of Saraguro is a wonderful place to spend a couple of days immersing yourself in traditional Andean culture. The proud inhabitants of the region originally lived near Lake Titicaca in Peru but ended up here in the 1470s as a result of the Inca Empire's system of resettlement, or mitimae.

Slow-paced and friendly, Saraguro town is a pleasant place to hang out, but the real highlights of a trip here are found in the surrounding mountains. The countryside still looks very much like it has for centuries, with mud-brick houses surrounded by diminutive plots of grains and tubers carefully tended by self-sufficient farmers. Beyond the villages, the rugged mountains provide endless opportunities for adventure, with graceful waterfalls and sweeping lookouts, as well as the chance to spot the largest flying bird in the Americas.

Villages of Saraguro

Travel the fascinating Andean heartland

Saraguro's innovative community tourism projects are renowned across Ecuador for their authenticity and sustainability.

GETTING AROUND

Fairly regular bus services run from the corner of the plaza to the community of Oñacapac via Tuncarta. Buses are generally not marked, so you'll have to ask locals which bus to take; pay the driver in cash. For Gera, irregular collective pickups leave from the Parque de Las Culturas, two blocks west of the plaza.

Shared taxis and pickups run to many other communities, including Las Lagunas and Ñamarin via the Baños del Inca trailhead – ask around at the main square.

Alternatively, you can reach all the surrounding communities by private taxi for a very reasonable price, which saves hanging around for a bus departure. Get the driver's phone number for the return trip – taxis are rarely found in villages.

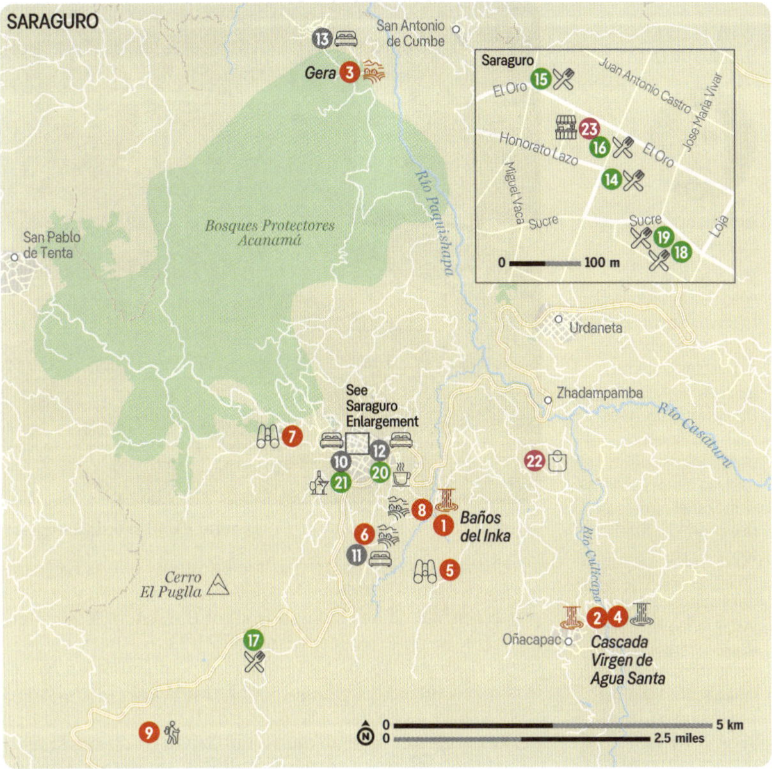

HIGHLIGHTS
1 Baños del Inka
2 Cascada Virgen de Agua Santa
3 Gera

SIGHTS
4 Cascada Sarashi
5 Centro Turistica El Gavilan
6 Las Lagunas
7 Mirador Yucucapac
8 Tuncarta

ACTIVITIES
9 Bosque Protegido Washapamba

SLEEPING
10 Hostal Achik Wasi
11 Inka Wasi
12 Sarakuru Hostal
13 Taski Wasi

EATING
14 La Casona del Sabor
15 La Muguna
16 Mercado Municipal
17 Quesos Saraguro/Pizza Contento
18 ShamuiCo
19 Tupay

DRINKING & NIGHTLIFE
20 La Casa del Cafe
21 Wawa Gallery

SHOPPING
22 Sombreros Sarango
23 Sunday Market

There are few better places in South America for independent travelers to escape the crowds and experience traditional highland culture.

All of the Kichwa villages around Saraguro have very distinct identities. Some stick steadfastly to indigenous traditions and don't permit outsiders to marry into the community, while others are more open. Travelers are, for the most part, universally welcome to visit and learn about the Kichwa culture, and a number of villages also have simple places to stay. In fact, the *saragureros* are so proud of their culture there's even a growing number of village YouTubers who provide unique insights into daily life.

WHY I LOVE SARAGURO

Alex Egerton, Lonely Planet writer

In a world of ever-more-packaged tourism experiences, Saraguro is a breath of fresh mountain air. Nowhere else in the country do I feel such a connection to Ecuador's rich Andean history than in the quiet streets of this charming little town. The lack of must-see sights is refreshing; here, the attraction is the town itself, or more to the point, its remarkable inhabitants. Whether you're sipping a fresh juice on the main plaza or shopping at the colorful market, in Saraguro, rich cultural heritage is all around.

MAJOPEZ/ALAMY

Loom at a workshop in Saraguro

Just a short walk from town, the community of **Las Lagunas** is known for its traditional textiles, and visitors can watch the process at the village loom in front of the school. The village *taita* (indigenous leader) weaves cloth here – both for local use and for sale to visitors. A formal demonstration can be organized through the adjoining **Inka Wasi** *(+593-99-036-3688, facebook.com/inkawasisaraguro)* lodge. It also organizes performances of Andean music and serves traditional meals.

Slightly further out in the foothills, **Tuncarta** is home to **Sombreros Sarango** *(+593-99-220-0398)*, which produces fine Saraguro hats. Pop in to check out the age-old process and pick up a perfectly fitted hat to take home.

Harder to get to, but well worth the effort, the village of **Gera** is one of the most traditional communities in the region and is set on the edge of a breathtaking canyon. Here, most houses are still built the traditional way, using earth and baked tiles, and the beautifully terraced farmlands below the town date to before European arrival. You can spend the night here and follow ancient mountain paths to unexcavated pre-Inca ruins, or try to spot majestic Andean condors soaring on the thermal winds.

If you can't make it out into the countryside, you can get a taste for the local culture on a Sunday in Saraguro itself,

EATING IN SARAGURO: OUR PICKS

Tupay: Hearty dishes with stacks of fresh organic produce. Mains of chicken and trout come served with delicious vegetable sides. *10am-9pm* $

ShamuiCo: A surprising find in tiny Saraguro, this sophisticated place in an arty courtyard on the main plaza adds a gourmet twist to traditional flavors. *noon-9pm Wed-Sun* $$

Quesos Saraguro/Pizza Contento: Try varieties of farm-fresh cheese then a pizza. Another branch is on the Panamericana south of town. *7am-9:30pm* $

Mercado Municipal: Breakfast at booths inside the municipal market: juices, traditional maize beverages, sandwiches with fresh Saraguro cheese. *7am-2pm* $

when villagers throughout the region – dressed elegantly for the occasion – descend on the town for the busy **market**. There is also a smaller fresh produce market on Fridays in the area known as Tres de Mayo that's worth a look.

COMMUNITY TOURISM

Very different Kichwa-speaking communities, sharing a common heritage with those of the southern highlands, are located along the banks of the **Río Napo** (p201) in the jungle-covered Oriente region.

Off-Piste Mountain Adventures

Waterfalls, lookouts and dramatic peaks

The countryside around Saraguro is not just a top cultural destination; it's an exceptional natural one as well.

East of town, accessible from a turnoff on the Panamericana, **Baños del Inka** has chilly waterfalls, shallow caves and pretty rock formations. It's a short but very steep and occasionally perilous hike up from the trailhead, just across the old bridge north of town. At the top of the trail there is a wooden walkway beside the rock face that leads to the base of the falls.

Even more spectacular cascades can be found a short walk from the community of Oñacapac, where the powerful **Cascada Virgen de Agua Santa** and **Cascada Sarashi** sit side by side. The former is known for a miraculous apparition but the currents are too strong for swimming, while the latter has an icy swimming hole.

Hiking around town is excellent, too. Trails from Saraguro also lead to a number of fine lookout points. Northwest of the center, the **Mirador Yucucapac** has great views over the town, while the **Centro Turistica El Gavilan** *(@el_vuelo_del_gavilan; $1)* has phenomenal panoramas of the surrounding countryside in addition to a vertigo-inducing giant swing. Just south of town, **Bosque Protegido Washapamba** is a community-run nature reserve that protects some of the region's most pristine Andean forest and has a number of great trails.

Intrepid hikers might like to hire a vehicle to travel west to the rarely visited **Cerro de Arcos**, one of the highest mountains in southern Ecuador, which is topped with archlike rock formations.

A CLASSIC LOOK

Even in other parts of Ecuador, it's easy to identify *saragureros* by their distinct traditional dress, which many members of the community continue to wear even when residing in larger cities and warmer climes. Women wear broad-brimmed black or white hats, long pleated skirts, ornate pins called *tupus* and elaborate beaded collars known as *chakiras*. Men wear fedora-like black hats, black ponchos and knee-length black shorts, and they may also don small white aprons and woven, double-pouch shoulder bags called *alforjas*. It's a style that has survived the test of time, and each part of the attire is an important craft tradition, with many items being handmade in communities around Saraguro.

EATING & DRINKING IN SARAGURO: OUR PICKS

La Casona del Sabor: Hugely popular for its filling, no-nonsense Ecuadorean staples, with a hot bowl of tasty soup. *7am-4pm* $

La Muguna: Run by a local tourism expert, this bright restaurant prepares traditional dishes and the house specialty, *trigotto* – a type of wheat risotto. *8am-9pm* $$

Wawa Gallery: Bar and gallery on the outskirts of town is the best place to unwind. Live Andean music and house beers. *6pm-midnight Thu-Sat, noon-6pm Sun*

La Casa del Cafe: An unassuming shop front on the highway hides the best cup of coffee in town, made from small-batch Loja beans. *24hr*

Loja

FINE COFFEE | MUSEUMS | LUSH HIKES

GETTING AROUND

Loja's historic center, where most attractions lie, is easy to navigate on foot. Taxis are reasonably priced and are the most convenient way to visit outlying attractions or get to the bus terminal, which is 4km north of the center. You can hail one of the many passing cabs, or ask your hotel to call a driver. Minimum fare is $1.25.

Urban buses (per trip $0.30) run south to the Jardín Botánico Reinaldo Espinosa and Parque Universitario, but require the purchase of a prepaid card before boarding. Cards are sold at the main bus terminal and outlets around town.

The most southerly of Ecuador's major cities, Loja has a historic center and is well off the main travel trail, making it an authentic and relaxed base from which to explore the majestic scenery of the southern highlands.

The capital of the department of the same name, Loja hasn't always been a far-flung destination – it was once an important staging point where Spanish conquistadores launched expeditions to explore the immense jungles of Amazonia just over the mountains to the east. Proximity to pristine nature remains Loja's major drawcard today. It's the jumping-off point for the highland portions of the stunning Parque Nacional Podocarpus, one of Ecuador's most scenic and least-visited national parks, as well as adventurous hiking trails into the surrounding mountains. It's also the center of the country's coffee industry, making it the ideal place to sample some of Ecuador's best beans.

A Stroll Through Historic Loja

Admire elegant architecture

Loja's compact historic center is formed by a neat grid of narrow streets lined with colonial-era abodes and numerous leafy plazas fronted by elegant old churches. Despite seeing quite a lot of traffic, the pace here is slow, making it a pleasant place for a walk.

The best location to begin a tour of the city is the impressive city gates, known as the **Puerta de La Ciudad**, which are part of a sizable castle beside the Río Zamora. It has a large arch spanning Sucre, a busy street that heads toward the center of town. Inside you'll find rotating art exhibitions, a good cafe and stairs leading to several lookout points, which afford great views over town to the dramatic mountains beyond.

Follow Sucre south to reach the **Parque Central**, an expansive tree-filled plaza surrounded by some pretty early Republican-era mansions interspersed with less elegant modern constructions. It's the center of activity in town and a good spot to sit back on a bench and observe daily Lojan life. Just a couple of blocks away, the small **Plaza Santo Domingo** is dominated by the grand, pale-brick **Iglesia Santo Domingo**, which seems a little

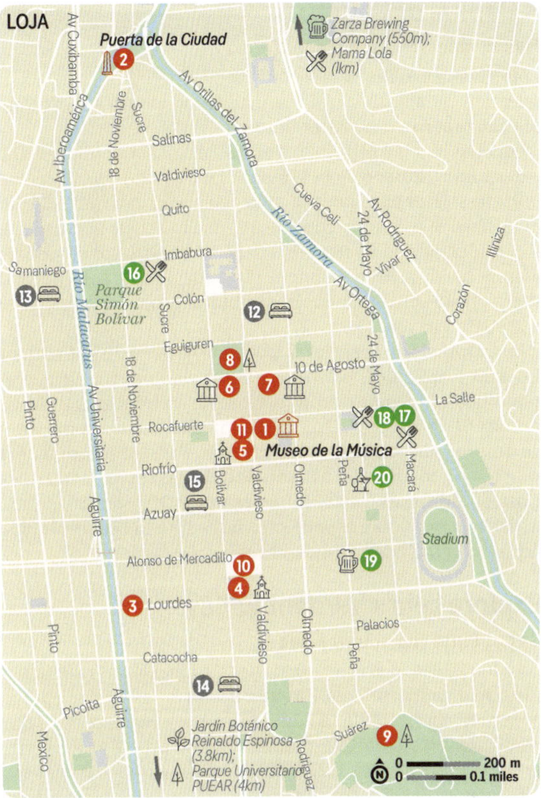

HIGHLIGHTS
1 Museo de la Música
2 Puerta de la Ciudad

SIGHTS
3 Calle Lourdes
4 Iglesia de San Sebastián
5 Iglesia Santo Domingo
6 Museo de la Cultura Lojana
7 Museo del Monasterio de Madres Concepcionistas
8 Parque Central
9 Parque Pucará
10 Plaza de la Independencia
11 Plaza Santo Domingo

SLEEPING
12 Hotel Grand Victoria
13 Hotel Virgen del Cisne
14 La Casa de Manuel
15 Zamorano Real Hotel

EATING
16 El Tamal Lojano
17 Maroma Cocina Creativa
18 Riscomar

DRINKING & NIGHTLIFE
see 10 Kaweh Coffee
19 La Huerta
20 Lecka Bistro Alemán

oversized for its surroundings. Its ornate gold and pale-blue interior is adorned with murals depicting the mysteries of the rosary.

Loja's prettiest plaza is found in the south of town, where the **Plaza de La Independencia** is surrounded by grand old buildings with pillared overhangs and shuttered wooden balconies. The center of the plaza is dominated by a giant 32m-high clock tower, while standing guard over the south side is the magnificent pale-yellow **Iglesia de San Sebastián** with its elegant wooden annex. A stage in the square is often used for live music. Just around the corner, narrow **Calle Lourdes** is the oldest alleyway in Loja and is lined with colorful old houses.

TOP TIP

Loja generally sees few visitors, but during celebrations for Easter as well as the Virgen del Cisne in August and the Independence of Loja in November, hotels across town fill to capacity. During these times, book well in advance to lock down a bed in the historic center in order to be close to the action.

EATING IN LOJA: OUR PICKS

Mama Lola: It's worth taking a taxi to this restaurant for large portions of well-prepared Ecuadorian favorites. *noon-10pm Mon-Sat, to 4pm Sun* $$

El Tamal Lojano: A local institution serving tasty traditional snacks, including *quimbolitos*, *humitas*, *empanadas de verde* and *tamales lojanos*. *8am-8pm* $

Riscomar: The best seafood in town, along with regular Ecuadorean fare served in an elegant dining room on the edge of the nightlife district. Good value. *noon-10pm* $

Maroma Cocina Creativa: It only has six tables but everything is top-notch at this modern fusion restaurant run by a talented young chef. *1-10pm Mon-Sat* $$

TRADITIONAL MOUNTAIN SNACKS

In the mountains of Ecuador, snacking is much the same as it has been for generations, with traditional maize- and plantain-based bites known as *delicias* (treats). Here are some popular varieties:

Humita: Corn dumpling steamed in a corn husk. The *sal* (salty) versions come with cheese; the *dulce* (sweet) versions are often flavored with anise.

Quimbolito: Light, sweet, corn-based cake steamed in *achira* leaves, usually topped with a raisin.

Tamales de Loja: Close to a *humita*, but usually stuffed with shredded chicken.

Empanada: Pocket of plantain or maize dough stuffed with sweet/savory fillings.

Bolón de verde: Fried ball of mashed green plantain, often with pork rinds.

A Capital of Culture

Music, mansions and monasteries

Loja's historical importance is reflected in the city's excellent selection of museums, which are all found within a short walk of each other in the center of town.

Located in a beautifully renovated old school building, the entertaining **Museo de la Música** *(7256-1342, admission free)* tells the stories of renowned musicians who have hailed from Loja, most of whom reached the pinnacle of their fame during the golden period of 1890–1940. In addition to photographs of impeccably attired crooners, there are old instruments and sheet music spread across a number of rooms opening onto a pretty courtyard.

Just around the corner, the polished **Museo de la Cultura Lojana** *(7257-0001, admission free)* is found in a graceful republican-era mansion and features exhibitions of local art, archaeology and ethnography in addition to some wonderful old photographs of the town. Fans of religious art won't want to miss the **Museo del Monasterio de Madres Concepcionistas** *(@museomadresconceptas, admission $3)*, which has two floors of works from the 16th to 18th centuries. Admission includes a guided tour.

Explore Loja's Verdant Valley

Get out into the countryside

You don't have to go far from Loja to immerse yourself in nature. Just south of town **Parque Pucará** has a trail leading up a pine-covered hillside to El Mirador, which presents fine views across the rooftops of town. Go in a group, as robberies are not unheard of, especially during the week when it's quieter.

There are longer trails through more remote parkland at the **Parque Universitario** *(PUEAR; unl.edu.ec; free)*, perched at an altitude of 2150m around 5km south of town on the road to Vilcabamba. Paths are well-marked and generally take 40 minutes to an hour to complete. Some paths are somewhat steep and may be slippery after rains, so bring good footwear.

Just across the highway, the **Jardín Botánico Reinaldo Espinosa** *(unl.edu.ec; $2)* is Ecuador's oldest botanical garden and has more than 1000 different species of flora, including sections dedicated to Andean species, fruit tress and traditional medicinal plants. There is also a bonsai garden and a fun maze.

DRINKING IN LOJA: OUR PICKS

La Huerta: Drink house beers in an enchanted garden or inside at the bohemian bar at this hip spot that wouldn't be out of place in trendier cities. *6pm-midnight Tue-Sat*

Zarza Brewing Company: Good ribs and Mexican plates, plus impressive house beers at this microbrewery on the north side of town. *4pm-midnight Mon-Sat*

Lecka Bistro Alemán: Quality beers, banging German food and a friendly welcome at this long-running bar/restaurant on main nightlife strip. *4-9pm Mon-Fri*

Kaweh Coffee: Cozy cafe preparing awesome coffee with beans from its farm in rural Loja. A variety of prep methods. *10am-noon & 4-9pm Mon-Fri, 3-9pm Sat*

Beyond Loja

Gorgeous countryside and low numbers of visitors make the rural areas of Loja department the ideal off-the-beaten-track nature destination.

Just outside Loja, Parque Nacional Podocarpus covers large swathes of stunning wilderness that run down the eastern flank of the Andes. North of the park, the winding highway that descends from Loja to the small town of Zamora is one of southern Ecuador's most scenic drives, with landscapes rapidly transitioning from windswept mountains covered with strands of cloud forest to jungle-covered foothills, passing countless impressive waterfalls along the way.

Straddling the biodiverse foothills between the southern highlands and the jungles of the Amazonia, Zamora is a nature lover's dream and a tourism hot spot waiting to happen. In addition to great hiking, bird-watching and cycling trips, the town also has delightful swimming holes and scenic river tubing.

Places

Parque Nacional Podocarpus p307
Zamora p308
Río Nangaritza p309

Parque Nacional Podocarpus

TIME FROM LOJA: **45MIN**

Two parks in one

Taking in swathes of Andean forest as well as vast expanses of humid tropical rainforest, the huge **Parque Nacional Podocarpus** *(free)* is one of Ecuador's most spectacular and biodiverse national parks. As a result of huge differences in altitudes, which range from as low as 900m to more than 3600m around the Andean peaks, the array of plants and animals found here is astonishing. More than 3000 plant species

GETTING AROUND

From Loja you can take any Vilcabamba-bound bus to the Cajanuma control point of Parque Nacional Podocarpus, but note that it's a stiff two-hour walk from the road up to the ranger station, where the trails begin. A taxi to the control point is around $6, or around $15 all the way to the trailheads, but not all drivers are willing to traverse the rough road.

Buses from Loja to Zamora leave regularly from the main terminal. Viajeros also has three direct buses from Cuenca to Zamora, otherwise changing at Loja is not much slower.

From Zamora, a taxi to the Bombuscaro car park is around $5; from here, it's a fairly gentle 20-minute walk to the ranger station. Many other attractions around Zamora can be reached on foot, but taxis will save energy for the trails proper.

TAKING THE BACK ROADS BACK

If you've come down to Loja along the spine of the Andes following the Pan-American Highway and need to head north again, it's not obligatory to retrace your steps. A long but exhilarating detour through the jungle will get you back to Quito or Cuenca via some of the country's most lush landscapes.

From Zamora the Troncal Amazonica highway heads north through the forested Andean foothills to San Miguel near the Colombian border.

To return to Cuenca, you can climb into the mountains via Yacuambi to Saraguro or take the road branching west near Gualaquiza that climbs through Sigsig.

For Quito, take the Troncal all the way to Baeza, then it's a short climb to the capital via the thermal springs at Papallacta.

and 600 different bird species have been recorded, and rare mammals include pumas, tapirs and spectacled bears.

The park's high sector is accessed from the **Control de Cajanuma**, 10km south of Loja, from where a sometimes rough dirt road leads 8.5km uphill to the ranger station and **refugio** where you can spend the night for a bargain $3 – you'll need to bring your own food and sleeping bag. To book space call the park administration in Loja on +593-99-286-0492.

From the station, several self-guided trails wind through cloud forest, including the scenic 5km, four-hour **Los Miradores** loop, which climbs up into the windy, ethereal *páramo* moors. Hardcore hikers can tackle the three-day trek to the remote lakes of **Lagunas del Compadre**.

In total contrast to the fog-covered plains at the top of the park, the lowland sector is blanketed with wet jungle punctuated by rushing streams and powerful waterfalls. It's accessed through **Control de Bombuscaro**, 6km south of Zamora, where there are several short and well-maintained (but sometimes muddy) trails into the forest and simple accommodations. The easiest and most popular trails lead to **Cascada Poderosa** and **Cascada Chismosa**, two beautiful waterfalls backed by walls of green foliage. The longer **Los Higuerones** trail reaches pockets of primary forest, while the short but brutally steep **El Mirador** trail leads to a panoramic lookout point.

The shortest of all the trails leads down to an absolutely stunning stretch of the **Río Bombuscaro**, where emerald-green waters thunder over massive boulders painted with splurges of moss, all backed by lush dense forest. It's beautiful at any time but especially attractive when it's dry and the water is translucent. It's wild, but strong swimmers are permitted to paddle in some of the pools.

There are also simple accommodations here (*cabañas* near the park office) and an open-air kitchen is nearby. Advanced reservations are not accepted, but call the friendly rangers (+593-07-303-9579) to check availability.

Zamora

TIME FROM LOJA: 1½HR

Off-the-beaten-path adventures

Straddling the boundary between the mountains of the southern highlands and the lowlands of the Oriente, diminutive Zamora doesn't get many visitors, but may just be one of Ecuador's best-kept secrets.

Known as the city of waterfalls and birds, the town doesn't disappoint on either front. The unique merging of ecosystems

EATING & DRINKING IN ZAMORA: OUR PICKS

El Señor Encocados: A small shop front on the *malecón* cooking up big flavors, this seafood joint does great soups, *encocados* and fried fish dishes. *9am-5pm* $

La Choza: A long-running place preparing great-value set meals that come with tasty soup and a fresh juice. Get in early. *7am-7pm* $

Asados del Manaba: An unpretentious *asadero* across from the river. Pick from barbecued chicken, pork or beef served with rice, plantains and beans. *6-11pm* $

Toxi: The best of the riverfront watering holes, Toxi has riverside seating, half a dozen craft beers on tap and an Argentinian barbecue. *6pm-midnight*

Zamora

means you'll find an impressive number of both mountain and lowland bird species just a short walk from town. And there are so many amazing waterfalls most locals have yet to see them all. Among those worth a visit are the high-volume **Cascada El Aventurero** on the road to Timbara, which fills a refreshing pool; and the towering **Cascada La Rosa**, which falls in two stages over a rock wall covered with ferns, moss and bromeliads.

With little traffic and glorious scenery around every bend, the area is great to explore on two wheels – rent bicycles at the ultra-helpful **Adventure Zamora** *(@adventurezamora)* by the river. It also hires out inner tubes for Zamora's ultimate DIY adventure – floating down the Río Bombuscaro, riding the rapids and taking in the spectacular sights and sounds of the jungle. The put-in point is the pretty pebble beach known as **El Arbol Que Chupa**.

For great views over town, climb the **Mirador Doña Dorita** *(facebook.com/mirador.dorita; adult/child $2/1)* just west of the center, or take on the tough climb to the **Mirador Tres Cruces** in the high mountains south of the plaza.

Río Nangaritza

TIME FROM LOJA: **3½HR**

A wild river trip

In the rarely visited lowlands east of Zamora, close to the Peruvian border, the Río Nangaritza flows beside the vast Cordillera del Cóndor. Traveling by boat along blackwater rivers, guests motor past odd rock formations, delicate waterfalls and cliffs covered in orchids. There are also caves and canyons frequented by bats and curious oilbirds to explore.

Several buses a day depart Loja for the river port of **Las Orquídeas**, where you can organize boat trips. Due to the distances involved, it's best to stay at least a night in the region. A good option is the family-run **Cabañas Yankuam** *(yankuamlodge.com)*, which also organizes tours upriver and throughout the region.

FURRY FRIENDS OF THE FOREST

Ecuador has an important population of the endangered Andean spectacled bear in its rugged mountains. Parque Nacional Podocarpus is one of the key habitats for the animal, which is the only bear species found in South America. Andean bears cover large distances in search of food – mainly fruits and bromeliads – with each animal requiring around 30 sq km to survive.

While foraging, the bears spread seeds over immense areas. They also open tracts of forest to sunlight and regeneration, forming a crucial cog in the mountain ecosystem.

The most peaceful of all bear species, they shun contact with humans and tend to take to the trees when feeling threatened.

Vilcabamba

MOUNTAIN TRAILS | HIP CAFES | HORSE-RIDING ADVENTURES

GETTING AROUND

Vilcabamba is very small and most places of interest are less than a 10-minute walk from the plaza. A fleet of taxis park on the main square and have fixed prices to points outside town, including various trailheads. Set a time for your return pickup or, if you have mobile data, get the number of the dispatcher and order a car with a quick message.

For destinations north near the Panamericana, it's also possible to jump on any Loja-bound bus, no matter how short the distance.

Tucked below towering mountains in Ecuador's deep south, the tiny town of Vilcabamba is known as the Ciudad de la Eterna Juventud (City of Eternal Youth), due to the high number of centenarians it has produced. Whether due to the balmy air, laid-back lifestyle or fresh mountain water, this magical reputation has attracted many expats, particularly retirees looking for healthy climes in which to stretch their pensions further. The hills around town are dotted with new homes, and the town has many foreign-owned businesses.

Vilcabamba is also a haven for artistic and new-age communities attracted by the barefoot lifestyle far from the rat race. This influx has created tensions, particularly concerning the cost of land and living, but has also created many jobs and has given the town a unique international atmosphere that makes it an entertaining base from which to explore the spectacular surrounding landscapes.

Trekking in the Magic Mountain Air

Tranquil trails and windy peaks

With magnificent mountains in all directions and a mostly dry, springlike climate, Vilcabamba is one of southern Ecuador's top hiking destinations. Trails lead out from the town in all directions, with short, scenic hikes and adventurous longer treks both on offer. Most hotels and hostels have hiking maps and some even have their own trails. Some treks pass through private property and you may be required to pay a nominal access fee.

An easy introductory hike leads from the northwest edge of town to a small spring known as **Agua de Hierro**. Even closer to the center, with a network of scenic trails, **Rumi Wilco** *(rumiwilco.com; $2)* is a private nature reserve running up a hillside from the Río Chamba. Self-guided map booklets are located – along with an honor box for admission fees – at the little hut by the entrance. For the hike with the best views, follow the trail to the top of **Cerro Mandango**, Vilcabamba's distinctive peak, which resembles a sun-drenched stone palace perched on the summit of a steep green mountain. Most visitors just hike the first part of the trail – the one-hour climb to a *mirador* (lookout) marked by a slightly psychedelic mirrored cross, which gives panoramic views of the town and surrounding mountains.

The second part of the trail to the rocky summit is a tricky further hour and should be avoided when it's windy. It requires hauling yourself up steep rock faces while clinging to steel cables, but those who make it to the top are rewarded with even more breathtaking panoramas. For long stretches of the journey, there is not much shade, so leave early to avoid the heat.

TOP TIP

Being a new-age center, Vilcabamba has plenty of advertisements for spiritual retreats, many of which include ceremonies with *ayahuasca*, a psychotropic plant used ritually in Amazon cultures. Note that only an authentic indigenous shaman should prepare and administer *ayahuasca* to avoid dangerous side effects that could ruin your trip.

Refreshing Cascades

Hike to hidden falls

For a strenuous hike that ends with a towering prize, follow the Río Yambala to the **Cascada El Palto**, an elegant 30m-high waterfall in a pretty valley lined with lush greenery.

From town, it's a five-hour, 15km round-trip trek along a fairly easy-to-follow path, but you can cut the journey in half by taking a taxi to the trailhead at the concrete bridge in Yamburara Alto. Be careful on the last stretch down to the waterfall, which is steep and can be slippery, especially after heavy rains.

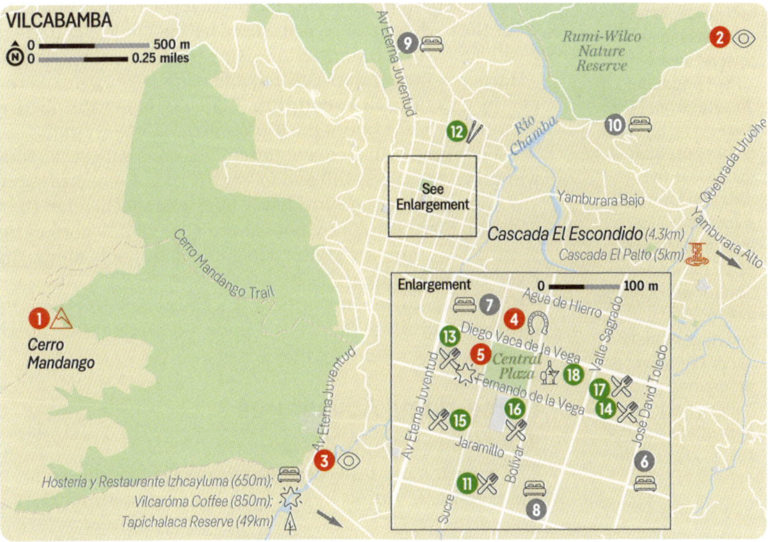

HIGHLIGHTS
1 Cerro Mandango

SIGHTS
2 Agua de Hierro
3 Doña Julita

ACTIVITIES
4 Caballos Gavilán
5 La Tasca Tours

SLEEPING
6 Avalon B&B
7 Hostal Jardín Escondido
8 Hostal Las Palmas
9 Hostería Paraiso
10 Rumi Wilco

EATING
11 ACWA
12 Dumplings & Noodles
13 La Baguette
14 Maricel Pasteleria
15 Restaurante Katherine
16 United Falafel Org
17 Vilcabrunch

DRINKING & NIGHTLIFE
18 Juice Factory

MOUNTAINS OF DIVERSITY

Rising up between the eastern Andes and the lowlands of the Amazonia in southern Ecuador and northern Peru, the Cordillera del Cóndor mountain range is a wonderland of cloud forests and one of the most biodiverse places in the world, with many endemic plant and animal species. However, population growth and economic pressures are taking their toll on the range, with deforestation and illegal mining encroaching on pristine areas.

The **Fundación Jocotoco** *(jocotoco.org.ec)* manages a number of nature reserves in the area that form a wildlife corridor linking the forests of Cordillera del Cóndor with national and regional parks, and runs a variety of conservation programs aimed at holding back the agricultural frontier.

CURIOSO.PHOTOGRAPHY/ALAMY

Cascada El Palto (p311)

Beyond the waterfall, the trail continues up into remote reaches of Parque Nacional Podocarpus, but park authorities discourage its use, as it's very overgrown and heads to a remote area of the park far from any facilities. If you're determined to enter the park from here, you'll need a local guide and to clear your plans with the Ministerio de Ambiente in Loja beforehand.

Harder to find, but less visited and equally beautiful, is the nearby **Cascada El Escondido**. To find it, follow the narrow path on the north side of the Río Yambala, skirting around the two locked gates. Immediately after the second gate, make your way down the grassy hill and follow the river 100m upstream.

While the falls here are lower and less spectacular than El Palto, there is a lovely pool at the base that is perfect for a refreshing dip, and there are additional pools along the river on the way up.

Note that, to reach the falls, it's necessary to cross the stream – and while there is a rope to aid getting over, it can be impassable after very heavy rains.

Horse-riding Adventures

Ride off into the hills

The rugged mountains around Vilcabamba provide some of the best horse riding in southern Ecuador, with numerous

EATING IN VILCABAMBA: OUR PICKS

Try the spicy tofu.

La Baguette: Great breakfasts and scrumptious French pastries made fresh daily at this corner bakery. Good for hiking snacks. Get in early. *7am-5pm* $

Restaurante Katherine: Unpretentious family-run place just off the park. Filling plates of tasty Ecuadorean fare served with soup and juice. *8am-3pm* $

Dumplings & Noodles: Delicious meat-free dishes along with iced tea at this relaxed place on the northern edge of town. *12:30-7:30pm Wed-Sun* $$

Maricel Pasteleria: Tasty all-day breakfasts and superb desserts make this cafeteria a top choice among Vilca expats. Carrot cake is especially good. *7am-6pm* $

quiet trails through spectacular scenery beginning just outside town. Most of the best rides head east, up into the buffer zone surrounding Parque Nacional Podocarpus, where there is little development, and wildlife sightings are common. Shorter adventures pass lookout points with panoramic views, while longer treks reach the sub-*páramo* plains bordering tracts of primary forest and include overnight stays in tents within basic shelters at the park's edge.

There are a number of highly experienced guides and tour companies around town that generally have strong and healthy mounts. **Caballos Gavilán** (+593-99-016-1759), founded by a Kiwi who has resided in Vilcabamba for years, offers excursions for riders of all levels with experienced local guides. Another accomplished operator is **La Tasca Tours** *(@latascatours; +593-98-556-1188)*, which also runs cycling trips and visits to local coffee farms. Expect to pay around $15 for a short ride and $40 for a half-day excursion.

Secrets of a Perfect Brew

From bean to cup

The department of Loja is widely regarded as Ecuador's best coffee-growing region, and the undulating countryside around Vilcabamba is a key area, with many small farms producing fragrant arabica beans for both domestic and international consumption.

At family-run **Vilcaróma Coffee** *(vilcaromacoffeerutadelcafe.com; tour $15)* visitors can follow the process from bean to cup on a guided two-hour tour that begins in the plantation. After picking your own beans, you'll discover how they are dried, threshed and toasted before enjoying limitless farm-fresh cups of caffeinated goodness. Along the way, the enthusiastic guides will pluck ripe fruits from the many productive trees on the farm for visitors to sample. At the end, you can pick up some bags of beans to enjoy once you get home.

Tours are offered in Spanish and English at 10am and 2pm but advanced reservations are essential to make sure your choice is available.

Less visitor orientated, **Doña Julita** *(@cafedonajulita; +593-93-999-8723)*, open 8am to 6pm, processes beans from all over the region and sells bags of many varieties. The friendly management are happy to show visitors around the processing facility where raw beans are toasted and prepared for market.

THE MOUNTAIN ROAD TO PERU

For most visitors, Vilcabamba is the end of the road, but it's possible to continue south by bus along the spine of the Andes to **Zumba** and on to the Peruvian border in a tiring full day of travel. An important military outpost during the wars between Ecuador and Peru in the 1940s and 1990s, Zumba has now become somewhat of a backwater, with little to hold travelers' attention.

From Zumba, *colectivos* (shared taxis) head to the border at **La Balsa**, from where it's a short walk across the Puente Internacional. Shared taxis here will take you to the Peruvian town of **San Ignacio**, the best place to break the journey and spend the night before continuing deeper into Peru.

EATING & DRINKING IN VILCABAMBA: OUR PICKS

Vilcabrunch: Friendly place with just a few tables. One of the most interesting menus in town: Asian and Ecuadorean meals. *noon-8pm Sun-Thu, to 5pm Fri* $$

ACWA: A bright hangout spot serving great coffee, waffles, sandwiches and salads. The attached shop is a good spot to pick up local coffee beans. *9am-4pm Tue-Sat* $$

United Falafel Org: Sit outside on the plaza or inside in the garden with good Middle Eastern fare. Hang around for drinks afterwards . *11am-8pm Wed-Sun* $$

Juice Factory: Tasty juices made from fresh seasonal fruits and healthy bowls make this busy spot the place to go for extra vitamins. *8am-4pm, closed Mon*

Places We Love to Stay

$ Budget $$ Midrange $$$ Top End

Cuenca

MAP p288

Hostal Yakumama A popular no-frills hostel with a good central location, creaky but homely dorms and rooms, and an inviting courtyard. Awesome attached cafe. $

El Cafecito An old-school hostel that has changed little over the years. It has neat, if sometimes small, rooms set over two floors and very helpful management. $

Pepe's House Hostel A colorful hostel in a great location, with comfy rooms with quality bedding, a great in-house cafe, and a curvaceous pet cat. $$

La Posada del Rey The spacious and stylish balcony rooms at this little hotel near the plaza are some of the best deals in town, but avoid the tight 3rd-floor options. $$

Hotel Posada del Angel A corner colonial-era building in a quiet area near Plaza San Sebastián, with elegant, comfortable rooms set around an internal courtyard. Good restaurant, too. $$

Casa Montalvo With high ceilings, polished wooden floors and modern accoutrements, this midrange spot makes a comfortable base for exploring Cuenca. Rooms surround an attractive courtyard garden. $$

Hotel Los Balcones A converted colonial-era home with a remarkable chandelier in the central courtyard. Small but well-appointed rooms, and the rooftop terrace has fine views. $$

Casa Barranco With a privileged location on the Calle Larga and a terrace overlooking the Río Tomebamba, this small hotel has charm, but service is hit-and-miss. $$

Hotel Morenica del Rosario A series of stairs winds up around sizable, well-furnished, occasionally dingy rooms – evoking images of some aging aristocrat's once-grand quarters – to a nice roof terrace. $$

Nass Casa del Aguila Set around a pretty courtyard in the heart of town with fair prices. Service is patchy, and included breakfast is basic, but it remains good value. $$

Mansión Alcázar Cuenca's best high-end digs are in this historic building, decorated with artistic flourishes and a lush garden. Rooms are luxurious and service is first class. $$$

Hotel Victoria A grand 17th-century house on the Barranco overlooking the Río Tomebamba that oozes class and character. Worth a splurge to feel the history. $$$

Hotel Inca Real Aspirations are clearly grand, and the gorgeous tiled courtyard prepares you for stunning rooms; yet these are functional, rather than spectacular. $$$

Parque Nacional Cajas

Estancia Buganey A stylish modern chalet hotel tucked in the foothills near the remote southern recreation area at Soldados. $$

Hosteria Dos Chorreras A fancy, full-service mountain retreat, with open fires and big bathtubs, set in a gorgeous green valley just outside the park boundary. $$$

Molino del Puente Charming accommodations on a rural property beside a rushing stream near the Llaviuco turnoff, although it's quite close to the road. Busy on weekends. $$$

Ingapirca

Hospedaje El Castillo A good, peaceful budget option just a five-minute walk from the ruins, with comfy heated rooms and an on-site restaurant. $

Posada Ingapirca A brisk walk uphill from Ingapirca, this converted hacienda has pretty gardens, open fireplaces and plenty of rustic charm, but doesn't skip on comfort either. $$$

Saraguro

MAP p301

Taski Wasi Right on the edge of Gera, overlooking the majestic valley below, this wonderful family-run lodge offers the rare combination of cultural immersion and privacy. One of Ecuador's best community guesthouses. $

Inka Wasi Attached to the home of the *taita* of the Lagunas community, this well-run lodge has traditional meals and interesting activities, including weaving workshops and music performances. $

Sarakuru Hostal Modern, clean and friendly – this spotless budget place with fast internet and cable TV is located between the bus offices and the plaza. $

Hostal Achik Wasi On a hillside on the edge of town, this tranquil, well-run lodge with good views is the best place to stay in Saraguro proper. $$

Loja

MAP p305

Hotel Virgen del Cisne Friendly and great value, this cheap and cheerful place is a short walk from the center and has bright, modern rooms. $

La Casa de Manuel Tucked away on the southern edge of town, this stylish guesthouse has a chic design and flourishes of art throughout. $$

Zamorano Real Hotel Modern and impeccably clean, this business-oriented place is a reliable choice in the heart of the town center. $$

Hotel Grand VIctoria Loja's only true boutique hotel has supremely comfortable rooms, charming common areas and top service. $$$

Zamora

Hotel Samuria Lots of comfort for a bargain price, with spacious air-con rooms, plenty of pillows, carpeted floors, work desks and modern bathrooms – all half a block from the plaza. $

Hotel Betania Friendly and great value, this spotless hotel has generous-sized rooms with good mattresses. $

Copalinga A bird-watchers' paradise surrounded by lush greenery beside the Río Bombuscaro just outside town; bookings essential. $$$

Vilcabamba

MAP p311

Avalon B&B Simple yet elegant accommodations, with a good kitchen, an inviting garden and great mountain views. $

Hostal Jardín Escondido Set behind high walls just a block from the plaza, the 'Hidden Garden' is spacious and tranquil. $

Hostal Las Palmas A warm welcome, comfortable rooms and a pleasant pool make this a popular budget choice in the middle of the town. $

Rumi Wilco A short walk from town across the river, this ecologically minded place has a series of remote rooms and *cabañas* with well-equipped kitchens spread through a private 40-hectare reserve. $

Hostería y Restaurante Izhcayluma Located 2km south of town, this elegant hilltop retreat is surrounded by nature and offers everything guests need for serious relaxation, including massages and a peaceful swimming pool. $$

Hostería Paraiso On the north side of town but still walking distance to the plaza, this cheerful place has rooms set around lovely gardens. $$

Calle Lourdes (p305), Loja

For places to stay in Galápagos Islands, see p347

BAILEY FREEMAN

Above: Iguana, Isla Isabela (p336); right: Puerto Baquerizo Moreno (p330)

Researched by
Bailey Freeman

Galápagos Islands

LIVING, BREATHING BIRTHPLACE OF DARWINISM

Follow Charles Darwin's footsteps in this wonderland of giant tortoises, sea lions, marine iguanas and finches that changed the way the world considered life itself.

A world away from mainland Ecuador at more than 1000km offshore, the Galápagos Islands have been a natural wonder ever since Charles Darwin's day. Ecuador has designated 97% of the islands as national park land, a testament to the country's commitment to preserving the invaluable heritage that changed humanity's understanding of evolution as we know it. Yet one of the wondrous realities of visiting the Galápagos is the relative harmony in which its human inhabitants exist alongside this rich biodiversity. Sea lions haul out each evening at busy harbors and beaches, while marine iguanas pile on top of each other along boardwalks and pedestrian-heavy pavements, all unperturbed enough to warrant watching your step to adhere to the legally mandated 2m distance from wildlife.

BETO SANTILLAN/SHUTTERSTOCK

Wandering further afield, the quotidian joy of encountering wildlife never dulls when the gaze of a blue-footed booby meets your own, a giant tortoise appears on your path, or an orca surfaces within spitting distance of your boat. As the islands' finches flit about, you may notice how their beaks and behaviors differ from island to island, as Darwin did. It'll take no time at all to fall in love with the real-world magic that spawned Darwin's theory of natural selection, and the place that continues to set the bar for conservation around the world.

THE MAIN AREAS

PUERTO AYORA (ISLA SANTA CRUZ)
Gateway to the Galápagos.
p322

PUERTO BAQUERIZO MORENO (ISLA SAN CRISTÓBAL)
Provincial capital with appealing *malecón*.
p330

PUERTO VILLAMIL (ISLA ISABELA)
The big island's breezy basecamp.
p336

PUERTO VELASCO IBARRA (ISLA FLOREANA)
The Galápagos' most rural escape.
p343

Find Your Way

Of the four inhabited Galápagos islands, Santa Cruz, San Cristóbal and Isabela are the main hubs for land-based visitors. These islands have accommodations, tour operators, airports and harbors for day trips to outlying islands.

Puerto Villamil, p336

Seahorse-shaped Isabela is the Galápagos' largest island, with peaceful Puerto Villamil at its south end serving as the jumping-off point for exploration, on and offshore.

BOAT

Ferries travel daily between the main islands, while smaller speedboats to Floreana follow a more irregular schedule. Ferry trips generally take between 1½ and two hours and are the most economical means of interisland travel.

TAXI

While buses ply regular routes on Santa Cruz and San Cristóbal, it's more efficient and convenient to hire a taxi to check out the sights on your own schedule. The going rate on each island tends to be quite consistent.

PLANE

If you're willing to spring for interisland flights, you'll save yourself time and possible seasickness by booking seats on the puddle-jumpers serving Santa Cruz, San Cristóbal and Isabela. There are no flights to Floreana, which can only be reached by boat.

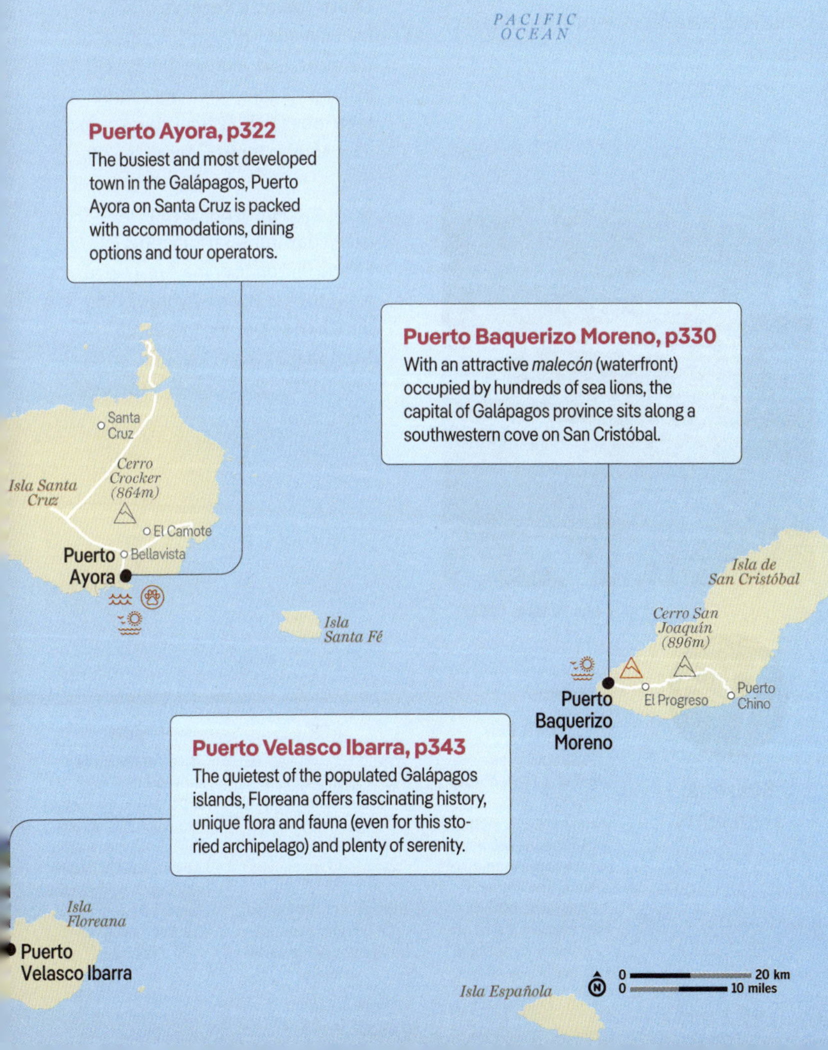

Puerto Ayora, p322

The busiest and most developed town in the Galápagos, Puerto Ayora on Santa Cruz is packed with accommodations, dining options and tour operators.

Puerto Baquerizo Moreno, p330

With an attractive *malecón* (waterfront) occupied by hundreds of sea lions, the capital of Galápagos province sits along a southwestern cove on San Cristóbal.

Puerto Velasco Ibarra, p343

The quietest of the populated Galápagos islands, Floreana offers fascinating history, unique flora and fauna (even for this storied archipelago) and plenty of serenity.

Plan Your Days

You've made the choice to come this far – even if you're limited to a few days on one island, you can get a taste of the biodiversity and isolated singularity of this storied place.

PAWEL CZUCZWARA/SHUTTERSTOCK

Los Túneles (p339)

Three Days to Travel Around

- Fly in and out of Isla Baltra to make the most of your days on **Santa Cruz** (p322). From the ferry landing on Santa Cruz, hire a taxi driver to take you to **Los Gemelos** (p327) trailhead to stretch your legs before heading on to **El Chato Tortoise Reserve** (p328) to commune with giant Galápagos tortoises. End your highlands visit with a walk through Chato's three **lava tubes** (p327), then check in to your hotel in **Puerto Ayora** (p322).

- Next, spend a day on an outer-island day trip – Bartolomé, Santa Fe and Pinzón to name a few – and a day back in Puerto Ayora visiting the **Charles Darwin Research Station** (p324) and lounging on the beach lining the gorgeous **Tortuga Bay** (p325).

Seasonal Highlights

JAN & FEB

Galápagos green sea turtles make landfall, laying eggs on their natal beaches. Isabela and Floreana are home to the biggest nesting sites. The Father of Evolution's birthday is commemorated on February 12, dubbed Darwin Day here.

APR

Waved albatross arrive on Española, much to bird-watchers' delight. Weather is pleasant, water is warm, and snorkeling opportunities are at their prime. This is also the best time to spot Galápagos penguins on Isabela.

JUN

Blue-footed boobies show off their dancing feet now that it's mating season. This is also the month the season known as *garúa* begins, bringing cool fog to the highlands and humid weather throughout the islands.

A Week to Explore

- Follow the Santa Cruz itinerary and then move on to Isabela. Enjoy the chill vibes of **Puerto Villamil** (p336) with a walk to **Concha de Perla** (p337), toting your snorkel gear for a dip with the colorful local wildlife. Next, rent a bike to ride to the **Muro de las Lágrimas** (p341), allowing for plenty of stops to lounge on empty beaches, peek at inland pools and mangrove coves and share unexpected run-ins with Isabela giant tortoises. If you have extra time, add in a day trip to **Los Túneles** (p339).

- End the trip by hopping over to San Cristóbal for an immersive **360° tour** (p333) and an evening on the buzzy *malecón*; then fly back to the mainland from San Cristóbal's airport.

10 Days or More

- Stretch out your multi-island tour with snorkeling day trips from each island, heading to more remote spots such as **Isla Bartolomé** (p329), **Isla Española** (p332) and **Isla Santa Fé** (p329).

- Recuperate back on your home-base islands with relaxed beach days.

- Lounge among the lizards at **Tortuga Bay** (p325) on Santa Cruz, meet the sea lions at **La Lobería** (p332) and **Playa Punta Carola** (p332) on San Cristóbal, or go on a walk down the wonderfully expansive **Puerto Villamil Beach** (p336) framing Isabela's southern shore.

- If you have the time, flee the mainstream crowd with a couple of days on **Floreana** (p343) to get a feel for what the original Galápagos settlers survived on this truly far-flung island wilderness.

JUL

Regional whale migration peaks, with humpback, blue, pilot and sperm whales among the cetaceans swimming through the currents converging around the Galápagos. Head out early in the morning for best chances of spotting one.

SEP

Lobster season officially begins and runs through the end of December, making this the time to taste the bounty of spiny lobsters that live in the Galápagos waters. Don't forget the garlic sauce!

DEC

The rainy season sets in, greening the islands in lush foliage and filling dry watering holes. Temperatures also begin to warm up, and giant tortoise eggs begin hatching.

Puerto Ayora (Isla Santa Cruz)

BUZZY TOWN | MISTY HIGHLANDS | SWIMMING HOLES

TOP TIP
Bring plenty of US dollars with you. To start, you'll need $200 in cash to pay the national park fee on arrival. Santa Cruz has a couple of ATMs near the main dock and along Avenida Charles Darwin across from Fishermen's Pier. Bills with small tears will often not be accepted.

Puerto Ayora is where the action is, with the Galápagos' most organized infrastructure. If you arrive in the Galápagos without plans already in place, Puerto Ayora is your best bet for figuring it out over a craft beer or a breakfast *bolón* (plantain ball). Tour operators all over town can help you find availability on outlying island adventures, whether you're looking to dive with hammerhead sharks, spy blue-footed boobies or swim among placid sea turtles – or all of the above.

From Puerto Ayora, several of Santa Cruz's many snorkeling spots are within walking distance, as are a handful of wild beaches and the Charles Darwin Research Station. Catch a taxi to the highlands' Jurassic Park–like *ranchos* (rural properties), where giant tortoises roam, and to misty twin craters and craggy lava tubes. Puerto Ayora makes an excellent starting point for launching your Galápagos adventure.

Darwin's Living Legacy

Evolutionary theory and wildlife walk

Take yourself on a real-world walking primer on the theory of evolution. While you may not be following in Darwin's literal footsteps, you'll pass a bust of the venerable man, marking the intersection of his namesake street – Avenida Charles

GETTING AROUND

Flights to Santa Cruz actually land on Isla Baltra, just off Santa Cruz's northern tip. Catch a bus from Baltra airport ($5) to the ferry dock for the five-minute ride across Itabaca Canal ($1) to Santa Cruz, where taxis and buses wait to take you to Puerto Ayora (buses $5, taxis $25 to $30). Puerto Ayora is small enough to explore on foot, with loads of dining options, shops, bars and tour offices clustered around the *malecón* (shoreline promenade) along Avenida Charles Darwin. Nearby beaches are mostly walkable (some with assistance from water taxis), with Playa de la Estación being the most accessible to those with mobility needs.

HIGHLIGHTS

1 Charles Darwin Research Station

SIGHTS

2 Galápagos Conservancy
3 Laguna de las Ninfas
4 Playa de la Estación
5 Playa Ratonera

SLEEPING

6 Alma de Cedrela
7 Casa del Lago
8 Galapagos Morning Glory
9 Hotel Fiesta

EATING

10 1835 Restaurant & Coffee
11 Agave Studio
12 Almar
13 Art Coffee
14 Calle de los Kioskos
15 Galápagos Deli
16 Midori
17 Nazca Esencia
18 ØY
19 Tropic Bird Café

DRINKING & NIGHTLIFE

20 Bohemian Cocktail Bar
21 Gelato Bar
22 Santa Cruz Brewery

SHOPPING

23 Aymara Art & Jewelry
24 Book Shop
25 Iguanas Bananas
26 Opuntia Ceramics
27 Samay Latin Art

SUSTAINABILITY IN NATURE & COMMUNITY

Ivonne Torres, conservation partnerships coordinator at Galápagos Conservancy, names a few ways to support its WISE program (Women in Sustainable Entrepreneurships). *galapagos.org*

Sin Latas: Lucia Galarza buys tuna from local fishers – sustainably caught, of course – and smokes it on invasive tree wood. Then she sells it in glass jars, and when you bring back your glass jar, she discounts 50c from the next buy. You can pick some up at **Art Coffee**.

Book Shop: The idea was to have a place where Ecuadorian authors could display their work. And you'll find books by *galápageños,* Ecuadorians and foreigners there, all sorts in English and Spanish, so everyone can access the information.

UNIVERSAL IMAGES GROUP NORTH AMERICA LLC/DEAGOSTINI/ALAMY

Charles Darwin Research Station

Darwin – and the national park's open-air post where **guided walking tours** *($10)* begin. They are led by knowledgeable rangers who will enlighten you on the islands' geology, wildlife and human history.

The tours take about an hour and a half, stopping at the **Galápagos Conservancy** *(galapagos.org)*, which offers a number of interpretive displays and spontaneous encounters with chatty Galápagos mockingbirds, brave little finches and the ubiquitous vermilion-throated lava lizards. You'll end up at the giant tortoise-breeding center, seeing babies and elders up close, when walks conclude at the **Charles Darwin Research Station** *(darwinfoundation.org)*. Pop into the exhibition hall for a look at the Bryde's whale skeleton and other natural-history displays, and grab a coffee or a snack at the little outdoor cafe if you're feeling peckish.

From the research station, take the path to **Playa Ratonera**, where you'll share the beach with sunning marine iguanas. Closer to town on the return walk, take the turnoff for **Playa de la Estación**, where you can snorkel and swim with a view of the Puerto Ayora harbor. If you've already taken the ranger walk, you can stroll along the main road to visit the beaches independently.

EATING IN PUERTO AYORA: OUR PICKS

Calle de los Kioskos: Delicious local eats on this street lined with mom-and-pop restaurants: ceviche, grilled meat, lobster. Daily specials offer great deals. *hours vary* $

Galápagos Deli: Cozy spot providing a break from heavy *almuerzos* (lunches), with light sandwiches, pizzas and ice cream, all in sunny surrounds. *10am-9:30pm* $

ØY: Beautiful restaurant serving Asian/Ecuadorian/Mediterranean fusion dishes with panache. Don't miss the melt-in-your-mouth Ceviche Jipijapa. *9am-noon & 4-9pm Thu-Mon* $$

Almar: Sustainably sourced spot with an excellent wine list. The outdoor deck above the water shows off sparkly evening views of Puerto Ayora. *noon-11:30pm* $$$

After you've spent a couple hours soaking up the beauty of the station's beaches, end your day with dinner along Avenida Charles Darwin and a walk back to the harbor, where the evening lights along the dock attract whitetip and blacktip sharks.

Cove & Crevasse

Snorkeling Santa Cruz's sweet-salty water

You don't have to stray far from central Puerto Ayora to find some of Santa Cruz's special corners – take a couple of afternoon hours to snorkel the crevasse of **Las Grietas**.

Begin this little adventure by hopping on a water taxi from the *muelle* (dock) at Puerto Ayora (one-way $1); the five-minute trip across the harbor drops you at a trail leading to the mangrove-fringed **Playa Los Alemanes**, where you can sun and swim before or after your Las Grietas visit. Continue along the boardwalk, skirting inns and homes as you walk through the lava-rock landscape dotted with palo santo trees, opuntia cactus and lava lizards.

In about 15 minutes, you'll come to a check-in hut where national park guides lead groups every half-hour ($10) – arrive before 4pm for the last trip. On the short hike to Las Grietas, you'll pass a salt pond and learn about the local ecology before reaching the stairs leading down to the brackish transitional zone within the steep-sided crack in the earth. The cool, deep water isn't as full of sea life as other sites, but the unique environment makes for a refreshing dip, even without snorkeling gear. You'll have about 45 minutes here, which is plenty, before hiking back out.

Wrap it up with a harbor-view cocktail at one of the peninsula's dockside bar/restaurants before catching a water taxi back to town.

The Path to Tortuga Bay

National park hike to wild beach

Take a free-flowing beach day with a national park walk out to wild, blue **Tortuga Bay**. From town, the pavement of Avenida Charles Binford turns into a path uphill that leads into national park land; the way is well signed. On the way down the road (before you enter the park itself), look for the signs pointing to **Laguna de las Ninfas**, a peaceful lagoon-side quest, should the gate be open (the lagoon was closed for repairs at the time of writing).

BEST PLACES TO SHOP IN PUERTO AYORA

Opuntia Ceramics *(9am-2pm, 3-9pm Mon-Sat, 4-9pm Sun)* Lovely pottery, prints and textiles from a small Galápagos-based artist collective.

Samay Latin Art *(9am-8pm Mon-Sat, 10am-7pm Sun)* Stunning collection of high-end art and jewelry from Ecuadorian artists around the country.

Aymara Art & Jewelry *(9am-noon, 3-8pm Mon-Sun)* Gallery featuring gorgeous textiles, woven masks and collection of retablos, an Andean diorama-style art form.

Book Shop *(10am-8:30pm Mon-Sat, 2-8:30pm Sun)* Established in partnership with the Galápagos Conservancy, the Book Shop highlights titles with insight into the islands and Ecuador as a whole.

Iguanas Bananas *(10am-noon, 4-8pm Mon-Sat)* Family-run gallery with high-quality watercolors, embroidery art and jewelry.

EATING IN PUERTO AYORA: OUR PICKS

Midori: Sashimi and Asian fusion in a darkly romantic garden setting at Avenida Charles Darwin's east end, with equally creative cocktails. *5-11pm Mon-Sat* $$$

Agave Studio: Mexican-inflected menu with thoughtful specialties, including vegan options. Near turnoff to Laguna las Ninfas, on south end of town. *1-9pm Mon-Sat* $$

Tropic Bird Café: Humble corner restaurant hidden in a row of flashy tourist spots. Some of the best fried *brujo* (scorpion fish) on the island. *7am-10pm* $$

Nazca Esencia: Local favorite injecting Peruvian flavor into Puerto Ayora's food scene. Classics like *lomo saltado* alongside Asian and Ecuadorian dishes. *7am-11pm* $$

UNMISSABLE GALÁPAGOS DISHES

Julio Teodoro Gallegos Sun, founder and owner of ØY, recommends Galápagos menu items. *@oy.rest*

Cod (bacalao) While we call it cod, it's actually *mero* (grouper) and is endemic to the Galápagos. It's really tender, and less fishy than cod. But they call it that because the first people that came here were Norwegians and they used to salt it. And when Ecuadorians see salted fish, it's usually cod!

Lobster The season opens from November to the first day of January, and it's one of the most common and best managed fisheries we have.

Tuna While it's not endemic – it's pelagic – the tuna here is huge and fresh. It's amazing.

Brujo Also known as scorpion fish, *brujo* is endemic from a deep fishery here.

NATURE PICTURE LIBRARY/ALAMY

Blacktip shark, Tortuga Bay (p325)

At the crest of the hill, climb the **lookout platform** for a great view of Puerto Ayora before following the paved path through the dry lava rock-scape. You'll pass huge thick-trunked opuntia cactus, candelabra cactus and leatherleaf, as the route rises and falls on the 30-minute walk to the wide curve of Tortuga Bay's white sand.

The trail spills onto the gorgeous main bay, where flags will warn you of the conditions – if it's a red flag and you want to swim, turn right to walk along the beach to **Playa Mansa** beyond the rocky peninsula at the end. The current there is not as strong, so it's a safer beach for swimming. Bonuses include fish-filled tide pools, occasional appearances of baby hammerheads, and the opportunity to rent a kayak to ply the calm waters. Otherwise, Tortuga Bay's beautiful arc is prime territory for watching giant marine iguanas, and strolling lazily across the powdery sand. Just know that there are no bathroom or snack facilities here, so bring everything you need with you.

Note that the park closes at 5pm, so arrive early enough to accommodate an hour of walking (round trip). It's also possible to catch a water taxi back to the dock at Puerto Ayora, but note that the last ones leave around 5pm.

EATING & DRINKING IN PUERTO AYORA: OUR PICKS

1835 Restaurant & Coffee: Croissants, smoothies and house-roasted coffee draw a morning crowd. Avocado toast is a great lunch treat. *7am-10:30pm* **$$**

Santa Cruz Brewery: Galápagos' first craft brewery. Solid beer list includes the Volcánica, an inventive coffee cherry Gose. *1pm-1am Thu-Sat, 3pm-midnight Sun-Wed*

Gelato Bar: Offers good espresso alongside all-day brunch items like flaky pastries and eggs Benedict. *8:30am-10pm Mon-Fri, 9am-11pm Sat & Sun*

Bohemian Cocktail Bar: Artsy watering hole with coffee, kombucha and cocktails. Try the Negroni with olive brine and smoked olives. *5-10pm Tue-Thu, to 11pm Fri & Sat*

Beyond Puerto Ayora

Santa Cruz harbors geological splendor and free-range tortoises in its misty highlands, while outlying islands offer Galápagos microcosms to explore.

After you fly into Santa Cruz, you'll have the pleasure of traversing the island to Puerto Ayora, taking in the dramatically changing landscapes and microclimates over the 40km journey. From the arid plain of palo santo to the highland lushness of endemic *scalesia* trees, back down to the humid, busy port, the island shows off its richness in the north-to-south drive.

The islets and uninhabited islands off Santa Cruz offer more contrast, with their niche populations of nesting Nazca boobies or equatorial penguins. Day trips from Santa Cruz bring into dazzling focus the volcanic origins of these islands and the adaptations of the tough flora and fauna that have survived here.

Places

Highland Santa Cruz

TIME FROM PUERTO AYORA TO LOS GEMELOS: **25MIN**

Twin craters, tortoises and lava tubes

Hit the ground running after flying into Santa Cruz, and have a taxi driver make a few sightseeing stops on your way into Puerto Ayora (prices run $60 to $70, and your driver will wait for you at each stop). After crossing the dry plain of palo santo trees (that burst into a sea of white blossoms in August), you'll head uphill into the highlands, which, at only 700m above sea level, still embodies a distinctly different ecosystem. Your first stop will be a trailhead that winds around the twin craters known as **Los Gemelos** (The Twins), their sinkholes swathed in misty tropical green forest. The craters weren't created by volcanic explosions, but rather the collapse of underground magma chambers, and the result is two giant chasms draped in greenery with a distinctly primeval vibe. The short 10-minute trail through endemic *scalesia*, bromeliads and lichens is flat and follows the edge of each crater. Keep eyes and ears open for Darwin's finches, vermilion flycatchers and Galápagos doves. Things can get muddy, so wear good shoes, even though the walk is short.

Loop back to the trailhead, continuing the drive to the village of Santa Rosa, where you may spot a giant Galápagos tortoise or two ambling down the dirt road or fraternizing

GETTING AROUND

Go-getters can rent bikes in Puerto Ayora and cycle up to the highlands; it's a 16km ride one-way to the village of Santa Rosa. Otherwise, public buses ($1) run to Santa Rosa about every 20 minutes, from where you can walk the 4km to the tortoise *ranchos*. Hire a taxi to hit all the highland highlights – it's economical when you split the cost with others. Trips to outlying islands can be booked all over Puerto Ayora.

LET'S TALK TOURS

Booking a tour in the Galápagos is an art. If you're set on a specific itinerary or visiting in peak season – mid-December to January or June to September – booking ahead of arrival is a good idea. But if you're a low/shoulder-season traveler with flexible plans, you'll save money by shopping around in person.

How does one pick from all the tour operators available at the port cities? Many share boats, meaning you'll likely be on excursions with folks who have booked with different outfitters. In other words, the operator generally doesn't matter that much, unless they have their own vessel. Prices are similar across the board, with the exception of luxury operators, so go with the companies who have good gear and pre-excursion communication.

BAILEY FREEMAN

El Chato Tortoise Reserve

with local cows. Here you'll find two private tortoise sanctuaries that offer similar experiences to one another: **Rancho Primicias** *(ranchoprimicias.com; $10)* and **El Chato Tortoise Reserve** *(ranchoelchato.com; $10)* will reveal meadows of massive tortoises ambling through the grasses and chomping on guava – the first look is akin to entering a real-life Jurassic Park. You'll learn about these magnificent creatures (many of them 80 to 100 years old) and spend time observing them napping in ponds, grazing on grass and exhaling like landlocked whales. Note their unique shell shape, domed to fit under the wild brush of Santa Cruz' highlands.

Once you've communed with the tortoises, finish your respective *rancho* visit with a journey through their underground **lava tubes**; Primicias has one longer one, while Chato has three shorter ones. While most of the lighted tunnel at Primicias is cavernous, one spot requires crawling on your belly; the tubes at Chato can be navigated without getting your hands dirty. If you need a snack, both *ranchos* have cafes serving lunch and coffee.

Your taxi will be waiting when you climb the wooden stairs back into daylight, and from there you'll descend to the warmer lowlands into Puerto Ayora.

LONESOME GEORGE

The climate-controlled, taxidermied remains of Lonesome George, the last Isla Pinta tortoise, can be seen at Puerto Ayora's **Charles Darwin Research Station** (p324) – simultaneously depressing and morbidly hopeful in his *galapagueño* sanctification as a conservation icon.

Sunny seclusion at Playa El Garrapatero

Named for a black bird called the *ani*, **Playa El Garrapatero** makes a lovely getaway from the more popular and crowded beaches of Puerto Ayora. As it's 21km from Puerto Ayora, a taxi can drop you off and pick you up at a prearranged time (one-way $20 to $25). From the road, walk about 15 minutes through typical opuntia and palo santo to the wide, sandy beach. Sun yourself alongside the marine iguanas, or bring snorkeling gear and look for sea turtles or sea lions seeking playmates. You may also spot pelicans, blue-footed boobies or even flamingos, with some casual beach bird-watching.

Offshore Islands

TIME TO ISLA BARTOLOMÉ: **40MIN**, **2HR**

Wildlife in diverse, uninhabited landscapes

Journeying to at least one of the uninhabited Galápagos islands is a must in order to see a broader range of animals in widely varying landscapes.

About two hours northwest of Santa Cruz is **Isla Bartolomé**, a satellite to neighboring Isla Santiago and the island that's widely regarded as the most photogenic in the archipelago. The journey is just as interesting as the destination; on your way, keep your eyes peeled for dolphins, sea turtles, jellyfish and manta rays as your boat slices through kilometers of deep blue sea. Once you arrive, Bartolomé impresses – the austere landscape is dotted with sculptural spatter cones amid the ropey pahoehoe lava, with hardy tequila plants splashing the hillsides in silver. Lava lizards may be the only terrestrial wildlife you see as you climb to the stunning **viewpoint,** affording a look down its dramatic peninsula and over **Pinnacle Rock** and Santiago's red cinder cones. When snorkeling here, you might catch flashes of Galápagos penguins zipping through the water, though you're more likely to see rays, sharks, sea turtles and schooling reef fish.

Around 1½ hours southeast from Puerto Ayora, attractive **Isla Santa Fe** presents opportunities to see blue-footed boobies, frigate birds, red-billed tropic birds and night herons as you explore the opuntia cactus forest. Pale, golden-hued Barrington land iguanas (Santa Fe land iguanas) are found only here and are the biggest in the Galápagos. Interestingly, they enjoy a symbiotic relationship with Darwin's finches, which pick them free of parasites. Offshore you'll see reef sharks, rays and sea lions.

Isla Seymour Norte, formed by uplift and thus flat like Santa Fe, has the largest frigate-bird colony in the Galápagos, as well as breeding colonies of swallowtail gull and blue-footed boobies, and land and marine iguanas. Trips to Seymour Norte take about 45 minutes from Santa Cruz, with snorkeling stops at beautiful beaches with similar reef life to that at Santa Fe.

BEYOND THE BEYOND

Though they often harbor singular wildlife-watching experiences, many further-flung islands visited by cruises and dive liveaboards don't appear on day-trip menus for land-based tours.

From Santa Cruz, the central but not commonly visited **Isla Pinzón** is more about shark diving than the island geography itself.

Of the trio of far-northern islands, **Isla Pinta** bears distinction as home to Lonesome George, the last known individual of his species. **Isla Marchena** attracts divers for schooling hammerheads and sometimes Galápagos dolphins, while **Isla Genovesa** is the best place to see nesting colonies of red-footed boobies, plus Nazca boobies, red-billed tropic birds and storm petrels.

The northernmost **Islas Darwin** and **Wolf** are known as deep-water dive sites, though photogenic Darwin's Arch collapsed from erosion in 2021.

Puerto Baquerizo Moreno (Isla San Cristóbal)

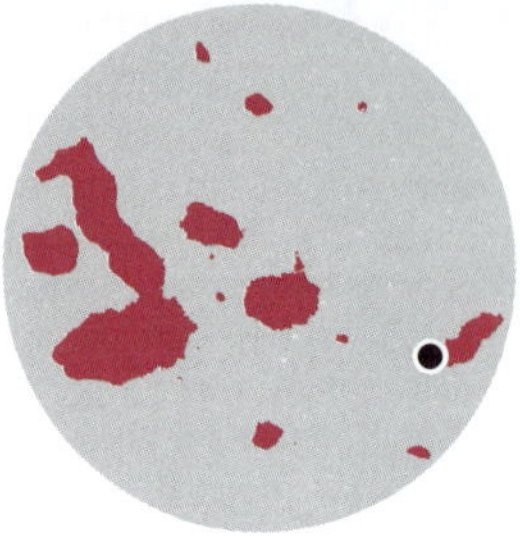

LOVELY MALECÓN | SEASIDE DINING | NEARBY BEACHES

If you have only a few days in the Galápagos, consider basing yourself on Isla San Cristóbal. Fly into Puerto Baquerizo Moreno, from where it's an easy five-minute taxi ride or 20-minute walk into town, and go from there. The capital of Galápagos Islands province has a lovely seaside promenade, Malecón Charles Darwin, that curves around the protected bay, with hundreds of sea lions cozy-ing up together on the beach right downtown. Puerto Baquerizo Moreno feels less dense and commercial than Puerto Ayora, but has loads of tour offices, sweet accommodations, and quality food and drink to restore your swim-weary spirit after adventures launched from town.

Take a day circling the island by boat to look for hammerhead sharks and orcas, and crisscross the island from pristine snorkeling bays to a highland crater lake. Sprinkle liberally with walks along the *malecón,* where you can enjoy passion-fruit sorbet and post-snorkeling cocktails in a hammock chair, all the while tuned to the sea-lion serenade.

GETTING AROUND

Pint-sized Puerto Baquerizo Moreno is small enough that you can leave the airport on foot, walk into town, check into your hotel and stroll to the nearest beach in an hour. Its small, human-scale downtown, fronted by an attractive *malecón,* has lots of cafes and bars offering sips and eats as you make your way from sea-lion beach to fishers' dock. Taxis are plentiful, too, offering short jumps across town and to La Lobería for under $5.

TOP TIP

The ferry between San Cristóbal and Santa Cruz can be a wild, choppy ride. Travelers prone to seasickness should take all the precautions – anti-nausea meds, acupressure bands, prayer – and book the earliest ferry; conditions are usually calmer in the mornings.

Treasures of Tijeretas Hill

A crash course in Puerto Baquerizo Moreno's wild side

Enjoy a classic Galápagos day, with a walk through national park land to hike lava rocks, snorkel a sparkling bay and loll with sea lions on a serene beach. Pack a lunch and take your time – this is the kind of day you savor.

From town, walk north along Avenida Alsacio Northia, following the signs past Playa Mann. Take a peek, but save it for another day – we foresee less-crowded beaches in your future. The road leads up to the **Centro de Interpretación Ambiental Gianni Arismendy** *(free),* a multiroom complex

HIGHLIGHTS
1 Las Tijeretas Overlook
2 Playa Mann

SIGHTS
3 Centro de Interpretación Ambiental Gianni Arismendy
4 Playa Punta Carola

ACTIVITIES
5 Muelle Tijeretas

SLEEPING
6 Casa Blanca
7 Casa Playa Mann
8 Hostal Romy
9 Hotel Mar Azul

EATING
10 El Descanso Marinero
11 Kachi Tanta
see 6 Pāhoe
12 Restaurante D'Coco Junior

DRINKING & NIGHTLIFE
13 Pier

with excellent displays on the natural history of the Galápagos Islands, a detailed history of their human habitation and a look at the islands' current environmental concerns. Hit the bathroom here if you need to, as these are the last facilities available before making your way into the park.

If you're looking for adventure, we suggest starting with the destination that's most challenging to reach – **Playa Baquerizo** – and working your way back; head out in the morning for optimum solitude and cooler temps, and don't forget your close-toed shoes for this one. To get here, make a beeline up the paved trail from the interpretive center to **Las Tijeretas overlook**, where you'll have a spectacular view of the bay and the gradations in its jewel-toned water. If you look closely, you may even be able to spot sea turtles gliding beneath the snorkelers. After admiring the soaring vista, carefully pick your way along the well-signed trail through lava boulders and palo santo for about 45 minutes to peaceful Playa Baquerizo, where you can watch sea turtles bob in the surf and nap with the sea lions, all with hardly another human in sight. Large marine iguanas also dot the beach, so you may have to share the small rim of shade

AN ISLAND OF FIRSTS

El Junco, San Cristóbal's water-filled crater lake, is the only permanent source of fresh water in the archipelago – a fact that led to the island's significant role in the Galápagos' early settlement. San Cristóbal was home to one of the Galápagos' earliest permanent settlements (following Patrick Watkins and General Villamil's efforts on Floreana) and it was the first one visited by Darwin and his crew in 1835. Today, Puerto Baquerizo Moreno functions as the capital of the Galápagos province and is home to an Ecuadorian navy facility.

WAVED ALBATROSS ON ISLA ESPAÑOLA

Isla Española is a popular day trip from San Cristóbal, and here you'll find something unique to the planet: its breeding colony of waved albatross, here from April to December. At its peak, 25,000 to 30,000 of these rare birds are in mating, nesting or chick-rearing mode. As the albatross are Española's main attraction, tours give plenty of time to commune with these amazing distance-flying avians. You're also likely to see Nazca and blue-footed boobies, swallowtail gulls, red-billed tropic birds, Española mockingbirds and possibly Galápagos hawks and turtledoves. The pretty pigmentation of bright red-and-green marine iguanas will also catch your eye, and the snorkeling is spectacular. Trips don't necessarily run daily, so serious bird-watchers should book ahead.

with your reptilian neighbors. As a note, Playa Baquerizo is a wild beach; there are no swim-safety flags, so take care if you want to hit the water, as the waves here can be large and dangerous.

Cool off after your return trip by heading down to **Muelle Tijeretas** (as seen from the overlook) and launching your underwater foray. Here, sea lions show off among colorful reef fish, sea turtles and whitetip sharks. Snorkeling is relaxed and informal, with lots of space to float around, even on crowded days.

From there, circle back and take the spur leading to **Playa Punta Carola**, a lovely crescent home to even more sea lions and the perfect spot for enjoying a San Cristóbal sunset. Pro tip: bring some insect repellent for maximum enjoyment. Wrap up your journey with an evening cocktail and ceviche at the Pier (p334) on the walk back into town, and you'll have completed a perfect Puerto Baquerizo Moreno day.

Beaches & Local Color

Sunning, swimming and wildlife-watching beaches

You can't come this far without a chill beach day or two. Start off by visiting the masses of sea lions at the **playa de los lobos** (sea lion beach) along the *malecón,* where pups nurse and males scrap over territory; a fence separates the beach from the pavement, but you can observe close-up (touching is still off-limits, of course).

Do some swimming and sunbathing yourself at the appealing **Playa Mann**, an easy 10-minute walk north of town. It's popular with families for its close location, shade, toilets and showers. Sea lions and marine iguanas hang here, and there's a beachside cafe and restaurants along nearby Avenida Alsacio Northia. Walk another 10 or 15 minutes through the interpretive center and on to Playa Punta Carola, which is usually less crowded and has similar wildlife.

Beautiful **La Lobería**, sits on the opposite side of town; it's a long walk past the airport or a $4 taxi ride to get there. Arrive at high tide, when the sea lions trade lounging on the sand for slicing through the water and launching into the air, dolphin-style. You'll also spot tons of sea turtles in the small protected bay. If you fancy a mosey, take the trail beyond the beach to the **Acantilado La Lobería** (La Lobería Cliff) to glimpse nesting shorebirds and sea turtles surfing the waves.

EATING IN PUERTO BAQUERIZO MORENO: OUR PICKS

Kachi Tanta: Fresh pastries, sandwiches and vegan options – the coconut-cream cinnamon roll is the stuff of dreams. *8am-8pm* $

Pāhoe: Beautiful *malecón*-side spot; highlights include an inspired tuna tartare, smoked mains, and an ooey gooey lava cake. *3-10pm* $$

Restaurante D'Coco Junior: Serves all things Galápagos, with a standout $6 *asado* special. *1-11pm* $

El Descanso Marinero: So well lit you can see it from space, this kitschy spot is best known for its *pescado a lo macho* (fish in a shellfish sauce). *9am-9pm* $$

Beyond Puerto Baquerizo Moreno

Head for the hills of San Cristóbal's highlands, visit a pristine east-coast beach and make a daylong circumnavigation of the entire island.

Places

Coastal Highlights p333
Interior Tour p335

As on other inhabited islands, the raw beauty of San Cristóbal generally doesn't lie in its port town. The highlands here include a crater lake – from the rim, you can bask in the cooler breezes while you look down the verdant volcanic slopes to where island meets ocean. Further along the road is San Cristóbal's tortoise-breeding center, where you can see baby and adult tortoises roaming freely.

You'll find abundant marine adventures offshore at Kicker Rock and elsewhere, with surf breaks at walkable spots and plenty of dive sites along the coastline. The island is small enough that you can even circumnavigate it in a day via boat, with excellent snorkeling stops along the way.

Coastal Highlights

TIME TO CERRO BRUJO: **45MIN**

Snorkeling and bird-watching around San Cristóbal

Squeeze the most from your day with a **360° tour** *(from $190)* of San Cristóbal. The beaches where you stop may vary depending on conditions, but you'll embark at the dock in Puerto Baquerizo Moreno in the morning and return in the late afternoon after making a circuit of the island. It's an excellent opportunity to check out San Cristóbal's coastal geology as you speed by, and there are several opportunities to hop out for a hike or snorkel. This is the primary tour on the island and almost all operators offer a version of it; shop around for a deal.

Trips run in both directions around the island, split evenly between boats to balance the distribution and timing of visitors; whether the routes go clockwise or counterclockwise varies, depending on schedules and conditions. Traveling counterclockwise, you'll do a wet landing at the white-sand **Bahía Rosa Blanca** for a short hike across the lava looking for blue-footed boobies and the opportunity to snorkel a protected lagoon that's home to sea turtles, sharks, eagle

GETTING AROUND

You can only access the highlands via taxi booked in Puerto Baquerizo Moreno; marine highlights like Kicker Rock and Bahía Rosa Blanca can only be reached via a guided 360° tour.

When traveling interisland to/from San Cristóbal, consider flying if your budget allows. The ferry crossing is consistently rough enough that seasickness is the norm. Twice-daily ferries cost around $35 one-way and take about 2½ hours; the 30-minute flights run between $160 and $190, depending on baggage weight.

SITE-SPECIFIC WILDLIFE TOURS

While the 360° tour gives you a taste of everything, those with specific interests should consider separate in-depth tours. Bird-watchers might consider a Punta Pitt tour for a closer encounter with avian life. Instead of cruising past the cliff in just a few minutes, you'll hike up to the top and are likely to see blue-footed, red-footed and Nazca boobies; in breeding season, you may glimpse mating dances. You'll also have some time to snorkel here.

Those wanting to see hammerhead sharks will love a dedicated Kicker Rock tour, which allows for more time and multiple swims or dives to see these unique predators, as well as eagle and manta rays, and whitetip and blacktip reef sharks.

rays and lobsters. Don't miss the easy walk through the mangroves to the wider side of the beach, where the blue water laps at the postcard-worthy sand. From here, your boat will cruise on to the dramatic **Punta Pitt** to look for roosting blue- and red-footed boobies, frigate birds and swallowtail gulls; serious bird-watchers should book a separate tour to see this spot in detail. Next, take another swim at **Bahía Sardina**, where you may see silvery clouds of schooling sardines in addition to the usual rays, sharks and sea turtles swimming with you.

The last stops in this direction are **Cerro Brujo**, a rock bridge that frames a fantastic view of Kicker Rock through its central arch, and **Kicker Rock** itself (aka León Dormido, or Sleeping Lion). Both of these formations are eroding tuff cones of volcanic origin that stand alone in the cerulean waters offshore of San Cristóbal. Swimming with the current around Kicker Rock gives you a taste of deep-water snorkeling, and you'll marvel at the steep wall dropping deep into the dark blue ocean. Scan for sea turtles and Kicker Rock's famous hammerhead sharks before returning to Puerto Baquerizo Moreno.

DRINKING IN PUERTO BAQUERIZO MORENO: OUR PICKS

Post Office: With a prime location on the *malecón*, this is the perfect bar for a sunset caipirinha. *4-11pm Mon-Thu & Sun; to midnight Fri & Sat*

Pier: Sip a margarita in a hammock chair with a view of boats anchored just offshore. Ceviche and seafood are specialties. *9am-9pm Wed-Mon, 2-9pm Tue*

Sea Garden: A breezy two-tiered cafe with coffee, juices, and delicious breakfast and lunch items – the tender sashimi toast is a winner. *8am-10pm Mon-Sat*

Green Coffee: A sweet, quiet spot next to jovial Playa Mann, with a shady patio, good *batidos* (fruit shakes) and surprisingly strong wi-fi. *7am-7pm*

JO CREBBIN/ALAMY

Cerro Brujo

Interior Tour

TIME TO PUERTO CHINO: **45MIN**

Crater lake, tortoises, beach oasis

Explore the island from west to east, hiring a taxi in Puerto Baquerizo Moreno to shuttle you from place to place ($60 to $80, depending on the number of people; most taxis accommodate around four). From town, the road climbs through cultivated orchards of oranges, bananas, plantains and passion fruit to the foot of **El Junco**, the island's 650m extinct volcano. Wooden stairs lead up through gorgeous Miconia groves to the crater's rim, with a trail along the edge. You'll see frigate birds coasting and dipping above the crater lake, one of the very few (and certainly most abundant) permanent sources of fresh water in the Galápagos. Take in the panoramic views, notice the tiny wildflowers in this lusher highland zone and descend back to the car. Note: the weather is cooler and mistier here, so the trail might be muddy.

A few minutes down the road brings you to the **Galapaguera de Cerro Colorado**, San Cristóbal's tortoise refuge, which is not only free to visit, but has mature tortoises freely trundling around between lovely trees draped in moss; this is one of the most 'natural' feeling reserves in the Galápagos, so it's worth a stop, even if you've visited other sanctuaries. Once you've had your giant-tortoise fix, continue the descent to the southeast coast to the trailhead for **Puerto Chino**, the final point on your island traverse. The paved path through opuntia cactus takes about 10 minutes before the beachside trees open onto a beautiful little white-sand cove, with turquoise waters beyond. Sunning sea lions and marine iguanas may be scattered about, and there's a short trail up and around the rocky point, where you can get a bird's-eye view of the waves crashing on lava rock and spot the occasional booby. Take your time relaxing at the tranquil beach and enjoy a delicious dip.

SEA LION SPECTACULAR

While sea lions are present throughout the Galápagos, the archipelago's biggest colonies reside on San Cristóbal, a fact that's evident upon arrival: sea lions drape themselves over benches, lie in the streets and even walk through restaurants along Puerto Baquerizo Moreno's *malecón*. (Note: if you book a hotel along the boardwalk, you will hear them all hours). And though these pinnipeds seem plentiful in number, they're actually an endangered species, with only around 20,000 individuals in the archipelago.

With this many up close, you'll be able to see family dynamics in detail: keep an eye out for tiny pups and see if you can spot the alpha male, indicated by his large size, domed forehead and somewhat aggressive behavior.

Puerto Villamil (Isla Isabela)

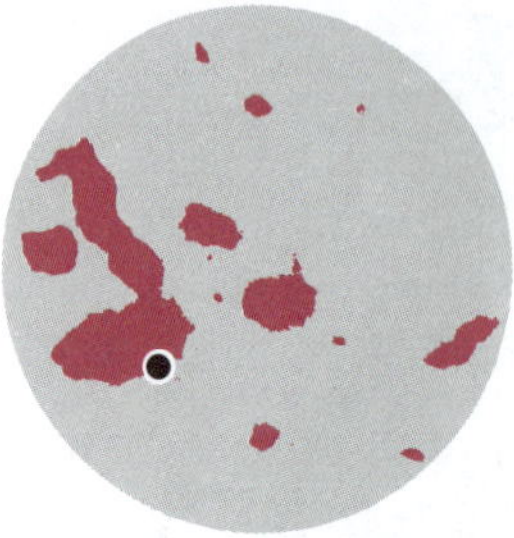

BEACHY VIBES | DIY ADVENTURES | WILDLIFE

GETTING AROUND

Puerto Villamil is quite small and pleasantly walkable. The airport is only 1.5km or so from town, but a $5 truck taxi (best booked in advance) will save you the not terribly attractive walk. It's a pleasant 1.2km amble from Puerto Villamil's plaza to the boat dock and entrance to Concha de Perla, but if you're in a hurry, a taxi will cost $2 per person.

Isla Isabela is its own wild and wonderful animal, even shaped like a seahorse, which, incidentally, you may see when snorkeling here. Of the main three islands where most land-based visitors set up camp, Isabela is the one with a downtown – Puerto Villamil – that's only partly paved, and a tourism infrastructure that feels very mom-and-pop (in a good way). Yet it's the biggest of the Galápagos Islands, formed from a connected chain of six volcanoes.

Here, the world operates in superlatives. Giant tortoises cross bike paths, enormous manta rays are often spotted in the nearby sea, and larger-than-life sea turtles rival the size of a Volkswagen. Top it all off with a still-steamy trip to the beautiful Sierra Negra and Volcán Chico, and you've got an adventure for the ages.

Daily ferries run from Santa Cruz, or you can fly to Isabela from Santa Cruz or San Cristóbal – a good option for those who are less seaworthy.

Tintoreras, Isabela's Natural Aquarium

Sleeping sharks and waking seabirds

Many people take a quick look at Isabela on a long day trip from Santa Cruz, which is certainly doable if you're short on time, and one of the advantages of visiting the island is its number of accessible half-day activities, of which **Las Tintoreras** reigns supreme. Depending on the tides, you could fit in the lovely half-day snorkel at Las Tintoreras between your arrival on the morning ferry and departure in the afternoon, but book ahead to ensure this is possible on your date. This excursion is also an excellent choice for those who may turn a little green from the waves on longer boat trips; this journey is a relaxed one. Rates run from $50 to $70, depending on the outfitter.

Pangas (small open-sided boats) leave from the Isabela dock, which is a bit of a destination in its own right; just off the pier sea lions loll about on a small, peaceful beach, and a handful of vendors sell empanadas, lunch plates and popsicles nearby. The boat ride takes about 15 minutes, beginning with a cruise

TOP TIP

If you can, plan more days than you think you'll need here. With fewer visitors in a less commercial setting, community life is more accessible. Isabela's low-speed appeal is good therapy for any wandering soul.

HIGHLIGHTS
1 Puerto Villamil Beach

SIGHTS
2 Centro de Crianza Arnaldo Tupiza Chamaidan
3 Poza de los Flamencos

ACTIVITIES
4 Las Tintoreras

SLEEPING
5 Cartago Bay
6 Cormorant Beach House
7 Hotel Loja
8 Iguana Crossing Boutique Hotel
9 Wooden House

EATING
10 Lonesome George G
11 Mercado Municipal
12 Tania y Lucho
13 Yummy Yummy

around the protected bay to look for whimbrels, blue-footed boobies and, if luck is on your side, the occasional Galápagos penguin. Then you'll take a relaxed hike around one of the **lava islets** that make up Las Tintoreras.

Take your time comparing the leaves of the ubiquitous red-and-white mangroves, and discerning the difference between the 'a'a and pahoehoe lava formations; the marine iguanas are perfectly camouflaged here, so watch your step as you move through the otherworldly landscape. Further observations will reveal Sally Lightfoot crabs in bright colors that shift with their age, green sea turtles surfacing in the pools, and sea lions on little mangrove-backed beaches. You'll also have a great opportunity to see the dozens of whitetip reef sharks *(tintoreras)* for which the islet is named, sleeping suspended in a crevasse.

To finish this low-effort, high-reward half-day, you'll snorkel around an area sheltered from wave action by the lava islets, following colorful parrotfish, schooling yellowtail surgeonfish, sea stars of varying sizes and algae-grazing sea turtles. If you're lucky, you may even spot a mammoth marbled ray, a sea-monster-esque species that can grow up to 2m across. All in all, it's not a bad roster of sightings before you return to the Isabela dock.

Slow Wildlife Stroll

Tortoises, flamingos and marine iguanas

You don't have to go out of town to see a little bit of Isabela's wildlife. On the west end of Puerto Villamil, look for the little Los Flamencos hotel (Avenida 16 de Marzo) to find the road to the boardwalk above the **Poza de los Flamencos** (Flamingo Pond). There's usually a lone flamingo stranded here due to a broken wing, and it sometimes has company also feeding in the shallows. Leaving the pond at the west end of the boardwalk,

CONCHA DE PERLA

The perfect add-on to a visit to Las Tintoreras is a visit to Concha de Perla. If you can, come early in the morning when you won't jostle for space with other humans – sea lions may still block your path and marine iguanas may take a nap on your flip-flops. Protected by a lava barrier reef, less confident swimmers can gently push off the deck steps into the calm bay and circle the edge to see fish swimming around mangrove roots, sea turtles slowly looming into view and the odd marine iguana swimming across. Even at its busiest, it's an easy spot for a quick, wildlife-cameo dip.

IGUANA CROSSING

Around dusk, stroll along the beach toward the west, to the point where lava rock meanders across the sand and forms a sort of natural jetty into the ocean. At this time of day, marine iguanas head out of the water in an extended scramble over the sand, rock hopping and slithering up the beach – the witching hour for these little seafaring Godzillas. A good landmark you can spot from the road is the aptly named Iguana Crossing Boutique Hotel (p347). Fun fact about the island's signature lizards: Isabela is home to the largest marine iguana colonies in the Galápagos, and the subspecies here is among the largest physically as well (adult males can grow up to 1.5m long!).

ZOLTAN BAGOSI/ALAMY

Centro de Crianza Arnaldo Tupiza Chamaidan

continue west along the main drag, Avenida Antonio Gil, until the signed fork in the road. The boardwalk to the breeding center is under construction, so continue on the main road around the bend until you reach the stand where you pay for entry. From there, it's another 10 to 15 minutes' walk up the road to the center.

Centro de Crianza Arnaldo Tupiza Chamaidan *($10)*, Isabela's tortoise-breeding center, has informative tours that will take you around the pens separating differing subspecies of Galápagos tortoises specific to Isabela of breeding age and younger, including babies of varying ages and sizes. In addition to the babies, you can spot the breeding center's original tortoise population in the first enclosure upon entry, a group that's been monitored since the establishment of the national park. Interesting fact: the lava flows from Isabela's many volcanoes separated the island's tortoise populations into lots of small groups, leading to evolutionary differences between the communities. Wild!

Exit to the road and walk northward another minute to the **viewpoint** over a clean, green pond surrounded by reeds and mangroves. There's a good chance you'll spot some flamingos in this more pristine setting, stepping delicately on stilt legs through the water, stretching rosy wings and craning curved necks to clean their feathers.

Backtrack to town via the northernmost section of the boardwalk (more attractive than the road), cutting back to the road about halfway through.

EATING IN PUERTO VILLAMIL: OUR PICKS

Lonesome George G: Plaza-side cafe offers *bolones* of all kinds – with seafood, peanut sauce, beef stew – for breakfast and a lunch special. *7am-4pm* $

Mercado Municipal: Food court hosting small restaurants serving Ecuadorian plates and grilled skewers; favorites Albita and Artardecer d' Yiya are here. *hours vary* $

Yummy Yummy: Flaky empanadas are the name of the game, and don't forget the Yummy sauce. *4-8pm* $

Tania y Lucho: Ecuadorian cuisine done well, especially when the restaurant does Sunday barbecue. The *corviches* are an indulgent appetizer. *3-11pm* $

Beyond Puerto Villamil

On the island and offshore, Isabela encourages clicking down into lower gear and wide-angle wildness.

While many local tours offer day trips to Isabela, making time to spend a few nights on the archipelago's largest island gives you the chance to experience the more mythic Galápagos you have imagined. It's a place as leisurely as the bike ride you might take over sandy spots on your way to wild beaches, or the tortoise moving steadily along the dirt road.

Once you leave the limits of Puerto Villamil, it doesn't take long for things to get wild. Be sure to set aside a day to enjoy one of the island's supreme highlights: snorkeling a sheltered lava maze – known as Los Túneles – that feels a bit like an underwater speakeasy known only to sea turtles, sleeping sharks and seahorses. Isabela is also some to some steamy geography: if you fancy getting some steps in, hike to the rim of an active volcano and witness the raw landscape of collapsed lava tubes, cones and craters created by the even slower geologic forces that have shaped this archipelago.

Places

GETTING AROUND

You can technically walk to the Wall of Tears from downtown Puerto Villamil, but cycling is the ideal way to go, as it allows for time to check out the many lovely detours along the journey. We recommend spending a little extra cash to get a mountain bike, as the way is rocky and hilly. Adventures beyond, to Sierra Negra and Los Túneles, require guides, as they enter national park lands.

Los Túneles

TIME FROM PUERTO VILLAMIL: **45MIN**

Wildlife in an underwater maze

The Galápagos Islands seem especially imbued with magic in places such as **Los Túneles**, off Isabela. Exploring this labyrinth of islets from above and below gives a firsthand look into the island's unique volcanic land formations and the flora and fauna flourishing within.

Tours – which run between $130 and $180, depending on boat type (standard or premium) – depart from the Isabela dock for the 45-minute trip to Los Túneles, which can be categorized as medium-choppy on the seasickness scale. They'll usually make a brief stop along the way to see black-and-white Nazca boobies roosting on a wave-lashed rock emerging from the ocean, or if significant sea life is spotted – huge manta rays and occasional pods of orcas pass through the area. You may also spot a rare fur seal, a separate species from the ever-present sea lions that was hunted to near extinction by early settlers.

When the boat arrives at Los Túneles, you'll transfer into a small glass-bottom boat that will carefully motor into the shallow-water landscape of candelabra cactus standing tall

FERNANDA LA PHANTASTICA

Isla Fernandina, one of the youngest Galápagos Islands, remains the most volcanically active, with eruptions every few years. Because of its geologic action, not much colonizing flora or fauna has had a chance to gain traction, but incredibly, a single Fernandina giant tortoise – previously believed extinct – was discovered on the island in 2019. DNA sequencing proved that the petite tortoise, dubbed Fernanda, was a genetic match to the last known individual of her species found on the island in 1906. The Galápagos Conservancy has conducted visits to Fernandina to search for other surviving individuals in hope of saving the species from extinction, but as yet have not found a mate for Fernanda.

and mangroves growing like giant bonsai on tiny islets. The black lava contrasts beautifully against deep turquoise water and, now and then, you'll find fluffy adolescent blue-footed boobies or some basking Galápagos penguins.

Hiking at Los Túneles allows you a booby's-eye view of the islets' arches, bridges, tunnels and caves that extend underwater, and the excursion also allows you to explore the terrestrial lava environment. Sea turtles gliding beneath or surfacing for a quick breath hint at what awaits for your swim.

The best of Los Túneles resides below the surface. First, your guide will lead you on a swim around the maze of lava caves, and while you can spot blacktip sharks and some other fish life, the real stars of the show are the fascinating underwater geological formations. The light passes through the water around you like columns as you swim through the cave network, and the feeling is extraterrestrial. And if the tide is low, you'll be able to swim between even more cave rooms and tunnels.

At the second stop, you'll snorkel among mangrove roots in search of wildlife, including whitetip reef sharks, colorful reef fish, golden or eagle rays and hopefully the tiny delight that is the Galápagos seahorse. This is also where you'll spot some of the biggest sea turtles of your Galápagos experience, which can often be found napping in the shallows.

Cruise back to the pier as the orange sun sinks toward the horizon, having soaked in one of the best wildlife-watching experiences in the archipelago.

The Interior

TIME TO MURO DE LAS LÁGRIMAS: **30MIN**

Bike ride, wild tortoises, Isabela history

Rent a bike in Puerto Villamil and go on a rare Galápagos adventure that you can DIY almost for free. Though your ultimate destination is the Wall of Tears 6km from downtown, you can make this journey as long or short as you like.

From town, ride west along Avenida Antonio Gil to the signed fork in the road, taking the left-most path along the beach. You may have to walk the bike through deeper sand here and there, but it soon becomes a graded dirt road. The road has about a dozen signposted spur trails to explore, but the ranger at the entrance will advise you to head to the wall first and work your way back.

Make like Mario Kart and wind through the tree tunnels, dodging wild Isabela tortoises, marine iguanas and potholes

DRINKING ON ISABELA: OUR PICKS

Beach: Park yourself on the beach berm with a fresh juice or cocktail to celebrate the sunset in simple style. *11am-2pm & 4-9:30pm Mon-Sat*

Pink Iguana: Though casual, this bar feels more hip than the rest, with vibey lights, games and a danceable energy. *10am-midnight Mon-Thu, to 2am Fri & Sat, 1-9pm Sun*

Zaroa Brewery: Isabela's only brewery, serving creative lemongrass, coconut and passion-fruit varieties in a spacious outdoor taproom. *5pm-midnight Mon-Sat*

Iguana Point Bar: This double-decker bar overlooking the *malecón* park serves drinks, food and excellent *batidos*. *9am-8pm Mon-Sat, to 5pm Sun*

Muro de las Lágrimas

until the road ends. Here, steps lead to the stacked-stone **Muro de las Lágrimas** (Wall of Tears). A sign memorializes the many prisoners of the former Isabela penitentiary who perished while building it as punishment for often quite minor crimes. In the inland heat, the length of this purposeless wall mutely embodies the despair of its construction. Fortunately, the penal colony closed in 1959.

On your way back, stops vary. First up is one of the most magical spots along the route: the short trail to El Estero (The Estuary). Wander through the fairyland gateway created by the ropey majagua tree, which in turn leads to a hidden 'beach' that connects to the coastline via a mangrove forest. During high tide, it's a magical swimming hole; during low tide, it's an atmospheric pathway to the coastal shallows, where sea turtles and marine birds visit in abundance.

Next, peer into iguana-covered lava tunnels, making sure not to miss the succulent-strewn meadow nearby, showing off in various shades of vermilion and ochre. You can see where the lava flowed straight into the ocean in the clashing of ecological worlds that built the very island you stand on.

Finally, lounge on near-empty beaches like the inviting **Playa del Amor**, which is actually a beach in progress – where smoothed-out seashells and urchin spines haven't yet broken down into sugary sand.

Volcán Sierra Negra

TIME TO NATIONAL PARK ENTRY BUILDING: **30MIN**

Hiking Volcán Sierra Negra

Feel the hot breath of the Earth and marvel at the impressive expanse of one of the world's largest volcanic calderas on a hike up **Volcán Sierra Negra**.

GET INSPIRED ON ISABELA

Caroline Marmion, local watercolor painter, shares her favorite places to find inspiration for her pieces.

Concha de Perla and the dock. You've got some beautiful views, even just the walkway down to the water. There you find iguanas, sea lions and turtles in the water, so that, to me, is inspiration. And animals are easy to paint here because they don't move!

My favorite place is **La Playita**. Every day the sun shifts, the clouds are different. So every day is a perfect day, and you see the most extraordinary things when you're not even looking for them. It's the scenery, it's the mangroves, it's the color of the ocean, it's the waves, it's the way the sun shifts; always something to see.

WHY I LOVE ISLA ISABELA

Bailey Freeman,
Lonely Planet writer

Isabela lures you in with its wide, sparkling beach, then hooks you with larger-than-life wildlife and landscapes that redefine your perspective as a being on this planet. I felt like I was dropped into a gigantic world much bigger and more resonant than my own. Nothing compares to the thrill of watching meters-wide manta rays doing acrobatics in the deep blue sea off Isabela's coast, snorkeling above sea stars as big as bike tires, or peering into the black expanse of Sierra Negra's crater barely obscuring the rumbling earth beneath. Isabela humbles you with its creative power – it's a place of life, in every sense of the word.

EDUARDO CABANAS/SHUTTERSTOCK

Volcán Chico

The largest of Isabela's six sister volcanoes, and the closest to Puerto Villamil, Sierra Negra is one of the Galápagos Islands' most active, last erupting as recently as 2018. You'll be hiking across some of the youngest land on Earth and seeing the geologic variety of color, texture and lava-scape in this blip of geologic time.

Taking the 14.5km hike is a five- to six-hour journey, but not particularly strenuous, and you'll experience several seasons and ecosystems along the way. Guided hikes often begin in foggy conditions that may leave the trail a bit muddy – the moisture sustains the welcome greenery of ferns, wildflowers and brush. Darwin's finches and Galápagos mockingbirds will likely make appearances and, with some luck, so might the more elusive Galápagos hawk.

When you arrive at the kilometers-wide caldera, it's a wonder to gaze across the expanse of black lava and contemplate the heat not far below. Fissures formed by rapidly heating and cooling lava stretch across the smooth surface, giving a nod to the seismic movement that happened not that long ago. After resting here, your tour will continue up through the rocky moonscape of multicolored volcanic formations to **Volcán Chico**, considered a parasitic cone of Sierra Negra. Here you'll have a chance to get close to fumaroles, where you can actually feel the heat emanating from geology in progress, and you may spot a couple of bright-yellow land iguana among the brush. The highest point of the hike, a cliff of twisted red rock, gives sweeping views of Isabela's unpopulated northern half.

Bring a weatherproof jacket for mist and rain, and wear sturdy, closed-toe hiking shoes for maximum hiking happiness.

Puerto Velasco Ibarra (Isla Floreana)

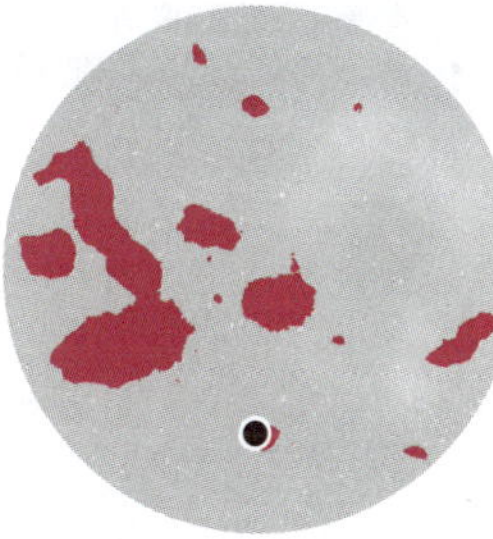

NATURAL BEAUTY | SNORKELING | FLAMINGOES

Puerto Velasco Ibarra welcomes visitors with blasé sea lions and huge, red-scaled marine iguanas sunning on the concrete dock. From the port, the village's main dirt road stretches a few blocks past a national parks office, a couple of restaurants and the local grocery store before hitting rural Floreana. Along the coastline in either direction, trails follow the island's edge to various lava and beach coves. All in all, it only takes about 10 minutes to walk from one side of town to the other, so you're never far from your destination.

Lava Seashore Walking Meditation

Birds and bones

Heading north from the port, the dirt road ends at the **Sendero Los Pulpos** (Octopus Trail), which traces a path about 1.5km through the rocky lava – chances are good that you'll have the trail to yourself along this empty, jagged lava coastline.

Keep your eyes peeled at the start of the trail for the wing-fruited lecocarpus – aka the Floreana daisy – a fascinating relative of the sunflower that's only found in one place in the world: right here in Floreana. As you move on, endemic painted locusts startle from basalt nooks, adding color to the path that changes in character and hue as it curves through varying states of lava erosion. Sinkholes give way to black pebbles mixed with shells and urchin spines, with the odd giant opuntia anchoring some favorable hill. Pause to observe bright-red Sally Lightfoot crabs, Floreana lava lizards and Galápagos brown pelicans.

As the trail approaches its terminus near the small **lagoon** on your right, the stones smooth out and you'll come to a few organic collections of seashell arrangements and found bones, sun-bleached and informally enshrined. Depending on the season and partly on luck, there may be flamingos feeding in the lagoon, creating a bright pop of pink in contrast to the lava landscape. If you don't see them here, keep an eye toward the sky around dusk, when you might spot their long silhouettes flying near the coastline.

continues on p346

GETTING AROUND

Floreana ferry schedules vary weekly and can change without notice. If staying overnight, leave a couple of buffer days in your schedule.

TOP TIP

Book all your meals on Floreana at least a few hours in advance, as the handful of little restaurants may be full with group reservations or closed altogether if no one inquires ahead. It's a good idea to sort out your first meal as soon as you've checked into your room.

KAROL KOZLOWSKI PREMIUM RM COLLECTION/ALAMY

Asilo de la Paz

TOP EXPERIENCE

Isla Floreana

Isla Floreana retains an air of wild mystique. Some of the island's first permanent residents inspired intrigue, settling here with visions of utopian health or disappearing without a trace beyond whispers of romance gone awry. The island remains blissfully undeveloped, with no flight service or daily ferries. Visit as a day trip from Santa Cruz or spend a night or two.

DID YOU KNOW?

The Floreana giant tortoise went extinct around 1850, due to overhunting by pirates and whalers, but see the 'Reversing Extinction' sidebar (p346) for exciting developments.

Exploring Floreana's Highlands

Before German settlers established lasting roots on Floreana, they were preceded by involuntary two-year resident Patrick Watkins, an Irish pirate abandoned on the island in the 1780s who survived by sheltering in a cave and bartering his cultivated crops for booze from passing ships. At **Asilo de la Paz** (Haven of Peace), you can sit in the shallow caves he likely occupied and among the surrounding mist-shrouded, labyrinthine rock formations bedecked in velvety mosses and lichens.

PRACTICALITIES

- Confused about ferry schedules? Floreana lodgings can usually help with boat bookings.

The local communal truck – *la chiva* (round trip $5) – departs daily from the main road in Puerto Velsaco Ibarra at 6am and 3pm, returning two hours later to collect you. Hop on for the 15-minute ride up the road into the lush highlands, where you'll be dropped off at the trailhead for Asilo de la Paz. The walk winds through cool *scalesia* forest, where reintroduced hybrid tortoises (Floreana tortoises went extinct around 1850) roam through their low-walled **tortoise sanctuary**, munching on greenery and relaxing in dug-out nests.

From here, the trail continues upward to the life-giving spring that made Floreana habitable, dripping down a fern-laden rock face; it may not look like much, but it's the water that kept Floreana's first settlers alive. The trail leads onward to the **stone labyrinth** of mysterious walls, small caves and an impassive carved stone face laced with delicate greenery. The Wittmers also sheltered here while they built their more permanent home, and many of the modifications and carvings in the caves are their handiwork. Turn around and you'll be treated to stunning views onto Cerro Pajas that are enhanced by the chirps of charmingly sociable Darwin's finches and yellow warblers, and if you're lucky, you may spot Floreana's top predator: its native short-eared owl.

Floreana's Furthest Reaches

Those visiting Floreana on a charter or liveaboard will have unique access to some of Floreana's most remote points of interest – the northern side of the island, which offers gorgeous desolation.

Remnants of maritime passersby speak to the island's isolation, such as the famous **mail barrel** at Post Office Bay. Long-distance whalers knew Floreana for its ad-hoc postbox. Passing sailors would peruse the barrel for mail addressed in their direction and, on arriving home, would deliver letters to their intended recipients.

While the original barrel at Post Office Bay still stands – it may or may not be in a state of repair, but it's still used for exchanging missives all over the world – there's now a replica near the town dock. Pop a postcard in and see if anyone's left one addressed near your home – dreamy traditionalists still hand-deliver.

Devil's Crown, an extinct volcanic caldera that's eroded down to jagged points looming out of the water, harbors a plethora of reef fish and colorful sea stars in its shallows. The ocean's current sweeps around the crater with enough strength to make for a fun drift dive or snorkel for confident swimmers. As you let the current carry you along, watch for whitetip reef sharks, hammerheads, manta rays and showy spotted eagle rays.

A visit to the mainland near Devil's Crown complements this boat dive. At **Punta Cormorant**, the unusual hue of the greenish-gold sand comes from volcanic olivine. A hike inland to the nearby **lagoon** often reveals flamingos in possibly the greatest numbers you'll see in the Galápagos – their pink legs and feathers stand out against the brackish water.

TROUBLE IN PARADISE

The 1930s brought epic drama to Floreana. German doctor Friedrich Ritter and partner Dore Strauch arrived in 1929 with a vision of cultivating an Eden. Three years later, intrigued by Dr Ritter's writings, Heinz and Margret Wittmer ventured from Germany to a homestead on Floreana with their son. Next, the self-proclaimed Baroness Eloise von Wagner Bosquet and her two lovers landed, bringing with them scandal that culminated in the sudden and unsolved disappearance of the baroness and one lover in 1934, as documented in the 2014 documentary *A Galápagos Affair.*

TOP TIPS

- Drones are not allowed.
- If you miss the *chiva* back from the highlands, it's possible to walk the 7km back to town, but it's not advisable when night falls.

SIGHTS
1 La Lobería
2 Lagoon
3 Playa Negra
4 Post Office Bay

ACTIVITIES
5 Sendero Los Pulpos
6 snorkel gear rental

SLEEPING
7 El Pajas

REVERSING EXTINCTION

The Floreana tortoise, notable for its saddleback-shaped carapace and long neck, went extinct around 1850. In 1994, researchers discovered similar tortoises on Isabela's Wolf Volcano, and DNA analysis revealed partial Floreana ancestry. A 2015 airlift brought 19 tortoises to Santa Cruz's breeding center in hope that selective breeding will yield descendants with high percentages of Floreana DNA.

continued from p343

Black-Sand Beaches, Snorkeling Bliss

DIY snorkeling with sea lions

Grab your snorkel and head towards Hotel Wittmer, of historic fame; walk through the open gate to access **Playa Negra** (Black Beach), a lovely cove of black sand with plenty of space to lay out your beach towel. You may spot a great blue heron or lava heron.

If you continue past Playa Negra, you'll find a trail at the end of the cove that follows the coastline's lava edge. The occasional Floreana marine iguana will cross your path, resplendent in red; if you visit during dry season, the plentiful Sesuvium framing the trail will also be a vivid crimson. About 1.5km along, the path ends at **La Lobería**, a small peninsula that forms a protected string of tiny beaches where sea lions congregate. The well-marked trail leads to a couple of coves, but the best spot for entering the water will be obvious for its sandy approach between the lava rock. Even if no sea lions are out, you'll likely encounter a surprising number of grazing sea turtles, in addition to hogfish, parrotfish and other colorful reef fish.

Sea lions often haul out on the white beach at the far end of the peninsula; snorkel along the edge of the cove to find some.

Places We Love to Stay

$ **Budget** **$$** **Midrange** **$$$** **Top End**

Puerto Ayora

MAP p323

Hotel Fiesta Quiet, comfortable rooms surround a pool at the southwestern end of town; serves excellent breakfasts. **$$**

Casa del Lago A sculptural, eco-conscious spot next to the Laguna de las Ninfas path, with plant-draped balconies and a decor theme that can be described as Tropical Hobbit. **$$**

Galapagos Morning Glory A friendly hostel that has it all: comfy beds, clean rooms and a nicely curated public space with plenty of hammocks for lounging. Also works with a great local laundry service that picks and up delivers your clothes back to you same-day. **$$**

Alma de Cedrela A small family-run hotel on the western side of town with extremely kind hosts – little touches like personalized welcome signs and a stocked community drinks fridge add to the overall hospitable feel. **$$**

Puerto Baquerizo Moreno

MAP p331

Hotel Mar Azul Conveniently located budget spot with an open-air hammock lounge and breakfast included. Rooms are basic, but the service from the staff is spectacular. **$**

Hostal Romy Set on the far side of the *malecón,* this family-run hotel charms with large rooms, a welcoming courtyard and a place to do your own washing. The owners will also give you a complimentary lift to the airport if schedule permits. A great choice for groups. **$$**

Casa Blanca This relaxed, elegant waterfront refuge has an excellent location, breezy terraces and architectural charm. The downstairs restaurant is one of the best on the island. **$$**

Casa Playa Mann An eco-minded, family-owned inn on the quiet road to Playa Mann, with a gorgeous courtyard featuring a historically recognized cactus, lovely hosts and great breakfasts. Rooms are spotless and tastefully decorated. **$$**

Puerto Villamil

MAP p337

Cartago Bay A small, budget-friendly inn on the edge of town, with clean rooms and a well-curated courtyard. If you speak Spanish, be sure to chat with Sr Celso about his scientific work on the island over a fresh coconut. **$**

Hotel Loja A centrally located hotel with spacious rooms (and bathrooms!), a pool, an attached coffee shop and excellent breakfasts. Management is friendly and proactive, and willing to assist with excursion arrangements, restaurant suggestions and any other travel needs. **$$**

Wooden House This sweet, family-run inn on the way to the dock offers quiet seclusion and a variety of rooms with – you guessed it – lovely wooden accents. Has an in-house restaurant and a pool, too. **$$**

Cormorant Beach House Set directly on Puerto Villamil's enormous beach, this modern hotel sports clean lines, ocean views and a rooftop terrace for breakfast. **$$**

Iguana Crossing Boutique Hotel This low-scale luxury choice features a nice outdoor pool and deck across from the beach; rooms vary in size and price, but the oceanfront balcony rooms steal the show. **$$$**

Puerto Velasco Ibarra

MAP p346

El Pajas An atmospheric treehouse-like stay a few blocks up from the main pier; cozy rooms, good hot water, and a flexible checkout on ferry days. **$**

Skybike, Mashpi (p132)
COURTESY OF METROPOLITAN TOURING

TOOLKIT

The chapters in this section cover the most important topics you'll need to know about in Ecuador. They're full of nuts-and-bolts information and valuable insights to help you understand and navigate Ecuador and get the most out of your trip.

Arriving

Ecuador is most commonly accessed by air. International flights arrive in either Quito or Guayaquil. Other travelers may choose to cross one of the land borders from Colombia or Peru, while the most adventurous travelers will enter the country on an Amazon riverboat.

Airports

The main international airports in Ecuador are in Quito and Guayaquil. If you're planning to visit the Galápagos, choose Guayaquil; it's the only Ecuadorian airport with direct flights to the islands.

Visas

Most nationalities can stay for up to 90 days visa-free. Remember that it's 90 days per calendar year, so cross-border visa runs won't help extend your stay.

SIM Cards

Only those with a local *cédula* (ID card) number can activate a SIM card, so if you don't have an Ecuadorian host, pay for a pre-activated SIM card at the airport.

ATMs

Ecuador uses the US dollar as currency, so many travelers arrive with cash on hand. You can change money at the airport, or withdraw money from an ATM with an international bank card.

Transport from Airport to City Center

	Quito	Guayaquil
TRAIN	$4–8	$0.50 (+ $2 bus pass)
BUS	$25–35	$5–10
TAXI	$15 per person	From $10 per person

BORDER CROSSING

Crossing land borders between Ecuador and Peru is simple. The main crossing is on the west coast of El Oro province in Huaquillas, and this is considered to be fastest and easiest; La Tina in Macará and La Balsa, near Zumba, are alternative crossings. Rumichaca is the official border for regular transit between Ecuador and Colombia. There's also the option to cross over the Río San Miguel, close to the Yasuní Nature Reserve, and through the Paso Internacional Tufiño in Tulcán. Huaquillas and Rumichaca are open permanently, but visitors must verify the availability of other crossings, as they may close due to security concerns.

Getting Around

Ecuador is a relatively small country and getting around is easy. There are ample transportation options for all types of travelers, no matter which region you're exploring.

TRAVEL COSTS

Car rental per day
small car/4WD $20–56/$71–99

Petrol
$0.75 per liter

Bus tickets
short-/long-haul $1-7/$12-40

Flight Guayaquil-Galápagos return
$290

City Transportation

The main cities have extensive and inexpensive bus lines. Guayaquil and Quito have integrated rapid bus systems; Quito's Trolebus goes to most of the tourist spots. In the capital, the new subway system, Metro de Quito, connects shopping and financial hubs with the historic center, while Cuenca boasts an ultramodern urban tram line called the Tranvía.

Intercity Buses & Vans

From no-frills to ultra-lux, dozens of intercity bus companies operate in Ecuador. Online ticketing works differently for each company, but the standard practice is to buy tickets at the station (*terminal terrestre*). You can also opt for transfer vans and private transportation companies. These are pricier, but faster.

TIP

Be cautious when traveling in coastal zones. Don't stop by isolated places, try not to veer away from main roads and, if possible, avoid driving at night.

PEAK & PLATE

To manage traffic congestion, Quito only allows certain cars on the streets from 6am to 9am and 4pm to 8pm on weekdays. The rule is based on the last number of your license plate: if that number is 1 or 2, you can't drive on Monday; if it's 3 or 4, you can't drive on Tuesday, and so on. Rental cars count, and you're open to fines if you break the law.

DRIVING ESSENTIALS

50

Speed limits for passenger cars: 50 km/h in urban zones, 90 km/h on perimeter roads and 100 km/h on straight roads.

18

The minimum driving age is 18.

Visitors can legally drive for 30 days on an International Driver's License.

Internal Flights

Most major cities in Ecuador are an hour apart by plane. If you have a flexible budget, plenty of domestic flights are available. It's always important to weigh the impact of air travel versus land transport, but in some cases, such as traveling to Galápagos, your options are limited.

Taxis

Taxis are widely available and the minimum short-range fare fluctuates between $1.50 and $1.75 in major cities. The vehicles are standard yellow and must operate with a meter in big cities. In small towns, you can agree on a fixed price before leaving. For safety, verify that they have a license plate.

Driving

Unsafe driving habits such as speeding and unnecessary honking are common, weather conditions vary and there are always obstacles – living and constructed – to avoid. If you're comfortable with defensive driving, a car will give you the autonomy to explore at your own pace.

Money

CURRENCY: US DOLLAR ($)

Credit Cards

International credit cards may carry a fee as high as 8%. Remember to always carry ID, as establishments may ask you to verify your identity.

Cash Is King

In smaller towns, rural areas and the Galápagos, cash is still king. Many small businesses and tour operators only accept cash, and some road tolls are cash only.

Spend Small

Big notes aren't often accepted with a smile – they are difficult to use and hard to change. Whenever possible, pay with small bills and coins. If you get larger bills from an ATM, aim to spend them at a big store, hotel or higher-end restaurant.

Ecuadorian Coins

Although Ecuador uses the US dollar, the country mints its own coins in values of one, five, 10, 25 and 50 cents. These are used in circulation for the corresponding value in dollars, but be sure to spend them in Ecuador, as they can't be exchanged or used outside.

HOW MUCH FOR...

Road tolls (approx)
$1

National park entry
$5–20

Galápagos entry fee
adult/child $200/100

Museum entry
$2–6

HOW TO... Tip

Ecuador doesn't have a standardized tipping culture. By law, restaurants include a 10% service fee on the bill, which is distributed between the establishment and staff. Full-day tour guides are often offered extra cash as a courtesy – if you're in a group, each person tips individually. If you're ever in doubt, remember that Ecuadorians tie tipping to satisfaction, so you can leave an extra sum to show your appreciation for good service.

LOCAL TIP

If you're driving around Ecuador, be sure to keep coins in your car to pay for road tolls. They're usually no more than $1, but generally, there's no option to pay by card.

WHY DOES ECUADOR USE US DOLLARS?

In 2000, Ecuador switched from the Ecuadorian sucre to the US dollar in an attempt to calm its volatile economy and inflation rates. The change was a disputed last resort, but it eventually led to economic stability. While the dollar's strength can make the cost of living in Ecuador more expensive and the country loses the economic autonomy of being able to print its own currency, most Ecuadorians consider the change to have been a positive fiscal move.

Accommodations

Nature & Ecolodges

Ecolodges are common offerings in areas where tourism relies on preserving diverse ecosystems. These places pioneer conservation and community sustainability programs. Mashpi (p132) lodge outside Quito and the Napo Wildlife Center (p185) ecolodge in Yasuní National Park are good examples.

Colonial Mansions

In the UNESCO World Heritage cities of Quito and Cuenca, many hotels are built in restored colonial mansions, with interior courtyards, baroque ceilings and wooden features. La Casona del Ronda in Quito and the Hotel Boutique Santa Lucia in Cuenca are two options.

Wildlife Reserves

Ecuador is one of the world's most biodiverse countries, and wildlife reserves help keep it that way. Some reserves have a small number of rooms available to those who want to visit. Maquipucuna Lodge (p131) and San Isidro Lodge (p181), a couple of hours from Quito, are private nature reserves ideal for wildlife-watchers.

Where a Hostel Isn't a Hostel

In Ecuador, a hostel isn't necessarily a hostel. The word can refer to anything from a no-frills guesthouse to a small hotel. They may offer typical hostel amenities, or you might just get a room and a shower. Other hostels are strangely magical, such as the Secret Garden (p244) hostel in Cotopaxi, where you can stay in a hobbit's house.

ACCOMMODATION PRICE RANGES

$ less than $30

$$ $30–75

$$$ more than $75

HOW MUCH FOR A NIGHT IN A...

Cozy hacienda **$80**

Colonial mansion **$100**

Chill hostel **$20**

Highland Haciendas

In the highlands, under the watchful glare of the country's volcanoes, you can stay at beautiful haciendas (colonial country estates). They are often homey and offer options for trekking, horse riding, learning crafts and enjoying regional culinary specialties. The luxurious suites at Hacienda Pinsaqui (p133) are steeped in history, while cozy rooms as Hacienda Cusín (p109) bring you close to nature.

GALÁPAGOS IMPACT

Tourism in the Galápagos Islands is a tricky balance. The industry is an important source of income for island residents, but tourism's impact negatively affects wildlife and fragile environments. Tourists who choose to stay on the islands produce waste that must be managed at increasing rates, while those who stay on boats may contribute to water contamination if engines aren't properly maintained. When choosing where to stay on the Galápagos, the ethos of the accommodation providers is more important than whether they're on land or sea. Remember to always do your research and favor local, smaller providers over large and international corporations.

Family Travel

Ecuador has a family-friendly culture and children are welcomed. The country is full of natural wonders, spectacular national parks and enchanting wildlife – excellent for entertaining kids. While Ecuadorians are generally welcoming to children of all ages, certain activities, such as Amazon treks and Galápagos snorkeling, are better suited to older children.

Best Family Destinations

This will depend on your children's ages and interests. The coast offers year-round warm weather and beautiful beaches with child-friendly activities. Meanwhile, the Amazon, Galápagos and mountain trekking are best for pre-teens and teens interested in adventure, nature and wildlife. Strolling around historical cities such as Quito and Cuenca can be a joy for the whole family.

Traveling with Babies

Babies are welcome in Ecuador, though some destinations in the Andean region might be off your list due to high altitude. Many Amazonian activities are also less recommended due to the risk of bites and mosquito-borne diseases or the risk of bringing common infant diseases such as chickenpox, viral colds or influenza to isolated communities.

Breastfeeding

Ecuador is a maternity-friendly country, where three-plus months of paid maternity leave is the minimum and lactation rooms are increasingly common. Ecuadorian women breastfeed in public with no restriction, so no worries if you're going to be breastfeeding on your visit.

Pram-Friendly? Probably Not

While Ecuador is family-friendly, streets aren't ideal for prams. In certain areas, sidewalks can be too narrow or uneven for easy wheeling. Take a page from the local book and opt for baby-carrying or folding strollers, especially outside big cities.

TOP FAMILY ATTRACTIONS

Zip through the cloud forest (p122)

Where waterfalls, wildlife and zip-lining adventures await.

Visit the Otavalo Market (p108)

Discover Ecuador's creative heritage at this world-class market.

Relax in a highland hacienda (p103)

Recharge in historic properties as you engage in cooking classes and horse riding.

Explore the Galápagos (p317)

An amazing adventure, especially with kids old enough to snorkel.

See a volcano (p212)

Parque Nacional Cotopaxi has family-friendly hikes with volcano views.

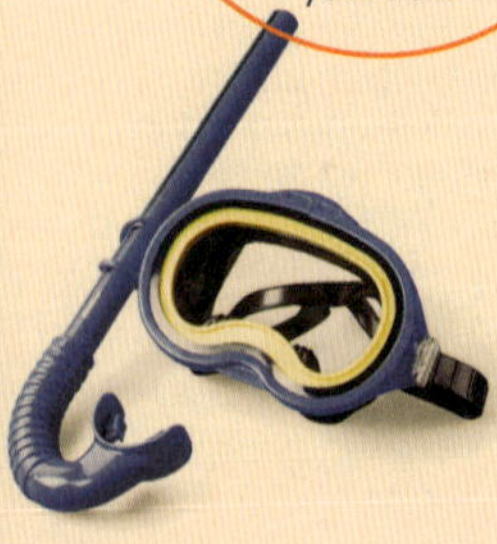

TRAVEL LIGHT

Family travel often means lugging a bunch of extra stuff around with you. Luckily for families traveling in Ecuador, you don't need to bring everything from home. Diapers (nappies), medicine, clothes, toys and healthy snacks are easily available in most locations. Purchasing the essentials as you travel helps support the local economy and keeps you from having to carry all that extra stuff in your carry-on luggage. Don't forget to restock your supplies in major cities and bigger towns, as availability might be limited in smaller towns, and places like the Galápagos Islands charge higher prices due to transportation fees.

Health & Safe Travel

TAP WATER

Tap water is safe to drink in major cities. However, for good measure, follow the local habit of boiling water or carrying water bottles – favor non-disposable bottles as a sustainable practice. In rural and remote areas, you might not have access to potable water at all, so plan accordingly.

Changing Altitudes

Ecuador is a country of many altitudes. One day you can be swimming in the ocean in the Galápagos Islands, and the next day strolling the streets of Quito, 2850m up in the Andes. These drastic changes can easily lead to altitude sickness (p43), so make sure to take time to acclimate at each higher destination.

Mosquito-Borne Diseases

Mosquito-borne diseases such as dengue and malaria are not widespread, but might be present in the coastal and Amazonian regions, especially during the rainy season. Be sure to wear long sleeves and pants, keep your vaccines up to date and invest in a good mosquito repellent if you're planning jungle treks.

VOLCANIC ERUPTIONS

There have been no notable eruptions in decades. However, inform yourself about local eruption procedures if you're in a volcano zone.

VOLCANO WARNINGS

White No chance of eruption, but still technically active

1

Yellow Increased seismic activity, stay alert

2

Orange Time to evacuate

3

Red Volcano has erupted

4

Urban Safety

Ecuador has undergone public-safety issues in recent years. While the majority of the country is still considered safe, there has been a rise in crime, largely due to an increase in drug-gang activity (previously, there were few such issues). Extra caution is recommended in coastal zones and borders.

VACCINES IN THE AMAZON

While keeping your vaccines up to date is a measure of self-protection, for inhabitants in remote villages and the Amazon region, it can make the difference between life and death. Native communities, who live deep in the forest with scarce access to health care, don't generally develop immunity to certain diseases. Make sure you're in good health when visiting, as something as simple as a flu can cause great damage to their communities.

FROM LEFT: BILLION PHOTOS/SHUTTERSTOCK, MATYAS REHAK/SHUTTERSTOCK

Food, Drink & Nightlife

When to Eat

Breakfast (*desayuno*; 7am to 9am) Ranges from a quick bread with cheese or jam, to a meal with meat, eggs, rice and/or plantains.

Lunch (*almuerzo*; noon to 2pm) Usually a main animal protein plus rice, potatoes, beans or plantains, and a salad.

Dinner (*cena*; 6pm to 8pm) Much like lunch. In cities, it's also the time to taste sweet delicacies with a hot drink.

Where to Eat

Market Food Courts Inside central markets are a host of food stands that fill up at lunchtime. Bigger lines often mean larger portions.

Huecas Generally inexpensive food made with regional ingredients. Ask for the special of the day.

Kiosk Often, roadside joints that sell only a single local specialty, whether it's *encebollado*, empanadas or otherwise.

Restaurants National and international restaurants can be found across the country.

EATING PRICE RANGES

$ less than $10

$$ $10–25

$$$ $25 and over

MENU DECODER

Ecuadorian menus are easy to read if you have some basic Spanish under your belt. Some key terms:

Entrada Starter

Plato principal Main dish

Postre Dessert

Casero Homemade

Frito Fried

Pollo Chicken

Gallina Generally, free-range chicken

Verde Green plantain

Cuy Guinea pig

Pescado Fish

Huevos Eggs

Cebolla Onion

Camarón Shrimp

Jugo natural Fresh juice

Menu del día Today's menu

Seco Stewed meat dish

Carne Meat

Chivo Goat

Maduros Fried ripe plantains (sweet)

Patacones Flattened and fried green plantains (savory)

Locro de papa Potato soup

Papas fritas French fries

Caldo Broth

Aji Hot sauce (often mild)

HOW TO... Enjoy Holiday Meals Like a Local

A food-centered culture makes Ecuadorians innate foodies. Many of the country's landmark dishes are tied to the holidays and specific times of the year. Between March and April, restaurants offer *fanesca*, a creamy pumpkin soup featuring 12 grains symbolizing the Twelve Apostles and meant to be eaten during Holy Week, more specifically on Good Friday. Between October and November, locals flock to their favorite *panadería* (bakery) for a taste of *guaguas de pan* (roughly translated as 'baby bread') and *colada morada* (red fruit and black corn drink), a treat with origins in the pre-Hispanic era, originally shared by indigenous people in honor of the dead. The meal is now a seasonal specialty and a must-have on November 2, Día de los Difuntos (Day of the Dead), when families reunite to visit cemeteries and mausoleums.

HOW MUCH FOR A...

Beer
$2–4

Soft Drink
75¢–$3

Meal at an inexpensive restaurant
$5

Meal for two with starters and drinks at a fine restaurant
$35–70

Cocktail in a downtown club
$10

Bottle of red table wine
$18

Mote con chicharron in a traditional market
$1–2

HOW TO...

Drink Like a Local

Ecuadorians know how to party. Here's what to have in your cup if you want to drink like a local.

Ecuador's national liquor, *aguardiente* ('fire water' in Spanish), is an exceptionally strong spirit made from fermented sugarcane. Popular throughout South America, *aguardiente* can be up to 100 proof. If you're in the Andes, you might encounter a drink called *canelazo* (not to be confused with the Colombian recipe of the same name), made of sugarcane alcohol mixed with *naranjilla* juice, sugar, orange juice and cinnamon; or *guarapo*, another spirit made from fermented sugarcane.

In the Andes, you'll also encounter *chicha*, a homemade beer brewed from fermented corn, while communities in the Amazon region have a drink of the same name made out of fermented yucca. You'll be able to get a pilsener, the national beer of Ecuador, everywhere.

Cocktail drinkers should try *mistela*, an *aguardiente*-based concoction infused with coffee, orange peel, cinnamon and clove, while eggnog lovers will adore *rompope*, a Latin American version of the Christmas classic.

Agave enthusiasts should sample *miske*, an ancient distilled liquor that stands out from all other agave-based spirits in the world for using the plant's sweet sap (*chawarmishki* or *aguamiel*) instead of its roasted heart.

Aguardiente

Aguardiente is Ecuador's most popular alcoholic drink, which some mistakenly refer to as rum. While both are made of sugarcane, *aguardiente* uses the cane's juice for fermenting, rather than the cane itself, as rum does.

BANANA CULTURE

Ecuador exports more bananas than any other country, though that doesn't mean there aren't enough to go around on the home front. In Ecuador, the banana has been used with impressive creativity in numerous traditional dishes, and you'll likely find a banana (or a plantain, which in Ecuador is considered a variety of banana) in almost anything you eat. There are a heap of popular street-food dishes that use bananas, including *emborrajados* (ripe plantains filled with cheese, covered in dough and fried), *plátanos asados* (grilled ripe plantains, often filled with cheese), *bollos de pescado* (a tamale-like food using green plantains instead of corn, with fish) and *corvíches* (green plantain and peanut-butter dough stuffed with cheese, fish or meat, then fried). Then you can find *chifles* (banana chips), or *empanadas de verde (*empanadas made with green plantain dough), *maduros con queso* (fried ripe plantains with cheese), *caldo de bolas de verde* (green plantain ball soup), *repe lojano* (green banana or plantain soup), *majado de verde* (mashed green plantains), *patacones* (mashed and fried green plantains) and *bolon de verde*, a very traditional dish where a green plantain dough is molded into a giant ball and stuffed with meat and cheese. The list could go on and on.

As you're enjoying, remember to thank the Afro-Ecuadorian and *montubio* community for creating most of the banana-based dishes.

Responsible Travel

Climate Change & Travel

It's impossible to ignore the impact we have when travelling; Lonely Planet urges all travelers to engage with their travel carbon footprint, which will mainly come from air travel. While there often isn't an alternative, travelers can look to minimise the number of flights they take, opt for newer aircrafts and use cleaner ground transport, such as trains. One proposed solution – purchasing carbon offsets – unfortunately does not cancel out the impact of individual flights. While most destinations will depend on air travel for the foreseeable future, for now, pursuing ground-based travel where possible is the best course of action.

The **UN Carbon Offset Calculator** shows how flying impacts a household's emissions.

The **ICAO's carbon emissions calculator** allows visitors to analyse the CO_2 generated by point-to-point journeys.

The Galápagos

The Galápagos National Park Directorate (GNPD) requires all businesses to take steps to conserve energy and water, recycle, source products locally, hire locally and pay fair wages. Travel with licensed tour providers that also support conservation or community projects.

The Amazon

Ecuador is one of the most biodiverse countries on Earth, and many tourism operators work hard to protect endemic species. In sensitive areas such as the Amazon, choose ecofriendly accommodations that are committed to preserving the area's exceptional biodiversity and helping indigenous communities.

Some sites are considered sacred by the indigenous people, and should be visited with care. The Cascada de Peguche (p111) waterfall, for example, is a sacred place for the Kichwa-Otavalo people, who hold ancient rituals here.

Ecuador has seen its peace interrupted by violence related to drug gangs and cartels in recent years. Before consuming, consider the negative impact that the demand for illegal drugs has on the country.

SUSTAINABLE AIR TRAVEL?

To minimize the impact of air travel on delicate environments, Ecuador built the world's first sustainable airport in the Galápagos. It was designed with bioclimatic architecture, built with reused materials and is completely powered by wind and solar energies.

GETTING AROUND

While air travel may be the easiest way around, Ecuador has plenty of land transportation options to reduce your carbon footprint. Use public transportation whenever possible.

Biodiversity

Ecuador may only occupy 0.2% of the Earth's landmass, but it has one of the highest rates of endemic species anywhere on the globe, and is home to 6.1% of the world's animal species.

Wildlife Interaction

Interaction with wildlife is a part of many Ecuadorian adventures, so be sensible during encounters. Don't feed or aggravate wild animals.

Cultural Conservation

There are 14 distinct indigenous groups in Ecuador, with the Kichwa being the largest. Whether you visit a shamanic ceremony or an annual festival such as Inti Raymi, be respectful of their traditions.

Chocolate Farming

While chocolate is one of Ecuador's main exports, traditional cacao farming harms natural habitats. Choose local brands supporting sustainable growers, such as República del Cacao, Indemini Baez or even To'ak (if you can swing the price tag).

Local Artisans

Ecuador's artisans have existed since pre-Inca times. Supporting their creative heritage means souvenir shopping at artisan-supporting markets and shops such as Casa de Arte Talleres (p119) in San Antonio de Ibarra or the famous Otavalo Market (p108), as well as choosing handmade goods over factory-produced souvenirs.

Ecuador has 11 national parks, nine ecological reserves, four biological reserves and 10 wildlife refuges.

Ecuador has the fourth-highest number of bird species of any country in the world.

The Rights of Nature

In 2008, Ecuador became the first country to recognize the 'rights of nature' in its constitution, protecting the rights of ecosystems to flourish and of people to petition on behalf of nature.

RESOURCES

amazonfrontlines.org
Indigenous-founded organization with info about conservation and justice programs.

galapagosconservation.org.uk
UK-based charity with conservation projects in the Galápagos.

tma.earth
Forest conservation nonprofit with info about regenerative agriculture.

LGBTIQ+ Travelers

Ecuador is ahead of the pack on LGBTIQ+ rights. Marriage equality, sexual orientation and gender-identity rights are all legally protected, though the country is not free of homophobia. Due to the dominating Catholic faith, Ecuadorians can be conservative, which means that while the LGBTIQ+ community is safe and thriving, it's often discreet in public.

Quito's Zona Rosa

Ecuador's urban zones and younger generations are typically accepting and open-minded, and cities such as Cuenca, Guayaquil and especially Quito have gay-friendly hotels, bars and restaurants from which to choose. Head to the Plaza Foch in Quito, best known as the city's Zona Rosa, or Pink Zone. Although its name comes from being the nightlife center (not necessarily for being a gay zone), it's gay-friendly, with nearby gay bars such as Radar and clubs like Kika Danzatoria and Tercer Milenio Discoteca central to the scene.

ANNUAL EVENTS

Quito hosts two LGBTIQ+ events every year. The first is Orgullo, the city's Gay Pride Festival, held on the last Saturday of June since 1998. The parade runs through the streets of Mariscal, ending at Parque La Carolina with live concerts and events. In November, the city also holds the two-week queer film festival, El Lugar Sin Limites (The Place Without Limits).

LEGAL STATUS

Ecuador was one of the first South American nations to make discrimination based on sexual orientation illegal (1998) and to protect marriage equality (June 2019). It also passed the Gender Identity Law in 2016, which gives transgender people the right to change their legal gender based on self-determination.

Saunas

Gay saunas are popular in Quito, though they are constantly opening and closing. Check out Sauna Jinetes, the city's longest-standing gay sauna, open since 1999. You'll need to remember to bring your passport so that you can get in.

Gay Travel Agencies

There are several travel agencies catering to the gay community (though the majority cater more specifically to gay men). Check out Ecuador Pride Travel *(ecuadorgaytravel.com)*, based dually out of Fort Lauderdale and Quito, or luxury provider Out Nomad *(outnomad.com)*.

PDAS

While Ecuador is ahead of the game in legal protections, the country retains Catholic and conservative influences. This means that while younger generations and urban dwellers are typically open-minded, older and more rural populations may be less familiar with conversations about sexuality and gender identity. While the worst you'll get is uncomfortable glares, the local LGBTIQ+ community typically opts against over-the-top displays of affection in public.

Accessible Travel

Despite Ecuador's progress in this area, accessible options in day-to-day life are almost non-existent in the country. Assistance is almost always necessary, especially outside major cities.

Accessible Bathrooms

Accessible bathrooms are increasingly common in urban areas. By law, all gas stations must offer accessible restrooms, meaning they're typically the most reliable (and the most common) place to find accessible restrooms.

Accommodations

Accessible accommodation isn't the rule in Ecuador, and even hotels that say they're accessible might be missing certain features. Search carefully and ask plenty of questions before booking.

Airport

Both Quito and Guayaquil airports have escalators and elevators, as well as adapted toilets, sinks and drinking fountains. Quito is somewhat more accessible, with fewer slopes and stairs and more extensive signage in braille.

RESOURCES

If you have any mobility, sight or hearing limitations, you might choose to join an adapted tour. **Latin America for All** *(latinamericaforall.com/destinations/ecuador-galapagos)* is one of the best disability-friendly tour operators in the country. **Red de Turismo Accesible Ecuador** *(REDTAEC; turismoaccesibleec.org/en/home-e)* is a national travel provider promoting accessibility. It considers itself a social enterprise to boost accessibility for people with disabilities in the tourism sector.

Transportation

Adapted public transportation in Ecuador is limited. Although taxi drivers will take any passenger regardless of disability, there are no specially adapted vehicles. The best option for the mobility impaired is private transfers.

Wheelchair Travel

Wheelchair travelers in Ecuador will almost always require assistance. Stores and eateries seldom have wheelchair-accessible entrances, and sidewalks are often narrow and uneven. When in the countryside, accessible tour operators such as REDTAEC have off-roading wheelchairs available.

PARKING

Parking for disabled motorists is widely available. You should have a sticker from CONADIS to use the spots, but that's rarely enforced, especially if you have a visible handicap. Adapted cars aren't available for rent in the country.

CONADIS

Ecuador's Consejo Nacional para la Igualdad de Discapacidades (CONADIS; National Council on Disability Equality) is charged with improving accessibility and providing Ecuadorians with disabilities with the tools they need to be active and participating members of society.

Cruise Around

One of the most accessible ways to experience Ecuador's star attraction, the Galápagos Islands, is to hop on a cruise ship. Cruising gives mobility-impaired travelers spectacular views of the islands, and up-close encounters with wildlife, without worry.

Women Travelers

Female travelers don't have much to worry about in Ecuador. The country is widely considered safe for solo women, and friendly locals and the country's compact size makes it easy to navigate on your own.

Dress the Part

Ecuador has a conservative Catholic influence and thus Ecuadorians tend to dress fairly conservatively. In the colder mountain regions, this isn't so evident, but along the coast, you'll see few Ecuadorians in bikinis (though this has as much to do with them not wanting to get dark from too much sun). Although locals have no problem with tourists dressing as they please, taking a page from local women's lookbook is an option if you're worried about attracting extra attention.

Sexual Safety

The responsibility of sexual safety in Ecuador generally falls on the woman. While condoms are widely available in pharmacies, emergency contraceptives without a prescription are only available at a public hospital (with a prescription, they're available over the counter). You can also easily get medicine for yeast infections or urinary infections at any pharmacy. Abortion is illegal.

Nightlife

As a single female traveler, you should always pay more attention at night. While partying in Ecuador is amazingly fun, follow a few standards to keep yourself safe. Don't go out alone – it can be easy enough to find a friend if you're staying at a hostel, so you're on the buddy system. Take trusted company taxis or an Uber if it's late, and don't overindulge if you're alone. Drug-related crime has increased in Ecuador, so not using drugs can also help you avoid trouble. Otherwise, trust your instincts.

Machismo

Machismo, a form of toxic masculinity and sexism, is a common pattern in certain Hispanic countries, especially among older men. This toxic mindset negatively enforces traditional gender roles, often placing unbalanced responsibilities and blame on women. While this is less likely to translate into sexual harassment than in some other countries, you may still experience some underlying (sometimes unconscious) discrimination or sexist remarks.

I'M FRIDAY/SHUTTERSTOCK

SEXUAL VIOLENCE

Ecuadorians are reserved and mostly keep to themselves, so be wary of overly friendly people or groups that appear way too eager to establish a connection. As you would anywhere else in the world, don't leave drinks unattended and be particularly careful when you go out at night. While criminal activity predominantly revolves around material objects, sexual violence cannot be entirely ruled out.

Nuts & Bolts

OPENING HOURS

Opening hours may vary, and are less regular in rural zones. Generally speaking, however, they are as follows.

Banks 8:30am to 4pm Monday to Friday

Restaurants Breakfast 7am to 11am, lunch noon to 4pm, dinner 6pm to 10pm

Coffee and sweet shops 7am to 6pm

Nightlife Bars 4pm to midnight, clubs and discos 8pm to 3am Thursday to Saturday (open most days in tourist zones)

Central markets 7am to 4pm Monday to Friday; some may open Saturday mornings

Churches 8am to noon and 2pm to 6pm

Shops Clothing shops 9am to 5pm, souvenir shops 10am to 7pm

Public Toilets

Public toilets will either be paid or devoid of things such as soap and toilet paper. Be prepared and keep a pack of tissues and hand sanitizer in your bag. Remember not to flush your toilet paper; it should go in the bin next to the toilet.

Smoking

Smoking is not allowed indoors, in shared spaces or in public transportation zones (such as bus stations).

GOOD TO KNOW

Time zone
Continental (UTC/GMT-5), Galápagos Islands (UTC/GMT-6)

Country calling code
+593

Emergency number
911

Population
17.7 million

Cell Phones & Internet Access

Cell-phone coverage in Ecuador is generally good, except high in the Andes and Galápagos, where coverage is notoriously spotty. Internet access is widespread and speeds are fast enough for most digital workers.

Electricity

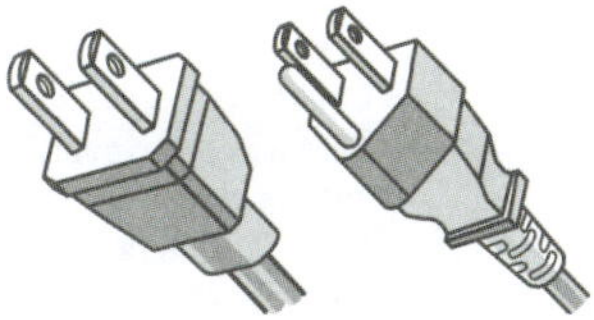

Type B
120V/60Hz

PUBLIC HOLIDAYS

Año Nuevo (New Year's Day) January 1

Día de la Provincia de Galápagos (Galápagos Day) February 12

Carnaval (Carnival) February/March

Viernes Santo (Good Friday) March/April

Día del Trabajo (Labor Day) May 1

Batalla de Pichincha (Battle of Pichincha) May 24

Primer Grito de Independencia (Independence of Quito) August 10

Independencia de Guayaquil (Guayaquil's Independence Day) October 9

Día de los Difuntos or Día de Muertos (Day of the Dead) November 2

Independencia de Cuenca (Cuenca's Independence Day) November 3

Día de Navidad (Christmas) December 25

Language

Spanish is the national language of Ecuador, and knowing some very basic phrases is not only courteous but also essential, particularly when navigating rural areas.

Basics

Hello. Hola. *o·la*
Goodbye. Adiós. *a·dyos*
Yes. Sí. *see*
No. No. *no*
Please. Por favor. *por fa·vor*
Thank you. Gracias. *gra·syas*
Excuse me. Con permiso. *kon per·mee·so*
Sorry. Perdón. *per·don*
What's your name? ¿Cómo se llama usted? *ko·mo se ya·ma oo·ste*
My name is ... Me llamo ... *me ya·mo ...*
Do you speak English? ¿Habla inglés? *a·bla een·gles*
I don't understand. No entiendo. *no en·tyen·do*

Directions

Where's ...? ¿Dónde está ...? *don·de es·ta ...*
What's the address? ¿Cuál es la dirección? *kwal es la dee·rek·syon*
Could you write it down? ¿Puede escribirlo? *pwe·de es·kree·beer·lo*
Can you show me (on the map)? ¿Me lo podría indicar (en el mapa)? *me lo po·dree·a een·dee·kar (en el ma·pa)*

Signs

Abierto Open
Cerrado Closed
Entrada Entrance
Salida Exit
Servicios/Baños Toilets

Time

What time is it? ¿Qué hora es? *ke o·ra es*
It's (10) o'clock. Son las (diez). *son las (dyes)*
It's half past (one). Es (la una) y media. *es (la oo·na) ee me·dya*
Morning. Mañana. *ma·nya·na*
Afternoon. Tarde. *tar·de*
Evening. Noche. *no·che*
Yesterday. Ayer. *a·yer*
Today. Hoy. *oy*
Tomorrow. Mañana. *ma·nya·na*

Emergencies

Help! ¡Socorro! *so·ko·ro*
Go away! ¡Váyase! *va·ya·se*
I'm sick. Estoy enfermo/a. *es·toy en·fer·mo/a (m/f)*
I'm lost. Estoy perdido/a. *es·toy per·dee·do/a (m/f)*
Call ...! ¡Llame a ...! *ya·me a ...*
... a doctor. ...un médico. *oon me·dee·ko*
... the police. ...la policía. *la po·lee·see·a*

Eating & Drinking

Can I see the menu, please? ¿Puedo ver el menú, por favor? *pwe·do ver el me·noo, por fa·vor*
What would you recommend? ¿Qué me recomienda? *ke me re·ko·myen·da*
Cheers! ¡Salud! *sa·lood*
That was delicious! ¡Estuvo delicioso! *es·ta·bo de·lee·syo·so*
The bill, please. La cuenta, por favor. *la kwen·ta por fa·vor*

NUMBERS

1 **uno** *oo·no*
2 **dos** *dos*
3 **tres** *tres*
4 **cuatro** *kwa·tro*
5 **cinco** *seen·ko*
6 **seis** *says*
7 **siete** *sye·te*
8 **ocho** *o·cho*
9 **nueve** *nwe·ve*
10 **diez** *dyes*

DISTINCTIVE SOUNDS

The strong and rolled *r*, and *kh* (pronounced as in the Scottish loch).

DONATIONS TO ENGLISH

Numerous – you may recognize armada, aficionado, embargo, fiesta, machismo, patio, plaza...

Where the @!*# is it?

Spanish-language and English-language keyboard layouts differ because the two alphabets aren't quite the same. This shouldn't generally be a problem, but for one pesky – all too useful in the age of email – key. The @ ('at') symbol – in Spanish this symbol is called *la arroba* – isn't necessarily labeled on keyboards or may not be accessed by simply pressing the keys you're used to. Try the F2 key, use an ALT code – or ask for help:

Where's the @ key? ¿Dónde está la arroba? *don·de es·ta la a·ro·ba*

Street Talk

¡De ley! Absolutely!

Verás Used in a variety of contexts to mean 'You'll see', 'Watch out' or 'I told you so'.

¿Mande? 'Come again?', 'What?' *In the time of the Spanish conquerors, this was the correct way for a subject to address their ruler.*

Chévere Cool

Chapa acostado – Speed bump. *Literally, it means 'police officer laying down'.*

Chupado Drunk

La farra Party

Must-know grammar

Spanish has a formal and informal word for 'you' (*usted* and *tú* respectively). The verbs have a different ending for each person, like the English 'I do' vs 'he/she does'.

Word stress

Rule of thumb: when a word ends in n, s or a vowel, the stress falls on the second-last syllable. Otherwise, the last syllable is stressed. If you see an accent mark over a syllable, it cancels out these rules and you just stress that syllable instead.

FALSE FRIENDS

Beware of 'false friends' – words which look and/or sound like an English word but have a different meaning altogether.

SPANISH AROUND THE WORLD

THE ECUADOR

STORYBOOK

Our writers delve deep into different aspects of Ecuadorian life

Saraguro valley (p300)

MAJOPEZ/SHUTTERSTOCK

A HISTORY OF ECUADOR IN 15 PLACES

Home to indigenous cultures, the Inca empire, the Spanish conquest, African descendants and some of the most innovative conservation efforts in the world, Ecuador has a rich and varied history, and much of it endures today. See sites around the country to learn what this diverse nation was built on. By Joel Balsam

IN MOST COUNTRIES, history stays in the past. In Ecuador, the story of the country's formation is written into the day-to-day lives of its people.

In this former home of the mighty Inca empire, for example, more than 500,000 people still speak Kichwa, a dialect of the original Inca language. The same community also continues to celebrate Inca festivals such as Inti Raymi, while cities filled with architecture dating to early Spanish Conquest remain intact, and some pre-Inca indigenous groups still practice their traditional ways of life.

From the coast to the mountains, rich artisan traditions – with origins predating any of the empires – carry on; along the country's coastline, you'll find replicas of pottery made by some of the first recorded humans on the continent to create ceramics.

Distinct periods in Ecuador's history – pre-Inca, Inca, Spanish Conquest and post-independence to today – are represented in modern society, not as a relic, but as a true, living piece of history that helps to weave together the story of incredibly diverse peoples. There are vestiges of the past at every corner, and many who once hid their traditions have begun to celebrate their heritage with pride, allowing for others to enjoy their contributions to this incredible country.

1. Santa Elena

EVERLASTING LOVE

A tender embrace by two 20-somethings, preserved for thousands of years, is an endearing symbol of the Las Vegas, Ecuador's earliest-known indigenous group. Present on the desertlike Santa Elena peninsula in the South Coast from 8000 to 4600 BCE, the pre-ceramic people were among the first to begin farming on the continent and were skilled hunter-gatherers and fisherfolk.

The 'embrace' is one of 192 grave sites at Museo Los Amantes de Sumpa in Santa Elena. It also showcases artifacts from Las Vegas, Valdivia and Guangalabalsa cultures, such as balsa-wood boats used to navigate the coastline.

For more on Santa Elena, see page 266.

2. Valdivia

PRE-COLUMBIAN POTTERS

The Valdivia picked up where the Las Vegas left off, cultivating kidney beans, cassava, chili peppers, and cotton on the South Coast from 3500 to 1800 BCE. More famously, the Valdivia were some of the first ceramists in the Americas, and many of their ceramic bowls, urns and animal figurines are still intact. The most recognizable piece is the Venus de Valdivia, an upright standing female figure, often with crossed arms, that has been replicated ad infinitum.

The modern-day town of Valdivia has sellers hawking replicas of the Venus, and there a few museums with an extensive catalogue of Valdivian artifacts.

For more on Valdivia, see page 271.

3. Otavalo

THRIVING ARTISANSHIP

One small mountain town outside of Quito is home to what is often argued to be South America's largest and longest-running artisan market. Dating back to before the Incan takeover in the 15th century, the biweekly market has more than 200 stalls filled with alpaca wool sweaters, panpipes, ponchos and intricately woven blankets. If you're looking for something unique to the region, pick up a rainbow-colored Aya Huma (or Diablo Umo) mask, worn every June during Otavalo's Inti Raymi festivities. Another festival, September's Fiestas del Yamor, stems from indigenous harvest traditions and features parades, dancing and traditional food.

For more on Otavalo, see page 107.

Person in Aya Huma mask, Inti Raymi (p37)

MARTIN STOCK STUDIO/SHUTTERSTOCK

4. Valley of Saraguro

RESILIENT CULTURE

The valley of Saraguro, in the Andes near Cuenca, is home to one of the most traditional indigenous communities in Ecuador. The group, which actually originated from the shores of Lake Titicaca, is the only known indigenous community in Ecuador that survived both Inca and Spanish colonization. Today, the Saraguro people keep a traditional way of life alive, in the language and herbal healing; rituals and solstice festivals; food, drink, music and dance; and in myths and legends passed down through generations. Respectfully visit villages Gera, Tuncarta, Las Lagunas and the town of Saraguro itself to enjoy their local market.

For more on Saraguro, see page 300.

5. Ingapirca

CAÑARI-INCAN RUINS

Ecuador's largest and most important Inca ruin was actually first built by the Cañari civilization, which dates from the 6th century to the early 16th. Originally called Hatun Cañar by the Cañari, it was renamed Ingapirca by the Incas in the 15th century when they moved in. As the story goes, the Inca had so much trouble conquering the Cañari, they resolved to simply live together in peace.

The stone ruins seen here are a unique example of integrated building styles, showcasing how the groups lived side by side, even though records indicate they remained distinct.

For more on Ingapirca, see page 296.

6. Pambamarca

INCA STRONGHOLD

Pambamarca, built atop an eroded volcano, was an essential pre-Incan – and later Incan, when taken over in the 15th century – fortress. Actually a collection of 14 hilltop fortresses, or *pucaras,* Pambamarca was long considered to mark the Inca's northern border, and was the site of many a bloody battle between the Inca and the Pais Caranqui – a collective of four neighboring chiefdoms (the Caranqui, Cayambe, Otavalo and Cochasquí). Visitors can hike between the *pucaras*, along an 8km arc in the northern Andes.

In the 18th century, Pambamarca was used by French astronomers as a celestial observatory to calculate the equatorial line.

For more on Pambamarca, see page 105.

7. Plaza San Francisco

SPANISH RULE

UNESCO-listed central Quito is chock-full of sites that reveal the history of this small but mighty country. Among them are two dozen churches and more than 30 museums, with the most important sites found at Plaza San Francisco. There, Iglesia y Convento de San Francisco, built between 1534 and 1605, is a haunting memorial to the Incan defeat by Catholic Spaniards, with iconography from both adorning its gold-clad walls. The church served as the birthplace of the Escuela Quiteña (Quito School of Art) and grew to become part of a monastery complex that took 150 years to complete.

For more on Plaza San Francisco, see page 65.

8. Volcán Cotopaxi

ECUADOR'S SCARIEST ATTRACTION

One of Ecuador's most popular tourist destinations is also its most dangerous. With 87 recorded eruptions (the first of which was in 1534), Cotopaxi is Ecuador's most active volcano. Eruptions in the 18th century destroyed the colonial settlement of Latacunga, and a spate of seismic activity in October 2022 forced the volcano to close for summits until late 2024.

At the time of publishing, Cotopaxi is open and scary, but a beautiful sign of what it's like to live in a country with 20 active volcanoes. When Cotopaxi will erupt next is, terrifyingly, anyone's guess.

For more on Volcán Cotopaxi, see page 214.

9. Isla Portete

AFRO-ECUADORIAN BIRTHPLACE

Around the same time the Spanish were taking over Inca land, in 1553, there was a shipwreck off the coast of Ecuador. The enslaved Africans who survived managed to escape to a small island in Esmeraldas Province on the North Coast. There, on Isla Portete, the group led by Alonso de Illescas set up the first *palenque* (settlement of fugitive enslaved Africans and indigenous people), forming the first Afro-Ecuadorian population. These days, Esmeraldas province continues to have a thriving Afro-Ecuadorian presence, experienced especially in its seafood cuisine; and Isla Portete features a memorial to de Illescas.

For more on Isla Portete, see page 151.

10. Cuenca

PICTURESQUE TOWN

Cuenca's historical center is considered to be one of the most well-preserved remnants of the Spanish colonial period, although it wasn't the first city on the soil. The first settlement was built by the Cañari people around 500 CE, who named it Guapondeleg, meaning 'plain as big as the sky'. Later, it was taken over by the Inca and renamed Tomebamba, or Pumapungo, a city said to have once rivaled the splendor of Cuzco. The site was already abandoned when the Spanish arrived in 1557 and founded their own settlement, Cuenca, which is recognized as a UNESCO World Heritage Site.

For more on Cuenca, see page 286.

11. Volcán Pichincha

INDEPENDENCE WAR

In 1820, Guayaquil had already declared its independence from Spain in a bloodless revolt; Ecuador's Andean city, Quito, was aiming to follow suit. Unfortunately, the northerners had to fight for their freedom, which culminated on May 24, 1822 at the Battle of Pichincha, fought on the slopes of Volcán Pichincha, just outside of Quito, 3500m above sea level.

The improbable battle location was thanks to a miscalculation by patriot General Antonio José de Sucre; however, it ended in a victory over the royalist army, and is considered the battle in which Ecuador officially won its independence from Spain.

For more on Volcán Pichincha, see page 69.

12. Las Peñas

BOHEMIAN NEIGHBORHOOD

Despite being founded in 1535, Guayaquil, Ecuador's biggest city, hardly feels historic. It's better known for being the country's commercial transport hub, and unfortunately, crime. However, the city's oldest

Cuenca's historic center (p286)

neighborhood, Las Peñas (The Rocks), stands apart. Wander along its cobblestone streets, past colorful homes, street art, galleries and boutique hotels, for a taste of 19th-century bohemian life and tranquil views over the Río Guayas. According to local legend, Argentinian-born revolutionary Ernesto 'Che' Guevara lived here for more than a month, and both author Ernest Hemingway and Chilean poet Pablo Neruda were frequent visitors.

For more on Las Peñas, see page 252.

13. The Galapágos Islands

ORIGIN OF SPECIES

English naturalist Charles Darwin was in the middle of a five-year research trip when he landed on San Cristóbal Island, one of 19 islands that form the Galápagos. First encountered by humans in 1535, the Galápagos Islands began their history as havens for pirates and whalers who hunted the islands' unique wildlife to near extinction. What Darwin found here inspired his world-changing book, *Origin of Species* (1859), and the theory of evolution.

In 1959, the Galápagos became a protected national park, and the UNESCO site is now a model of conservation and sustainable travel.

For more on the Galapágos Islands, see page 317.

14. Montecristi

WORLD-FAMOUS HAT

In 1906, US President Theodore Roosevelt visited the Panama Canal, wearing what soon after became one of the world's most famous hats – the Panama hat. However, there was a mix-up, as the handwoven, toquilla-straw hat that adorned Roosevelt's head was actually made in Montecristi, Ecuador.

The hats are part of an age-old tradition in the villages around Montecristi, where locals have been handweaving toquilla straw for hundreds of years. There are still a handful of weavers capable of crafting genuine Montecristi *superfinos* – the crème de la crème of Panama hats – which can sell for upwards of $25,000.

For more on Montecristi, see page 164.

15. Parque Nacional Yasuní

CONSERVATION WIN

Ecuador is often called a 'banana republic,' because for much of its history its economy relied on the exportation of bananas and other fruits. Unfortunately for the environment, another large export is petroleum, drilled from fragile Amazon territory. The Parque Nacional Yasuní, which was opened for oil extraction in 2013, made history in 2023 when Ecuador's population overwhelmingly voted to 'keep the oil in the soil' and end petroleum production in the national park, helping to preserve the local ecosystem. The vote also marked the first time in history that a country has ever limited fossil-fuel extraction through direct democracy.

For more on Parque Nacional Yasuní, see page 184.

MEET THE ECUADORIANS

Ecuadorians pride ourselves on the diversity of our people, the stunning natural marvels that surround us even in urban settings and our food-based gatherings. Mayra Peralta introduces her people.

ALEXANDER VON HUMBOLDT, the German naturalist who embarked on an ambitious expedition through the Americas in 1799, is credited with a phrase that Ecuadorians have etched into their souls and often recall to describe the essence of our people. 'Ecuadorians are rare beings: they sleep peacefully amidst rumbling volcanoes, live in poverty amidst incomparable riches, and find joy in sad music.' Despite the slightly patronizing tone and though Ecuadorian identity is not a monolith, Humboldt's quote captures how Ecuadorians regard ourselves: people of contradictions, fiercely proud to be born and raised amid jaw-dropping landscapes, generous families and extraordinary traditions.

With people from four different regions coexisting in a compact territory, it's hard for Ecuadorians to be boxed into one category. Instead, the region we come from will likely define the way we glide through life. People from the highlands, best known as *serranos,* generally keep to themselves; polite but distant enough to surprise you with affection and unrivaled loyalty once they've warmed to you. They're quiet, early risers and hardworking to a fault.

On the other hand, *costeños* (people from the Coastal region) are easygoing, fun and will speak to you so fast you might need to ask them to slow down. Entrepreneurial and adventurous, they always go straight to the point and know exactly how to strike up a conversation.

You'll find a middle ground in the Oriente and the Galápagos, where people are modestly friendly, kind and helpful, and zealously guard the natural wonders that surround them.

Though Ecuadorians, particularly *costeños* and *serranos,* will seldom see eye to eye on trivial debates, like which region has the best food, what the best city to live in is, or the country's best football team – *costeños* will likely claim Barcelona or Emelec, while *serranos* will claim Liga de Quito or Independiente del Valle – we are all united by solidarity, resilience and love for our country.

Regardless of our differences, we come together to lend a hand to the needy or share a plate of food. Food is, in fact, our love language and the common thread that brings families and communities together regularly. Nearly all of our celebrations unfold around the table. That's why there will always be an extra seat for an unexpected guest, or why we might feel offended if you turn down an invitation to eat with us.

Always open and eager to show visitors the beauty of our country, the Ecuadorian people will make anyone feel welcome, at home and one of us, even if you can't speak our language. Try learning Spanish with us, though, and you will see just how colorful the language can get.

Ecuador in Numbers

Ecuador's population reached 17.7 million in 2024. *Mestizos* are the dominant demographic, followed by indigenous, Afro-Ecuadorian and *montubio* (rural coastal groups) people. There are 95 men per 100 women, and the median age is 29.

Pictured clockwise from top left: Dancers at Carnaval, Cuenca (p286); artisan displaying clay mask she made; Kichwa festival Pawkar Raymi, Otavalo (p107); Kichwa man holding up a piranha

CLOCKWISE FROM TOP LEFT: IRENEUKE/SHUTTERSTOCK, ANGELA N PERRYMAN/SHUTTERSTOCK, DGRAMAL/SHUTTERSTOCK, SL-PHOTOGRAPHY/SHUTTERSTOCK

I'M AN ECUADORIAN

I was born in Ecuador's capital, Quito, and grew up in a neighborhood in the northeast of the city. My maternal family, indigenous to the area, has inhabited those lands for more than two centuries. Originally forest and agricultural fields, their lands were already labeled as urban territory by the time I was born, but I still grew up watching my grandparents and mother cultivate the land and harvest the fruits of their hard work, literally and figuratively.

From my dad, a war veteran, I developed a taste for travel. He'd take the entire family – mom, sister and maternal grandparents – on long rides across the highlands and clear water beaches, where we'd indulge in endless treats.

At 17, I moved to France to pursue my undergrad studies and have since been moving between cities. But wherever I go, I remain a proud *quiteña* and a granddaughter of exemplary indigenous people, and credit my nationality for my resilient, stubborn and hardworking nature.

Waorani women

IRENEUKE/SHUTTERSTOCK

ECUADOR'S INDIGENOUS PEOPLE

Celebrate the country's first peoples. By Mayra Peralta

SPREAD OUT OVER the landscape from the coast to the Amazonian region, Ecuadorian indigenous groups are just as varied as the country's geography. Despite being a national minority today, they have heavily contributed to shaping the nation's identity and preserving its diversity, culture and languages.

Indigenous Ecuador at a Glance

According to the Council of Nationalities and Peoples of Ecuador (CODENPE), 14 indigenous nations and 18 indigenous peoples live on Ecuadorian territory. The most recent census revealed nearly 8% of the Ecuadorian population identifies as indigenous – 68% of this demographic is concentrated in the highlands, while 24% lives in the Amazon region and 8% on the coast.

Spread across the Pichincha and Imbabura provinces, Natabuela, Kitu Kara and Otavalo stand out in the northern highlights. *Otavaleños,* globally recognized for their involvement in the arts and crafts, host the largest indigenous textile and crafts market in South America in their namesake town. Their artistry is the continuation of a lengthy legacy that now translates into vibrant creations ranging from alpaca-wool sweaters and eclectic bags to wall hangings and table decor.

Otavalo and nearby towns in Imbabura are a prime destination during the summer-solstice celebrations, when indigenous people in the highlands celebrate Inti Raymi, a festival honoring Inti, the Sun God.

Meanwhile, the Panzaleo and Chibuleo people, along with other groups dedicated to agriculture and farming, inhabit the central highlands. In the southern region, the Cañari and Saraguro people spark attention with eye-catching traditional dress; Cañari women wear voluminous *polleras* (midi skirts), while Saraguros can be spotted anywhere due to their wide-brimmed hats adorned with cow print.

In Santo Domingo de los Tsáchilas and Esmeralda, the Épera, Tsáchila and Cachi people are the only remaining indigenous communities on the Ecuadorian coast. Their economy is predominantly based on crafts, agriculture and community tourism. Tsáchilas, colloquially known as *colorados* for their achiote hair-dye technique, host cultural tours that include energetic cleanses, hair dying and basket-weaving workshops.

Shuar, Achuar, Waorani and Cofán are some of the Indigenous communities watching over ancient territories and actively promoting natural resources and biodiversity conservation in the Oriente (Amazonian region). Nestled in remote villages deep in

PASTAZA
ARTESANOS
WAO
AMAZONÍA
ECUADOR
200 gr.

the forest, many of them receive visitors for tours and immersive cultural experiences.

The Oriente is also home to the Tagaeri and Taromenane, two of the last known peoples living in voluntary isolation in South America. They are organized in nomadic groups, moving between territories in the Yasuní National Park and its vicinities, although their survival has been endangered by oil extraction, mining and other exploitative practices.

Indigenous People's History & Resistance

The origins of indigenous communities in Ecuador can be traced to pre-Columbian societies, which makes them holders of millennia-old culture and history.

Museums and archaeological sites, including the National Museum, Museo Casa del Alabado and Parque Arqueológico Rumipamba, document this history, showcasing everyday objects, ceramics, ceremonial artifacts and art depicting ancient cultures' lifestyles and societal organization.

Clay pieces from the Valdivia culture, the first ceramist society in the western hemisphere (considered the 'cradle of American culture'), are some of the most culturally significant objects on display at the Museo Nacional and Casa del Alabado, both in Quito. Meanwhile, in situ archaeological museums such as Tulipe, La Florida and Rumipamba safeguard vestiges of ancient civilizations such as Quitus and Yumbos, who inhabited Quito and its vicinities.

Upon the arrival of Spaniards and throughout the Spanish colonial rule, indigenous peoples (especially those inhabiting the Andean region) were exploited and coerced to assimilate into the invaders' culture. The colonists used systems such as *mita, obraje* and *encomienda* to subject these communities to forced labor.

By the end of the 19th century and the beginning of the 20th century, indigenous uprisings, syndicates and early forms of political organization played a key role in the fight for indigenous rights. Activists such as Jesus Gualavisi, Dolores Cacuango and Tránsito Amaguaña – the latter two considered pioneers of feminism and bilingual education in the country – led social mobilizations demanding land-tenure reform and asserting the rights to salaries and education.

In Otavalo, Museo Viviente Otavalango serves as a landmark of indigenous resistance. Housed in what was once La Fabrica San Pedro, a textile factory where indigenous people were exploited and abused, the museum is now owned by a group of indigenous families. The site features traditional *otavaleño* objects: costumes, agricultural tools and textile-processing artifacts. The museum is also a community center of sorts, where the community displays art, dances and music.

Community-Based Tourism Initiatives

Although the contemporary extraction economy (oil exploitation, logging, mining) has endangered the livelihoods of indigenous groups in Ecuador, communities continue to practice their ancestors' traditions and protect the connection to their lands. Over the years, initiatives such as community-based tourism and agricultural and crafts projects have created sustainable economic alternatives for indigenous people.

In the Amazonian provinces, community hotels, cultural centers and reserves are designed to highlight the stories of indigenous nations such as Siona, Secoya, Kichwa and Shuar, among many others. In Misahuallí, women from the Kichwa nation run Sinchi Warmi, a community-tourism center and lodge where visitors can learn about their culture and traditions through cooking, dancing, wildlife photography and exploring the Amazon rainforest.

Similarly, in the central highlands, Chimborazo province offers plenty of options for tourists, from lodging at the Centro Cultural Pucará Tambo and trekking with guides from the Puruhá community, to visiting Centro Comunitario La Moya to enjoy traditional cuisine and learn about the customs, legends and cosmovision of its indigenous people.

Experiencing Ecuador guided by indigenous communities is a way of discovering their culture and supporting their economy, empowering their people and better understanding the social fabric that sets Ecuador apart. By learning about indigenous communities, visitors can gain a deeper appreciation of their contributions to shaping Ecuadorian culture. Looking at their history also means acknowledging their ongoing struggles for recognition and rights, and their efforts to safeguard their lands and traditions.

TORTOISE AS ALLEGORY & ORACLE

The Galápagos tortoise represents the majesty of the islands.
By Bailey Freeman

AFTER A FEW days in the Galápagos Islands, you may no longer be surprised by marine iguanas splayed in piles on beaches, eyes closed Zen-like in the sun, nor by sea lions swirling up in curiosity as you swim along the surface of a reef. Giant tortoises perambulating in the wild, however – this may remain an elusive delight. Spotting the dark dome of a Galápagos tortoise shell moving through highland grasses feels almost like glimpsing a dinosaur. In a way, it is – these strangely magnificent creatures are some of the oldest reptile species surviving today.

Shells & Speciation

The languidly charismatic icon and namesake of the islands (visitors thought the tortoises' shells resembled saddles – *galápagos* in Spanish), giant Galápagos tortoises are a stellar example of Charles Darwin's theory of natural selection. Darwin observed, as you can yourself at the main islands' tortoise-breeding centers, that the shape of Galápagos tortoise shells differed from island to island.

On some islands, the tortoises had rounder, domed shells and shorter necks, while on others, the shells were shaped more like saddles, flaring out at the bottom and affording space for those tortoises' more elongated necks to stretch higher. Pondering the reasons for these morphological differences, Darwin eventually concluded that the saddleback tortoises lived on more arid islands that necessitated a higher reach to find vegetation, with tortoises on those islands eventually evolving longer necks with shells to accommodate upward mobility. Tortoises that lived in more bountiful environments could forage low to the ground with their shorter necks and rounder shells.

So it happened that the giant tortoises, isolated as they were on their respective islands, evolved into at least 14 distinct subspecies. On some of the bigger islands, tortoise populations were isolated from one another by geography and thus diverged into separate subspecies on the same island. To witness the incredible uniqueness of endemic fauna and speciation in these remote islands is, of course, what draws visitors from around the world to this near-mythic archipelago. Amazingly, the terrestrial and marine biodiversity continues to thrive despite human impact on the island environment, though certainly human history has also negatively altered it.

Human Predation

Although it's believed that Inca people from mainland Ecuador managed to navigate to the Galápagos in the pre-Columbian era, the first human contact on record was by Fray Tomás de Berlanga, the Bishop of Panama, whose Peru-bound ship went adrift and landed at the islands. Though thereafter claimed nominally by Spain, the Galápagos did not hold much value to the empire over the next few centuries. However, their existence proved extremely valuable to roving 17th- and 18th-century buccaneers and pirates, who could escape to the islands' remote safety and reprovision with fresh water and tortoises between raids. In the 19th century, whalers followed suit as they plundered the rich waters around the islands, abundant with whales and fur seals.

Giant tortoises have the notable ability to live for up to a year without food or water, a boon for survival but making them ideal, slow-moving protein sources for mariners spending months at sea. These island giants were hunted almost to extinction by pirates, whalers and explorers, with scientists estimating that 100,000 to 200,000 tortoises were exterminated within a couple of centuries.

Unintended Consequences

Humans not only became the tortoises' sole predators but they also introduced species into the island ecosystems, both deliberately and inadvertently. Over time, traffic through and colonization of the islands brought in domesticated animals that went feral, such as goats, pigs, dogs and cats that preyed on tortoise eggs and babies whose shells had not yet hardened enough to protect them from predators. Rats introduced on passing ships continue to cause problems with iguana and tortoise nests to this day, though there are ongoing local efforts to eradicate their populations.

More recently, the accidentally introduced and ominously named vampire fly *(Philornis downsi)*, discovered on the islands in 1997, has wreaked devastation on the iconic Darwin's finch and flycatcher populations. Vampire flies lay eggs in the birds' nests, leaving the larvae to hatch and feed on the beaks and blood of the baby birds. Many nestlings perish as a result of the parasites' damage. The nestlings that survive often develop beak deformities that affect their songs and subsequently their mating patterns, hybridizing their offspring even if they manage to reproduce successfully.

Despite these horrific developments, evolution continues in real time. The finches, for example, have already exhibited changed behaviors in response to the vampire flies. Adult female finches stay in the nest longer than historically recorded, to preen the babies and consume the flies that appear in their nests, supported by the male finches who forage to feed the offspring. Though human intervention through insect control is likely necessary to mitigate the damage to the finch and other avian populations, the evolution in action illustrates the finch's resilience and rapid response.

Positive Intervention & Rewilding

Though finch behavior has changed to reduce harm to its offspring, the birds' own efforts may not be enough, and carefully considered human intervention seems to be helping without negatively affecting other species. Galápagos Conservancy scientists have implemented strategies to combat vampire-fly damage, such as setting insect traps and providing insecticide-treated nesting materials for finches and other birds to use.

These interventions appear to be yielding higher fledgling numbers on some islands, and captive breeding programs have produced healthy fledglings that were successfully released into the wild.

Similarly, decades-long efforts to rewild Galápagos tortoises aim to restore ecological balance by reintroducing subspecies to their legacy islands, a process that often goes hand in hand with other anti-invasive measures (specifically the elimination of rats and goats). Visitors to the breeding centers on Isla Santa Cruz and Isla Isabela learn about the natural history of the Galápagos tortoise and the restoration programs, while enjoying a look at multiple subspecies – babies to massive

Tortoise and egret, Isla Santa Cruz (p322)
MARIDAV/SHUTTERSTOCK

adults – trundling around. Because Galápagos tortoises don't reach sexual maturity until age 20 to 25, and can live for about 150 years in captivity, these programs are playing the long game.

Other research and conservation efforts are ongoing, led by organizations like the Galápagos Conservancy, the Charles Darwin Foundation and the Galápagos National Park: among them are habitat restoration for the waved albatross and the Galápagos petrel; the eradication of invasive guava and blackberry plants to restore endemic scalesia forests; and establishing and maintaining sustainable fisheries.

George, Diego, Fernanda...& Hope

For the Isla Pinta tortoise *(Chelonoidis abingdonii),* hopes for survival died in 2012 with Lonesome George, the last remaining creature of his species. But for all the loss that Lonesome George's passing represents, he has a foil in Diego, an Isla Española tortoise *(Chelonoidis niger hoodensis).* Since 1976, when only 15 of his species existed in the world, Diego has sired hundreds of offspring, bringing the current population to more than 2000 (earning him the nickname 'Super Diego') before retiring to Española to live out his golden centenarian years in the wild.

More recent discoveries, such as tortoises with DNA of the extinct Isla Floreana species, have resulted in a long-range selective breeding program to bring that species back from extinction, in a way; the first group of these hybrid Floreana tortoises was released in the wild in February 2026. And the incredible 2019 discovery of Fernanda, an exact DNA match to the Isla Fernandina species thought to have gone extinct in 1906, offers yet another glimmer of hope for reversing at least one species' extinction status.

Tortoises are not only the most iconic creature of the archipelago, but also an archetype representing all of the endangered endemic species connected by the Galápagos web. Conservation projects are working hard to protect endangered populations of rare endemics such as pink land iguanas on Isabela's Volcán Wolf, Galápagos penguins, marine iguanas and Galápagos flycatchers, among others.

Coexistence & Conservation

On a practical level, the victory of one species' 'de-extinction' doesn't cancel out the pressure that human activity and climate change place on the delicate balance of the islands.

Cruise visitor numbers have been tightly controlled since 1998, but land-based tourism has grown significantly in the years since. With 280,000 visitors to the Galápagos in 2024, the impacts on both marine and terrestrial environments are significant. Pollution from fuel, microplastics and plastic trash can be seen throughout the islands and detected in the bodies of whale sharks and other filter feeders. The sheer number of humans landing on islands that don't have abundant freshwater sources results in the generation of plastic waste, only one facet of human impact that ripples throughout the ecosystem.

Despite the challenges that come with balancing tourism with ecological protections, both private and state-sponsored bodies are working to preserve the islands and sustain continued visitation – tour operators adhere to strict timetables to avoid overpopulating Galápagos hot spots, licensed guides must be local to the archipelago, and many companies partner with local conservation organizations and the national park itself. Here at the wellspring of evolutionary theory, the vision of pristine, balanced biodiversity is what draws us all to experience it for ourselves. Who can resist this alluring kaleidoscope of swimming iguanas, mysterious albatrosses and hand-sized seahorses? Traveling thousands of kilometers to witness a blue-footed booby showing off a mating dance, or scalloped hammerhead sharks schooling below, is also what keeps the local human economy afloat. Sustainable tourism benefits Galápagos communities and drastically reduces exploitation of marine life. However, our best individual efforts to minimize our impact may also need to be mitigated by a reduction in visitor numbers in the future, for the sake of conserving this beautiful, fragile biodiversity.

ECUADOR'S HACIENDAS

These dignified countryside lodgings are epitomes of Ecuadorian history – good, bad, distant and recent. By Luke Waterson.

HACIENDAS HAVE SHAPED rural life in Ecuador since the 16th century. Often translated into English as 'ranches', in reality, these extensive and invariably gorgeously situated farms are much more. They are excellent ways for travelers to experience traditional country culture, are living pieces of history, offer vital employment in remote areas and help protect Ecuador from environmentally detrimental development.

A Checkered History

Ecuador's green northern sierra was the main fertile farmland for Spanish colonizers, with its rich volcanic soil and pleasant climate. So the Spanish Crown apportioned the land into manageable chunks from the 1500s onwards, with haciendas overseeing each.

As with most colonial-era constructions, Quito's UNESCO-listed center notwithstanding, their histories were often marred by the exploitation of Indigenous laborers, who were forced to work on these estates through debt bondage. But examining the entirety of hacienda history also shows that haciendas helped and housed South America's great freedom-fighter Simón Bolívar during his campaigns to liberate Ecuador

Hacienda Zuleta (p133)

CHAD CASE/ALAMY

from the Spanish. In fact, you can sleep in Bolívar's old room at at Otavalo's Hacienda Pinsaquí (p133).

Hacienda Zuleta (p133) near Ibarra conserves Carranqui culture ruins on its property, and champions its indigenous origins. The hacienda attached to the old San Pablo textiles factory in Otavalo, which once ran on exploited indigenous labor, has been taken over by a collective of indigenous Otavalo people and reborn as Museo Viviente Otavalango (p107), a space to showcase their history. After agrarian reforms in the 1960s, haciendas gave back many of their lands to local farmers (though opinions on how beneficial this was for the general populace differ), and today, they provide important local employment in rural areas. Haciendas have checkered pasts, but embody 400 years of how Ecuador's countryside has developed.

Windows into Rural Life

Most of Ecuador's remaining haciendas, enviably situated amid verdant Andean slopes, survive not solely as the large-scale farms they began as, but as places where visitors can stay to enjoy traditional country life. Haciendas were never simply farms, but rather collections of buildings sometimes surpassing many villages in size and facilities. They included worker accommodation, for example. Most had their own chapel, and food from hacienda estates rendered them essentially self-sufficient. To design its grounds, **Hacienda Piman** *(haciendapiman.com)* near Ibarra even employed the same landscape gardener who planned gardens at Versailles.

Some haciendas have amassed so many historical artifacts and memorabilia that they even sport dedicated museums. But every hacienda has an element of the living museum about it. Wander down their echoing tiled corridors, past creaky furniture, around cobbled courtyards and through prettily planted gardens, livestock-grazed fields, lakes and woods that make up their grounds, and you will see for yourself.

Hacienda Pinsaqui (p133)

LUKE WATERSON

Traditions Preserved

Haciendas still play an important role in preserving rural traditions. Horses have always been integral to hacienda life, and there are many opportunities to go horse riding, and to see horses being tended. Other animals from alpacas to *cuy* (guinea pigs) are invariably found on the premises.

Haciendas often operate classes teaching traditional textile-making or ancestral Andean cooking techniques. Traditional highland lunch at an atmospheric hacienda is rightly a highlight of even the swiftest Ecuador tours. Hacienda Zuleta, meanwhile, supports local women who produce exquisite embroidery and exhibit it in a workshop on the premises. It helps rehabilitate critically endangered Ecuadorean condors, too.

Springboards for Remote Adventures

Their bewitching rural locations make haciendas handy (if not ideal) for exploring Ecuador's remoter landscapes. Hacienda Piman is among the best lodgings from which to discover Chota Valley's Afro-Caribbean heritage. Hacienda El Porvenir (p217) makes a fine base for scaling Volcán Cotopaxi. And one or many volcanoes will likely form the view from a hacienda's windows.

Be they repositories of history, standard-bearers of countryside culture or bases for beautiful day trips, haciendas are defining elements of Ecuador's DNA. A great overview of Ecuador's haciendas can be found at **Haciendas Ecuador** *(haciendasinecuador.com)*.

ART OF THE PEOPLE

Splashing color across Quito, street art continues a long storytelling tradition informed by *indigenismo,* sociopolitical issues and cultural pride. By Wendy Yanagihara

THERE'S A SAYING that 'No wall is white' in Ecuador, referencing the sheer ubiquity of murals across the country. And while there are *barrios* in Quito particularly well-known for their street art by well-known local and international artists, colorful urban art brightens the landscape all over the city.

A Latin American Artistic Tradition

The roots of modern Latin American mural art can be traced to the Mexican *muralismo* (muralism) movement that directly followed the Mexican Revolution in 1920. The Mexican government commissioned some of the country's best artists – Diego Rivera, David Alfaro Siquieros and José Clemente Orozco most prominent among them – to paint murals that were meant to educate the majority rural and illiterate population of their shared history and to cultivate a shared sense of Mexican identity and cultural pride. Painted on the walls of educational institutions, the murals illustrated elements of Mexico's precolonial historical events and indigenous culture, celebrating the *mestizo* identity of Mexico as it moved towards industrialization. *Indigenismo,* the elevation and centering of indigenous people in these artworks, was central to Mexican muralism.

Muralism as an art form did not, however, originate after the Mexican Revolution – in Mayan temples such as at Bonampak, beautifully preserved murals from around 800 CE depict daily life, ritual and arts in great detail, making it one of the oldest examples of this artistic tradition. But in the modern era, the influence of Mexican muralism looms large, with the themes of *indigenismo* and sociopolitical issues remaining integral to much of the work that followed throughout Latin America.

Quito Muralism

Carrying the patriotic muralism tradition into midcentury, the Ecuadorian government commissioned the country's most esteemed artist, Oswaldo Guayasamín, to create artwork intended to unify a country demoralized by land skirmishes and territorial losses to Peru. Guayasamín answered with a 103-painting series called *Huacayñan,* Kichwa for 'The Way of Tears,' representing the social injustices, poverty and identity experienced by the *mestizo,* Black and indigenous peoples of Ecuador in his distinctive, expressionist style.

This first of several government commissions was bookended by his last in 1988, an enormous relief installation in Ecuador's Legislative Palace titled *Imagen de la Patria* (Image of the Homeland), which included representations of some of the country's national heroes but also its significant indigenous leaders, women activists, the working class and a rejection of militarism

STORYBOOK

EDUARDO GALEANO
LAS VENAS ABIERTAS DE AMÉRICA LATINA
"CADA PERSONA BRILLA CON LUZ PROPIA ENTRE TODAS LAS DEMÁS. NO HAY DOS FUEGOS IGUALES. HAY FUEGOS GRANDES Y FUEGOS CHICOS Y FUEGOS DE TODOS LOS COLORES."

and foreign intervention in its politics. This imagery bears unapologetic witness to the social injustices and not-always-rosy heritage of the homeland and acts as a silent reminder to Ecuador's National Assembly.

Taking It to the Streets

As Quito developed in the 1940s and '50s, public art and murals began to form part of the architectural plans of some modern buildings. These institutionally sanctioned artworks naturally formed a part of the city's vernacular, where artists made it a guerrilla medium for sociopolitical public messaging in the 1960s. But the '90s were really when the more contemporary tradition took hold here.

Nowadays, urban art is an inextricable and essential element of Quito's cityscape, where the satirical, political and beautiful often blend. While neighborhoods such as La Floresta or La Tola are known for their high concentration of colorful murals, the entire city is truly a canvas for a wide range of artistic styles and storytelling on walls, stairways, corridors and interiors. *Muralismo* speaks truth to power, or solidarity to the powerless, or superfluous cheekiness to everyone, creating a freedom of expression simultaneously joyous, politically strident and completely normalized as a part of the urban conversation. Quito would not be Quito without its sometimes inscrutable, usually artistically impressive and always fascinating street art, which can make any nondescript corner a thought-provoking opportunity.

Quiteño Artists

The breadth of local artists' styles is as diverse as in any medium, and their subject matter may be anything from *quiteño* culture and issues to free artistic expression. The *muralismo* tradition often uses surrealism or magical realism in its expression. Quiteño artists such as Apitatán take this approach in pieces such as *Tejiendo memoría* (Weaving Memory) at the corner of Los Ríos and Esmeraldas in La Tola. A face lies horizontally with both eyes closed, and an open third eye, with tears flowing out of one closed eye into a stream. Jungle greenery instead of hair creates part of the landscape, and a small figure sits on one end gazing downstream, while a small stone at the other end appears to be an ancient, worn-down face overgrown with roots. Apitatán explains the image as speaking to time concealing nature's sacred wisdom and connecting back to that generational inheritance.

Just down the same block, a local *chicha* (fermented corn or yuca drink) bar stands out with its bright-blue wall and yellow mural by *quiteño* artist Christian Tapia. The stylized graphic design pays homage to the tradition of the drink, gastronomic culture and the space's former life as a neighborhood cafe. Even next door, there's rainbow-hued psychedelia decorating the roll-up door (if it's shut, of course).

Women street artists also make their mark, including works like the ones by Belén Bike and Maria 'Too Fly' Castillo, who created Ecuador's first large-scale (40m tall) mural on the sciences building at Universidad Central del Ecuador (UCE) during the women-centered Festival WarmiPaint in 2015.

South American Collabs & Culture

The concentration of cool street art in La Floresta makes it an easy neighborhood art walk. In this artsy *barrio,* there's a street-art gallery where you can purchase prints by local and visiting street artists whose work enlivens the local walls, interiors and even street planters. Keep your eyes peeled to find works of international visiting artists, big and small – like the (small) rocket-riding rabbits by Colombian female artist ERRE, and the (big) neon-hued script of Peruvian Elliot Tupac, declaring *'Donde Hay Amor, Hay Vida'* (Where There Is Love, There Is Life).

Another notable piece in saturated yellow and pink depicts an indigenous girl reading Eduardo Galeano's seminal *Las venas abiertas de América Latina (The Open Veins of Latin America),* painted by visiting artist Toxicómano of Colombia.

Collaborations between local and international artists also appear up and down these streets, beautiful testament to the medium being a core art of the South American creative tradition.

***Las venas abiertas de América Latina* (The Open Veins of Latin America) by Toxicómano**

MURAL ARTIST: TOXICÓMANO CALLEJERO, PHOTO: WENDY YANAGIHARA

INDEX

Map Pages **000**

L

M

Map Pages **000**

N

Map Pages **000**